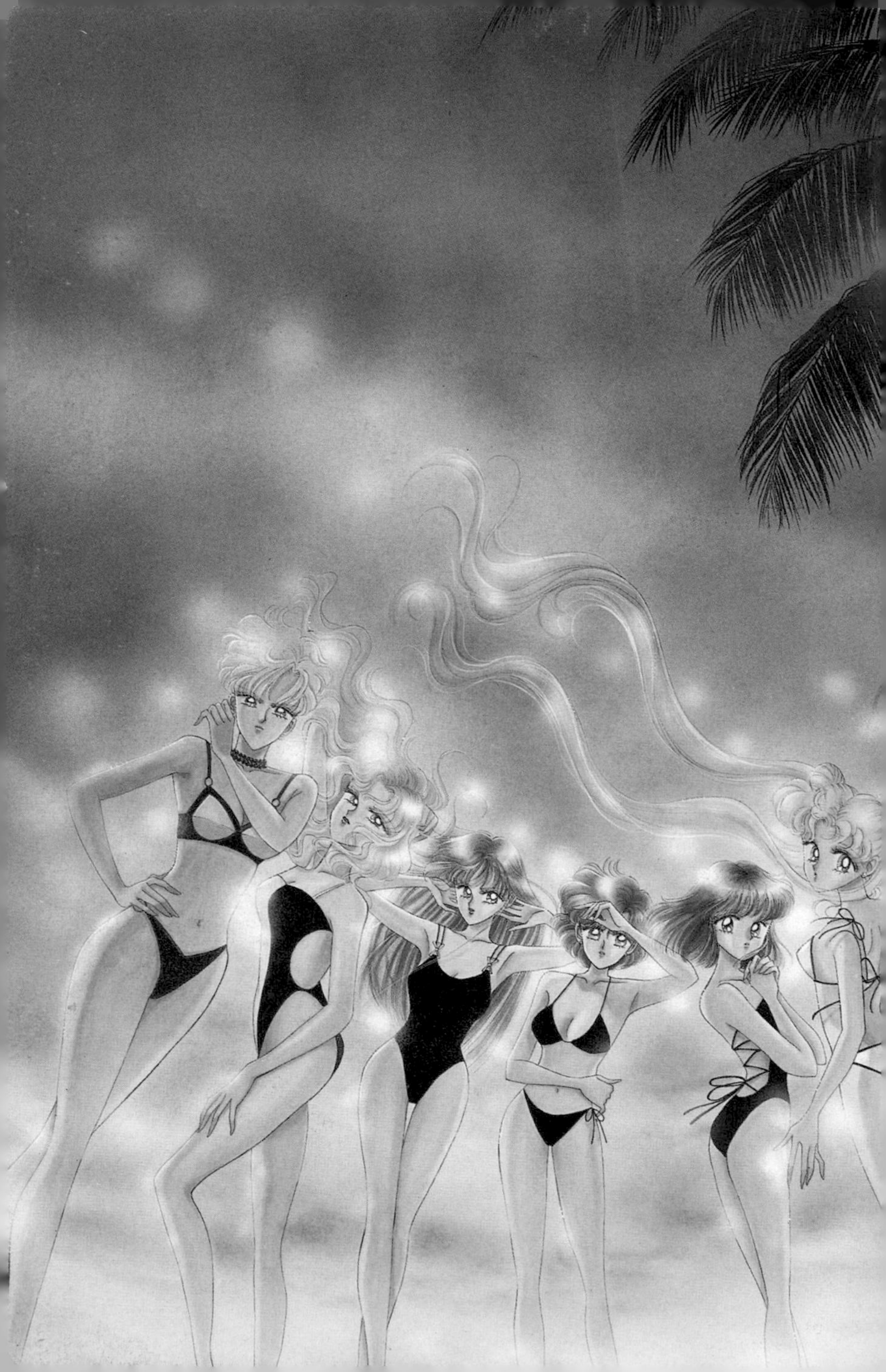

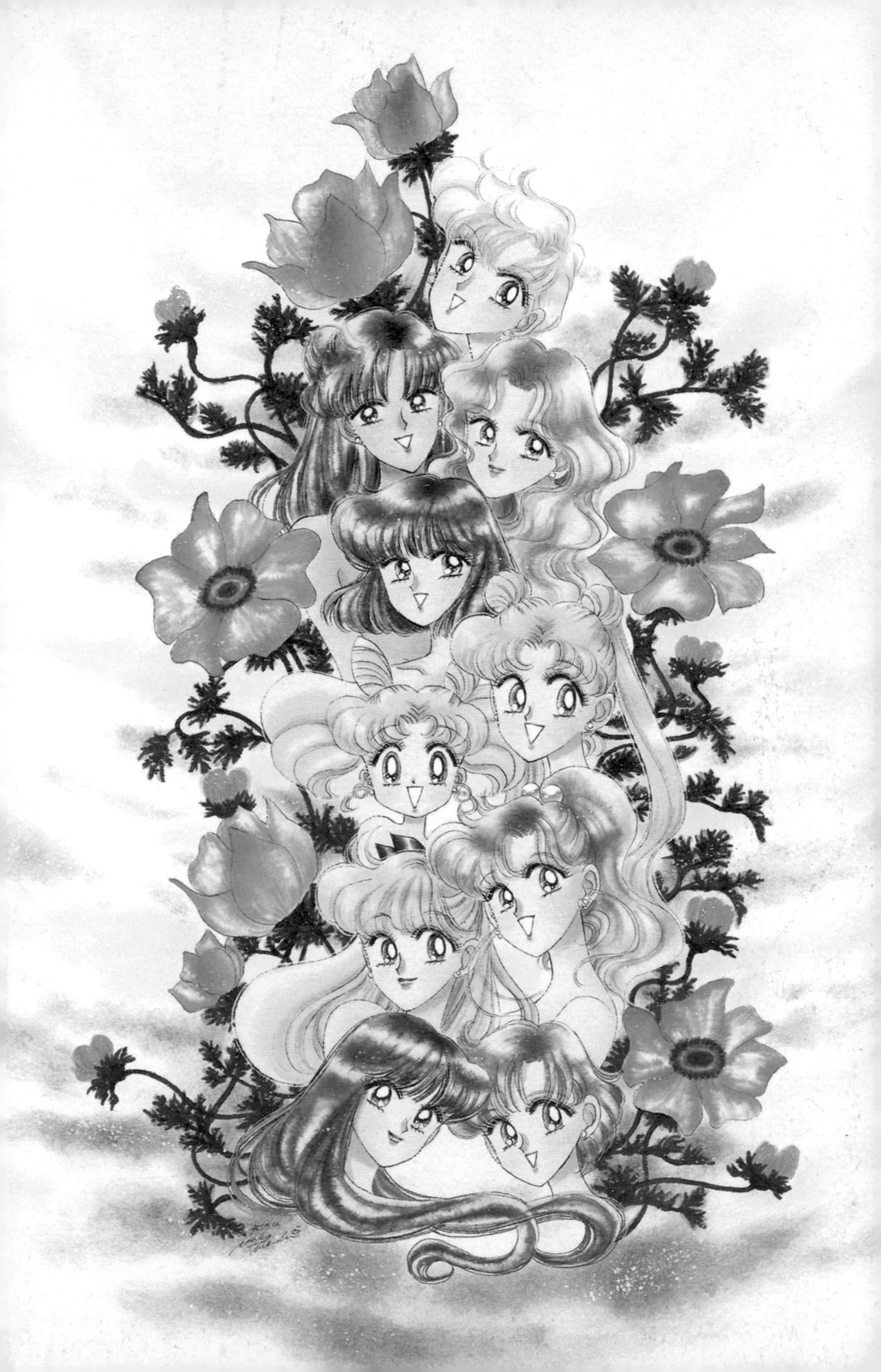

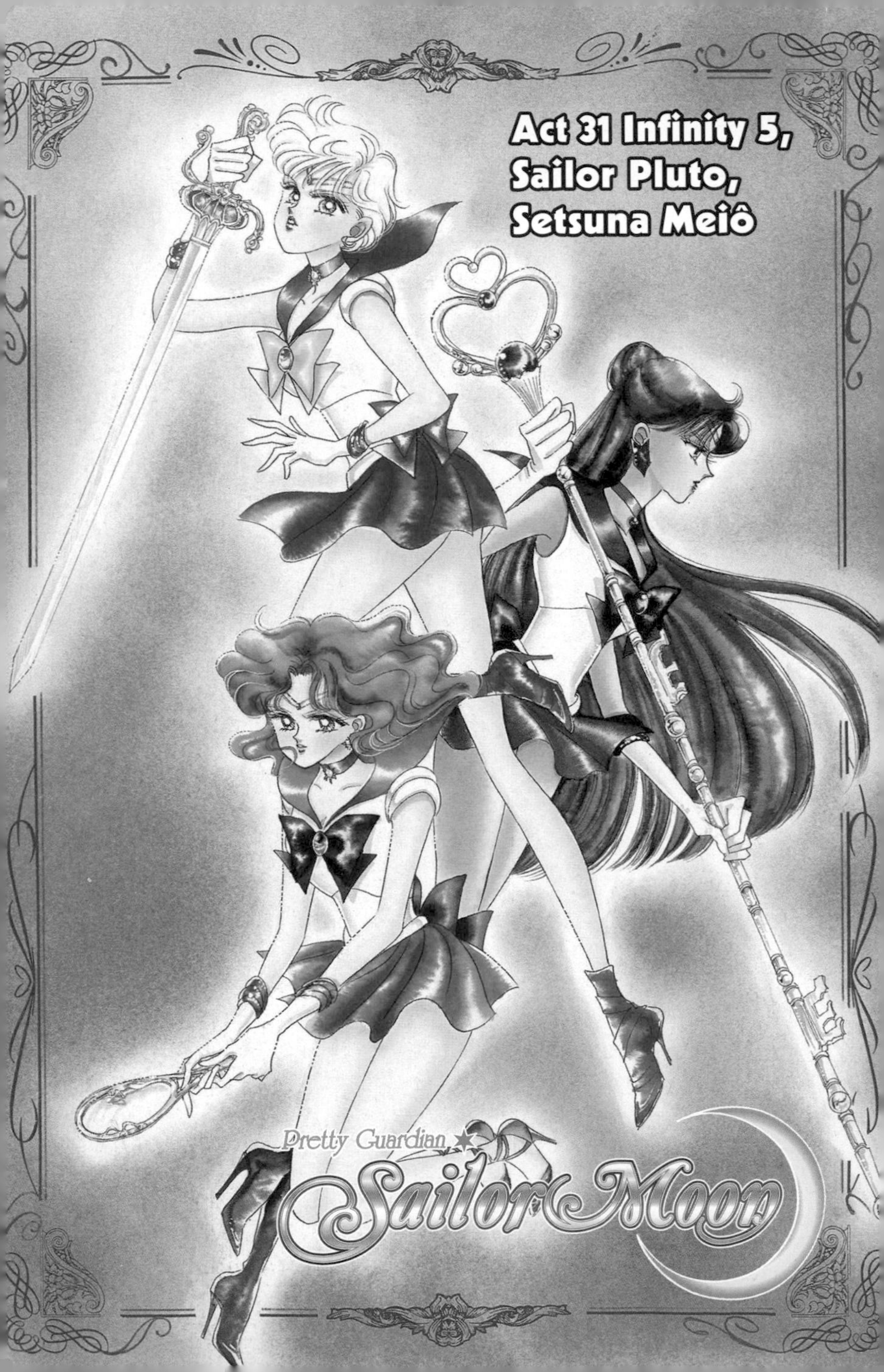
Act 31 Infinity 5,
Sailor Pluto,
Setsuna Meiô
Pretty Guardian
Sailor Moon

CONTENTS

Pretty Guardian SAILORMOON

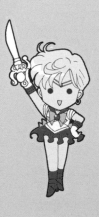

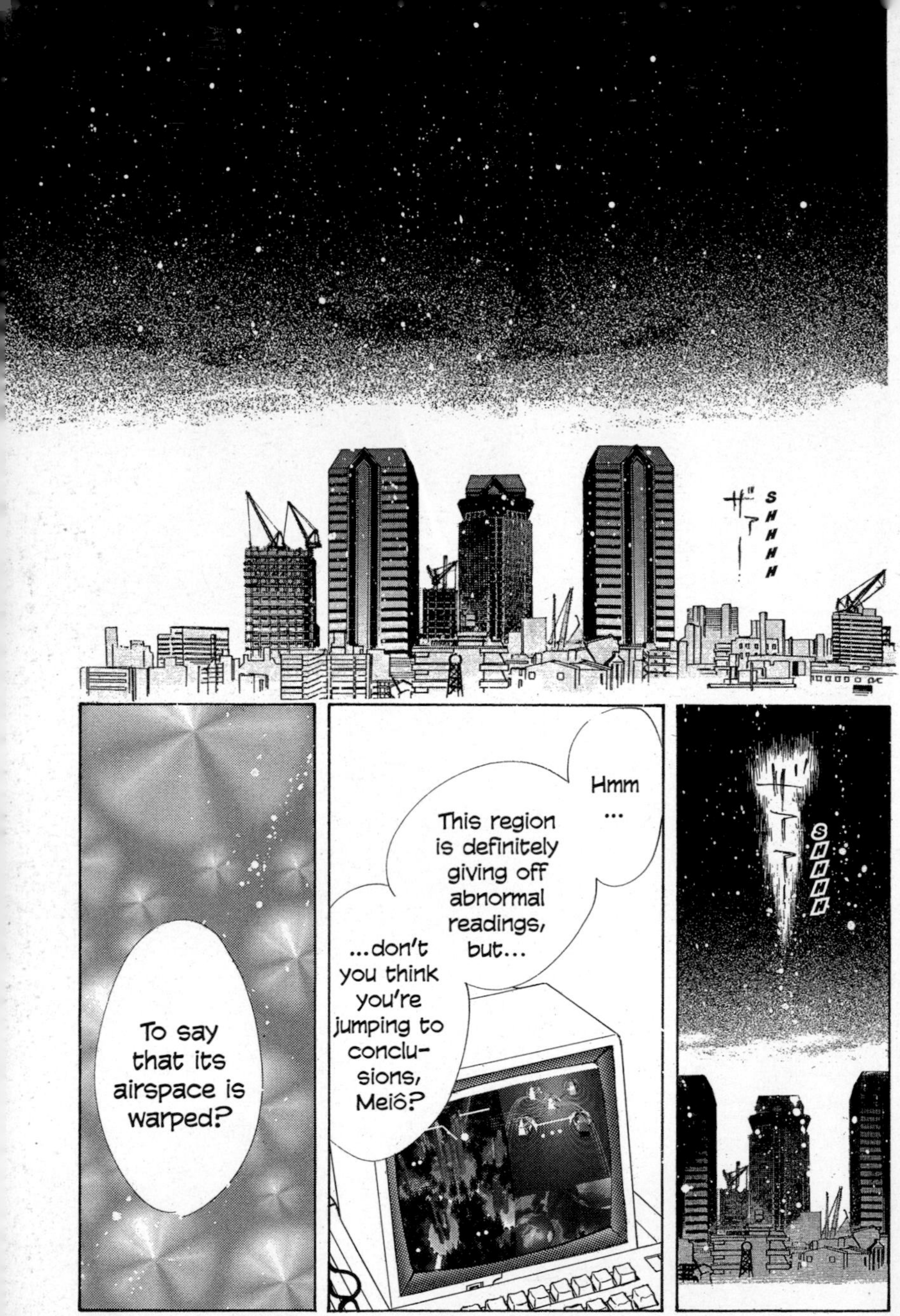
SHHHH
SHHHH
Hmm...
This region is definitely giving off abnormal readings, but...
...don't you think you're jumping to conclusions, Meiô?
To say that its airspace is warped?

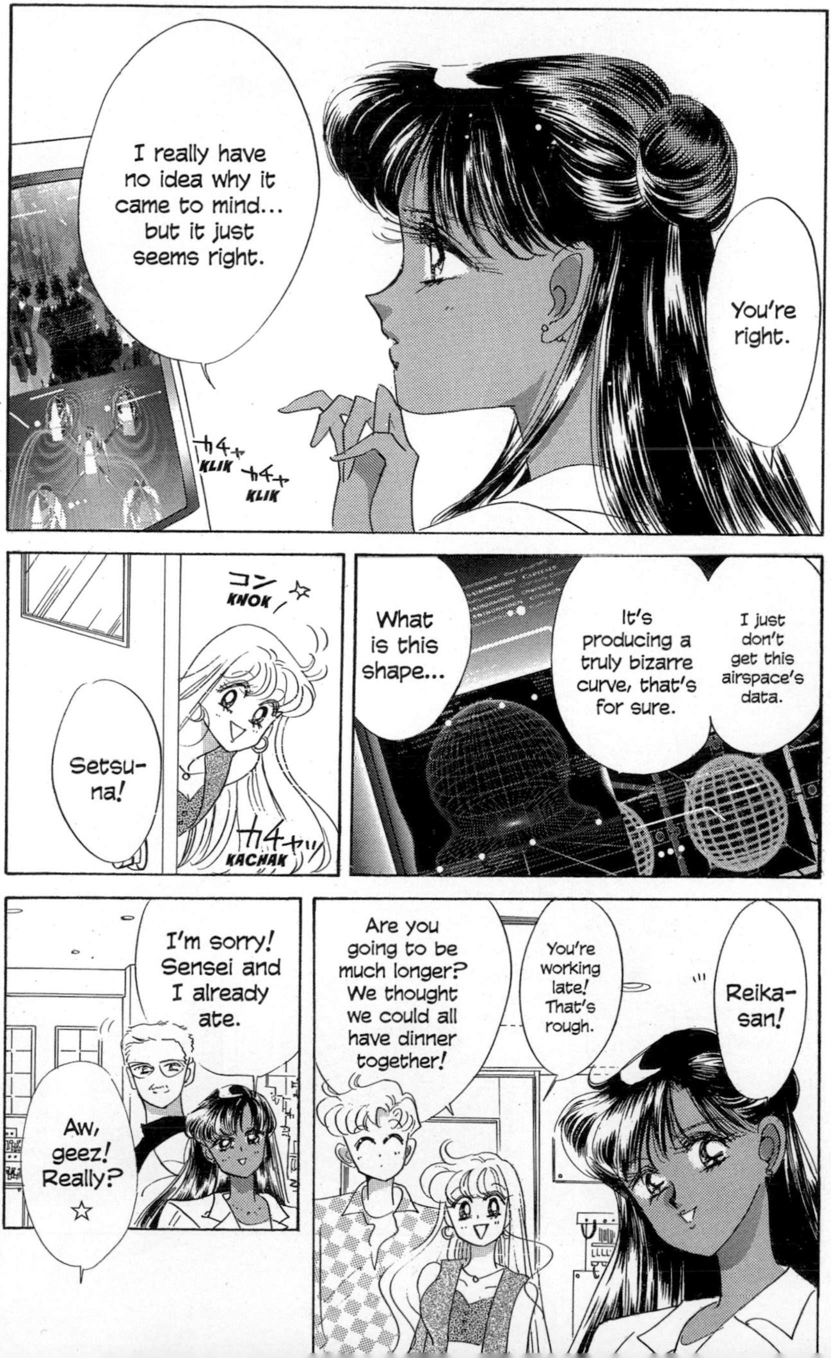
You're right.
I really have no idea why it came to mind... but it just seems right.
カチャ KLIK
カチャ KLIK
I just don't get this airspace's data.
It's producing a truly bizarre curve, that's for sure.
What is this shape...
コン KNOK
Setsu-na!
カチャッ KACHAK
Reika-san!
You're working late! That's rough.
Are you going to be much longer? We thought we could all have dinner together!
I'm sorry! Sensei and I already ate.
Aw, geez! Really? ☆

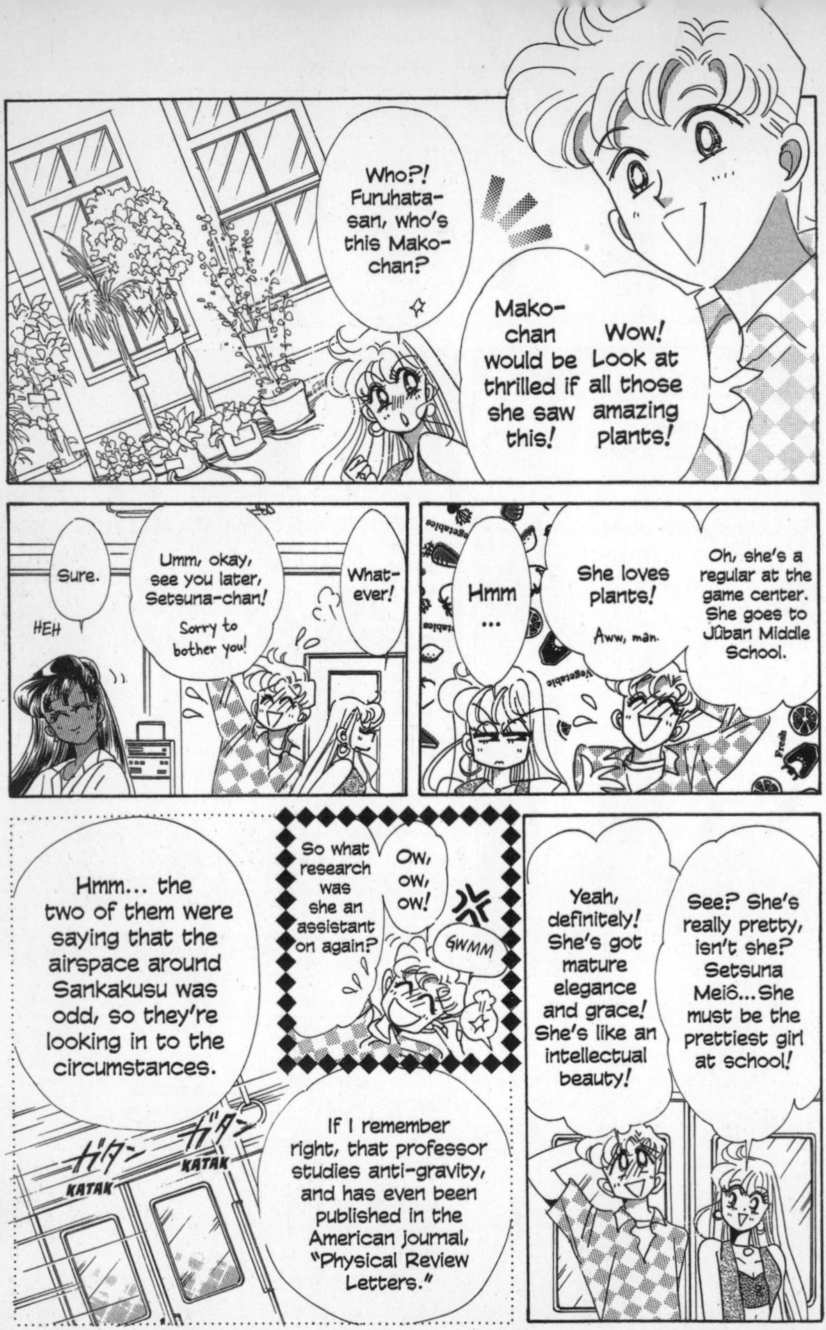
Wow! Look at all those amazing plants!
Mako-chan would be thrilled if she saw this!
Who?! Furuhata-san, who's this Mako-chan?
Oh, she's a regular at the game center. She goes to Jûban Middle School.
She loves plants!
Aww, man.
Hmm ...
What-ever!
Umm, okay, see you later, Setsuna-chan!
Sorry to bother you!
Sure.
HEH
See? She's really pretty, isn't she? Setsuna Meiô...She must be the prettiest girl at school!
Yeah, definitely! She's got mature elegance and grace! She's like an intellectual beauty!
Ow, ow, ow!
So what research was she an assistant on again?
GWMM
Hmm... the two of them were saying that the airspace around Sankakusu was odd, so they're looking in to the circumstances.
If I remember right, that professor studies anti-gravity, and has even been published in the American journal, "Physical Review Letters."
KATAK
KATAK

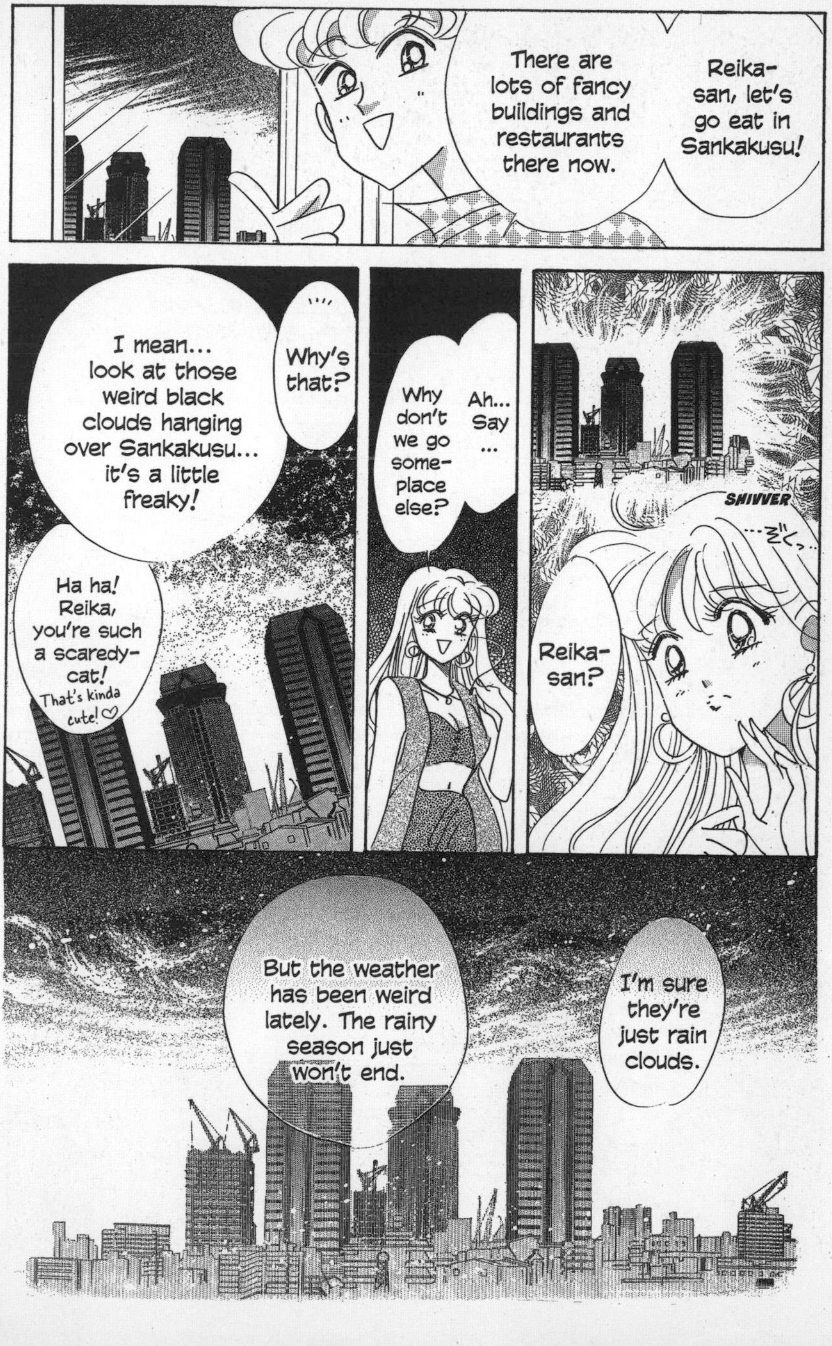
Reika-san, let's go eat in Sankakusu!
There are lots of fancy buildings and restaurants there now.
SHIVVER
...ぞくっ...
Reika-san?
Ah... Say ...
Why don't we go someplace else?
...!
Why's that?
I mean... look at those weird black clouds hanging over Sankakusu... it's a little freaky!
Ha ha! Reika, you're such a scaredy-cat! That's kinda cute! ♡
I'm sure they're just rain clouds.
But the weather has been weird lately. The rainy season just won't end.

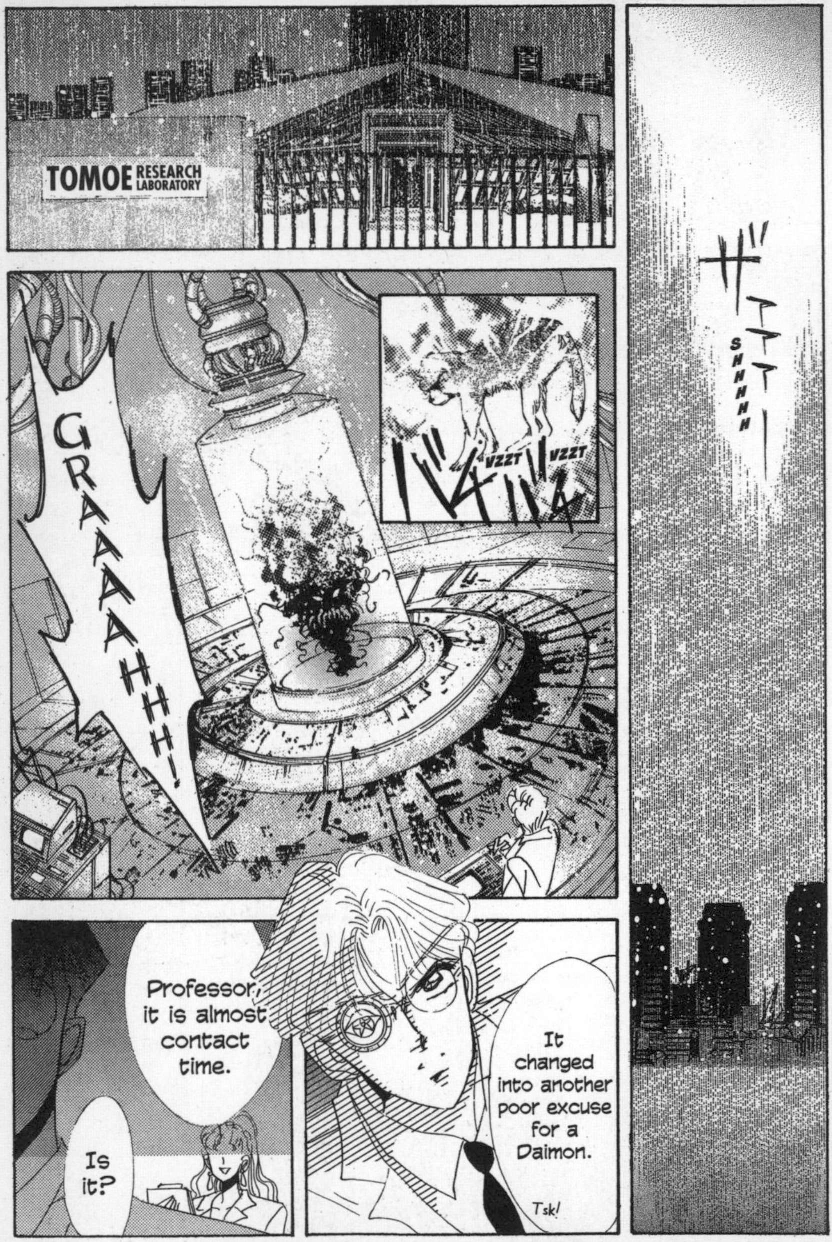
ザァァァー
SHHHHH
TOMOE RESEARCH LABORATORY
VZZT VZZT
GRAAAAHHH!
It changed into another poor excuse for a Daimon.
Tsk!
Professor, it is almost contact time.
Is it?

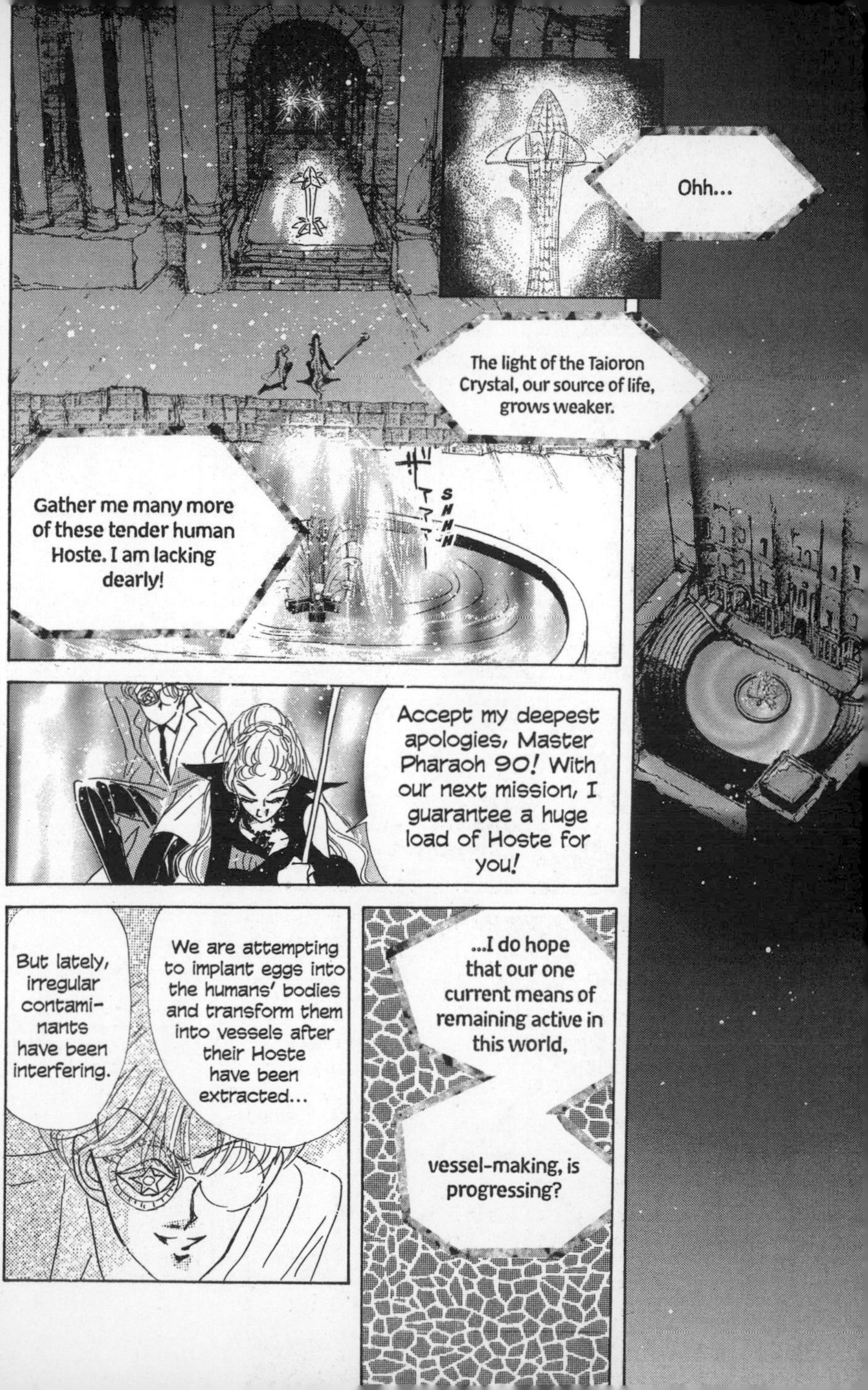
Ohh...
The light of the Taioron Crystal, our source of life, grows weaker.
Gather me many more of these tender human Hoste. I am lacking dearly!
SHHH
Accept my deepest apologies, Master Pharaoh 90! With our next mission, I guarantee a huge load of Hoste for you!
...I do hope that our one current means of remaining active in this world,
vessel-making, is progressing?
We are attempting to implant eggs into the humans' bodies and transform them into vessels after their Hoste have been extracted...
But lately, irregular contami-nants have been interfering.

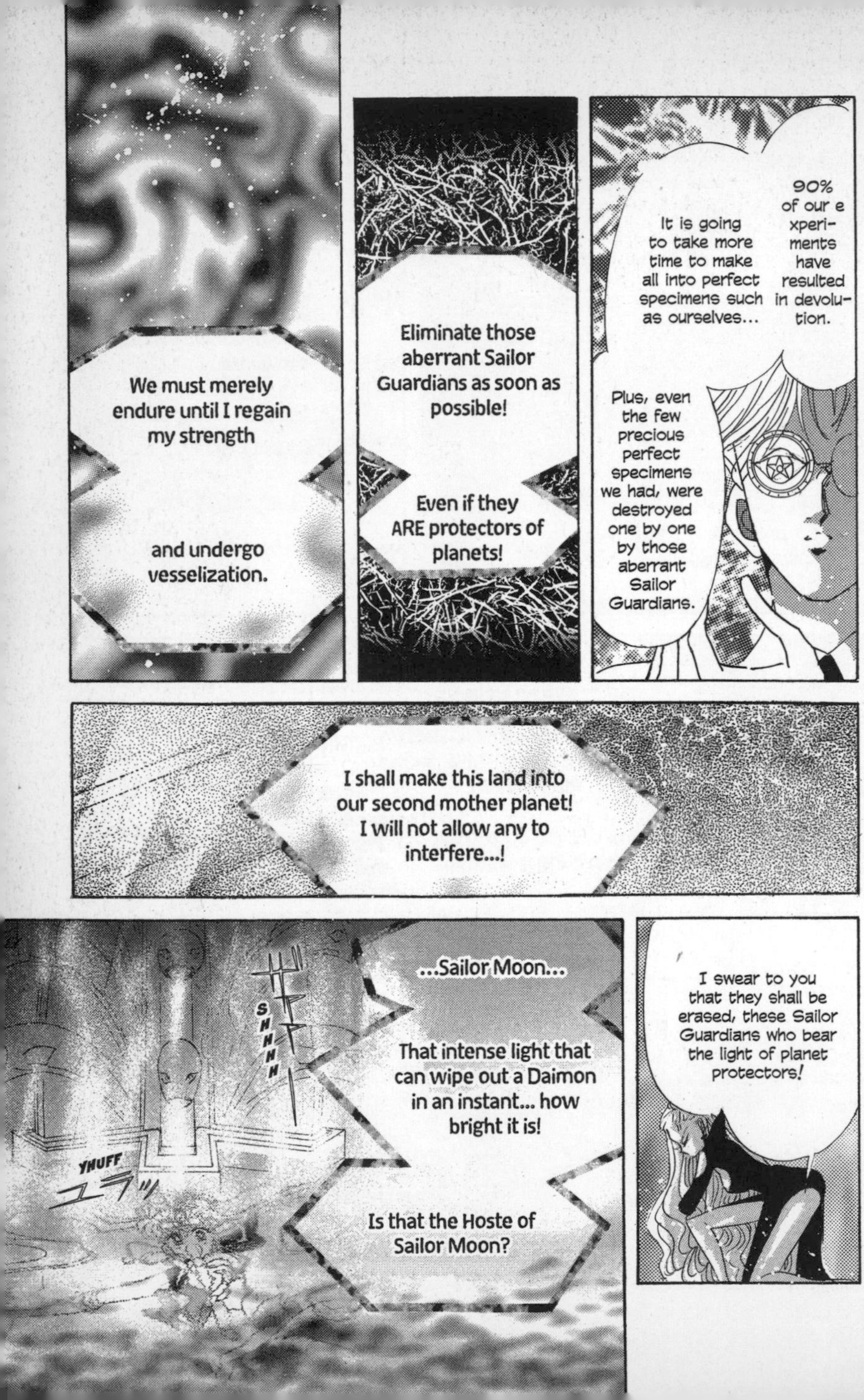
90% of our e xperi- ments have resulted in devolu- tion.
It is going to take more time to make all into perfect specimens such as ourselves...
Plus, even the few precious perfect specimens we had, were destroyed one by one by those aberrant Sailor Guardians.
Eliminate those aberrant Sailor Guardians as soon as possible!
Even if they ARE protectors of planets!
We must merely endure until I regain my strength
and undergo vesselization.
I shall make this land into our second mother planet! I will not allow any to interfere...!
I swear to you that they shall be erased, these Sailor Guardians who bear the light of planet protectors!
...Sailor Moon...
SHHHH
That intense light that can wipe out a Daimon in an instant... how bright it is!
YHUFF
Is that the Hoste of Sailor Moon?

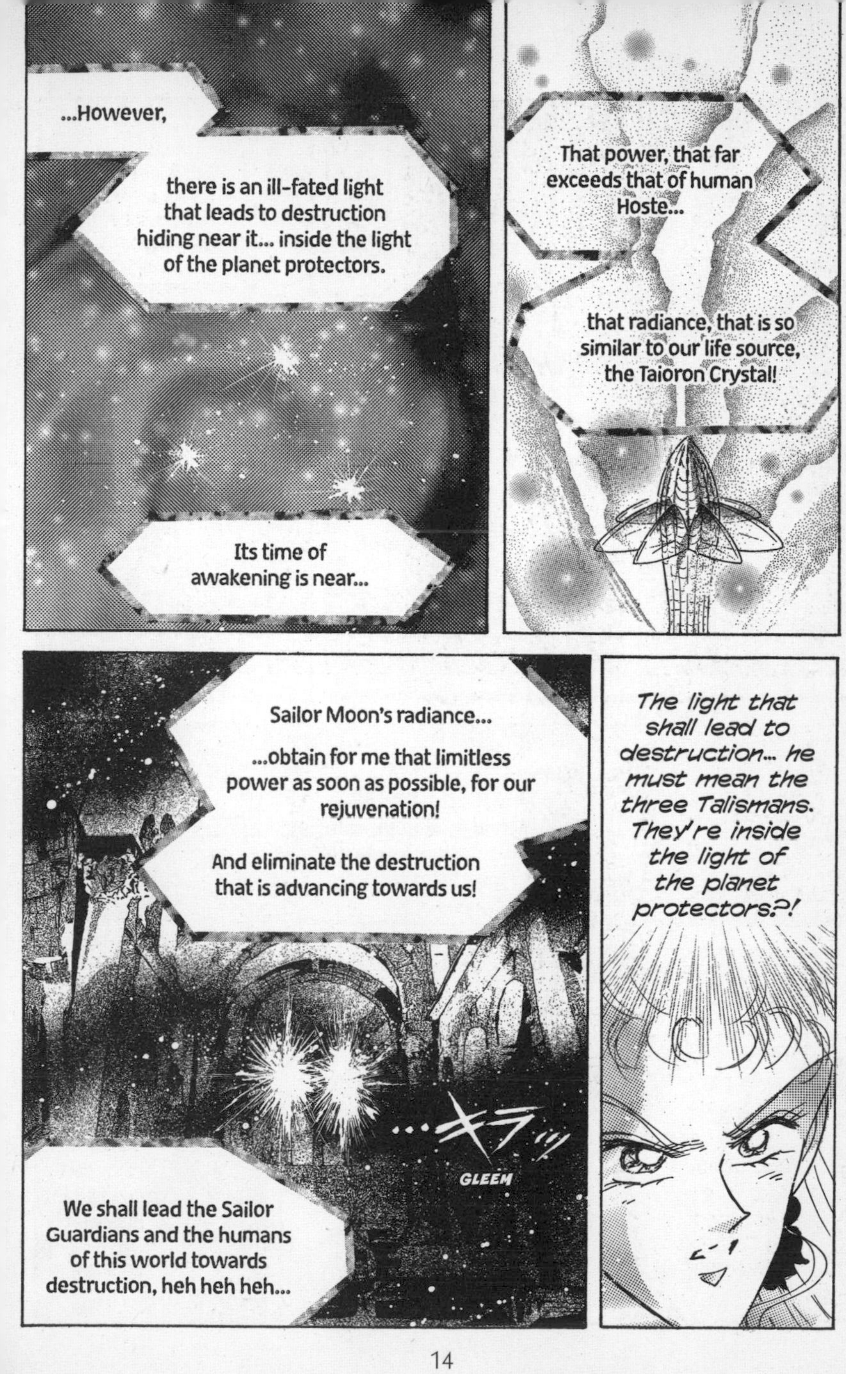
That power, that far exceeds that of human Hoste...
that radiance, that is so similar to our life source, the Taioron Crystal!
...However,
there is an ill-fated light that leads to destruction hiding near it... inside the light of the planet protectors.
Its time of awakening is near...
The light that shall lead to destruction... he must mean the three Talismans. They're inside the light of the planet protectors?!
Sailor Moon's radiance...
...obtain for me that limitless power as soon as possible, for our rejuvenation!
And eliminate the destruction that is advancing towards us!
GLEEM
We shall lead the Sailor Guardians and the humans of this world towards destruction, heh heh heh...

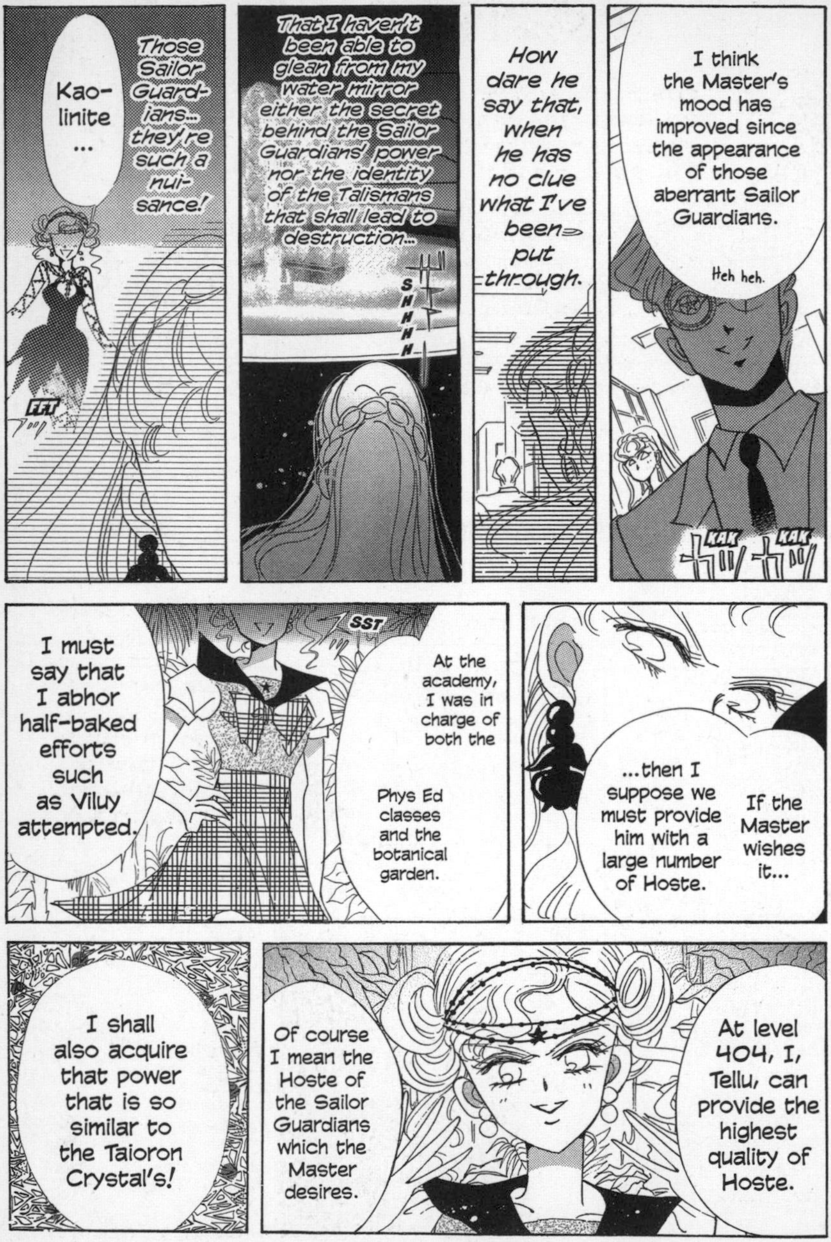
I think the Master's mood has improved since the appearance of those aberrant Sailor Guardians.
Heh heh.
KAK
KAK
How dare he say that, when he has no clue what I've been put through.
That I haven't been able to glean from my water mirror either the secret behind the Sailor Guardians' power nor the identity of the Talismans that shall lead to destruction...
SHHHH
Those Sailor Guardians... they're such a nuisance!
Kaolinite...
FFT
If the Master wishes it...
...then I suppose we must provide him with a large number of Hoste.
SST
At the academy, I was in charge of both the Phys Ed classes and the botanical garden.
I must say that I abhor half-baked efforts such as Viluy attempted.
At level 404, I, Tellu, can provide the highest quality of Hoste.
Of course I mean the Hoste of the Sailor Guardians which the Master desires.
I shall also acquire that power that is so similar to the Taioron Crystal's!

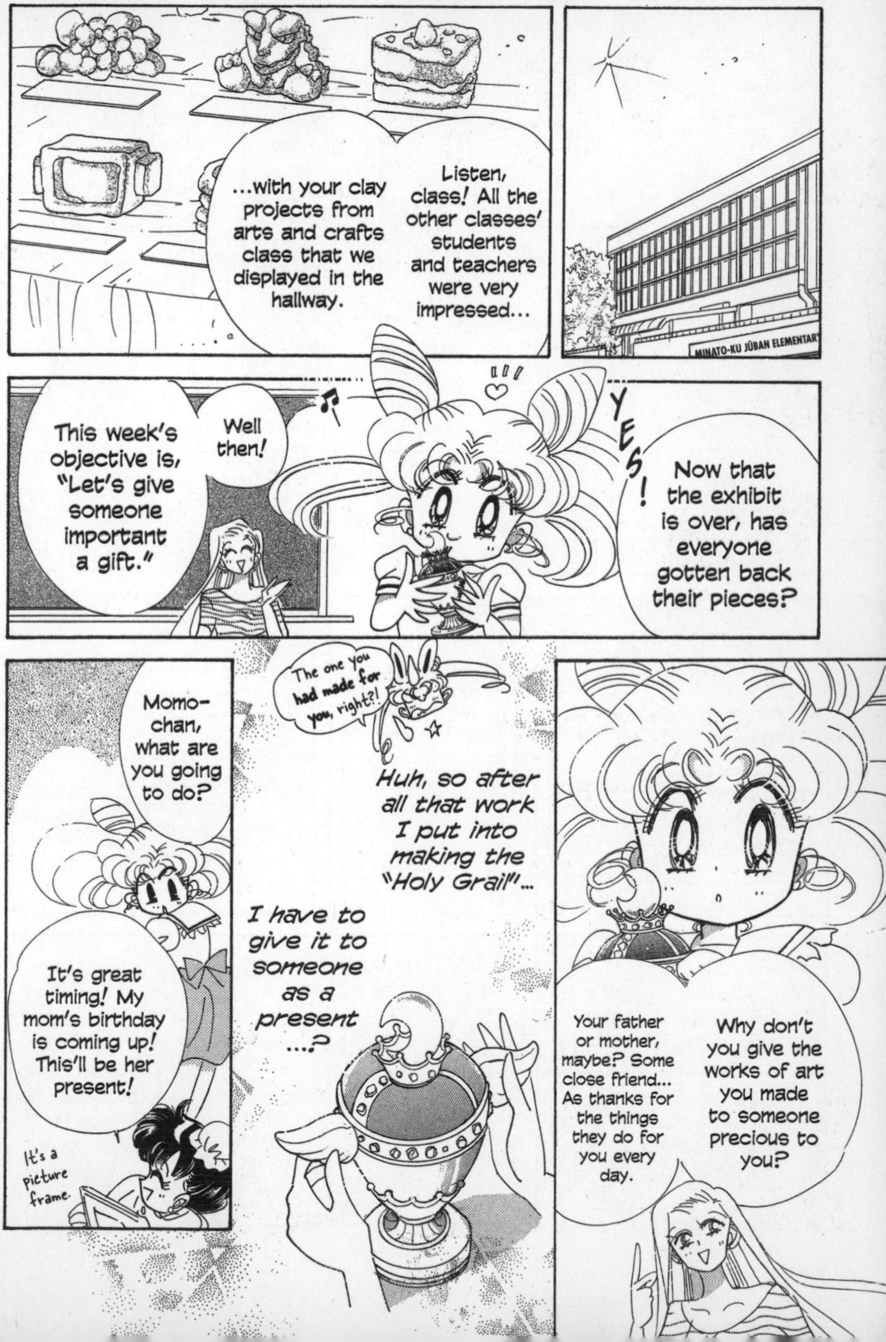
MINATO-KU JÛBAN ELEMENTAR
Listen, class! All the other classes' students and teachers were very impressed...
...with your clay projects from arts and crafts class that we displayed in the hallway.
YES!
Now that the exhibit is over, has everyone gotten back their pieces?
Well then!
This week's objective is, "Let's give someone important a gift."
Why don't you give the works of art you made to someone precious to you?
Your father or mother, maybe? Some close friend... As thanks for the things they do for you every day.
The one you had made for you, right?!
Huh, so after all that work I put into making the "Holy Grail"...
I have to give it to someone as a present ...?
Momo-chan, what are you going to do?
It's great timing! My mom's birthday is coming up! This'll be her present!
It's a picture frame.

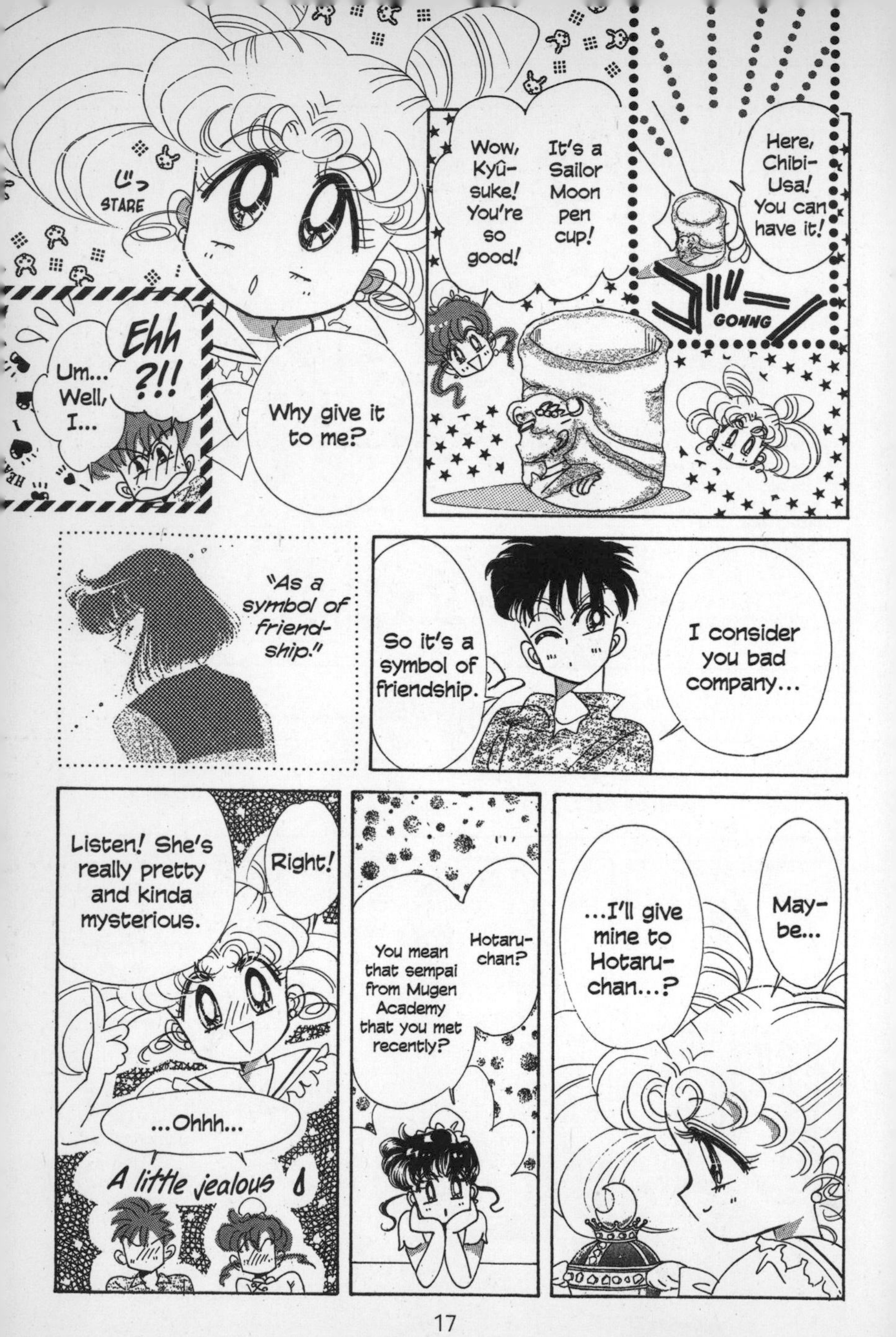
Here, Chibi-Usa! You can have it!
GONNG
It's a Sailor Moon pen cup!
Wow, Kyû-suke! You're so good!
STARE
Why give it to me?
Ehh?!!
Um... Well, I...
I consider you bad company...
So it's a symbol of friendship.
"As a symbol of friendship."
May-be...
...I'll give mine to Hotaru-chan...?
Hotaru-chan?
You mean that sempai from Mugen Academy that you met recently?
Right!
Listen! She's really pretty and kinda mysterious.
...Ohhh...
A little jealous

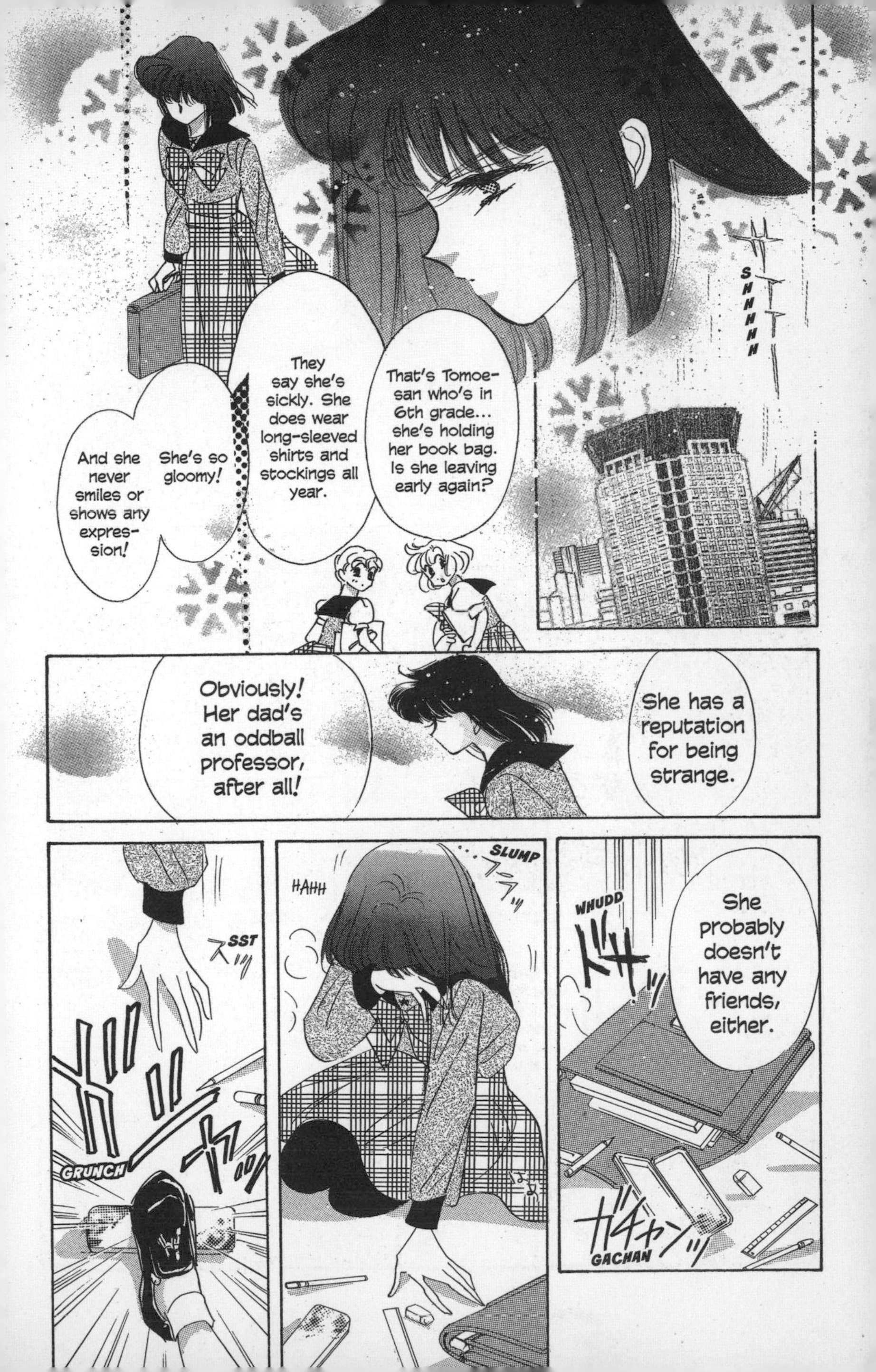
SHHHHH
That's Tomoe-san who's in 6th grade... she's holding her book bag. Is she leaving early again?
They say she's sickly. She does wear long-sleeved shirts and stockings all year.
She's so gloomy!
And she never smiles or shows any expression!
She has a reputation for being strange.
Obviously! Her dad's an oddball professor, after all!
WHUDD
She probably doesn't have any friends, either.
GACHAN
SLUMP
HAHH
SST
GRUNCH

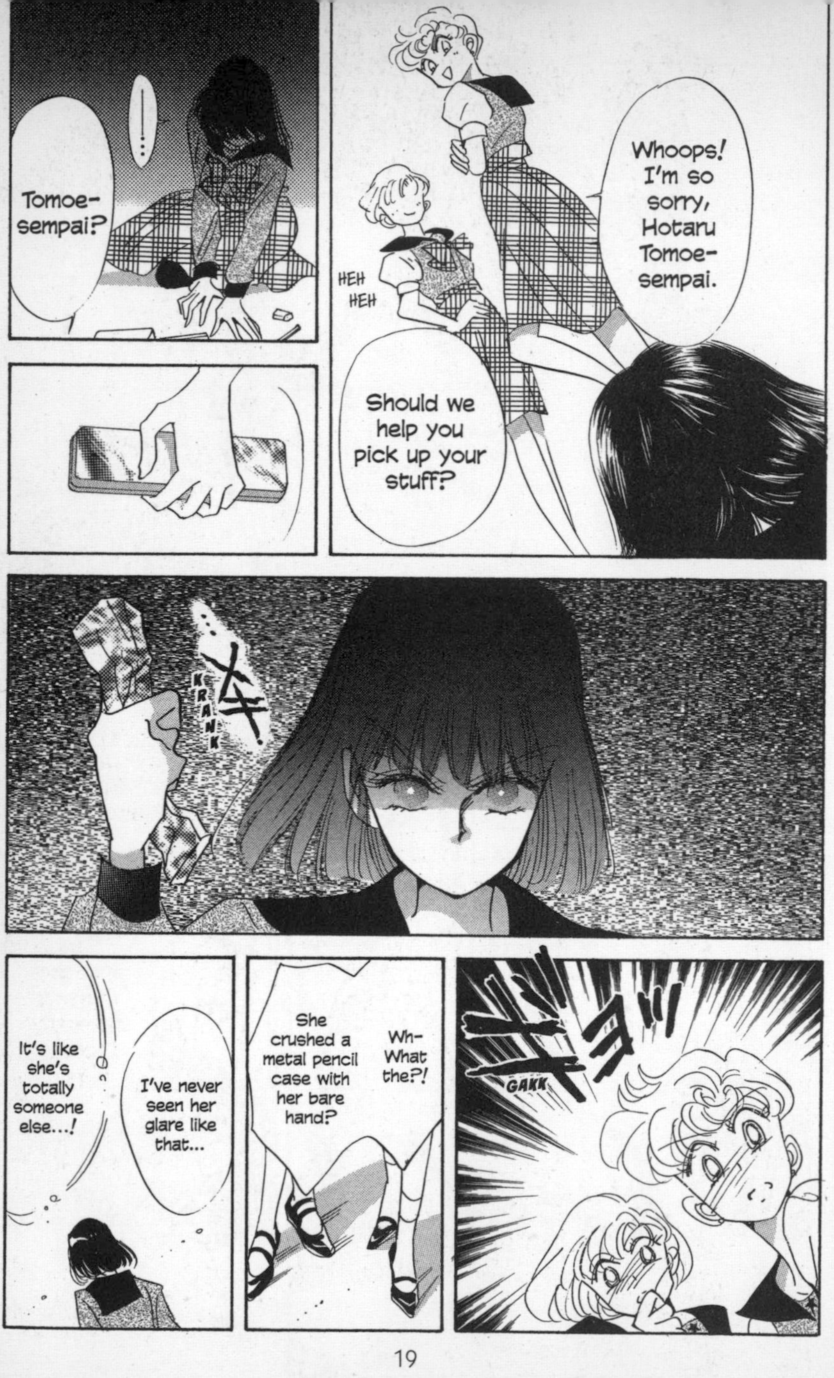
Whoops! I'm so sorry, Hotaru Tomoe-sempai.
HEH HEH
Should we help you pick up your stuff?
!...
Tomoe-sempai?
...
KRANK
GAKK
Wh- What the?!
She crushed a metal pencil case with her bare hand?
I've never seen her glare like that...
It's like she's totally someone else...!

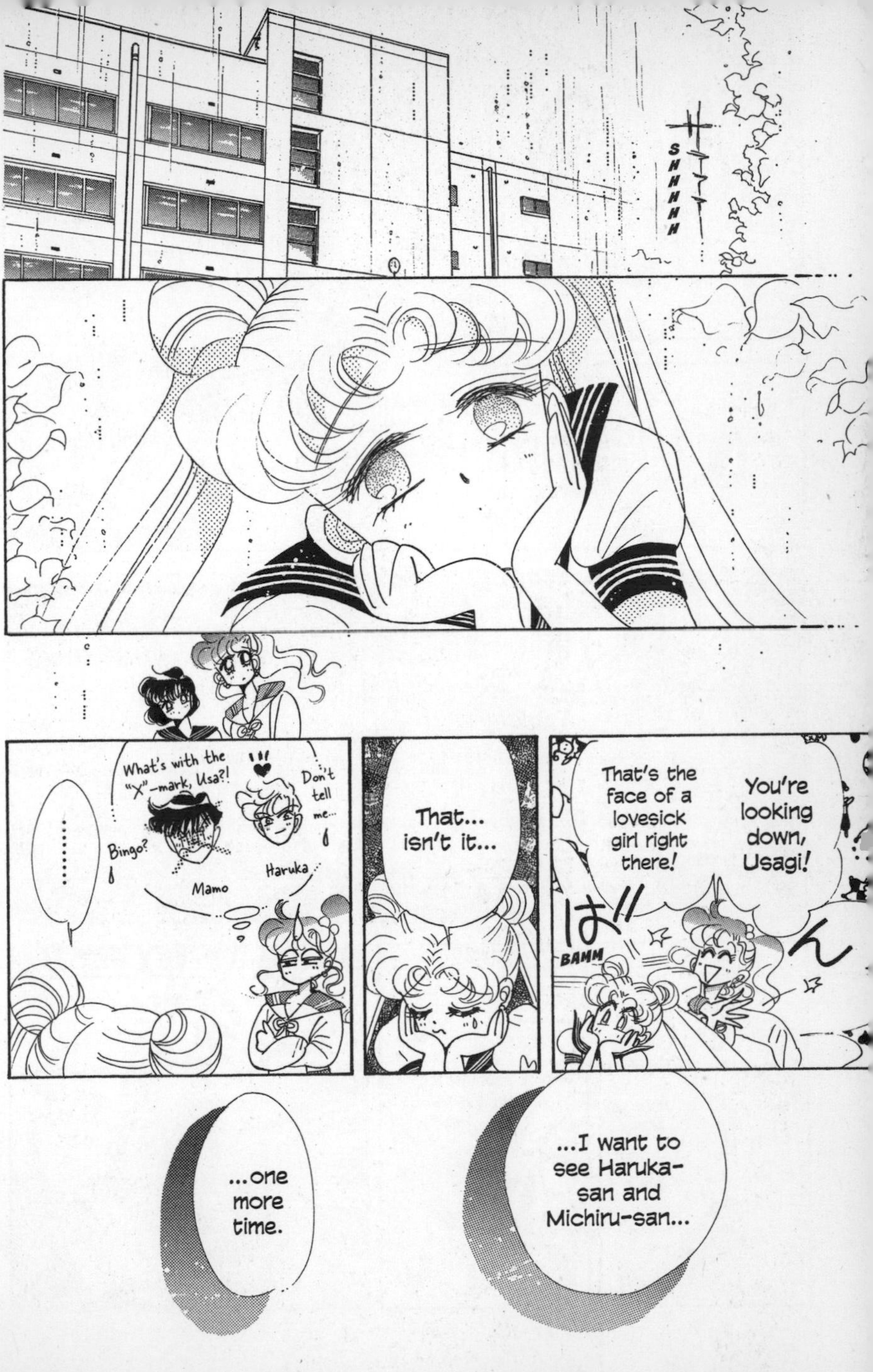
SHHHHH
You're looking down, Usagi!
That's the face of a lovesick girl right there!
は!!
BAMM
ん
That... isn't it...
Don't tell me...
Haruka
What's with the "X"-mark, Usa?!
Bingo?
Mamo
....
...I want to see Haruka-san and Michiru-san...
...one more time.

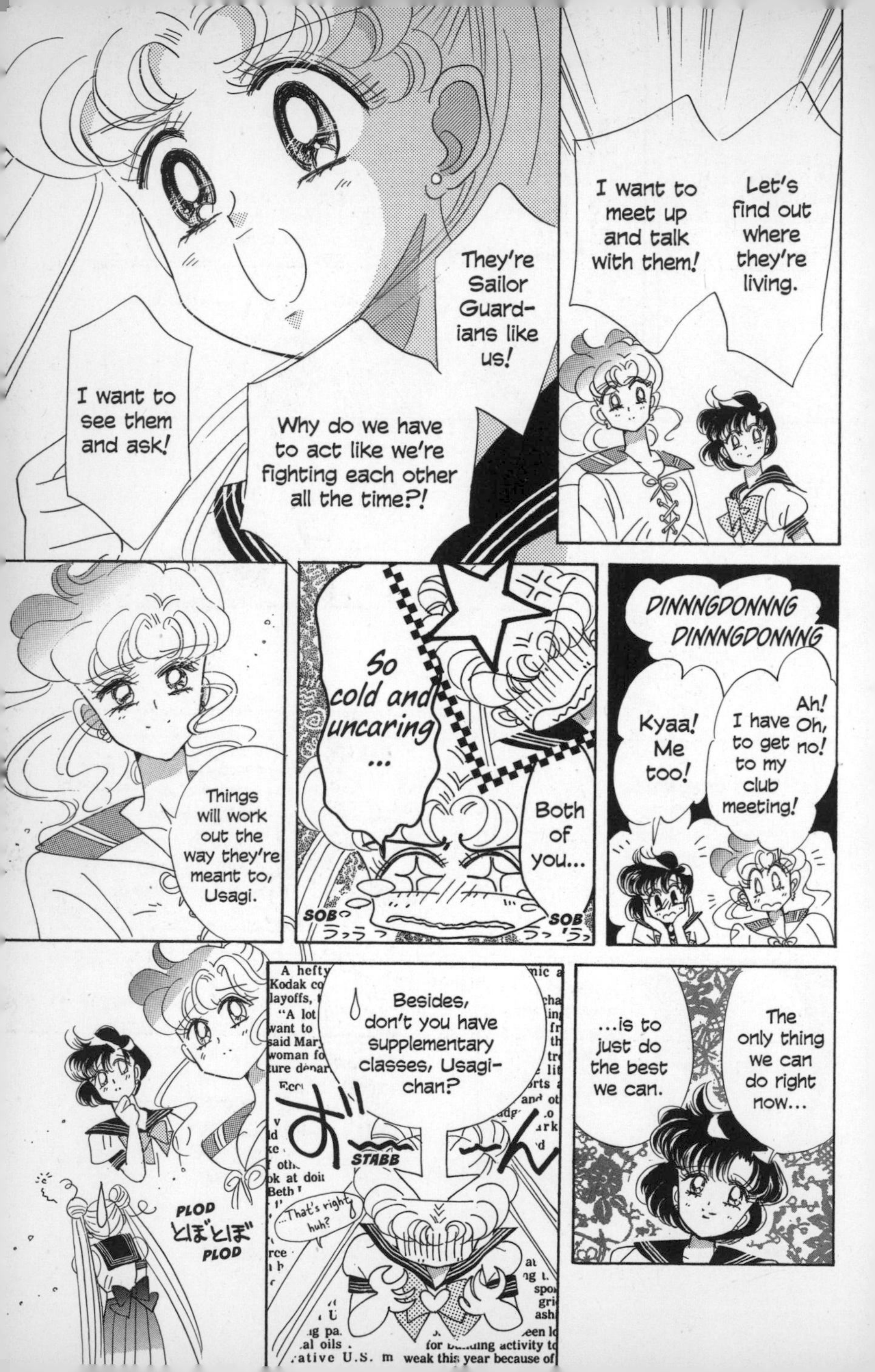
Let's find out where they're living.
I want to meet up and talk with them!
They're Sailor Guardians like us!
Why do we have to act like we're fighting each other all the time?!
I want to see them and ask!
DINNNGDONNNG
DINNNGDONNNG
Ah! Oh, no!
I have to get to my club meeting!
Kyaa! Me too!
Both of you...
So cold and uncaring ...
SOB
SOB
Things will work out the way they're meant to, Usagi.
The only thing we can do right now...
...is to just do the best we can.
Besides, don't you have supplementary classes, Usagi-chan?
STABB
...That's right, huh?
PLOD
とぼとぼ
PLOD

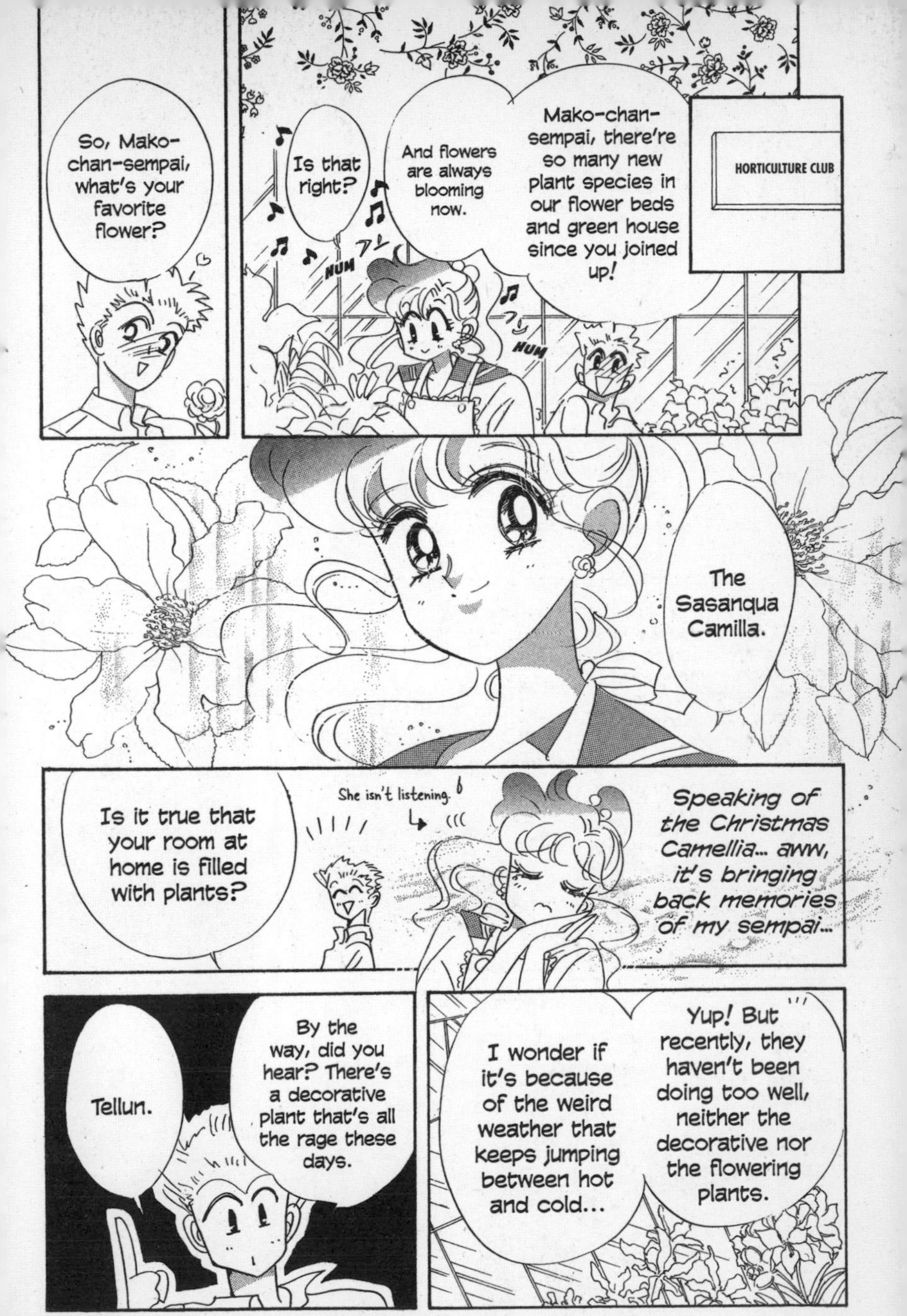
HORTICULTURE CLUB
Mako-chan-sempai, there're so many new plant species in our flower beds and green house since you joined up!
And flowers are always blooming now.
HUM
Is that right?
HUM
So, Mako-chan-sempai, what's your favorite flower?
The Sasanqua Camilla.
Speaking of the Christmas Camellia... aww, it's bringing back memories of my sempai...
She isn't listening.
Is it true that your room at home is filled with plants?
Yup! But recently, they haven't been doing too well, neither the decorative nor the flowering plants.
I wonder if it's because of the weird weather that keeps jumping between hot and cold...
By the way, did you hear? There's a decorative plant that's all the rage these days.
Tellun.

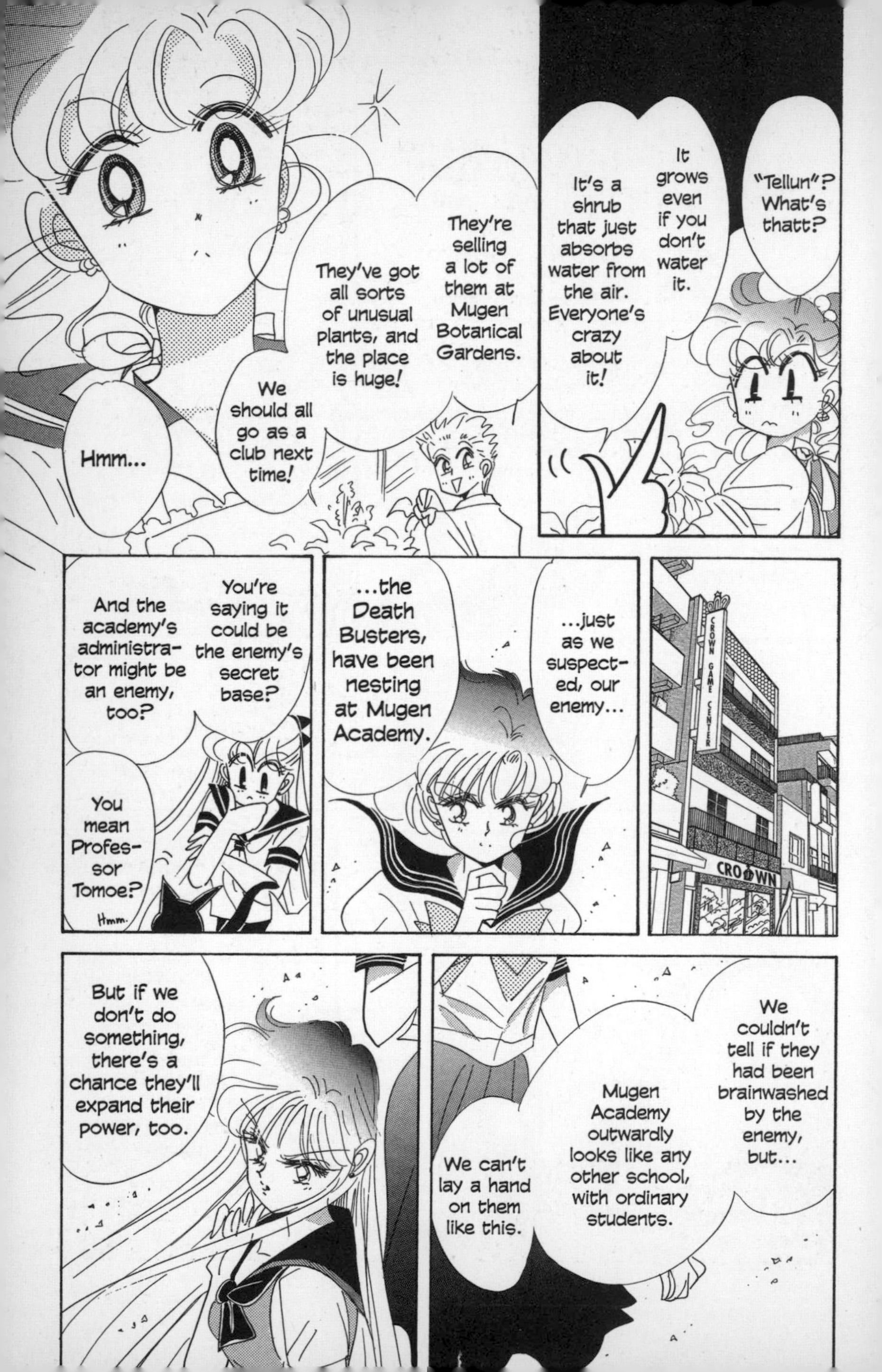
"Tellun"? What's thatt?
It grows even if you don't water it.
It's a shrub that just absorbs water from the air. Everyone's crazy about it!
They're selling a lot of them at Mugen Botanical Gardens.
They've got all sorts of unusual plants, and the place is huge!
We should all go as a club next time!
Hmm...
CROWN GAME CENTER
CROWN
...just as we suspected, our enemy...
...the Death Busters, have been nesting at Mugen Academy.
You're saying it could be the enemy's secret base?
And the academy's administrator might be an enemy, too?
You mean Professor Tomoe?
Hmm.
We couldn't tell if they had been brainwashed by the enemy, but...
Mugen Academy outwardly looks like any other school, with ordinary students.
We can't lay a hand on them like this.
But if we don't do something, there's a chance they'll expand their power, too.

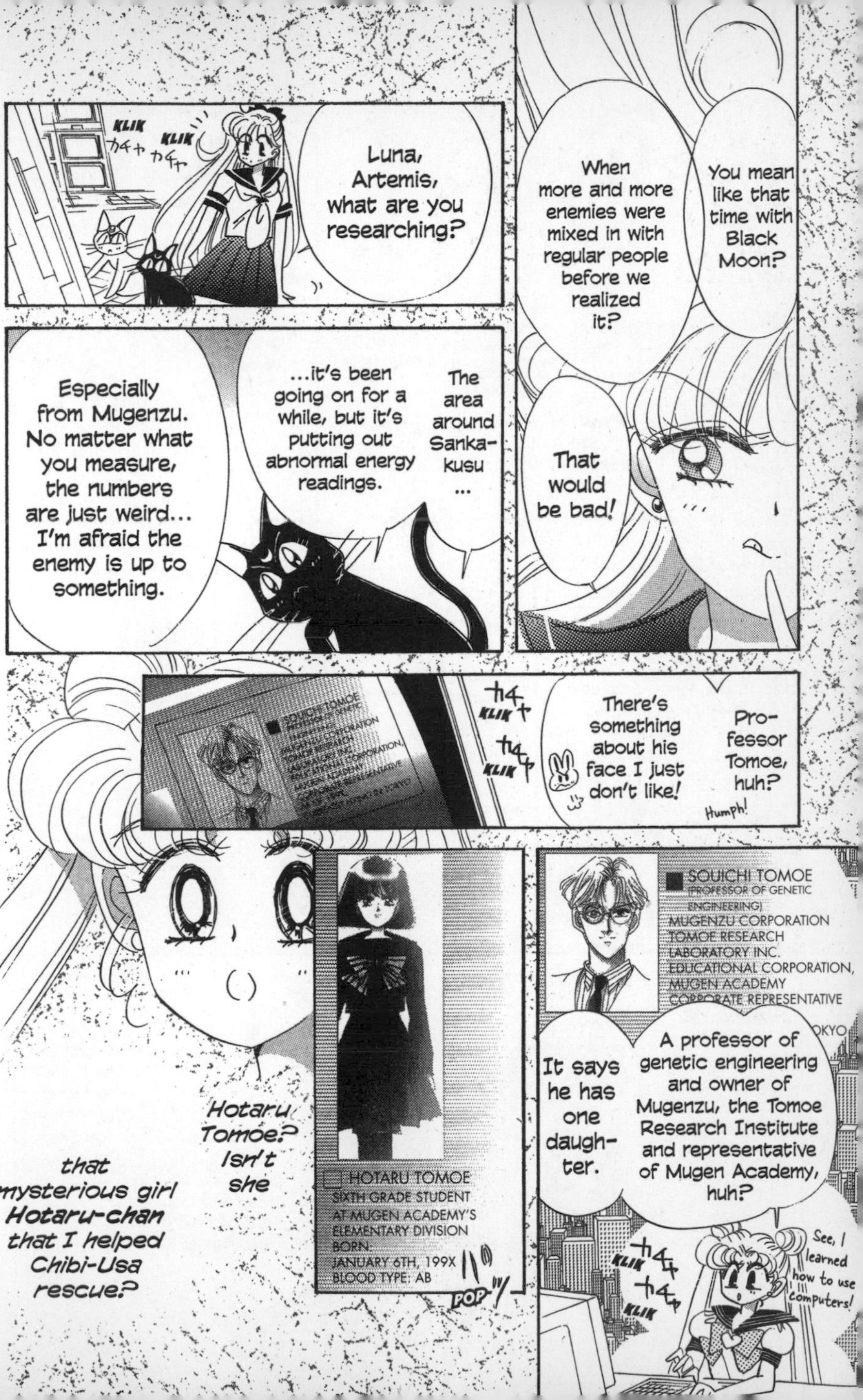
You mean like that time with Black Moon?
When more and more enemies were mixed in with regular people before we realized it?
That would be bad!
KLIK
KLIK
Luna, Artemis, what are you researching?
The area around Sanka-kusu ...
...it's been going on for a while, but it's putting out abnormal energy readings.
Especially from Mugenzu. No matter what you measure, the numbers are just weird... I'm afraid the enemy is up to something.
Pro-fessor Tomoe, huh?
Humph!
There's something about his face I just don't like!
KLIK
KLIK
SOUICHI TOMOE
(PROFESSOR OF GENETIC ENGINEERING)
MUGENZU CORPORATION
TOMOE RESEARCH LABORATORY INC.
EDUCATIONAL CORPORATION,
MUGEN ACADEMY
CORPORATE REPRESENTATIVE
A professor of genetic engineering and owner of Mugenzu, the Tomoe Research Institute and representative of Mugen Academy, huh?
It says he has one daugh-ter.
See, I learned how to use computers!
KLIK
KLIK
HOTARU TOMOE
SIXTH GRADE STUDENT AT MUGEN ACADEMY'S ELEMENTARY DIVISION
BORN: JANUARY 6TH, 199X
BLOOD TYPE: AB
POP
Hotaru Tomoe? Isn't she
that mysterious girl Hotaru-chan that I helped Chibi-Usa rescue?

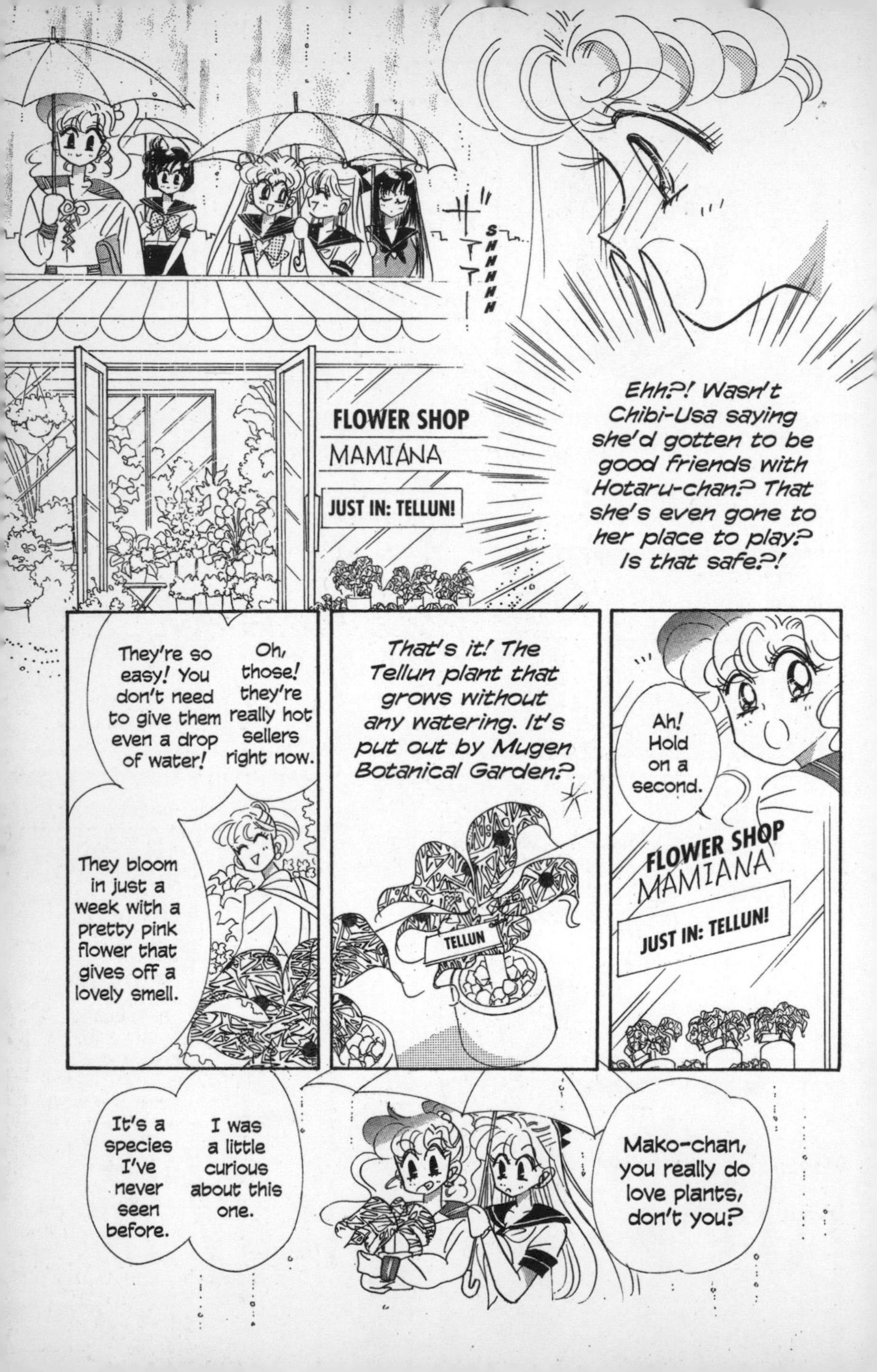
Ehh?! Wasn't Chibi-Usa saying she'd gotten to be good friends with Hotaru-chan? That she's even gone to her place to play? Is that safe?!
SHHHHH
FLOWER SHOP
MAMIANA
JUST IN: TELLUN!
Ah! Hold on a second.
FLOWER SHOP
MAMIANA
JUST IN: TELLUN!
That's it! The Tellun plant that grows without any watering. It's put out by Mugen Botanical Garden?
TELLUN
Oh, those! they're really hot sellers right now.
They're so easy! You don't need to give them even a drop of water!
They bloom in just a week with a pretty pink flower that gives off a lovely smell.
Mako-chan, you really do love plants, don't you?
I was a little curious about this one.
It's a species I've never seen before.

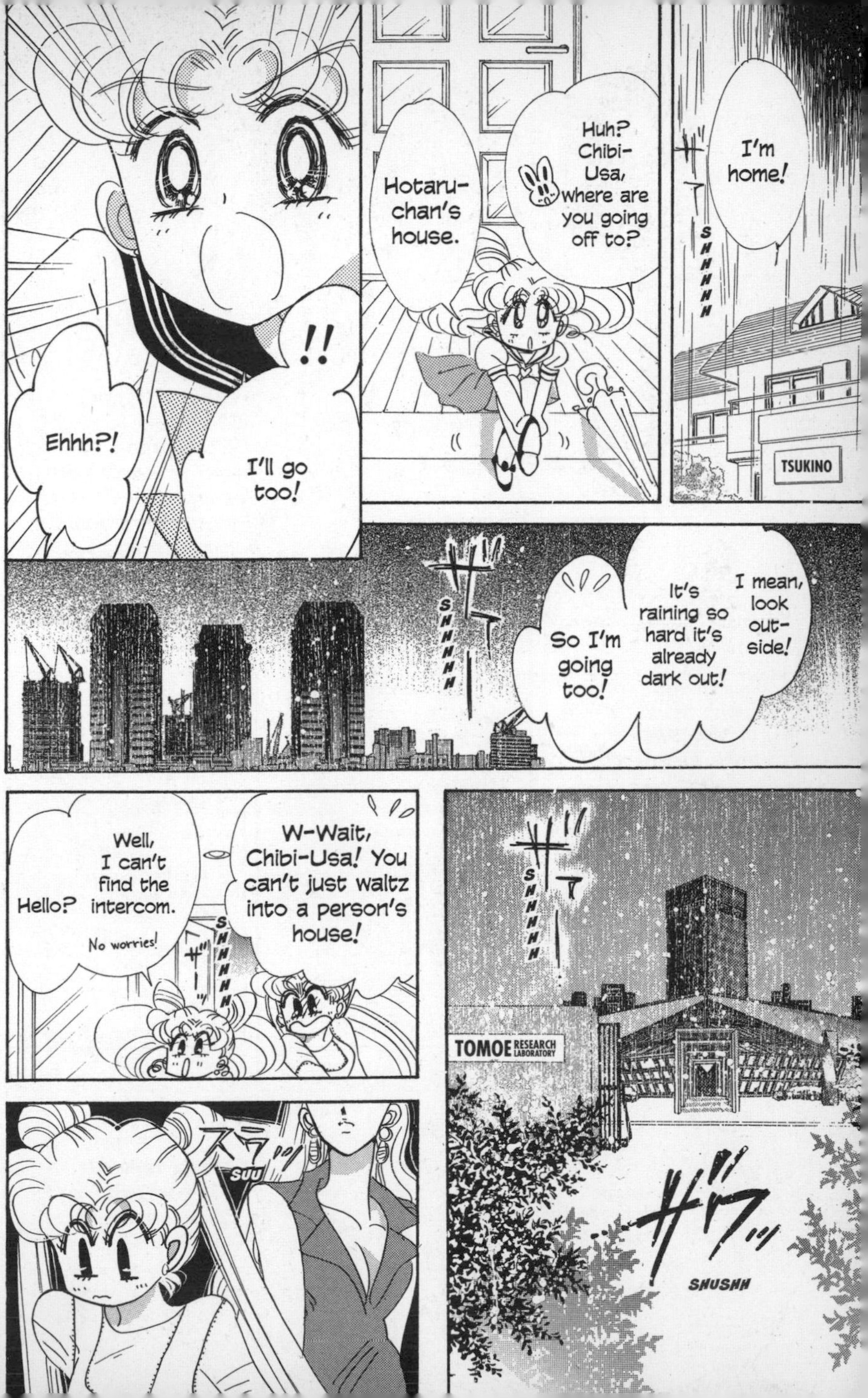
I'm home!
SHHHHH
TSUKINO
Huh? Chibi-Usa, where are you going off to?
Hotaru-chan's house.
!!
I'll go too!
Ehhh?!
SHHHHH
I mean, look out-side!
It's raining so hard it's already dark out!
So I'm going too!
SHHHHH
TOMOE RESEARCH LABORATORY
SHUSHH
W-Wait, Chibi-Usa! You can't just waltz into a person's house!
Well, I can't find the intercom.
Hello?
No worries!
SHHHHH
SUU

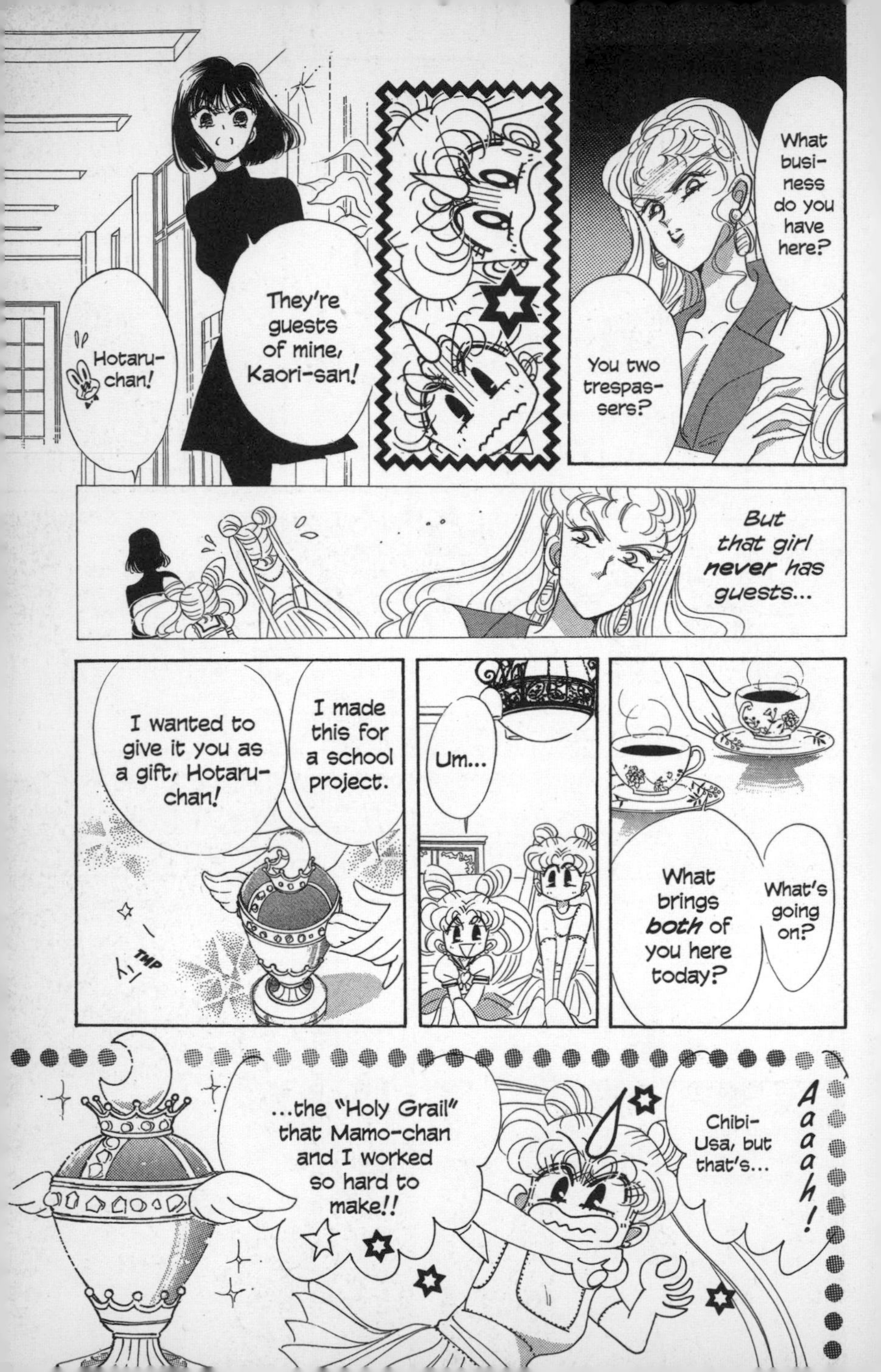
What business do you have here?
You two trespassers?
They're guests of mine, Kaori-san!
Hotaru-chan!
But that girl never has guests...
What's going on?
What brings both of you here today?
Um...
I made this for a school project.
I wanted to give it you as a gift, Hotaru-chan!
TMP
Aaaah!
Chibi-Usa, but that's...
...the "Holy Grail" that Mamo-chan and I worked so hard to make!!

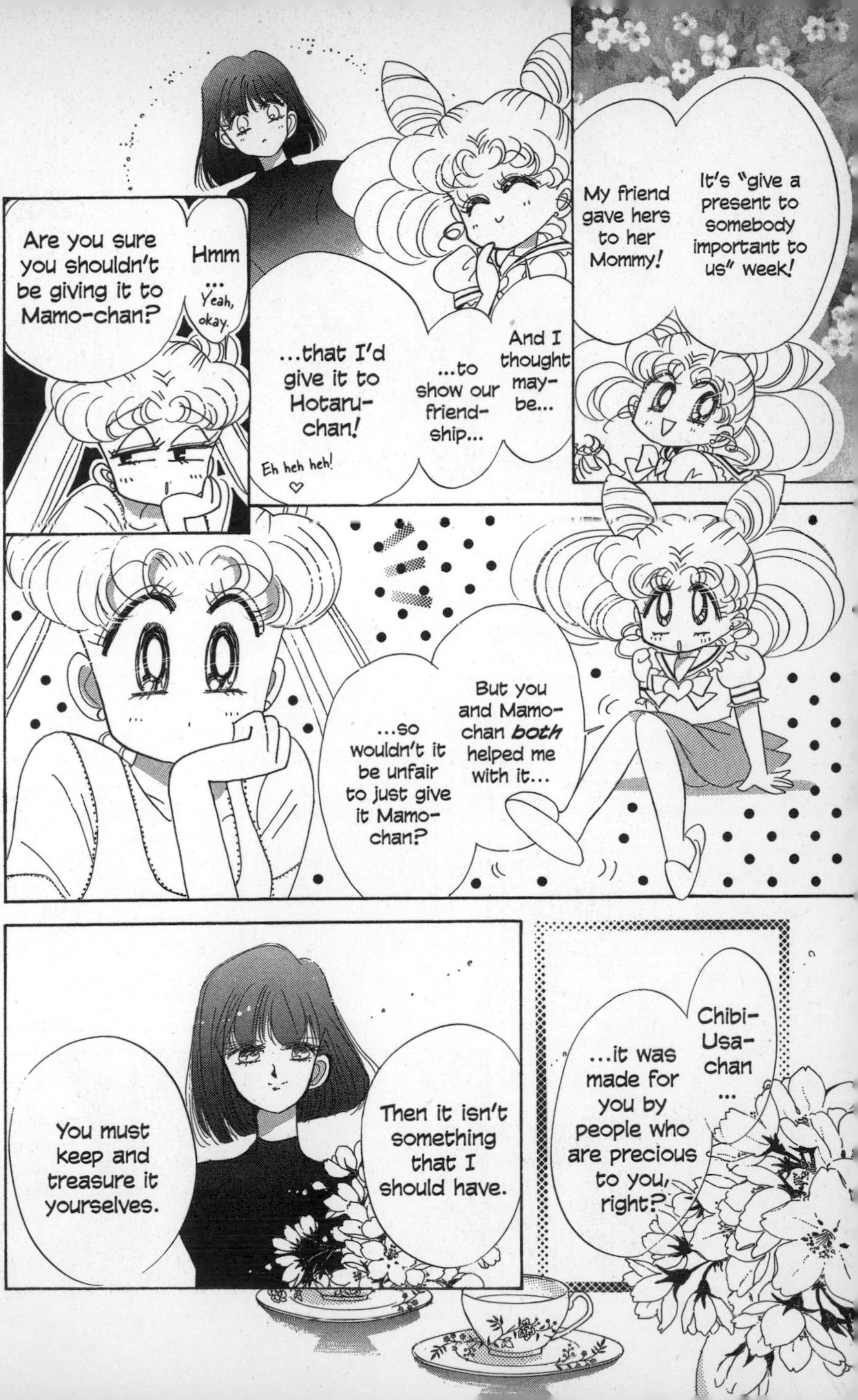
It's "give a present to somebody important to us" week!
My friend gave hers to her Mommy!
And I thought may-be...
...to show our friend-ship...
...that I'd give it to Hotaru-chan!
Eh heh heh! ♡
Hmm ... Yeah, okay.
Are you sure you shouldn't be giving it to Mamo-chan?
But you and Mamo-chan *both* helped me with it...
...so wouldn't it be unfair to just give it Mamo-chan?
Chibi-Usa-chan ...
...it was made for you by people who are precious to you, right?
Then it isn't something that I should have.
You must keep and treasure it yourselves.

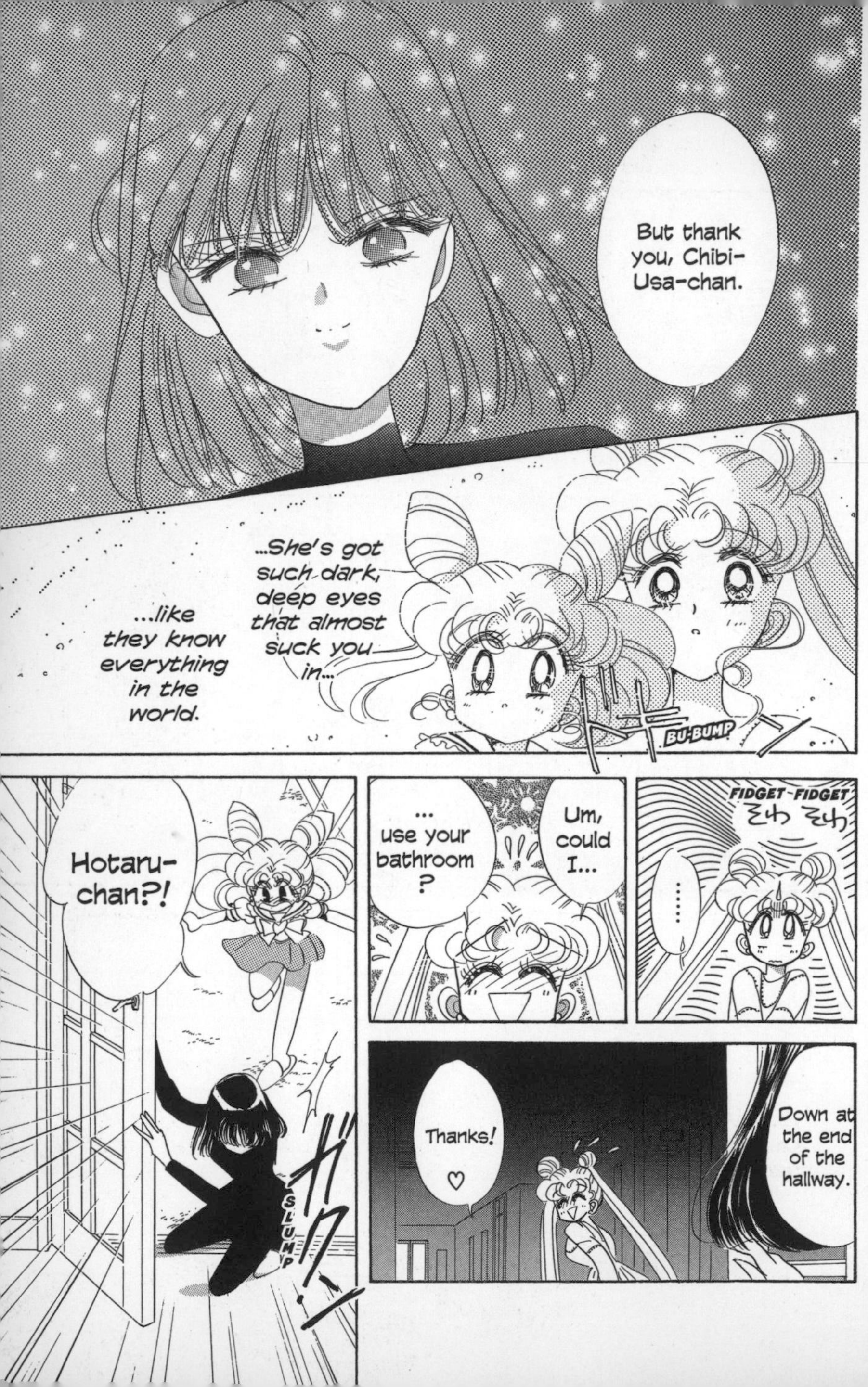
But thank you, Chibi-Usa-chan.
...She's got such dark, deep eyes that almost suck you in...
...like they know everything in the world.
BU-BUMP
FIDGET-FIDGET
そわ そわ
......
Um, could I...
... use your bathroom ?
Down at the end of the hallway.
Thanks! ♡
Hotaru-chan?!
SLUMP

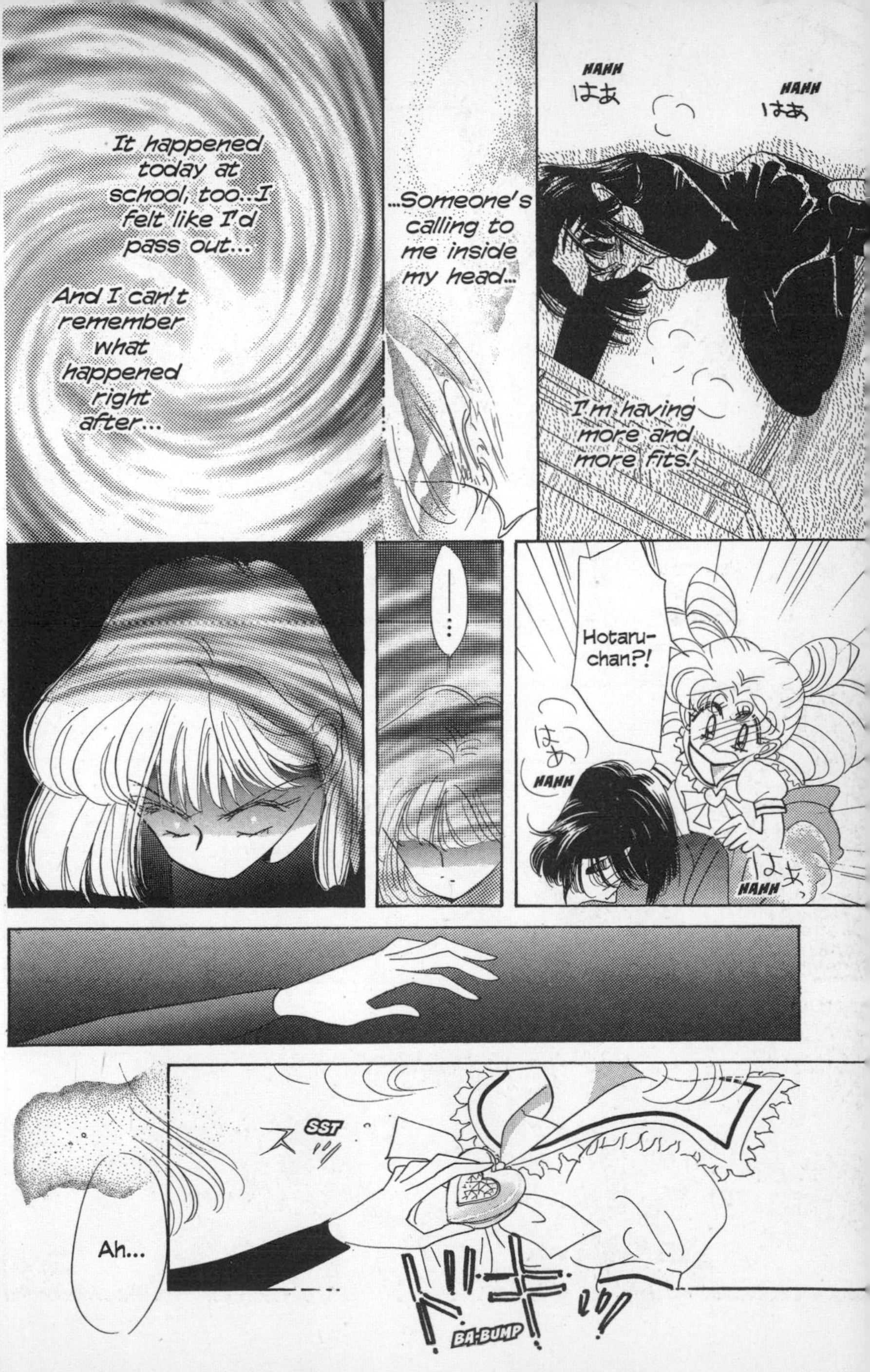
HAHN
はあ
HAHN
はあ
I'm having more and more fits!
...Someone's calling to me inside my head...
It happened today at school, too...I felt like I'd pass out...
And I can't remember what happened right after...
Hotaru-chan?!
はあ
HAHN
はあ
HAHN
...!
SST
スッ
Ah...
BA-BUMP

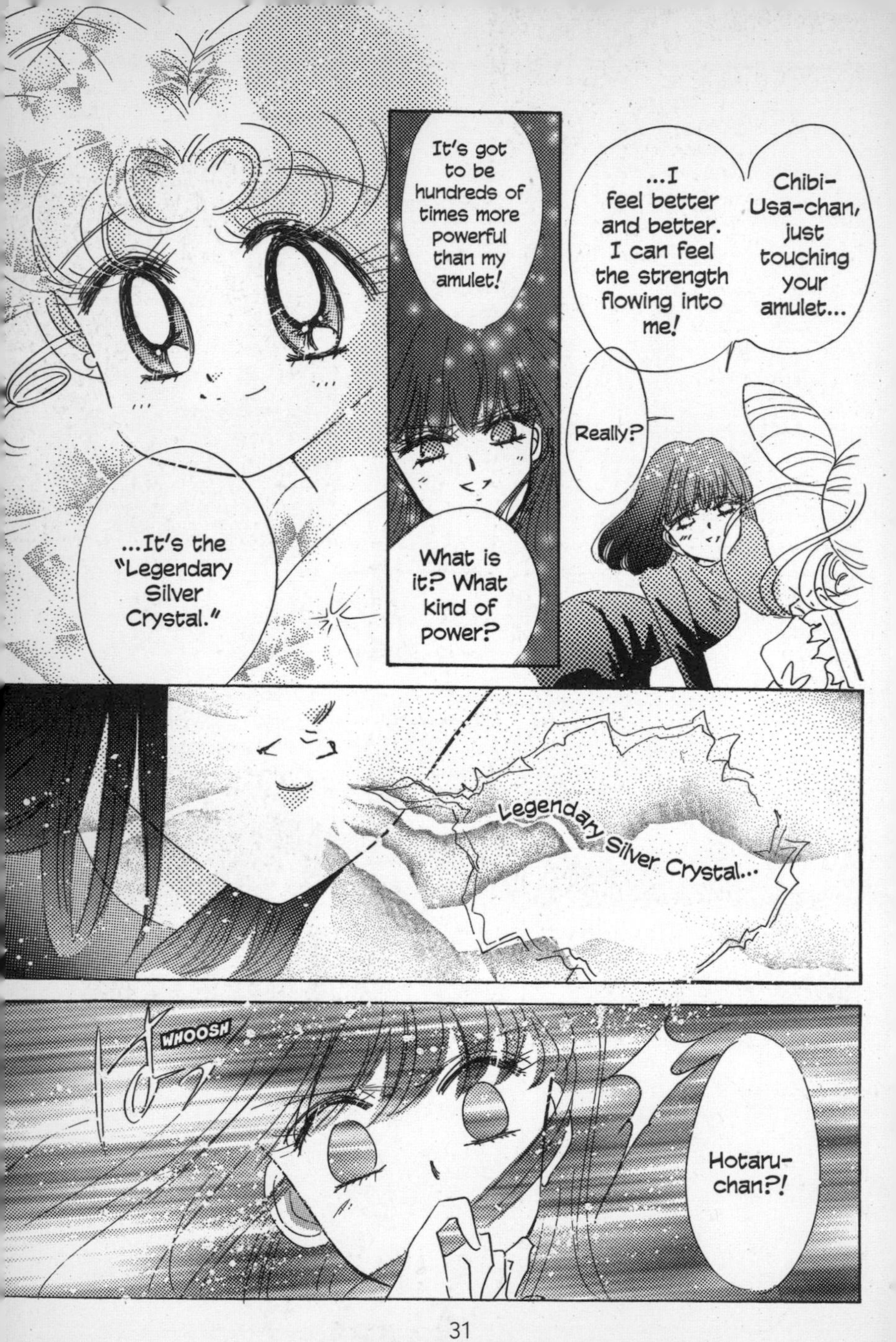
Chibi-Usa-chan, just touching your amulet...
...I feel better and better. I can feel the strength flowing into me!
Really?
It's got to be hundreds of times more powerful than my amulet!
What is it? What kind of power?
...It's the "Legendary Silver Crystal."
Legendary Silver Crystal...
Hotaru-chan?!
WHOOSH

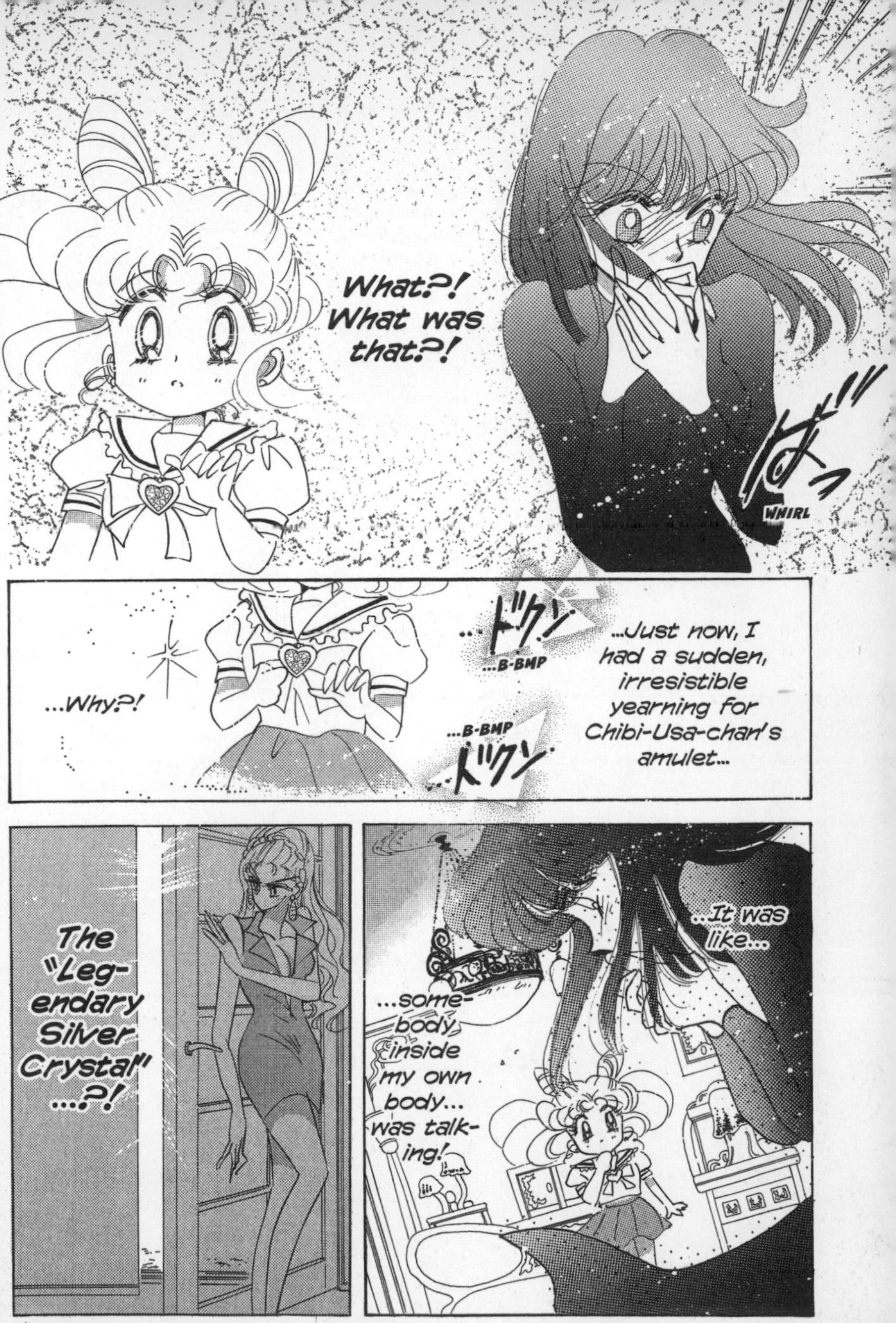
What?! What was that?!
ばっ
WHIRL
...Just now, I had a sudden, irresistible yearning for Chibi-Usa-chan's amulet...
...ドクン
...B-BMP
...B-BMP
...ドクン
...Why?!
...It was like...
...some-body inside my own body... was talk-ing!
The "Leg-endary Silver Crystal" ...?!

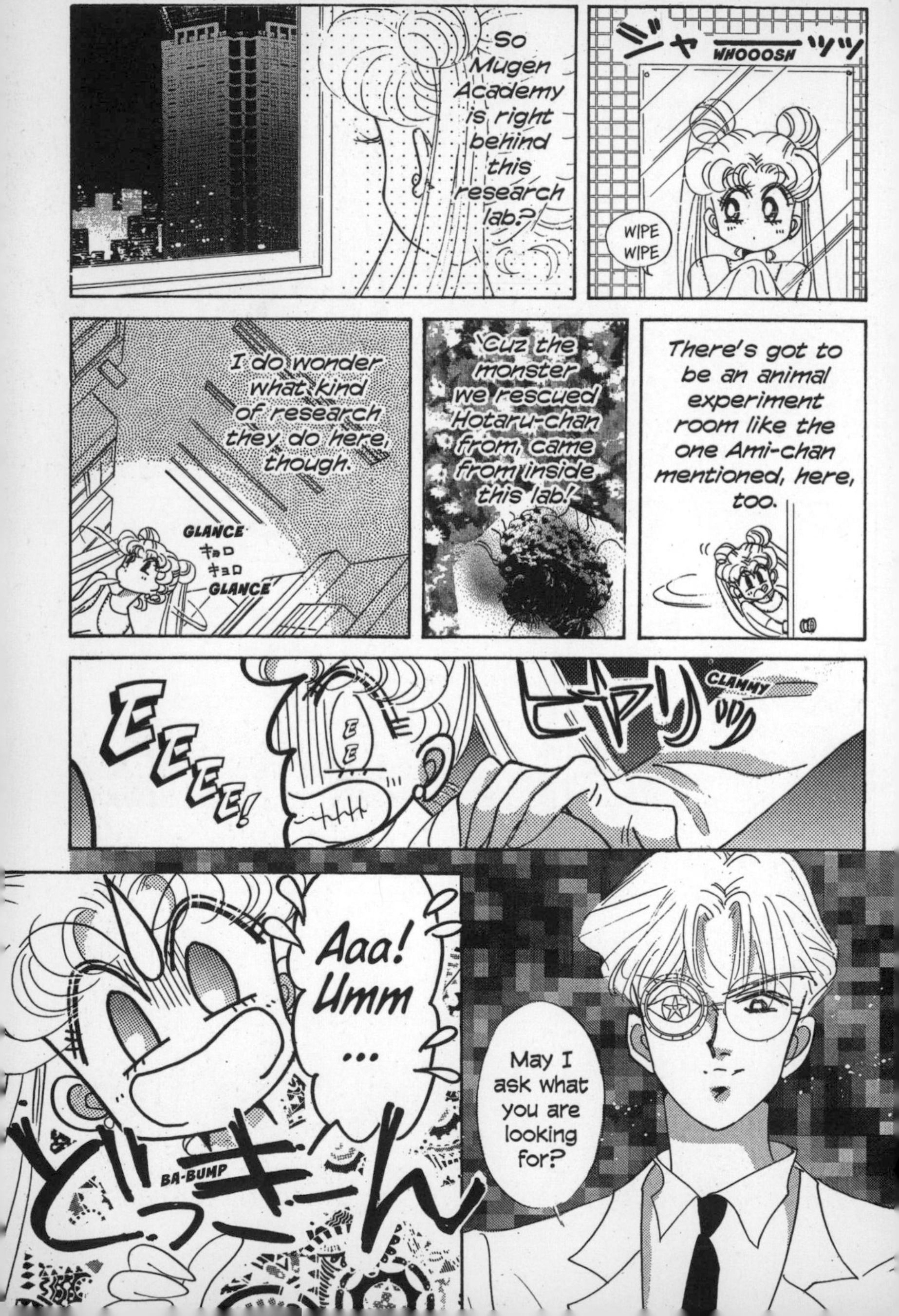
ジャッ
WHOOOSH
ッ
WIPE WIPE
So Mugen Academy is right behind this research lab?
There's got to be an animal experiment room like the one Ami-chan mentioned, here, too.
'Cuz the monster we rescued Hotaru-chan from, came from inside this lab!
I do wonder what kind of research they do here, though.
GLANCE
キョロ
キョロ
GLANCE
ヒヤリッ
CLAMMY
E
E
EEEEE!
May I ask what you are looking for?
Aaa! Umm ...
どっきーん
BA-BUMP

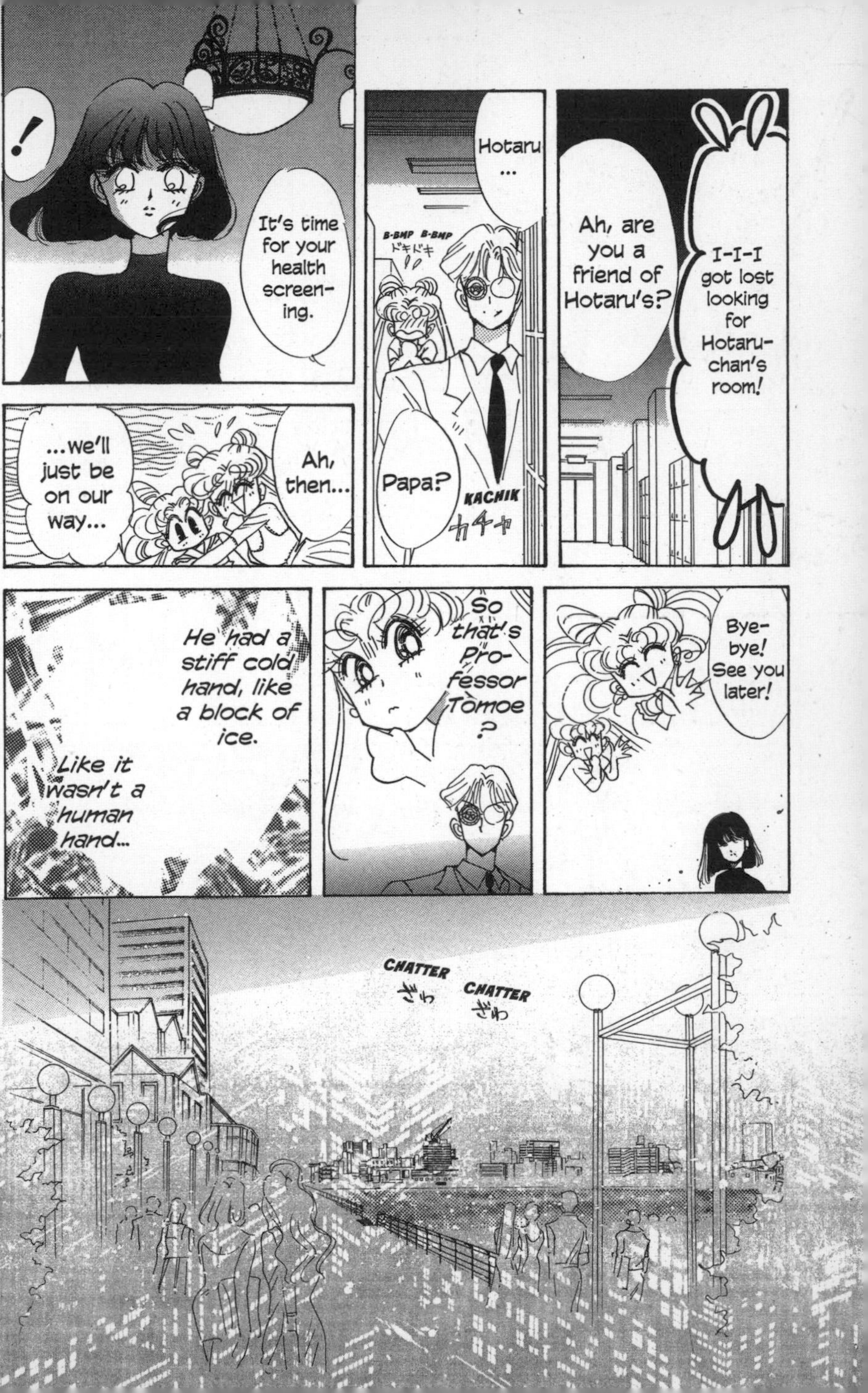
I-I-I got lost looking for Hotaru-chan's room!
Ah, are you a friend of Hotaru's?
Hotaru...
B-BMP B-BMP
ドキドキ
KACHIK
カチャ
Papa?
!
It's time for your health screening.
Ah, then...
...we'll just be on our way...
Bye-bye! See you later!
So that's Professor Tomoe?
He had a stiff cold hand, like a block of ice.
Like it wasn't a human hand...
CHATTER
ざわ
CHATTER
ざわ

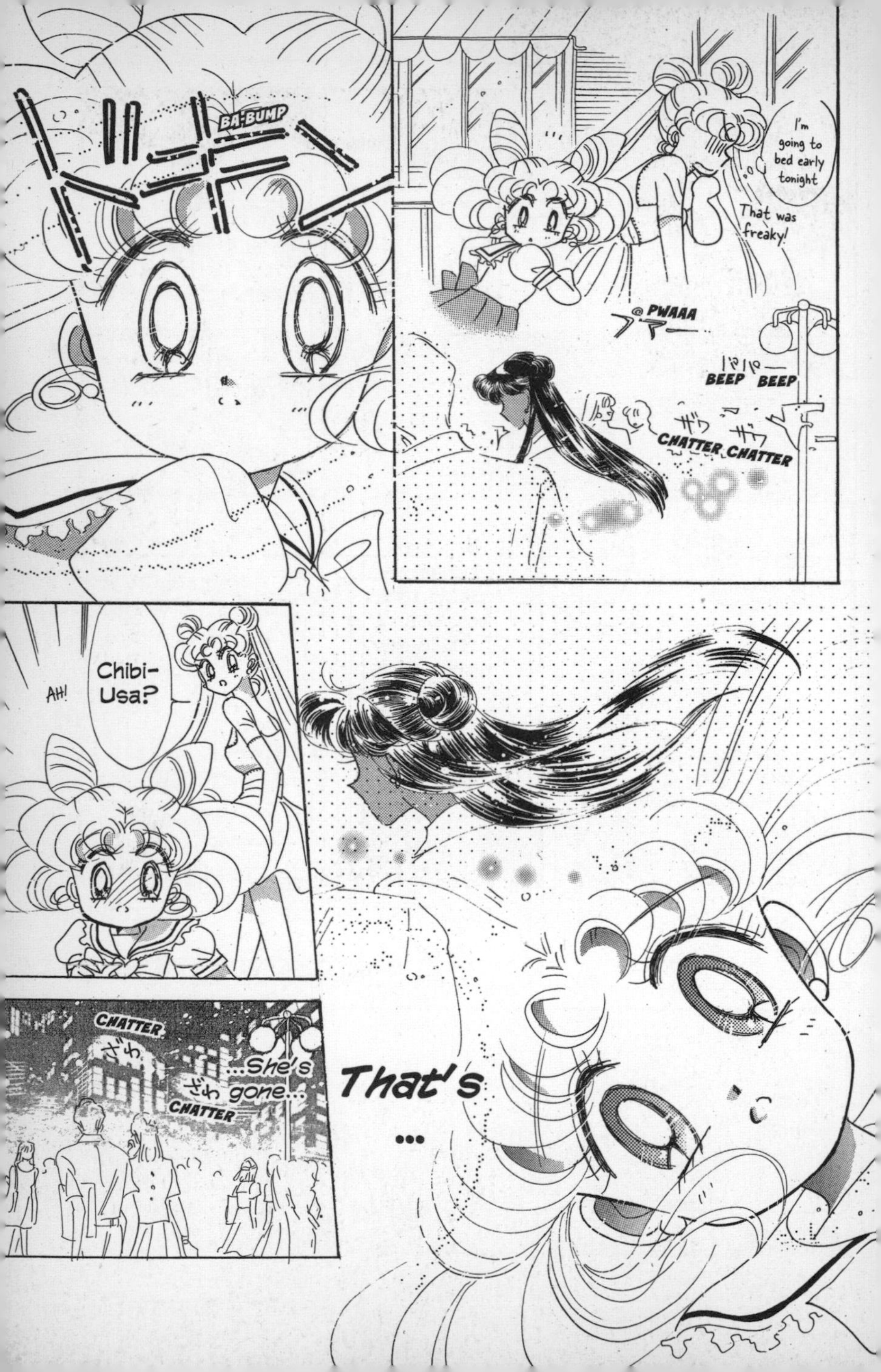
I'm going to bed early tonight
That was freaky!
PWAAA
BEEP BEEP
CHATTER CHATTER
BA-BUMP
That's ...
AH!
Chibi-Usa?
CHATTER
...She's gone...
CHATTER

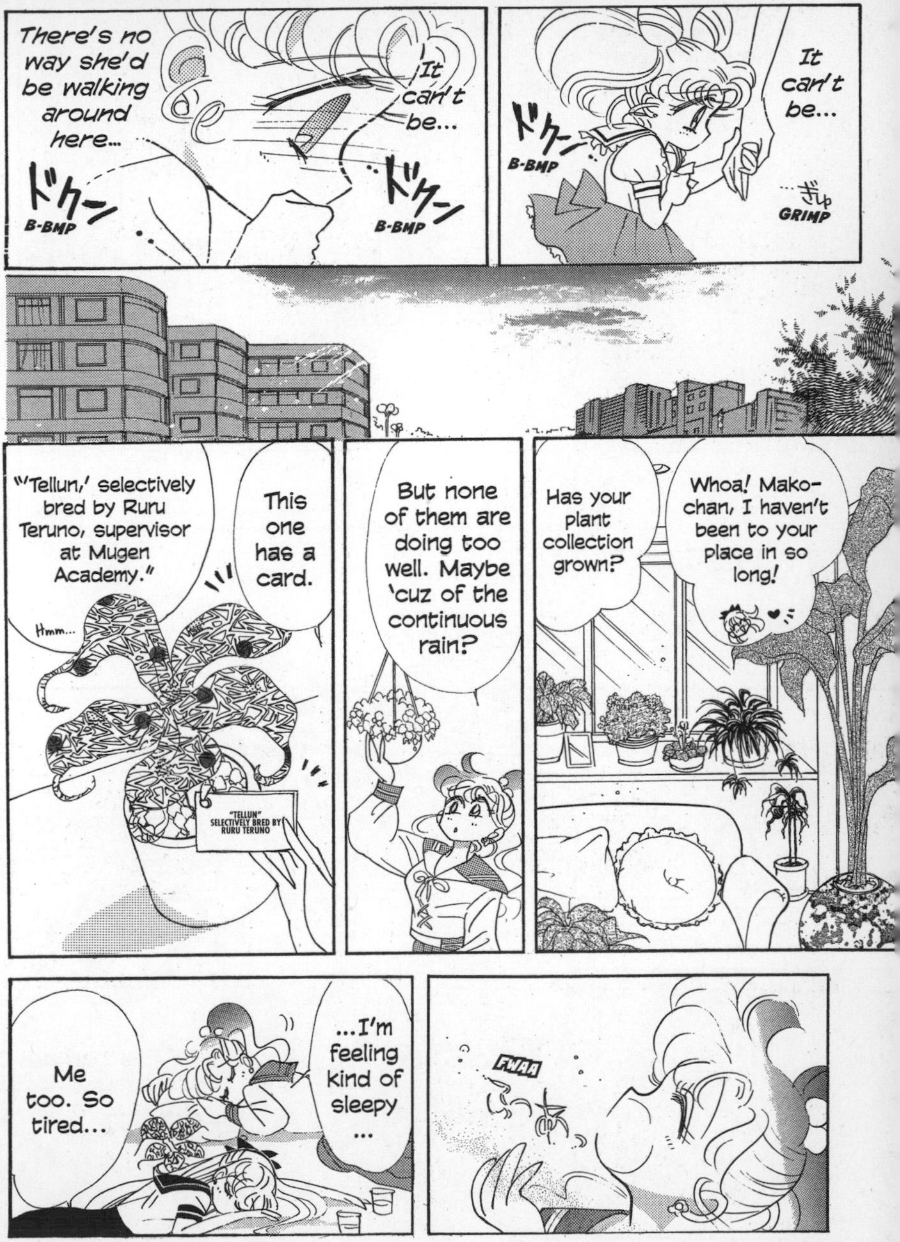
It can't be...
ドクーン
B-BMP
...ぎゅ
GRIMP
It can't be...
There's no way she'd be walking around here...
ドクーン
B-BMP
ドクーン
B-BMP
Whoa! Mako-chan, I haven't been to your place in so long!
Has your plant collection grown?
But none of them are doing too well. Maybe 'cuz of the continuous rain?
This one has a card.
"'Tellun,' selectively bred by Ruru Teruno, supervisor at Mugen Academy."
Hmm...
"TELLUN" SELECTIVELY BRED BY RURU TERUNO
FWAA
...I'm feeling kind of sleepy ...
Me too. So tired...

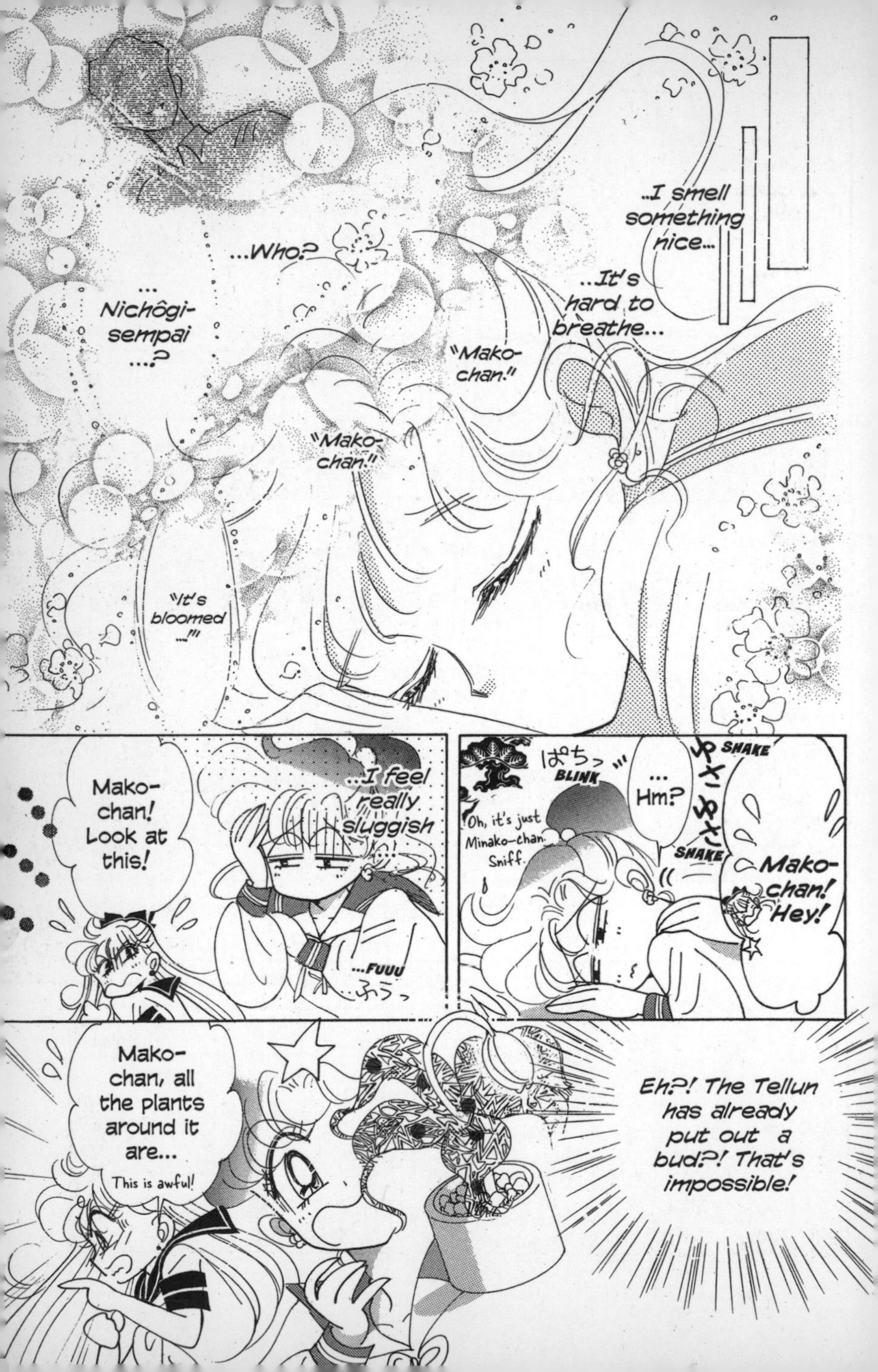

...I smell something nice...
...It's hard to breathe...
"Mako-chan."
...Who?
... Nichôgi-sempai ...?
"Mako-chan."
"It's bloomed ...!"
Mako-chan! Hey!
ゆさゆさ SHAKE SHAKE
... Hm?
ぱちっ BLINK
Oh, it's just Minako-chan. Sniff.
...I feel really sluggish ...!
Mako-chan! Look at this!
...FUUU ふうっ
Eh?! The Tellun has already put out a bud?! That's impossible!
Mako-chan, all the plants around it are...
This is awful!

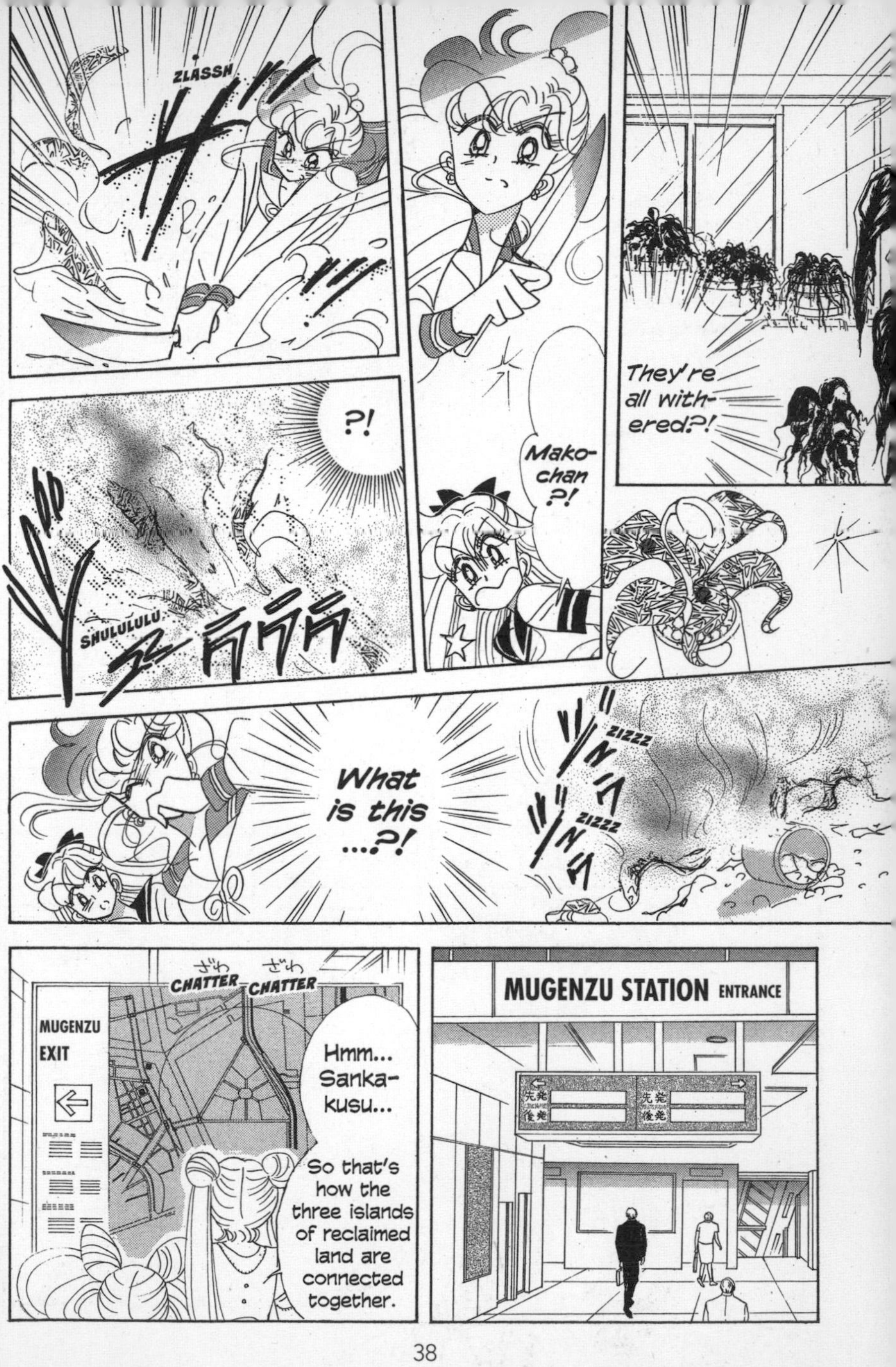
They're all withered?!
ZLASSH
Mako-chan ?!
?!
SHULULULU
ZIZZZ
What is this ...?!
ZIZZZ
MUGENZU STATION ENTRANCE
ざわ ざわ
CHATTER CHATTER
MUGENZU EXIT
Hmm... Sankakusu...
So that's how the three islands of reclaimed land are connected together.

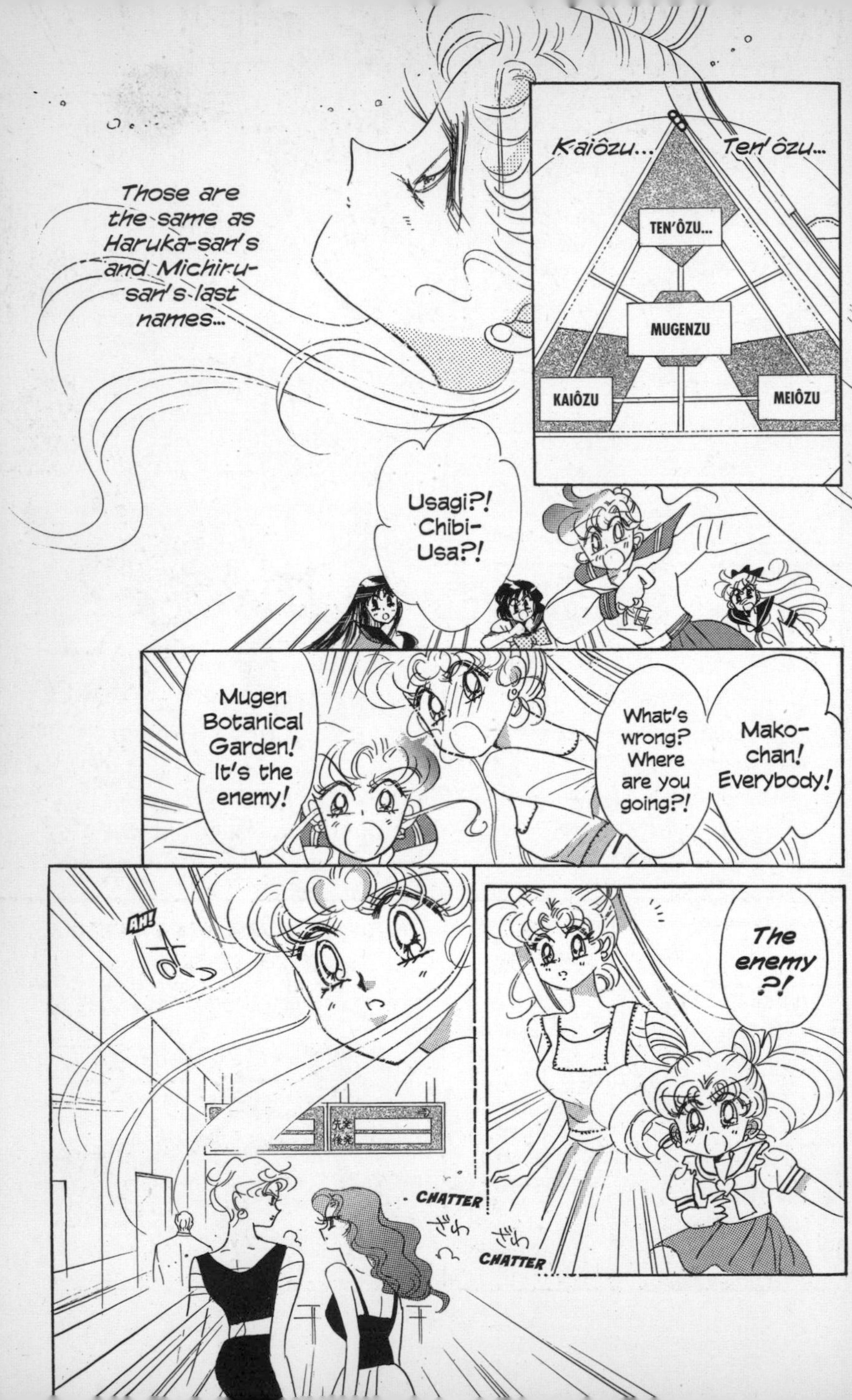
Kaiôzu...
Ten'ôzu...
TEN'ÔZU...
MUGENZU
KAIÔZU
MEIÔZU
Those are the same as Haruka-san's and Michiru-san's last names...
Usagi?! Chibi-Usa?!
Mako-chan! Everybody!
What's wrong? Where are you going?!
Mugen Botanical Garden! It's the enemy!
The enemy?!
AH!
CHATTER
ざわ
ざわ
CHATTER

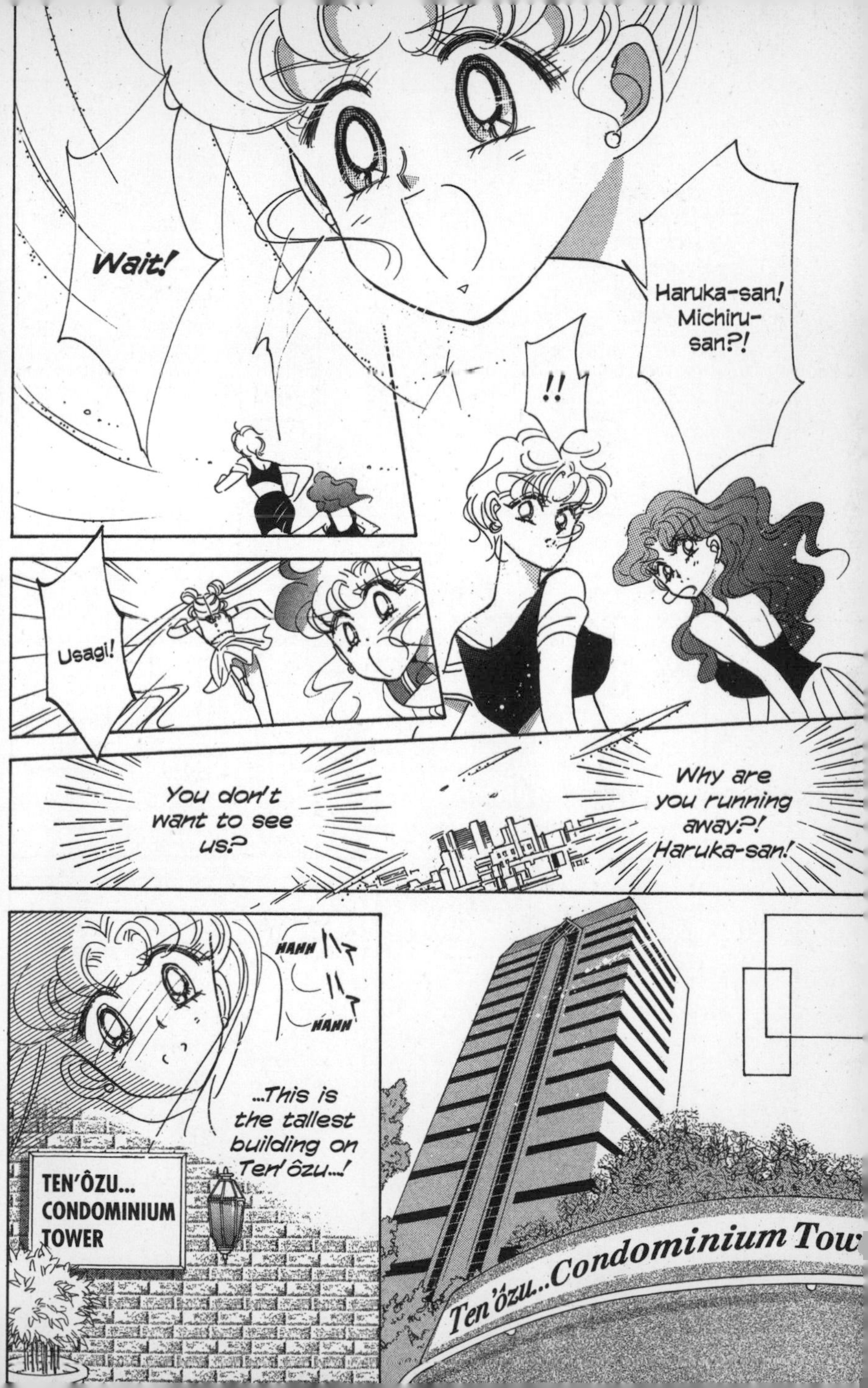

Haruka-san! Michiru-san?!
!!
Wait!
Usagi!
Why are you running away?! Haruka-san!
You don't want to see us?
Ten'ôzu...Condominium Tow
HANH
HANH
...This is the tallest building on Ten'ôzu...!
TEN'ÔZU... CONDOMINIUM TOWER

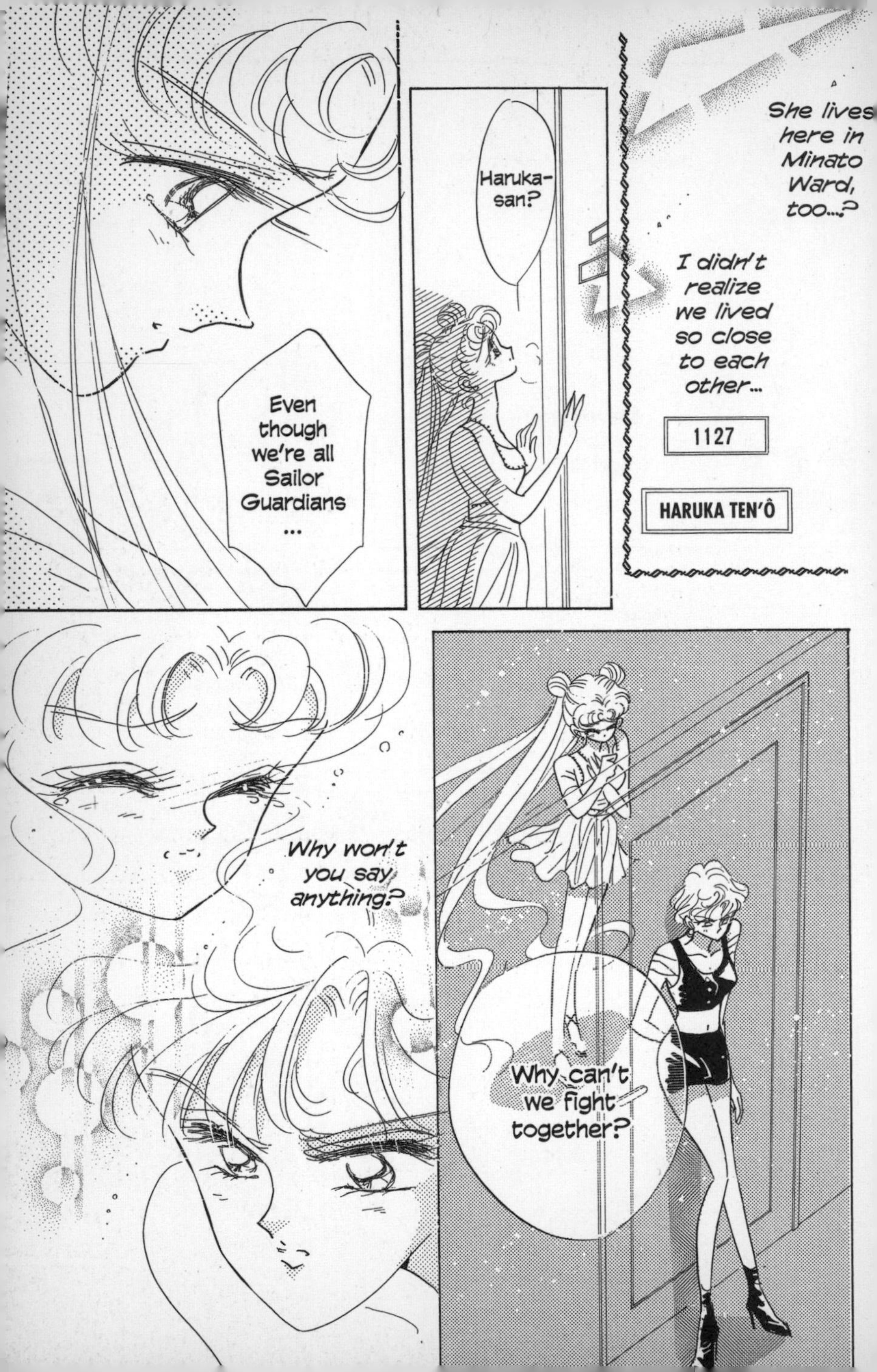
She lives here in Minato Ward, too...?
I didn't realize we lived so close to each other...
1127
HARUKA TEN'Ô
Haruka-san?
Even though we're all Sailor Guardians...
Why can't we fight together?
Why won't you say anything?

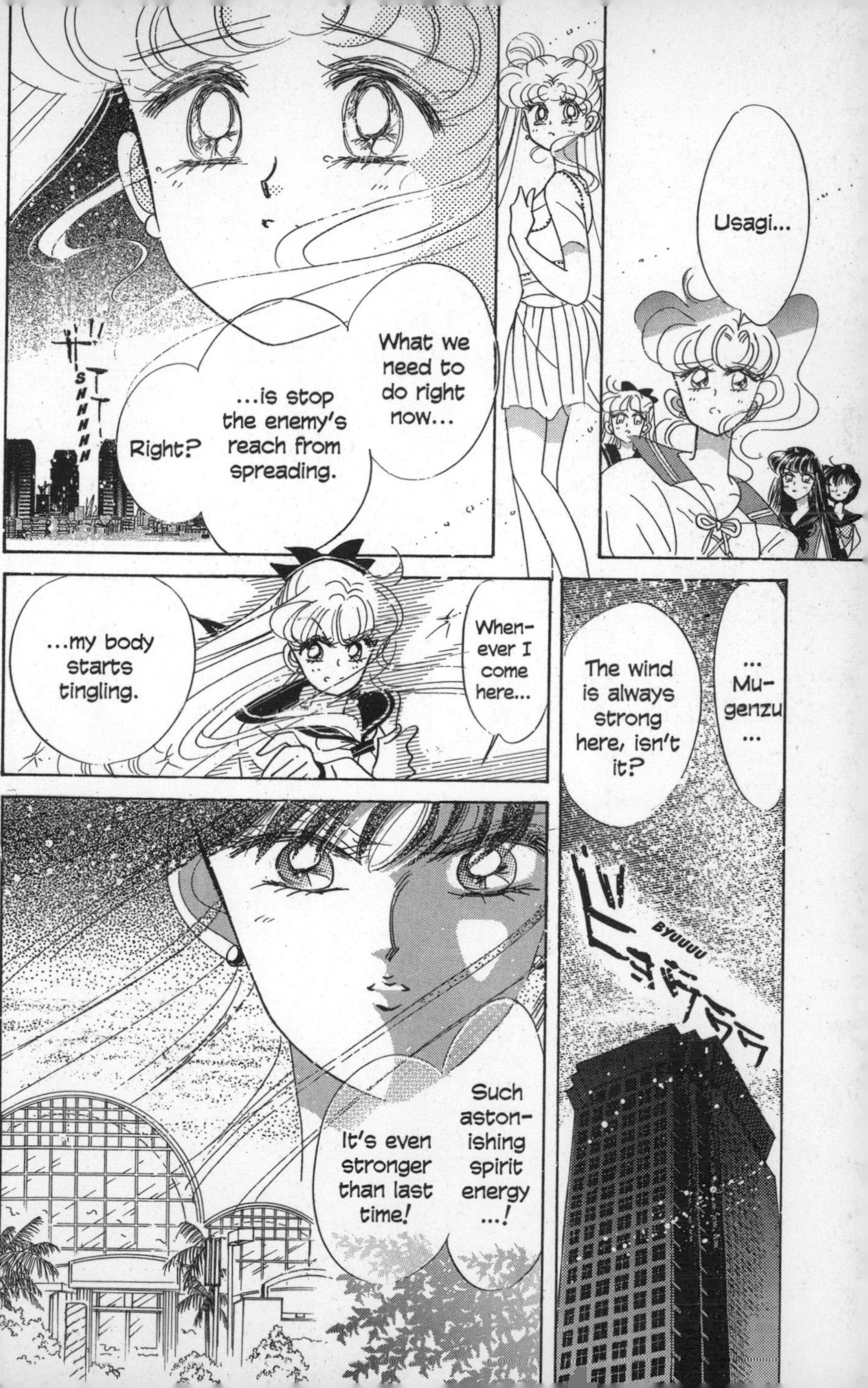
Usagi...
What we need to do right now...
...is stop the enemy's reach from spreading.
Right?
SHHHHH
... Mugenzu ...
The wind is always strong here, isn't it?
BYUUUU
When-ever I come here...
...my body starts tingling.
Such aston-ishing spirit energy ...!
It's even stronger than last time!

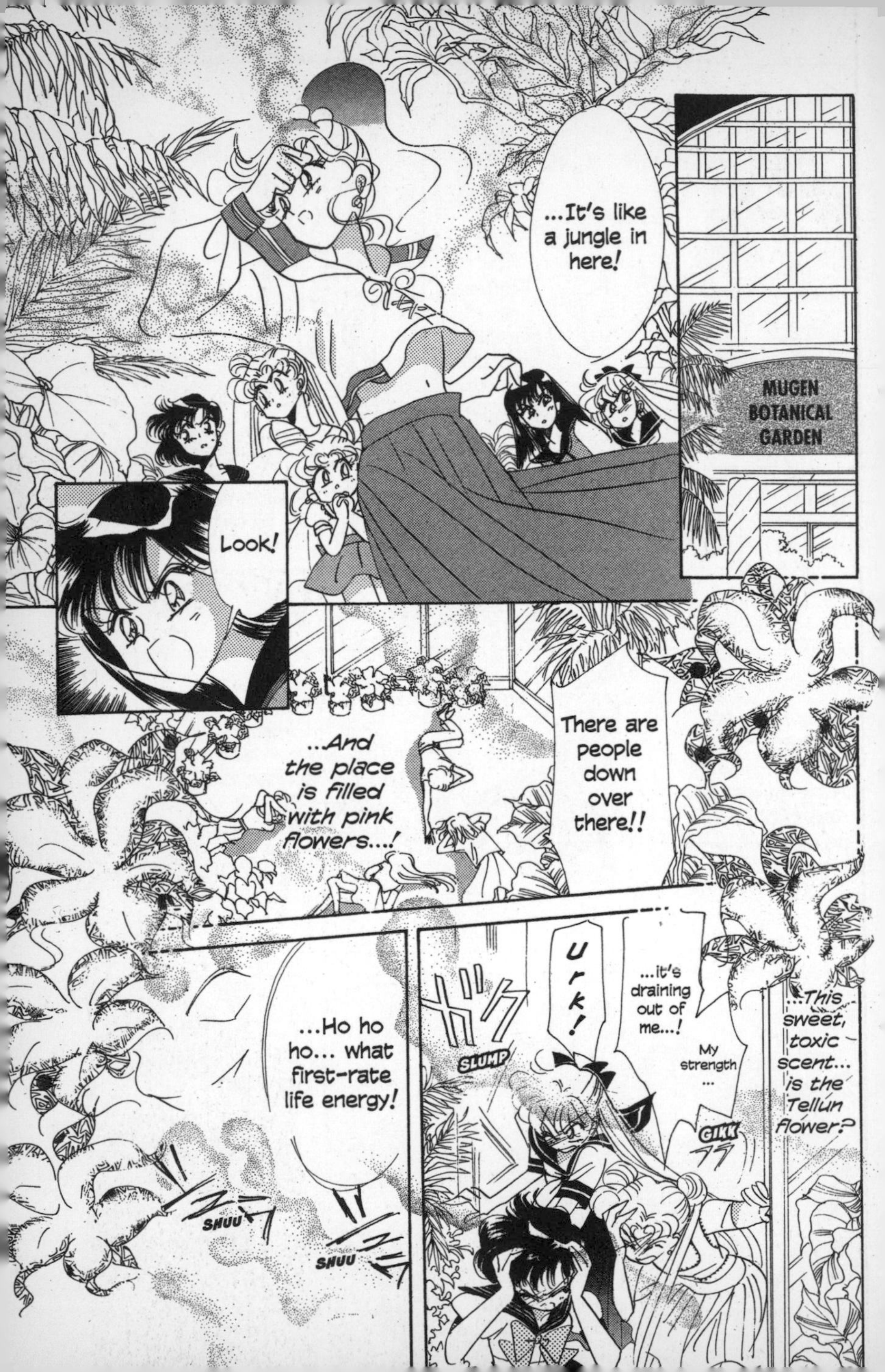
MUGEN BOTANICAL GARDEN
...It's like a jungle in here!
Look!
There are people down over there!!
...And the place is filled with pink flowers...!
...This sweet, toxic scent... is the Tellun flower?
My strength ...
...it's draining out of me...!
Urk!
ガク
SLUMP
GINN
...Ho ho ho... what first-rate life energy!
SHUU
SHUU

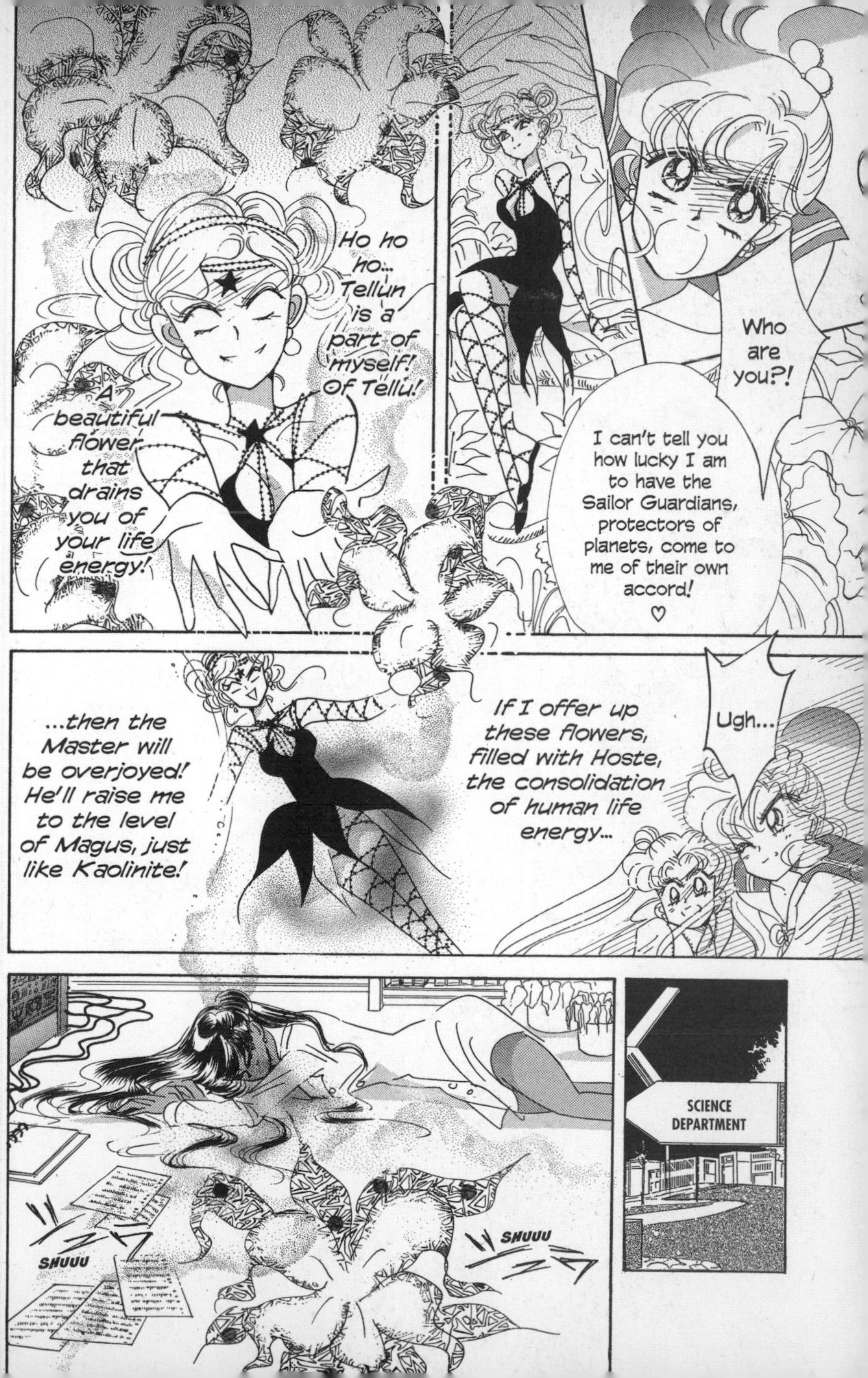
Who are you?!
I can't tell you how lucky I am to have the Sailor Guardians, protectors of planets, come to me of their own accord! ♡
Ho ho ho... Tellun is a part of myself! Of Tellu!
A beautiful flower that drains you of your life energy!
Ugh...
If I offer up these flowers, filled with Hoste, the consolidation of human life energy...
...then the Master will be overjoyed! He'll raise me to the level of Magus, just like Kaolinite!
SCIENCE DEPARTMENT
SHUUU
SHUUU

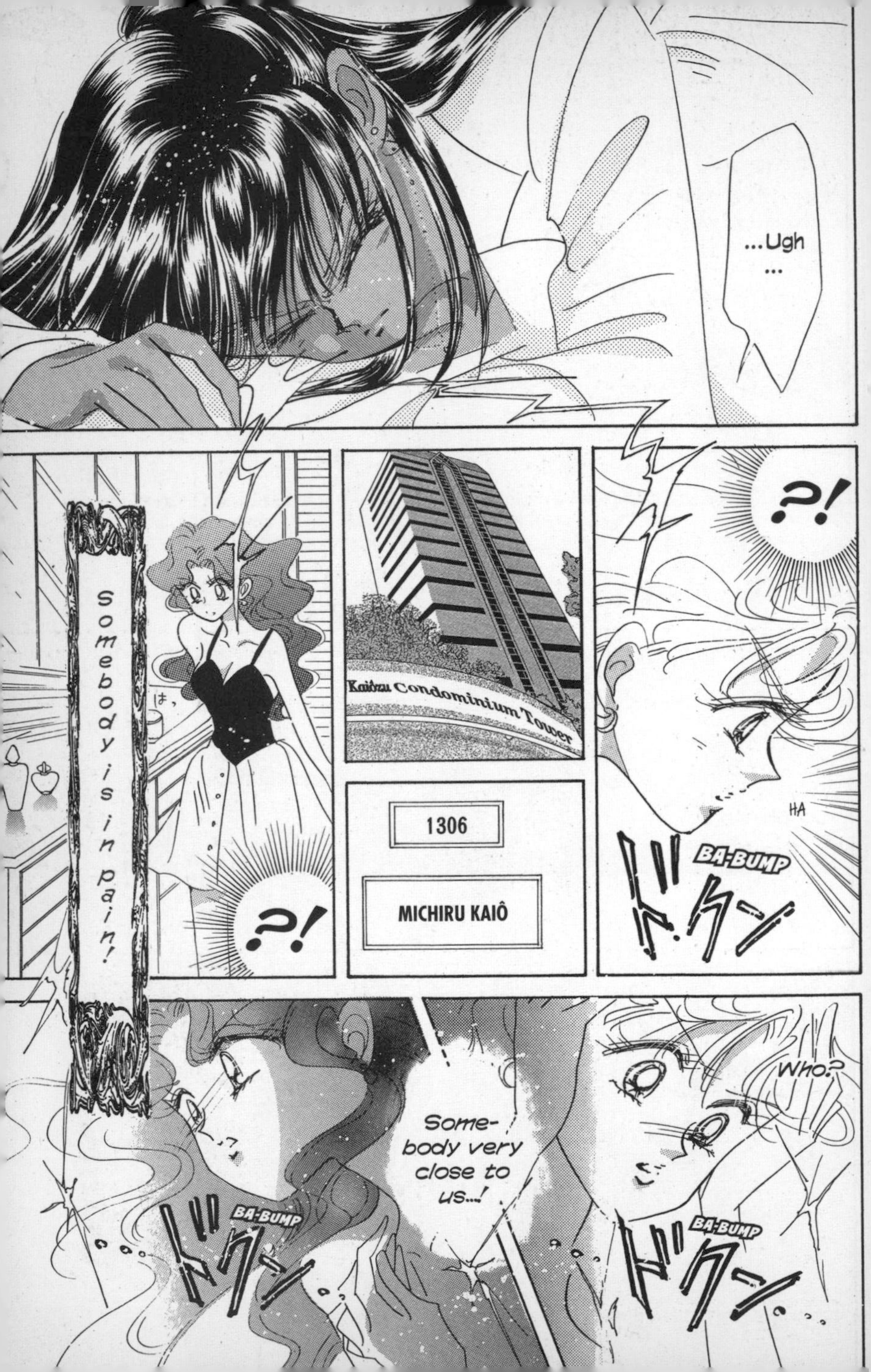
...Ugh
...
?!
HA
BA-BUMP
Kaidzu Condominium Tower
1306
MICHIRU KAIÔ
?!
Somebody is in pain!
Who?
BA-BUMP
Some-body very close to us...!
BA-BUMP

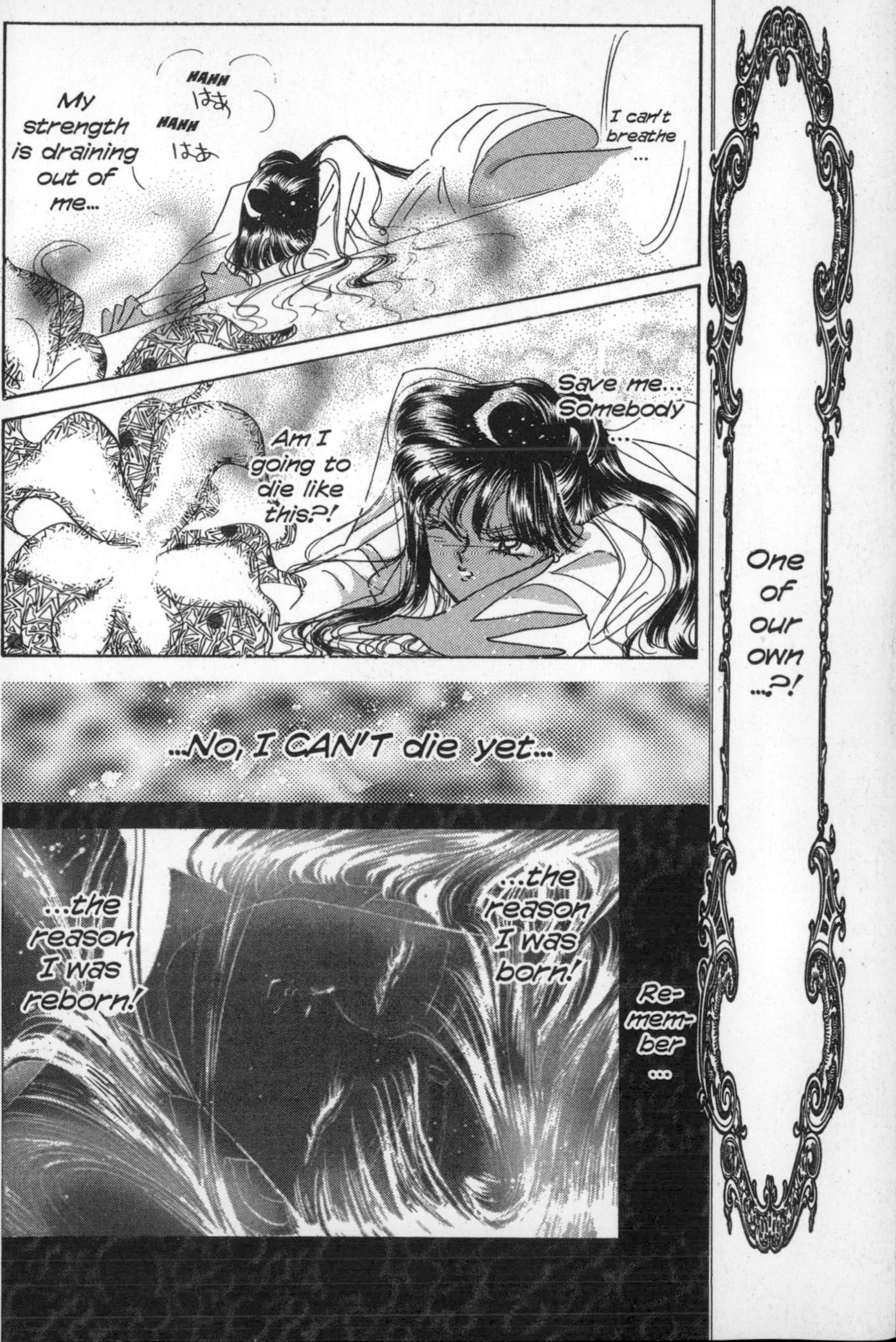
One of our own ...?!
I can't breathe ...
HAHN はあ
HAHN はあ
My strength is draining out of me...
Save me... Somebody ...
Am I going to die like this?!
...No, I CAN'T die yet...
Re-mem-ber ...
...the reason I was born!
...the reason I was reborn!

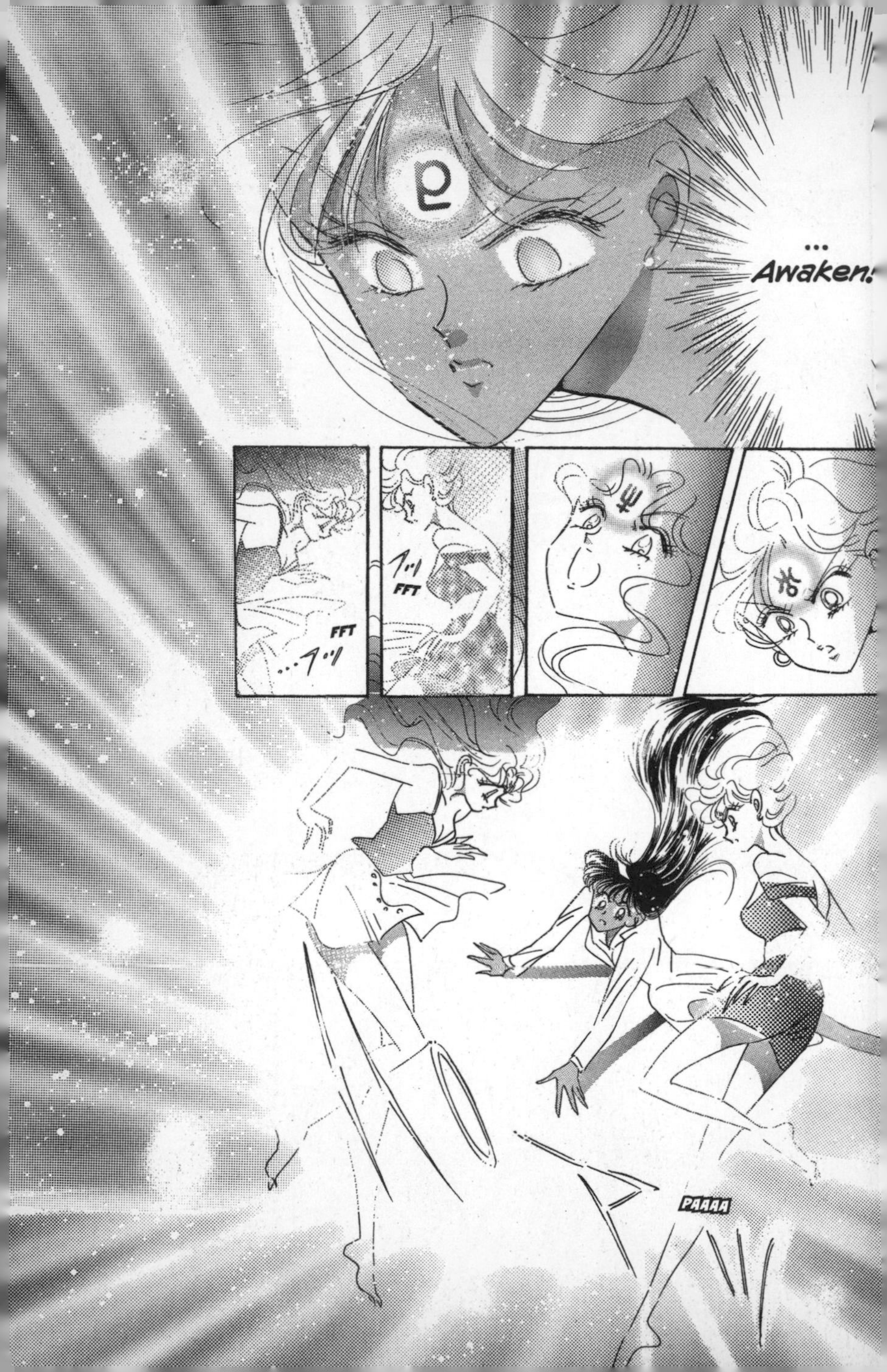
... Awaken!
フッ
FFT
FFT
...フッ
PAAAA

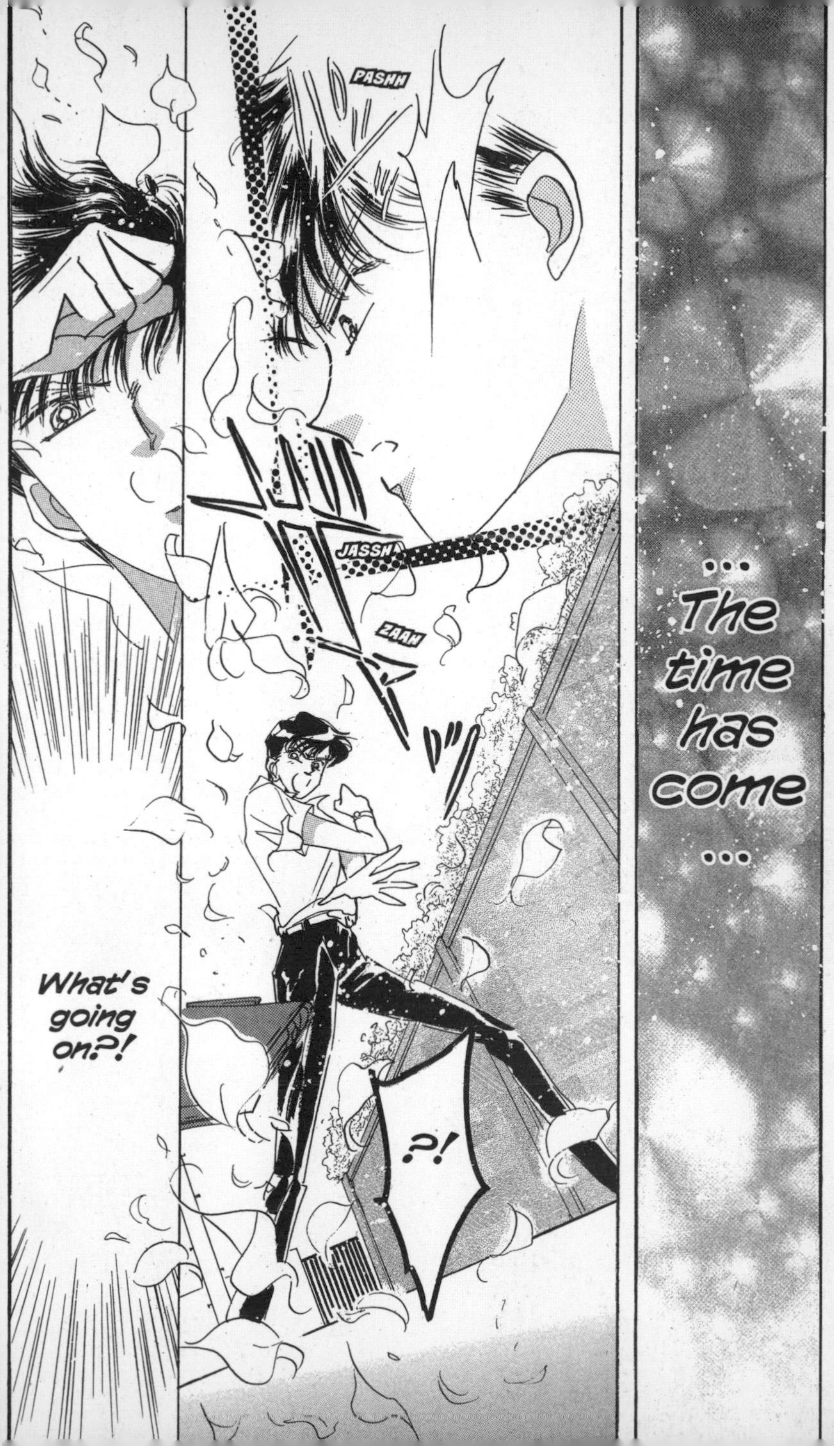
... The time has come ...
PASHH
JASSH
ZAAH
?!
What's going on?!

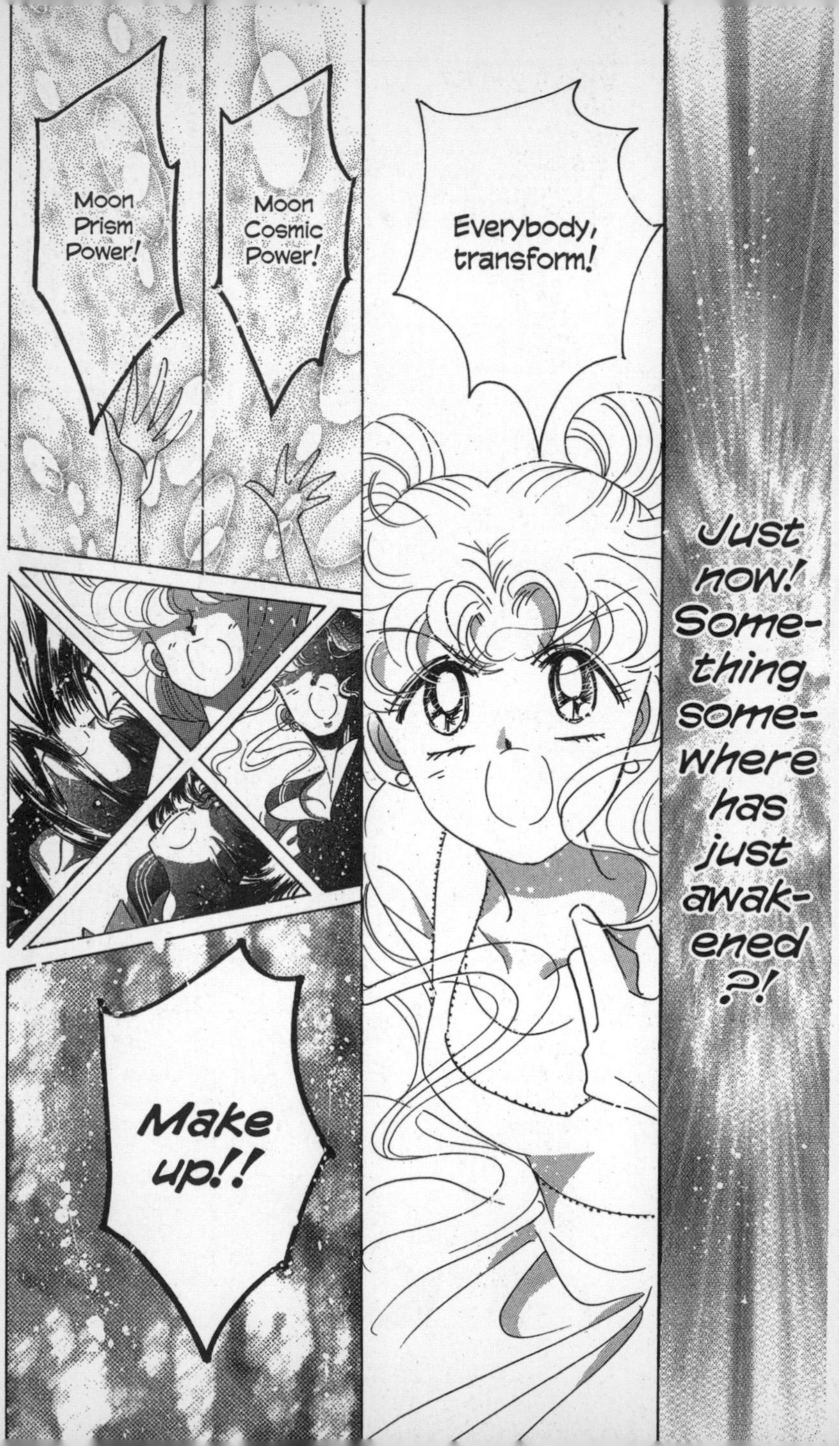
Just now! Some-thing some-where has just awak-ened?!
Everybody, transform!
Moon Cosmic Power!
Moon Prism Power!
Make up!!

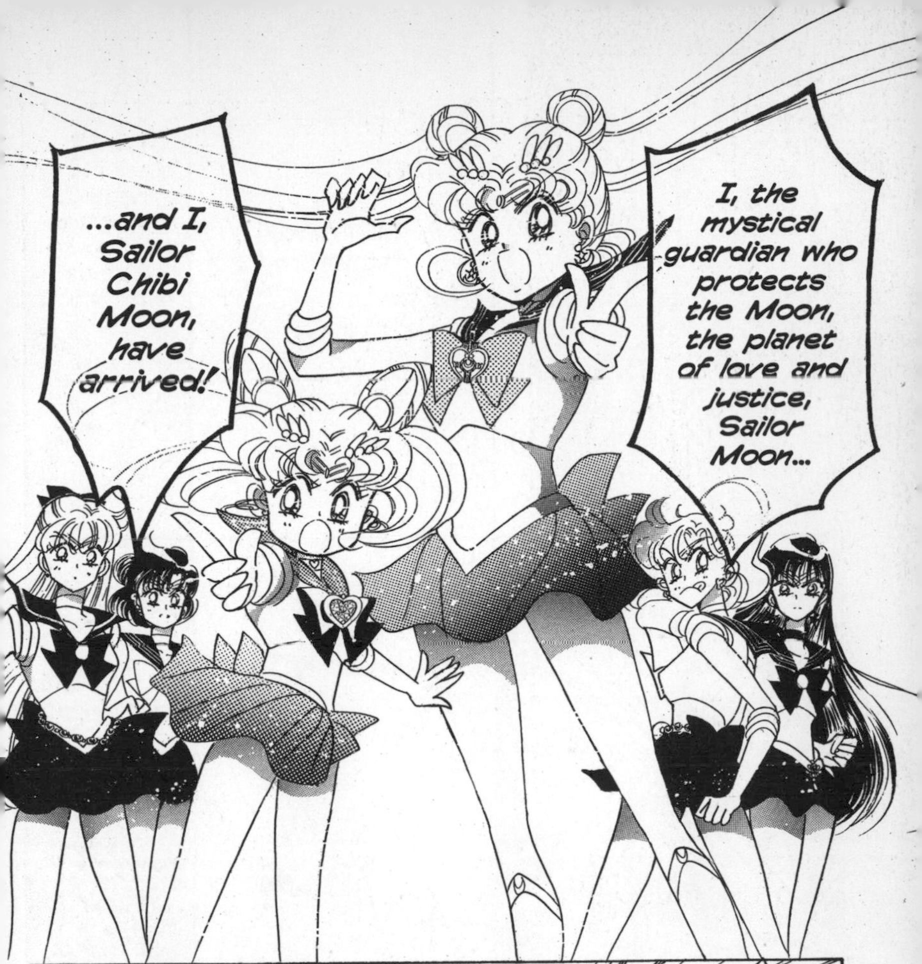
I, the mystical guardian who protects the Moon, the planet of love and justice, Sailor Moon...
...and I, Sailor Chibi Moon, have arrived!

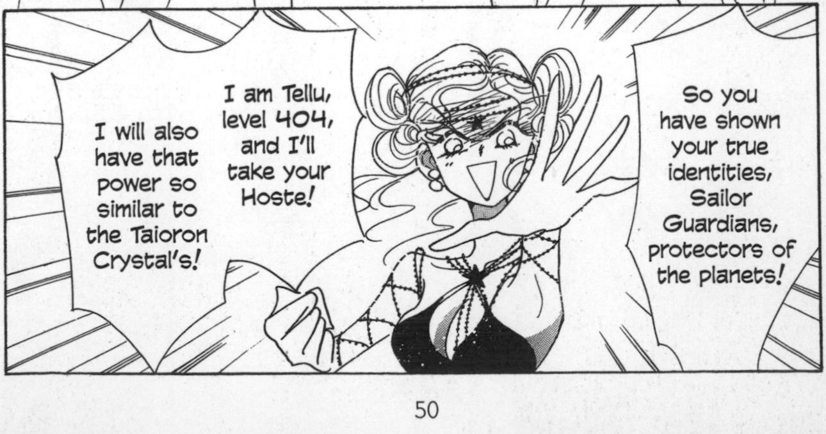
So you have shown your true identities, Sailor Guardians, protectors of the planets!
I am Tellu, level 404, and I'll take your Hoste!
I will also have that power so similar to the Taioron Crystal's!

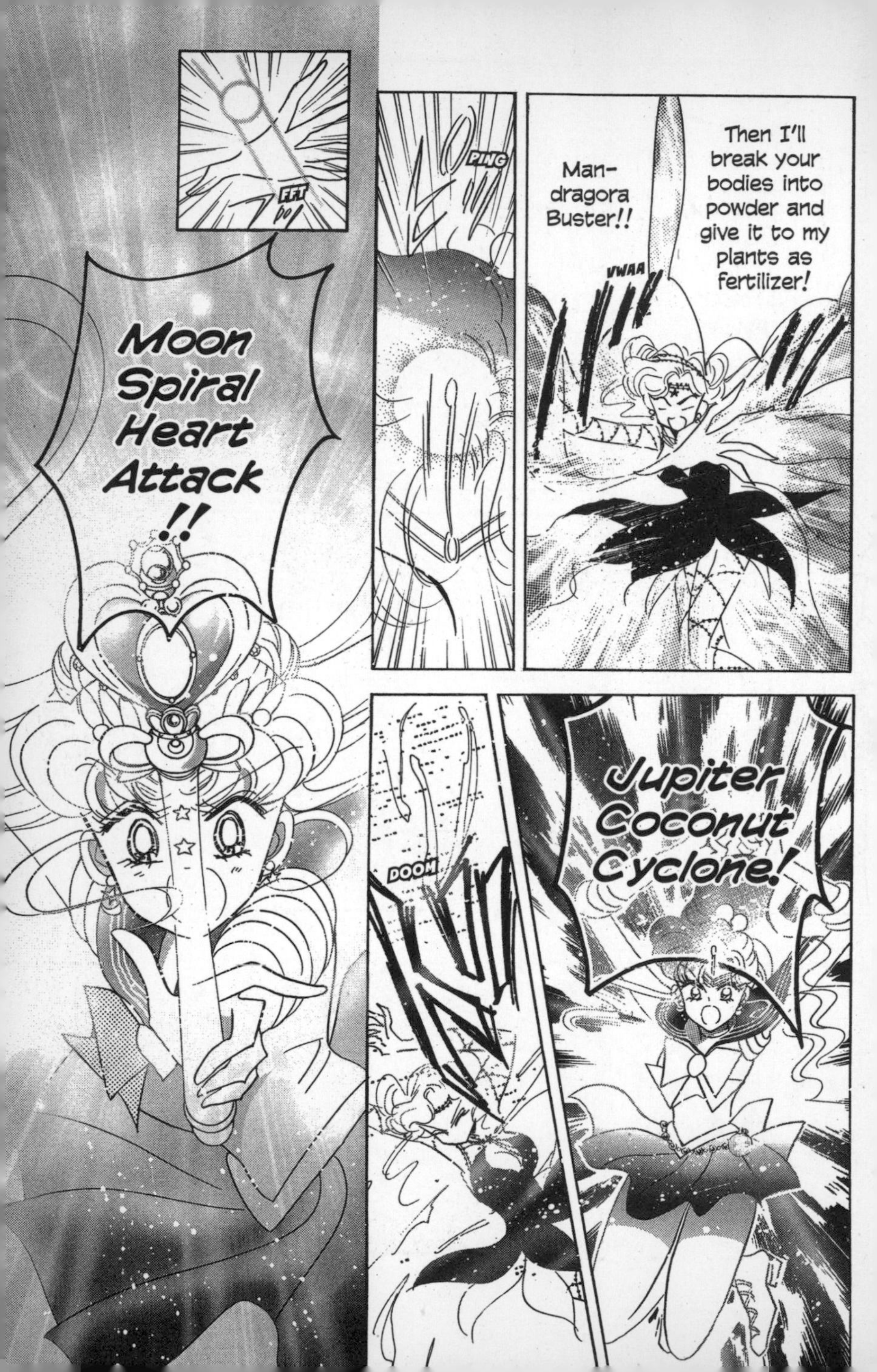

Then I'll break your bodies into powder and give it to my plants as fertilizer!
Man-dragora Buster!!
VWAA
PING
Jupiter Coconut Cyclone!
DOOM
FFT
Moon Spiral Heart Attack!!

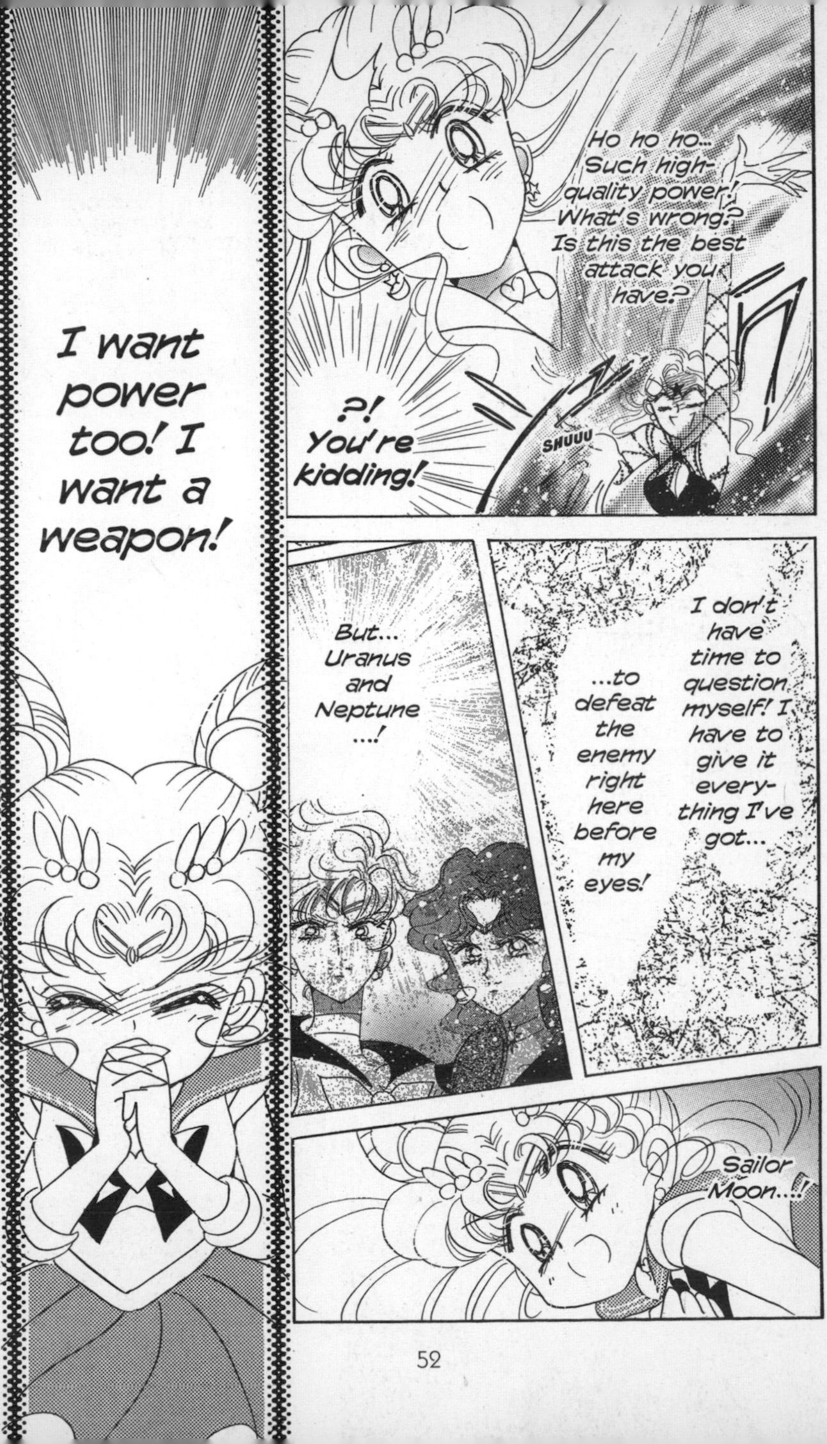
Ho ho ho... Such high-quality power! What's wrong? Is this the best attack you have?
SHUUU
?! You're kidding!
I don't have time to question myself! I have to give it everything I've got...
...to defeat the enemy right here before my eyes!
But... Uranus and Neptune ...!
Sailor Moon...!
I want power too! I want a weapon!

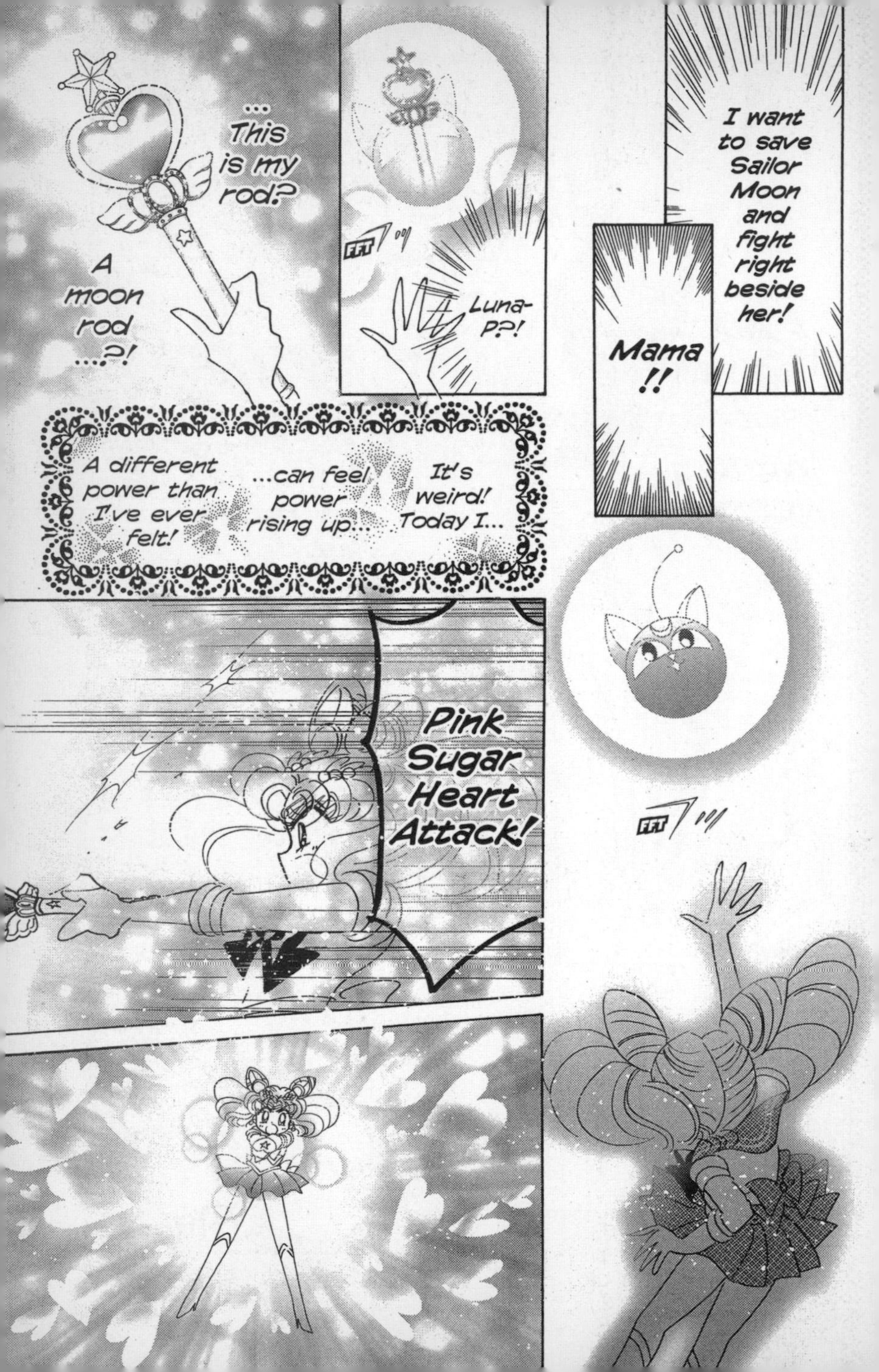
I want to save Sailor Moon and fight right beside her!
Mama!!
FFT
FFT
Luna-P?!
...This is my rod?
A moon rod...?!
It's weird! Today I...
...can feel power rising up...
A different power than I've ever felt!
Pink Sugar Heart Attack!

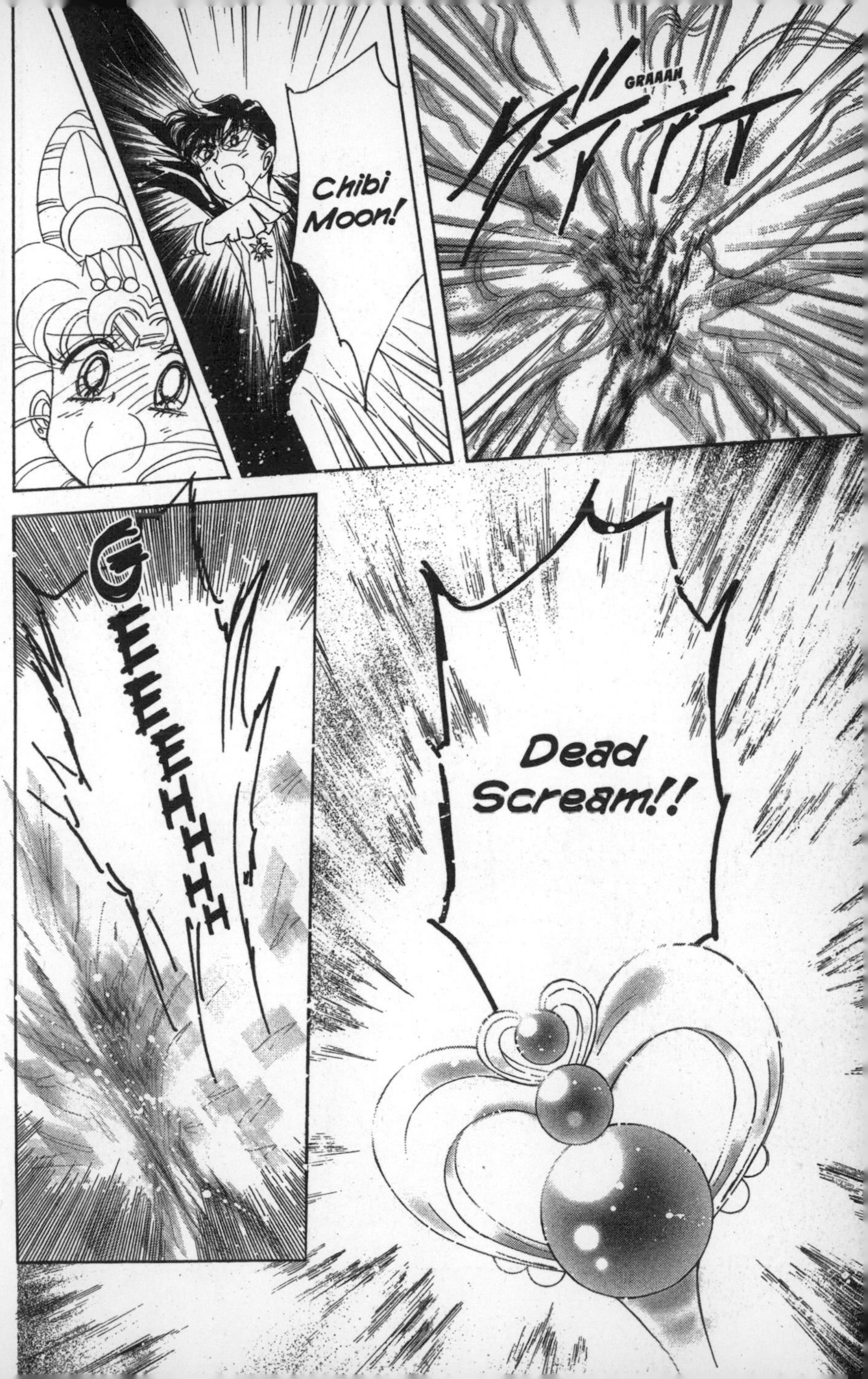
GRAAAH
Chibi Moon!
Dead Scream!!
GEEEHHHH

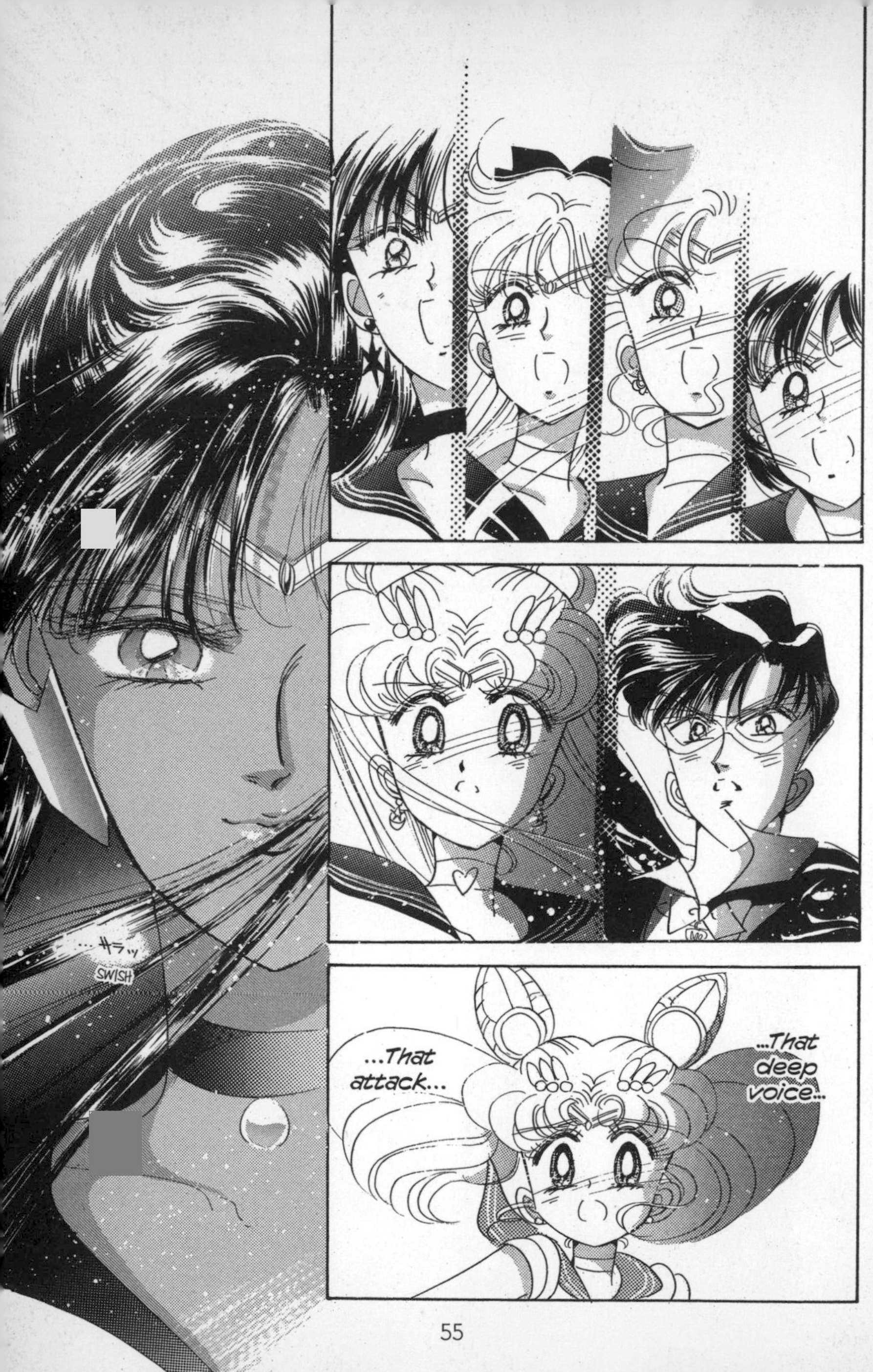
...That deep voice...
...That attack...
...キラッ
SWISH

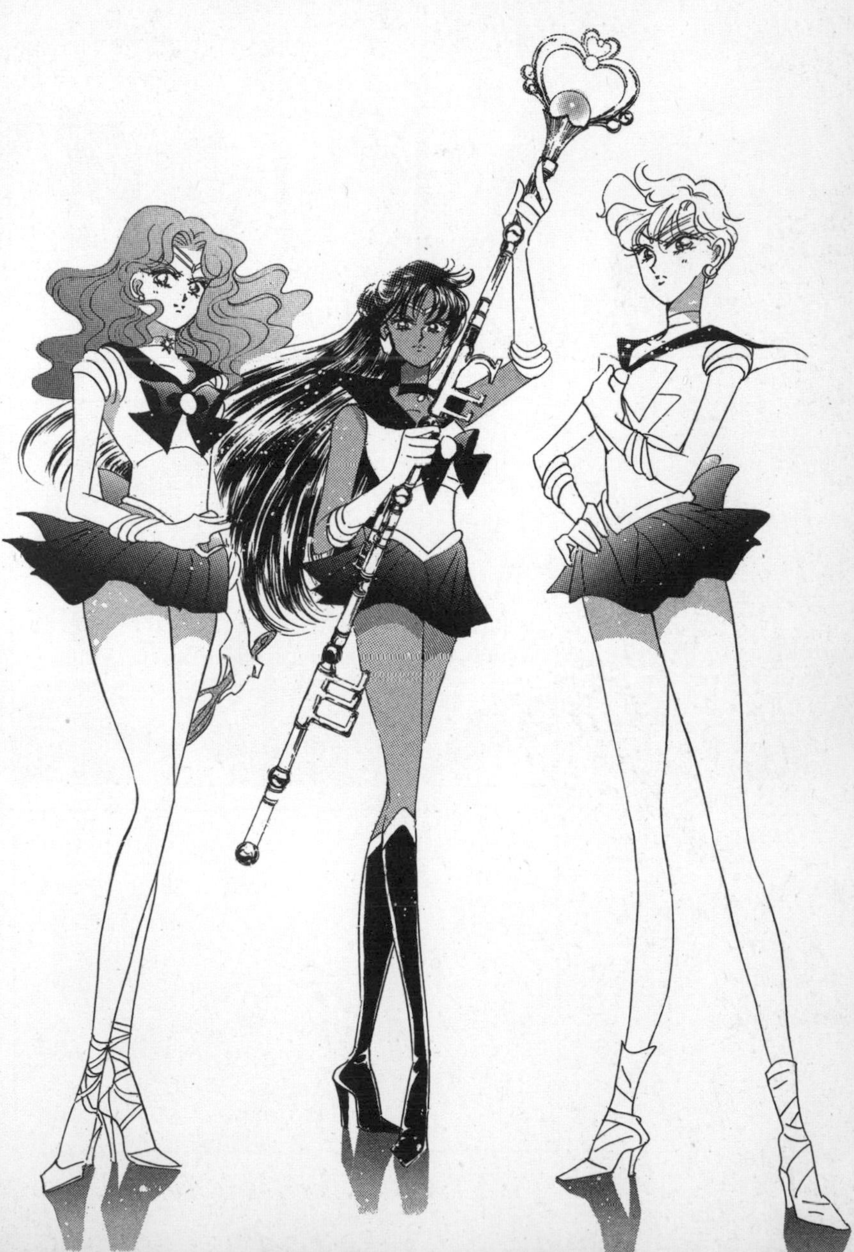

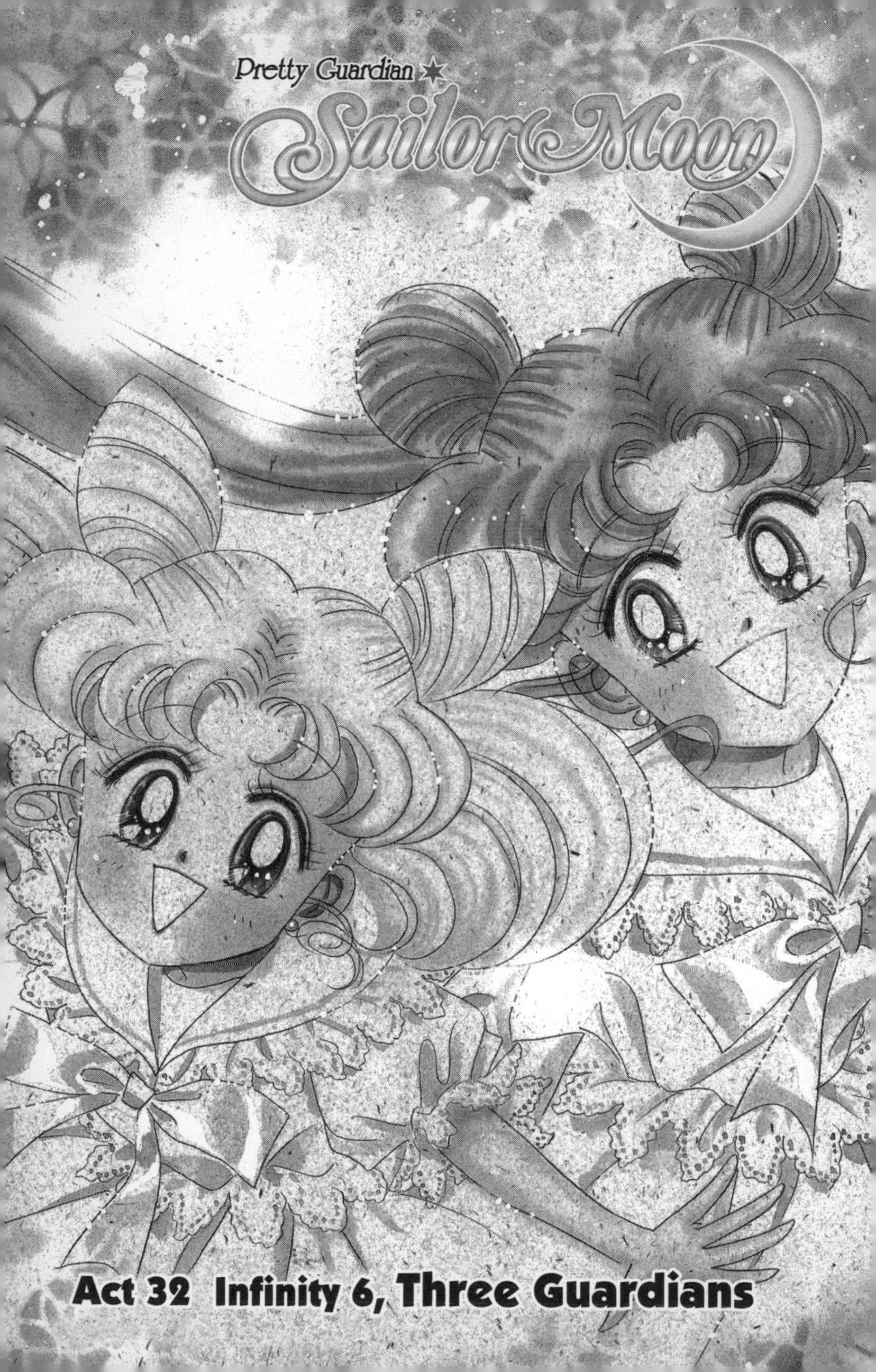
Pretty Guardian
Sailor Moon
Act 32 Infinity 6, Three Guardians

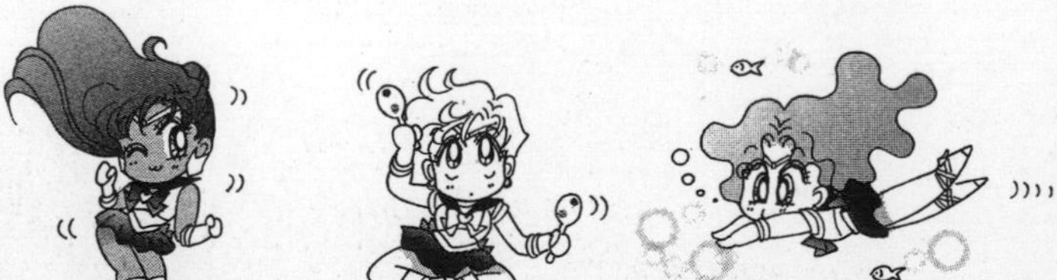

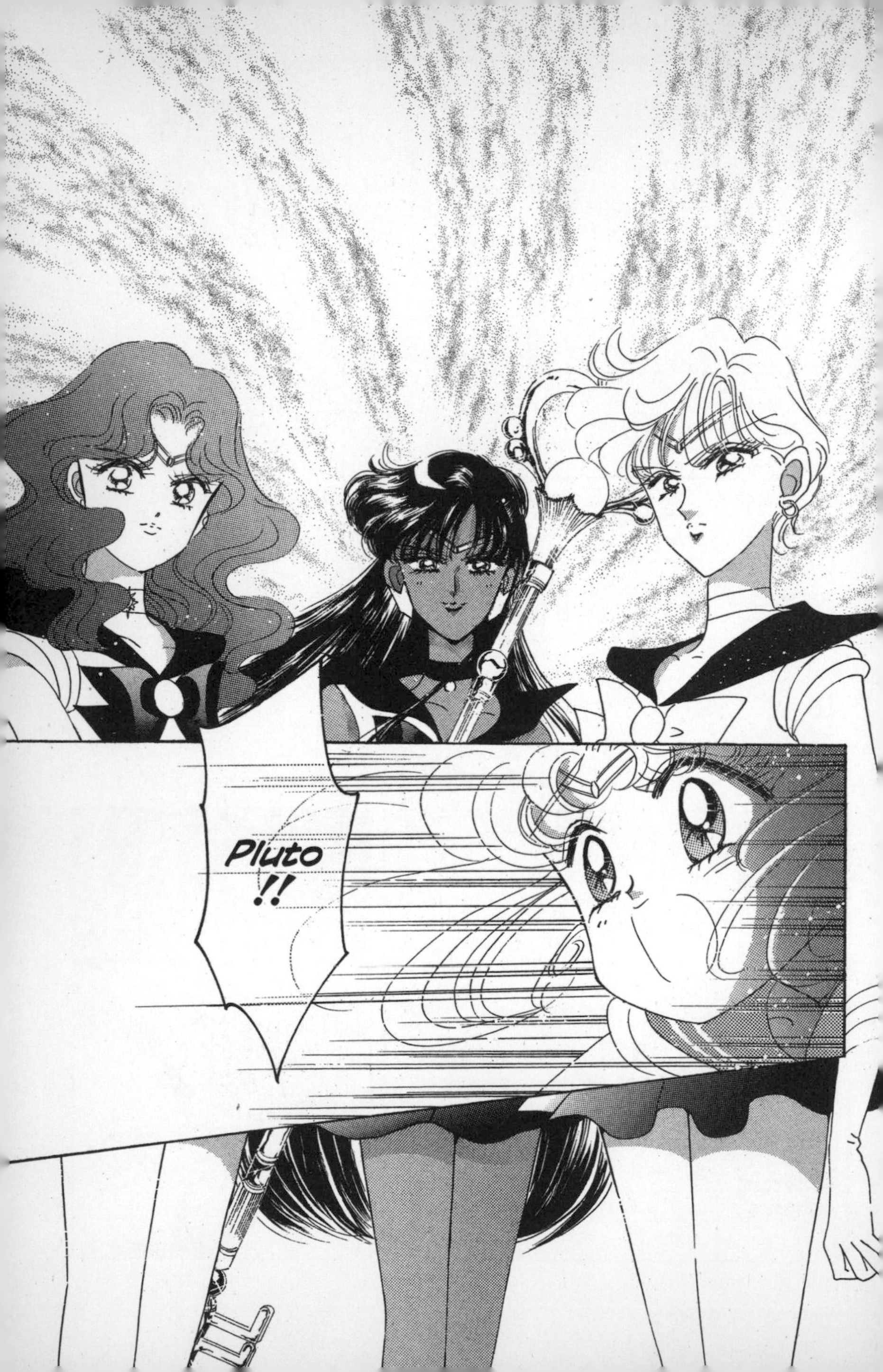
Pluto !!

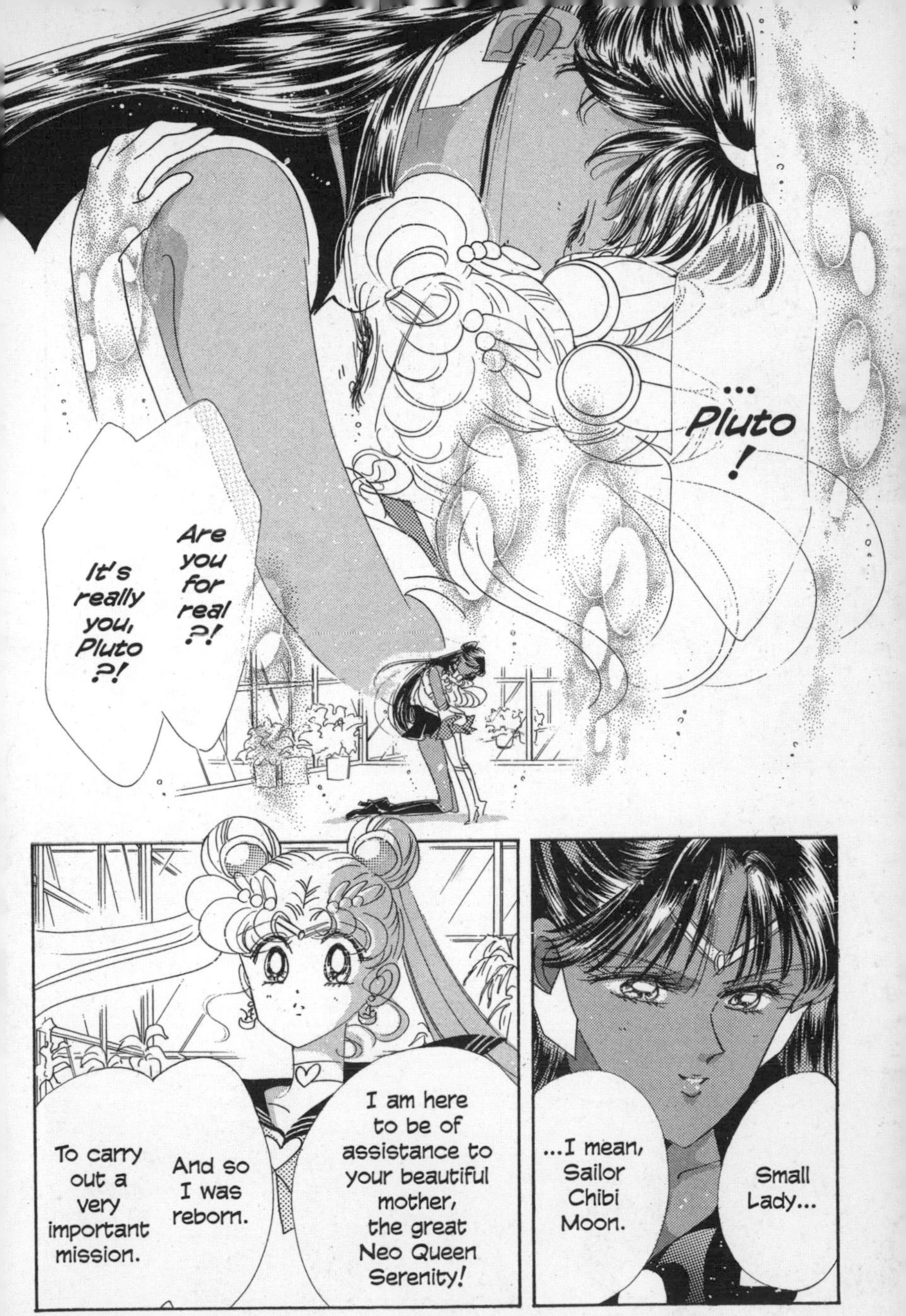
...Pluto!
Are you for real?!
It's really you, Pluto?!
Small Lady...
...I mean, Sailor Chibi Moon.
I am here to be of assistance to your beautiful mother, the great Neo Queen Serenity!
And so I was reborn.
To carry out a very important mission.

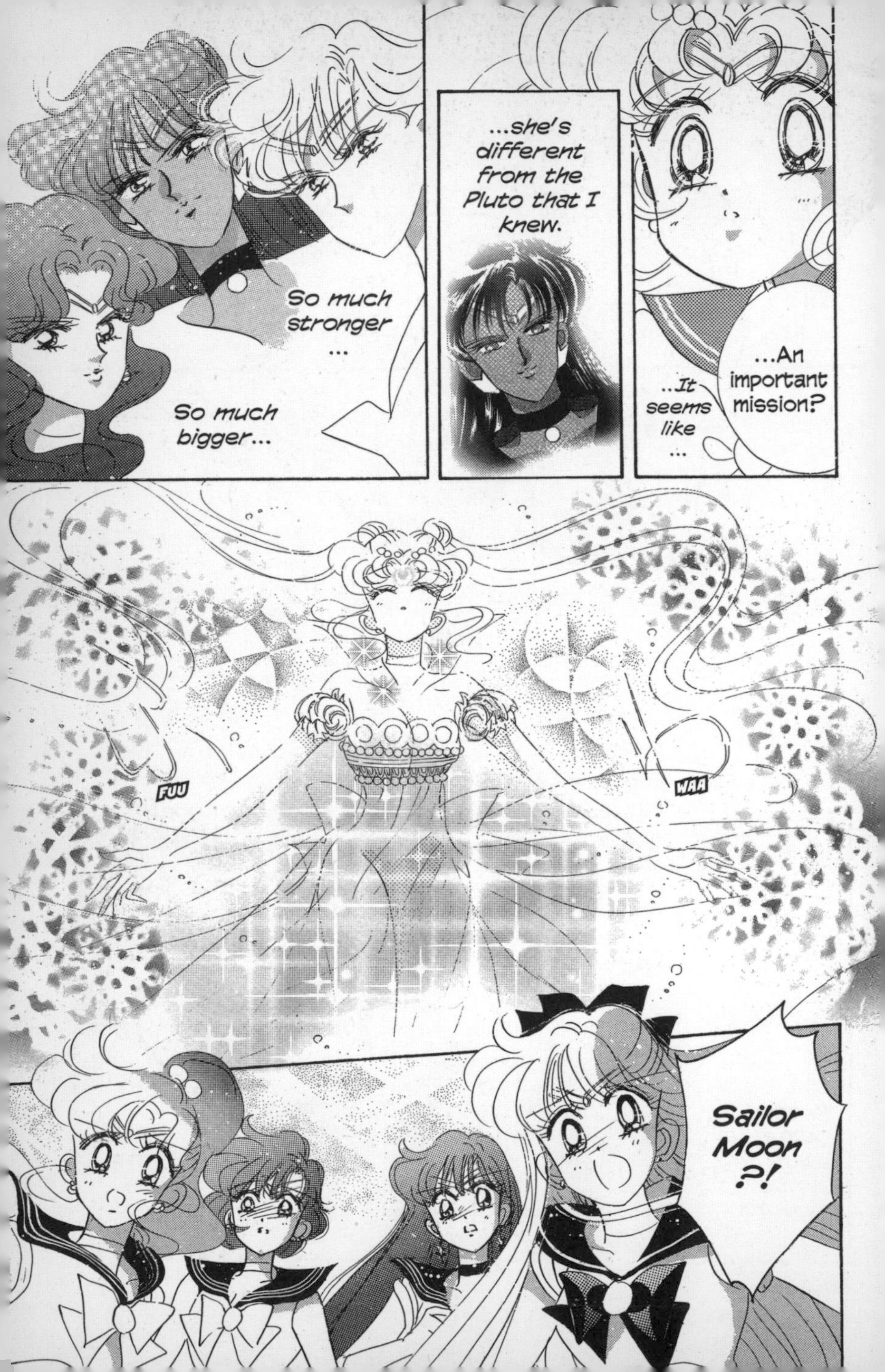
...An important mission?
...It seems like ...
...she's different from the Pluto that I knew.
So much stronger ...
So much bigger...
WAA
FUU
Sailor Moon ?!

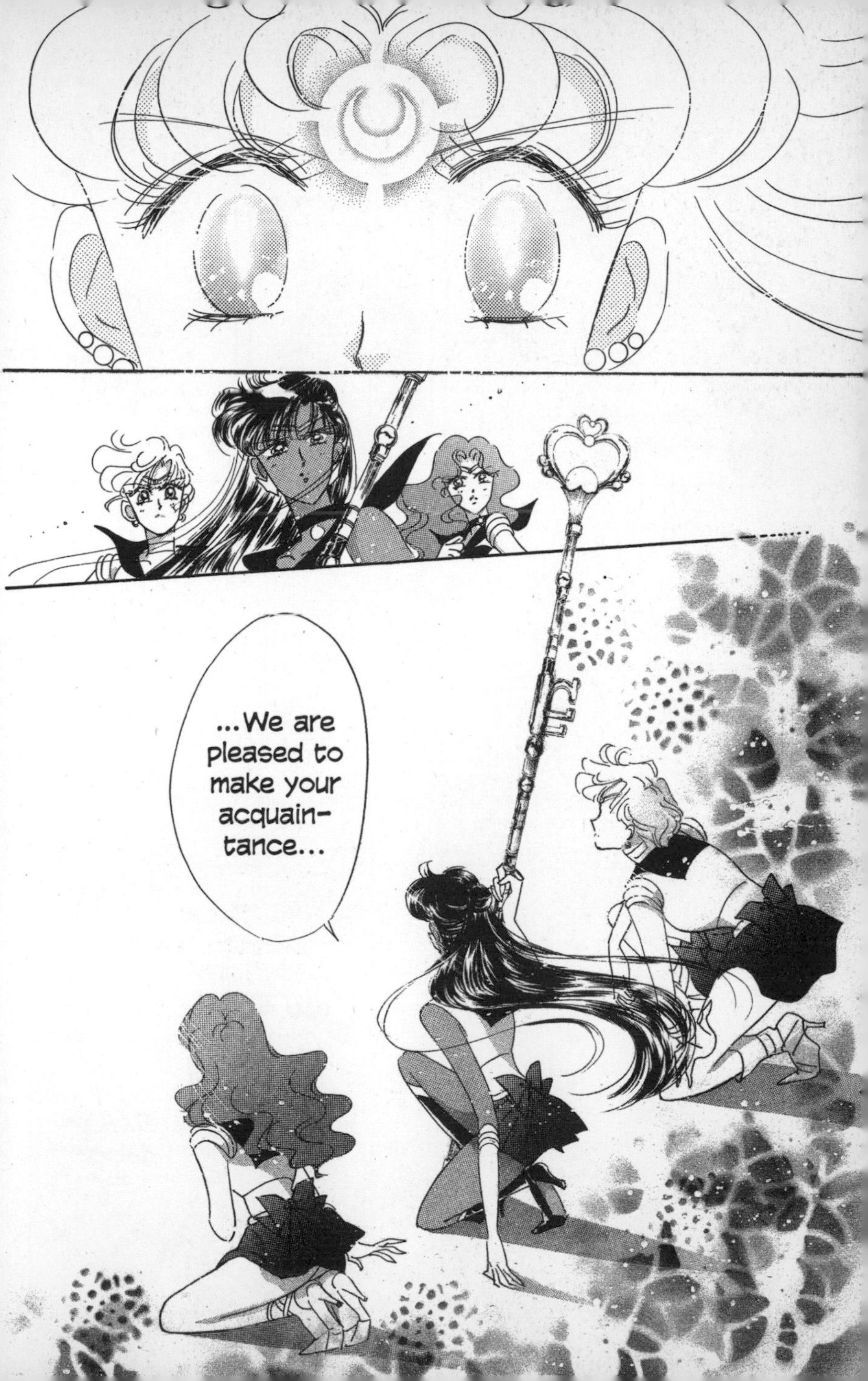
...We are pleased to make your acquaintance...

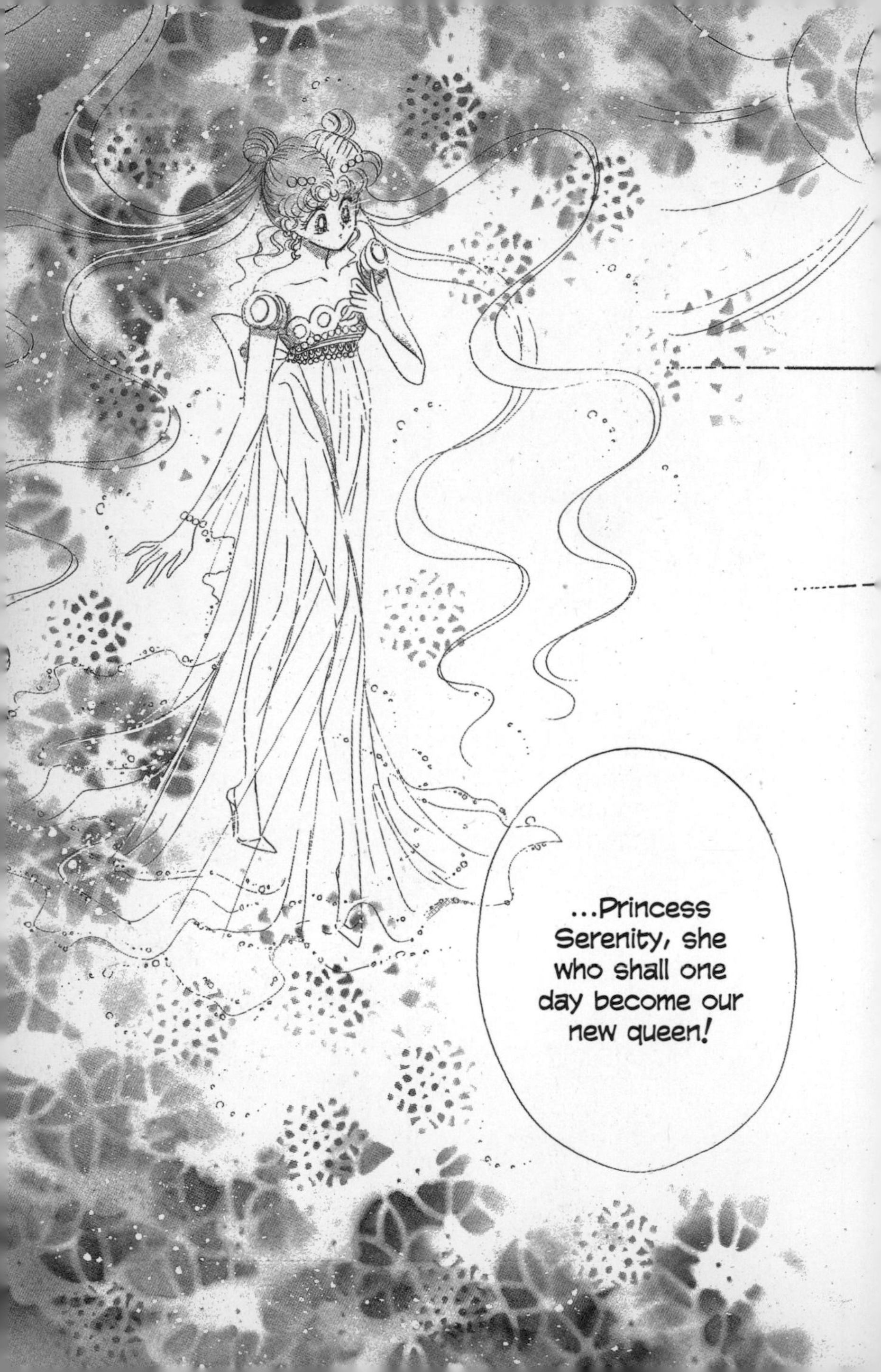
...Princess Serenity, she who shall one day become our new queen!

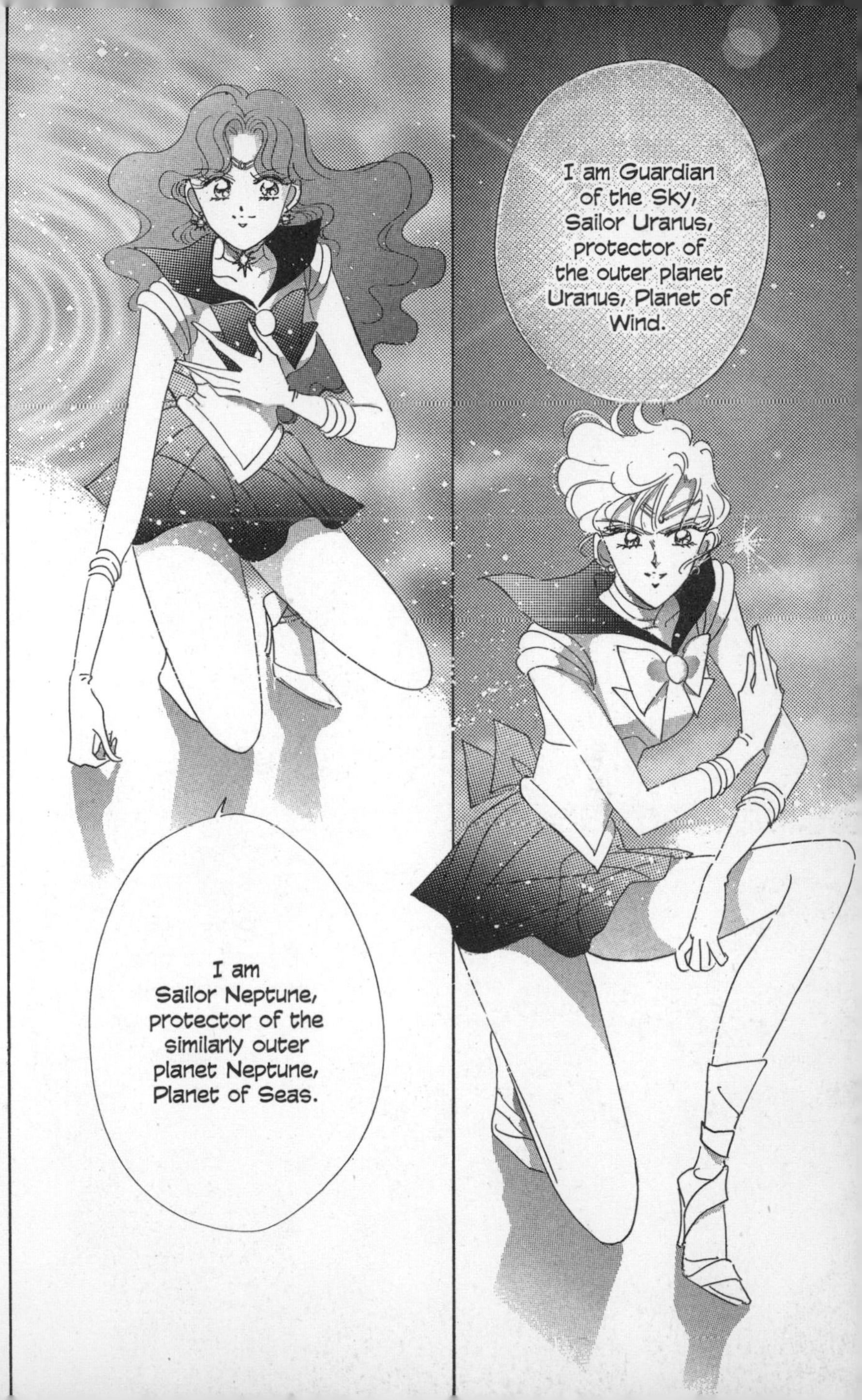
I am Guardian of the Sky, Sailor Uranus, protector of the outer planet Uranus, Planet of Wind.
I am Sailor Neptune, protector of the similarly outer planet Neptune, Planet of Seas.

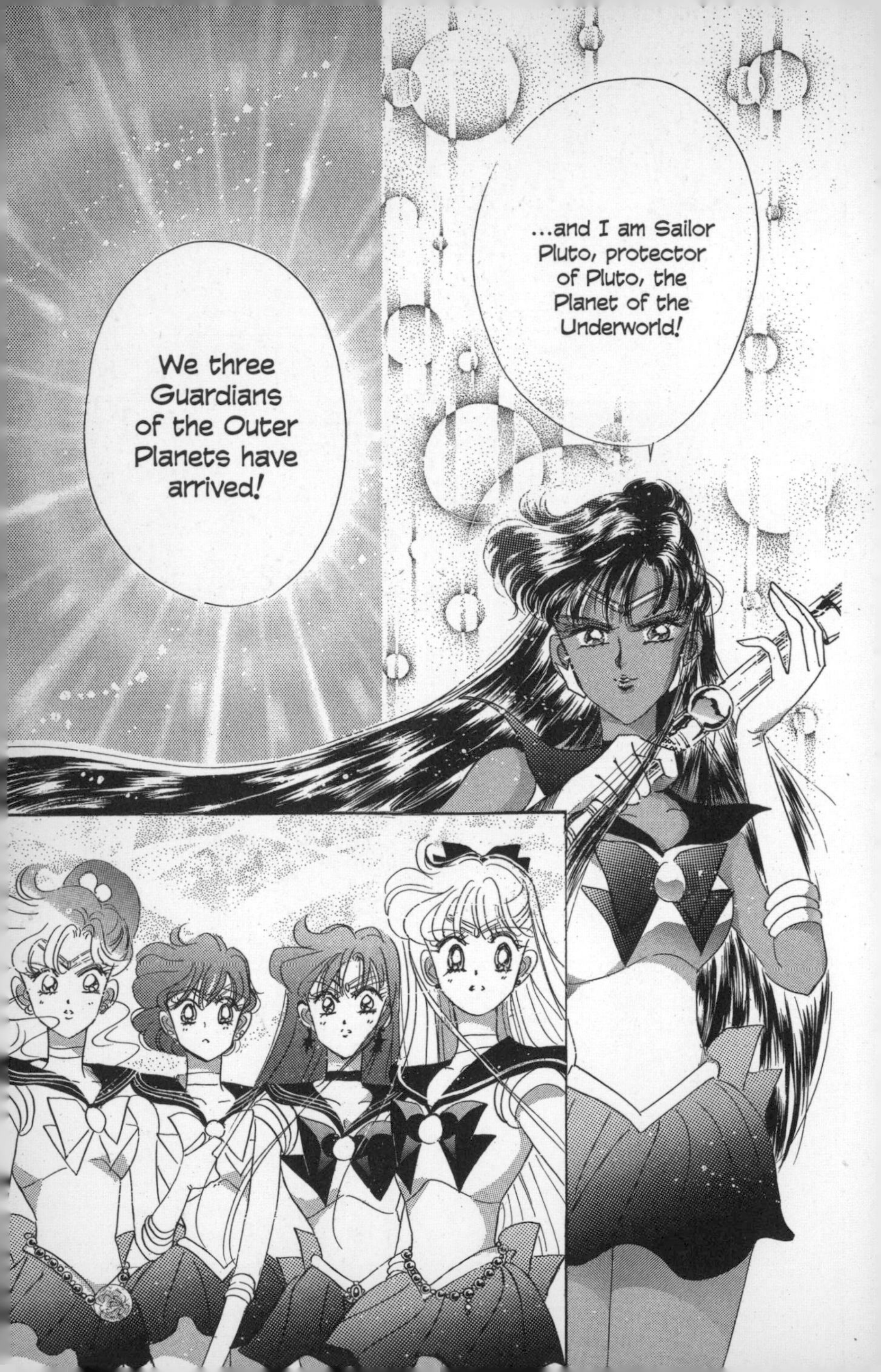
...and I am Sailor Pluto, protector of Pluto, the Planet of the Underworld!
We three Guardians of the Outer Planets have arrived!

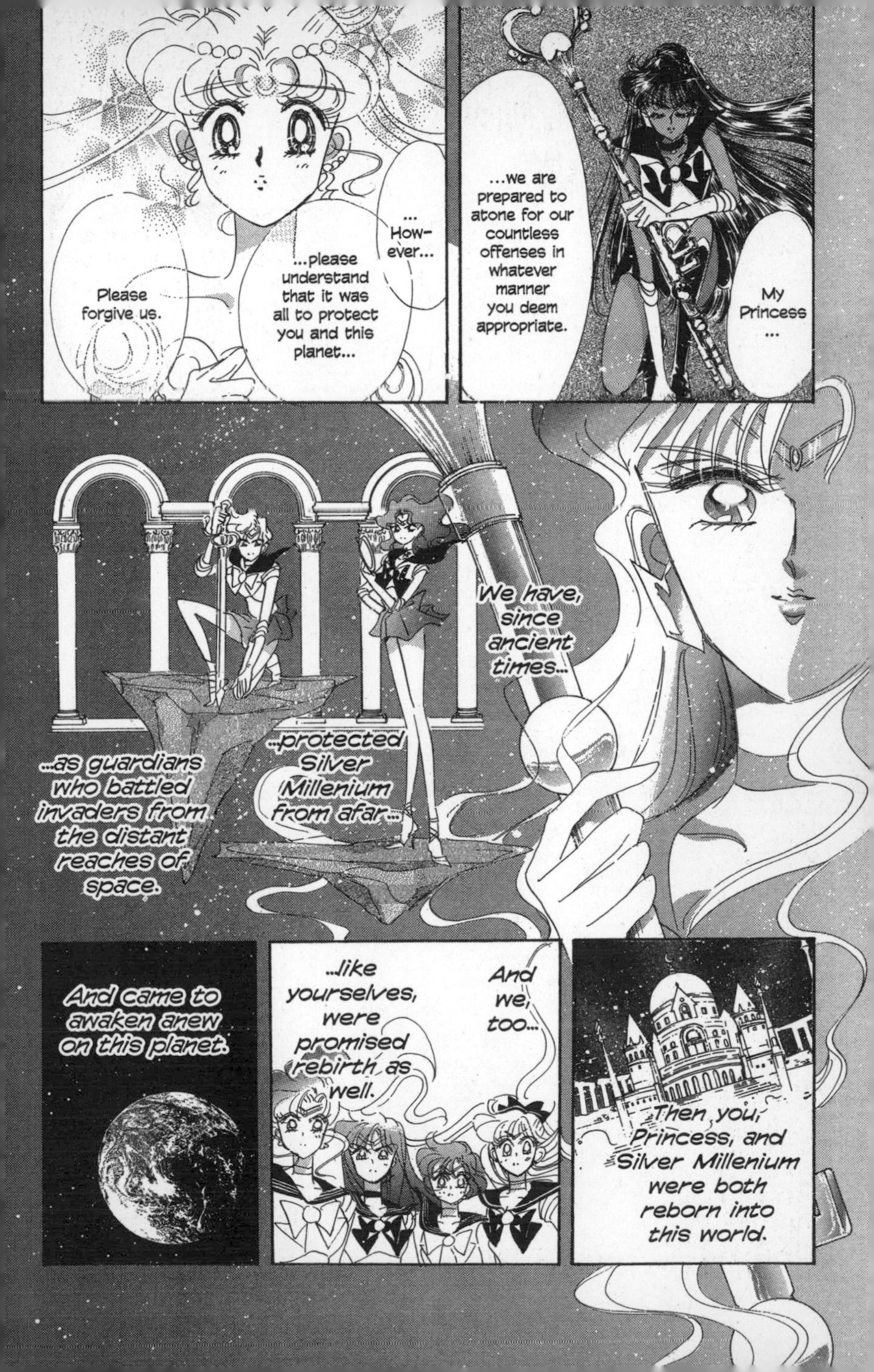
My Princess ...
...we are prepared to atone for our countless offenses in whatever manner you deem appropriate.
... How-ever...
...please understand that it was all to protect you and this planet...
Please forgive us.
We have, since ancient times...
...protected Silver Millenium from afar...
...as guardians who battled invaders from the distant reaches of space.
Then you, Princess, and Silver Millenium were both reborn into this world.
And we, too...
...like yourselves, were promised rebirth as well.
And came to awaken anew on this planet.

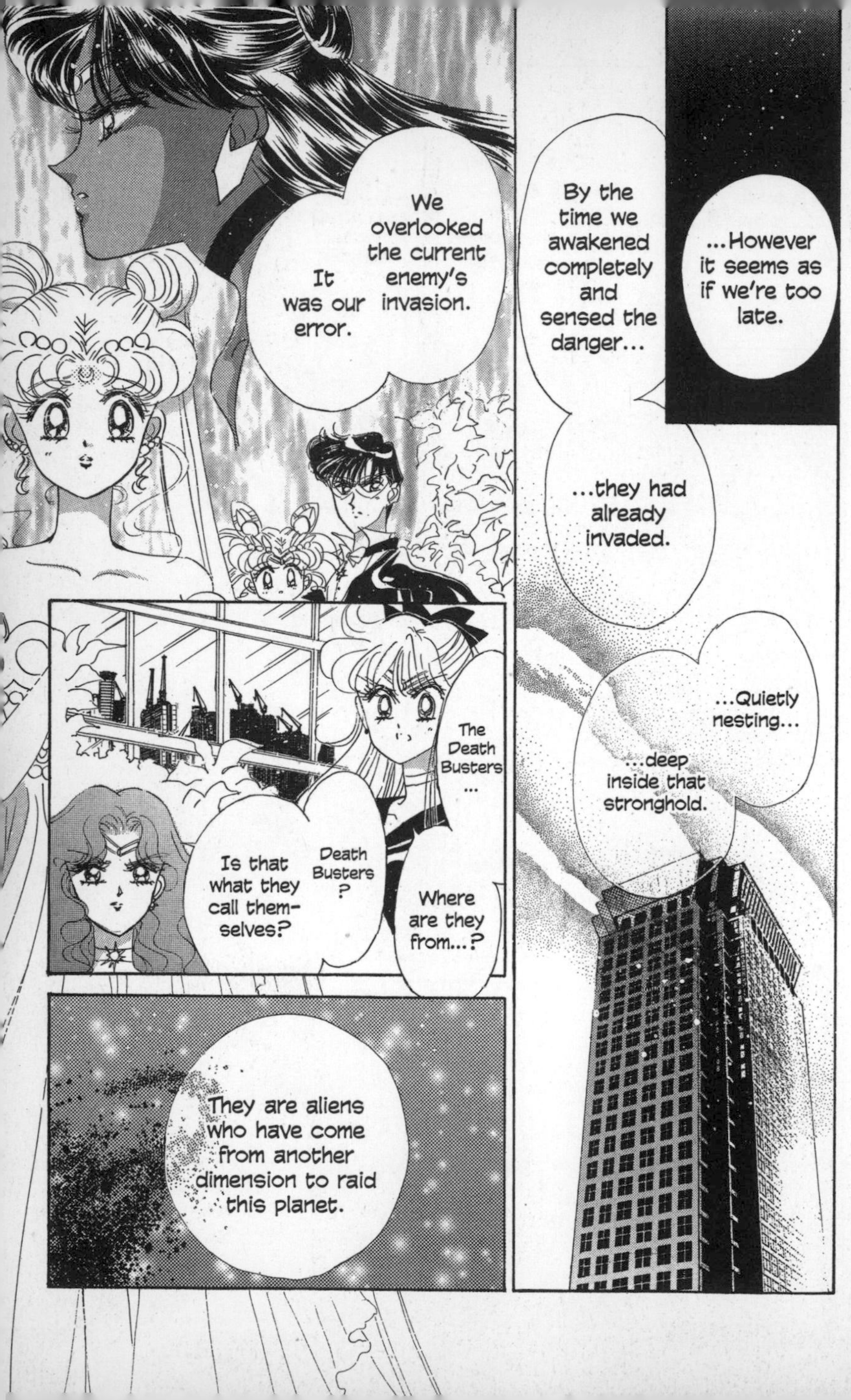
...However it seems as if we're too late.
By the time we awakened completely and sensed the danger...
...they had already invaded.
...Quietly nesting...
...deep inside that stronghold.
We overlooked the current enemy's invasion.
It was our error.
The Death Busters...
Death Busters?
Is that what they call them-selves?
Where are they from...?
They are aliens who have come from another dimension to raid this planet.

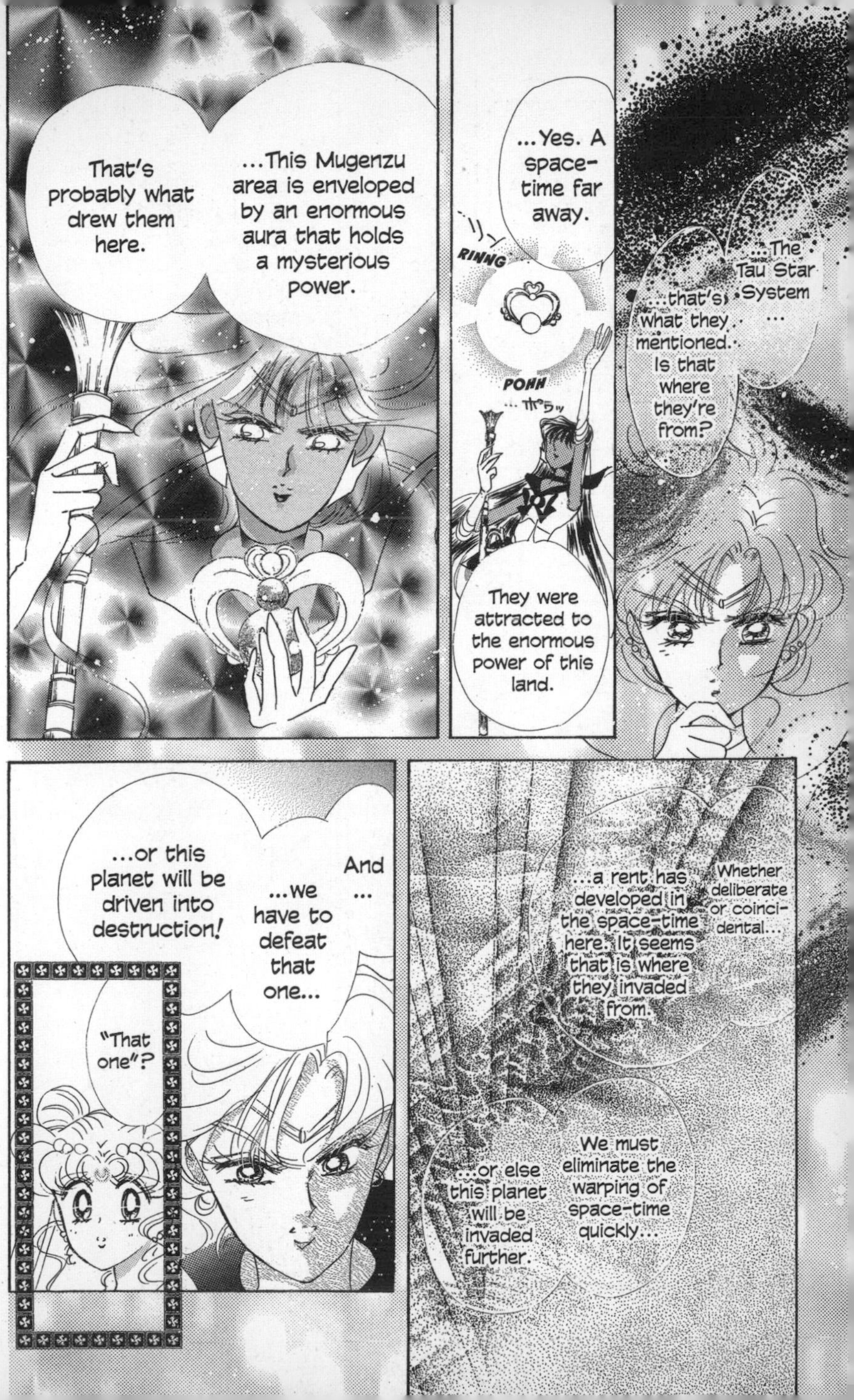
...The Tau Star System ...
...that's what they mentioned. Is that where they're from?
...Yes. A space-time far away.
RINNG
POHN
They were attracted to the enormous power of this land.
...This Mugenzu area is enveloped by an enormous aura that holds a mysterious power.
That's probably what drew them here.
Whether deliberate or coincidental...
...a rent has developed in the space-time here. It seems that is where they invaded from.
We must eliminate the warping of space-time quickly...
...or else this planet will be invaded further.
And ...
...we have to defeat that one...
...or this planet will be driven into destruction!
"That one"?

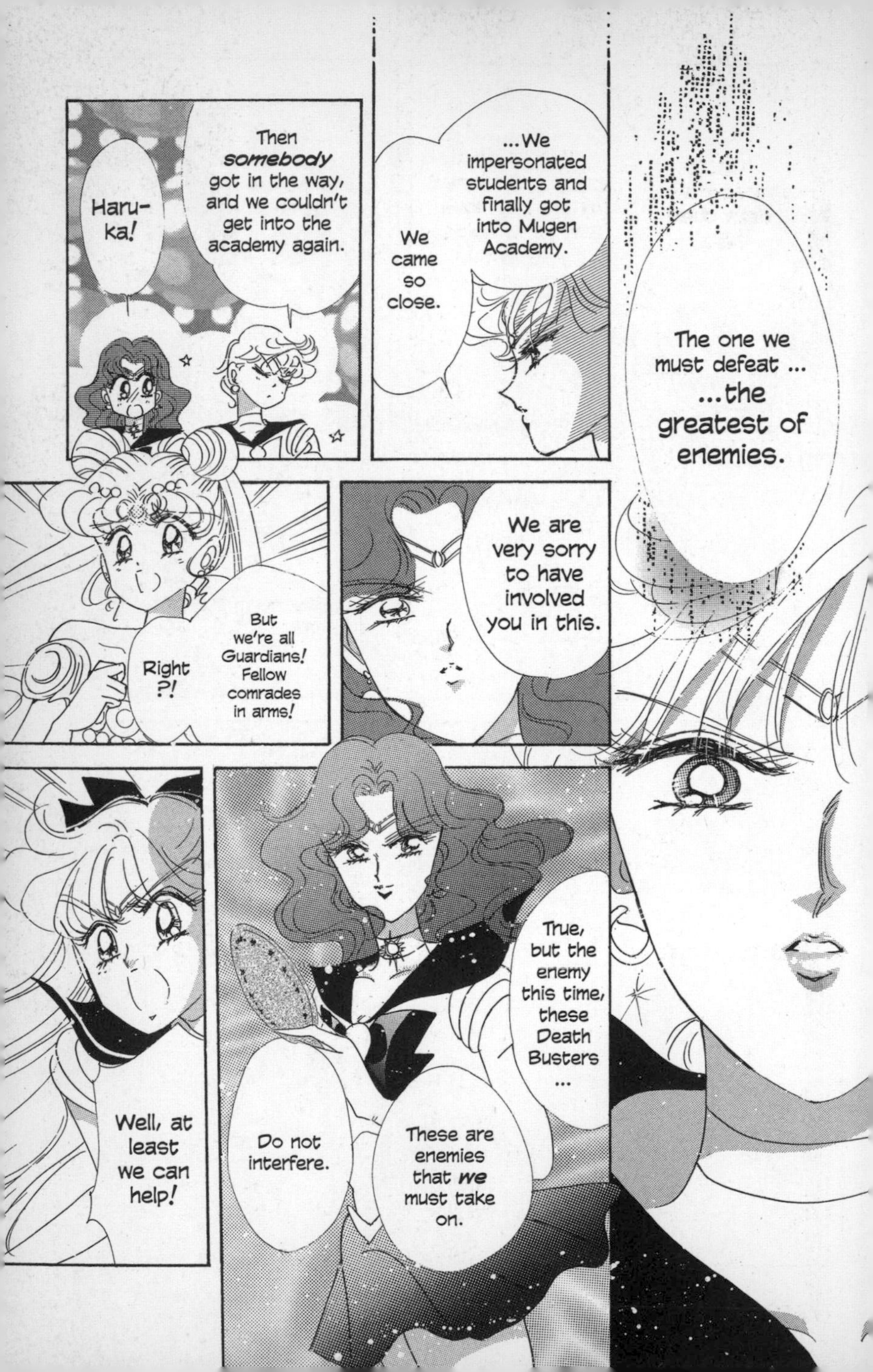
The one we must defeat ... ...the greatest of enemies.
...We impersonated students and finally got into Mugen Academy.
We came so close.
Then *somebody* got in the way, and we couldn't get into the academy again.
Haru-ka!
We are very sorry to have involved you in this.
But we're all Guardians! Fellow comrades in arms!
Right?!
True, but the enemy this time, these Death Busters ...
These are enemies that *we* must take on.
Do not interfere.
Well, at least we can help!

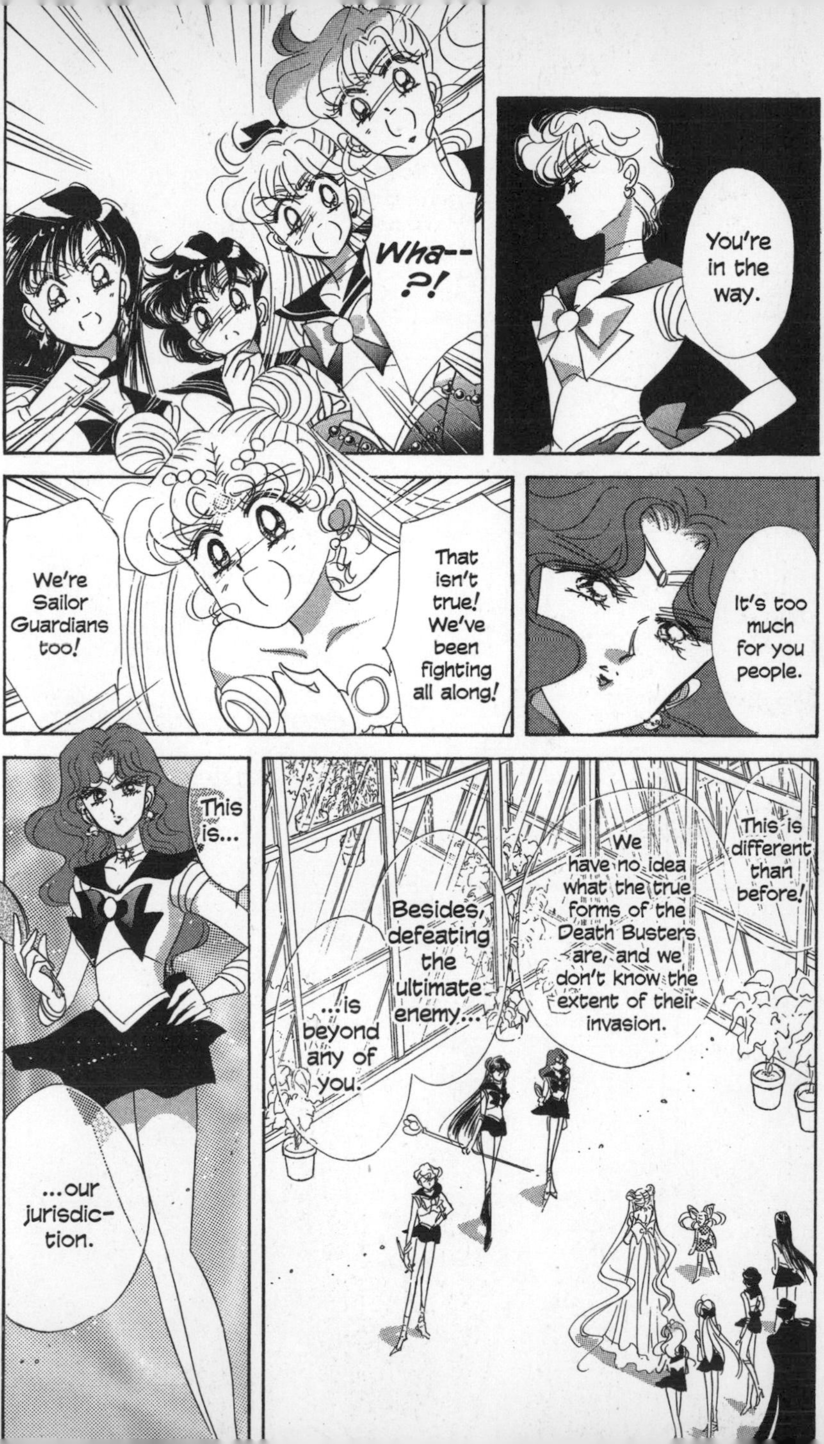
You're in the way.
Wha-- ?!
It's too much for you people.
That isn't true! We've been fighting all along!
We're Sailor Guardians too!
This is different than before!
We have no idea what the true forms of the Death Busters are, and we don't know the extent of their invasion.
Besides, defeating the ultimate enemy...
...is beyond any of you.
This is...
...our jurisdiction.

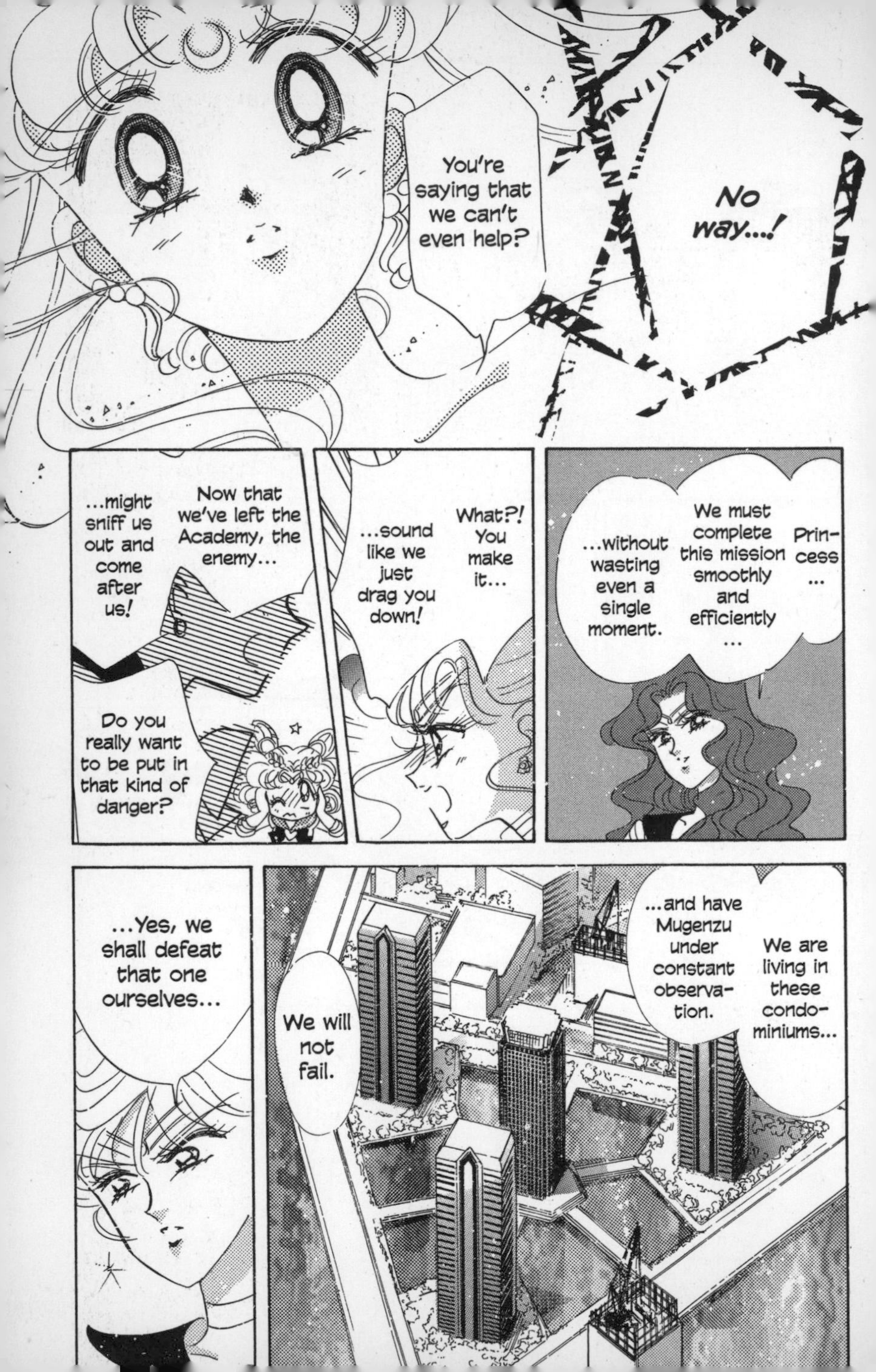
No way...!
You're saying that we can't even help?
Prin-cess...
We must complete this mission smoothly and efficiently...
...without wasting even a single moment.
What?! You make it...
...sound like we just drag you down!
Now that we've left the Academy, the enemy...
...might sniff us out and come after us!
Do you really want to be put in that kind of danger?
We are living in these condo-miniums...
...and have Mugenzu under constant observa-tion.
We will not fail.
...Yes, we shall defeat that one ourselves...

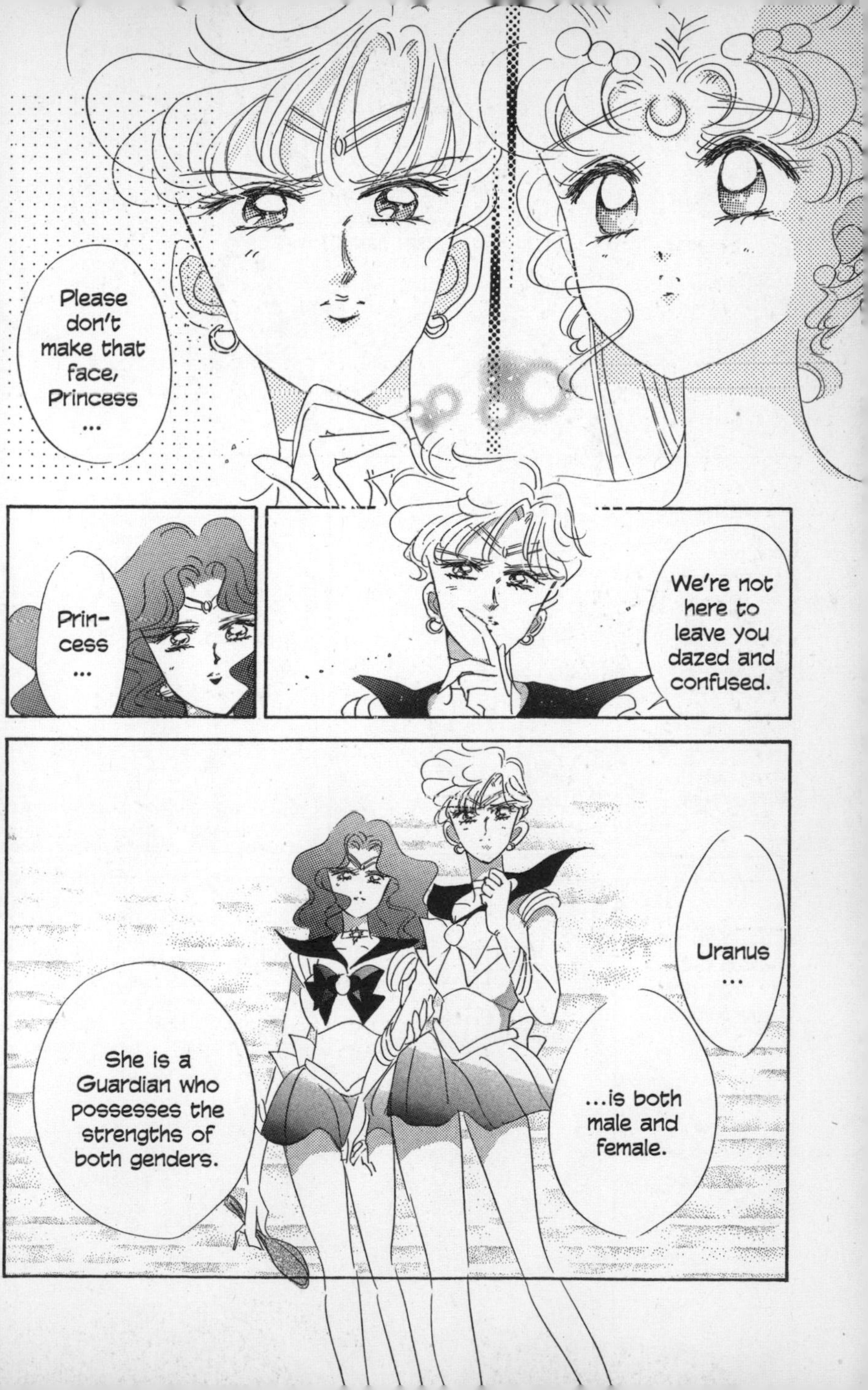
Please don't make that face, Princess ...
We're not here to leave you dazed and confused.
Prin-cess ...
Uranus ...
...is both male and female.
She is a Guardian who possesses the strengths of both genders.

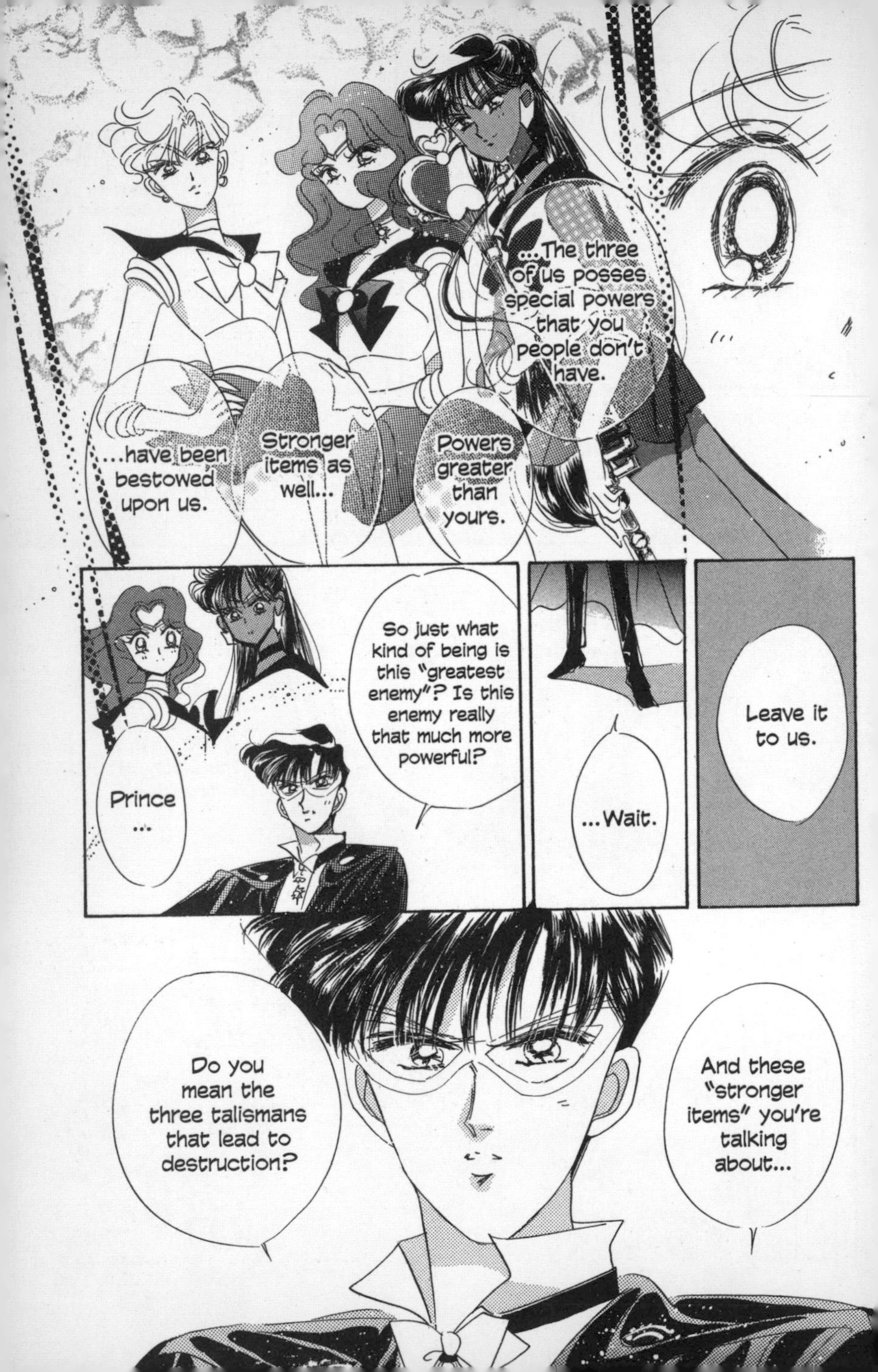
...The three of us posses special powers that you people don't have.
Powers greater than yours.
Stronger items as well...
...have been bestowed upon us.
Leave it to us.
...Wait.
So just what kind of being is this "greatest enemy"? Is this enemy really that much more powerful?
Prince ...
And these "stronger items" you're talking about...
Do you mean the three talismans that lead to destruction?

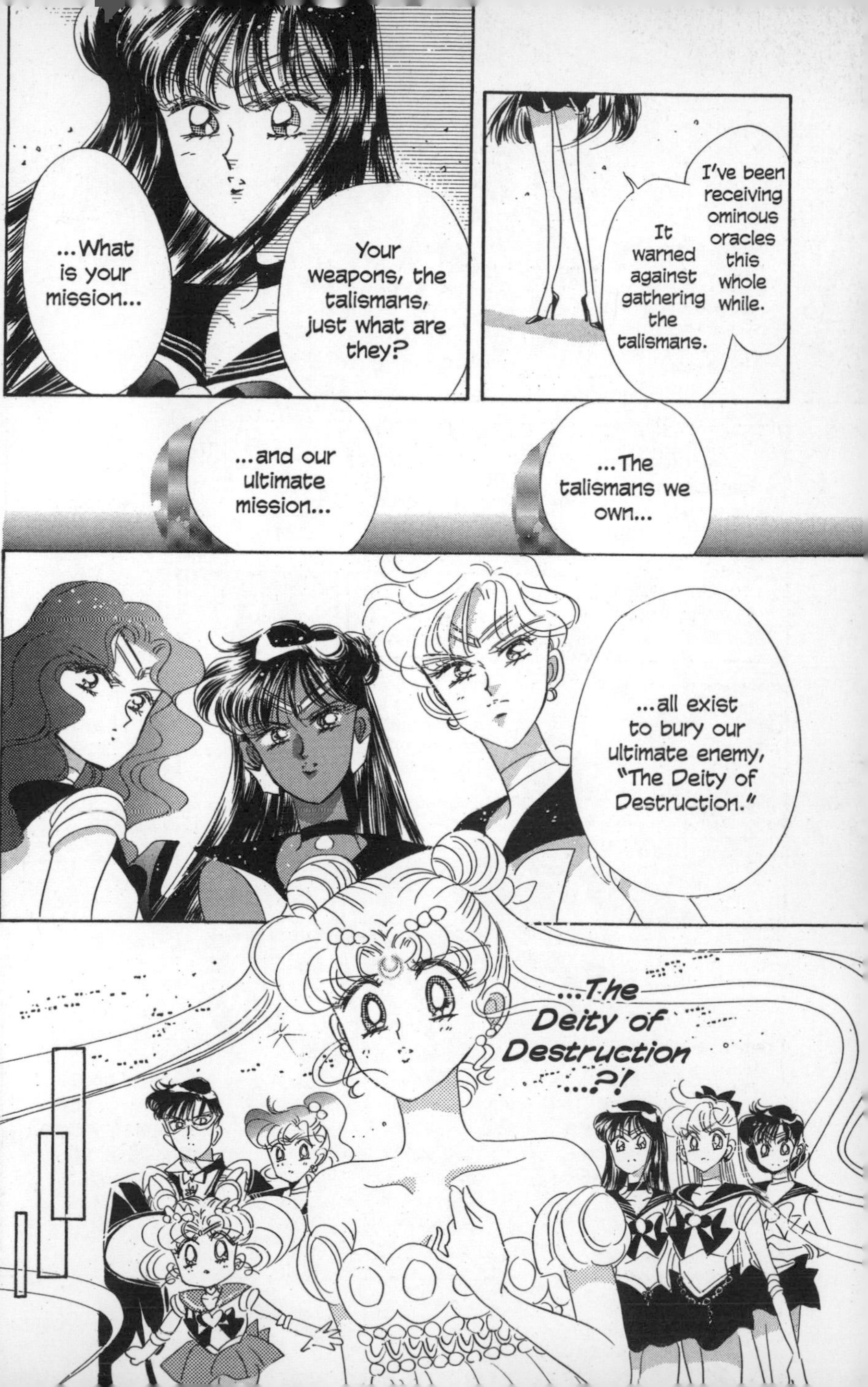
I've been receiving ominous oracles this whole while.
It warned against gathering the talismans.
Your weapons, the talismans, just what are they?
...What is your mission...
...The talismans we own...
...and our ultimate mission...
...all exist to bury our ultimate enemy, "The Deity of Destruction."
...The Deity of Destruction ...?!

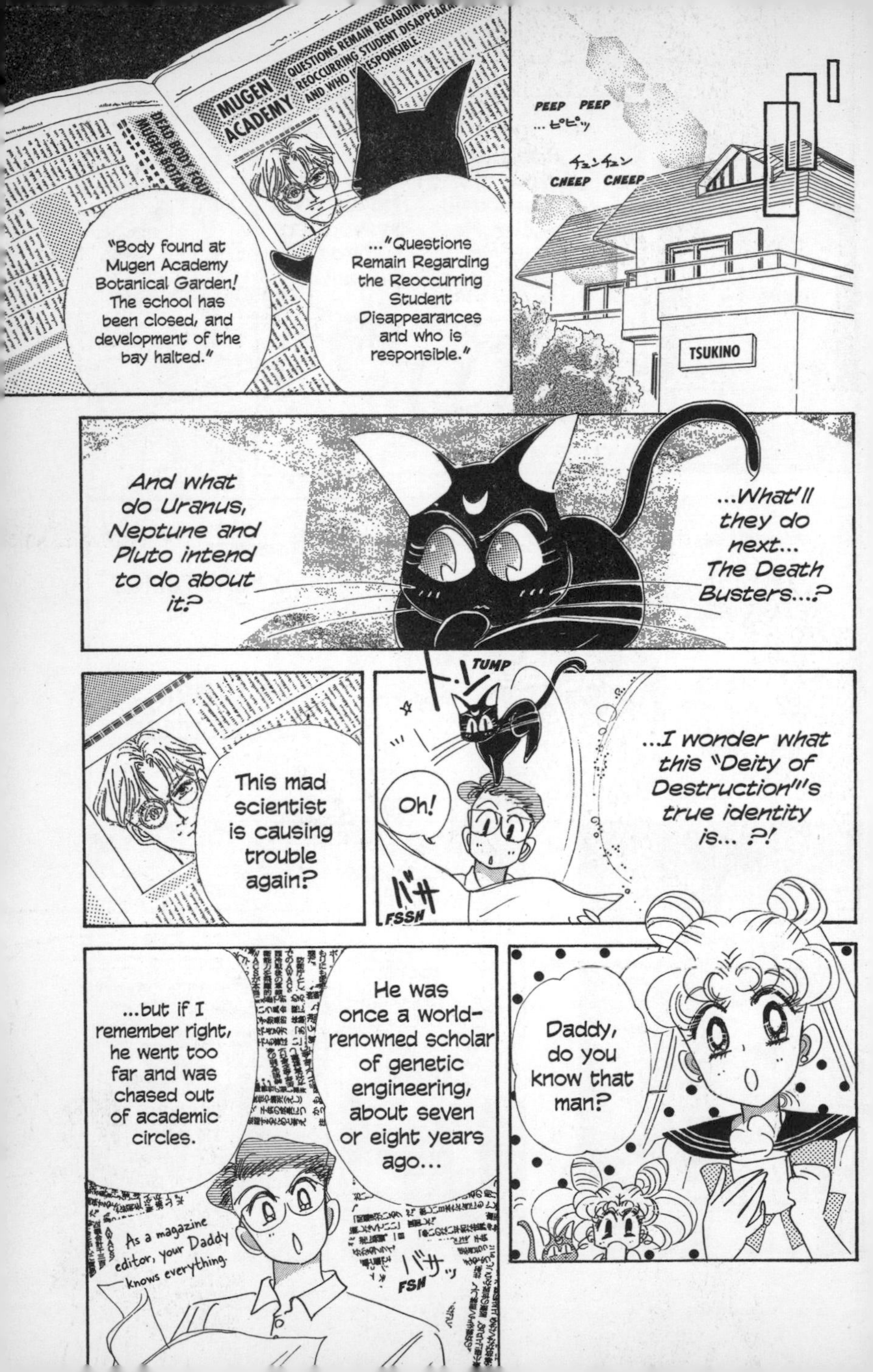
PEEP PEEP
... ピピッ
チュンチュン
CHEEP CHEEP
TSUKINO
MUGEN ACADEMY
..."Questions Remain Regarding the Reoccurring Student Disappearances and who is responsible."
"Body found at Mugen Academy Botanical Garden! The school has been closed, and development of the bay halted."
...What'll they do next... The Death Busters...?
And what do Uranus, Neptune and Pluto intend to do about it?
TUMP
...I wonder what this "Deity of Destruction"'s true identity is... ?!
Oh!
バサ
FSSH
This mad scientist is causing trouble again?
Daddy, do you know that man?
He was once a world-renowned scholar of genetic engineering, about seven or eight years ago...
...but if I remember right, he went too far and was chased out of academic circles.
As a magazine editor, your Daddy knows everything.
バサッ
FSH

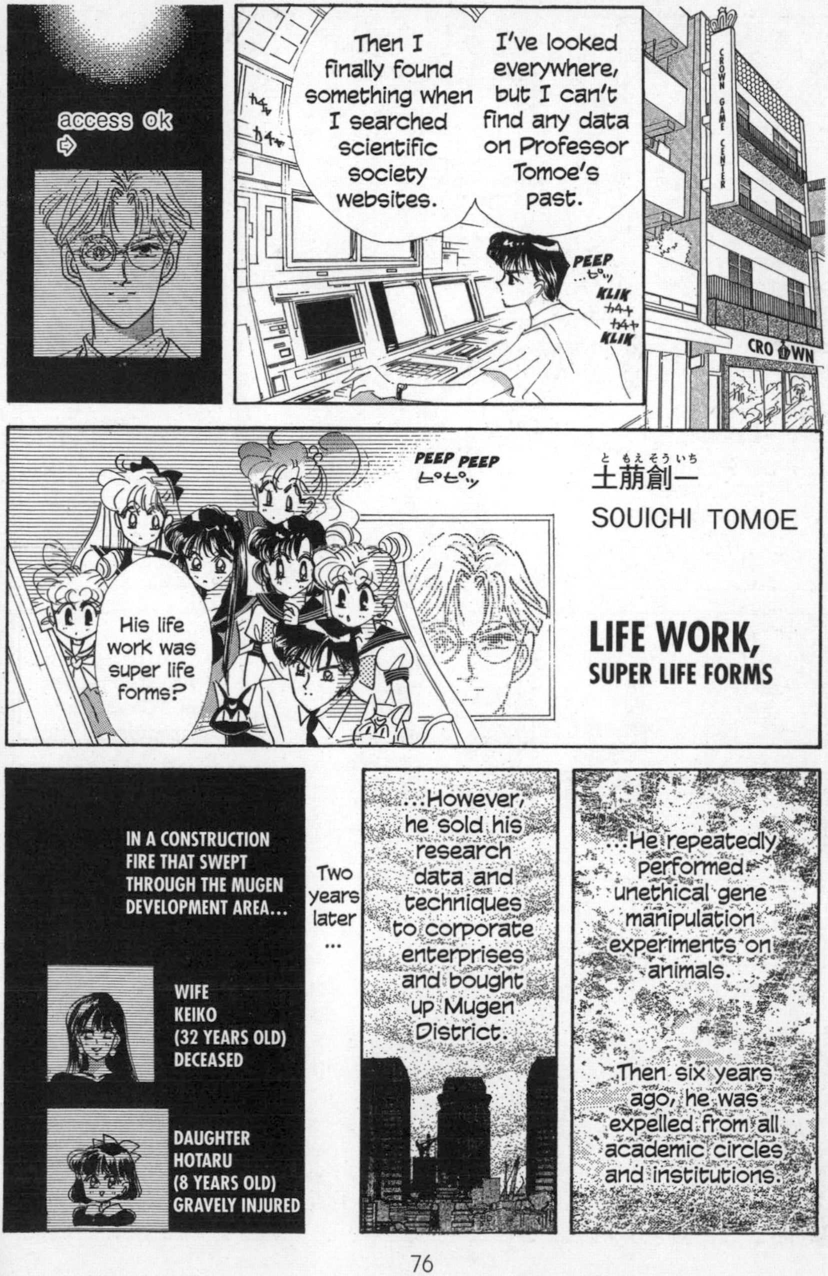

CROWN GAME CENTER
I've looked everywhere, but I can't find any data on Professor Tomoe's past.
Then I finally found something when I searched scientific society websites.
PEEP
KLIK
KLIK
CRO WN
access ok
PEEP PEEP
土萠創一
SOUICHI TOMOE
LIFE WORK, SUPER LIFE FORMS
His life work was super life forms?
...He repeatedly performed unethical gene manipulation experiments on animals.
Then six years ago, he was expelled from all academic circles and institutions.
...However, he sold his research data and techniques to corporate enterprises and bought up Mugen District.
Two years later ...
IN A CONSTRUCTION FIRE THAT SWEPT THROUGH THE MUGEN DEVELOPMENT AREA...
WIFE KEIKO (32 YEARS OLD) DECEASED
DAUGHTER HOTARU (8 YEARS OLD) GRAVELY INJURED

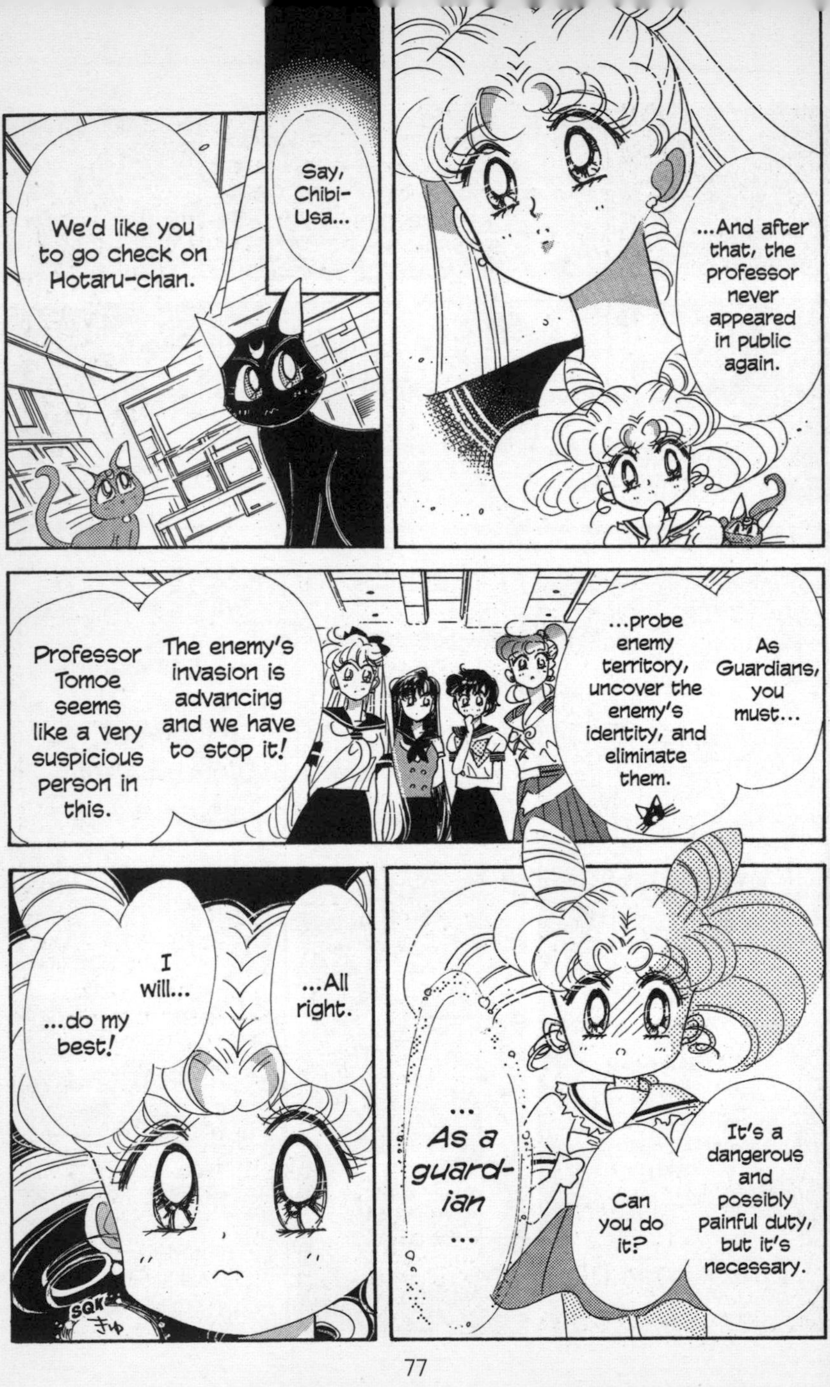
...And after that, the professor never appeared in public again.
Say, Chibi-Usa...
We'd like you to go check on Hotaru-chan.
As Guardians, you must...
...probe enemy territory, uncover the enemy's identity, and eliminate them.
The enemy's invasion is advancing and we have to stop it!
Professor Tomoe seems like a very suspicious person in this.
It's a dangerous and possibly painful duty, but it's necessary.
Can you do it?
...As a guardian...
...All right.
I will...
...do my best!
SQK きゅ

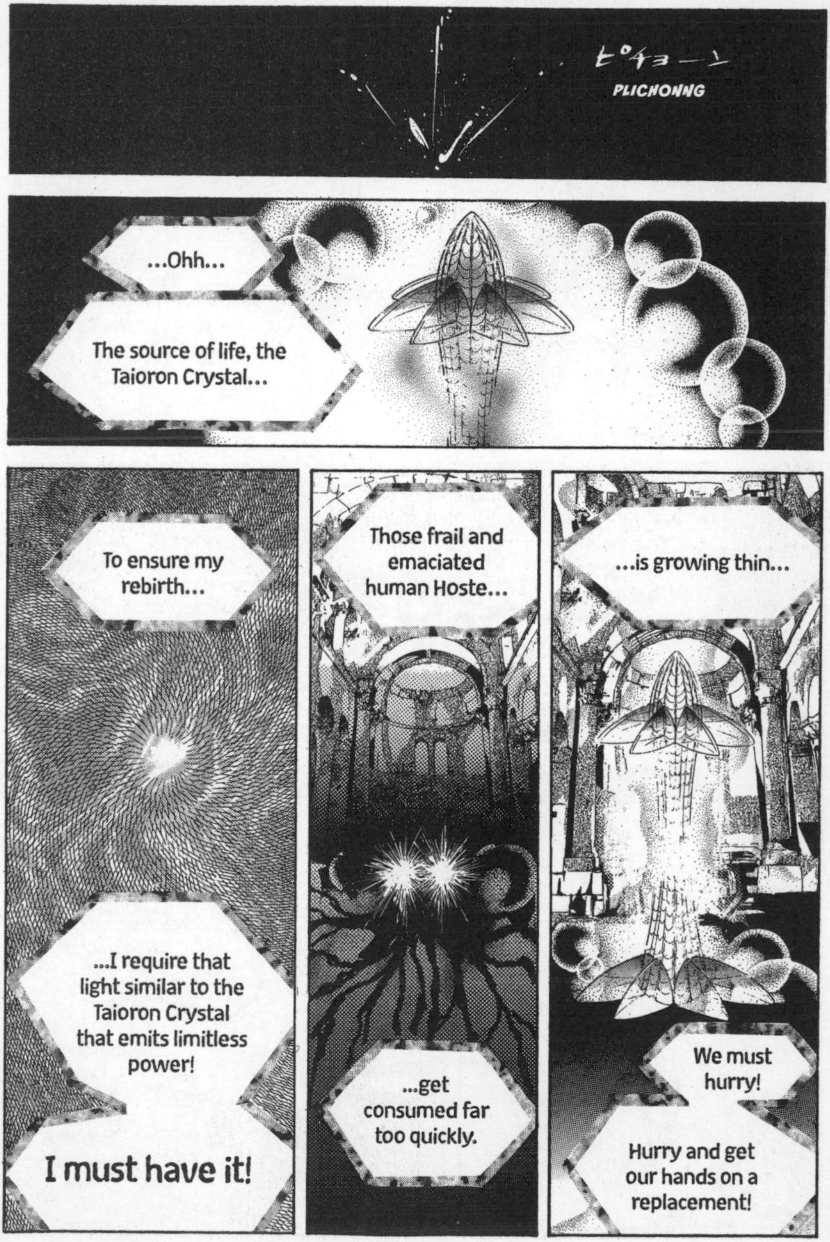
ピチョーン
PLICHONNG
...Ohh...
The source of life, the Taioron Crystal...
...is growing thin...
We must hurry!
Hurry and get our hands on a replacement!
Those frail and emaciated human Hoste...
...get consumed far too quickly.
To ensure my rebirth...
...I require that light similar to the Taioron Crystal that emits limitless power!
I must have it!

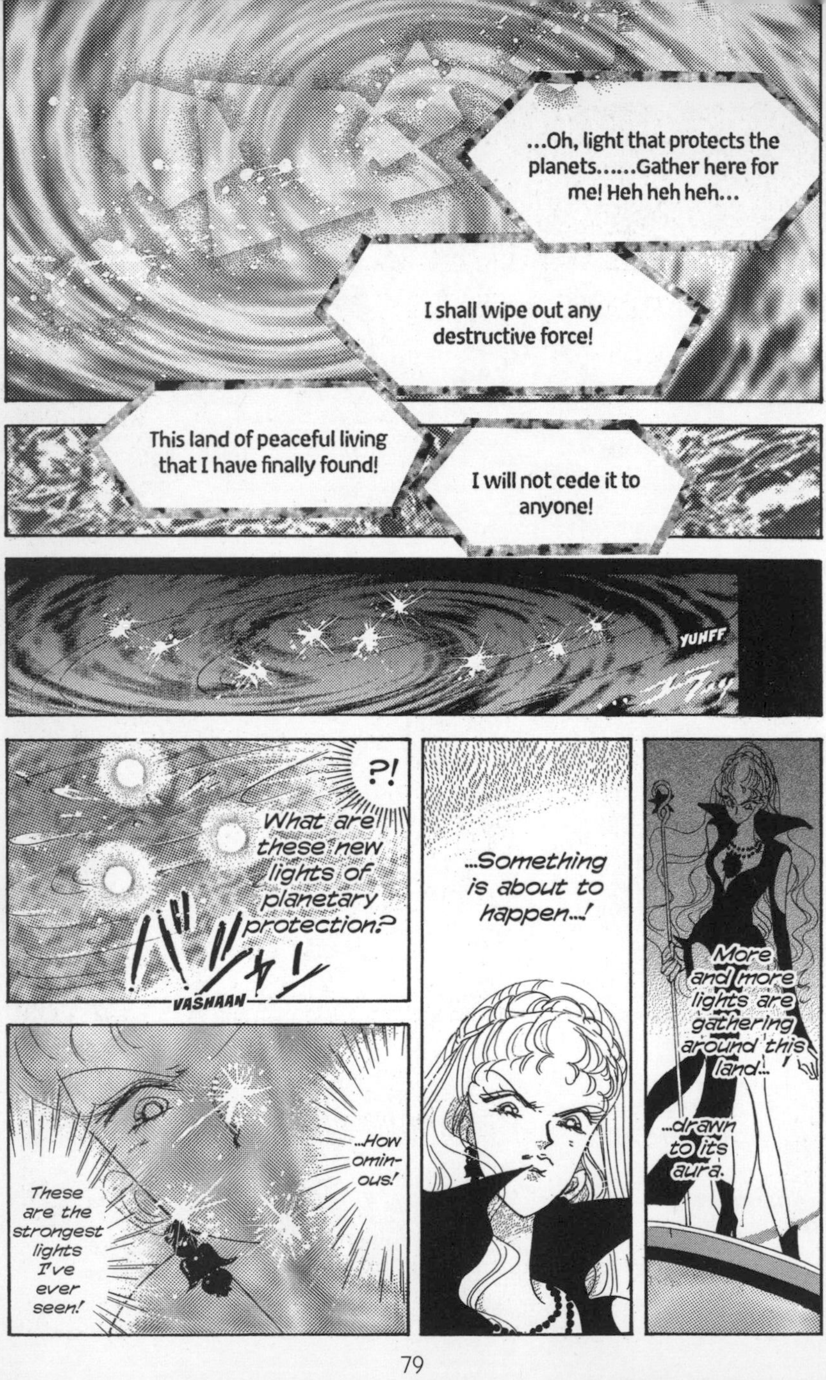
...Oh, light that protects the planets......Gather here for me! Heh heh heh...
I shall wipe out any destructive force!
This land of peaceful living that I have finally found!
I will not cede it to anyone!
YUHFF
More and more lights are gathering around this land...
...drawn to its aura.
...Something is about to happen...!
?!
What are these new lights of planetary protection?
VASHAAN
...How ominous!
These are the strongest lights I've ever seen!

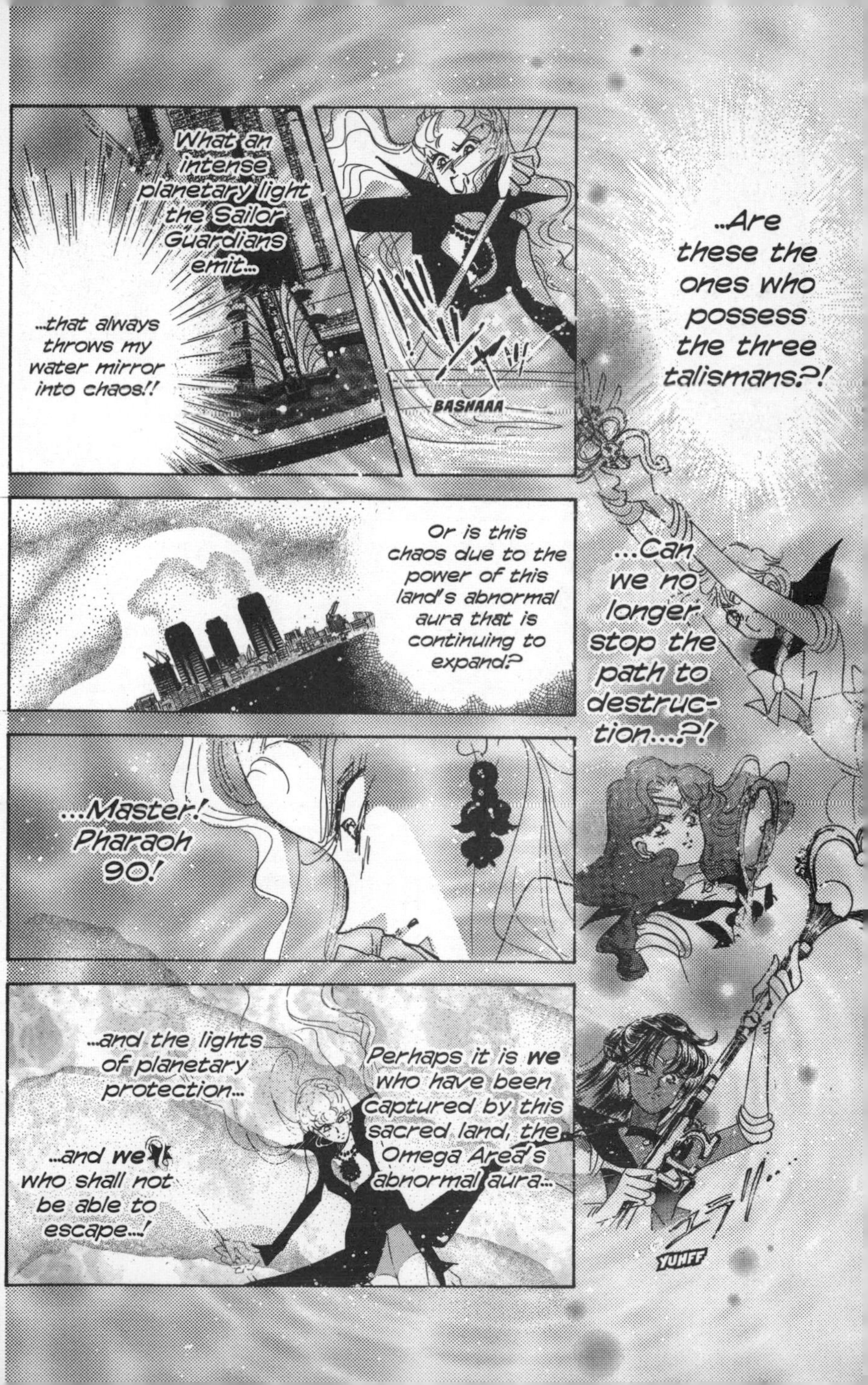

...Are these the ones who possess the three talismans?!
...Can we no longer stop the path to destruction...?!
YUNFF
BASHAAA
What an intense planetary light the Sailor Guardians emit...
...that always throws my water mirror into chaos!!
Or is this chaos due to the power of this land's abnormal aura that is continuing to expand?
...Master! Pharaoh 90!
Perhaps it is **we** who have been captured by this sacred land, the Omega Area's abnormal aura...
...and the lights of planetary protection...
...and **we** who shall not be able to escape...!

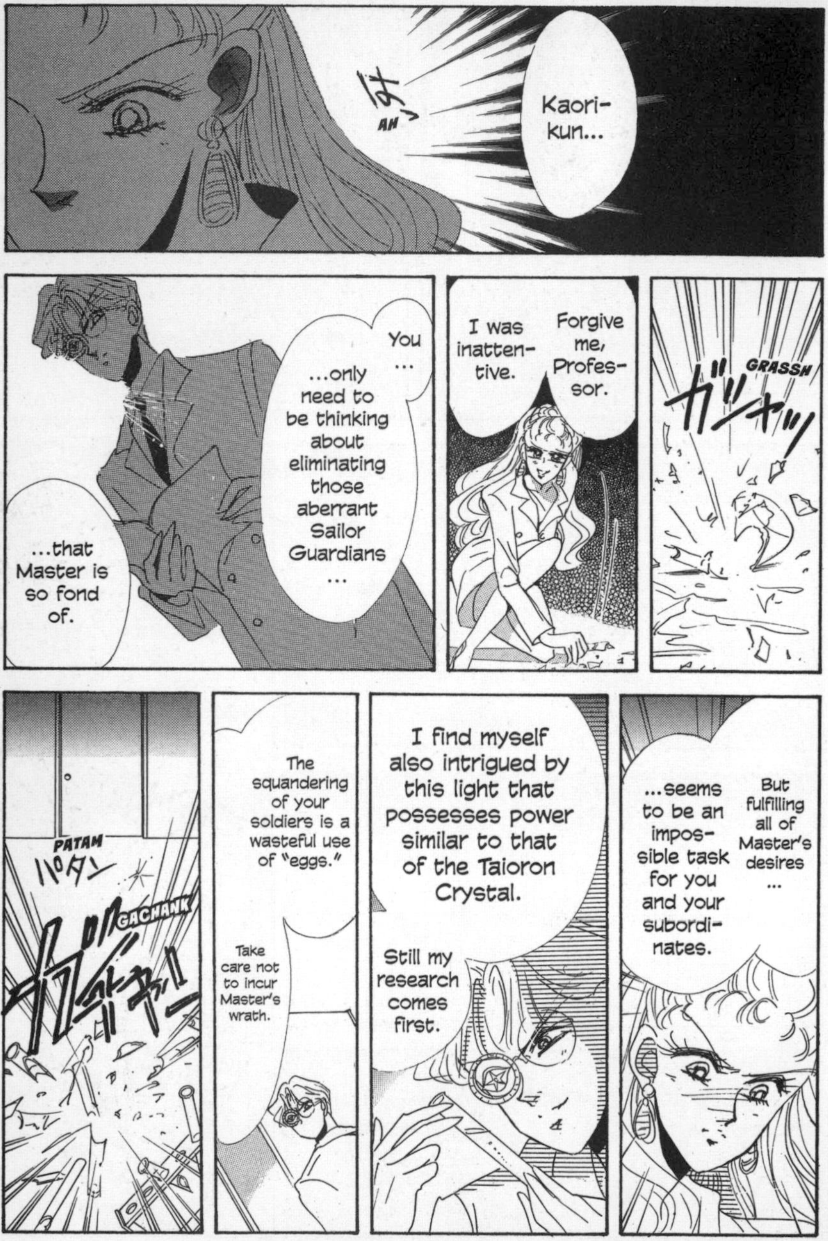
AH
Kaori-kun...
GRASSH
Forgive me, Professor.
I was inattentive.
You ...
...only need to be thinking about eliminating those aberrant Sailor Guardians ...
...that Master is so fond of.
But fulfilling all of Master's desires ...
...seems to be an impossible task for you and your subordinates.
I find myself also intrigued by this light that possesses power similar to that of the Taioron Crystal.
Still my research comes first.
The squandering of your soldiers is a wasteful use of "eggs."
Take care not to incur Master's wrath.
PATAM
GACHANK

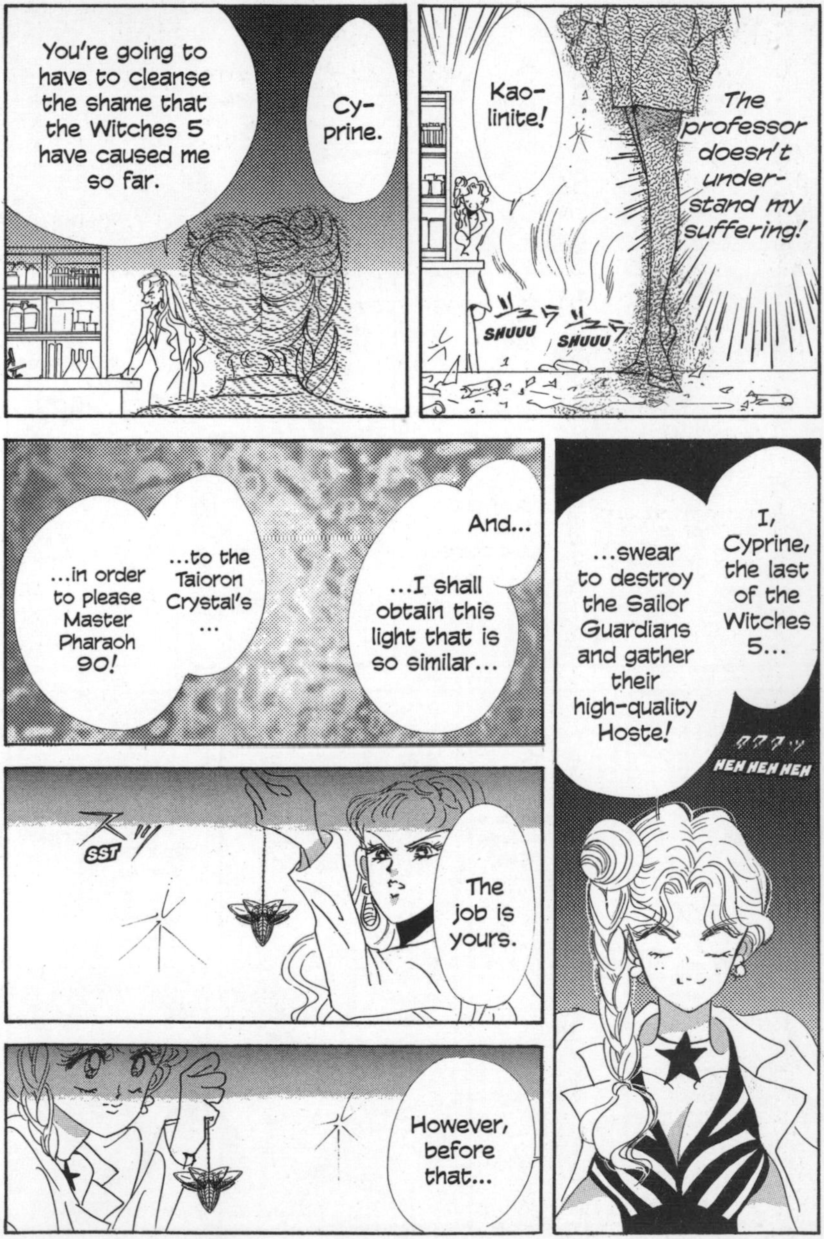
The professor doesn't understand my suffering!
Kao-linite!
SHUUU
SHUUU
Cy-prine.
You're going to have to cleanse the shame that the Witches 5 have caused me so far.
I, Cyprine, the last of the Witches 5...
...swear to destroy the Sailor Guardians and gather their high-quality Hoste!
HEH HEH HEH
And...
...I shall obtain this light that is so similar...
...to the Taioron Crystal's...
...in order to please Master Pharaoh 90!
SST
The job is yours.
However, before that...

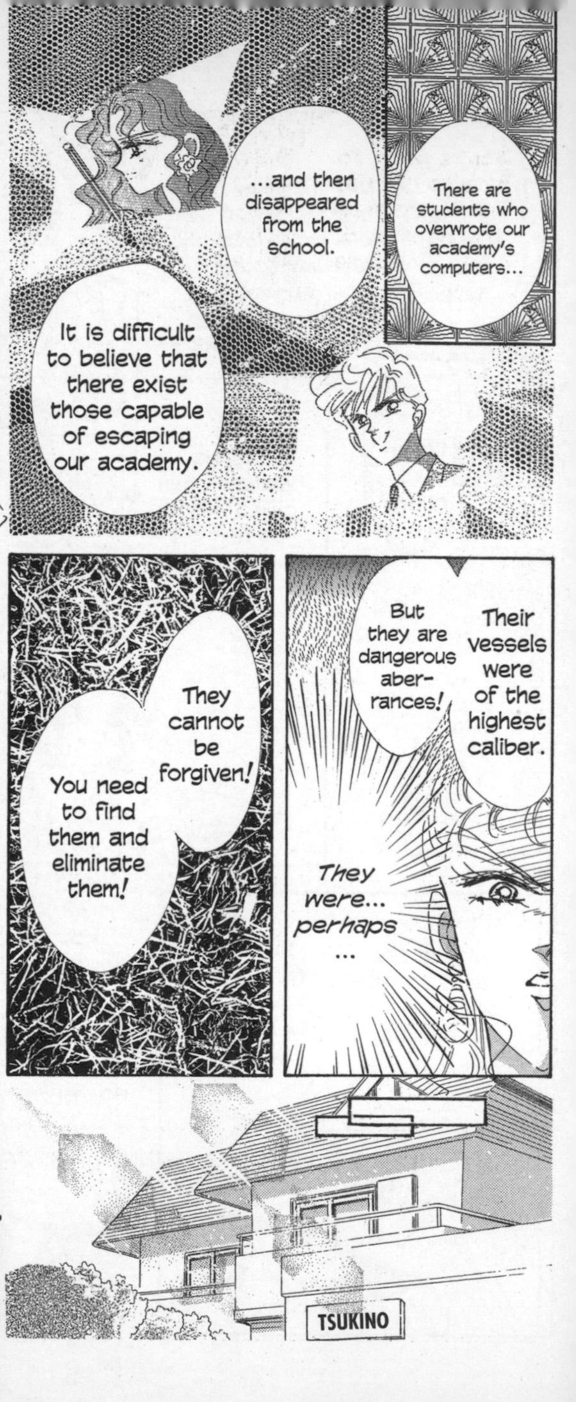
There are students who overwrote our academy's computers...
...and then disappeared from the school.
It is difficult to believe that there exist those capable of escaping our academy.
Their vessels were of the highest caliber.
But they are dangerous aber-rances!
They were... perhaps ...
They cannot be forgiven!
You need to find them and eliminate them!
TSUKINO

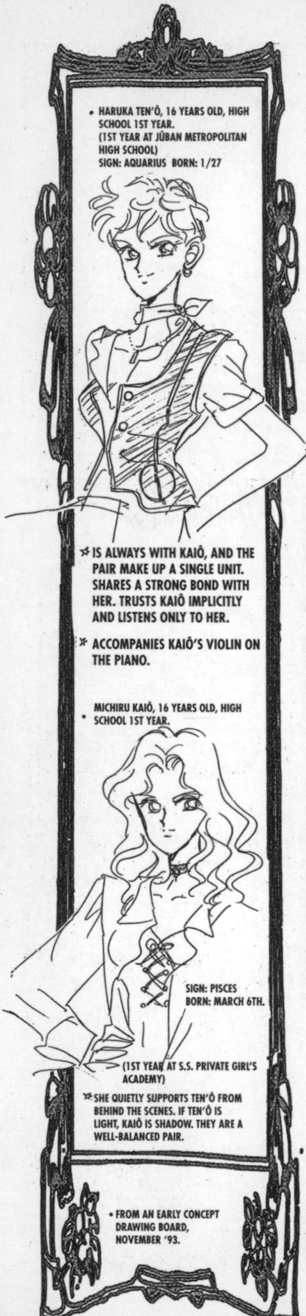
• HARUKA TEN'Ô, 16 YEARS OLD, HIGH SCHOOL 1ST YEAR.
(1ST YEAR AT JÛBAN METROPOLITAN HIGH SCHOOL)
SIGN: AQUARIUS BORN: 1/27
☆ IS ALWAYS WITH KAIÔ, AND THE PAIR MAKE UP A SINGLE UNIT. SHARES A STRONG BOND WITH HER. TRUSTS KAIÔ IMPLICITLY AND LISTENS ONLY TO HER.
☆ ACCOMPANIES KAIÔ'S VIOLIN ON THE PIANO.
• MICHIRU KAIÔ, 16 YEARS OLD, HIGH SCHOOL 1ST YEAR.
SIGN: PISCES
BORN: MARCH 6TH.
(1ST YEAR AT S.S. PRIVATE GIRL'S ACADEMY)
☆ SHE QUIETLY SUPPORTS TEN'Ô FROM BEHIND THE SCENES. IF TEN'Ô IS LIGHT, KAIÔ IS SHADOW. THEY ARE A WELL-BALANCED PAIR.
• FROM AN EARLY CONCEPT DRAWING BOARD, NOVEMBER '93.

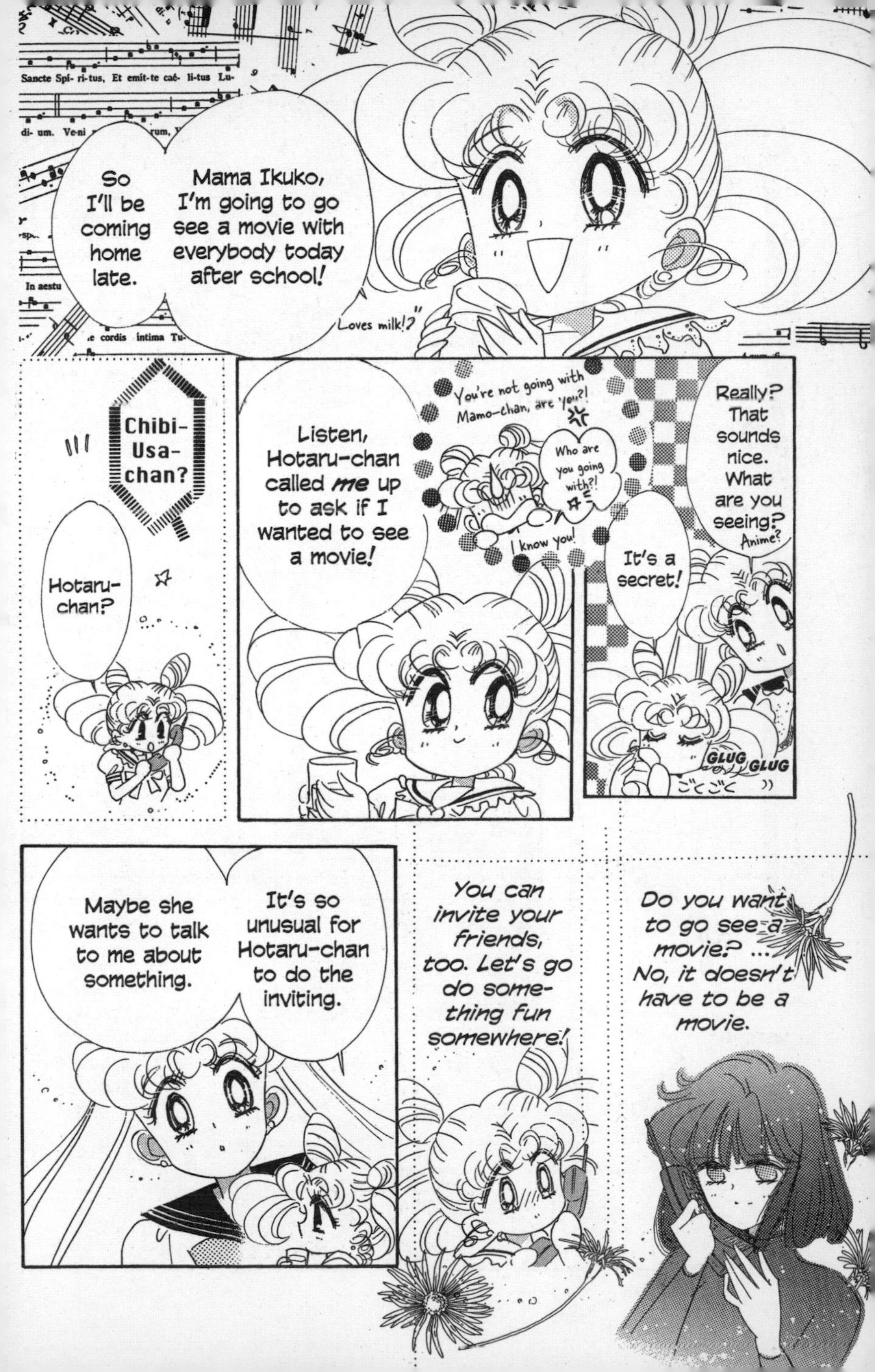
Sancte Spi-ri-tus, Et emit-te cae-li-tus Lu-
di-um. Ve-ni
In aestu
cordis intima Tu-
Mama Ikuko, I'm going to go see a movie with everybody today after school!
So I'll be coming home late.
Loves milk!?
Really? That sounds nice. What are you seeing?
Anime?
It's a secret!
GLUG GLUG
ごくごく
Listen, Hotaru-chan called *me* up to ask if I wanted to see a movie!
You're not going with Mamo-chan, are you?!
Who are you going with?!
I know you!
Chibi-Usa-chan?
Hotaru-chan?
Do you want to go see a movie? ... No, it doesn't have to be a movie.
You can invite your friends, too. Let's go do something fun somewhere!
It's so unusual for Hotaru-chan to do the inviting.
Maybe she wants to talk to me about something.

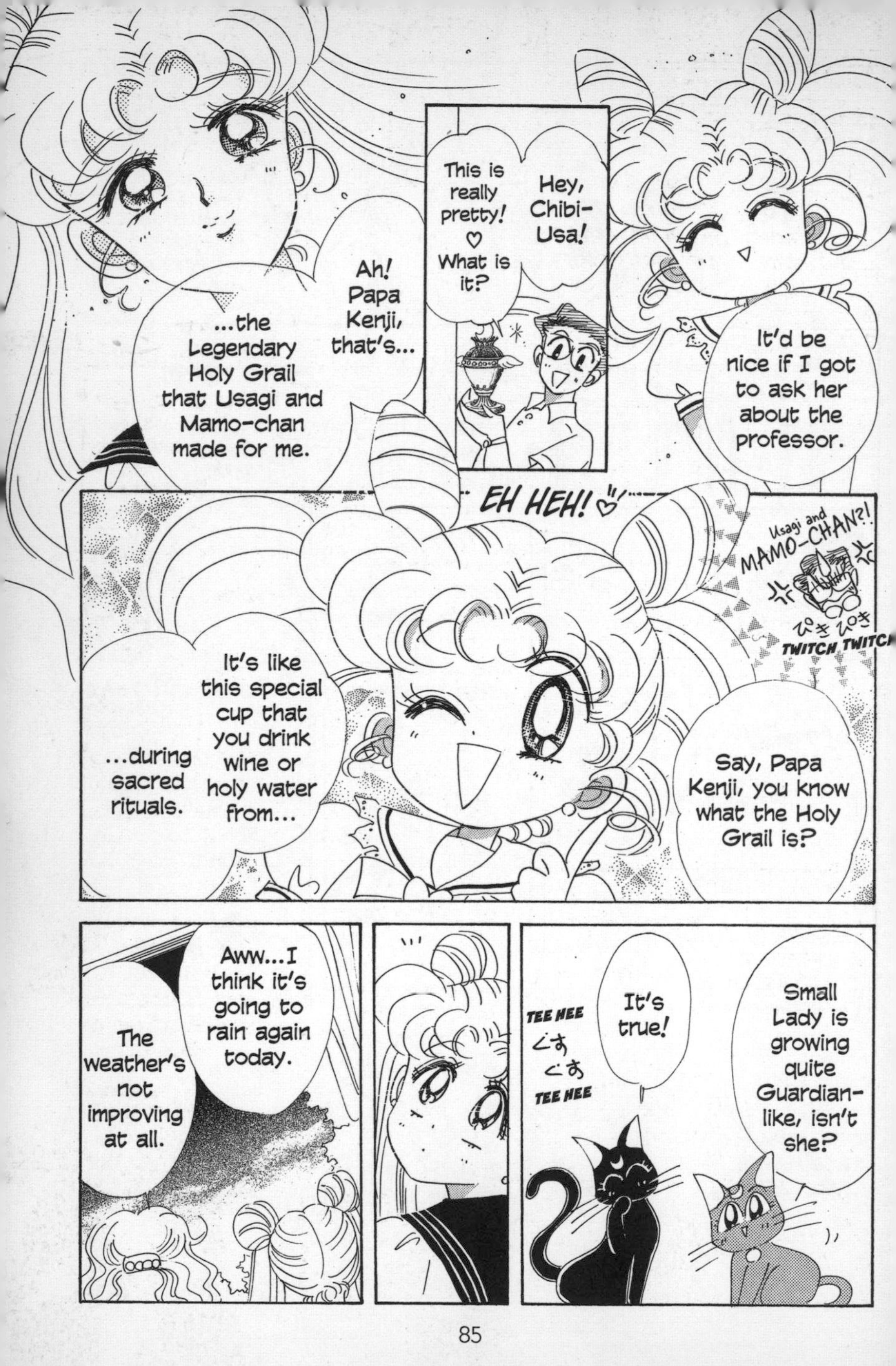

It'd be nice if I got to ask her about the professor.
Hey, Chibi-Usa!
This is really pretty! ♡ What is it?
Ah! Papa Kenji, that's...
...the Legendary Holy Grail that Usagi and Mamo-chan made for me.
EH HEH! ♡
Usagi and MAMO-CHAN?!
ぴきぴき
TWITCH TWITCH
Say, Papa Kenji, you know what the Holy Grail is?
It's like this special cup that you drink wine or holy water from...
...during sacred rituals.
Small Lady is growing quite Guardian-like, isn't she?
It's true!
TEE HEE
くす くす
TEE HEE
Aww...I think it's going to rain again today.
The weather's not improving at all.

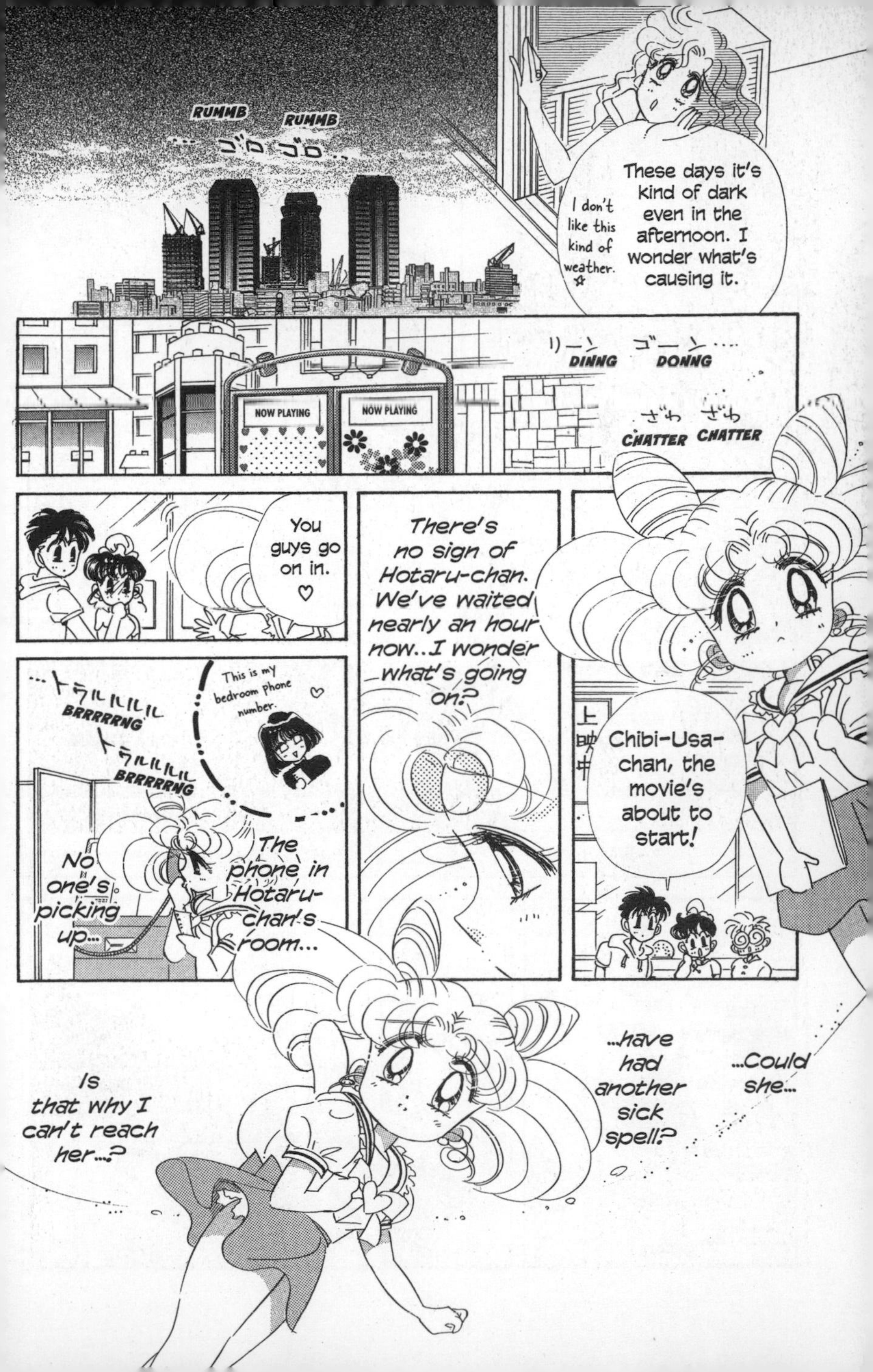
These days it's kind of dark even in the afternoon. I wonder what's causing it.
I don't like this kind of weather. ☆
ゴロゴロ..
RUMMB RUMMB
リーン ゴーン...
DINNG DONNG
NOW PLAYING
NOW PLAYING
ざわ ざわ
CHATTER CHATTER
Chibi-Usa-chan, the movie's about to start!
There's no sign of Hotaru-chan. We've waited nearly an hour now...I wonder what's going on?
You guys go on in. ♡
This is my bedroom phone number.
BRRRRRNG
BRRRRRNG
The phone in Hotaru-chan's room...
No one's picking up...
...Could she...
...have had another sick spell?
Is that why I can't reach her...?

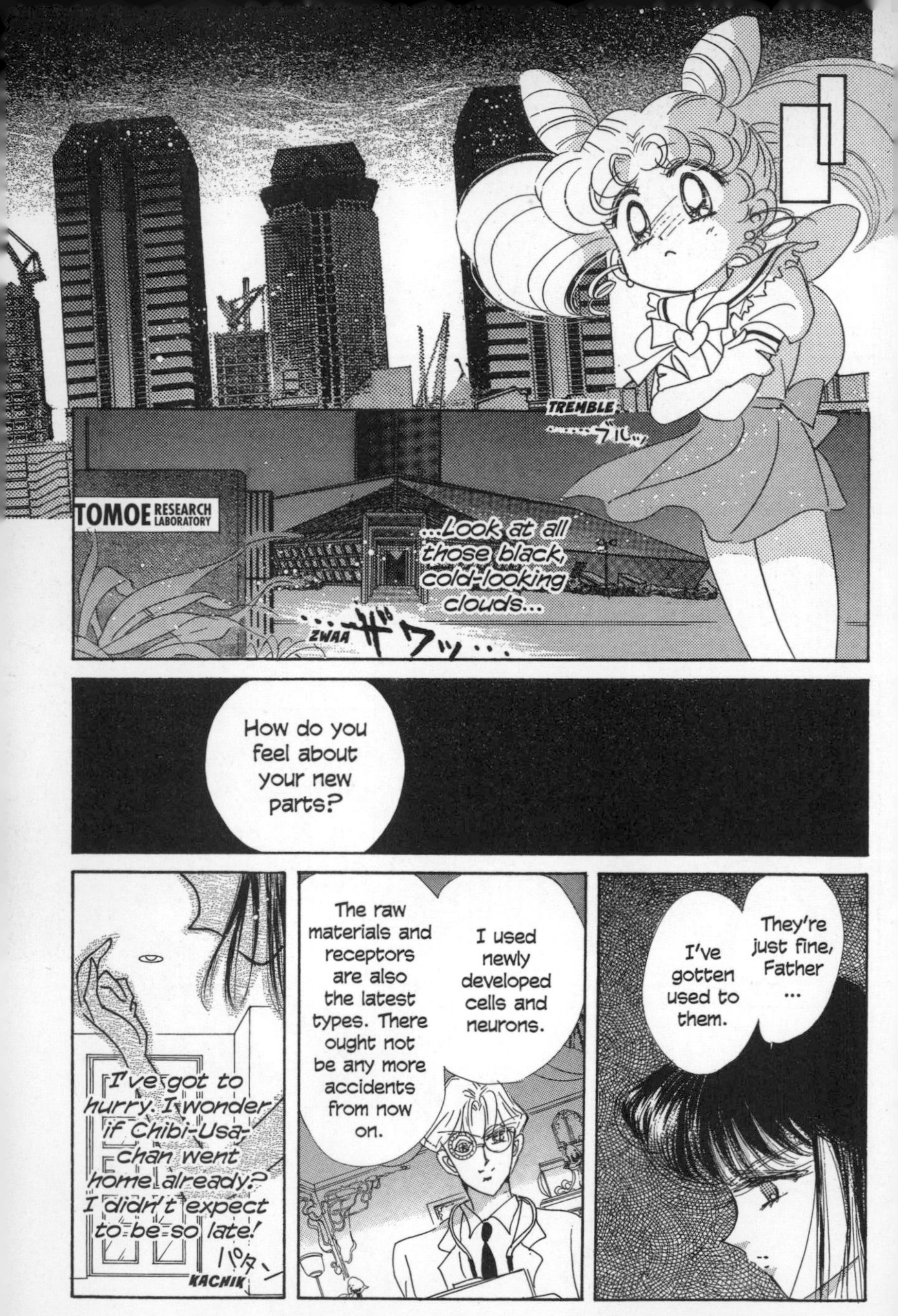
TREMBLE
...Look at all those black, cold-looking clouds...
ZWAA
TOMOE RESEARCH LABORATORY
How do you feel about your new parts?
They're just fine, Father ...
I've gotten used to them.
I used newly developed cells and neurons.
The raw materials and receptors are also the latest types. There ought not be any more accidents from now on.
I've got to hurry. I wonder if Chibi-Usa-chan went home already? I didn't expect to be so late!
KACHIK

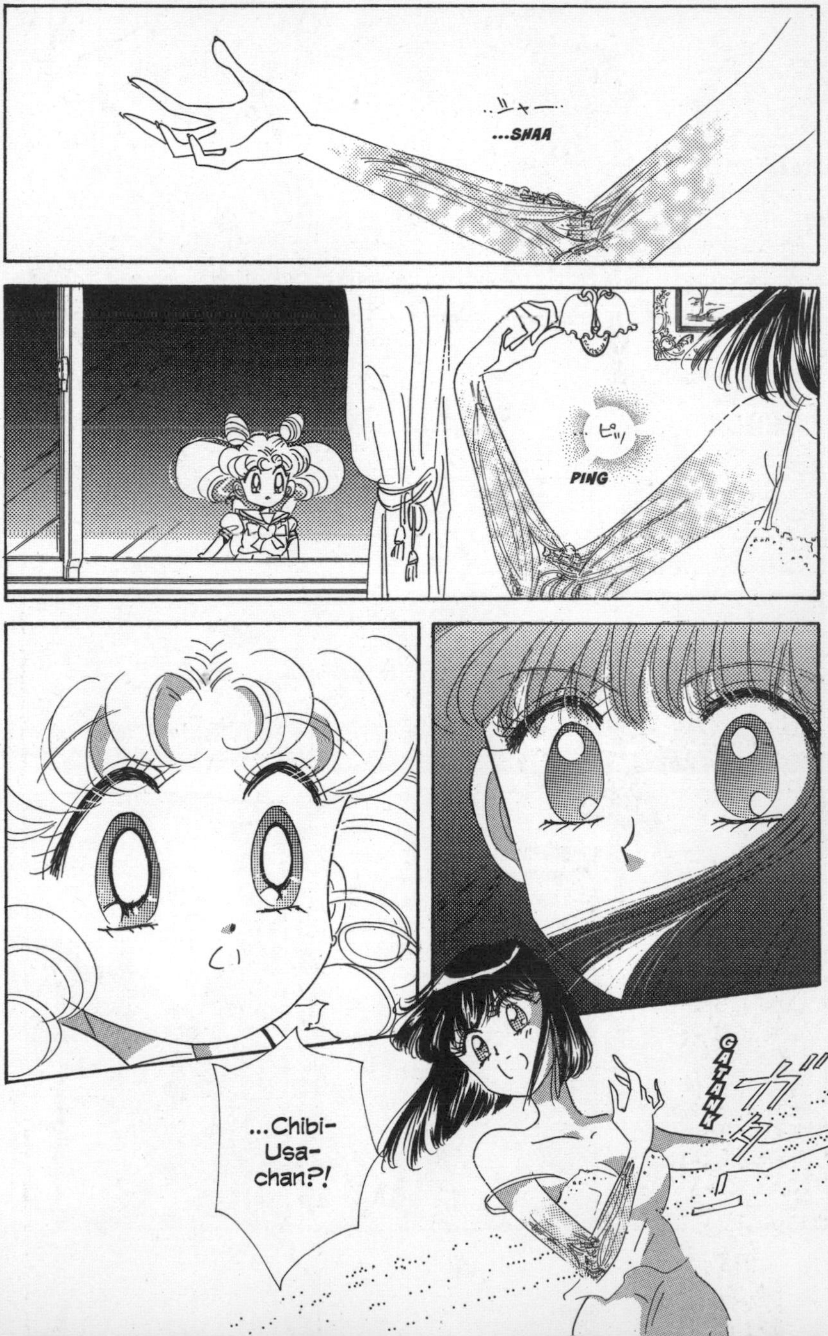
…シャー…
...SHAA
ピッ
PING
GATANK
ガタッ
...Chibi-Usa-chan?!

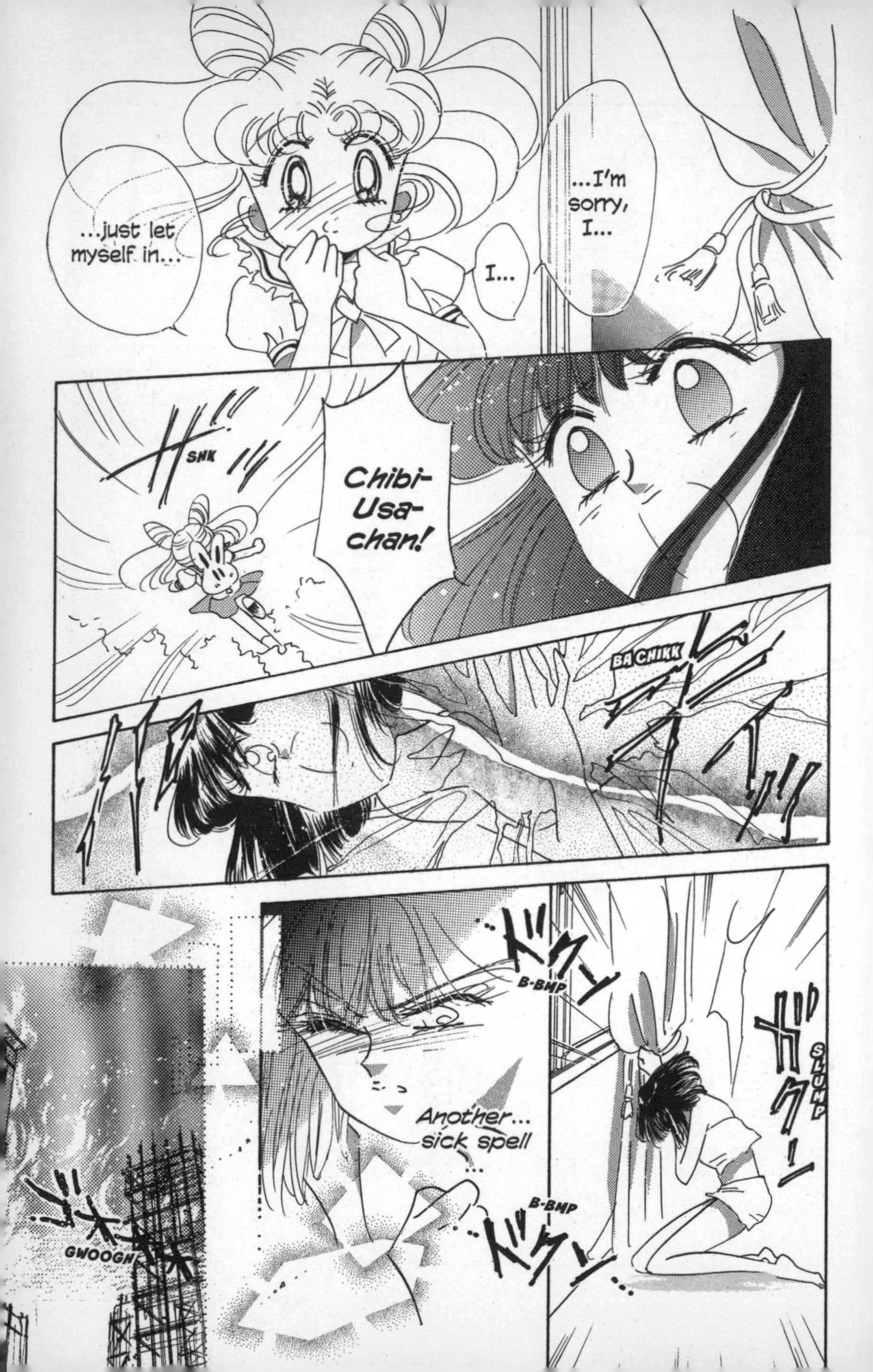
...I'm sorry, I...
I...
...just let myself in...
Chibi-Usa-chan!
SHK
BA CHIKK
SLUMP
B-BMP
Another... sick spell...
B-BMP
GWOOGH

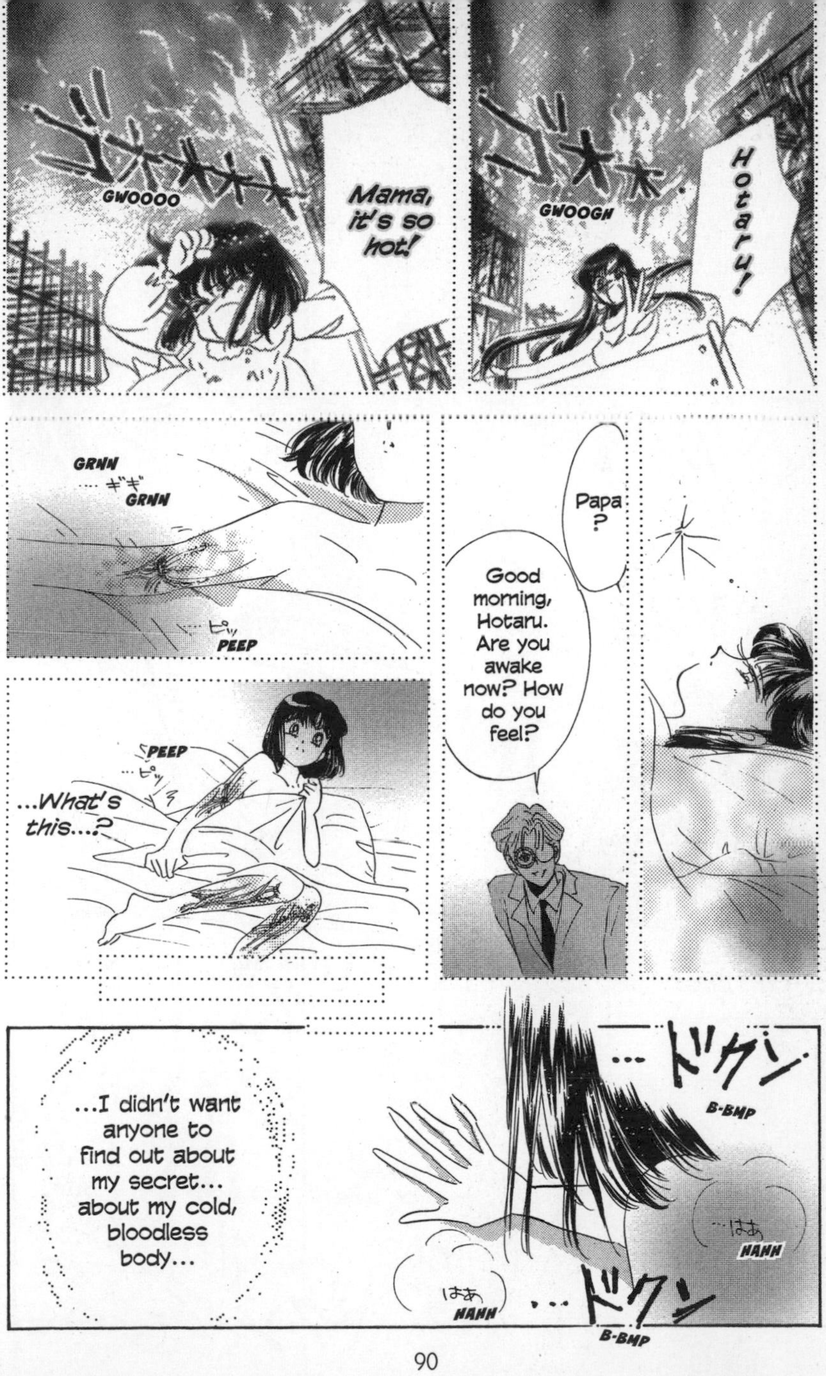
GWOOGH
Hotaru!
GWOOOO
Mama, it's so hot!
Papa?
Good morning, Hotaru. Are you awake now? How do you feel?
GRNN ...ギギ GRNN
...ピッ PEEP
PEEP ...ピッ
...What's this...?
...ドクン B-BMP
...はあ HAHN
...I didn't want anyone to find out about my secret... about my cold, bloodless body...
はあ HAHN
...ドクン B-BMP

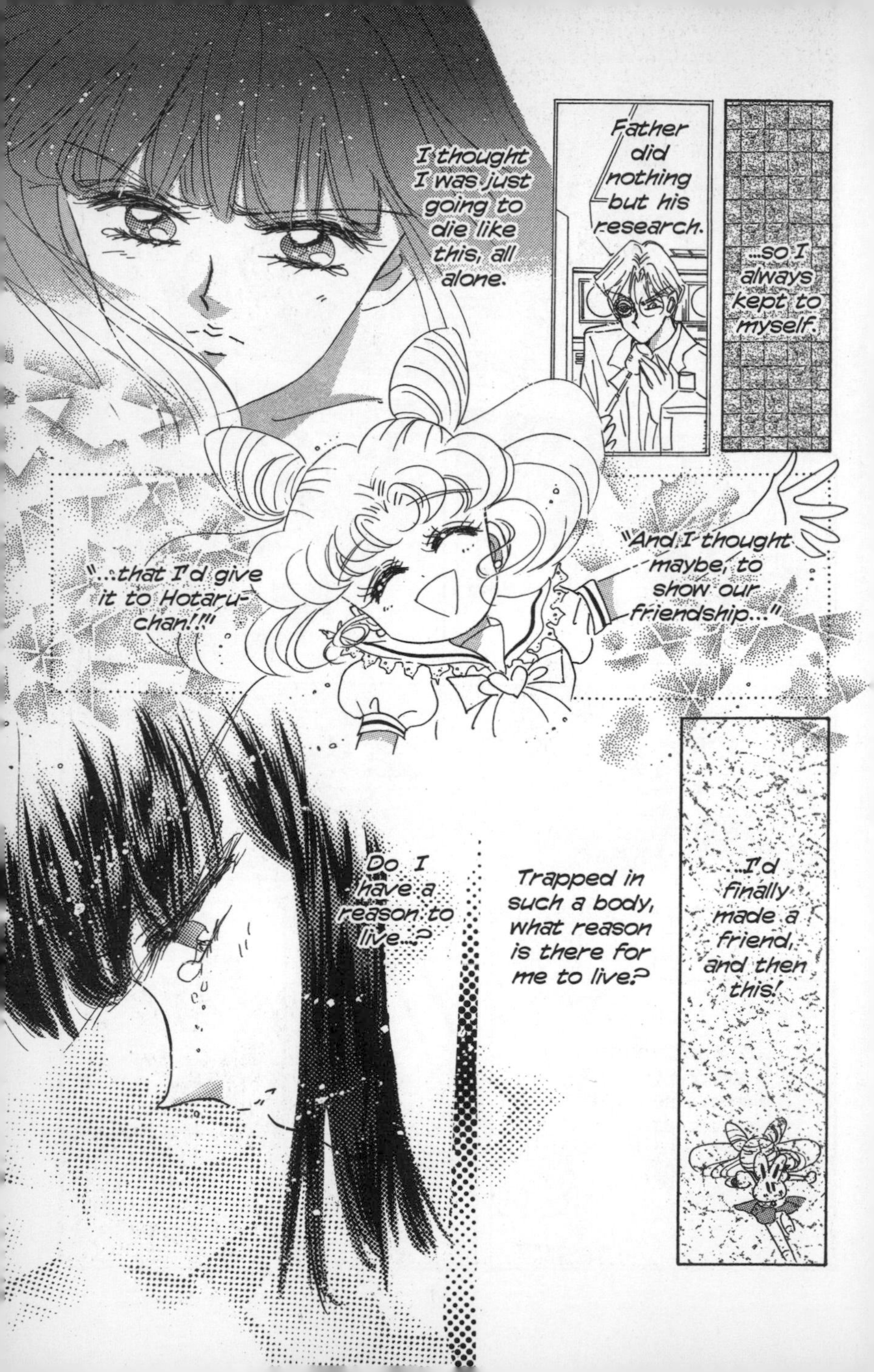
...so I always kept to myself.
Father did nothing but his research.
I thought I was just going to die like this, all alone.
"And I thought maybe, to show our friendship..."
"...that I'd give it to Hotaru-chan!!"
...I'd finally made a friend, and then this!
Trapped in such a body, what reason is there for me to live?
Do I have a reason to live...?

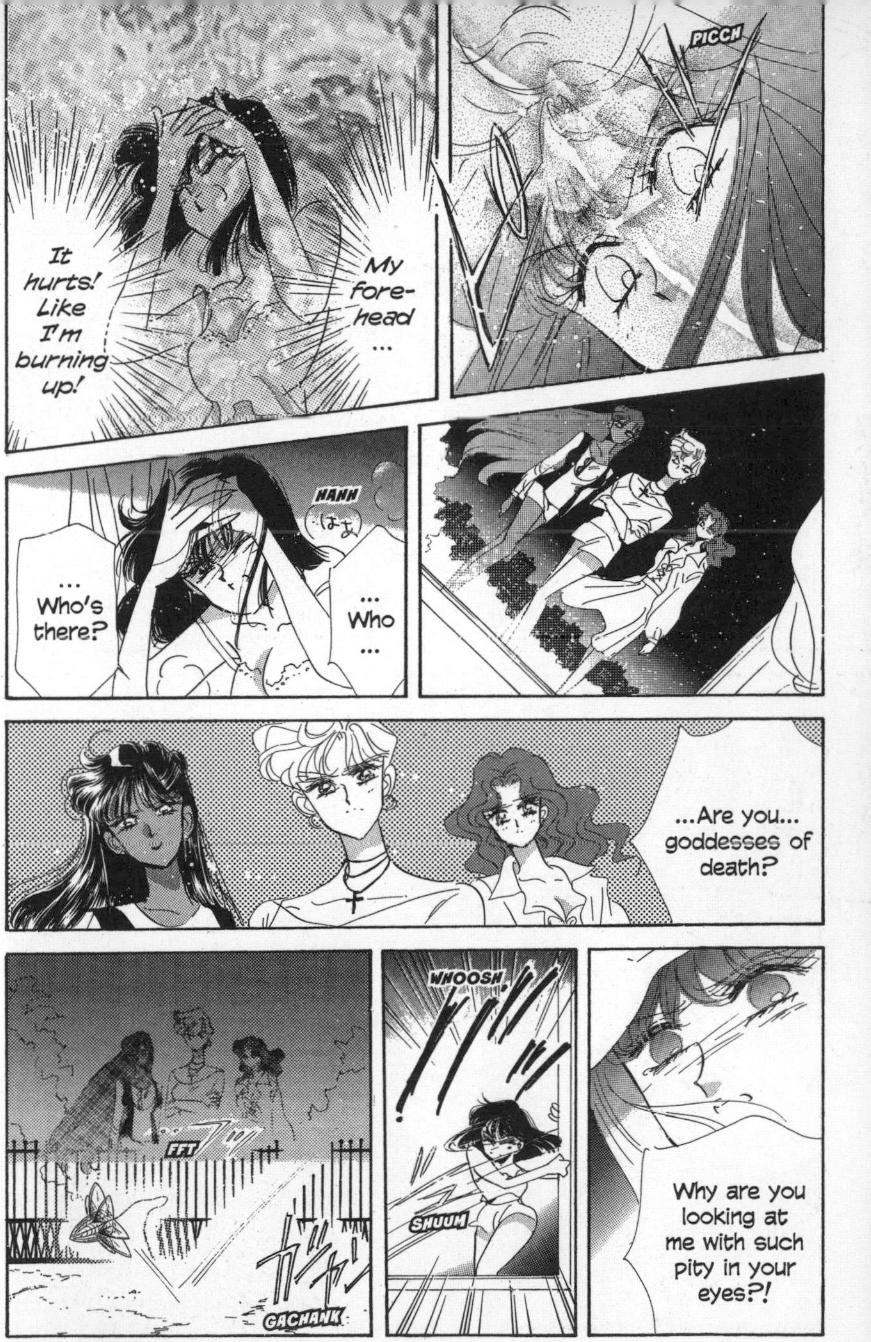
PICCH
My fore-head ...
It hurts! Like I'm burning up!
HANN
... Who ...
... Who's there?
...Are you... goddesses of death?
Why are you looking at me with such pity in your eyes?!
WHOOSH
SHUUM
FFT
GACHANK

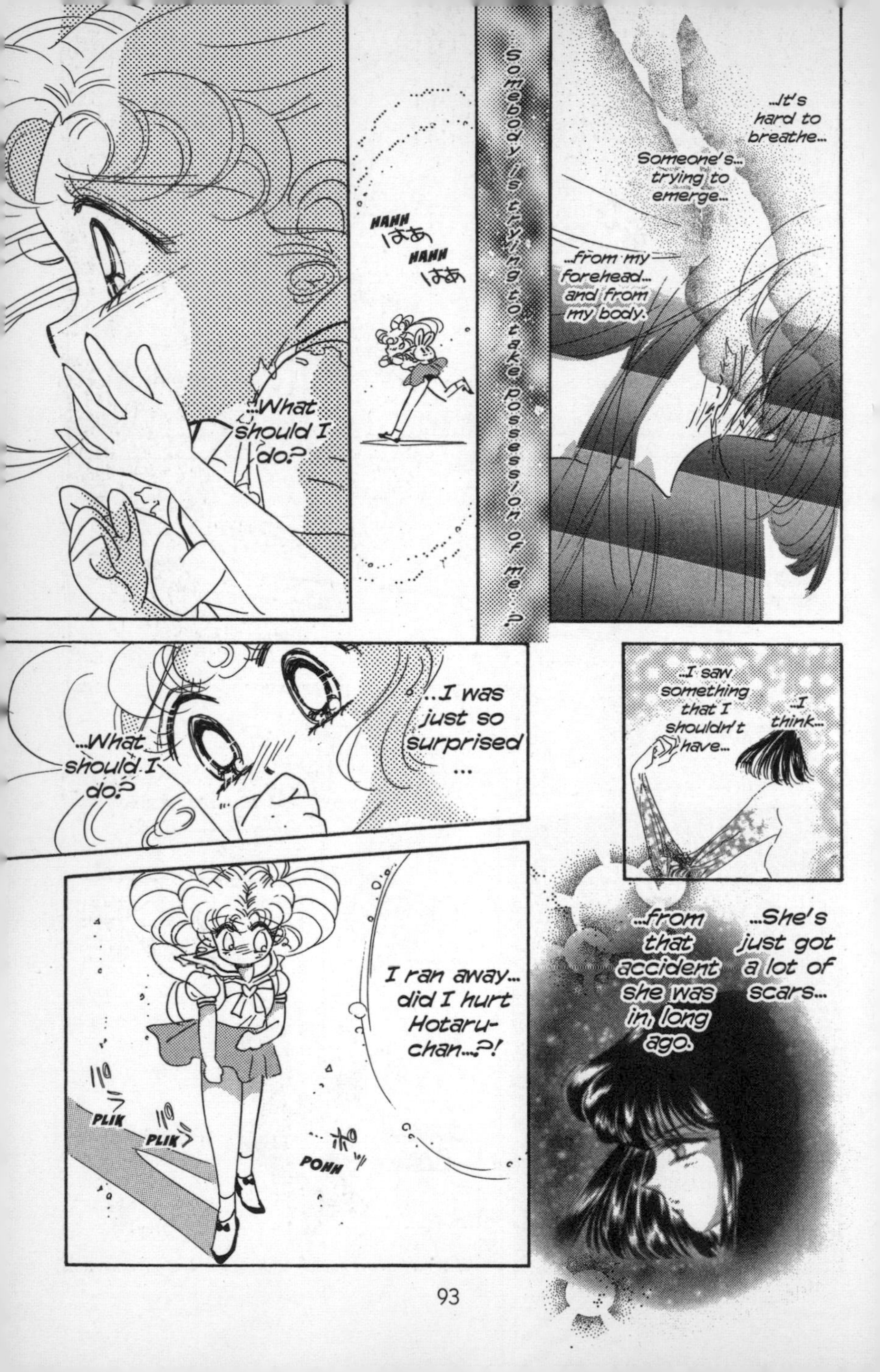
...It's hard to breathe...
Someone's... trying to emerge...
...from my forehead... and from my body.
Somebody is trying to take possession of me...?
HAHH はあ
HAHH はあ
...What should I do?
...I saw something that I shouldn't have...
...I think...
...I was just so surprised...
...What should I do?
...She's just got a lot of scars...
...from that accident she was in, long ago.
I ran away... did I hurt Hotaru-chan...?!
PLIK
PLIK
POHN

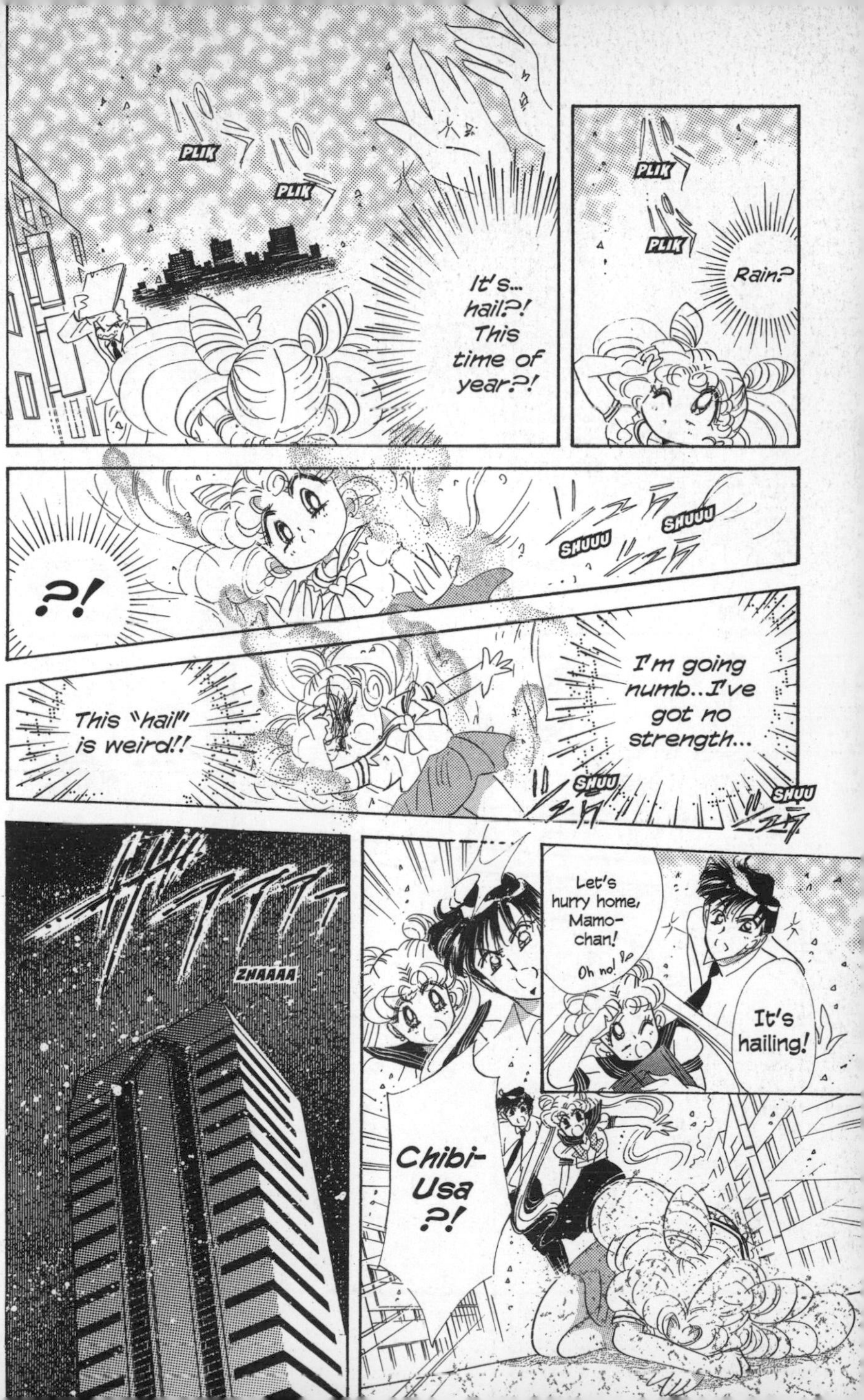
PLIK
PLIK
Rain?
PLIK
PLIK
It's... hail?! This time of year?!
SHUUU
SHUUU
?!
I'm going numb..I've got no strength...
This "hail" is weird!!
SHUU
SHUU
Let's hurry home, Mamo-chan!
Oh no!
It's hailing!
Chibi-Usa ?!
ZHAAAA

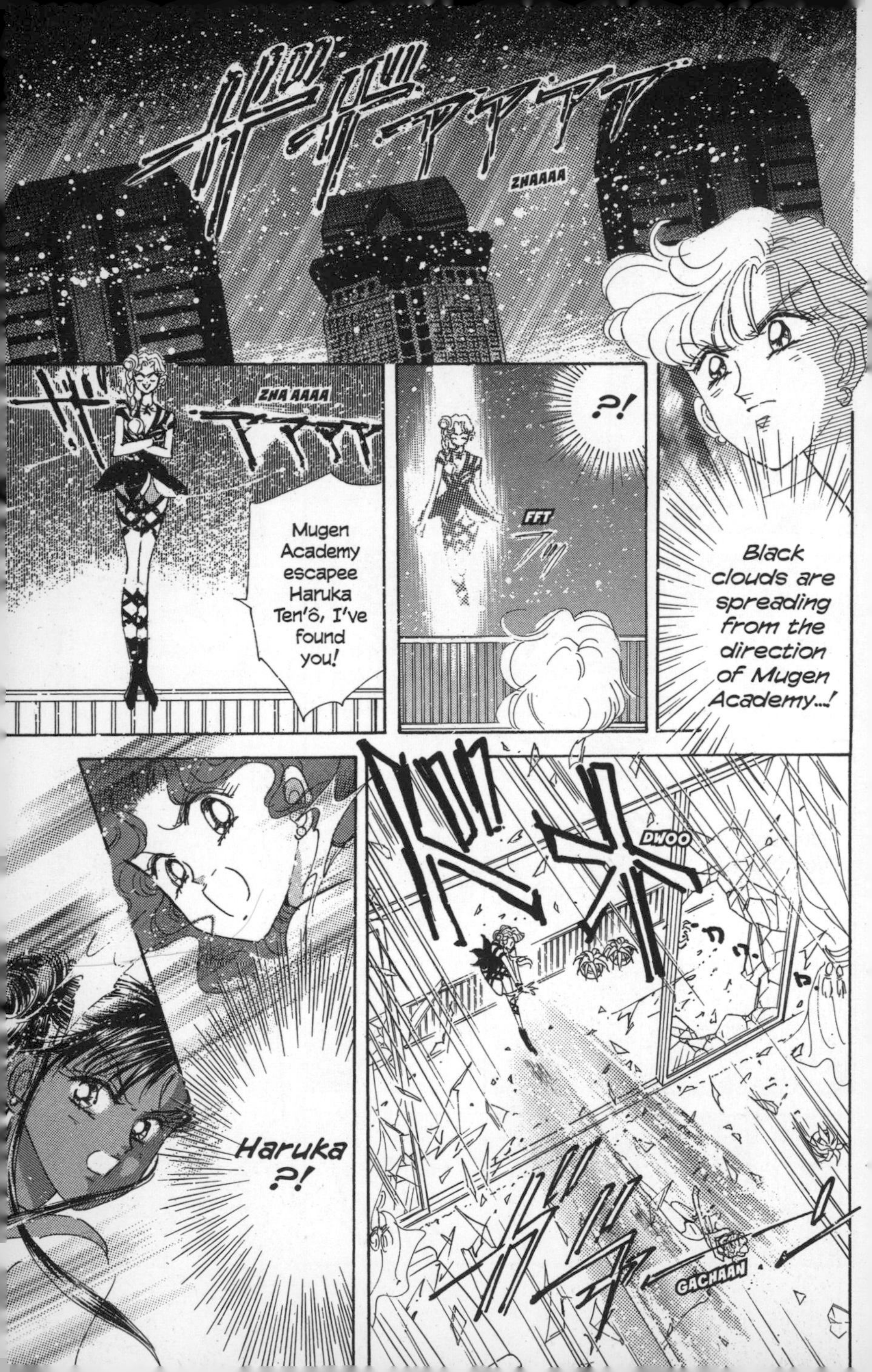
ZHAAAA
Black clouds are spreading from the direction of Mugen Academy...!
?!
FFT
ZHA AAAA
Mugen Academy escapee Haruka Ten'ô, I've found you!
DWOO
GACHAAN
Haruka ?!

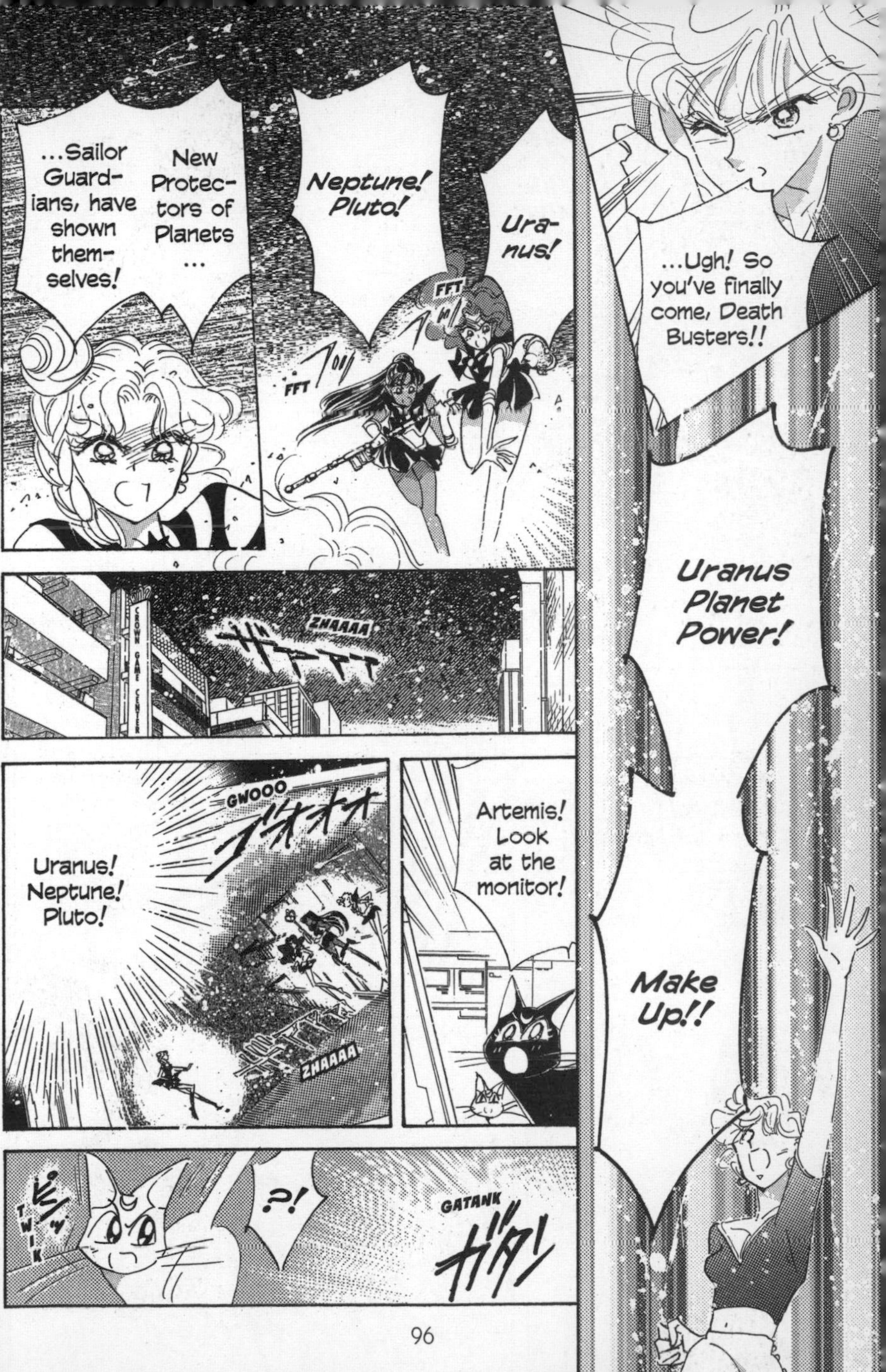
...Ugh! So you've finally come, Death Busters!!
Uranus Planet Power!
Make Up!!
Ura-nus!
Neptune! Pluto!
FFT
FFT
New Protec-tors of Planets ...
...Sailor Guard-ians, have shown them-selves!
ZHAAAA
CROWN GAME CENTER
Artemis! Look at the monitor!
GWOOO
Uranus! Neptune! Pluto!
ZHAAAA
GATANK
?!
TWIK

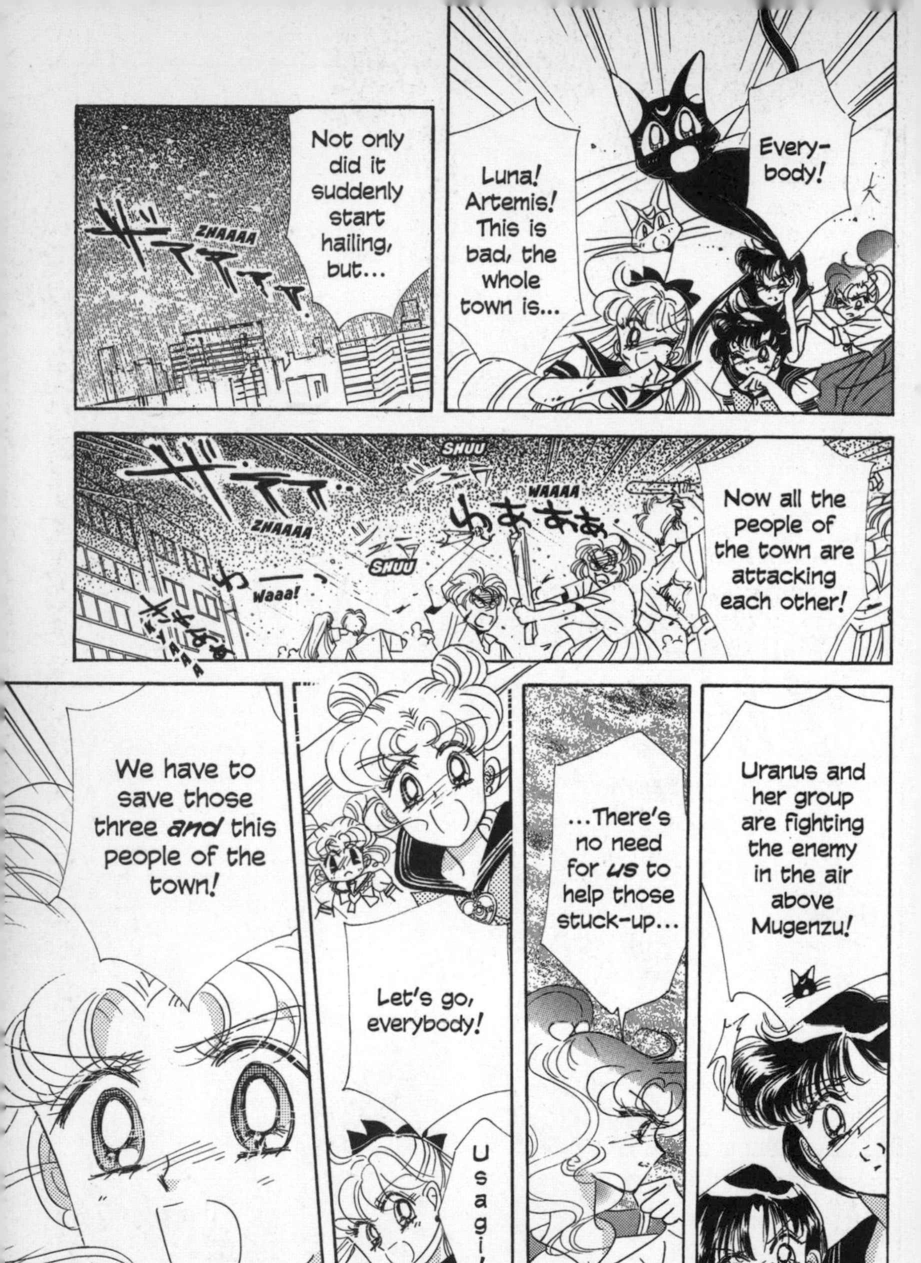
Every-body!
Luna! Artemis! This is bad, the whole town is...
Not only did it suddenly start hailing, but...
ZHAAAA
Now all the people of the town are attacking each other!
SHUU
WAAAA
ZHAAAA
SHUU
Waaa!
KYAAAA
Uranus and her group are fighting the enemy in the air above Mugenzu!
...There's no need for *us* to help those stuck-up...
Let's go, everybody!
Usagi...!
We have to save those three *and* this people of the town!

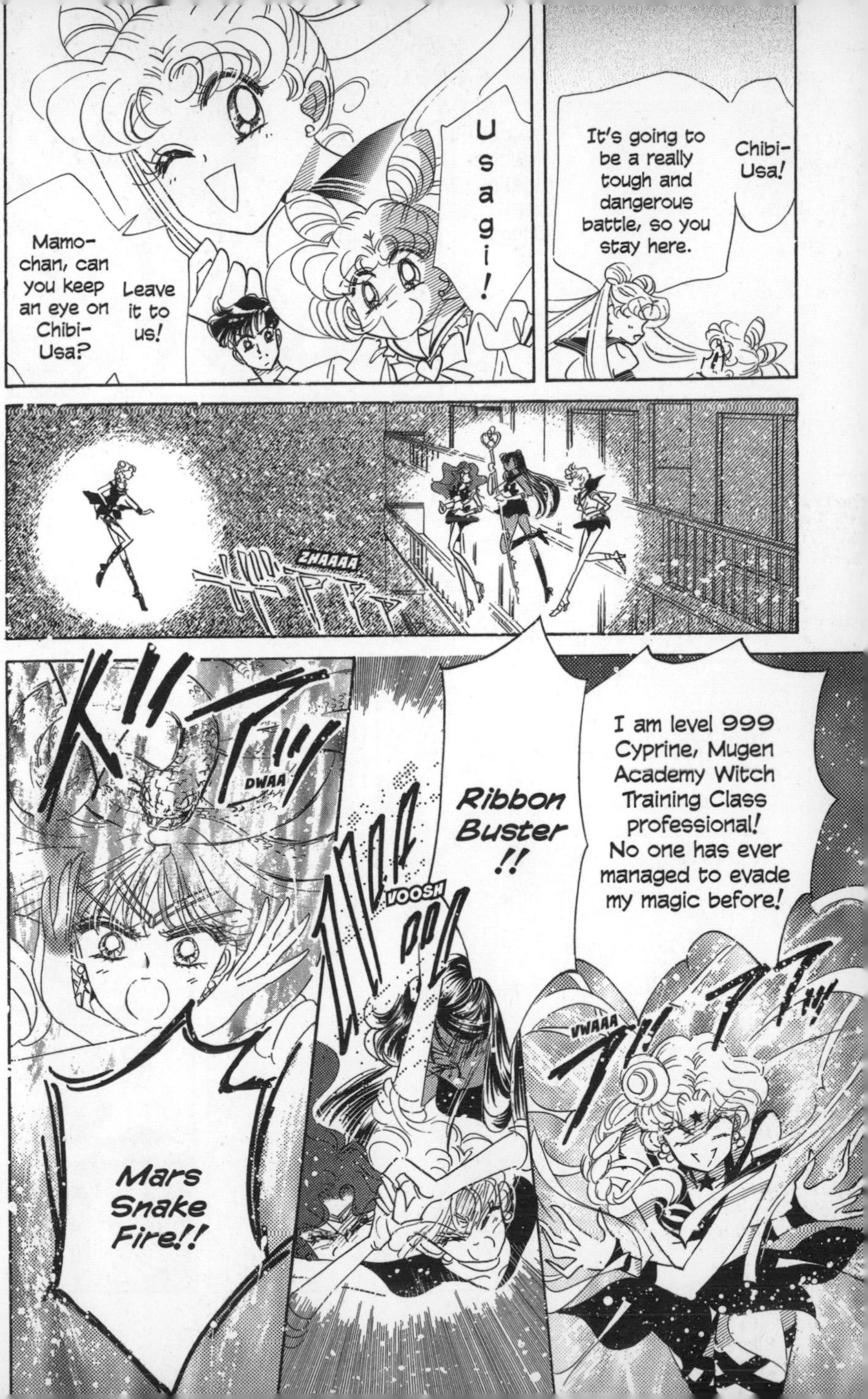
Chibi-Usa!
It's going to be a really tough and dangerous battle, so you stay here.
Usagi!
Mamo-chan, can you keep an eye on Chibi-Usa?
Leave it to us!
ZHAAAA
I am level 999 Cyprine, Mugen Academy Witch Training Class professional! No one has ever managed to evade my magic before!
VWAAA
Ribbon Buster!!
VOOSH
DWAA
Mars Snake Fire!!

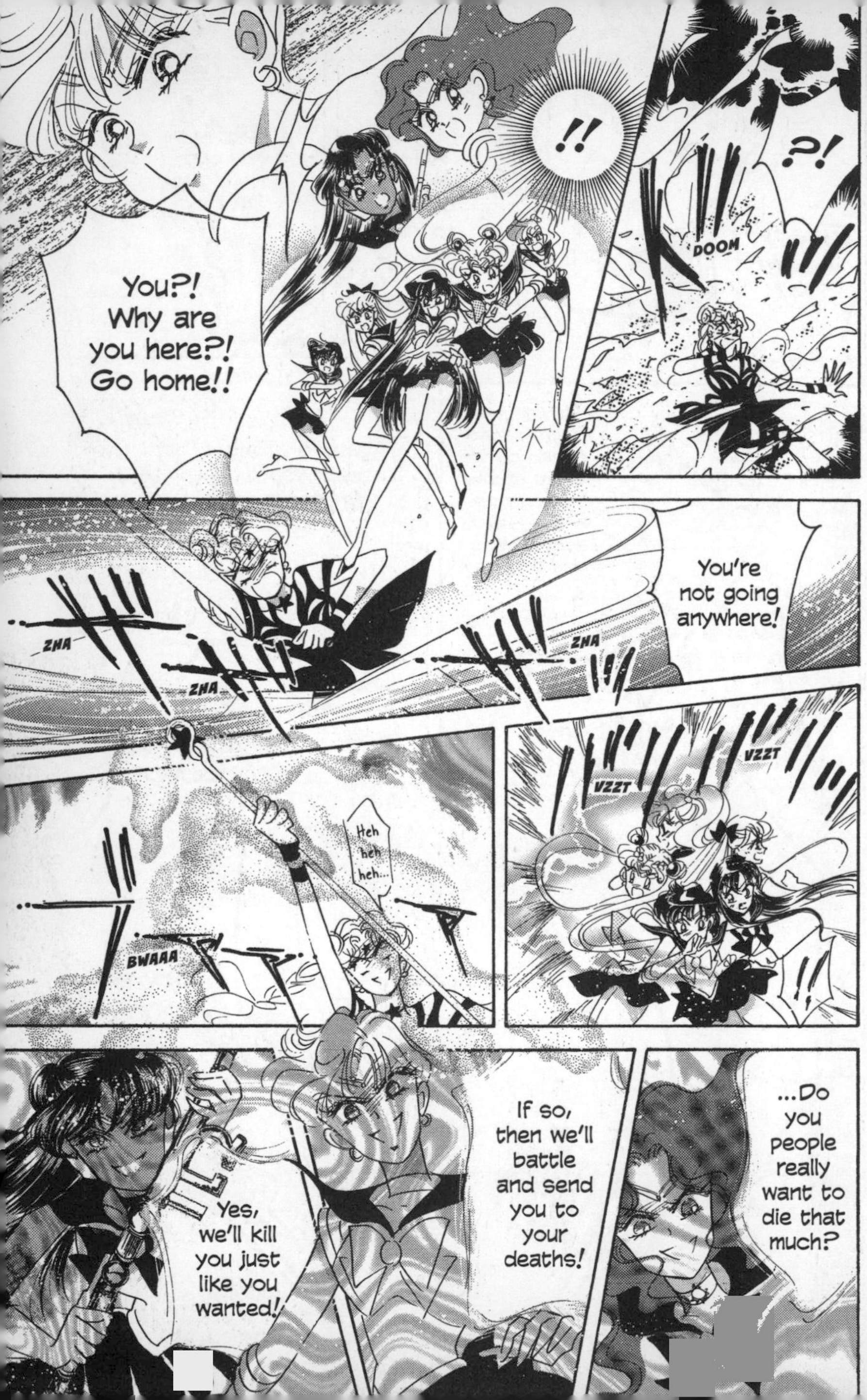
?!
DOOM
!!
You?! Why are you here?! Go home!!
You're not going anywhere!
ZHA
ZHA
ZHA
VZZT
VZZT
!!
Heh heh heh...
BWAAA
...Do you people really want to die that much?
If so, then we'll battle and send you to your deaths!
Yes, we'll kill you just like you wanted!

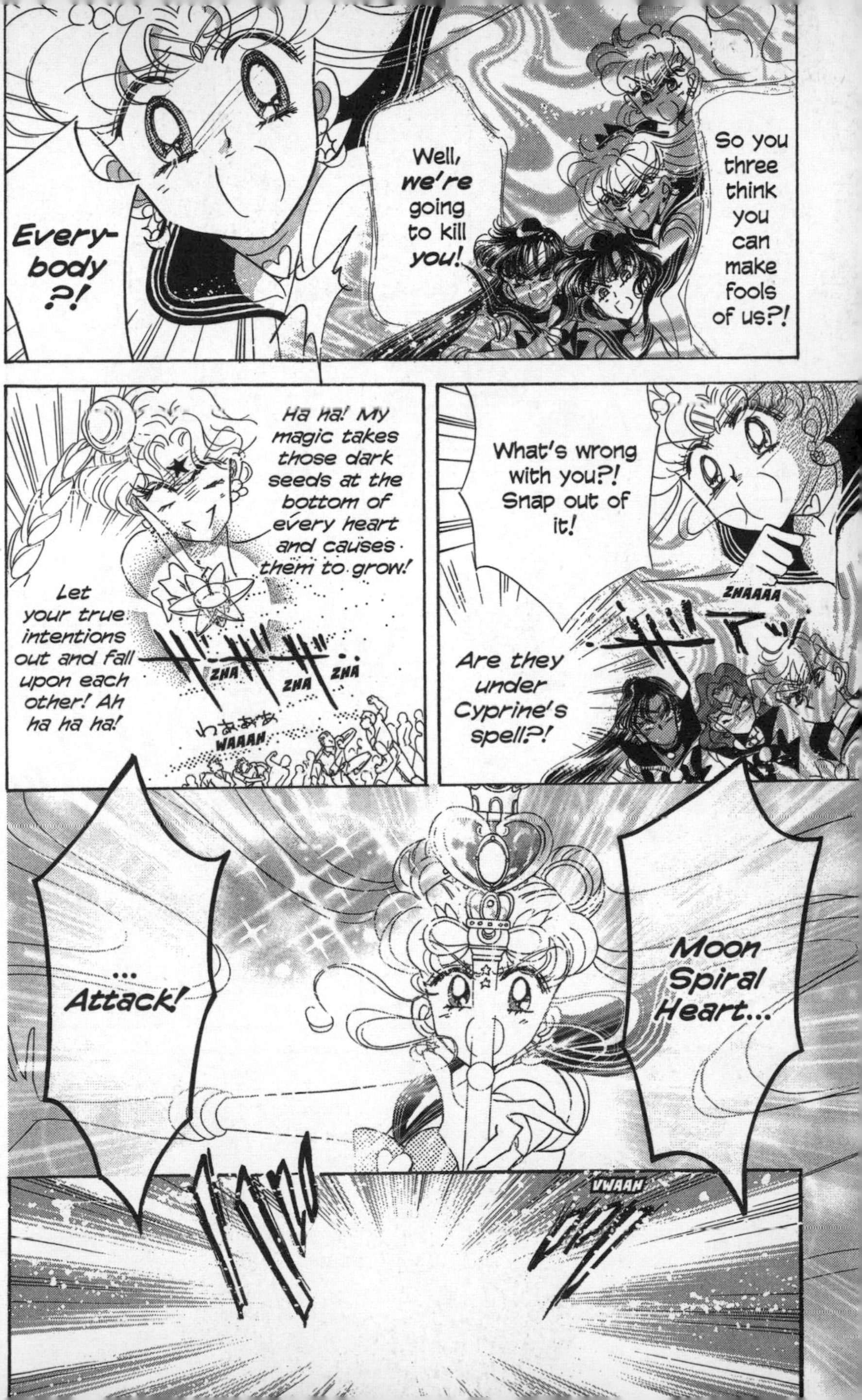

So you three think you can make fools of us?!
Well, we're going to kill you!
Every-body ?!
What's wrong with you?! Snap out of it!
ZHAAAA
Are they under Cyprine's spell?!
Ha ha! My magic takes those dark seeds at the bottom of every heart and causes them to grow!
Let your true intentions out and fall upon each other! Ah ha ha ha!
ZHA
ZHA
ZHA
WAAAH
Moon Spiral Heart...
... Attack!
VWAAH

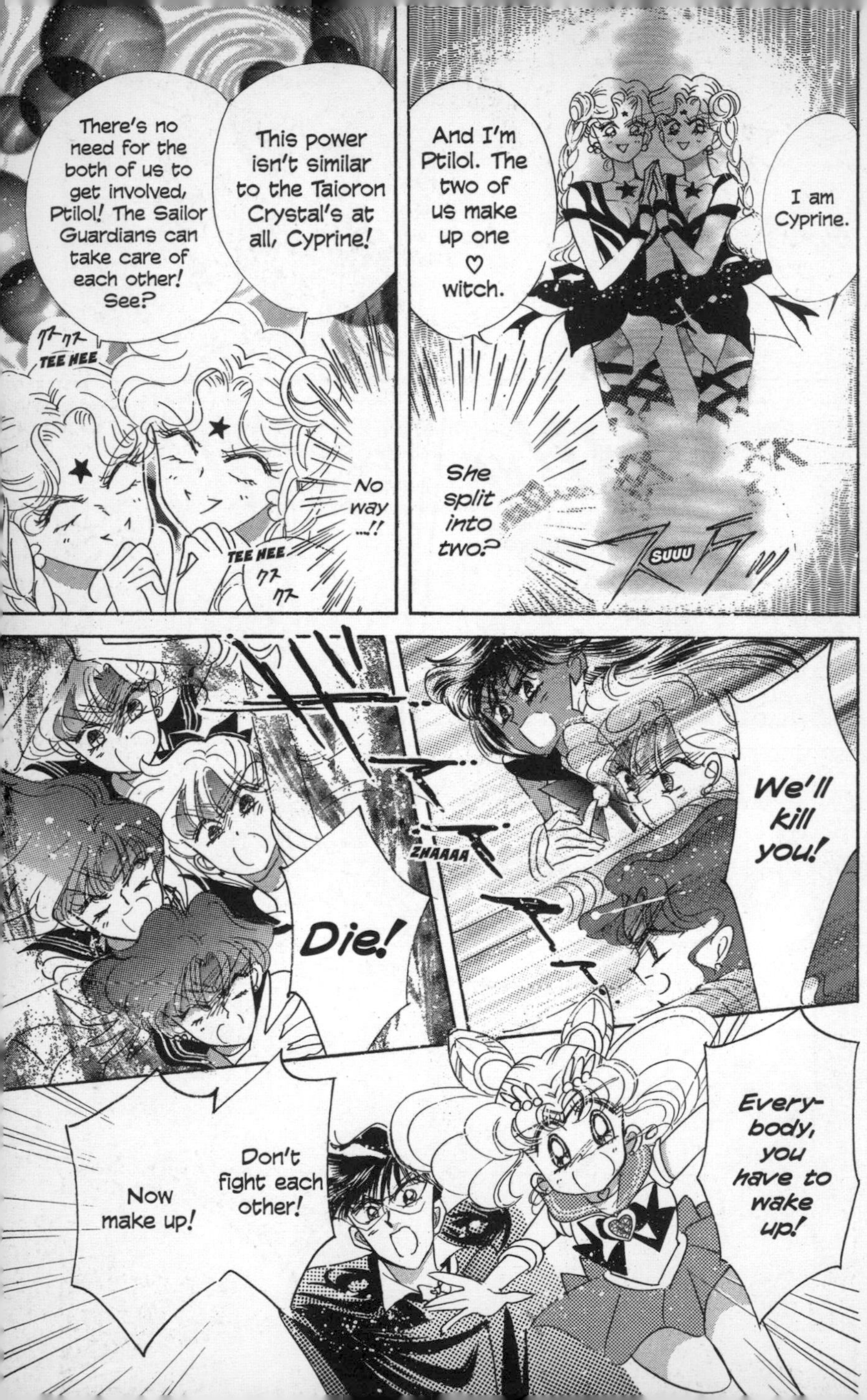
I am Cyprine.
And I'm Ptilol. The two of us make up one ♡ witch.
She split into two?
SUUU
This power isn't similar to the Taioron Crystal's at all, Cyprine!
There's no need for the both of us to get involved, Ptilol! The Sailor Guardians can take care of each other! See?
No way...!!
TEE HEE
クスクス
TEE HEE
クスクス
We'll kill you!
ZHAAAA
Die!
Every-body, you have to wake up!
Don't fight each other!
Now make up!

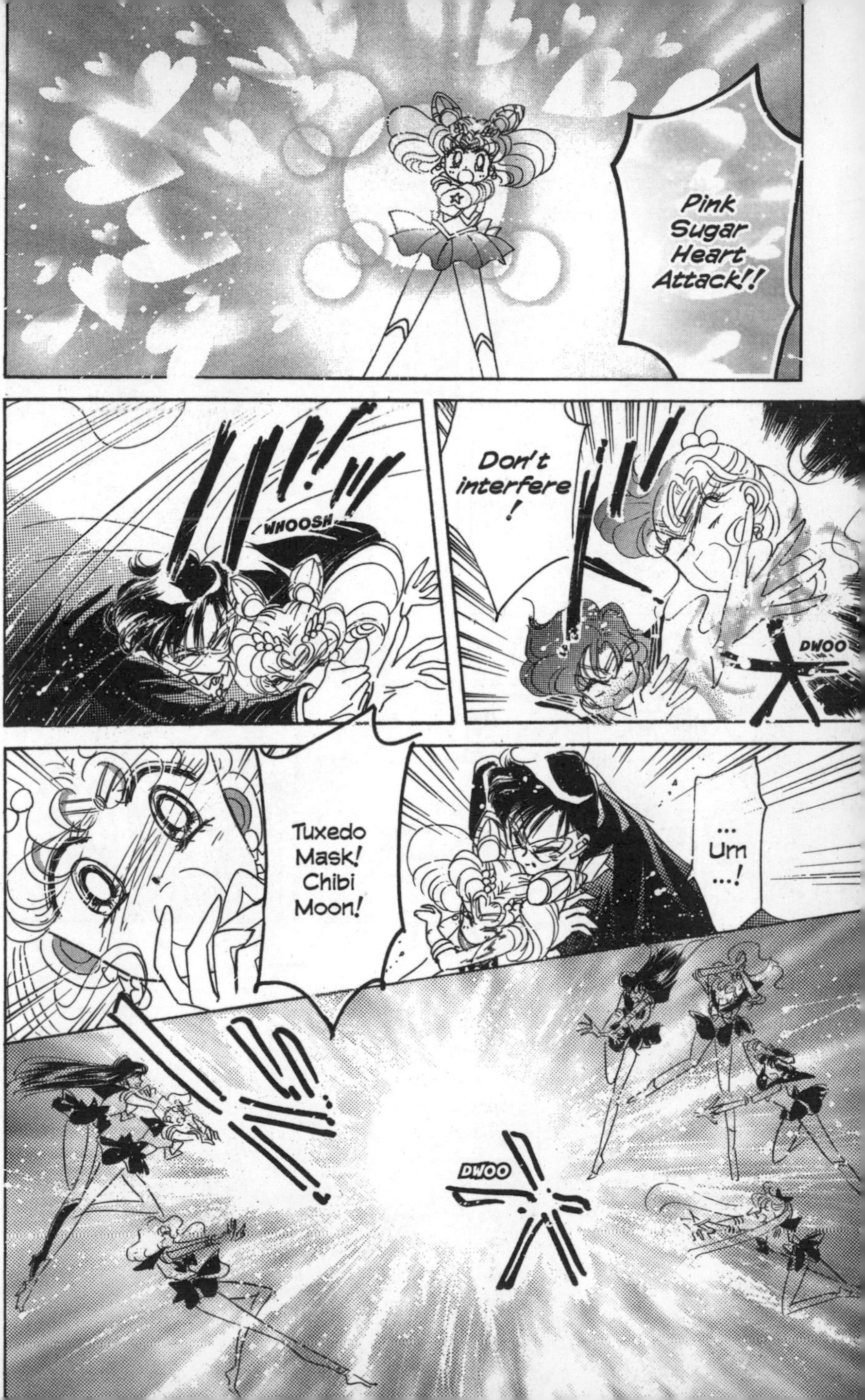
Pink Sugar Heart Attack!!
Don't interfere!
DWOO
WHOOSH
... Um ...!
Tuxedo Mask! Chibi Moon!
DWOO

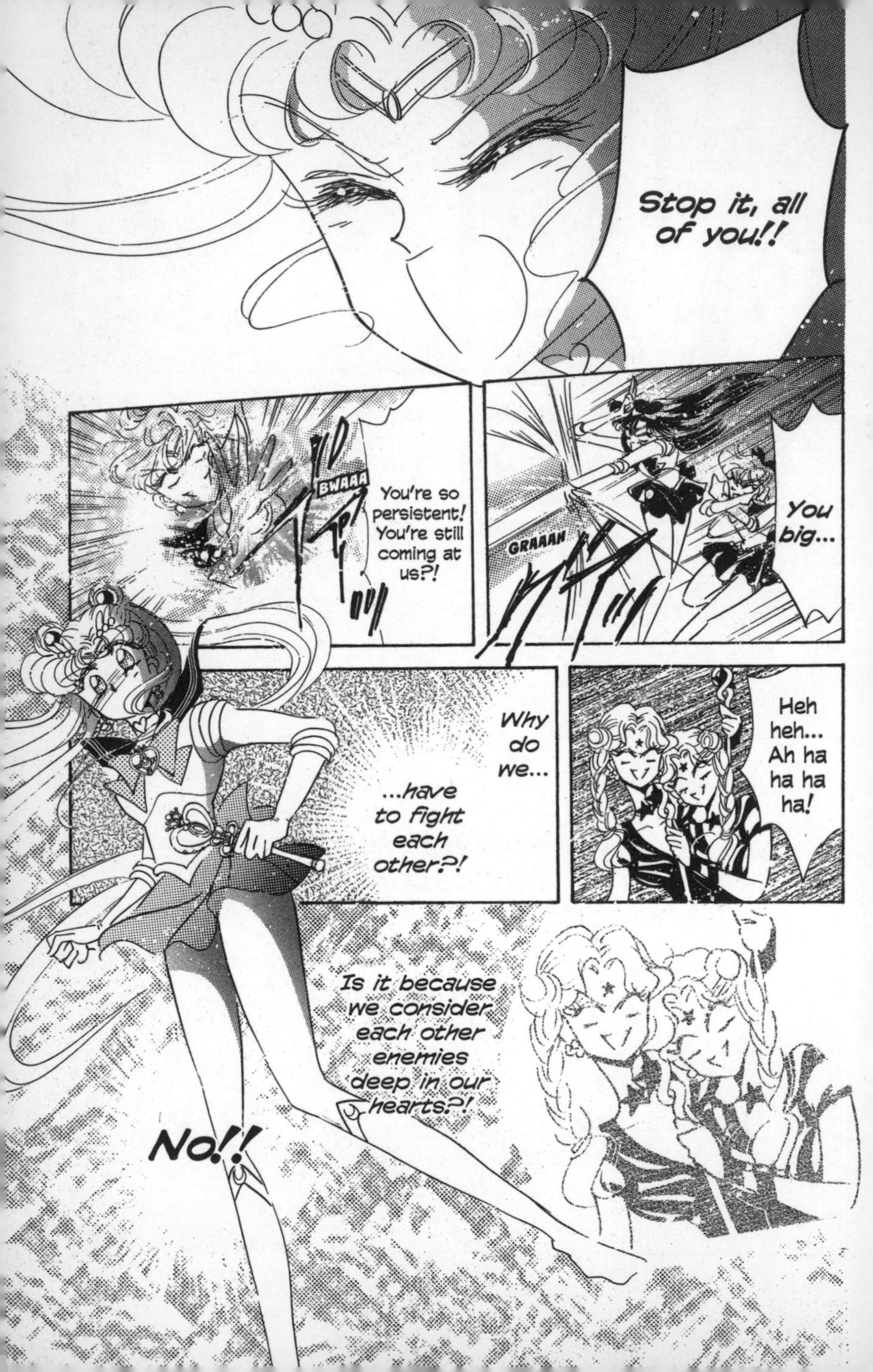
Stop it, all of you!!
You big...
GRAAAH
You're so persistent! You're still coming at us?!
BWAAA
Heh heh... Ah ha ha ha ha!
Why do we...
...have to fight each other?!
Is it because we consider each other enemies deep in our hearts?!
No!!

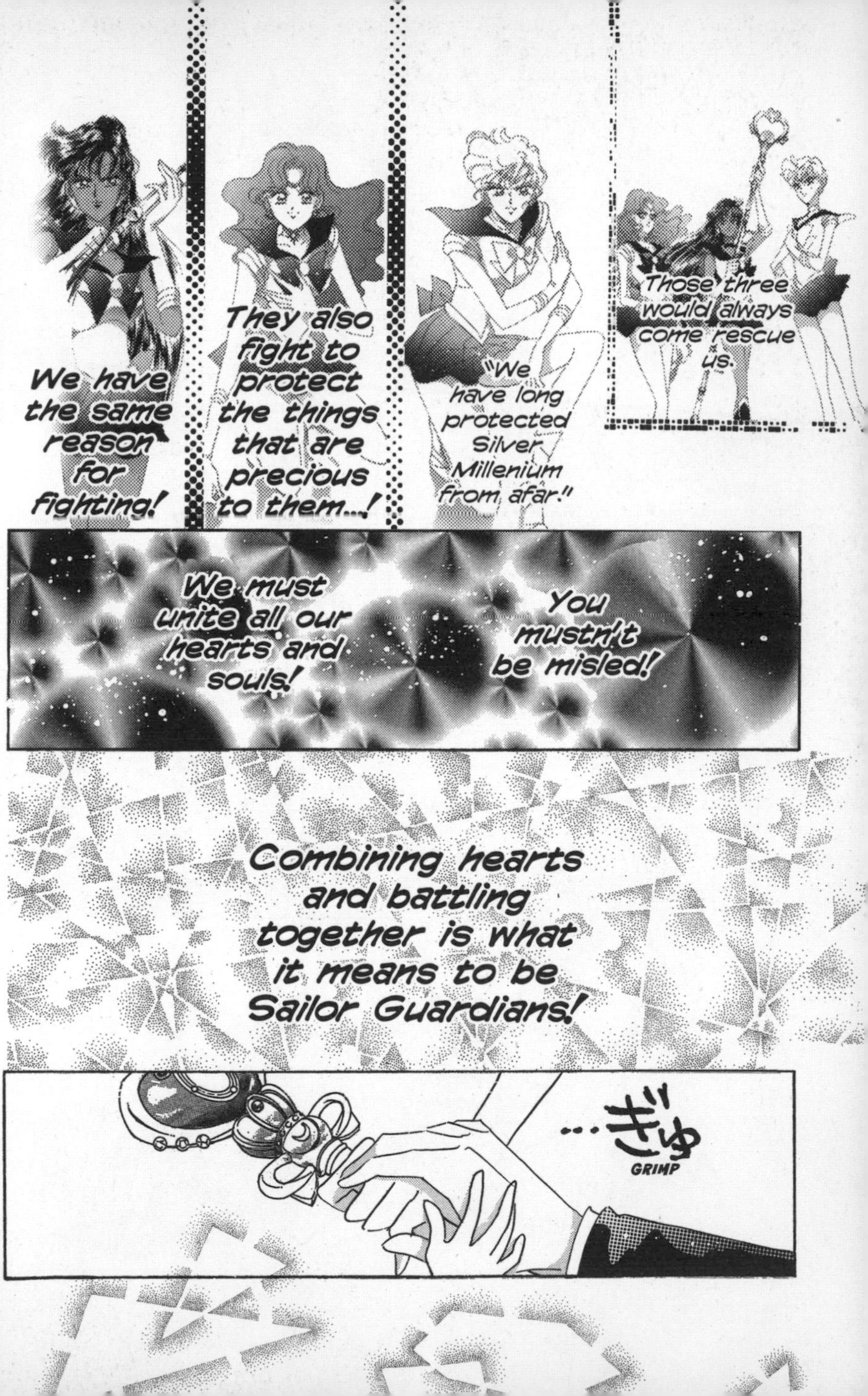
Those three would always come rescue us.
"We have long protected Silver Millenium from afar."
They also fight to protect the things that are precious to them...!
We have the same reason for fighting!
You mustn't be misled!
We must unite all our hearts and souls!
Combining hearts and battling together is what it means to be Sailor Guardians!
...ぎゅ
GRIMP

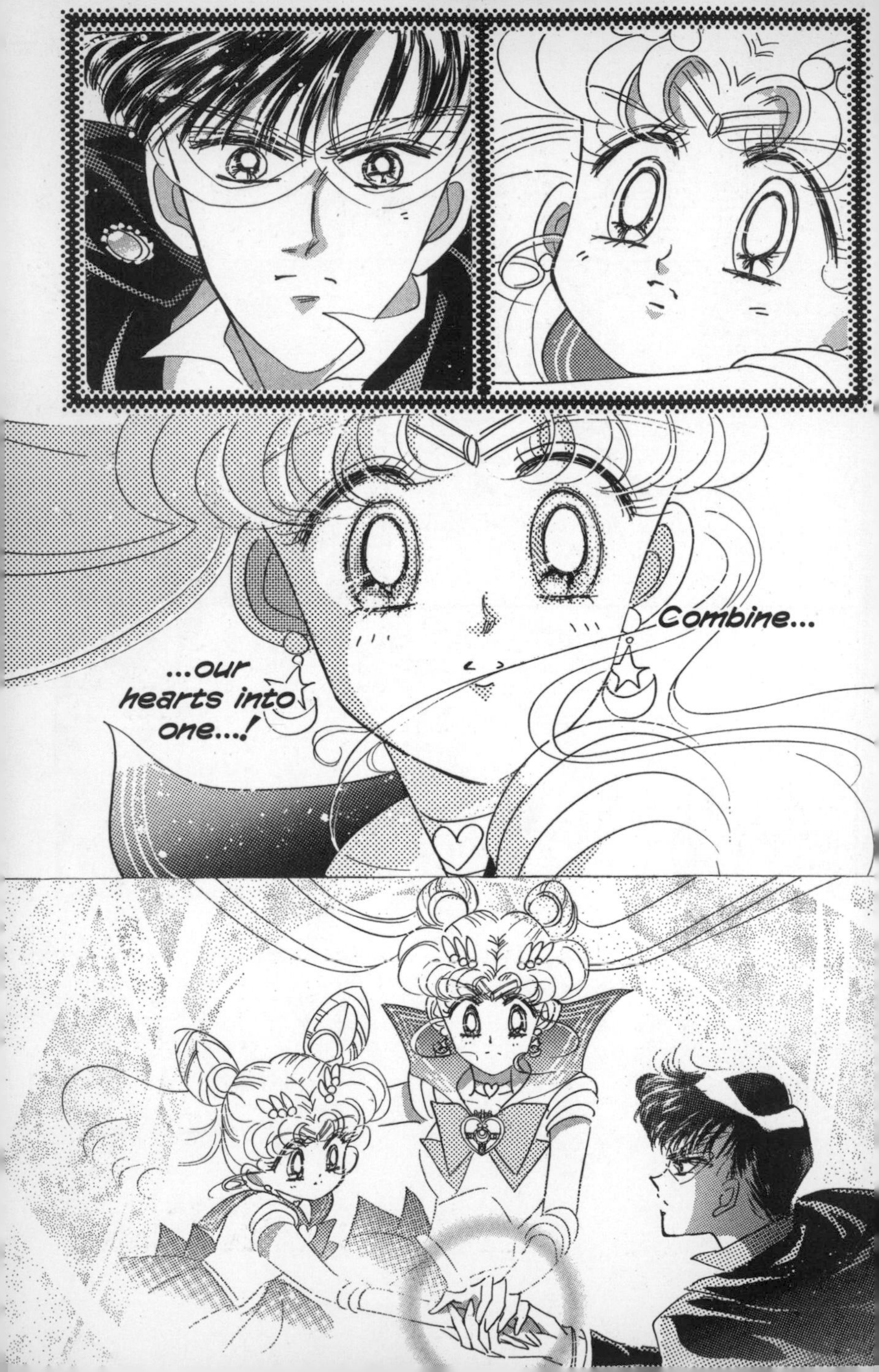
Combine...
...our hearts into one...!

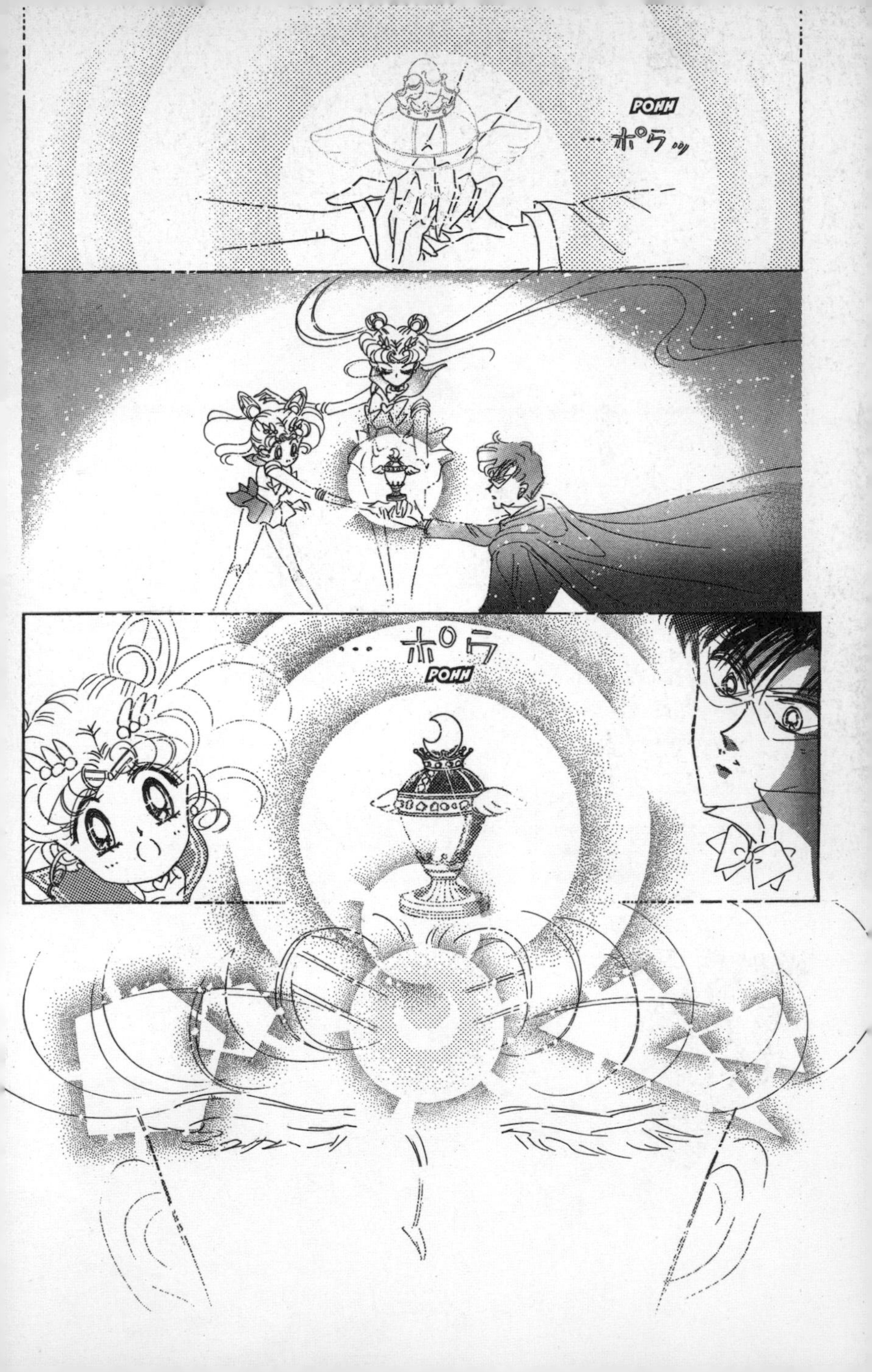
POHH
…ポワッ
…ポワ
POHH

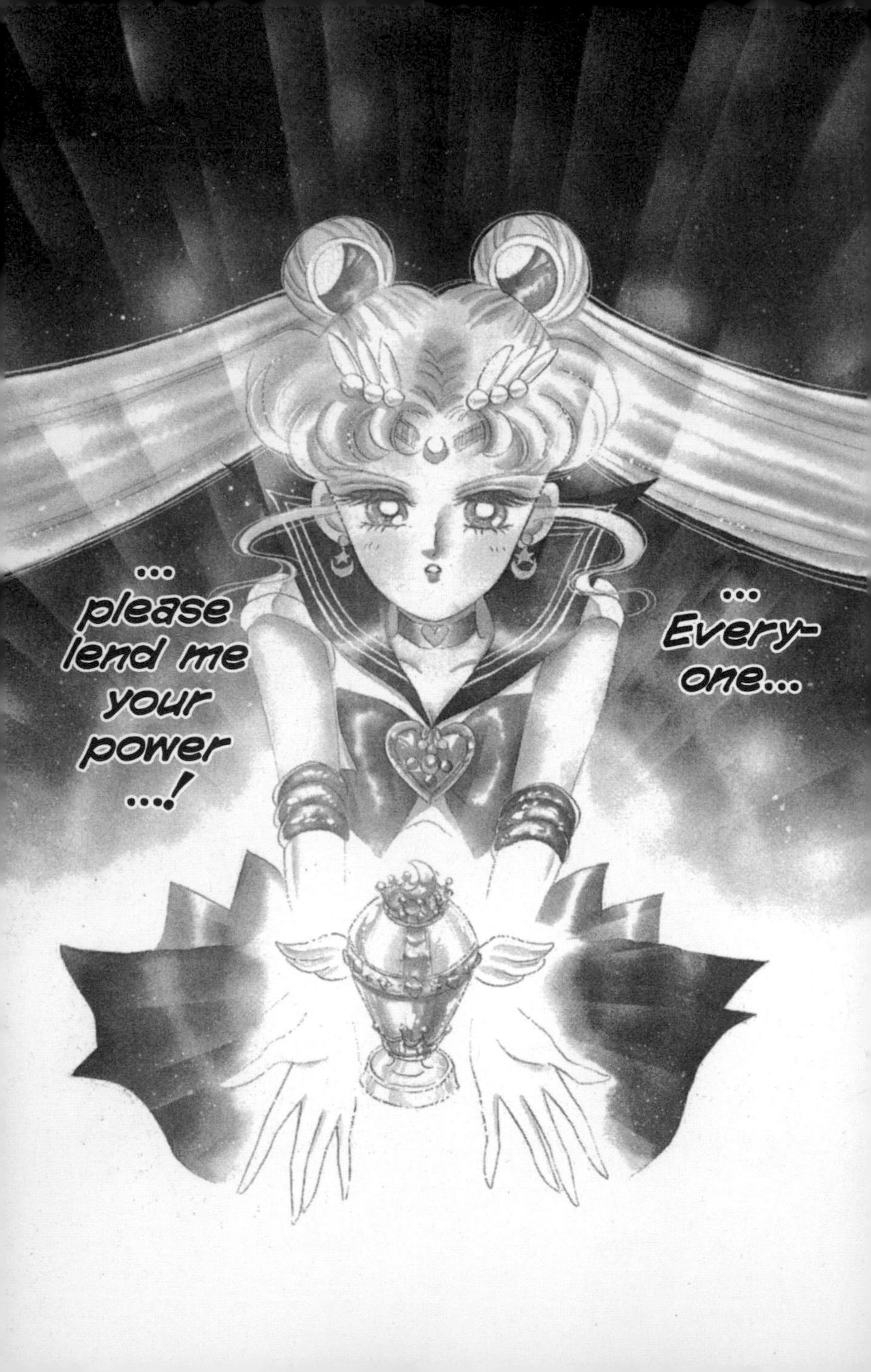
...Every-one...
...please lend me your power...!

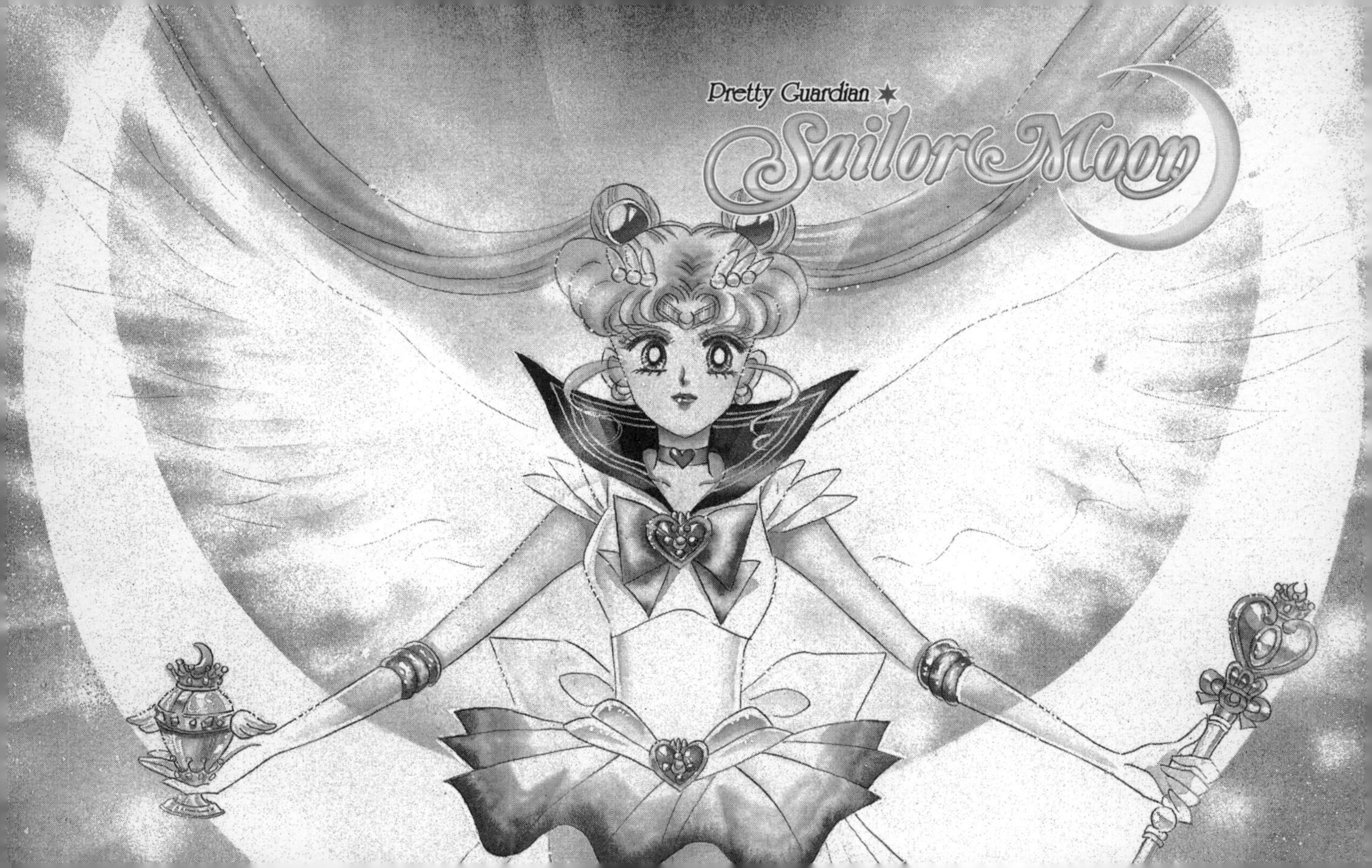
Pretty Guardian ★
Sailor Moon

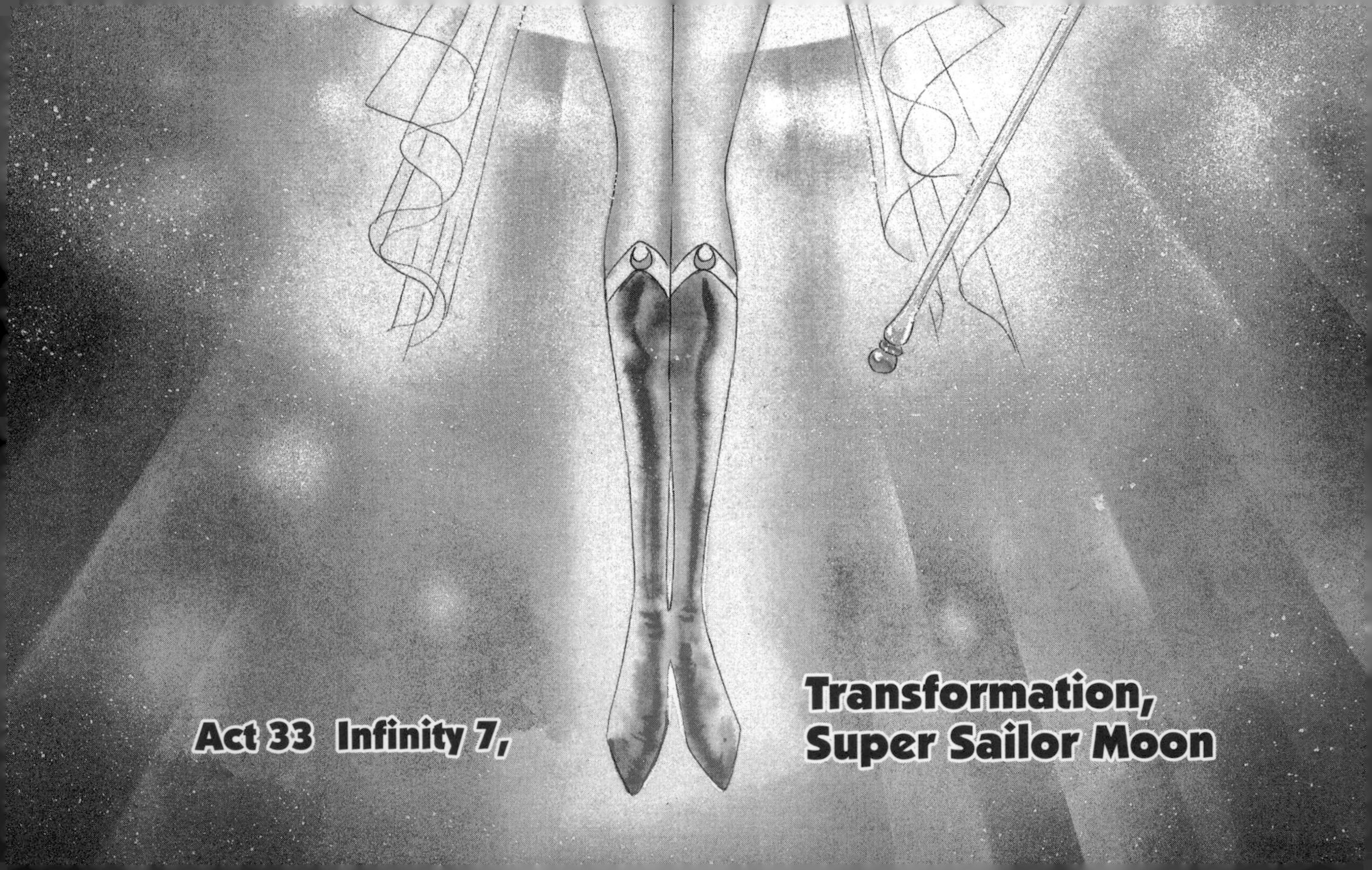
Act 33 Infinity 7,
Transformation,
Super Sailor Moon

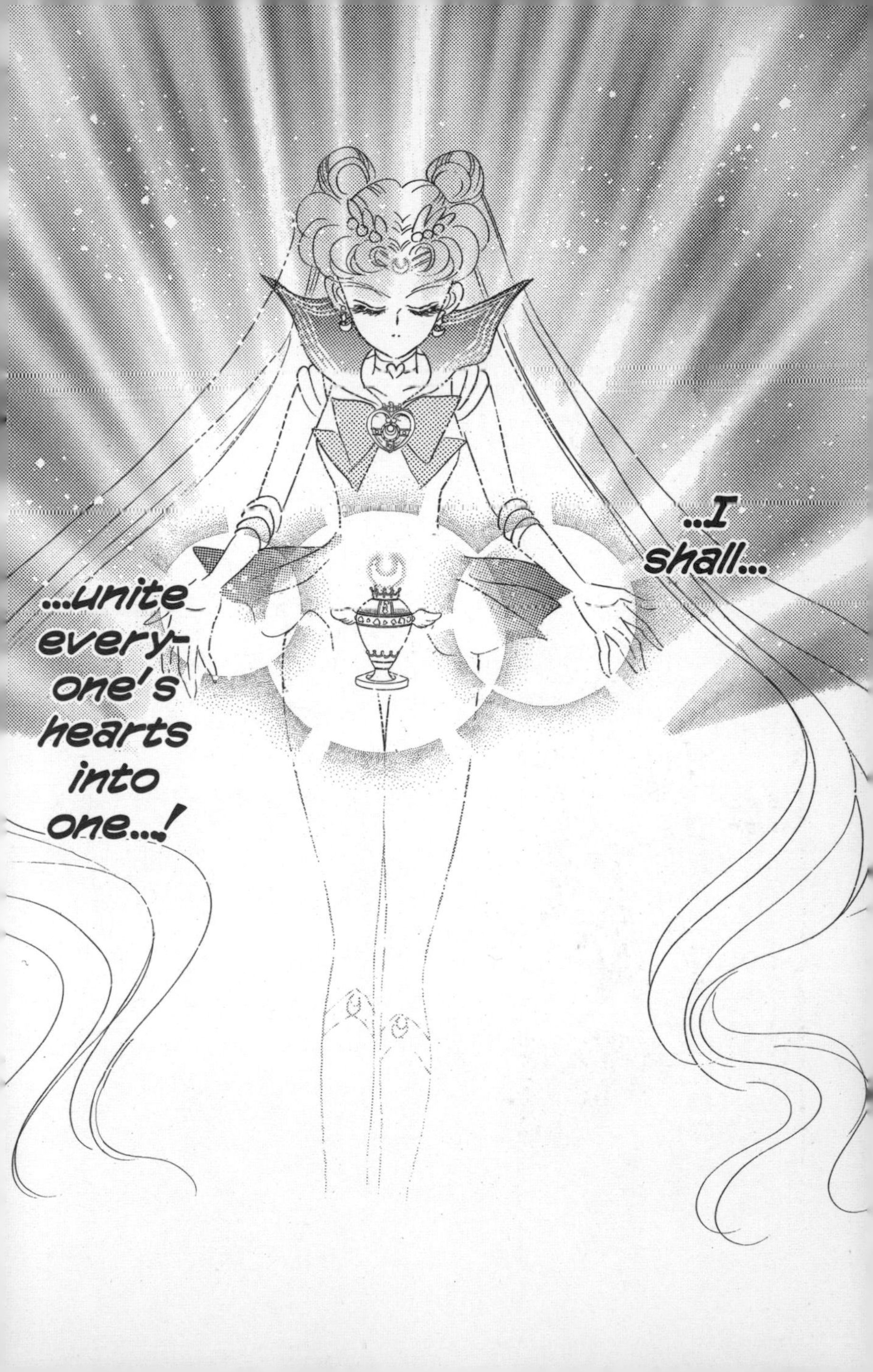
...I shall...
...unite every-one's hearts into one...!

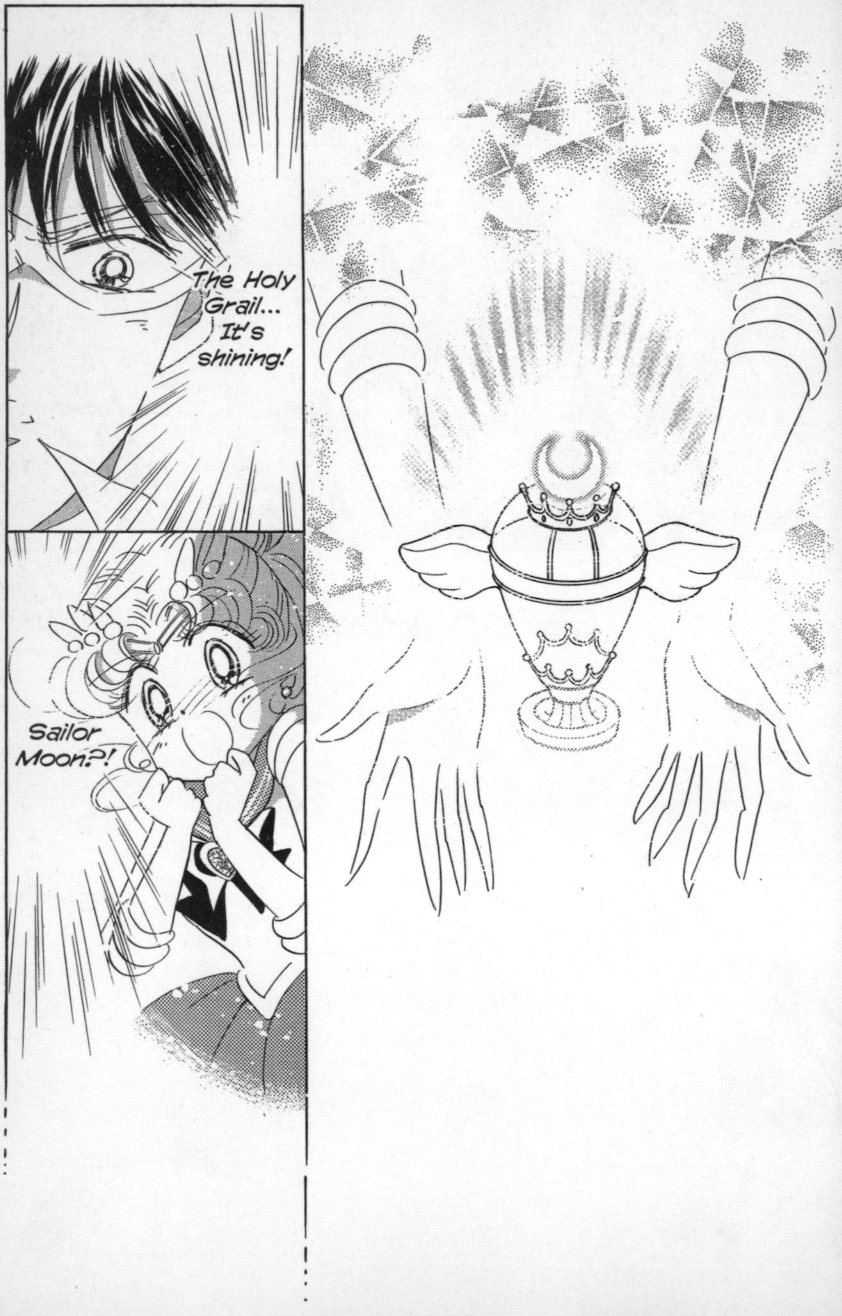
The Holy Grail... It's shining!
Sailor Moon?!

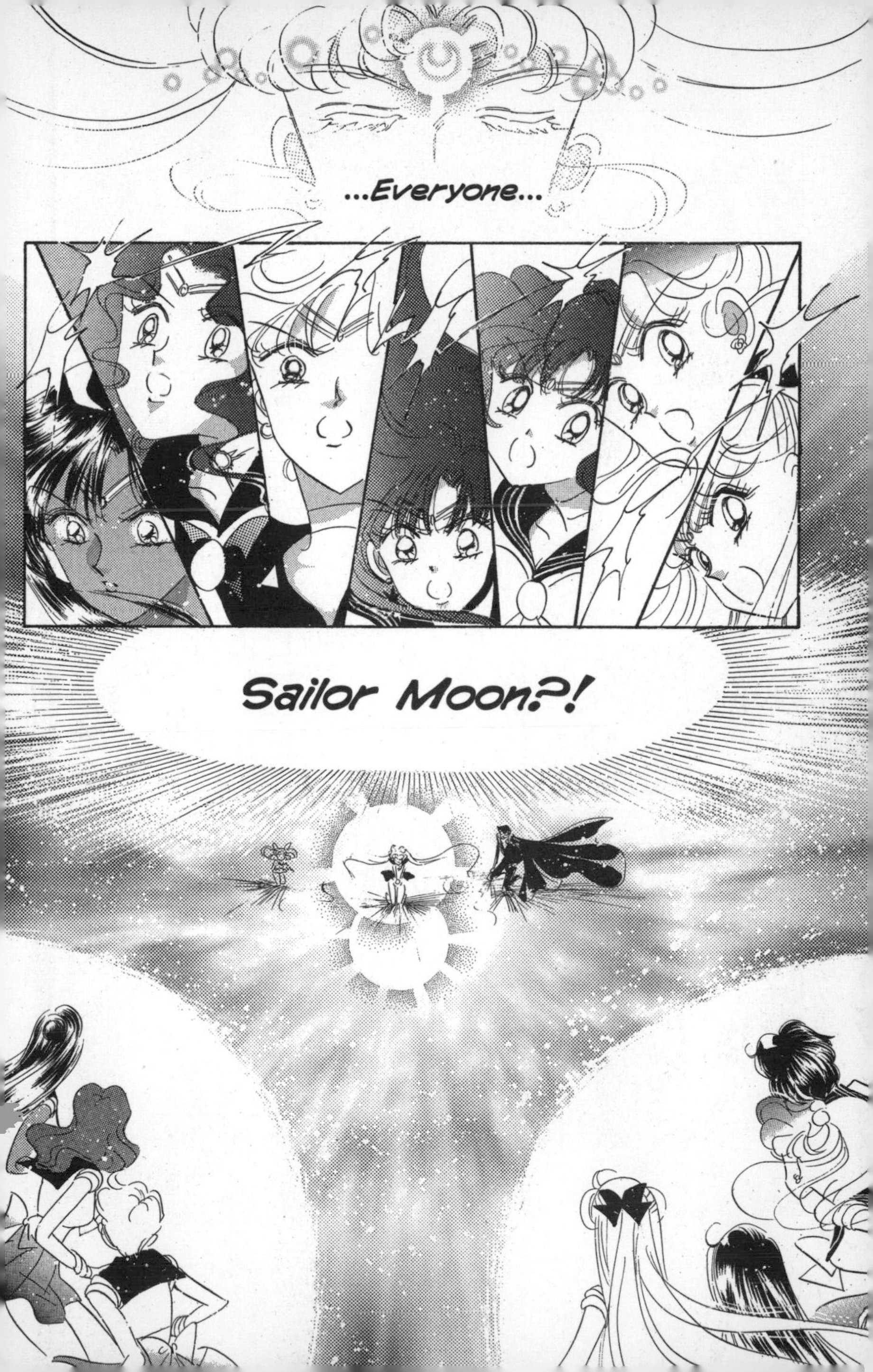
...Everyone...
Sailor Moon?!

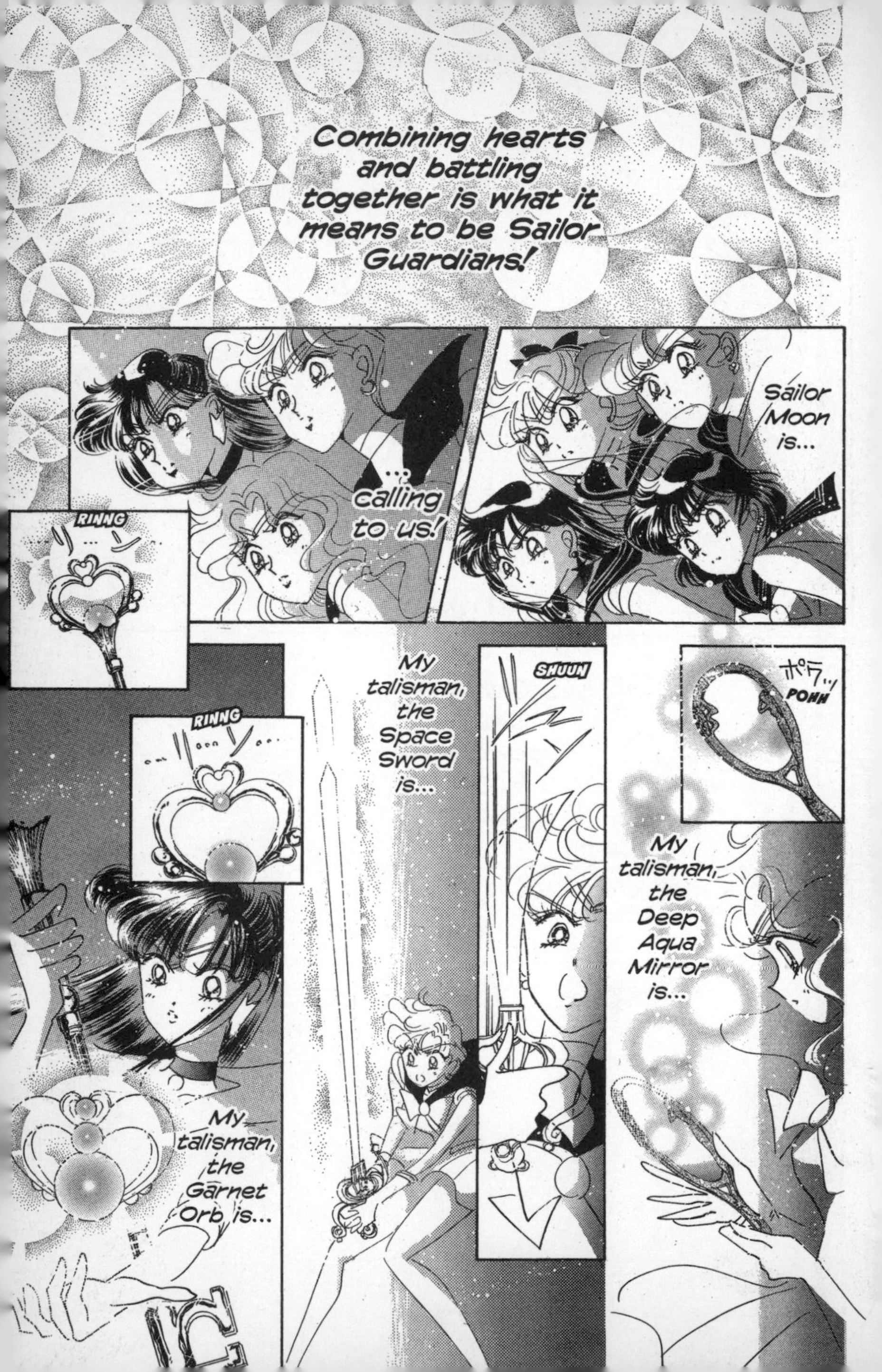
Combining hearts and battling together is what it means to be Sailor Guardians!
Sailor Moon is...
...calling to us!
RINNG
ポワッ
POHN
My talisman, the Deep Aqua Mirror is...
SHUUN
My talisman, the Space Sword is...
RINNG
My talisman, the Garnet Orb is...

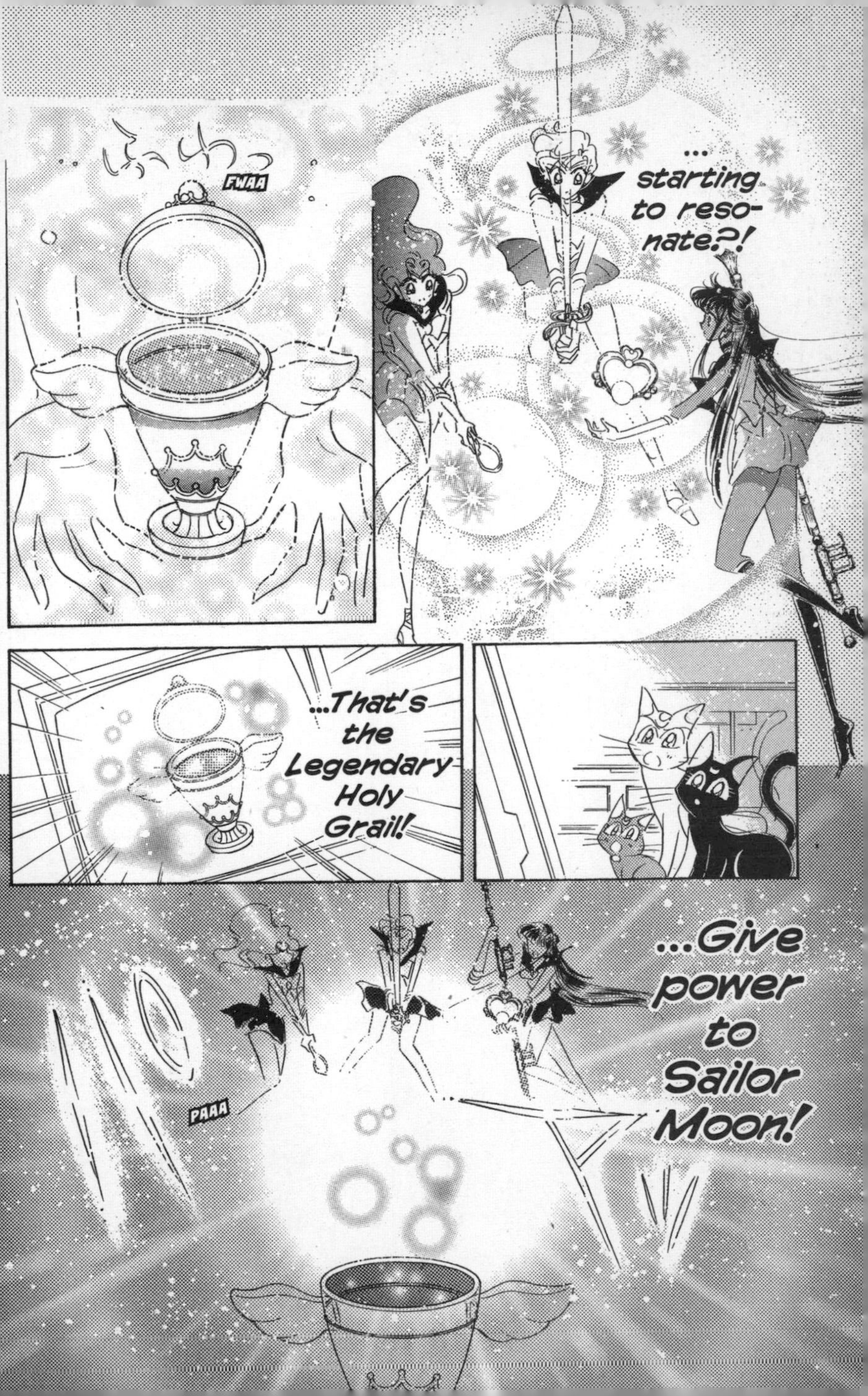

... starting to resonate?!
FWAA
...That's the Legendary Holy Grail!
...Give power to Sailor Moon!
PAAA

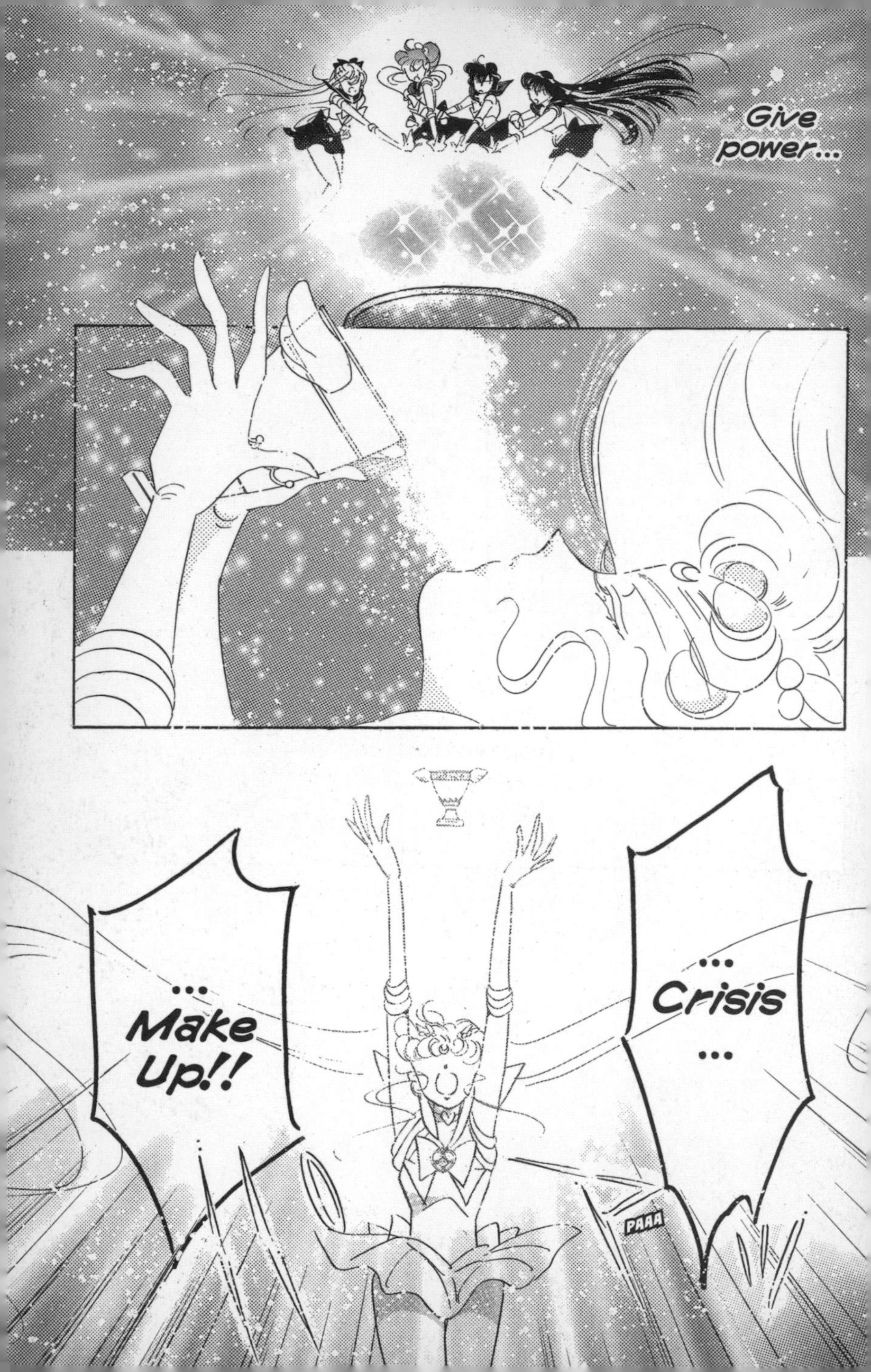
Give power...
... Crisis ...
... Make Up!!
PAAA

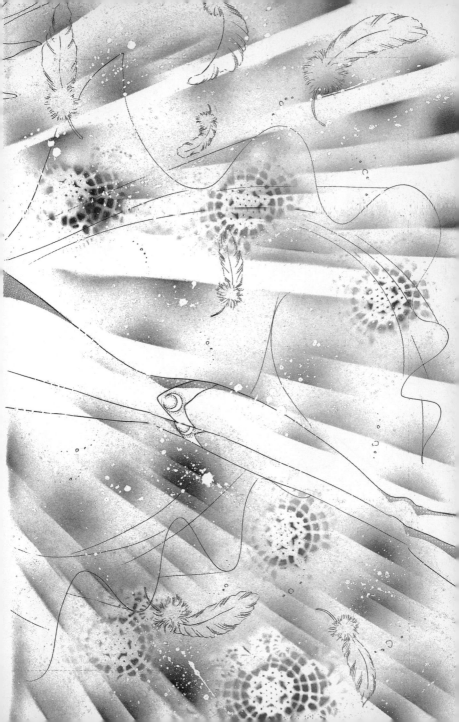

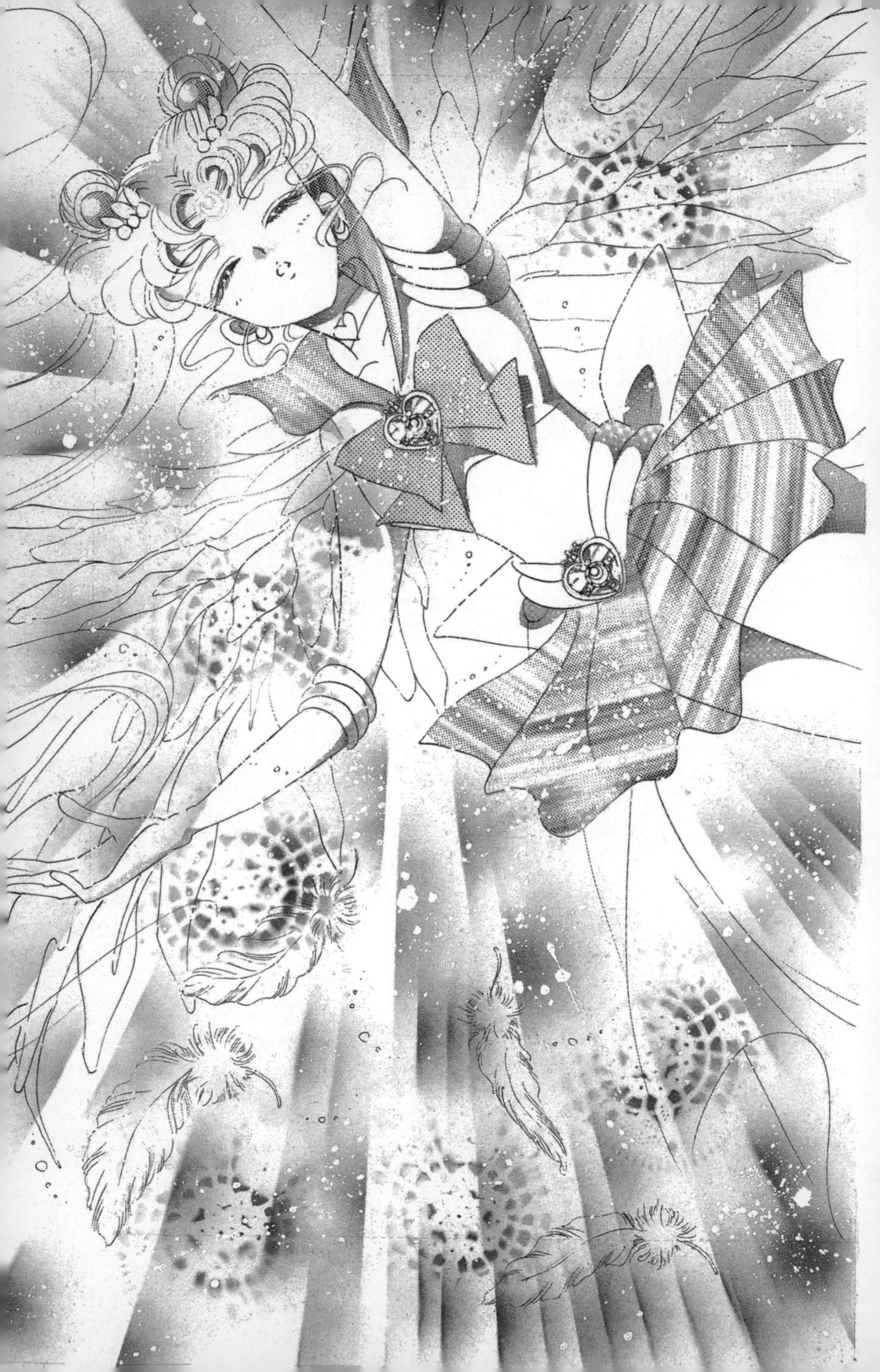

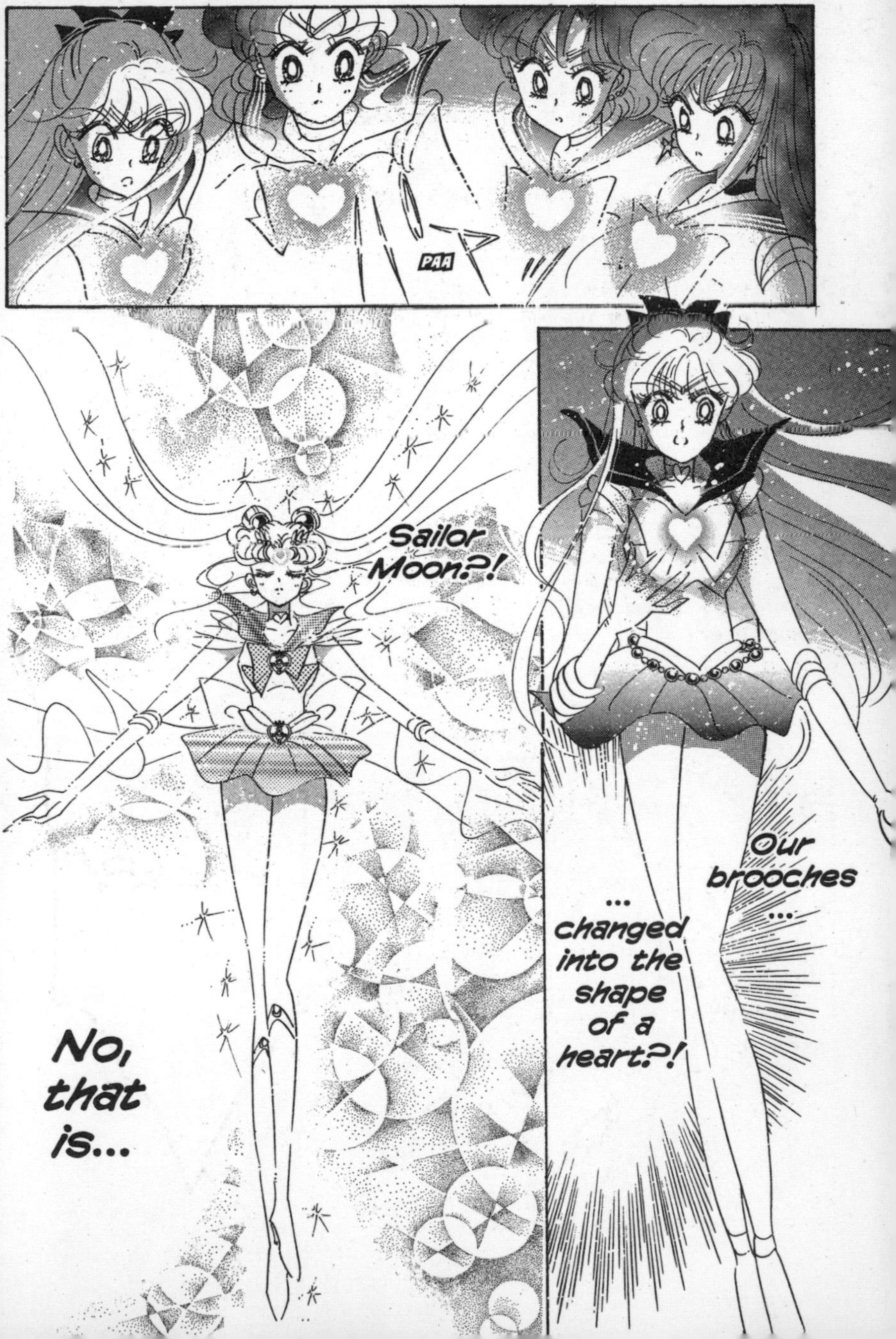
PAA
Our brooches ...
... changed into the shape of a heart?!
Sailor Moon?!
No, that is...

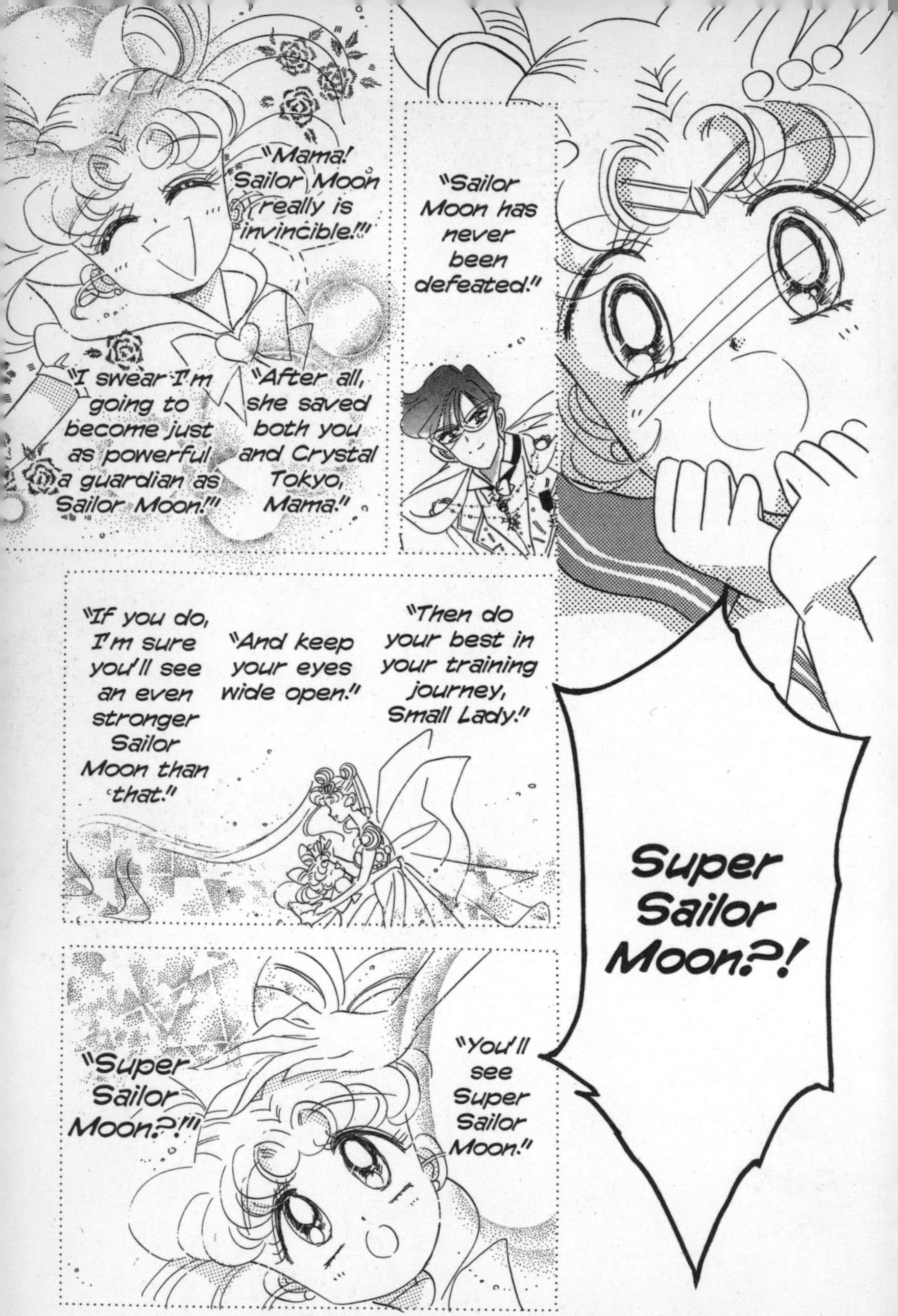
Super Sailor Moon?!
"Sailor Moon has never been defeated."
"Mama! Sailor Moon really is invincible!!"
"After all, she saved both you and Crystal Tokyo, Mama."
"I swear I'm going to become just as powerful a guardian as Sailor Moon!!"
"Then do your best in your training journey, Small Lady."
"And keep your eyes wide open."
"If you do, I'm sure you'll see an even stronger Sailor Moon than that."
"You'll see Super Sailor Moon."
"Super Sailor Moon?!"

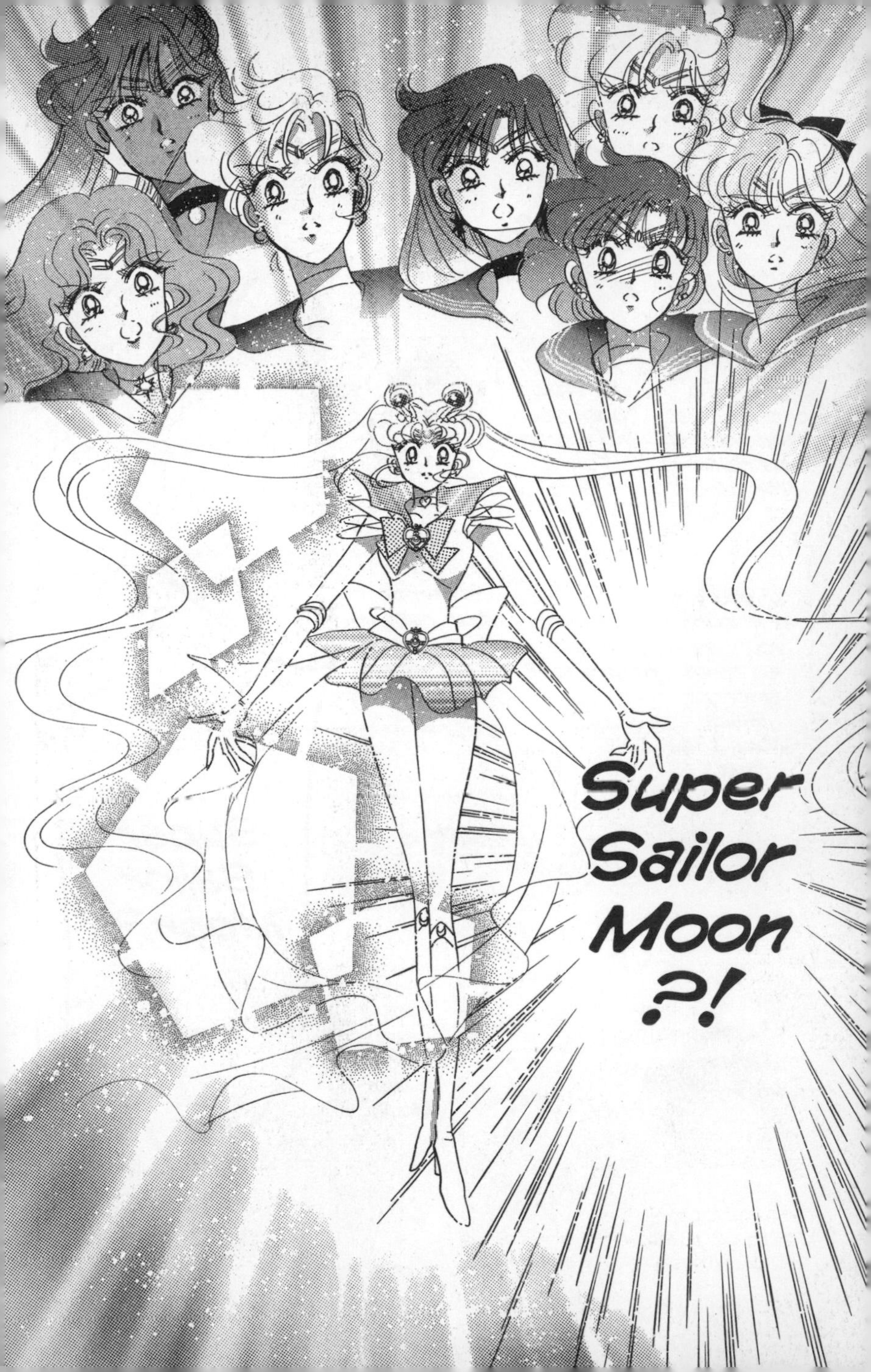
Super Sailor Moon ?!

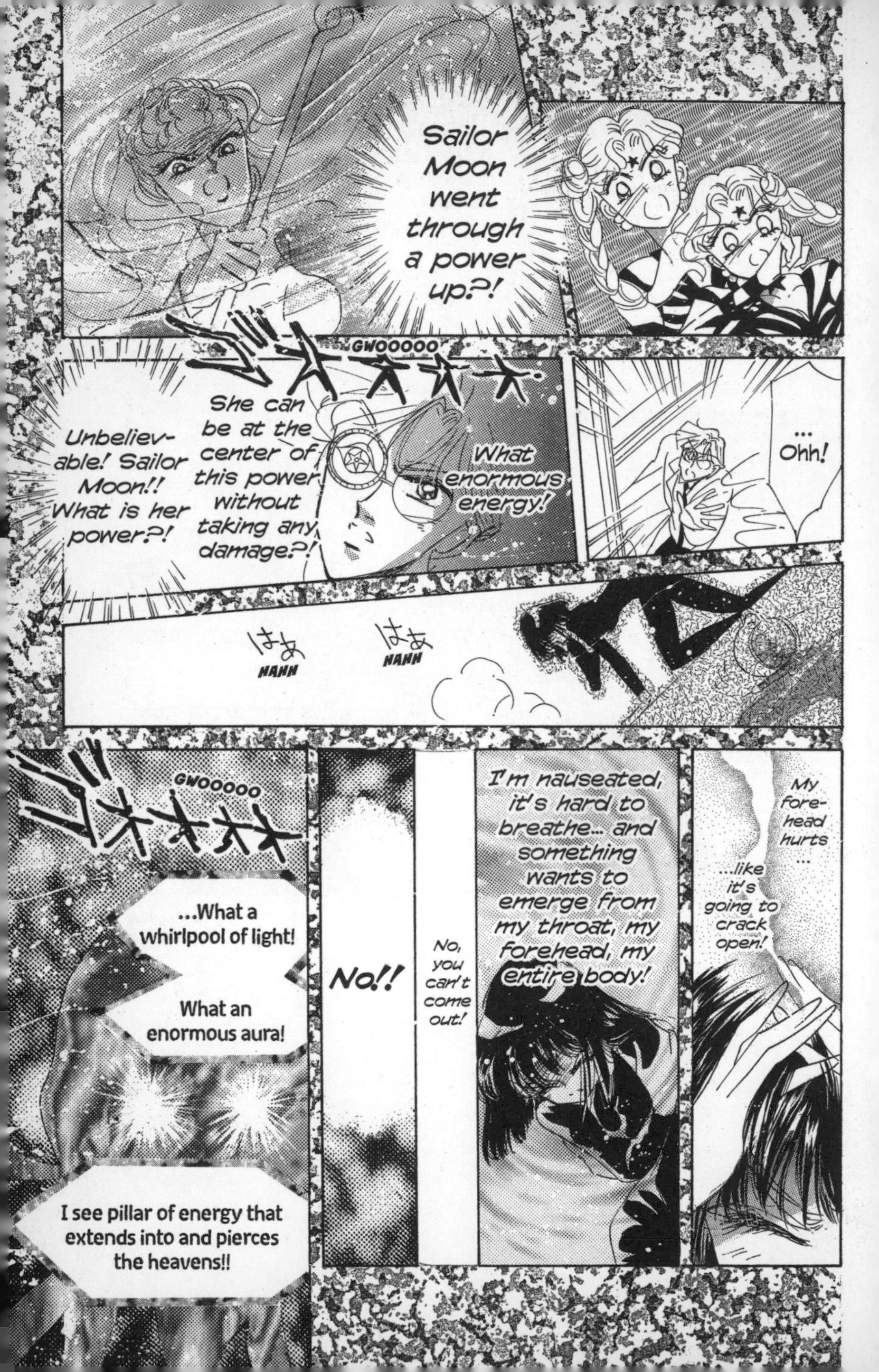
Sailor Moon went through a power up?!
...Ohh!
GWOOOOO
What enormous energy!
She can be at the center of this power without taking any damage?!
Unbeliev-able! Sailor Moon!! What is her power?!
はあ
HAHH
はあ
HAHH
My fore-head hurts ...
...like it's going to crack open!
I'm nauseated, it's hard to breathe... and something wants to emerge from my throat, my forehead, my entire body!
No, you can't come out!
No!!
GWOOOOO
...What a whirlpool of light!
What an enormous aura!
I see pillar of energy that extends into and pierces the heavens!!

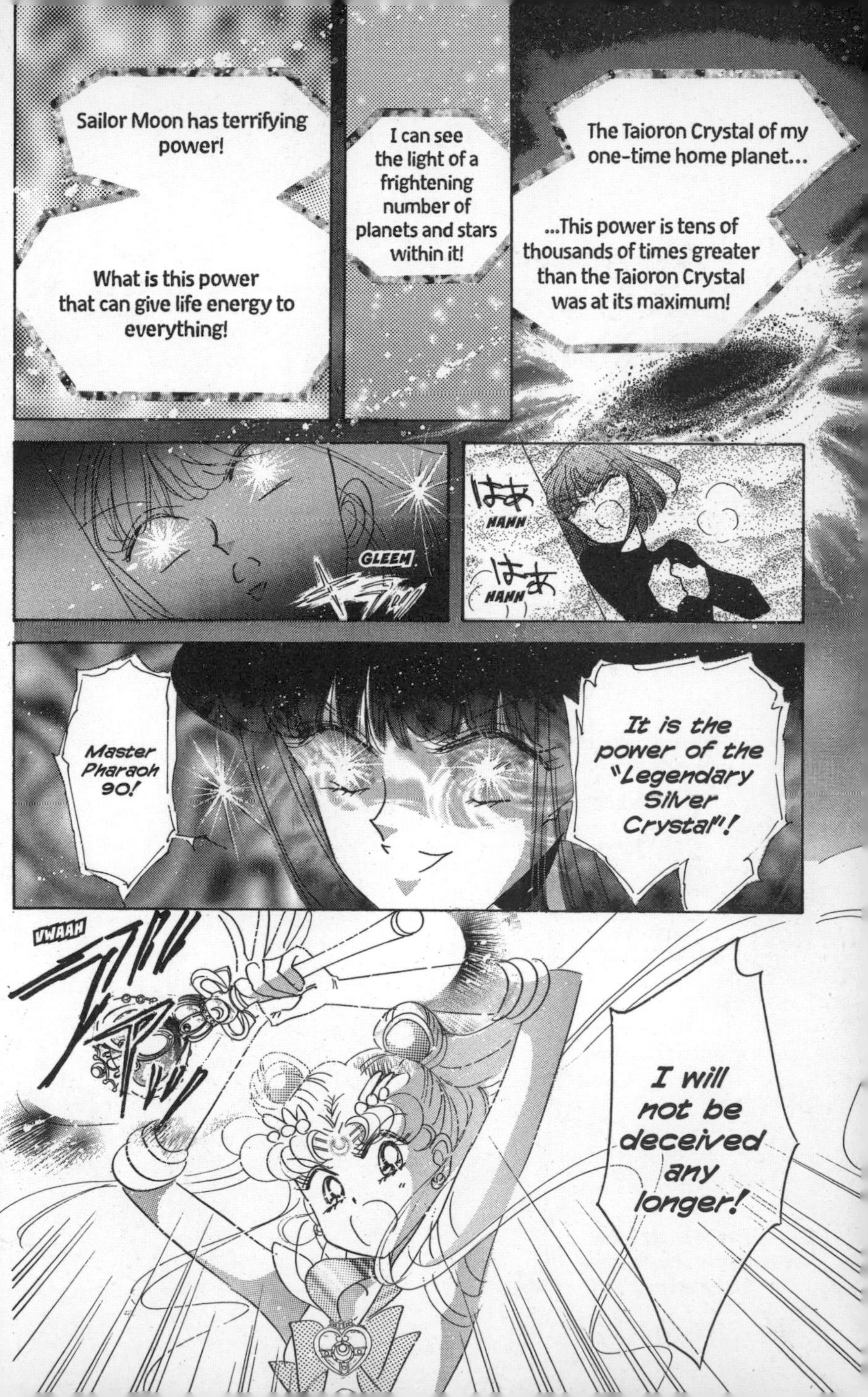
The Taioron Crystal of my one-time home planet...
...This power is tens of thousands of times greater than the Taioron Crystal was at its maximum!
I can see the light of a frightening number of planets and stars within it!
Sailor Moon has terrifying power!
What is this power that can give life energy to everything!
はあ
HAHH
はあ
HAHH
GLEEM
It is the power of the "Legendary Silver Crystal"!
Master Pharaoh 90!
VWAAH
I will not be deceived any longer!

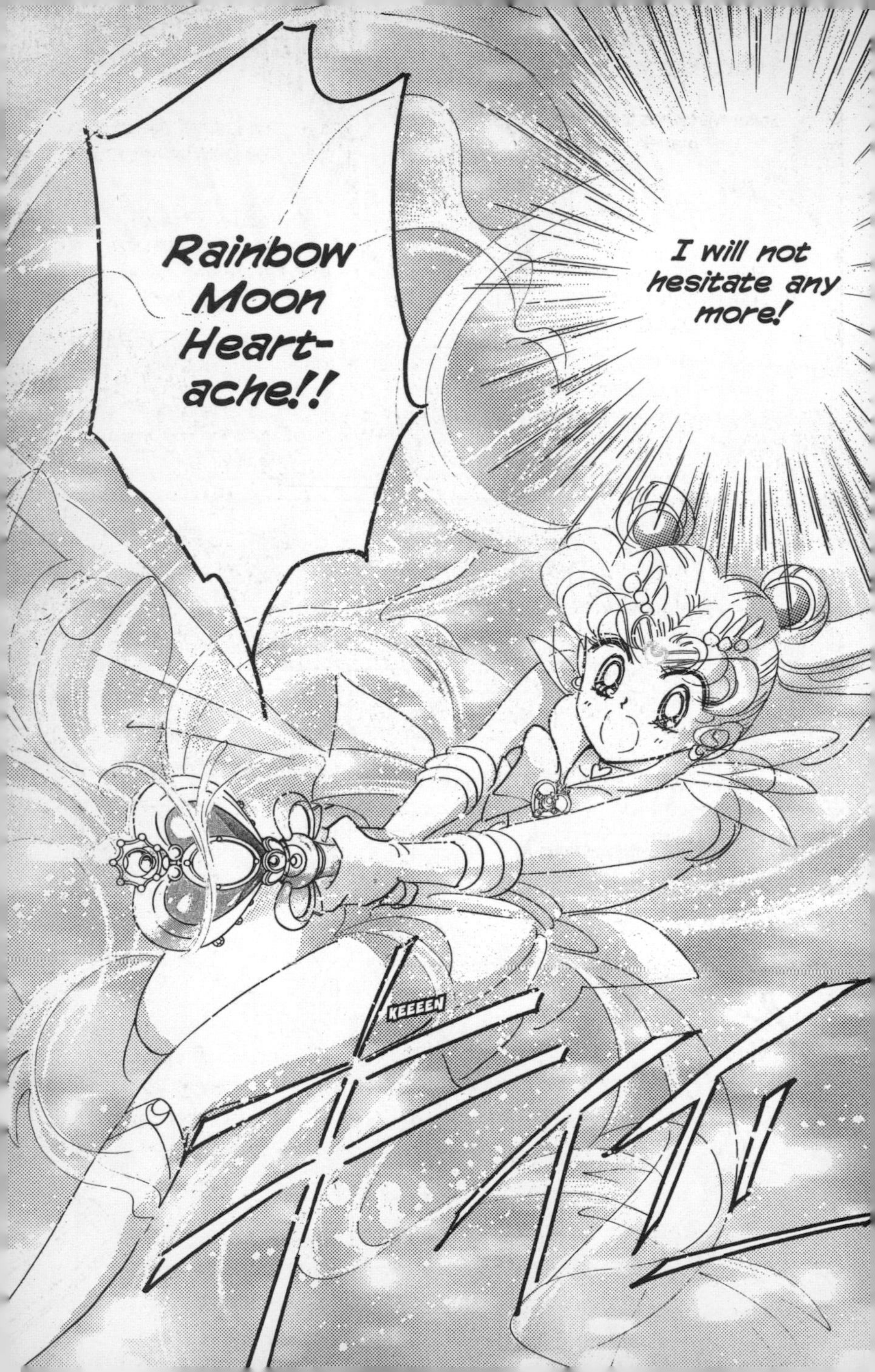
I will not hesitate any more!
Rainbow Moon Heart-ache!!
KEEEEN

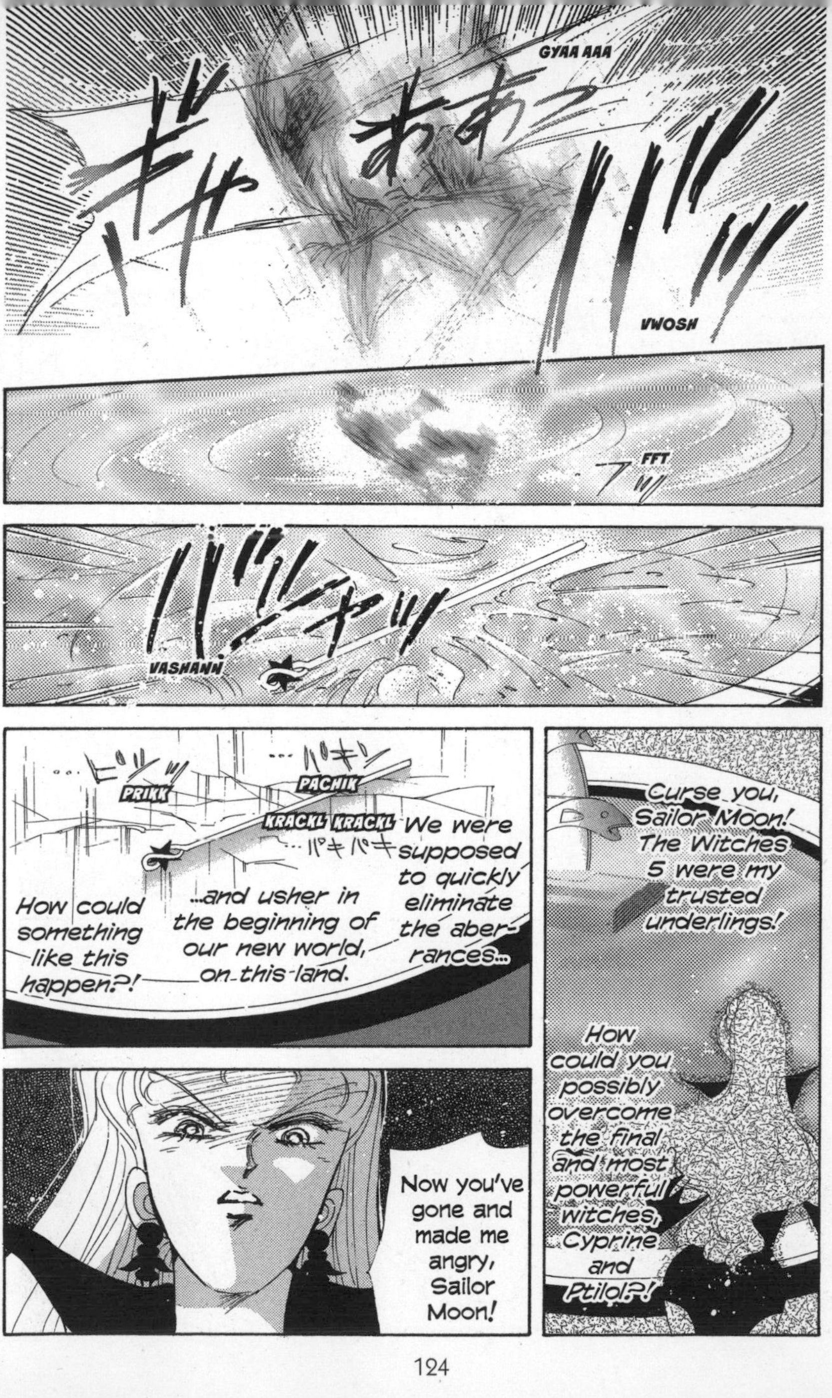
GYAA AAA
VWOSH
FFT
VASHANN
Curse you, Sailor Moon! The Witches 5 were my trusted underlings!
How could you possibly overcome the final and most powerful witches, Cyprine and Ptilol?!
PRIKK
PACHIK
KRACKL KRACKL
We were supposed to quickly eliminate the aberrances...
...and usher in the beginning of our new world, on this land.
How could something like this happen?!
Now you've gone and made me angry, Sailor Moon!

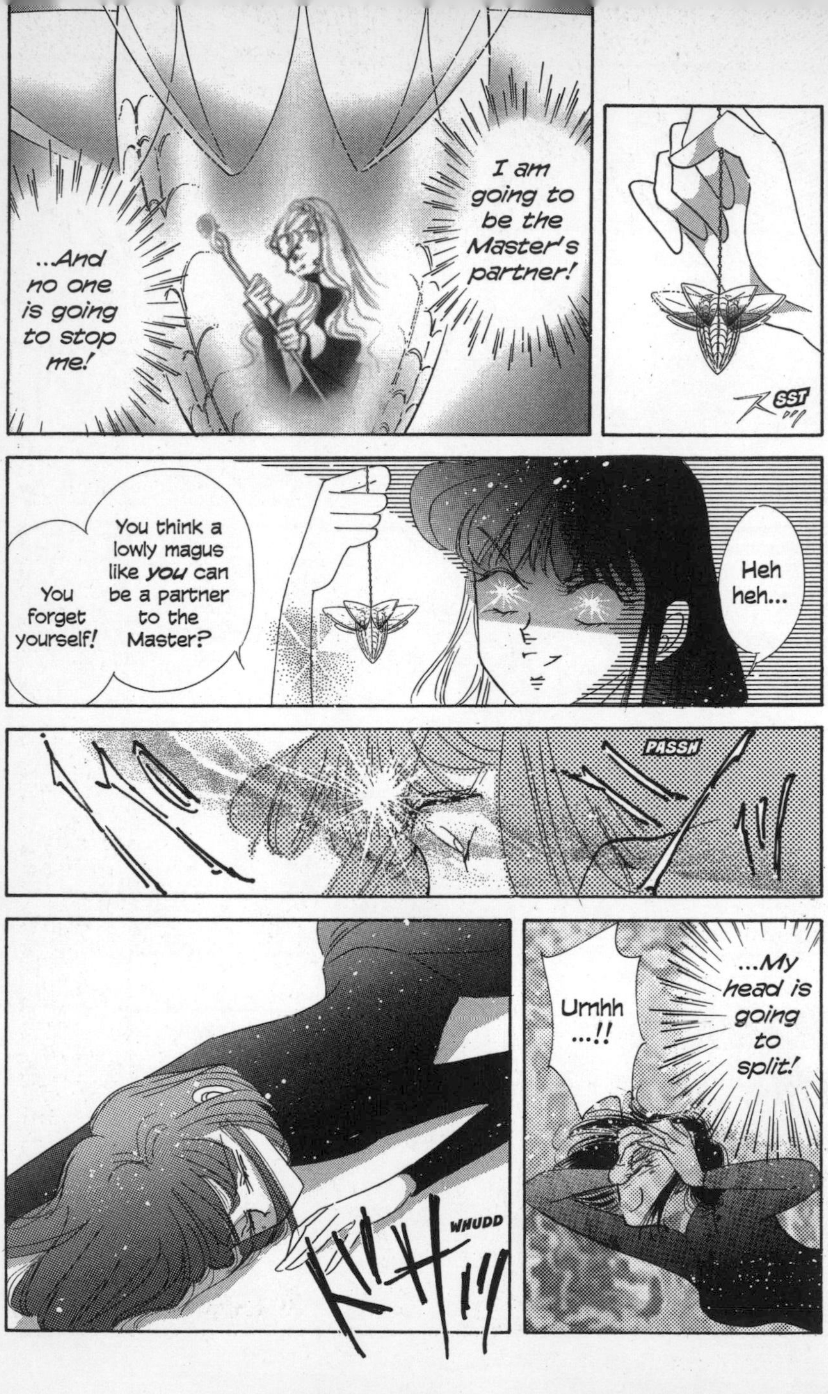
SST
I am going to be the Master's partner!
...And no one is going to stop me!
Heh heh...
You think a lowly magus like *you* can be a partner to the Master?
You forget yourself!
PASSH
...My head is going to split!
Umhh ...!!
WHUDD

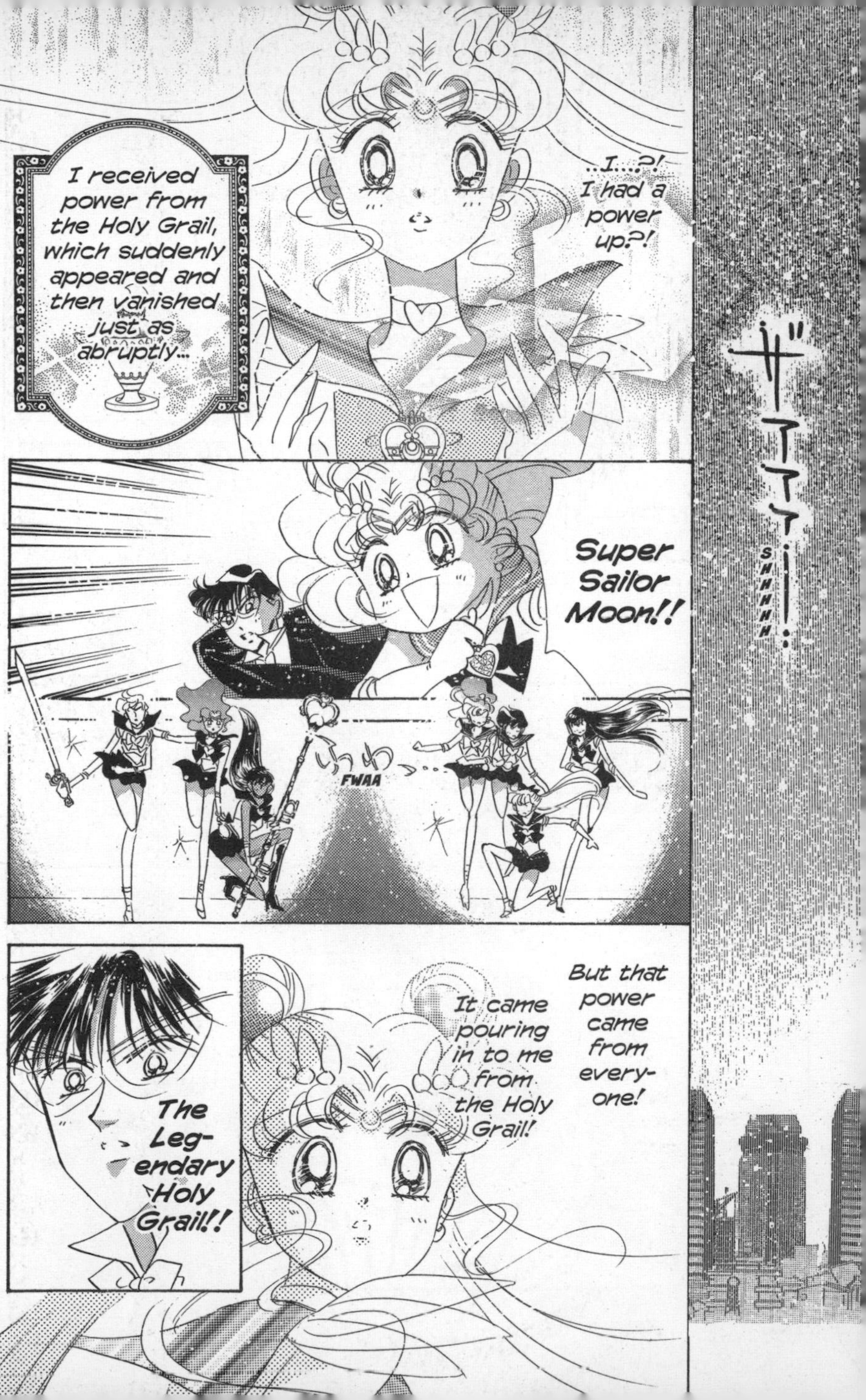
ザアアア
SHHHHH
...I...?! I had a power up?!
I received power from the Holy Grail, which suddenly appeared and then vanished just as abruptly...
Super Sailor Moon!!
FWAA
But that power came from everyone!
It came pouring in to me from the Holy Grail!
The Legendary Holy Grail!!

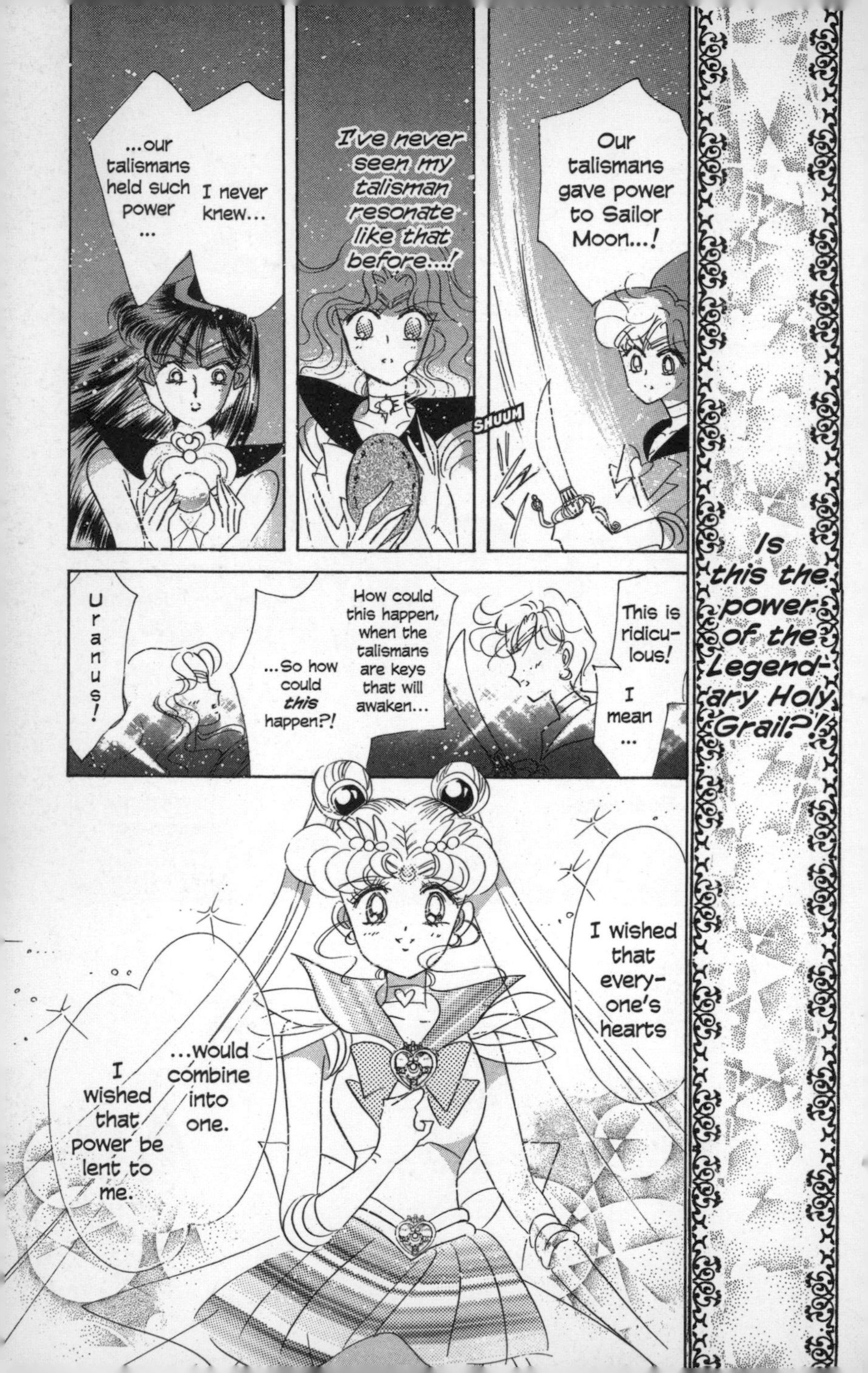
Is this the power of the Legendary Holy Grail?!
Our talismans gave power to Sailor Moon...!
SHUUM
I've never seen my talisman resonate like that before...!
I never knew...
...our talismans held such power...
This is ridiculous!
I mean...
How could this happen, when the talismans are keys that will awaken...
...So how could *this* happen?!
Uranus!
I wished that every-one's hearts
...would combine into one.
I wished that power be lent to me.

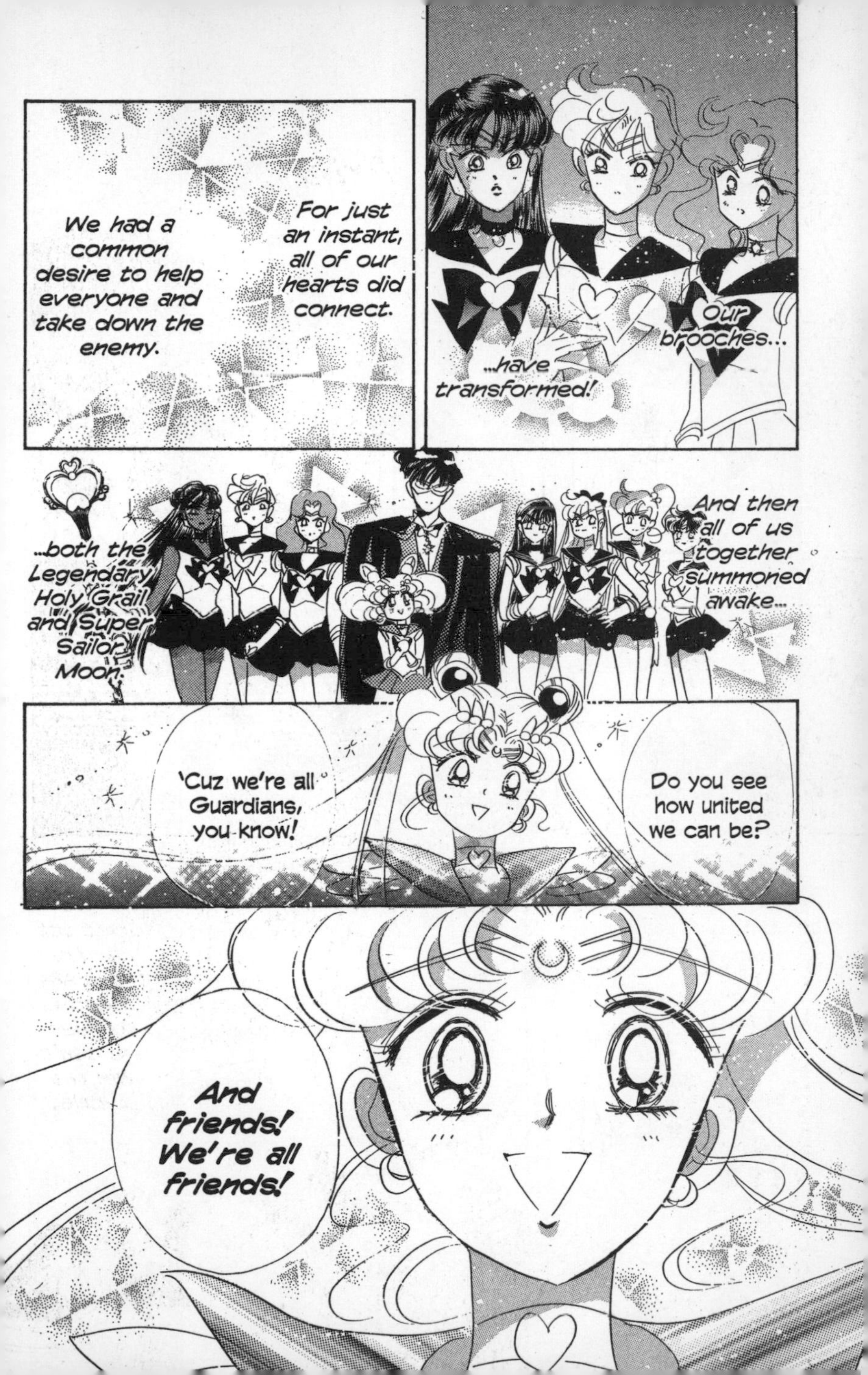
Our brooches...
...have transformed!
For just an instant, all of our hearts did connect.
We had a common desire to help everyone and take down the enemy.
And then all of us together summoned awake...
...both the Legendary Holy Grail and Super Sailor Moon.
Do you see how united we can be?
'Cuz we're all Guardians, you know!
And friends! We're all friends!

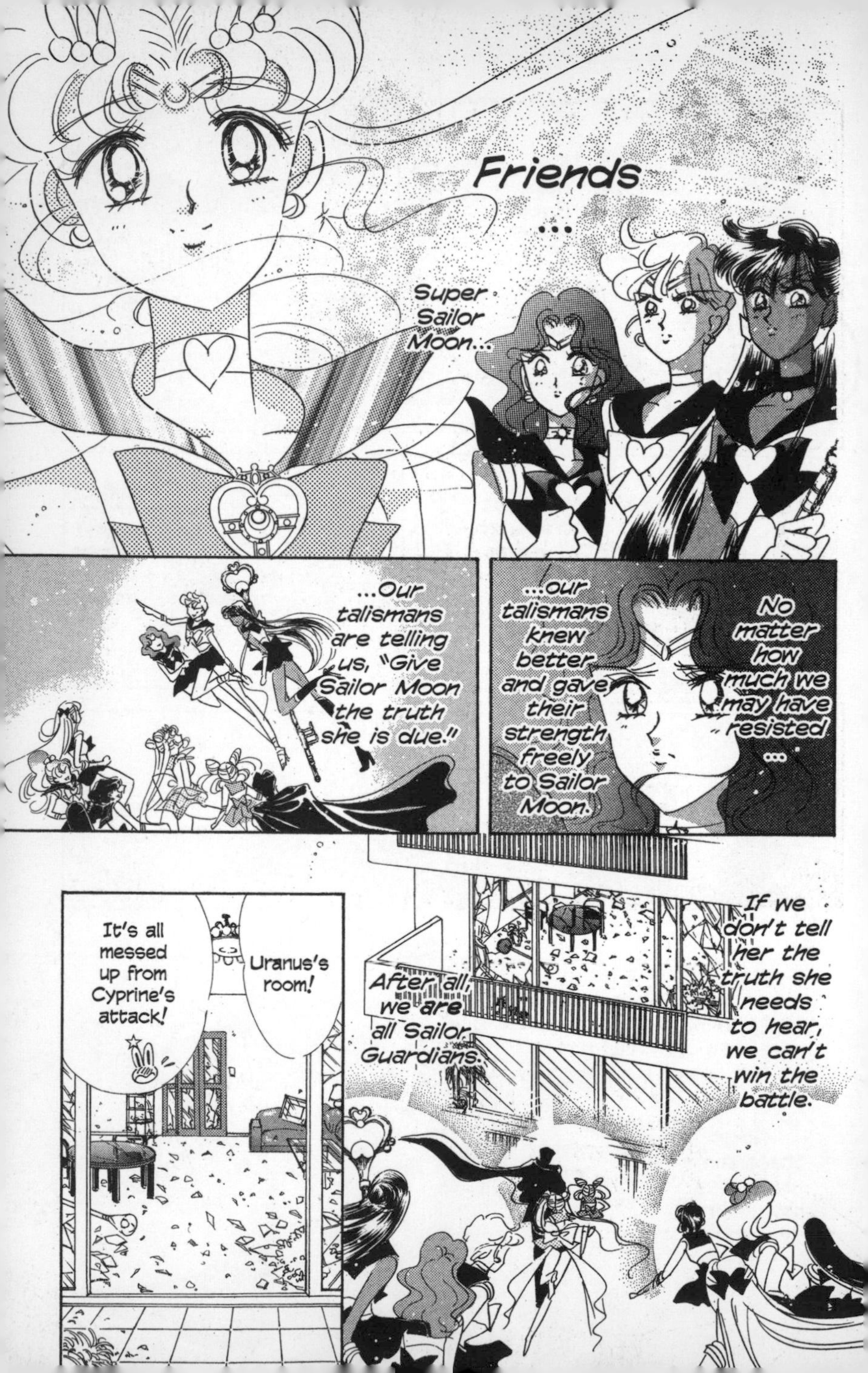
Friends ...
Super Sailor Moon...
No matter how much we may have resisted ...
...our talismans knew better and gave their strength freely to Sailor Moon.
...Our talismans are telling us, "Give Sailor Moon the truth she is due."
If we don't tell her the truth she needs to hear, we can't win the battle.
After all, we are all Sailor Guardians.
Uranus's room!
It's all messed up from Cyprine's attack!

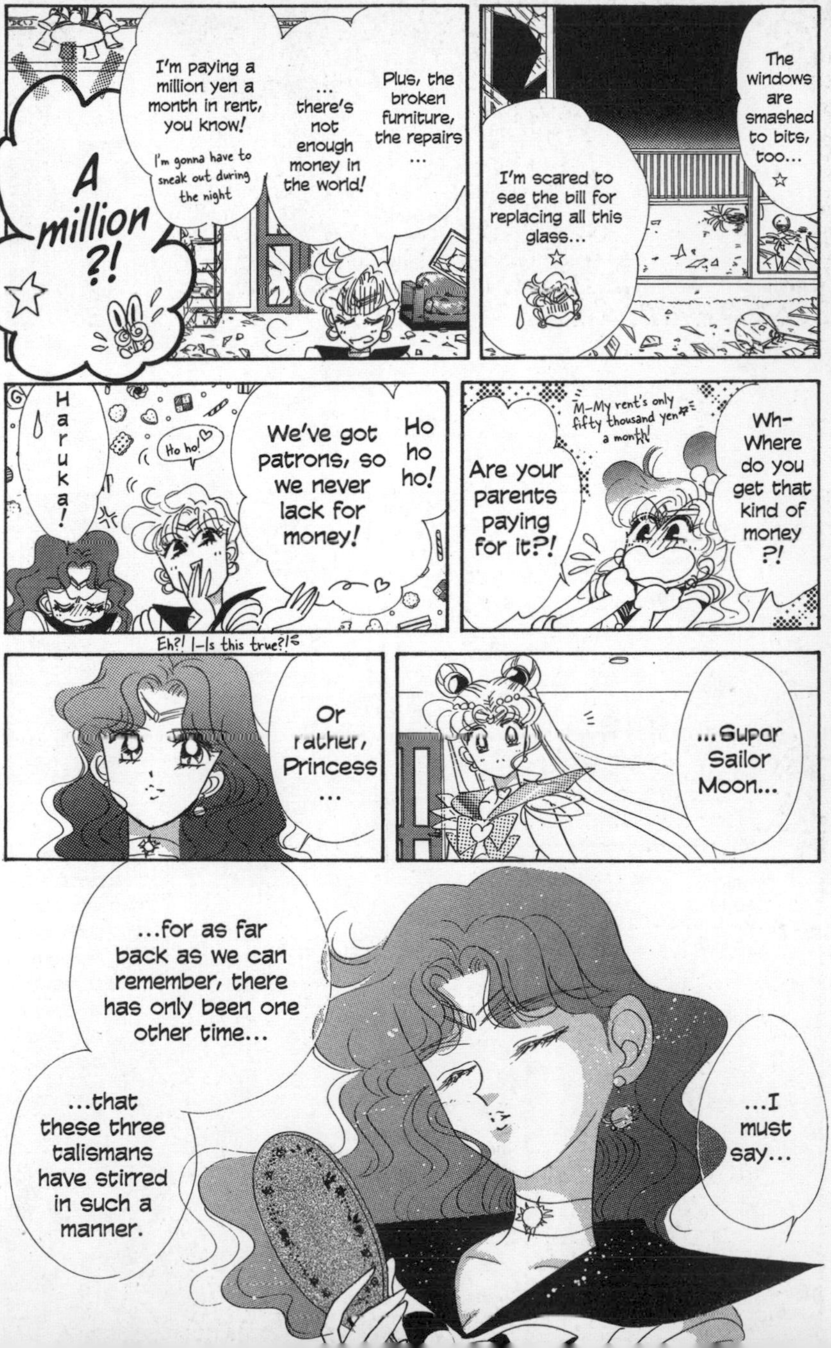
The windows are smashed to bits, too... ☆
I'm scared to see the bill for replacing all this glass... ☆
Plus, the broken furniture, the repairs ...
... there's not enough money in the world!
I'm paying a million yen a month in rent, you know!
I'm gonna have to sneak out during the night
A million ?! ☆
Wh- Where do you get that kind of money ?!
M-My rent's only fifty thousand yen a month!
Are your parents paying for it?!
Ho ho ho!
We've got patrons, so we never lack for money!
Ho ho!
Haruka!
Eh?! I-Is this true?!
...Super Sailor Moon...
Or rather, Princess ...
...I must say...
...for as far back as we can remember, there has only been one other time...
...that these three talismans have stirred in such a manner.

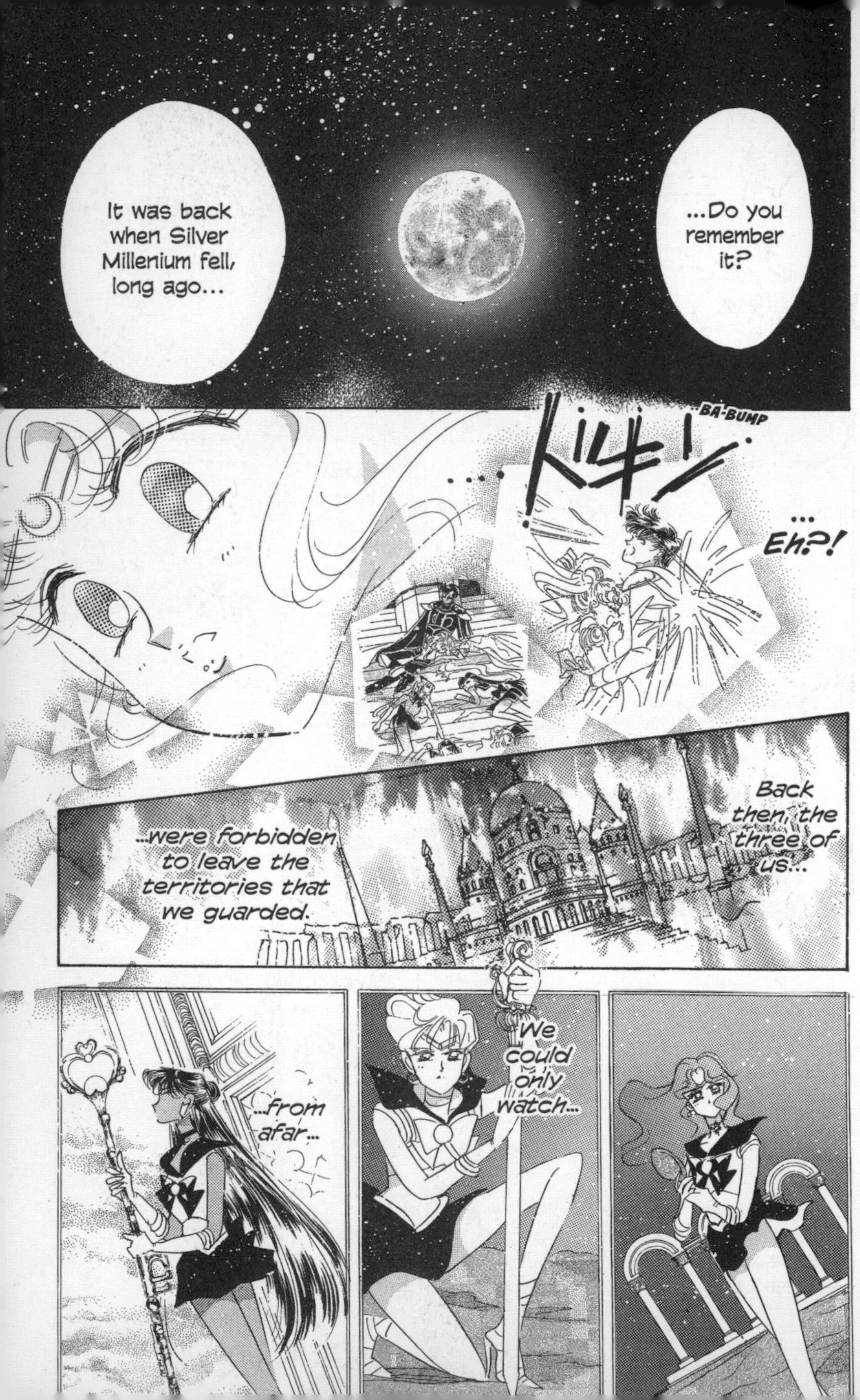
...Do you remember it?
It was back when Silver Millenium fell, long ago...
BA-BUMP
...Eh?!
Back then, the three of us...
...were forbidden to leave the territories that we guarded.
We could only watch...
...from afar...

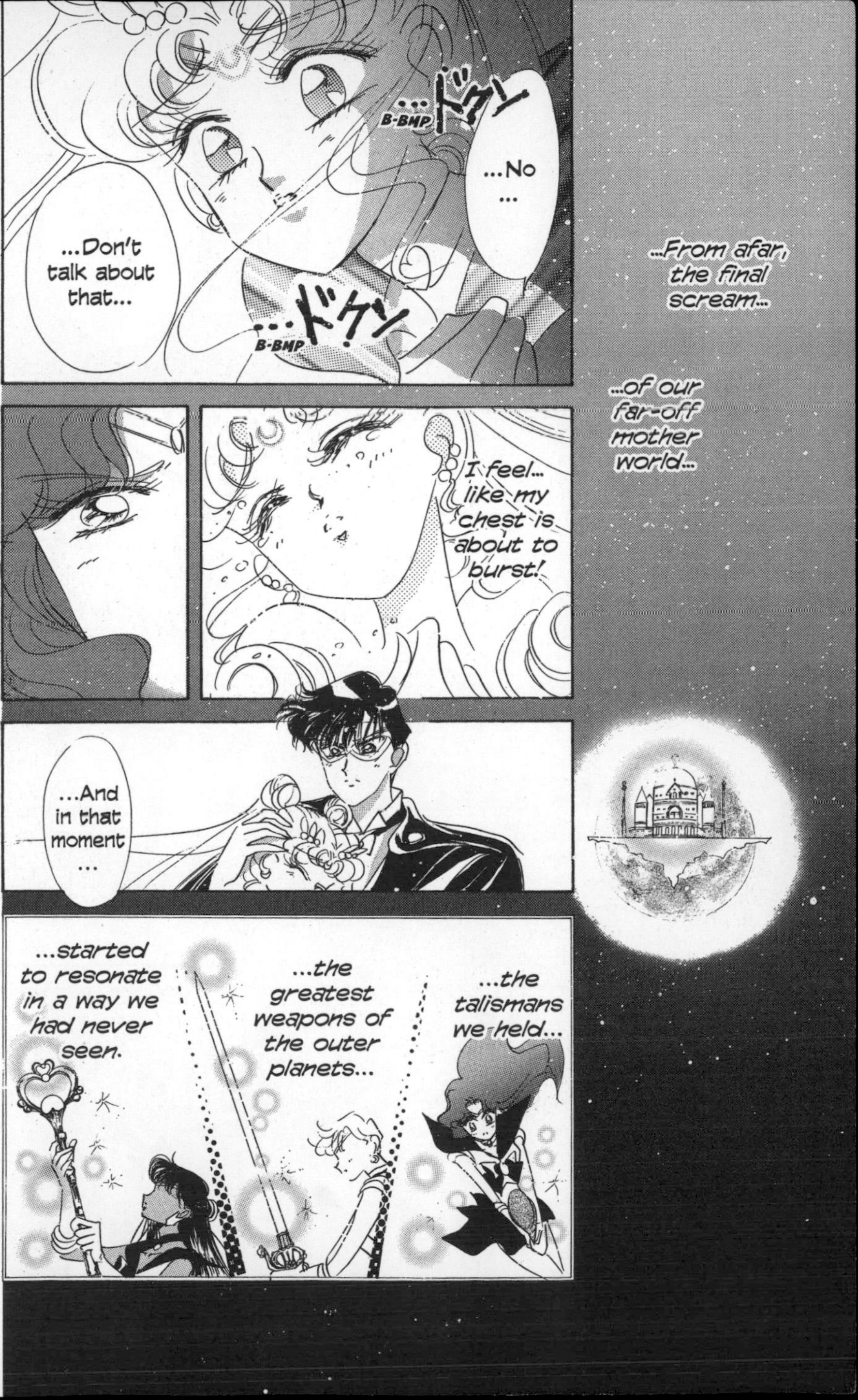

...From afar, the final scream...
...of our far-off mother world...
…ドクン
B-BMP
...No ...
...Don't talk about that...
…ドクン
B-BMP
I feel... like my chest is about to burst!
...And in that moment ...
...the talismans we held...
...the greatest weapons of the outer planets...
...started to resonate in a way we had never seen.

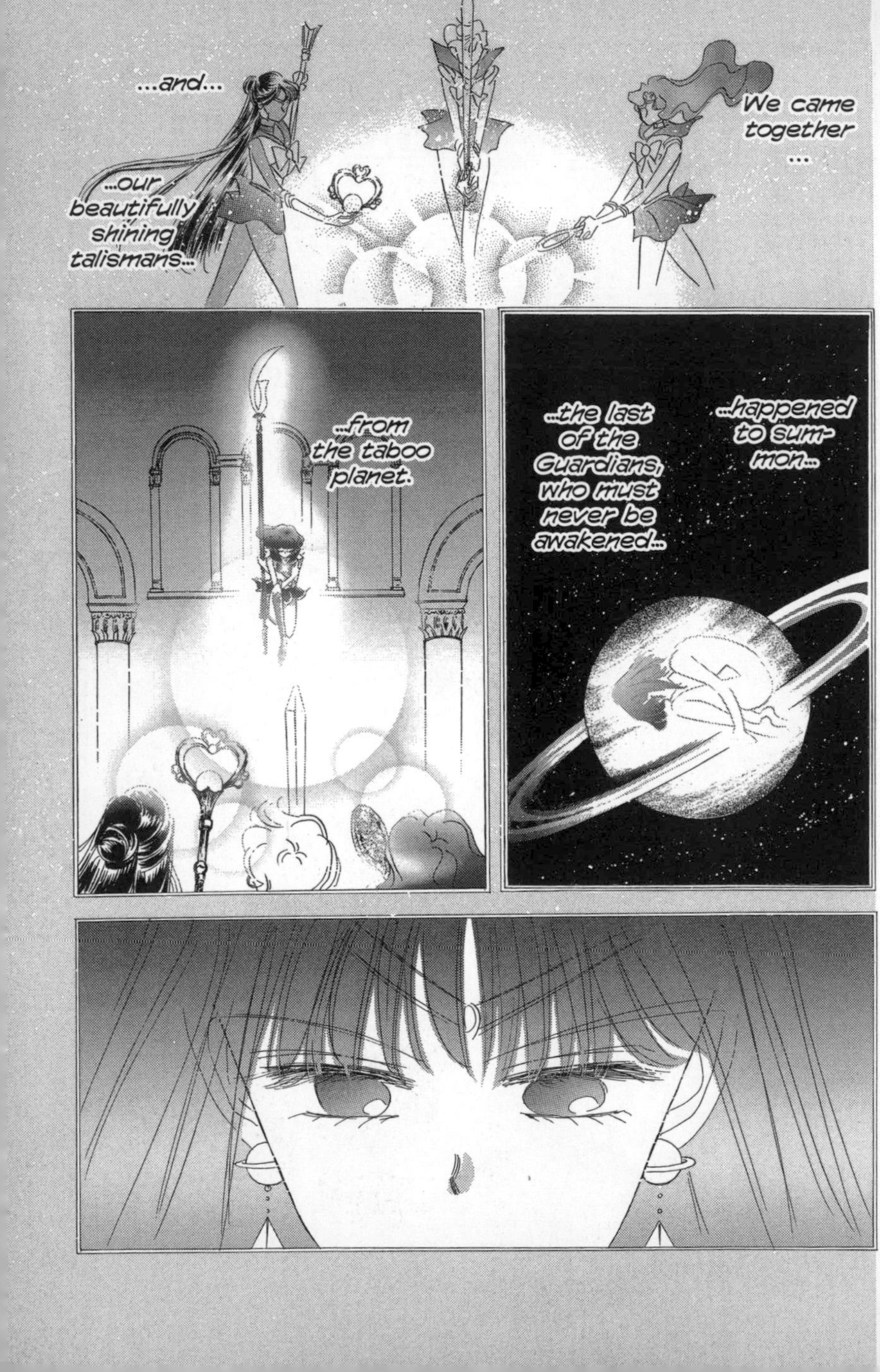
We came together ...
...and...
...our beautifully shining talismans...
...happened to sum-mon...
...the last of the Guardians, who must never be awakened...
...from the taboo planet.

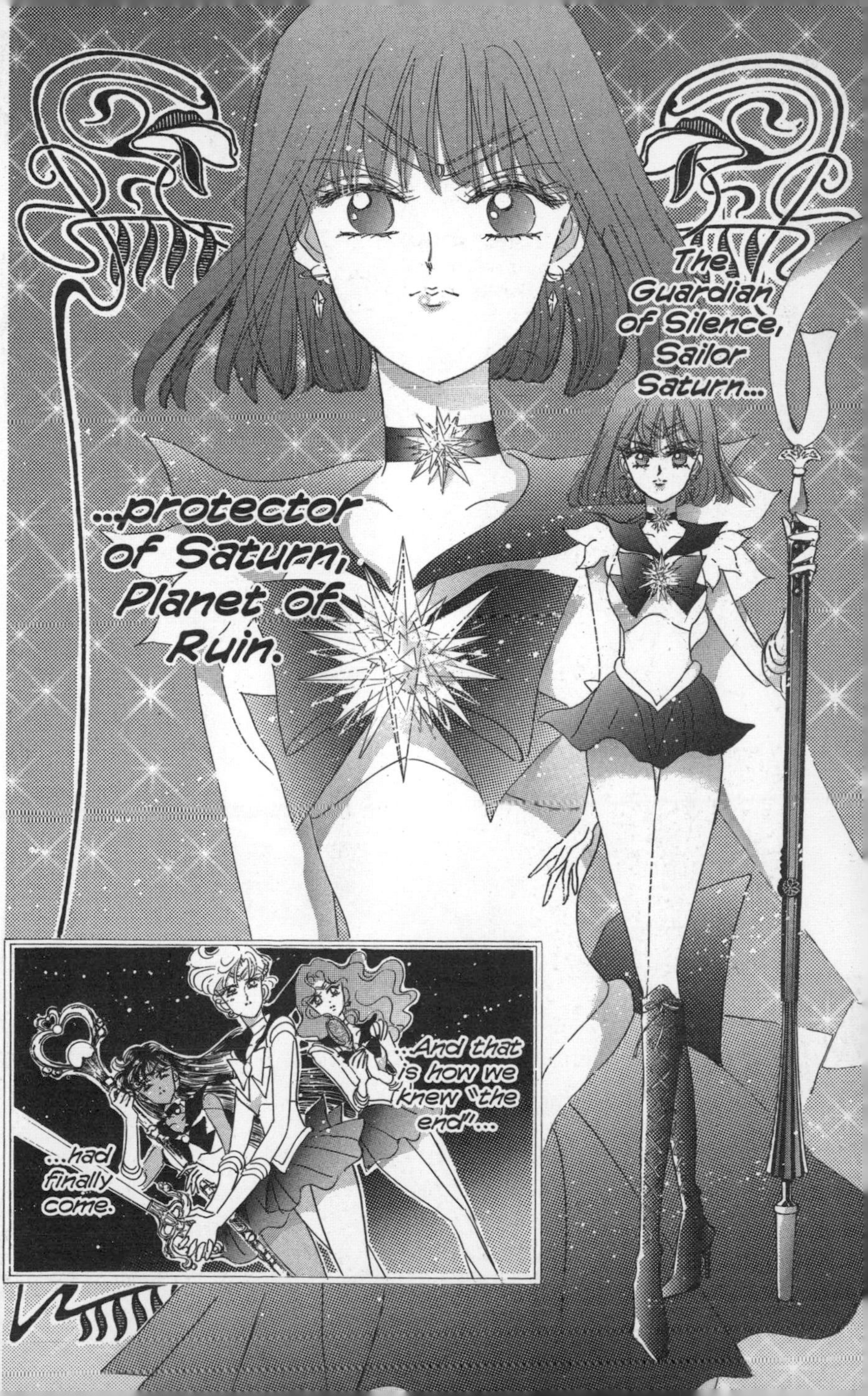

The Guardian of Silence, Sailor Saturn...
...protector of Saturn, Planet of Ruin.
...And that is how we knew "the end"...
...had finally come.

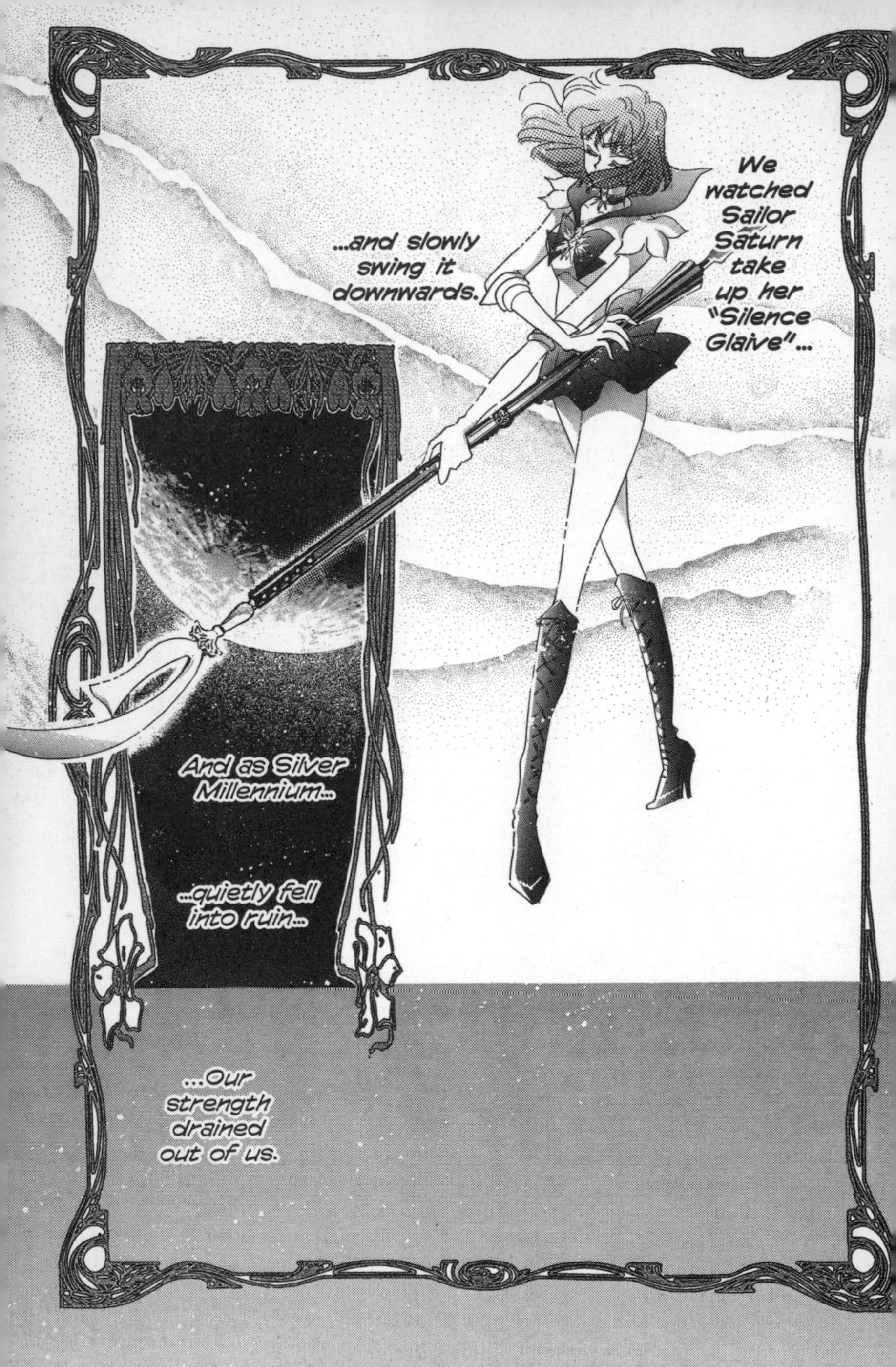
We watched Sailor Saturn take up her "Silence Glaive"...
...and slowly swing it downwards.
And as Silver Millennium...
...quietly fell into ruin...
...Our strength drained out of us.

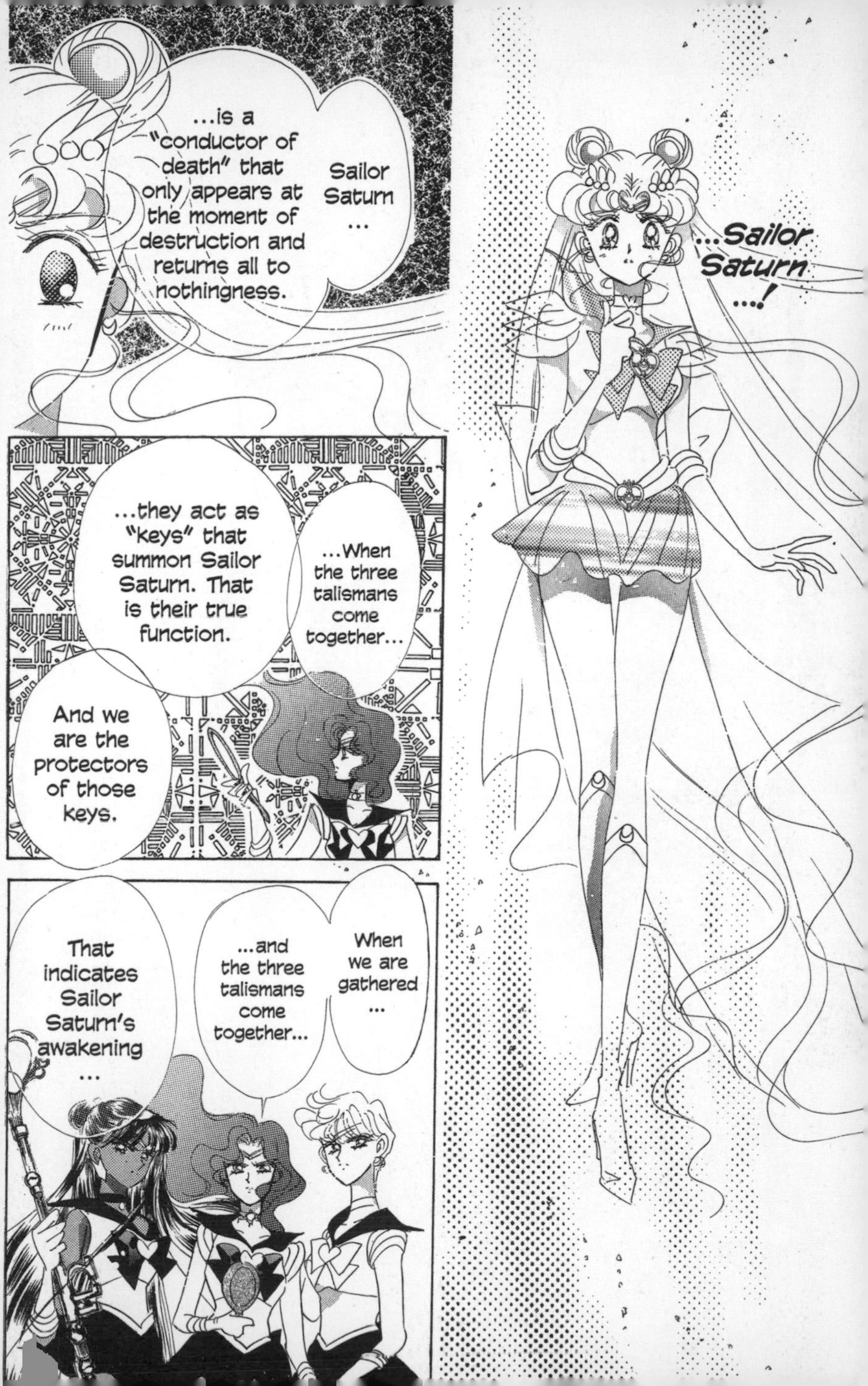
...Sailor Saturn ...!
Sailor Saturn ...
...is a "conductor of death" that only appears at the moment of destruction and returns all to nothingness.
...When the three talismans come together...
...they act as "keys" that summon Sailor Saturn. That is their true function.
And we are the protectors of those keys.
When we are gathered ...
...and the three talismans come together...
That indicates Sailor Saturn's awakening ...

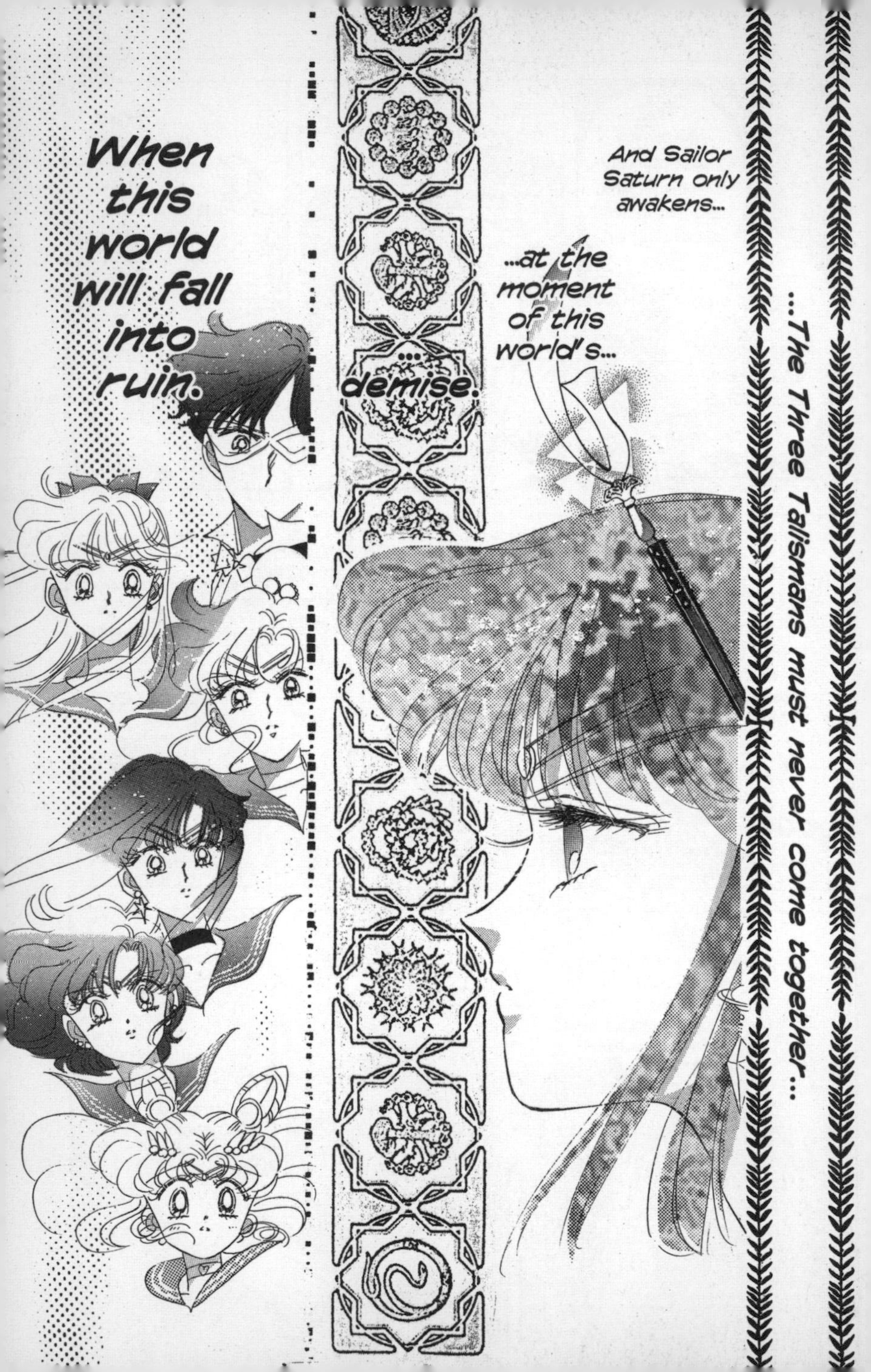

...The Three Talismans must never come together...
And Sailor Saturn only awakens...
...at the moment of this world's...
...demise.
When this world will fall into ruin.

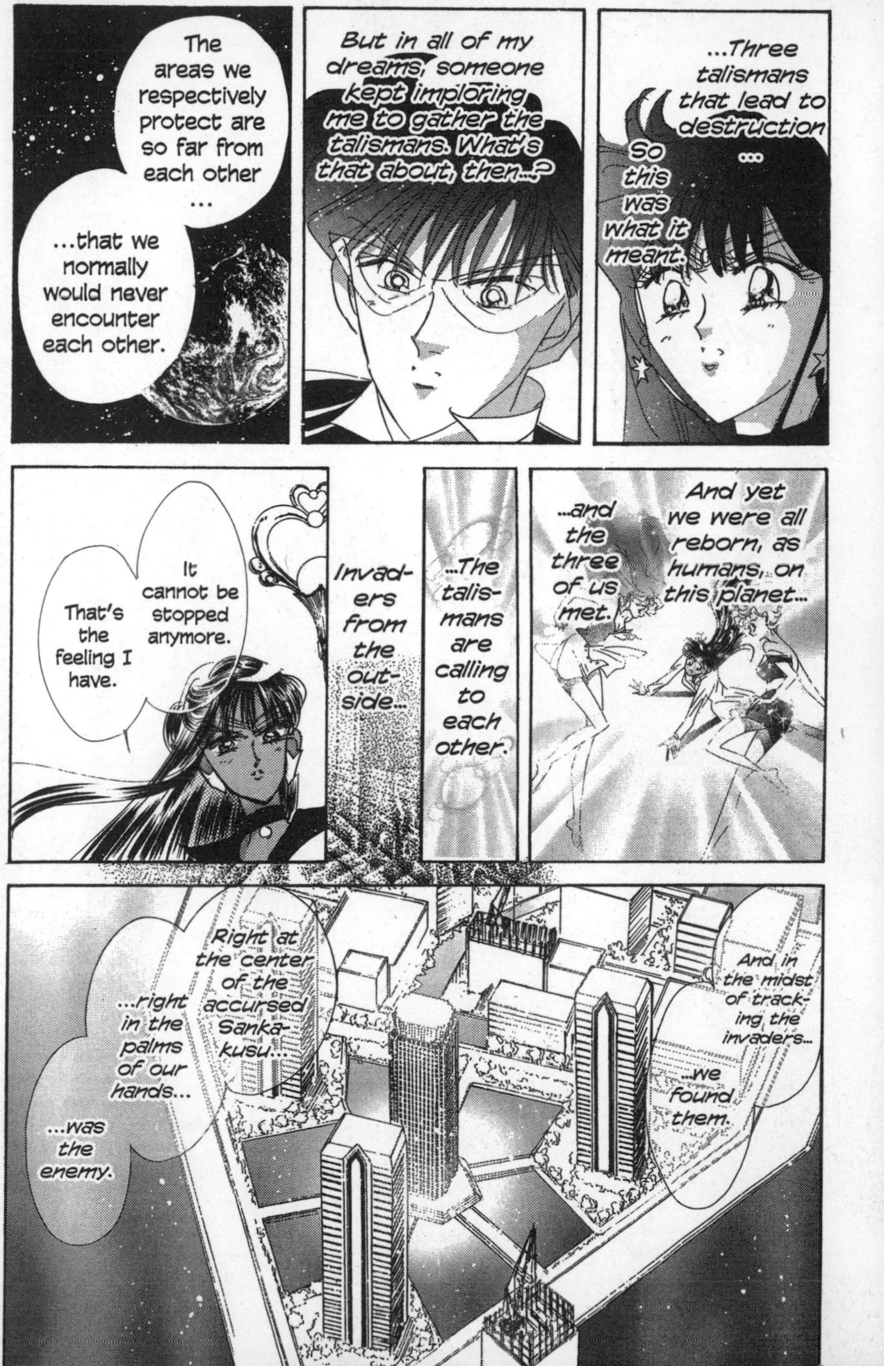
...Three talismans that lead to destruction ...
So this was what it meant.
But in all of my dreams, someone kept imploring me to gather the talismans. What's that about, then...?
The areas we respectively protect are so far from each other ...
...that we normally would never encounter each other.
And yet we were all reborn, as humans, on this planet...
...and the three of us met.
...The talismans are calling to each other.
Invaders from the outside...
It cannot be stopped anymore.
That's the feeling I have.
And in the midst of tracking the invaders...
...we found them.
Right at the center of the accursed Sankakusu...
...right in the palms of our hands...
...was the enemy.

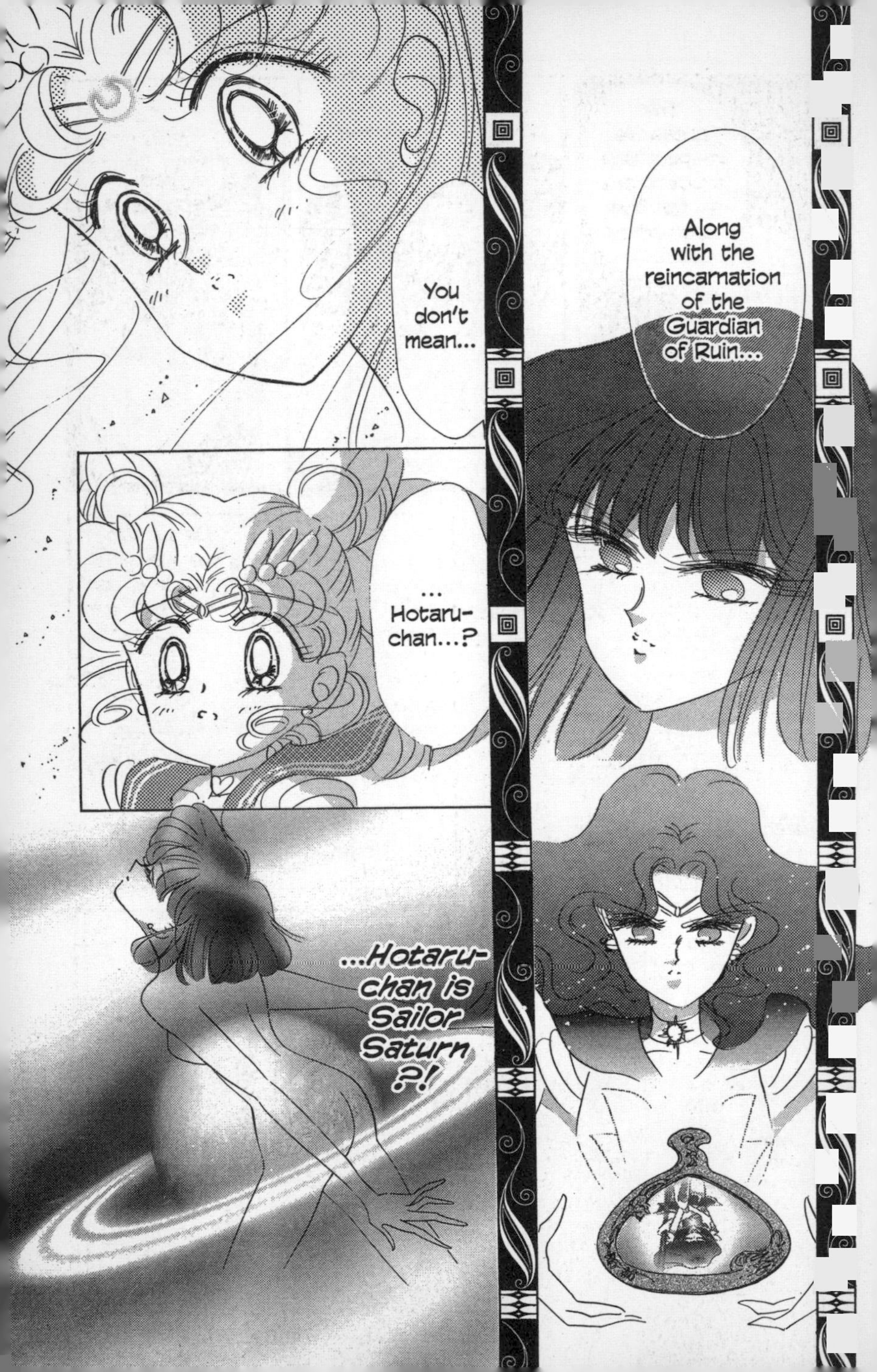
Along with the reincarnation of the Guardian of Ruin...
You don't mean...
... Hotaru-chan...?
...Hotaru-chan is Sailor Saturn ?!

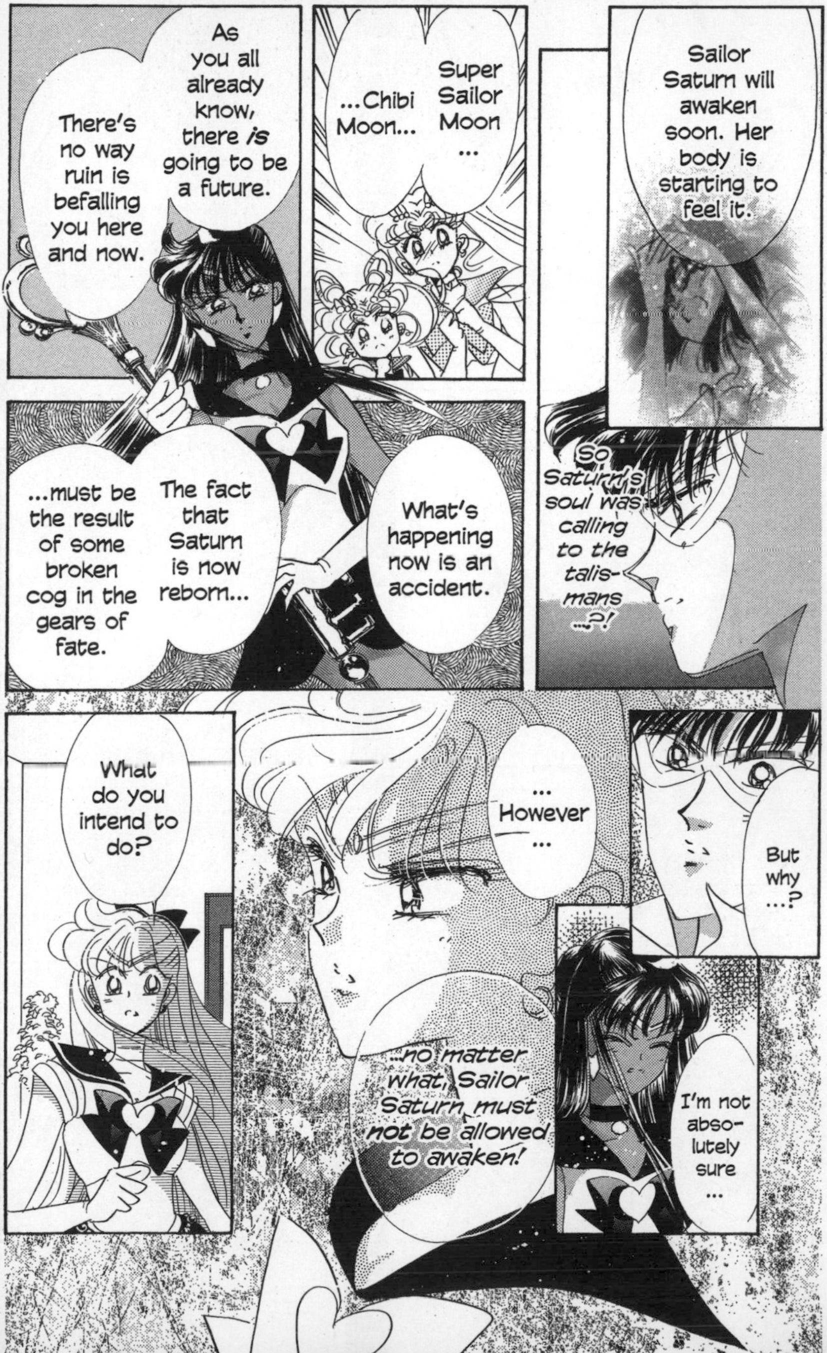

Sailor Saturn will awaken soon. Her body is starting to feel it.
So Saturn's soul was calling to the talismans ...?!
Super Sailor Moon ...
...Chibi Moon...
As you all already know, there *is* going to be a future.
There's no way ruin is befalling you here and now.
What's happening now is an accident.
The fact that Saturn is now reborn...
...must be the result of some broken cog in the gears of fate.
But why ...?
I'm not absolutely sure ...
... However ...
...no matter what, Sailor Saturn must **not** be allowed to awaken!
What do you intend to do?

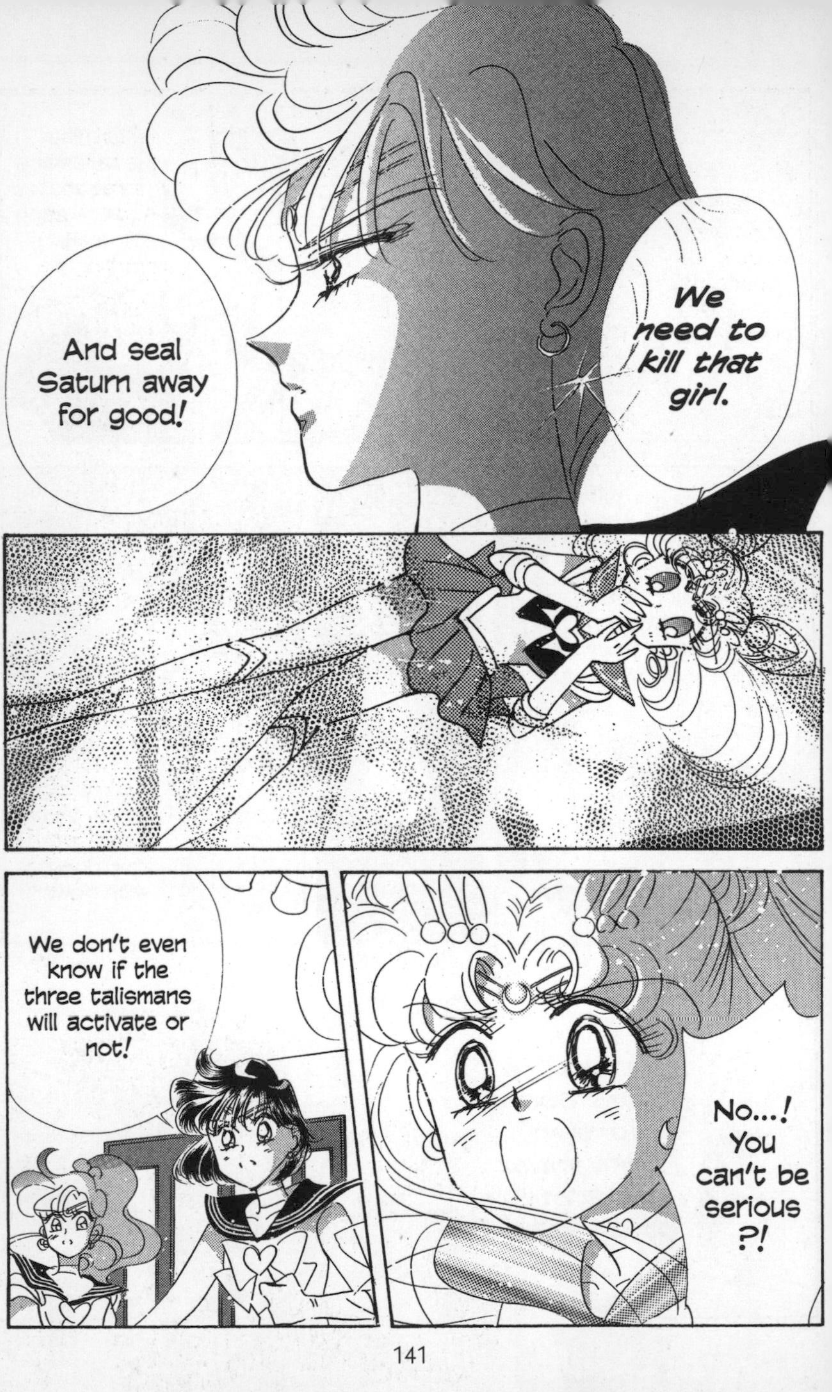
We need to kill that girl.
And seal Saturn away for good!
No...! You can't be serious ?!
We don't even know if the three talismans will activate or not!

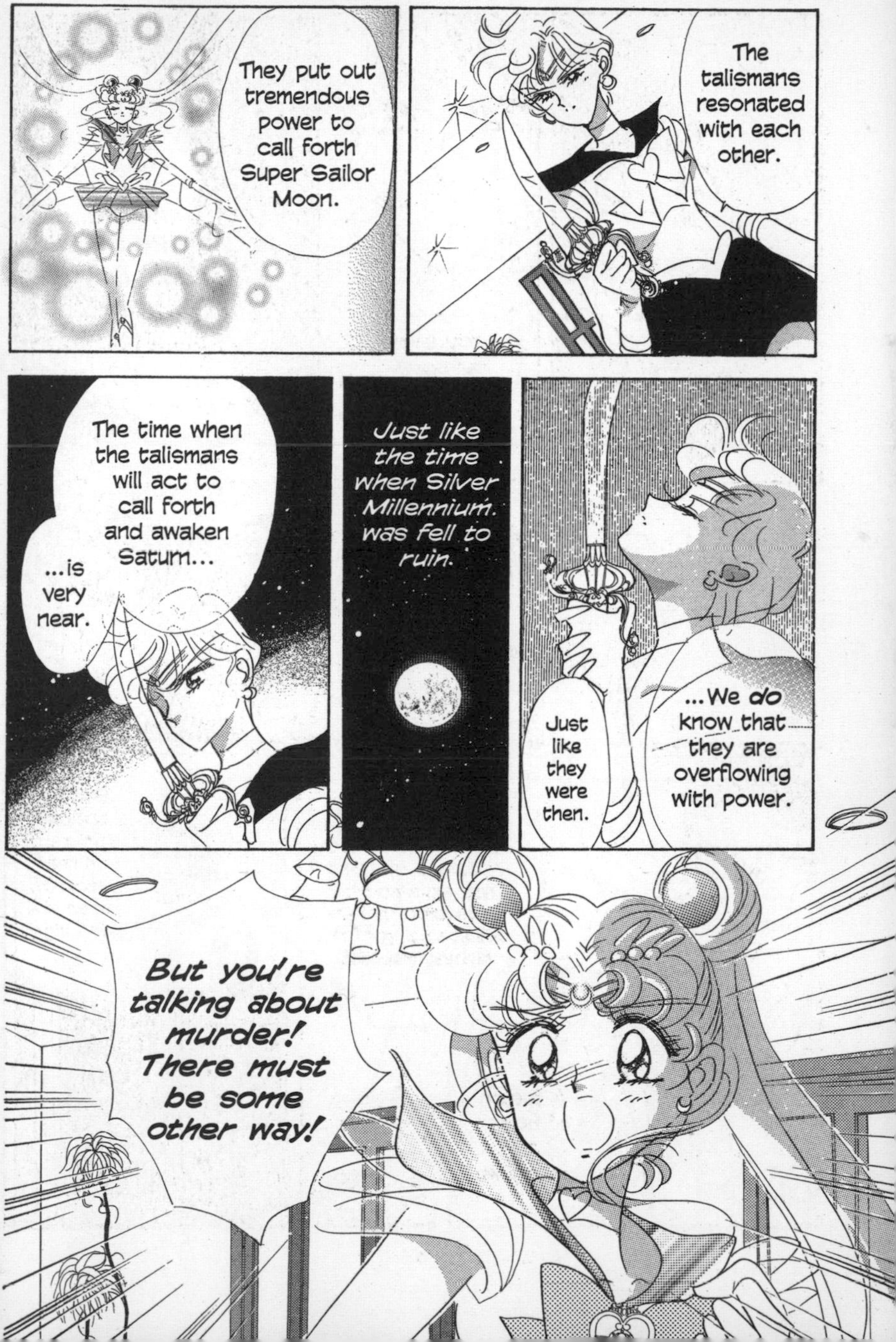
The talismans resonated with each other.
They put out tremendous power to call forth Super Sailor Moon.
...We do know that they are overflowing with power.
Just like they were then.
Just like the time when Silver Millennium was fell to ruin.
The time when the talismans will act to call forth and awaken Saturn...
...is very near.
But you're talking about murder! There must be some other way!

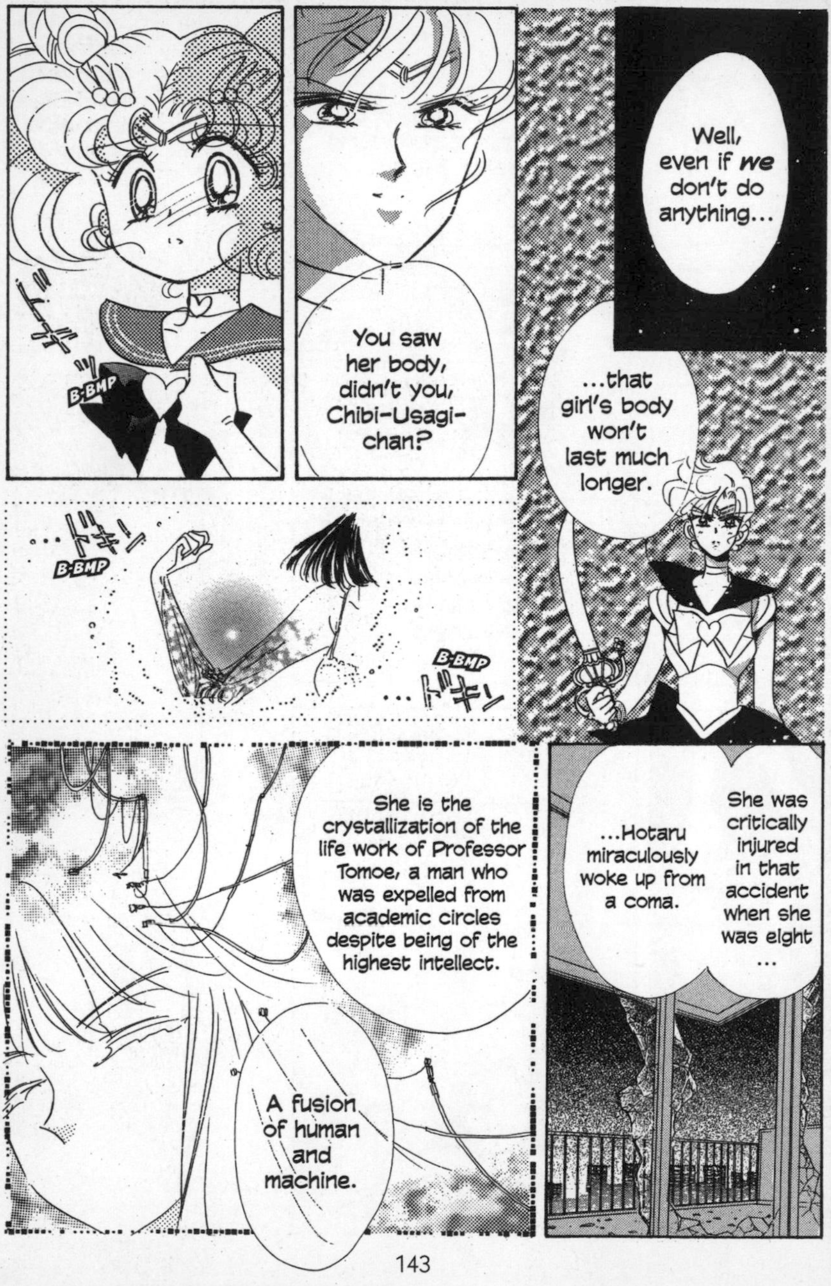
Well, even if *we* don't do anything...
...that girl's body won't last much longer.
You saw her body, didn't you, Chibi-Usagi-chan?
B-BMP
B-BMP
B-BMP
She was critically injured in that accident when she was eight ...
...Hotaru miraculously woke up from a coma.
She is the crystallization of the life work of Professor Tomoe, a man who was expelled from academic circles despite being of the highest intellect.
A fusion of human and machine.

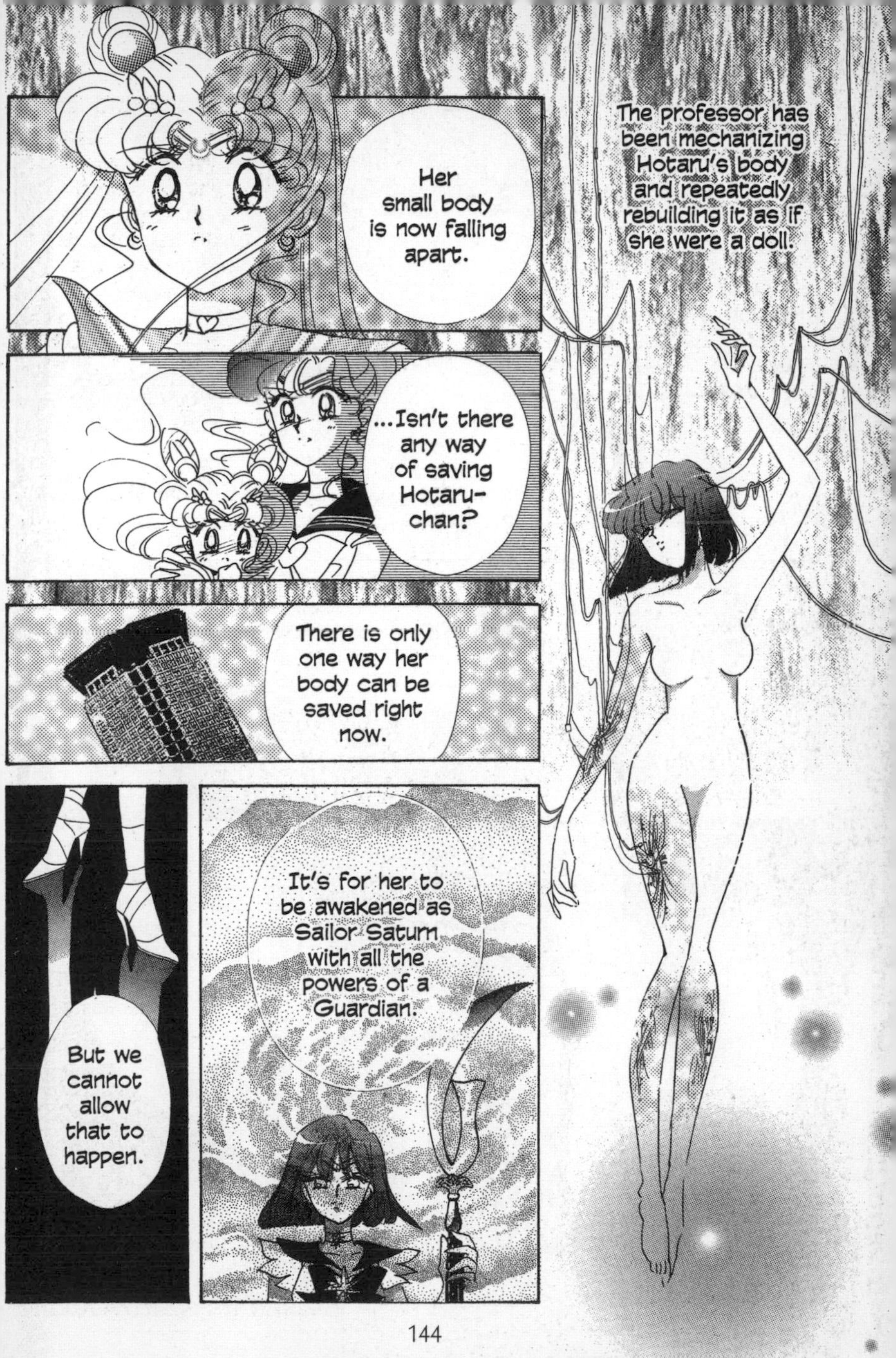
The professor has been mechanizing Hotaru's body and repeatedly rebuilding it as if she were a doll.
Her small body is now falling apart.
...Isn't there any way of saving Hotaru-chan?
There is only one way her body can be saved right now.
It's for her to be awakened as Sailor Saturn with all the powers of a Guardian.
But we cannot allow that to happen.

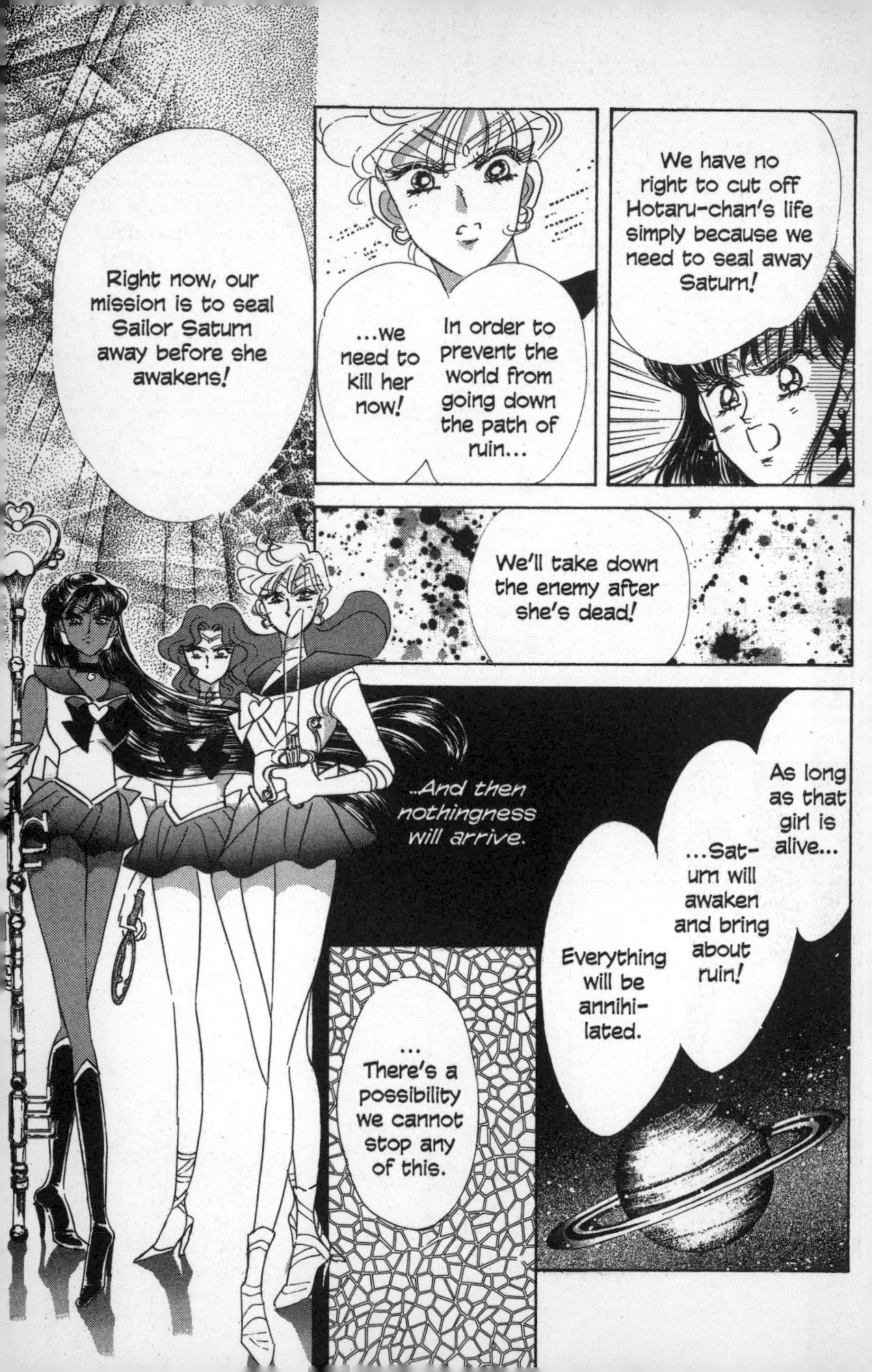
We have no right to cut off Hotaru-chan's life simply because we need to seal away Saturn!
In order to prevent the world from going down the path of ruin...
...we need to kill her now!
We'll take down the enemy after she's dead!
As long as that girl is alive...
...Sat-urn will awaken and bring about ruin!
Everything will be annihi-lated.
...And then nothingness will arrive.
... There's a possibility we cannot stop any of this.
Right now, our mission is to seal Sailor Saturn away before she awakens!

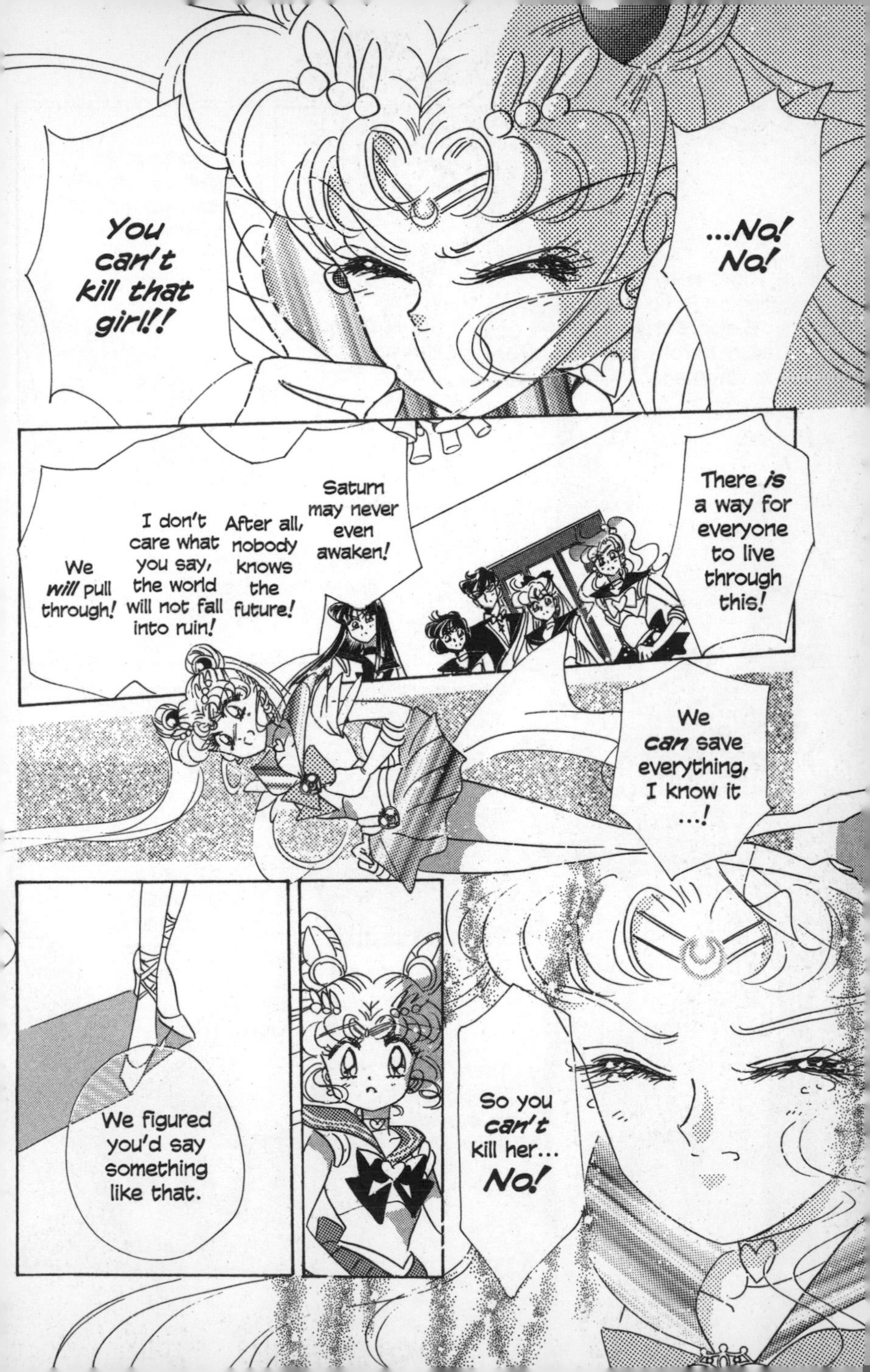
...No! No!
You can't kill that girl!!
There is a way for everyone to live through this!
Saturn may never even awaken!
After all, nobody knows the future!
I don't care what you say, the world will not fall into ruin!
We will pull through!
We can save everything, I know it ...!
So you can't kill her... No!
We figured you'd say something like that.

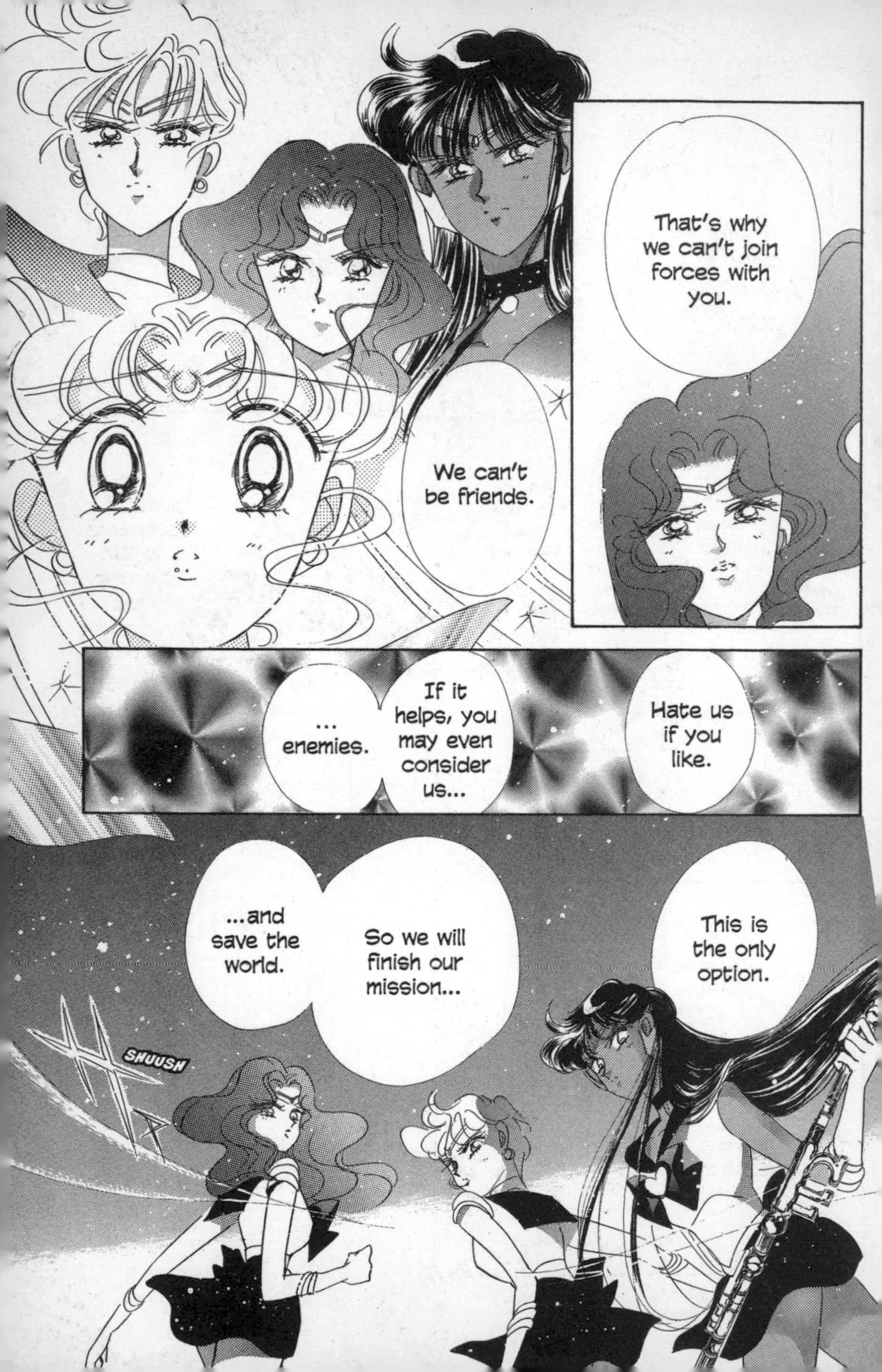
That's why we can't join forces with you.
We can't be friends.
Hate us if you like.
If it helps, you may even consider us...
...enemies.
This is the only option.
So we will finish our mission...
...and save the world.
SNUUSH

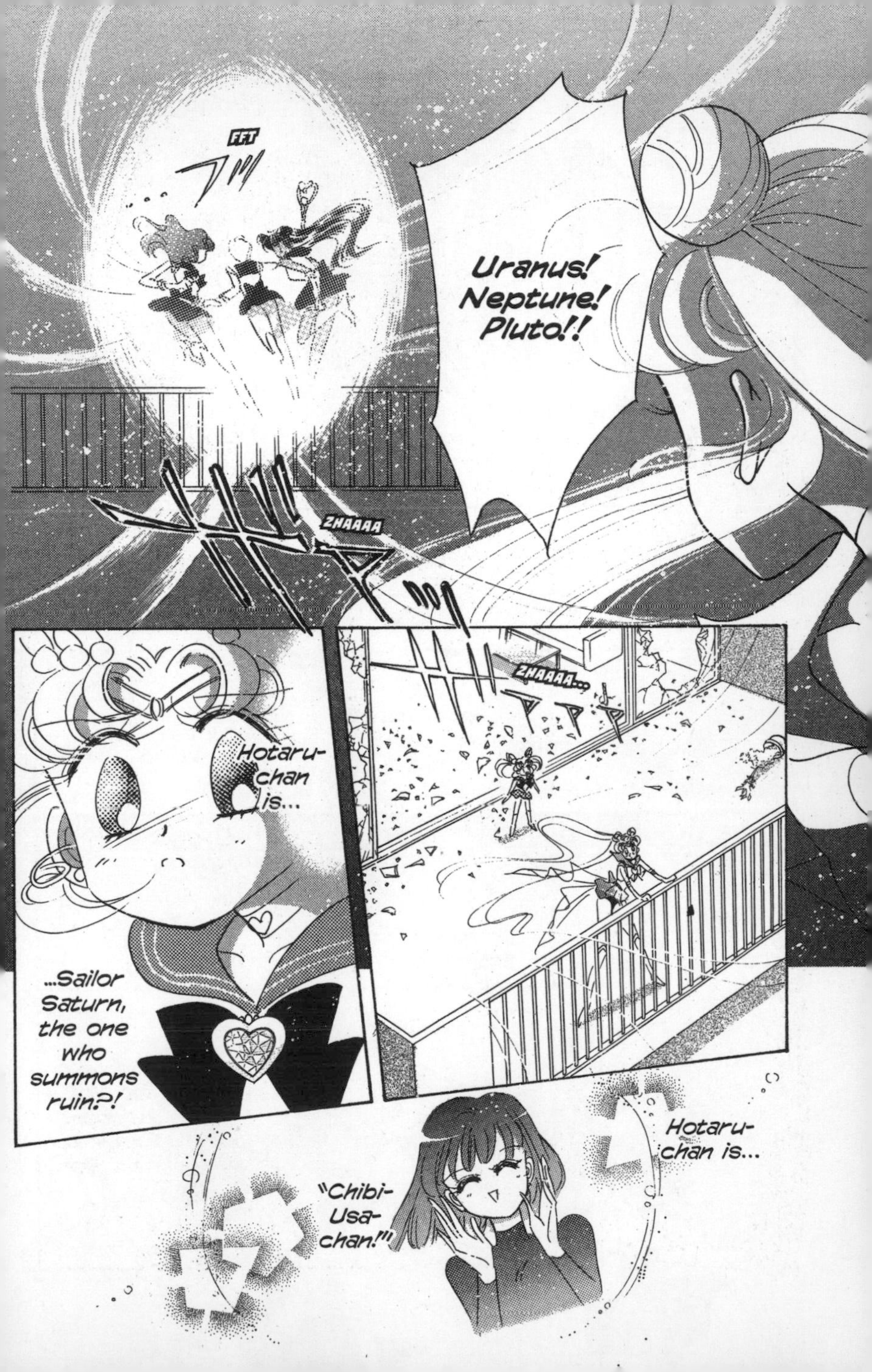

Uranus! Neptune! Pluto!!
FFT
ZHAAAA
ZHAAAA...
Hotaru-chan is...
...Sailor Saturn, the one who summons ruin?!
Hotaru-chan is...
"Chibi-Usa-chan!"

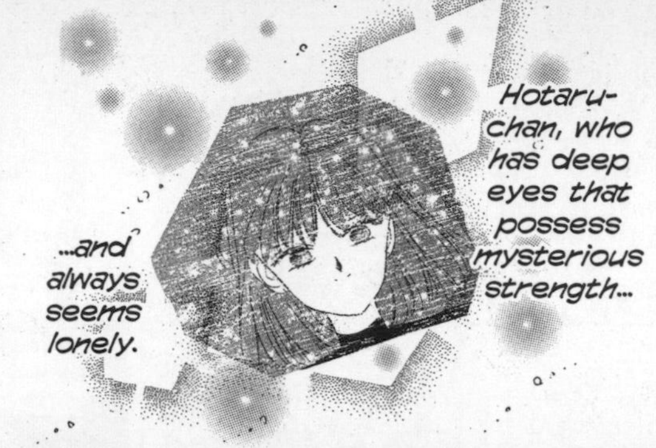
Hotaru-chan, who has deep eyes that possess mysterious strength...
...and always seems lonely.
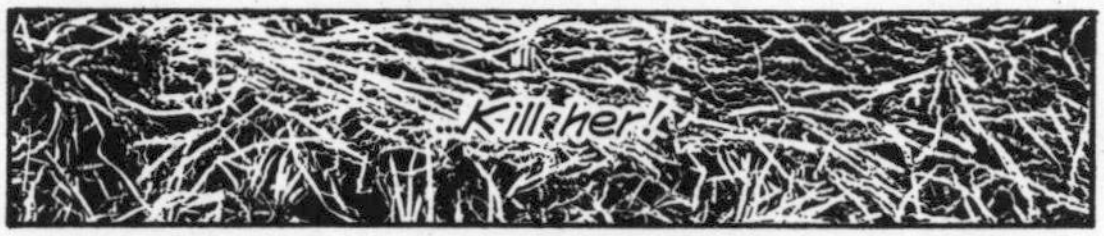
Kill her!
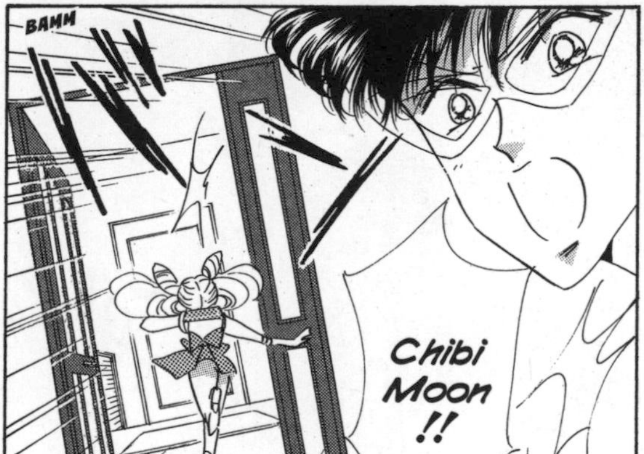
BAMM
Chibi Moon !!
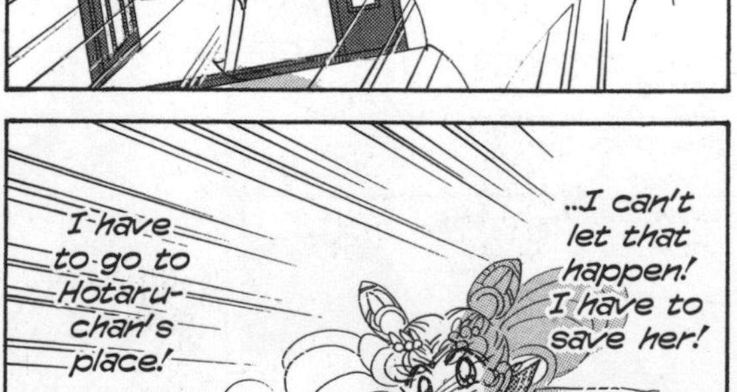
...I can't let that happen! I have to save her!
I have to go to Hotaru-chan's place!
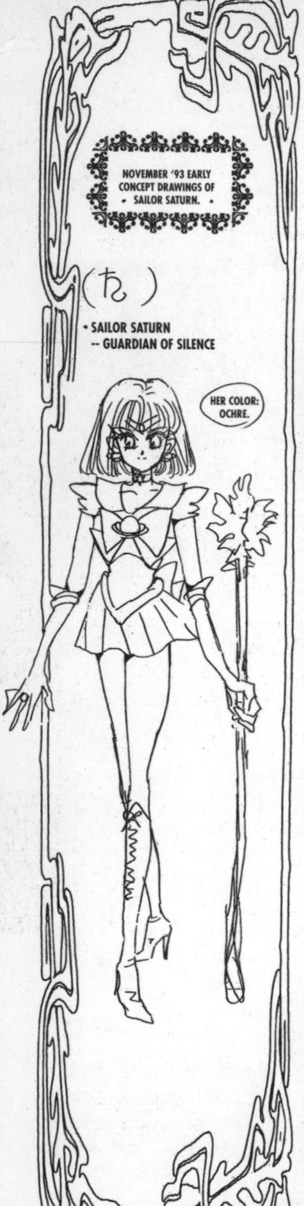
NOVEMBER '93 EARLY CONCEPT DRAWINGS OF • SAILOR SATURN. •
• SAILOR SATURN -- GUARDIAN OF SILENCE
HER COLOR: OCHRE.

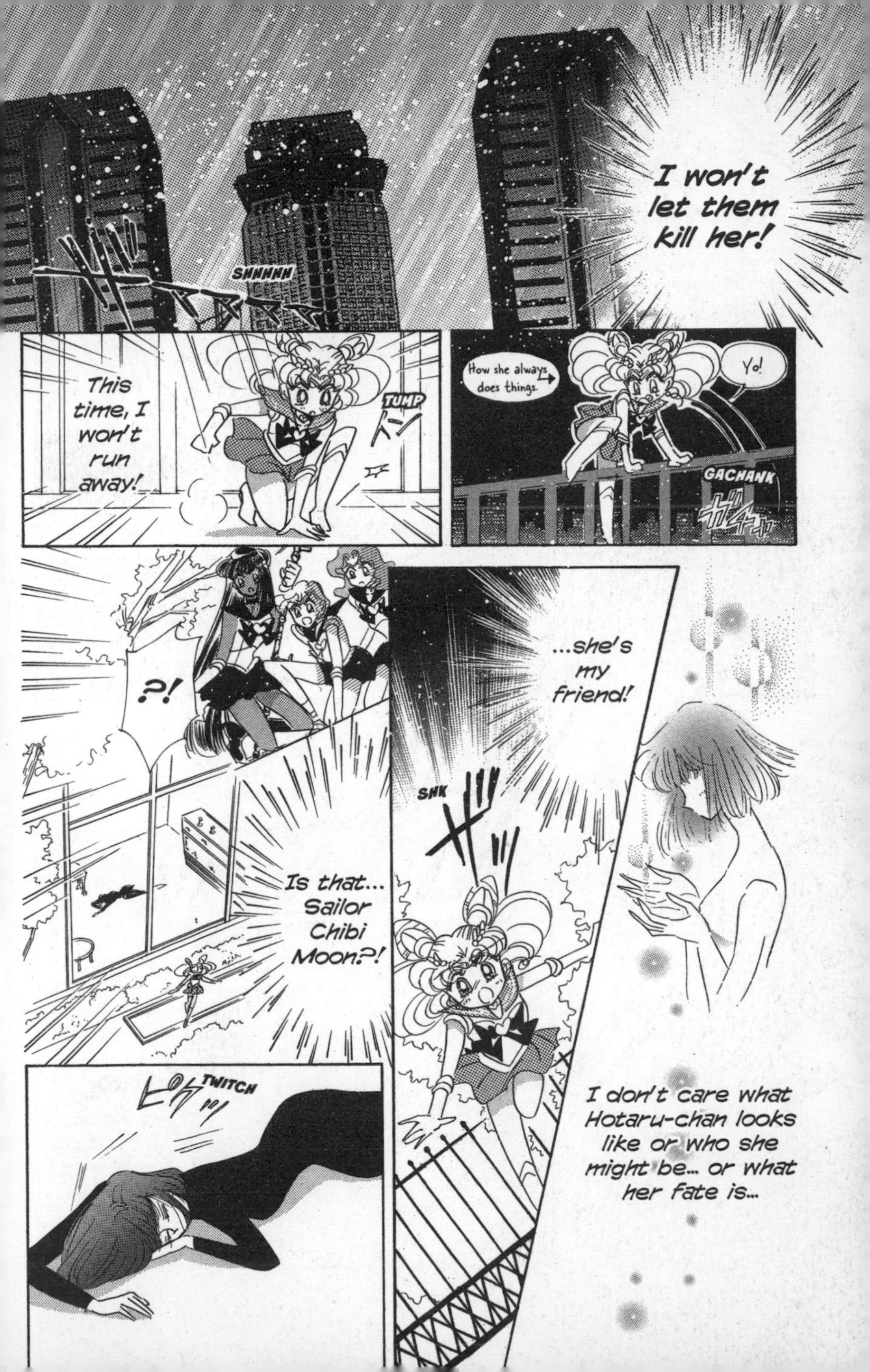

SHHHHH
I won't let them kill her!
How she always does things.
Yo!
GACHANK
This time, I won't run away!
TUMP
I don't care what Hotaru-chan looks like or who she might be... or what her fate is...
...she's my friend!
SHK
?!
Is that... Sailor Chibi Moon?!
TWITCH

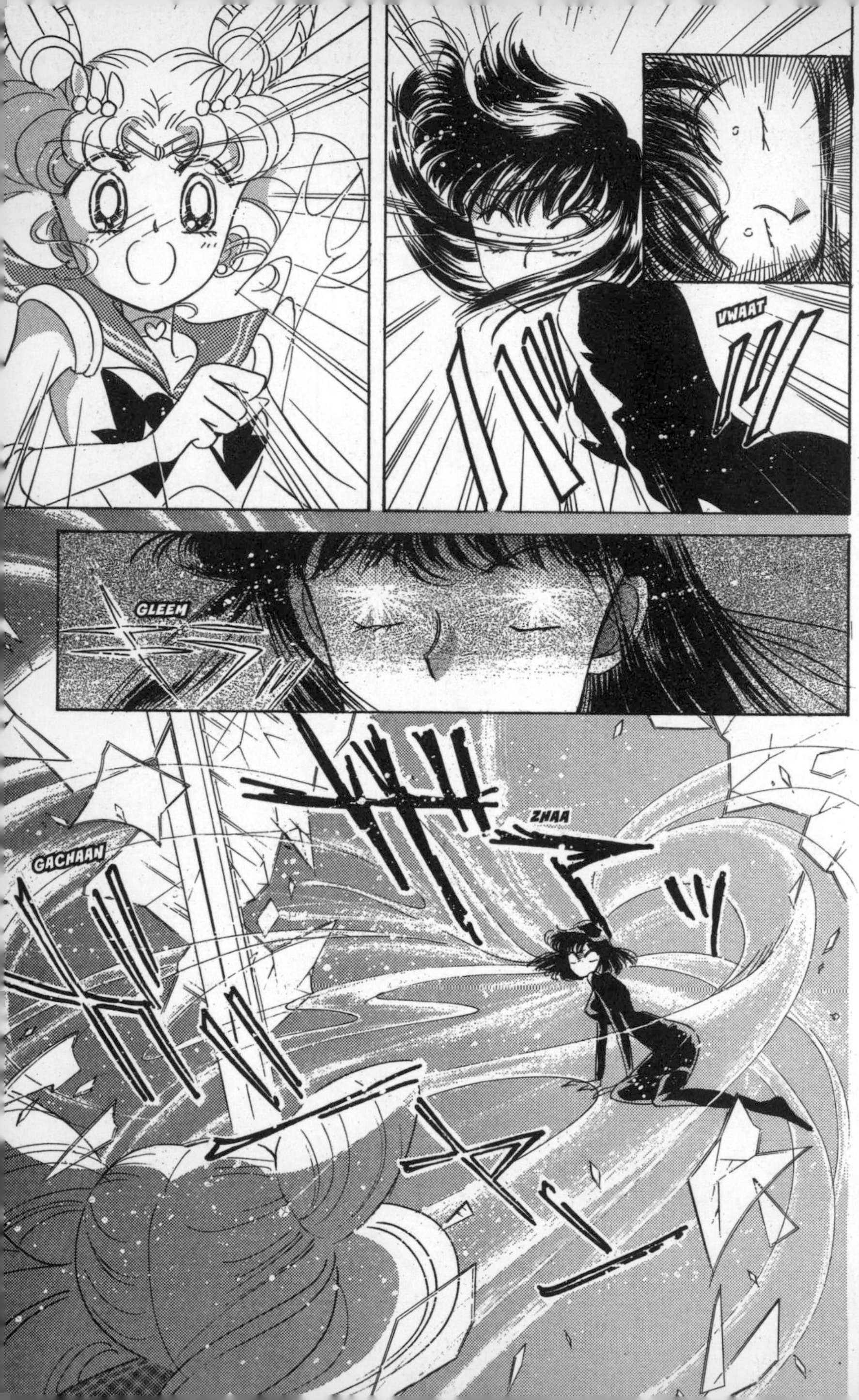
VWAAT
GLEEM
ZNAA
GACHAAN

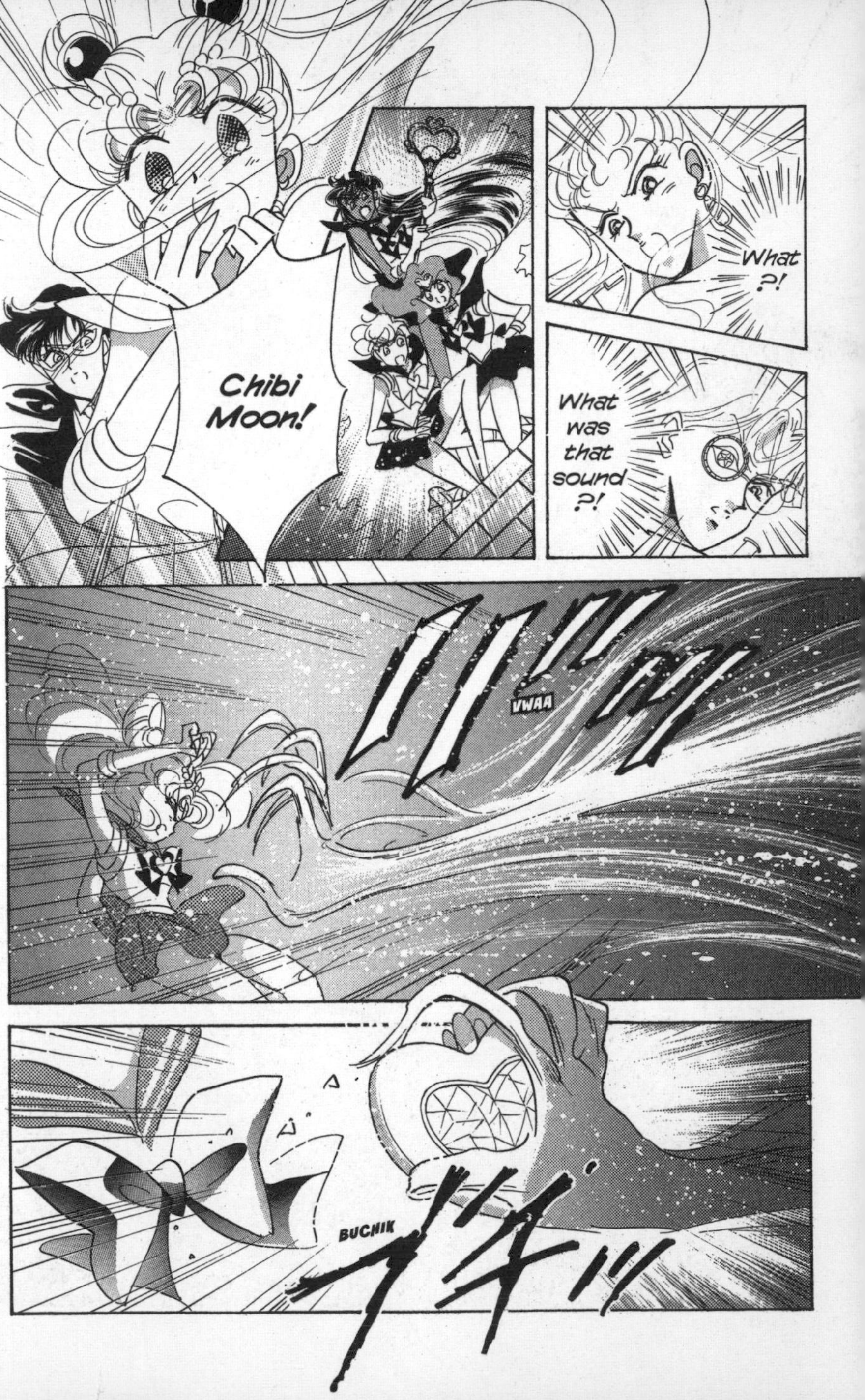
What ?!
What was that sound ?!
Chibi Moon!
VWAA
BUCHIK

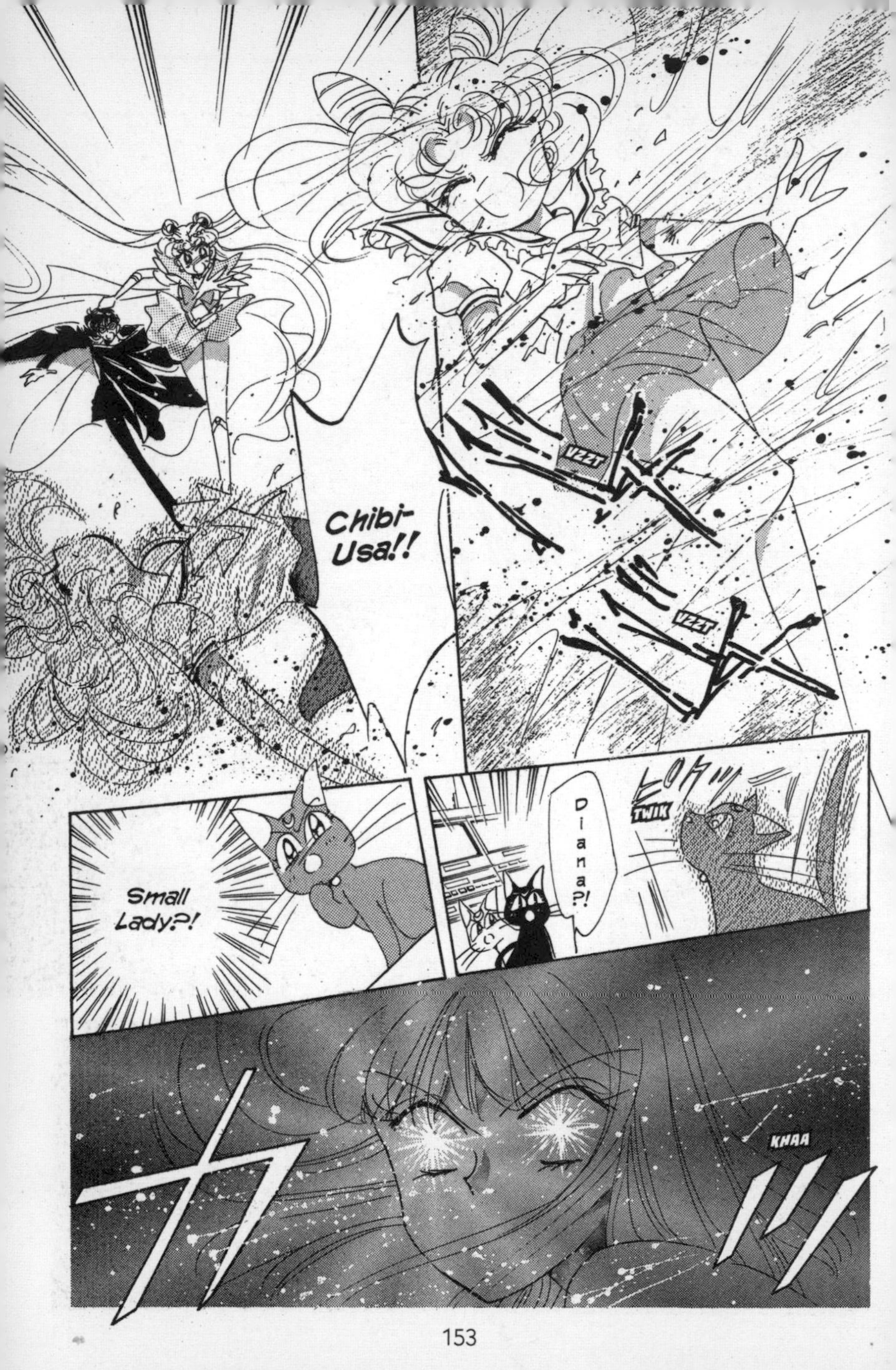
VZZT
VZZT
Chibi-Usa!!
TWIK
Diana?!
Small Lady?!
KHAA

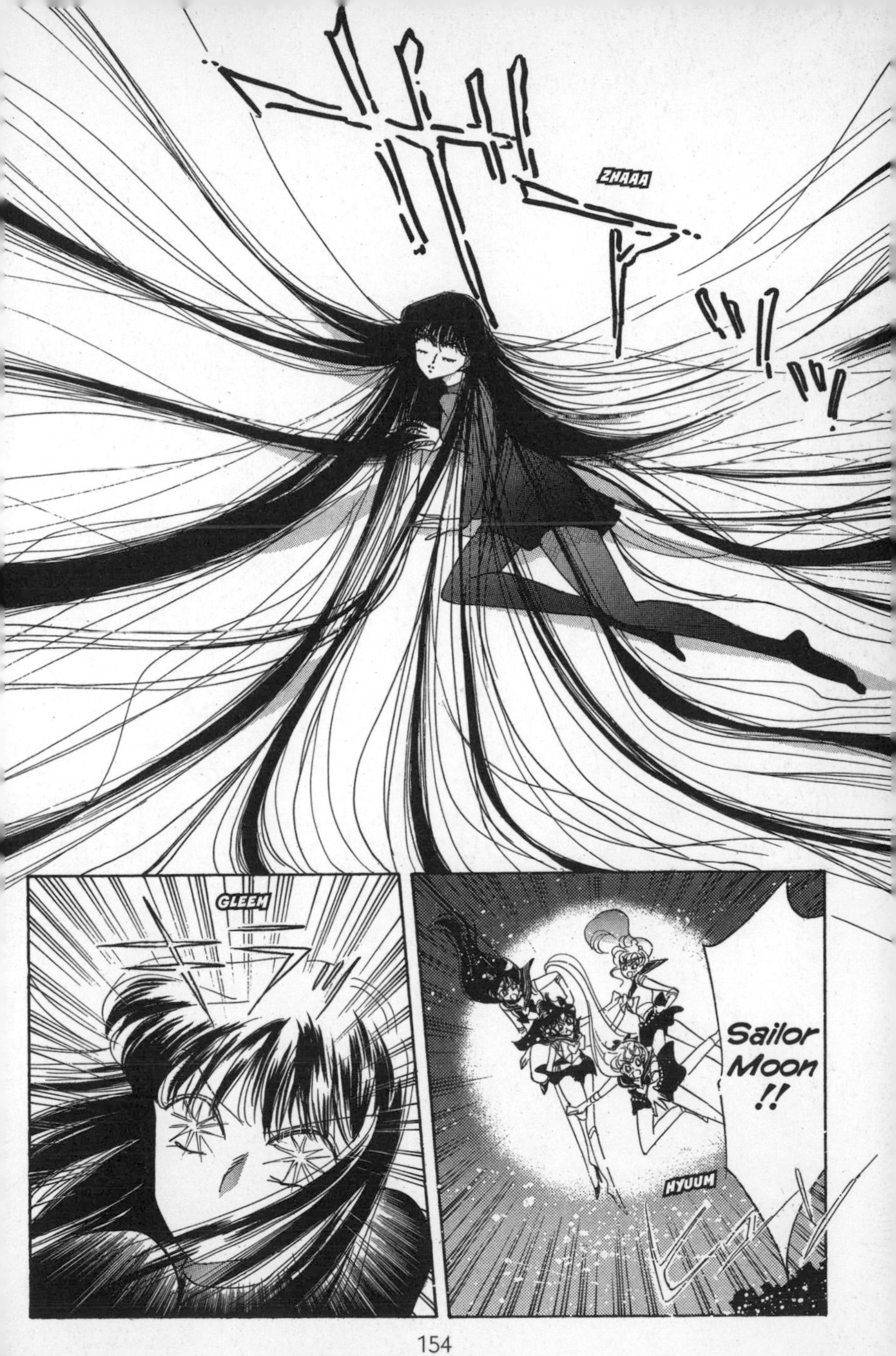
ZHAAA
Sailor Moon !!
HYUUM
GLEEM

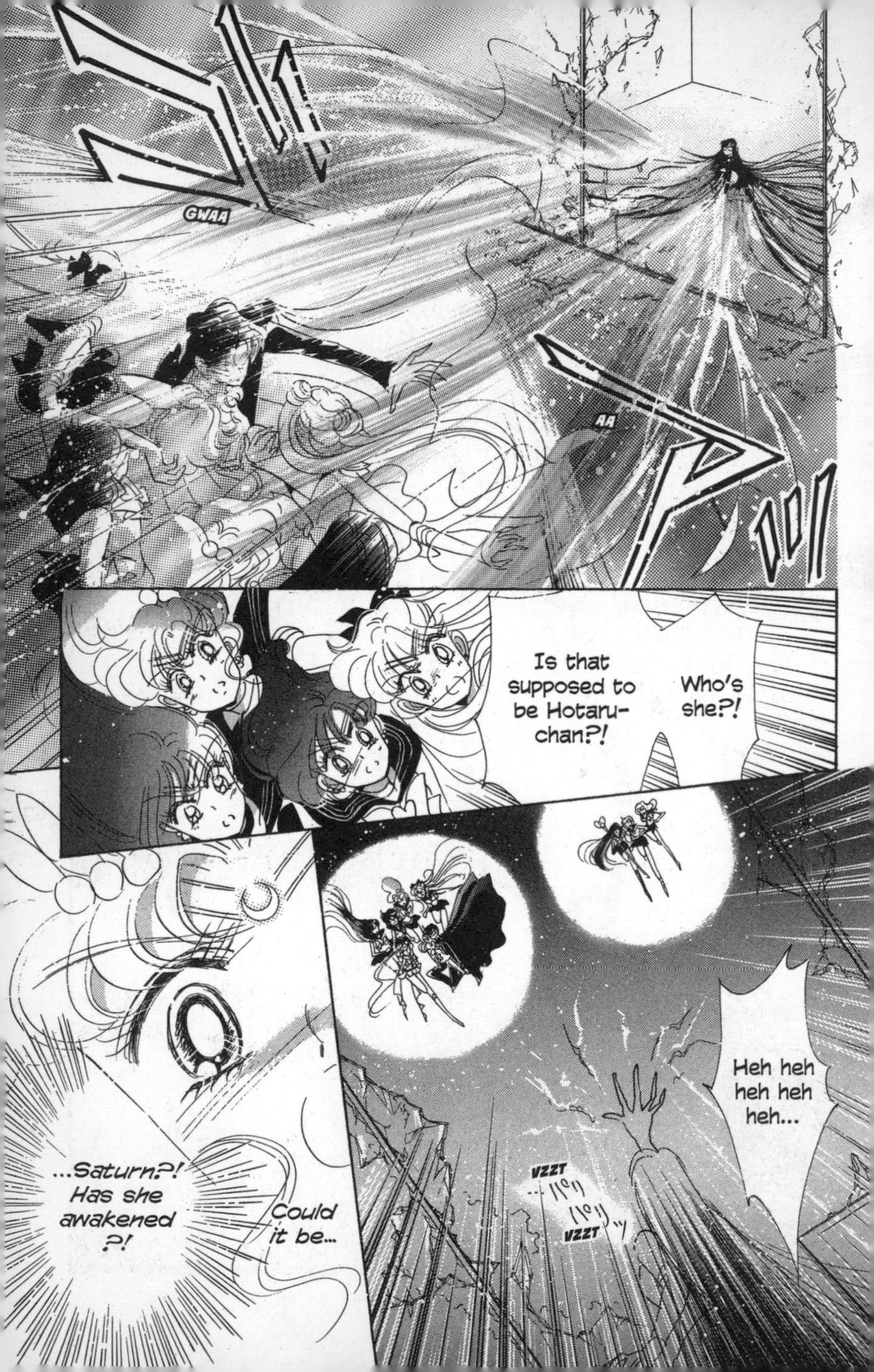
GWAA
AA
Who's she?!
Is that supposed to be Hotaru-chan?!
Heh heh heh heh heh...
VZZT
VZZT
Could it be...
...Saturn?! Has she awakened?!

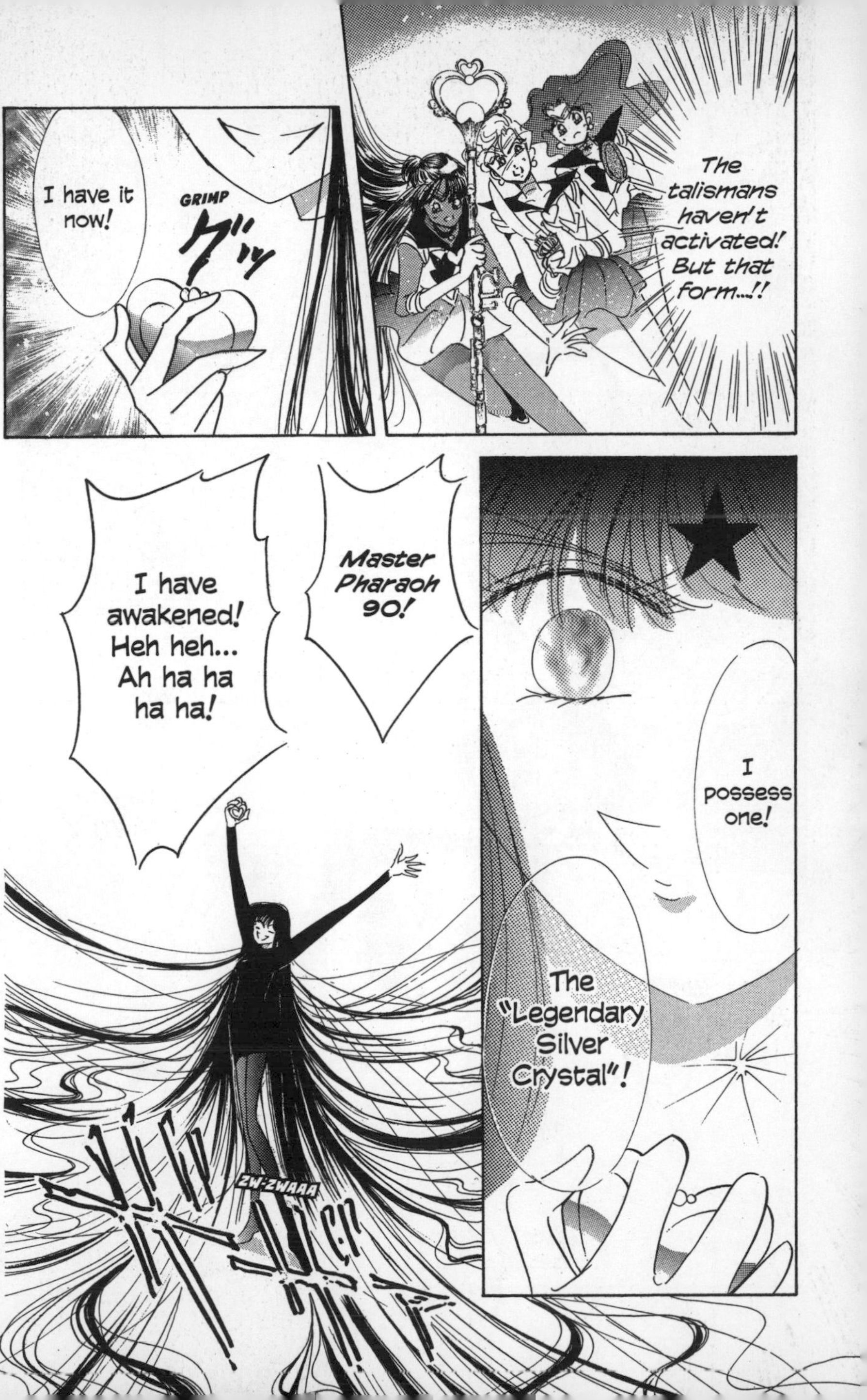
The talismans haven't activated! But that form...!!
I have it now!
GRIMP
グッ
I possess one!
The "Legendary Silver Crystal"!
Master Pharaoh 90!
I have awakened! Heh heh... Ah ha ha ha ha!
ZW-ZWAAA

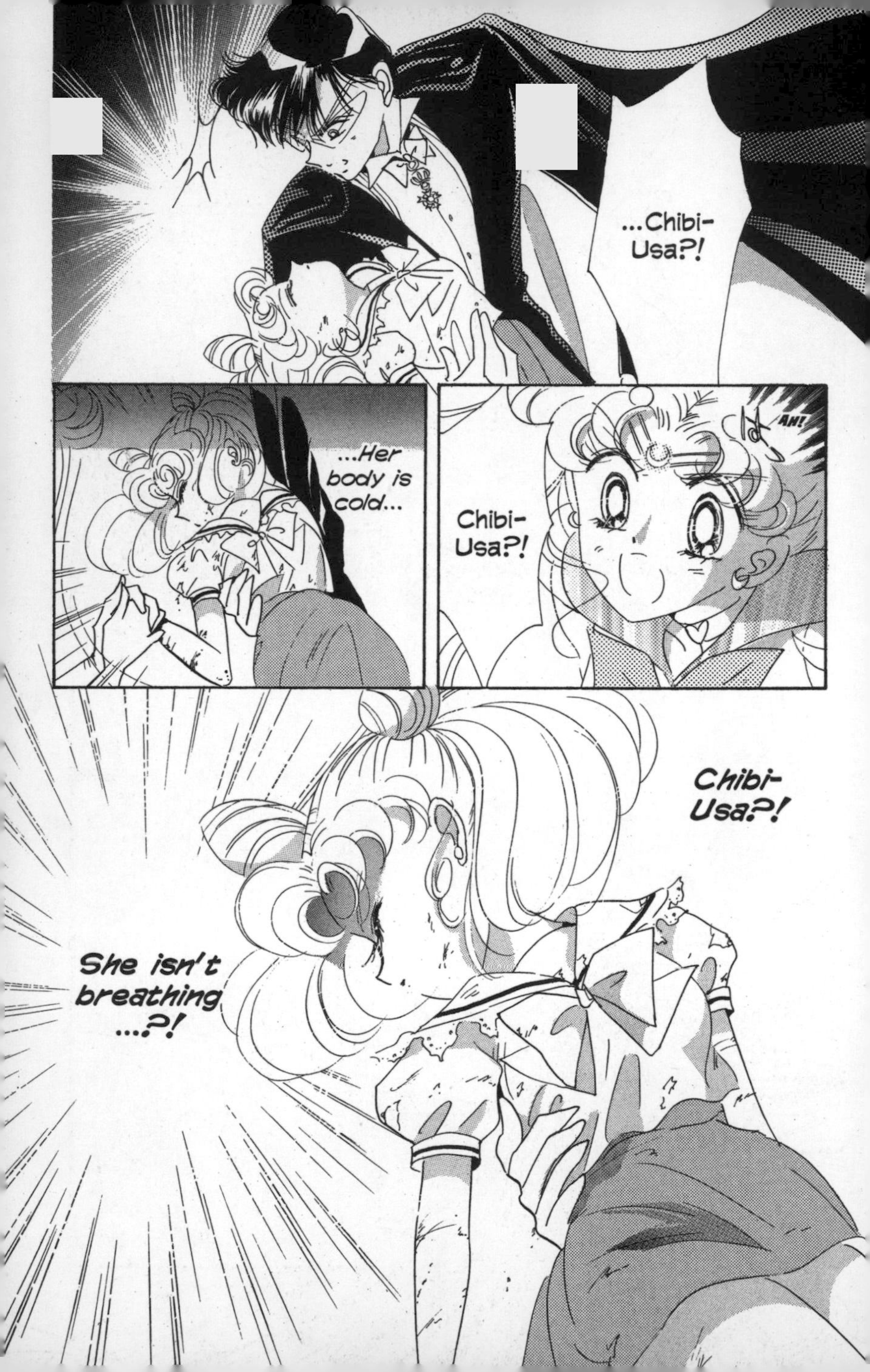
...Chibi-Usa?!
AH!
Chibi-Usa?!
...Her body is cold...
Chibi-Usa?!
She isn't breathing ...?!

Act 34 Infinity 8, Infinite Labyrinth 1

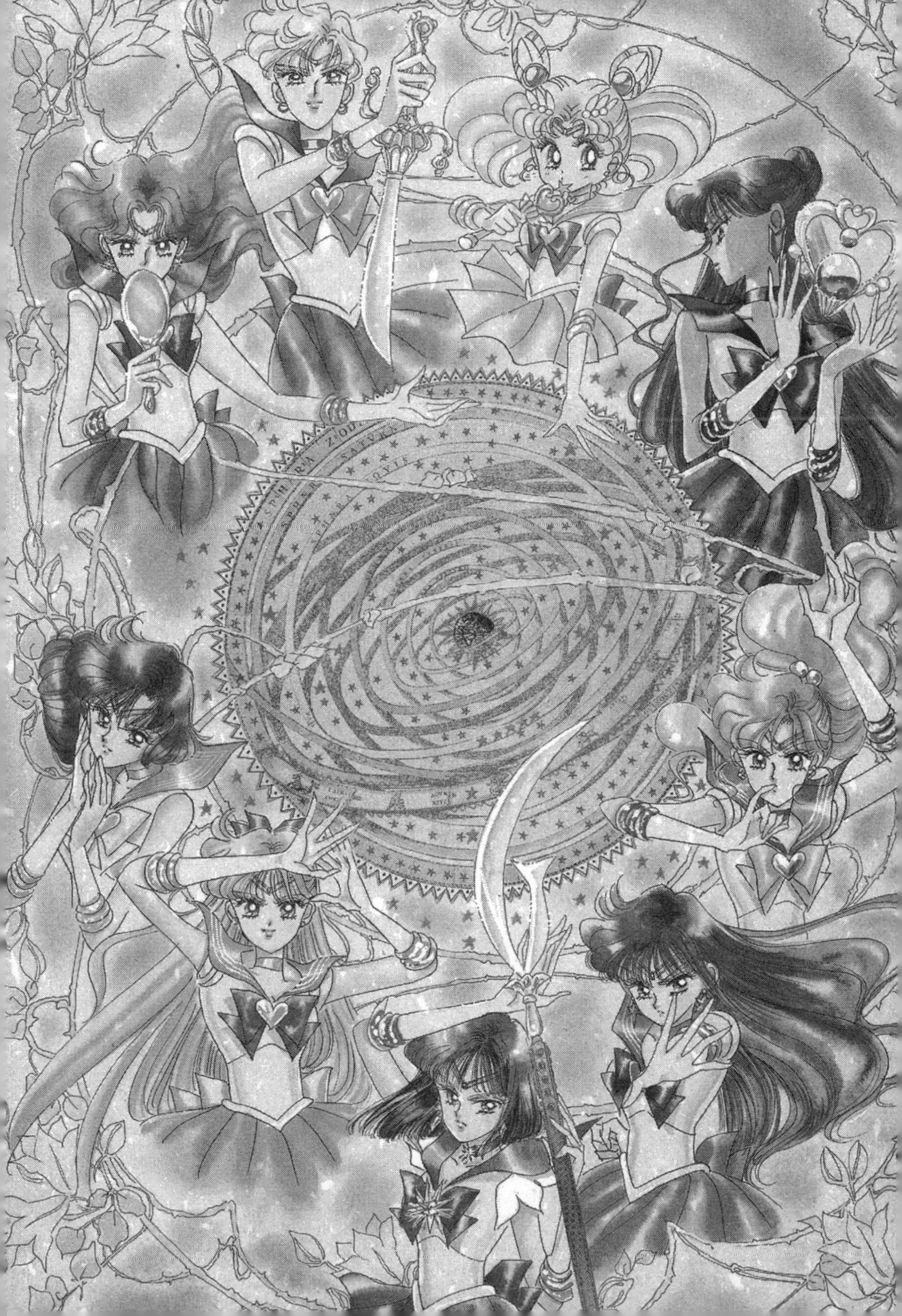

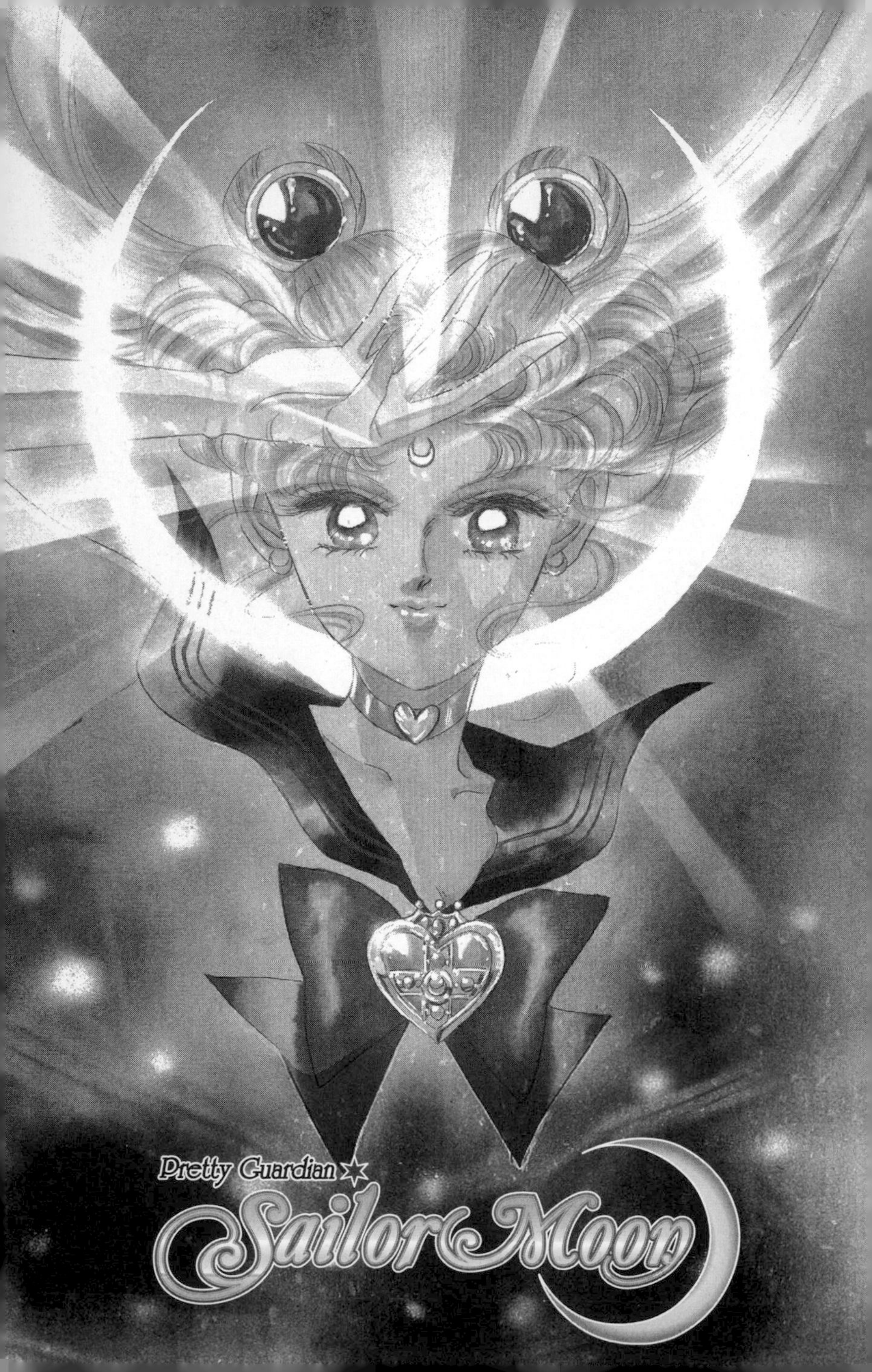
Pretty Guardian
Sailor Moon

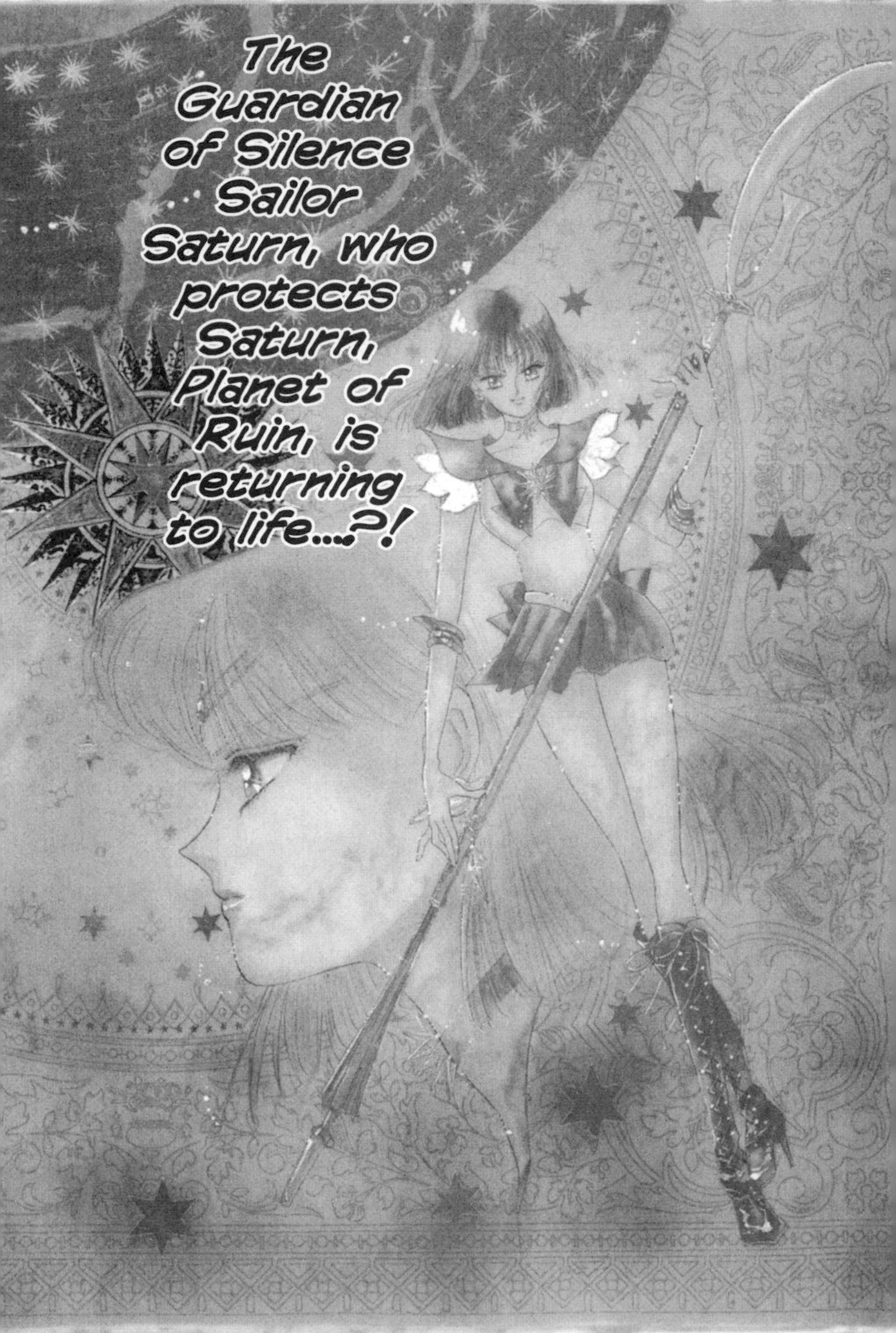
The Guardian of Silence Sailor Saturn, who protects Saturn, Planet of Ruin, is returning to life...?!

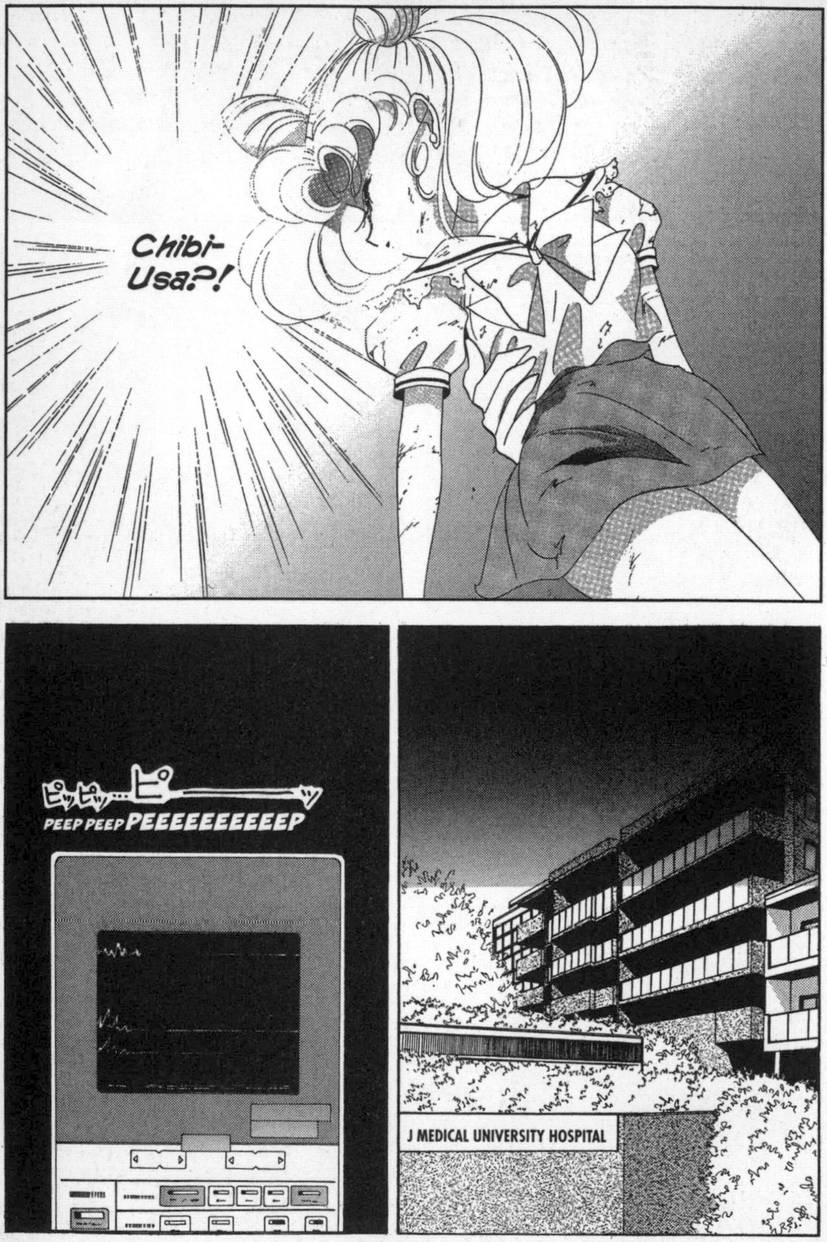
Chibi-Usa?!
J MEDICAL UNIVERSITY HOSPITAL
ピッピッ…ピーーーッ
PEEP PEEP PEEEEEEEEEEP

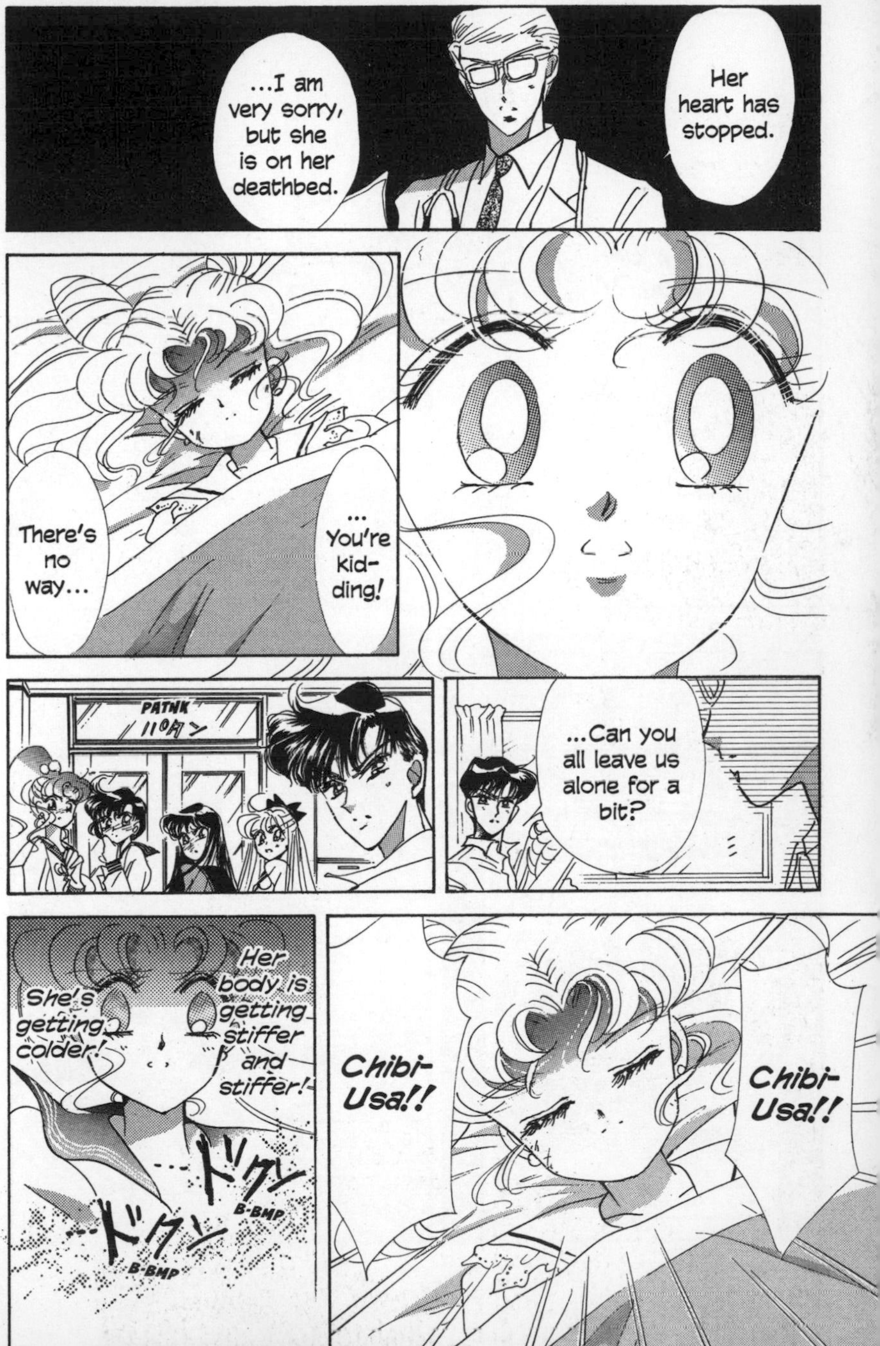
Her heart has stopped.
...I am very sorry, but she is on her deathbed.
... You're kid-ding!
There's no way...
...Can you all leave us alone for a bit?
PATNK
Chibi-Usa!!
Chibi-Usa!!
Her body is getting stiffer and stiffer!
She's getting colder!
ドクン
B-BMP
ドクン
B-BMP

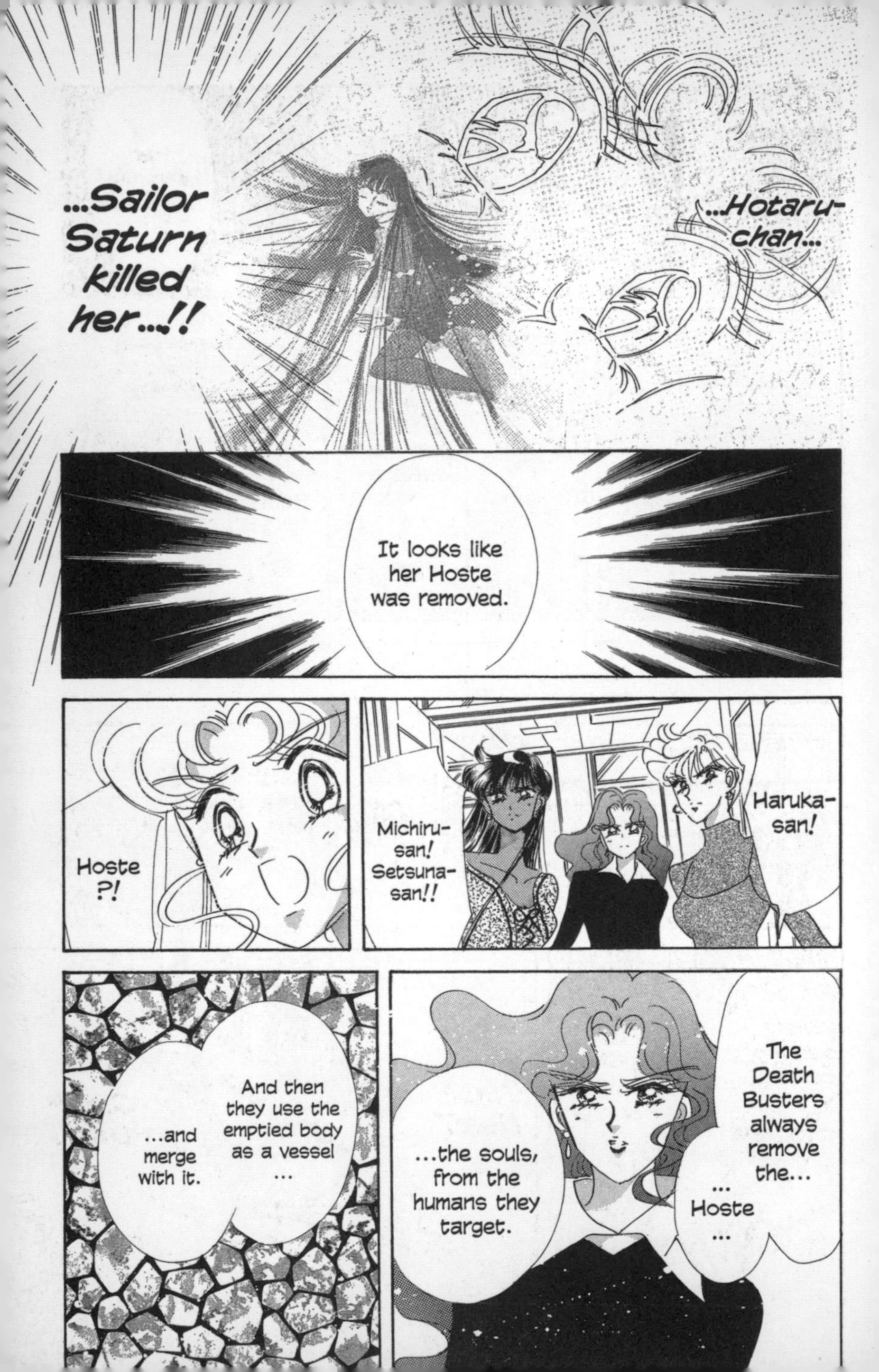
...Hotaru-chan...
...Sailor Saturn killed her...!!
It looks like her Hoste was removed.
Haruka-san!
Michiru-san! Setsuna-san!!
Hoste ?!
The Death Busters always remove the...
... Hoste ...
...the souls, from the humans they target.
And then they use the emptied body as a vessel ...
...and merge with it.

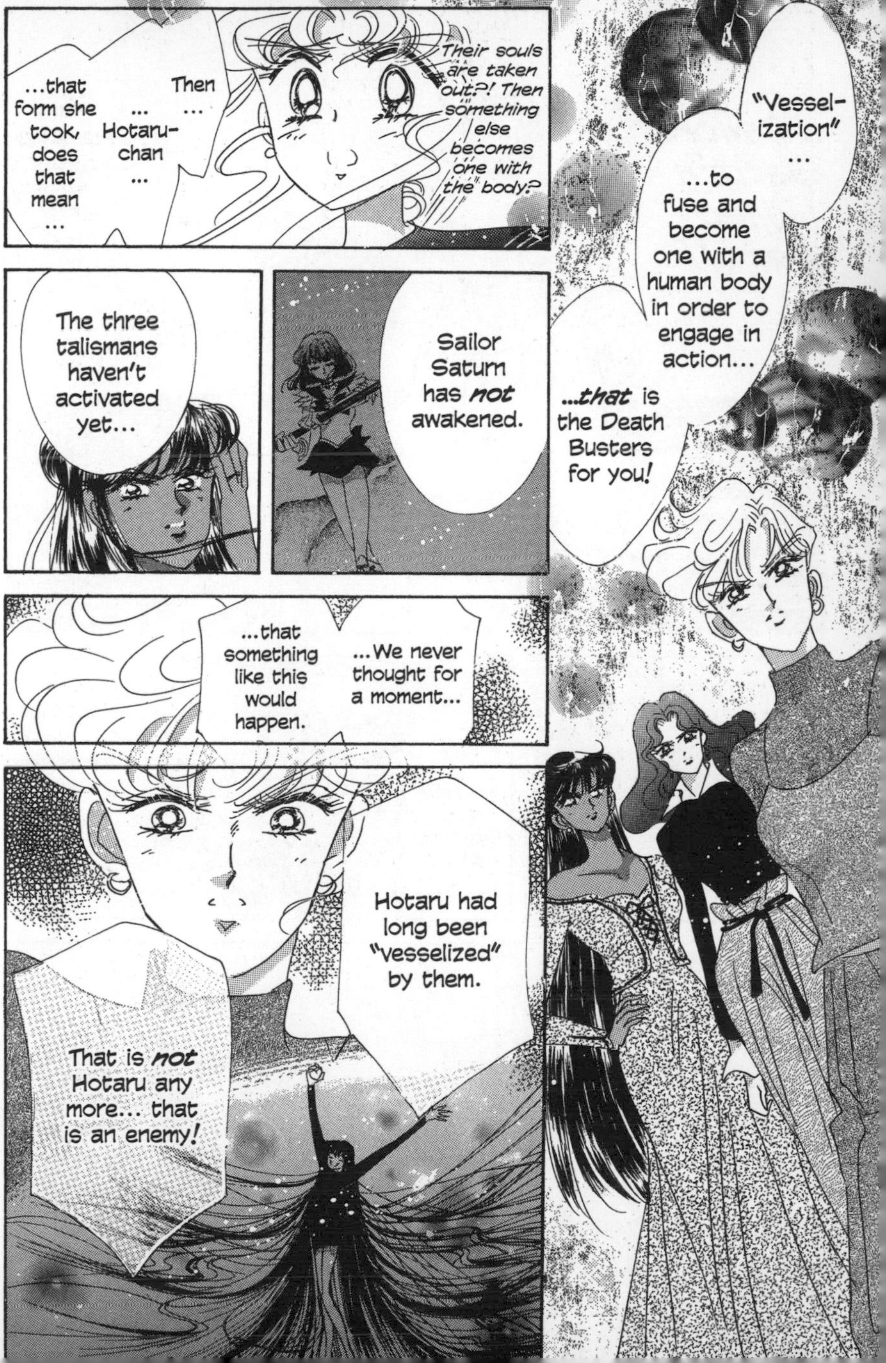
"Vessel-ization" ...
...to fuse and become one with a human body in order to engage in action...
...*that* is the Death Busters for you!
Their souls are taken out?! Then something else becomes one with the body?
Then ... Hotaru-chan ...
...that form she took, does that mean ...
Sailor Saturn has *not* awakened.
The three talismans haven't activated yet...
...We never thought for a moment...
...that something like this would happen.
Hotaru had long been "vesselized" by them.
That is *not* Hotaru any more... that is an enemy!

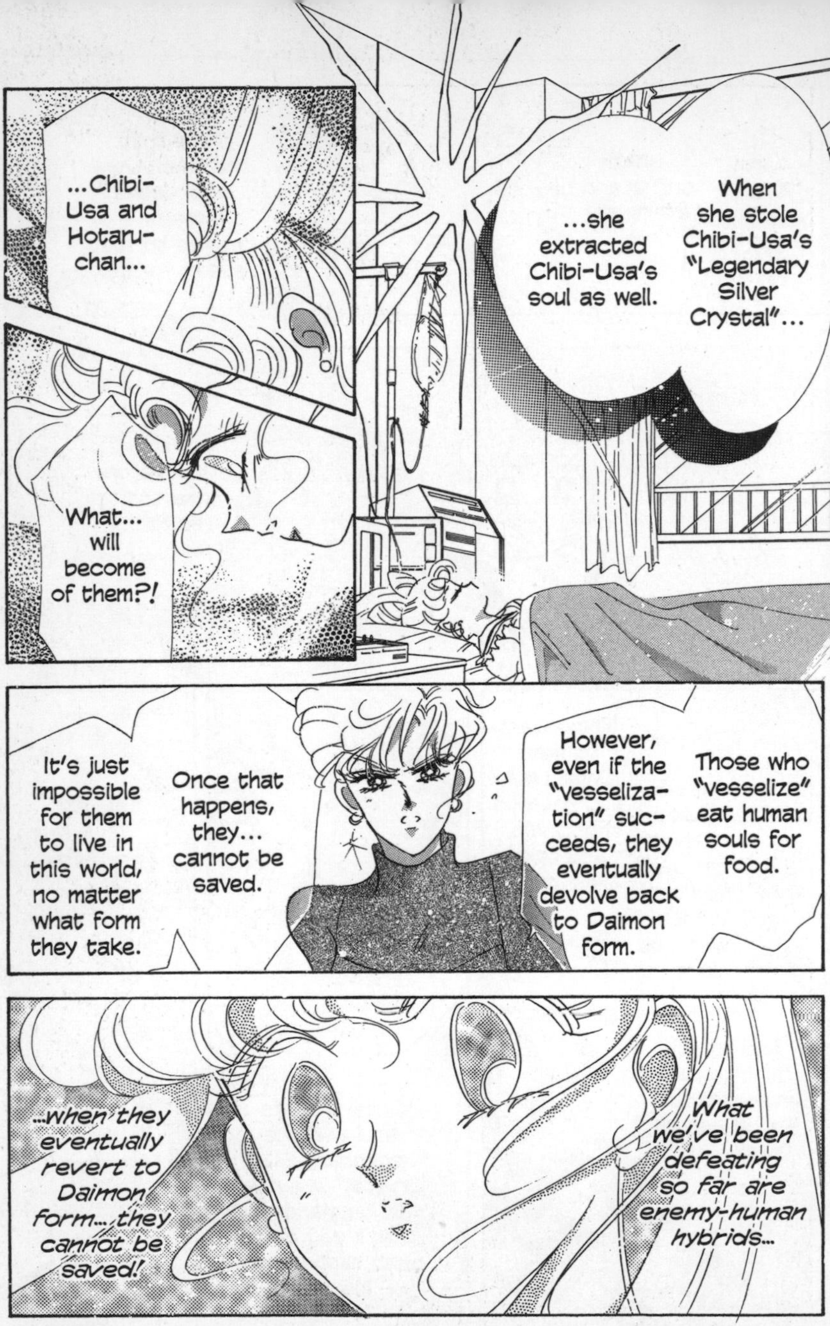
When she stole Chibi-Usa's "Legendary Silver Crystal"...
...she extracted Chibi-Usa's soul as well.
...Chibi-Usa and Hotaru-chan...
What... will become of them?!
Those who "vesselize" eat human souls for food.
However, even if the "vesselization" succeeds, they eventually devolve back to Daimon form.
Once that happens, they... cannot be saved.
It's just impossible for them to live in this world, no matter what form they take.
What we've been defeating so far are enemy-human hybrids...
...when they eventually revert to Daimon form... they cannot be saved!

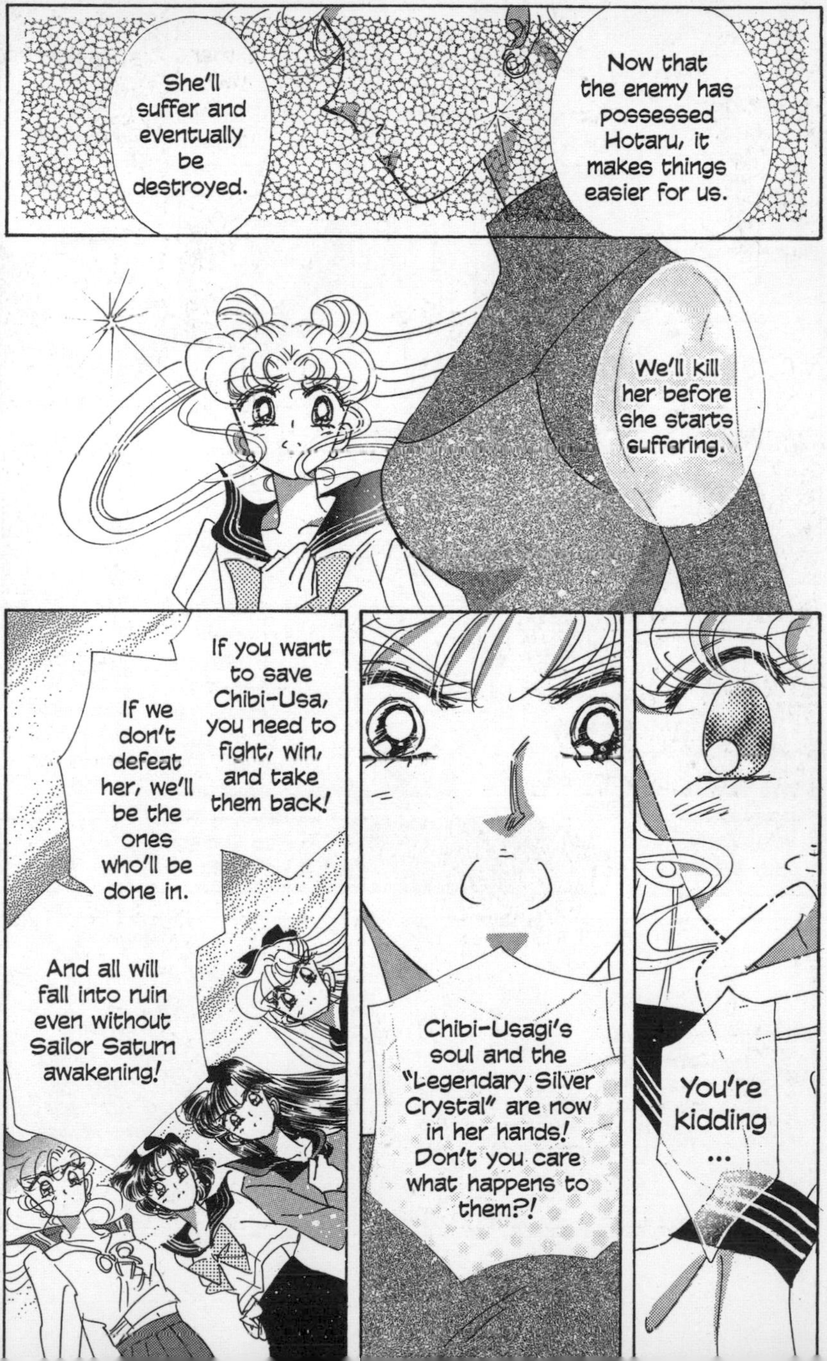
Now that the enemy has possessed Hotaru, it makes things easier for us.
She'll suffer and eventually be destroyed.
We'll kill her before she starts suffering.
You're kidding ...
Chibi-Usagi's soul and the "Legendary Silver Crystal" are now in her hands! Don't you care what happens to them?!
If you want to save Chibi-Usa, you need to fight, win, and take them back!
If we don't defeat her, we'll be the ones who'll be done in.
And all will fall into ruin even without Sailor Saturn awakening!

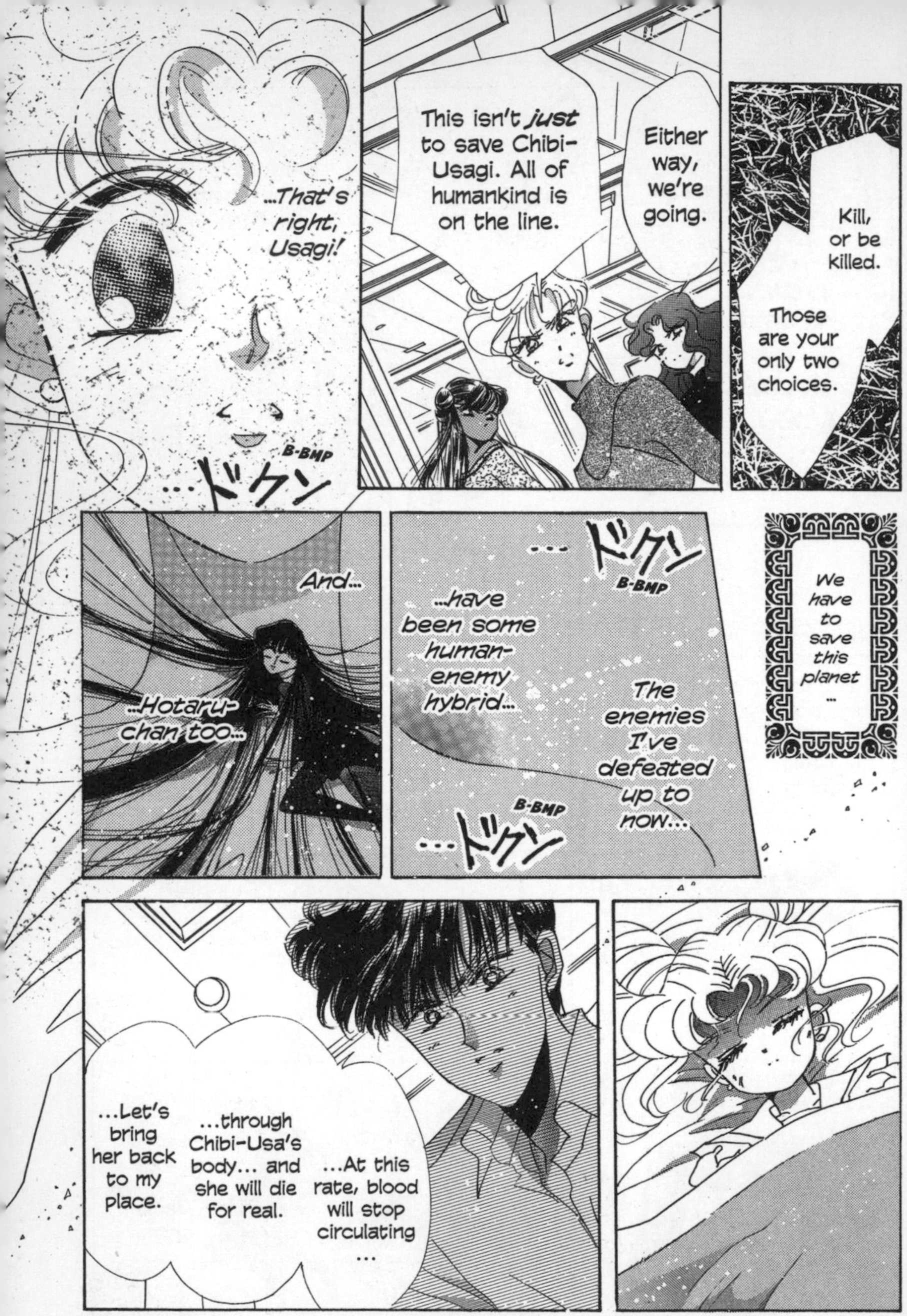
Kill, or be killed.
Those are your only two choices.
Either way, we're going.
This isn't *just* to save Chibi-Usagi. All of humankind is on the line.
...That's right, Usagi!
B-BMP
...ドクン
We have to save this planet ...
...ドクン
B-BMP
The enemies I've defeated up to now...
...have been some human-enemy hybrid...
B-BMP
...ドクン
And...
...Hotaru-chan too...
...At this rate, blood will stop circulating ...
...through Chibi-Usa's body... and she will die for real.
...Let's bring her back to my place.

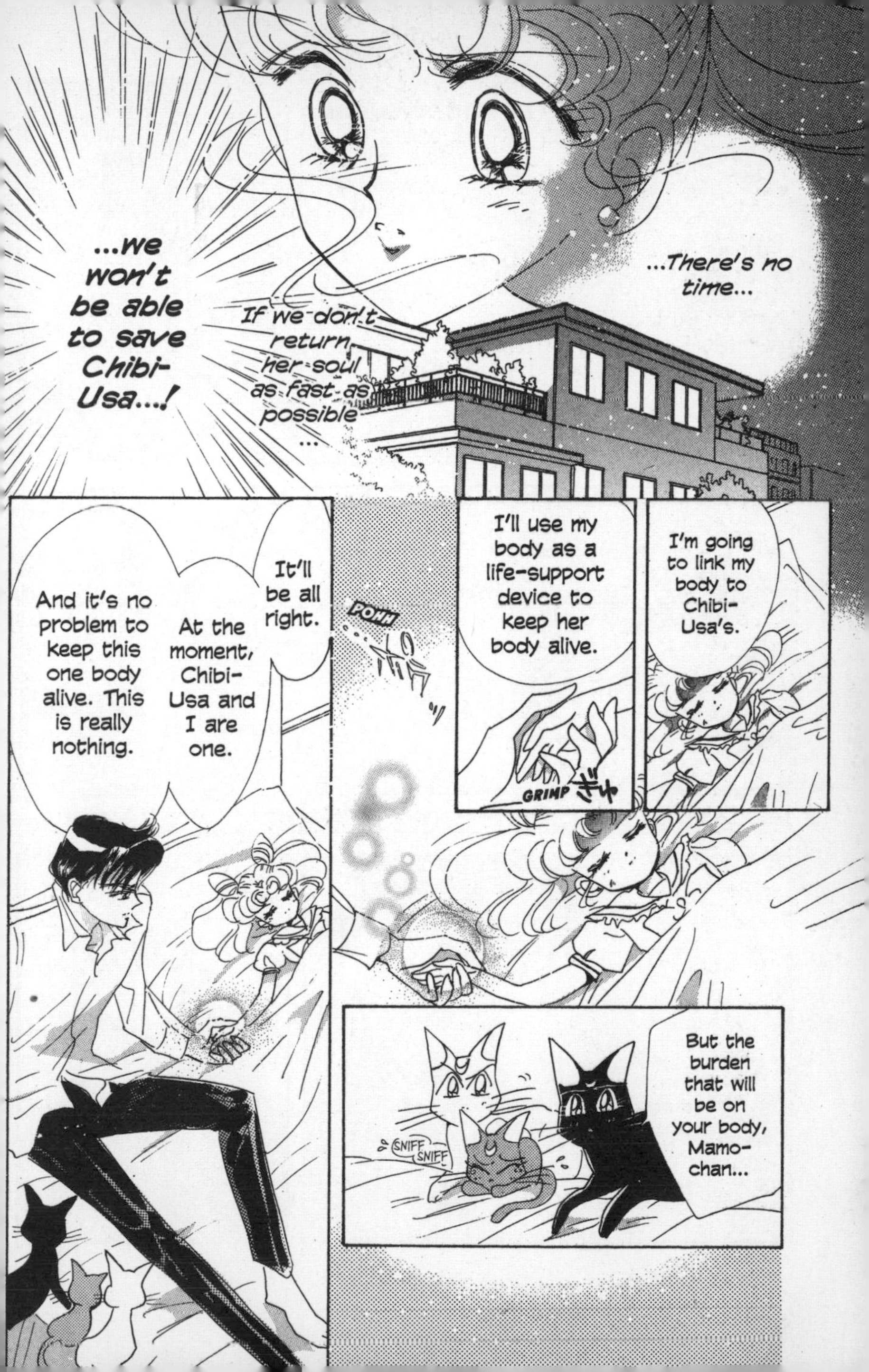
...There's no time...
If we don't return her soul as fast as possible...
...we won't be able to save Chibi-Usa...!
I'm going to link my body to Chibi-Usa's.
I'll use my body as a life-support device to keep her body alive.
GRIMP
POHN
It'll be all right.
At the moment, Chibi-Usa and I are one.
And it's no problem to keep this one body alive. This is really nothing.
But the burden that will be on your body, Mamo-chan...
SNIFF SNIFF

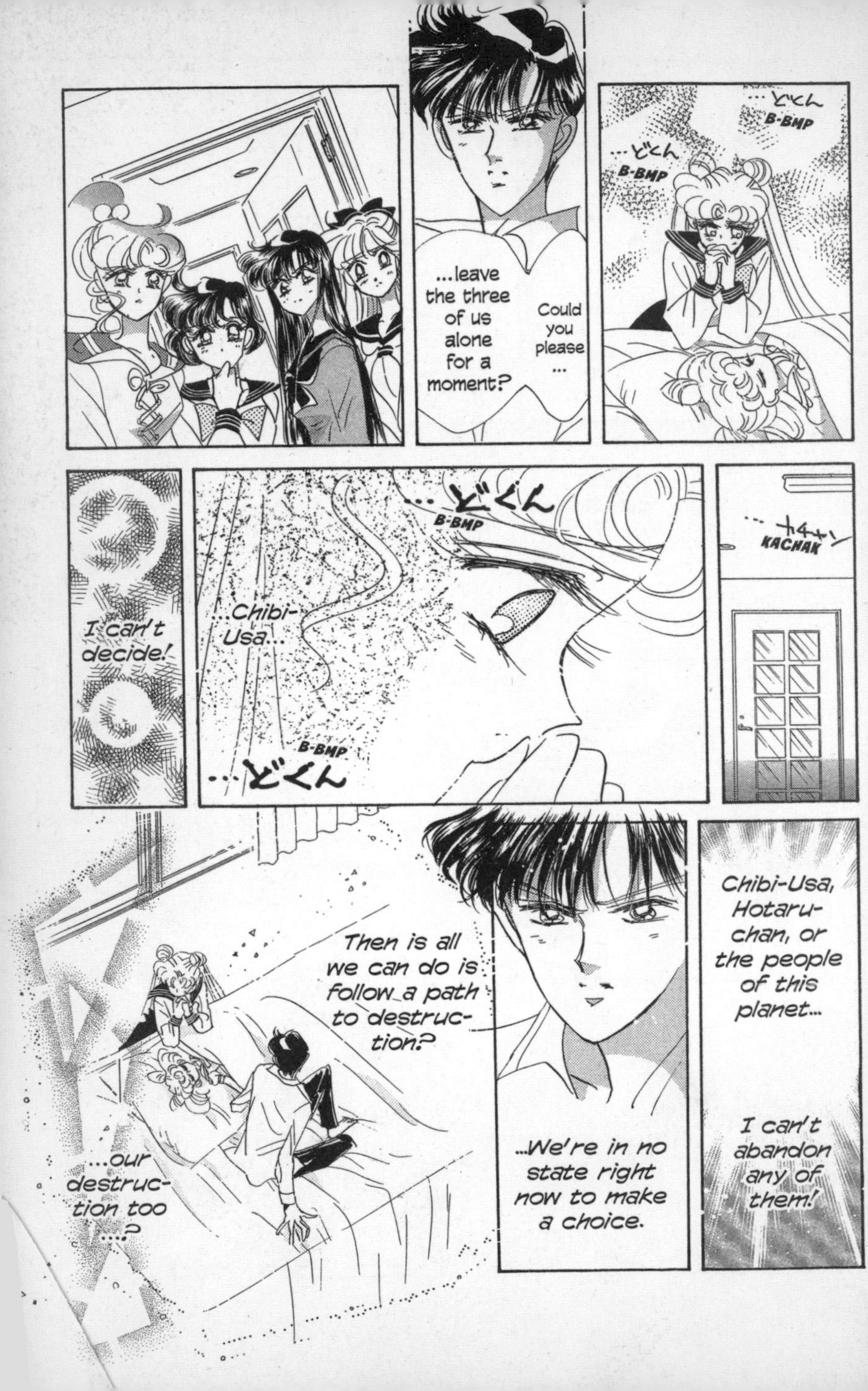

...どくん
B-BMP
...どくん
B-BMP
Could you please ...
...leave the three of us alone for a moment?
KACHAK
...どくん
B-BMP
...Chibi-Usa...
B-BMP
...どくん
I can't decide!
Chibi-Usa, Hotaru-chan, or the people of this planet...
I can't abandon any of them!
...We're in no state right now to make a choice.
Then is all we can do is follow a path to destruction?
...our destruction too ...?

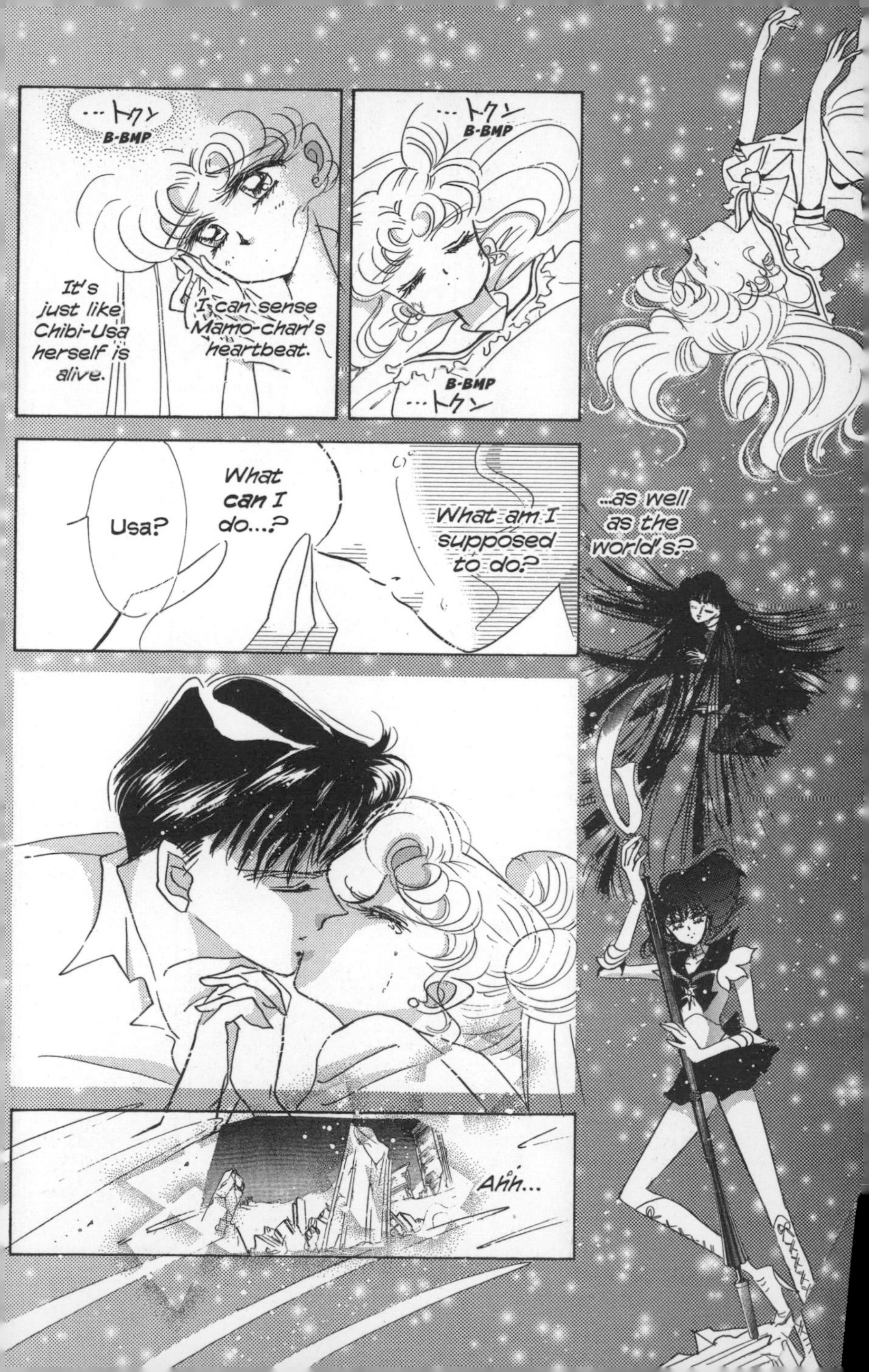
...as well as the world's?
...トクン
B-BMP
...トクン
B-BMP
B-BMP
...トクン
I can sense Mamo-chan's heartbeat.
It's just like Chibi-Usa herself is alive.
What am I supposed to do?
What can I do...?
Usa?
Ahh...

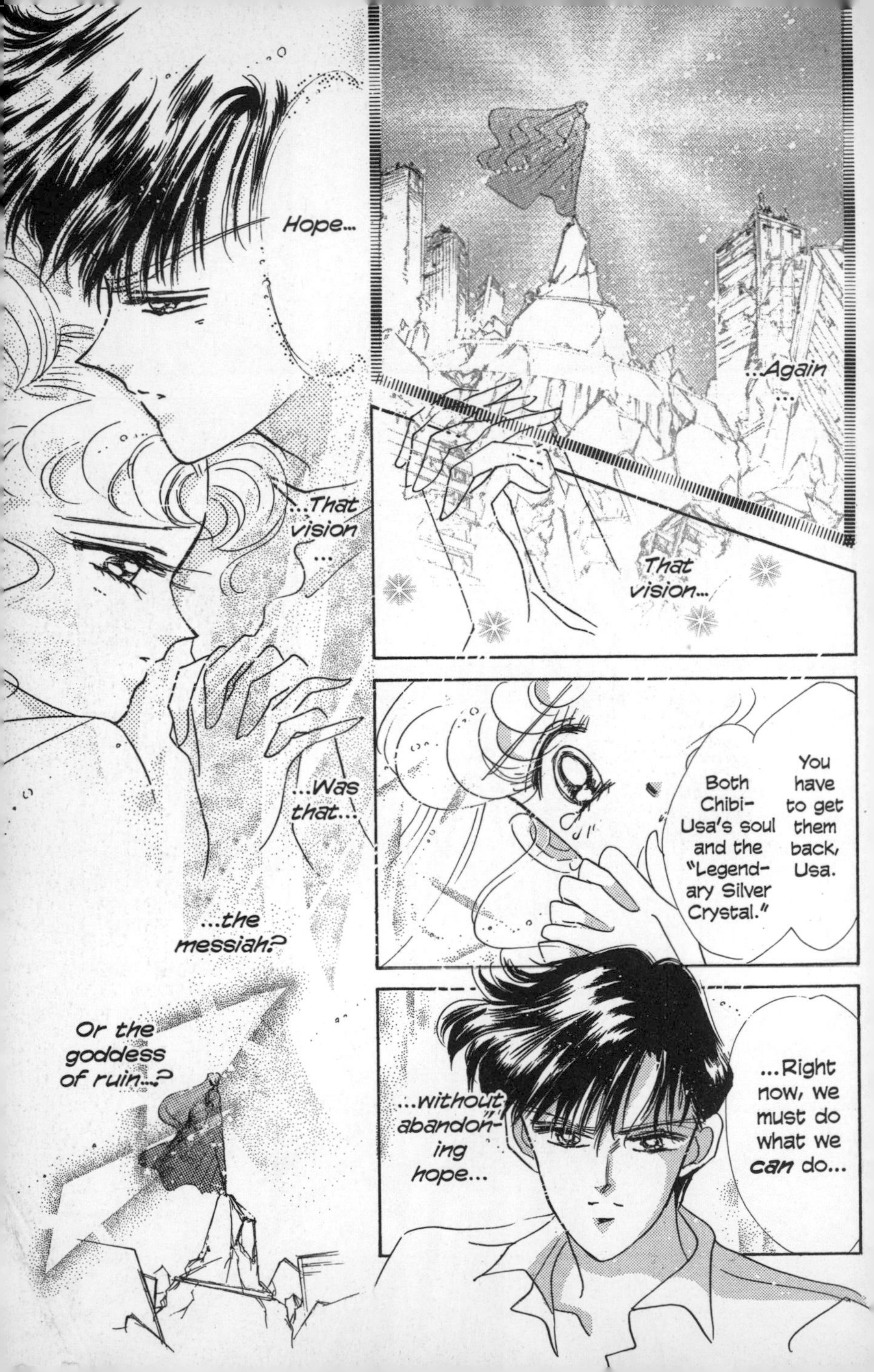
...Again...
That vision...
You have to get them back, Usa.
Both Chibi-Usa's soul and the "Legendary Silver Crystal."
...Right now, we must do what we *can* do...
...without abandoning hope...
Hope...
...That vision...
...Was that...
...the messiah?
Or the goddess of ruin...?

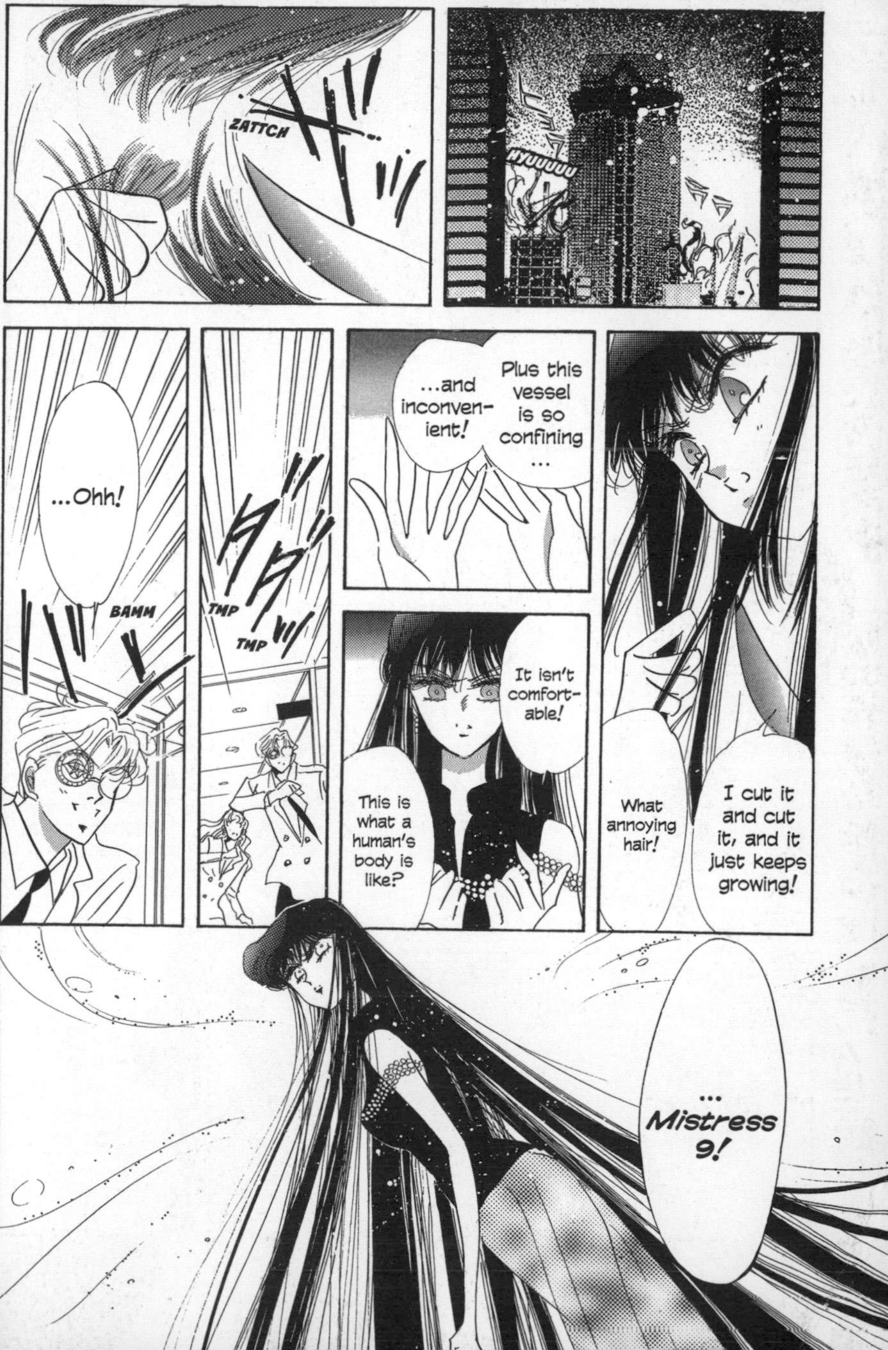
HYUUUUU
ZATTCH
I cut it and cut it, and it just keeps growing!
What annoying hair!
Plus this vessel is so confining...
...and inconvenient!
It isn't comfortable!
This is what a human's body is like?
TMP
TMP
...Ohh!
BAMM
... Mistress 9!

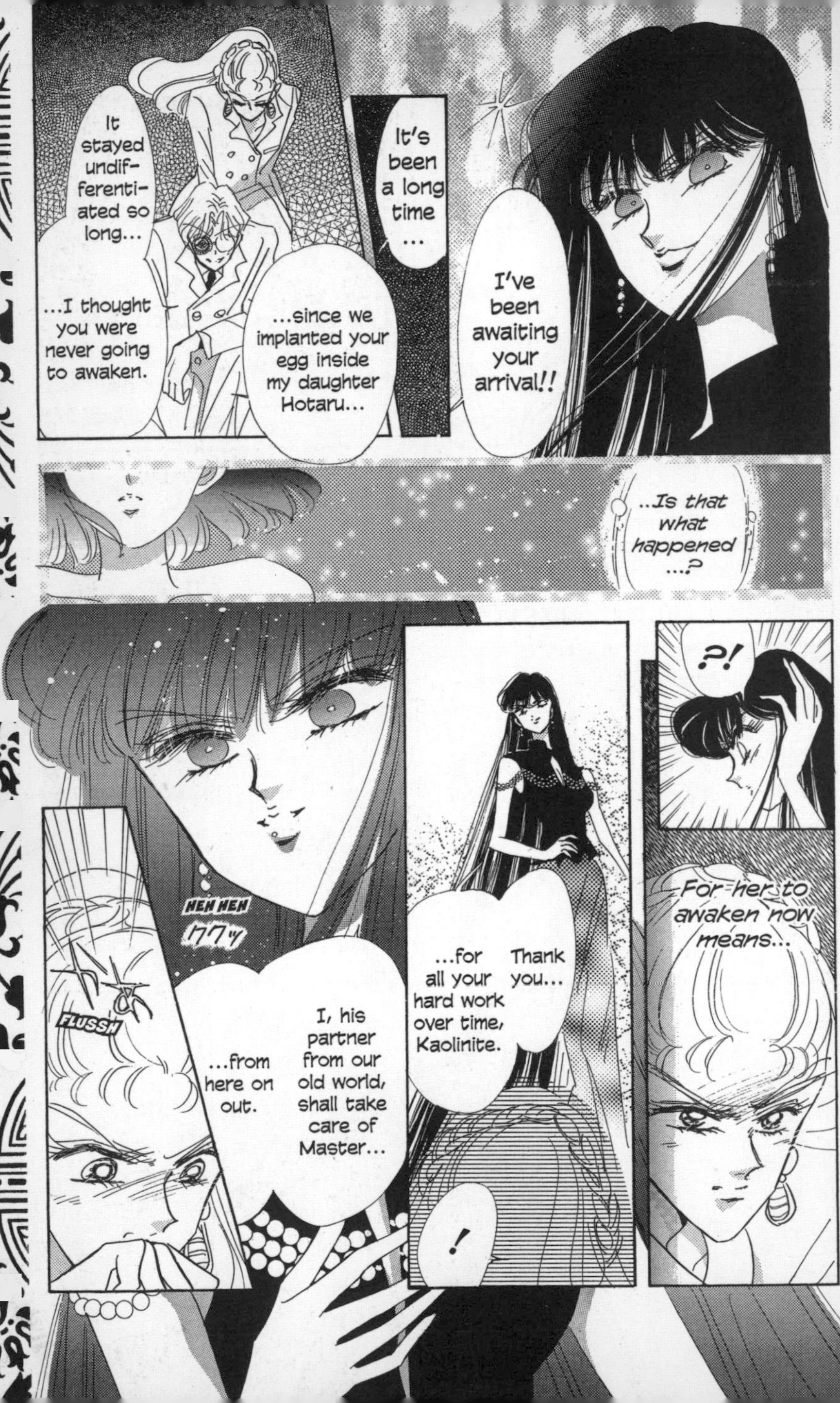
I've been awaiting your arrival!!
It's been a long time ...
...since we implanted your egg inside my daughter Hotaru...
It stayed undif-ferenti-ated so long...
...I thought you were never going to awaken.
..Is that what happened ...?
?!
For her to awaken now means...
Thank you...
...for all your hard work over time, Kaolinite.
!
HEH HEH
I, his partner from our old world, shall take care of Master...
...from here on out.
FLUSSH

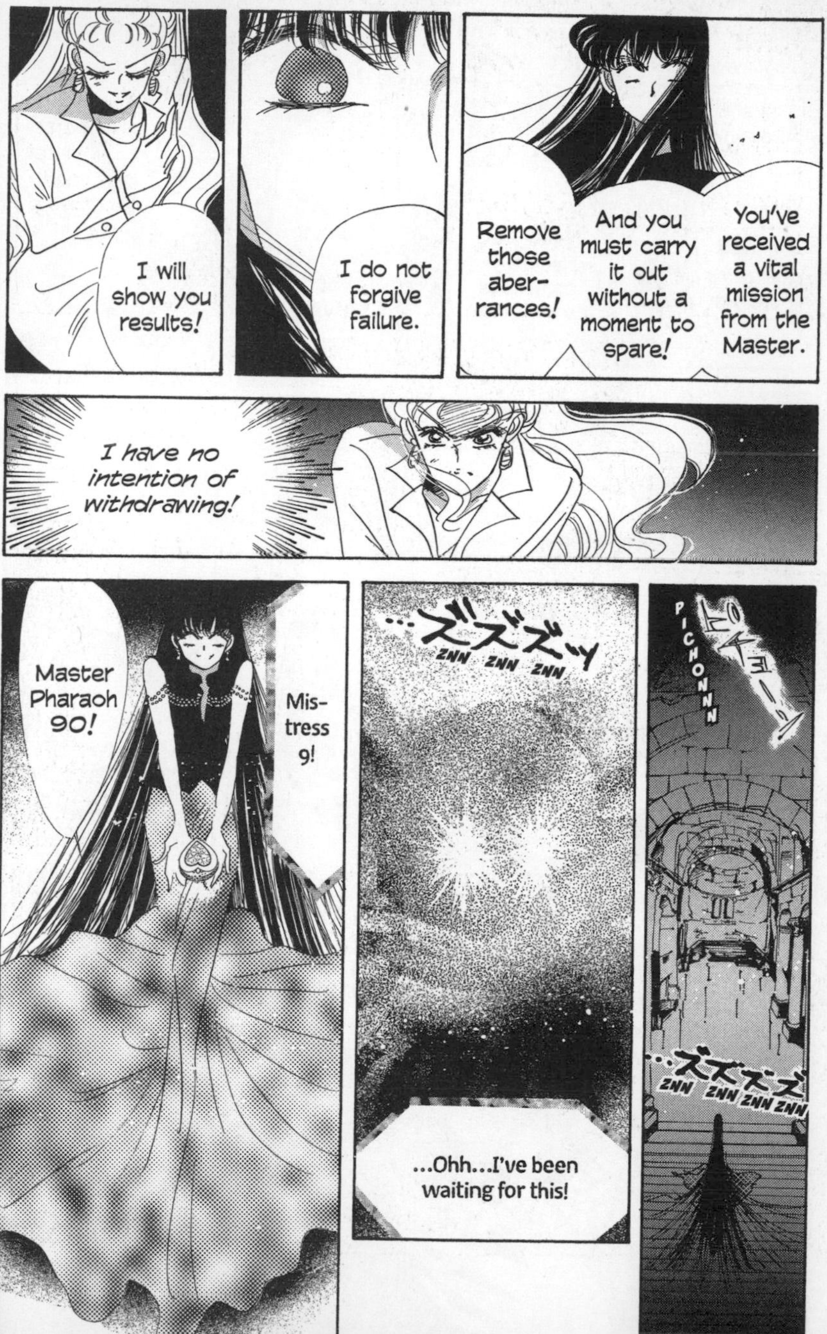
You've received a vital mission from the Master.
And you must carry it out without a moment to spare!
Remove those aber-rances!
I do not forgive failure.
I will show you results!
I have no intention of withdrawing!
ピチョーン
PICHONNN
…ズズズズ
ZNN ZNN ZNN ZNN
…ズズズッ
ZNN ZNN ZNN
...Ohh...I've been waiting for this!
Mis-tress 9!
Master Pharaoh 90!

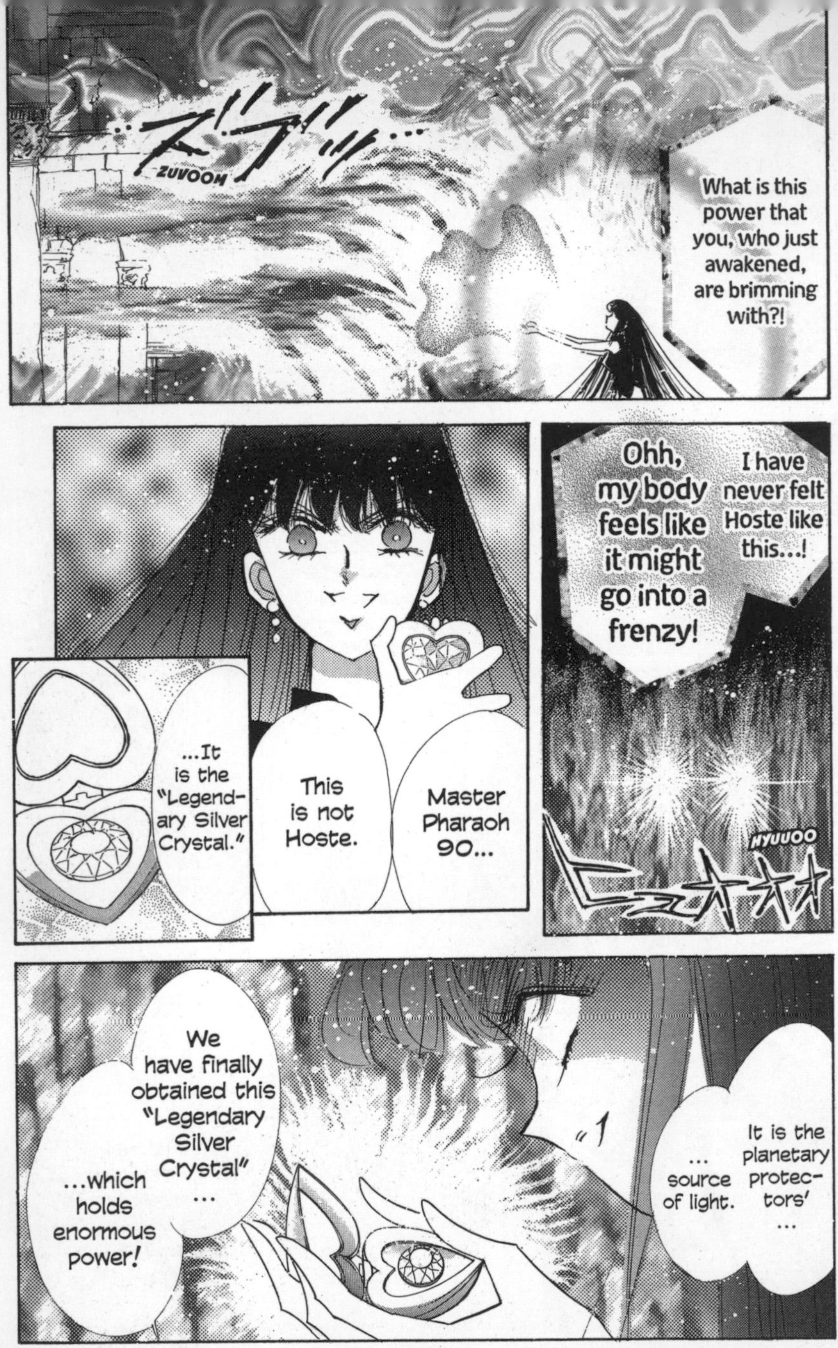
ZUVOOM
What is this power that you, who just awakened, are brimming with?!
I have never felt Hoste like this...!
Ohh, my body feels like it might go into a frenzy!
HYUUOO
Master Pharaoh 90...
This is not Hoste.
...It is the "Legendary Silver Crystal."
It is the planetary protectors' ...
... source of light.
We have finally obtained this "Legendary Silver Crystal" ...
...which holds enormous power!

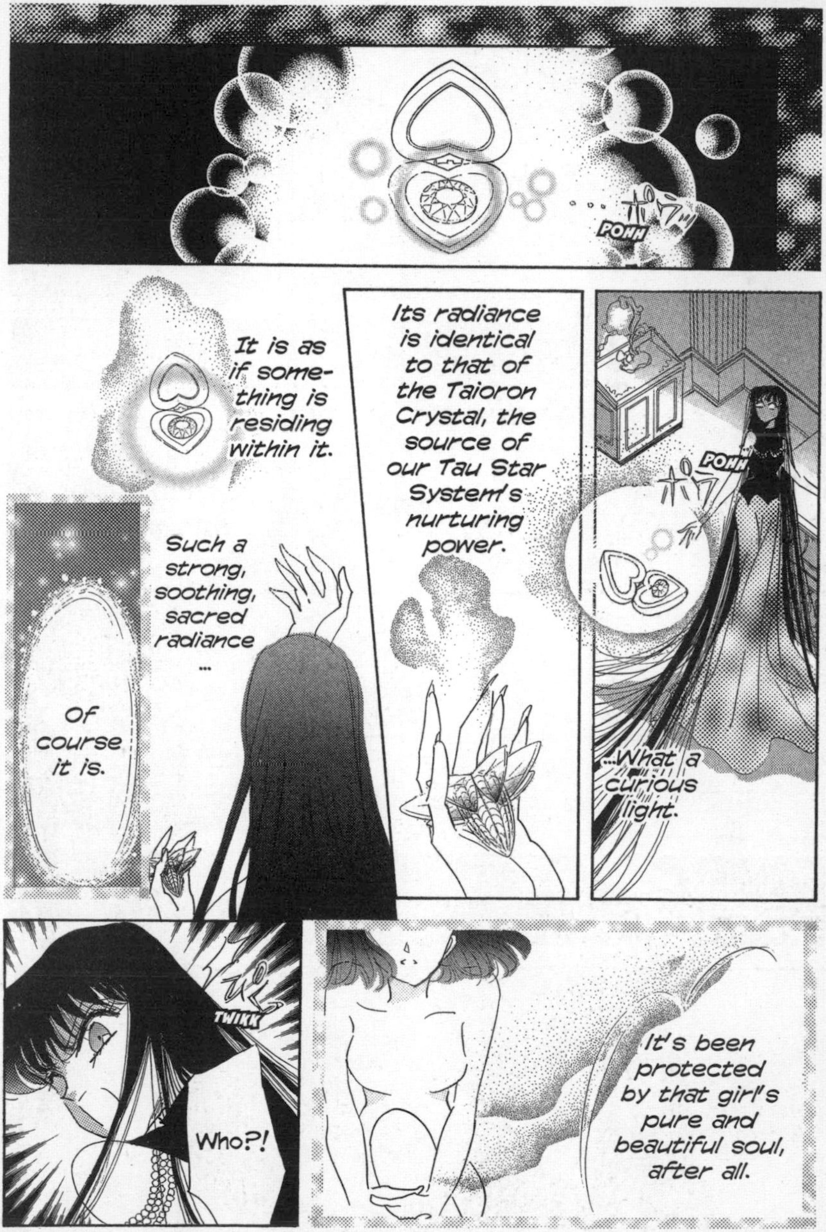
POHH
POHH
...What a curious light.
Its radiance is identical to that of the Taioron Crystal, the source of our Tau Star System's nurturing power.
It is as if some-thing is residing within it.
Such a strong, soothing, sacred radiance ...
Of course it is.
It's been protected by that girl's pure and beautiful soul, after all.
TWIKK
Who?!

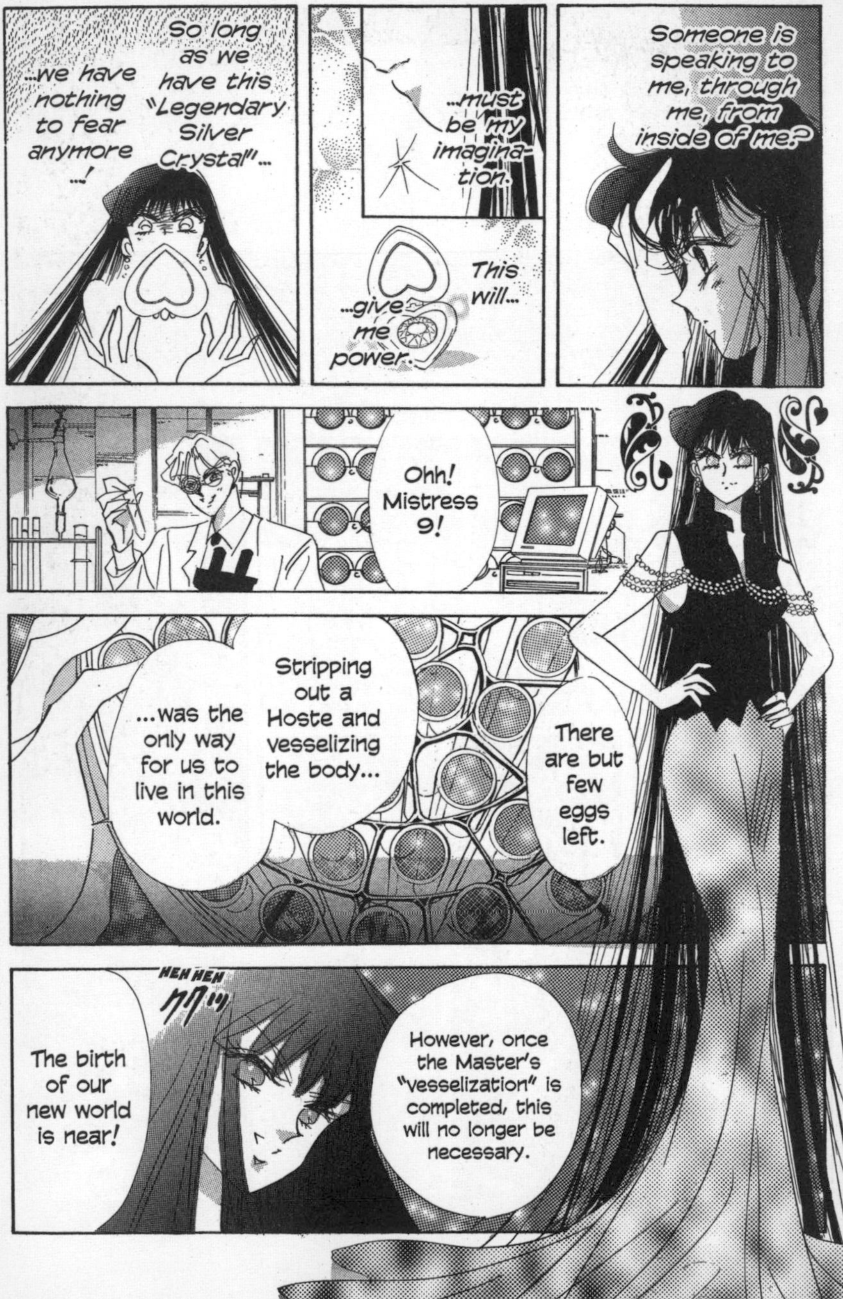
Someone is speaking to me, through me, from inside of me?
...must be my imagination.
This will...
...give me power.
So long as we have this "Legendary Silver Crystal"...
...we have nothing to fear anymore ...!
Ohh! Mistress 9!
There are but few eggs left.
Stripping out a Hoste and vesselizing the body...
...was the only way for us to live in this world.
However, once the Master's "vesselization" is completed, this will no longer be necessary.
HEH HEH
The birth of our new world is near!

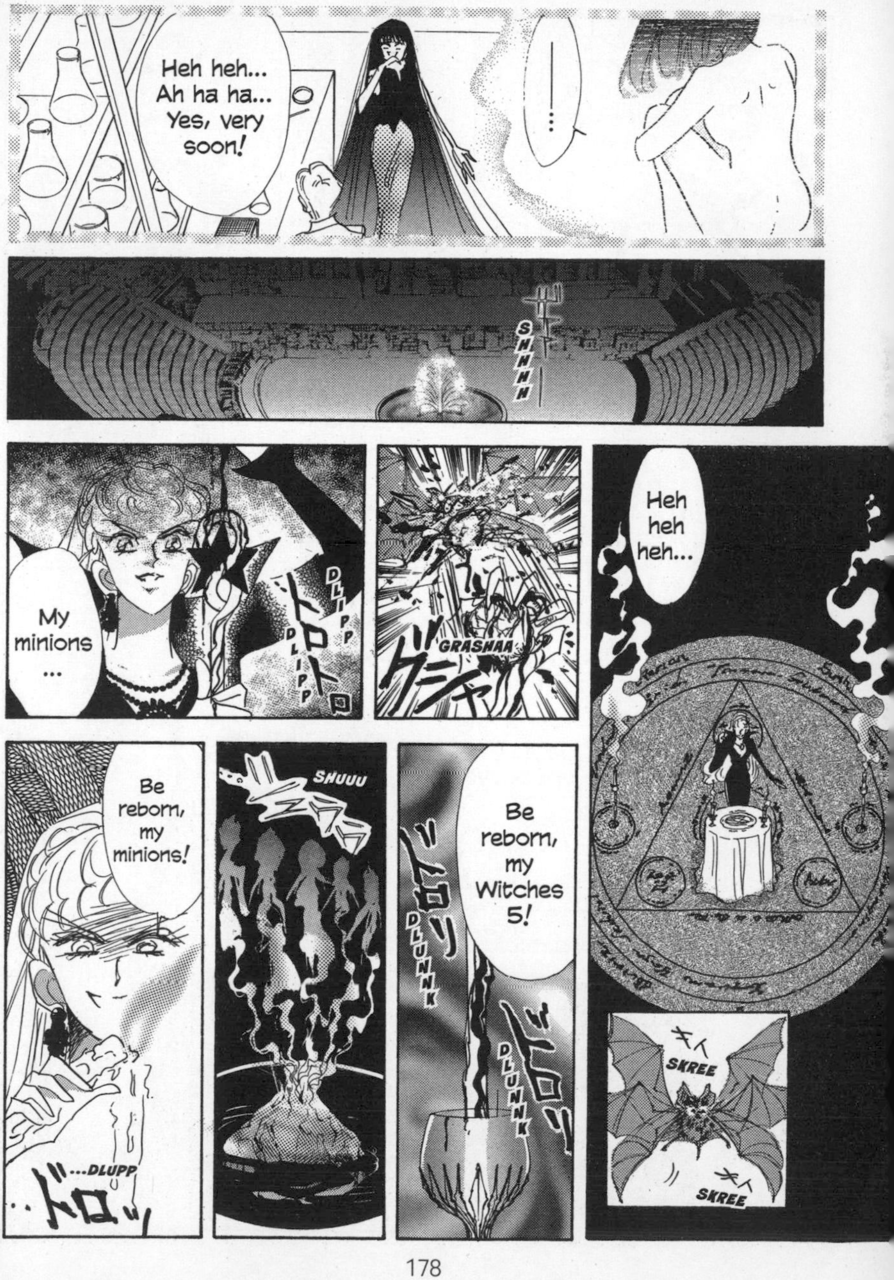
!...
Heh heh... Ah ha ha... Yes, very soon!
SHHHH
Heh heh heh...
SKREE
SKREE
GRASHAA
DLIPP
DLIPP
My minions ...
DLUNNK
Be reborn, my Witches 5!
DLUNNK
SHUUU
Be reborn, my minions!
...DLUPP

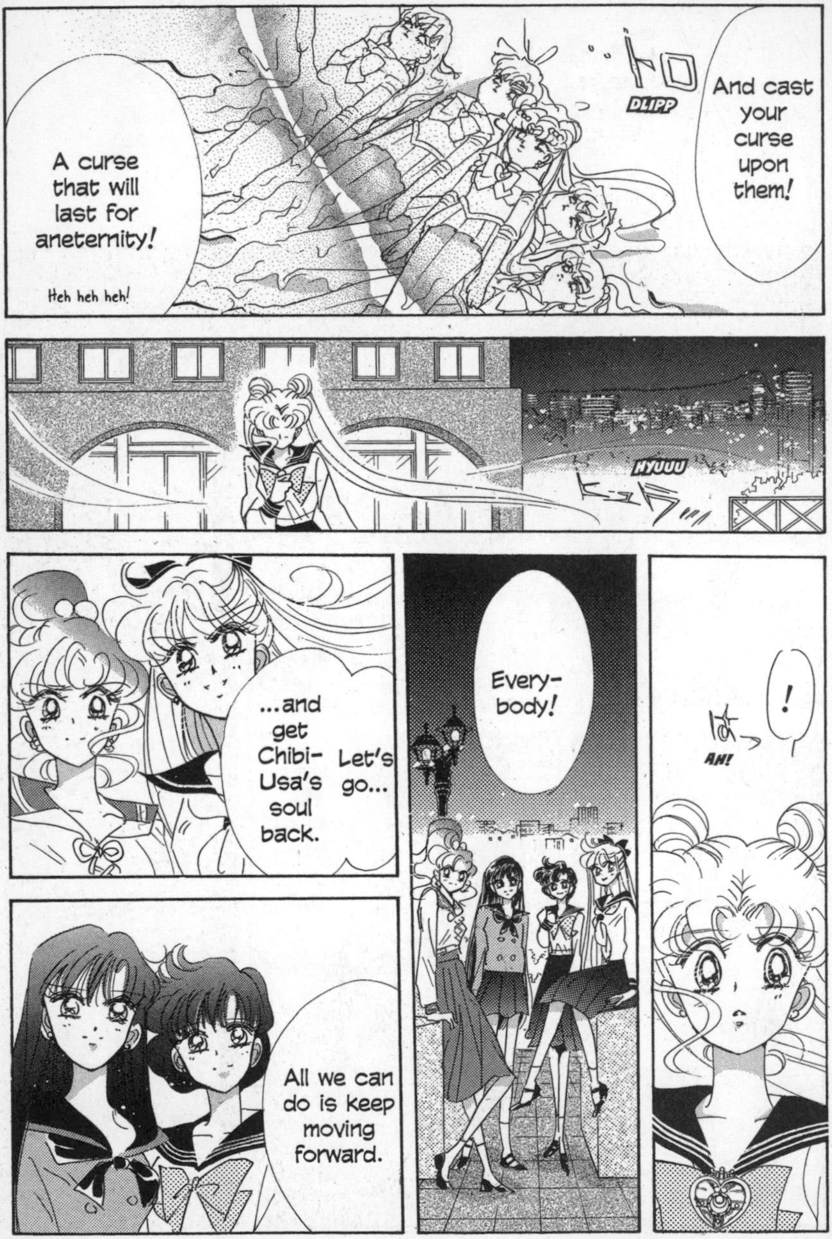
And cast your curse upon them!
DLIPP
A curse that will last for aneternity!
Heh heh heh!
HYUUU
!
AH!
Every-body!
Let's go...
...and get Chibi-Usa's soul back.
All we can do is keep moving forward.

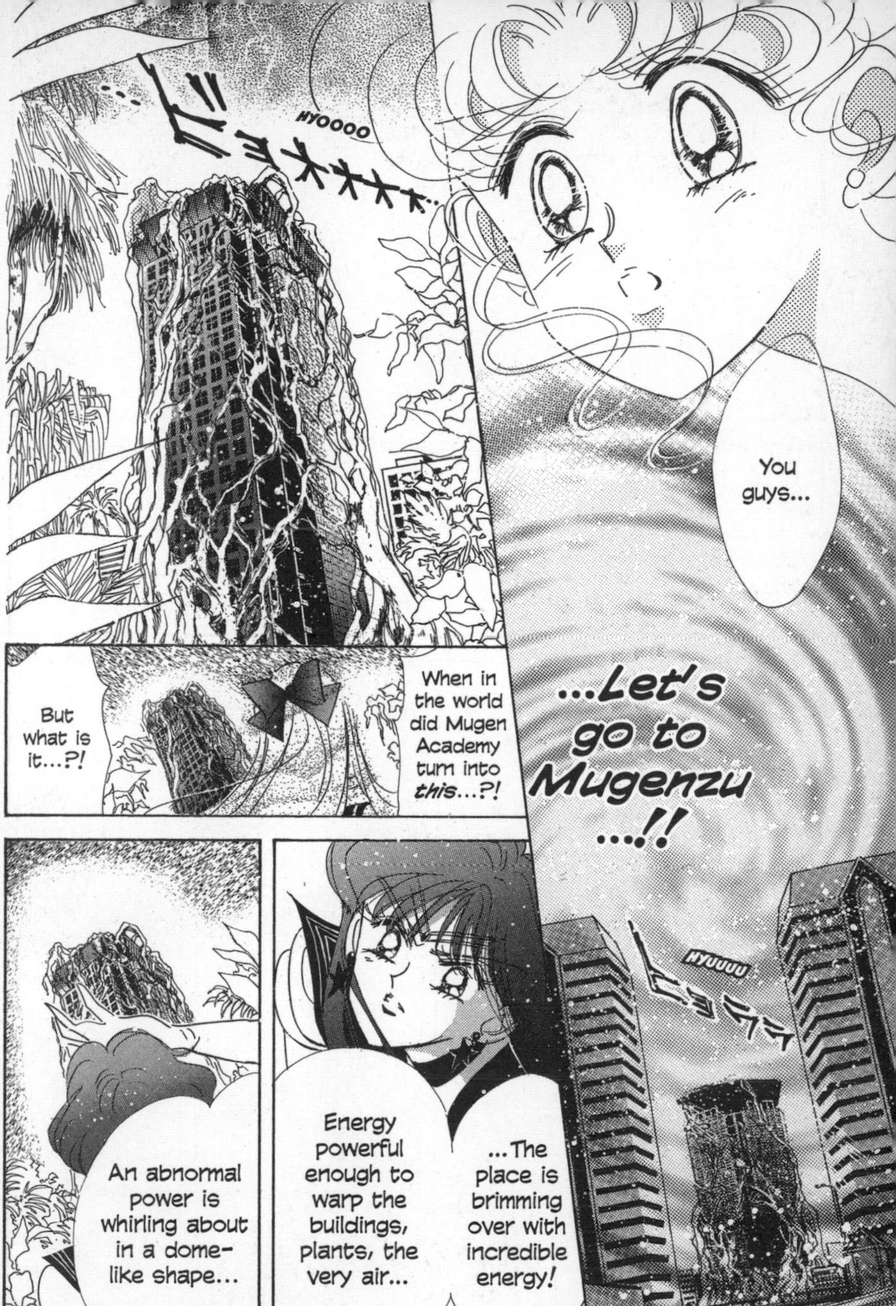
You guys...
...Let's go to Mugenzu ...!!
HYUUUU
...
HYOOOO
When in the world did Mugen Academy turn into *this*...?!
But what is it...?!
...The place is brimming over with incredible energy!
Energy powerful enough to warp the buildings, plants, the very air...
An abnormal power is whirling about in a dome-like shape...

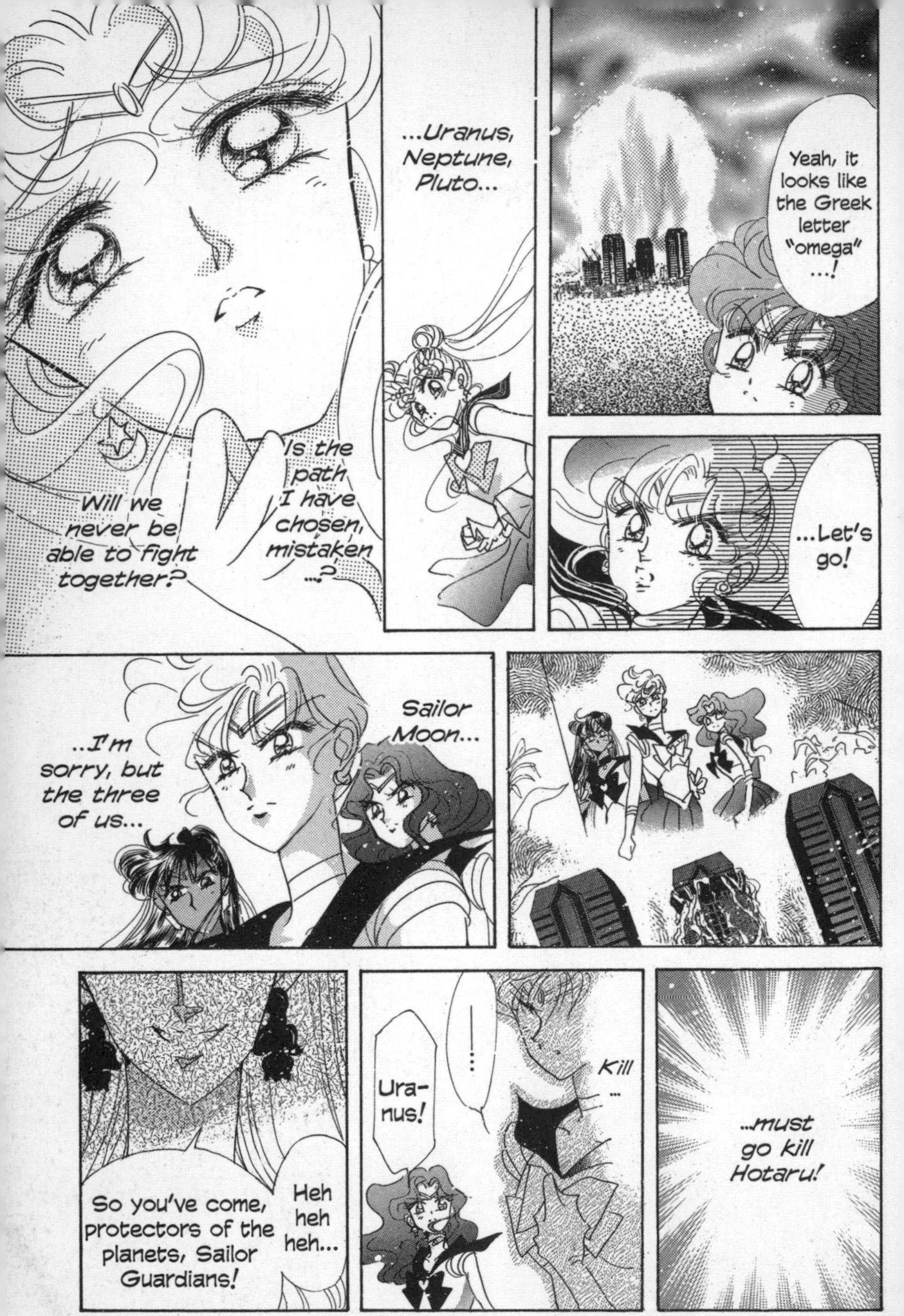
Yeah, it looks like the Greek letter "omega" ...!
...Let's go!
...Uranus, Neptune, Pluto...
Is the path I have chosen mistaken ...?
Will we never be able to fight together?
Sailor Moon...
...I'm sorry, but the three of us...
...must go kill Hotaru!
Kill ...
...!
Ura-nus!
Heh heh heh...
So you've come, protectors of the planets, Sailor Guardians!

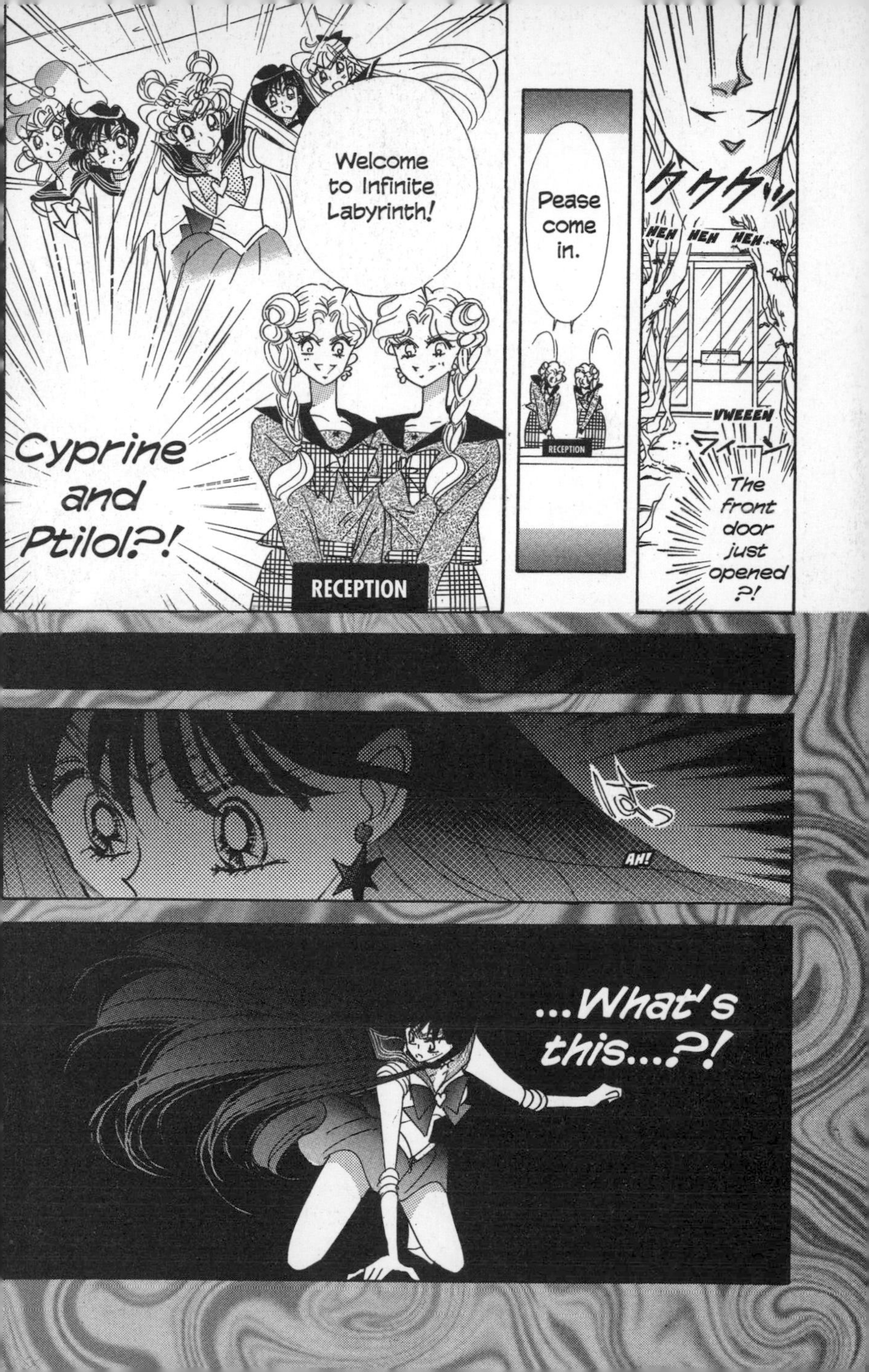

クククッ
HEH HEH HEH...
VWEEEN
ライーン
The front door just opened?!
Pease come in.
RECEPTION
Welcome to Infinite Labyrinth!
Cyprine and Ptilol?!
RECEPTION
AH!
...What's this...?!

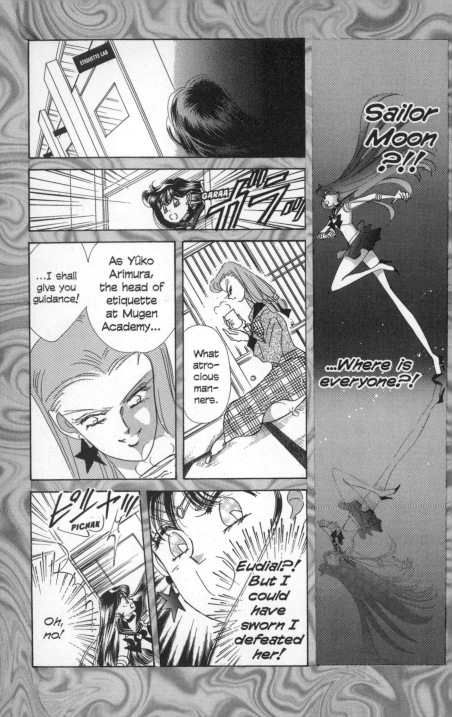

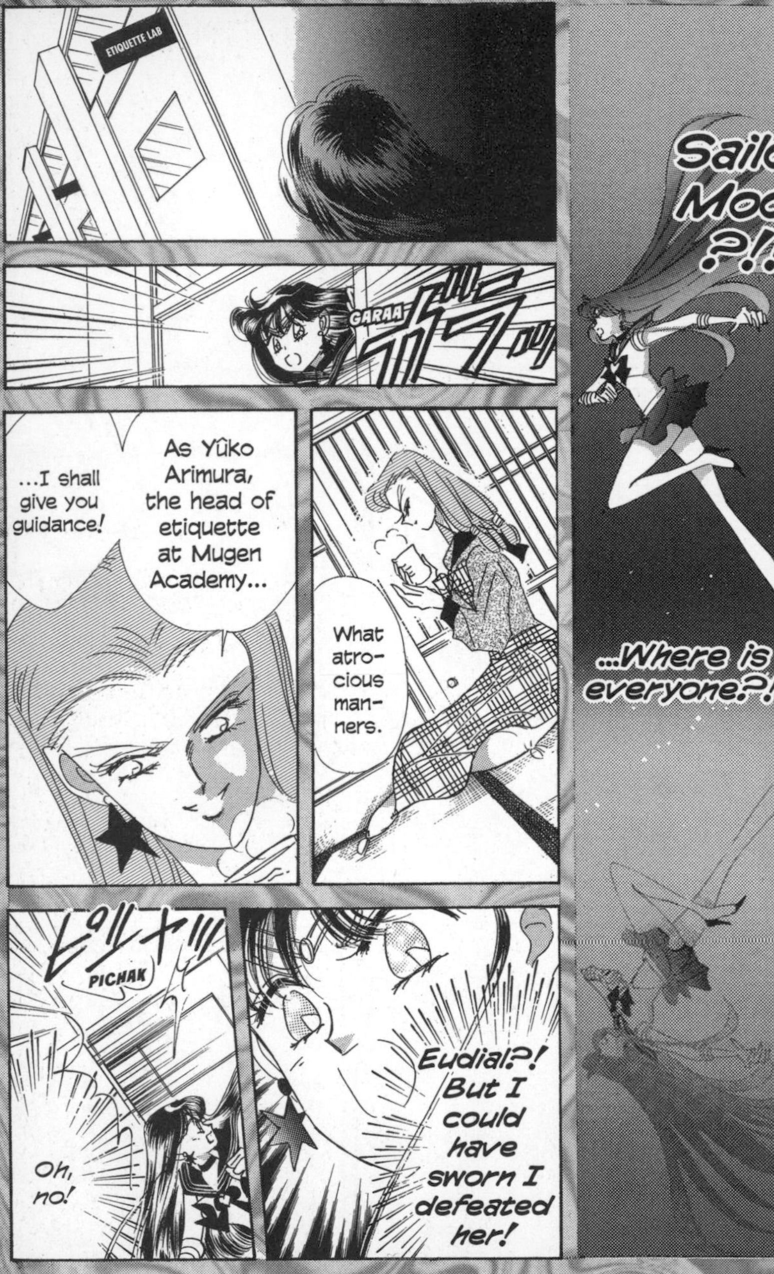
Sailor Moon ?!!
...Where is everyone?!
ETIQUETTE LAB
GARAA
What atrocious manners.
As Yûko Arimura, the head of etiquette at Mugen Academy...
...I shall give you guidance!
Eudial?! But I could have sworn I defeated her!
PICHAK
Oh, no!

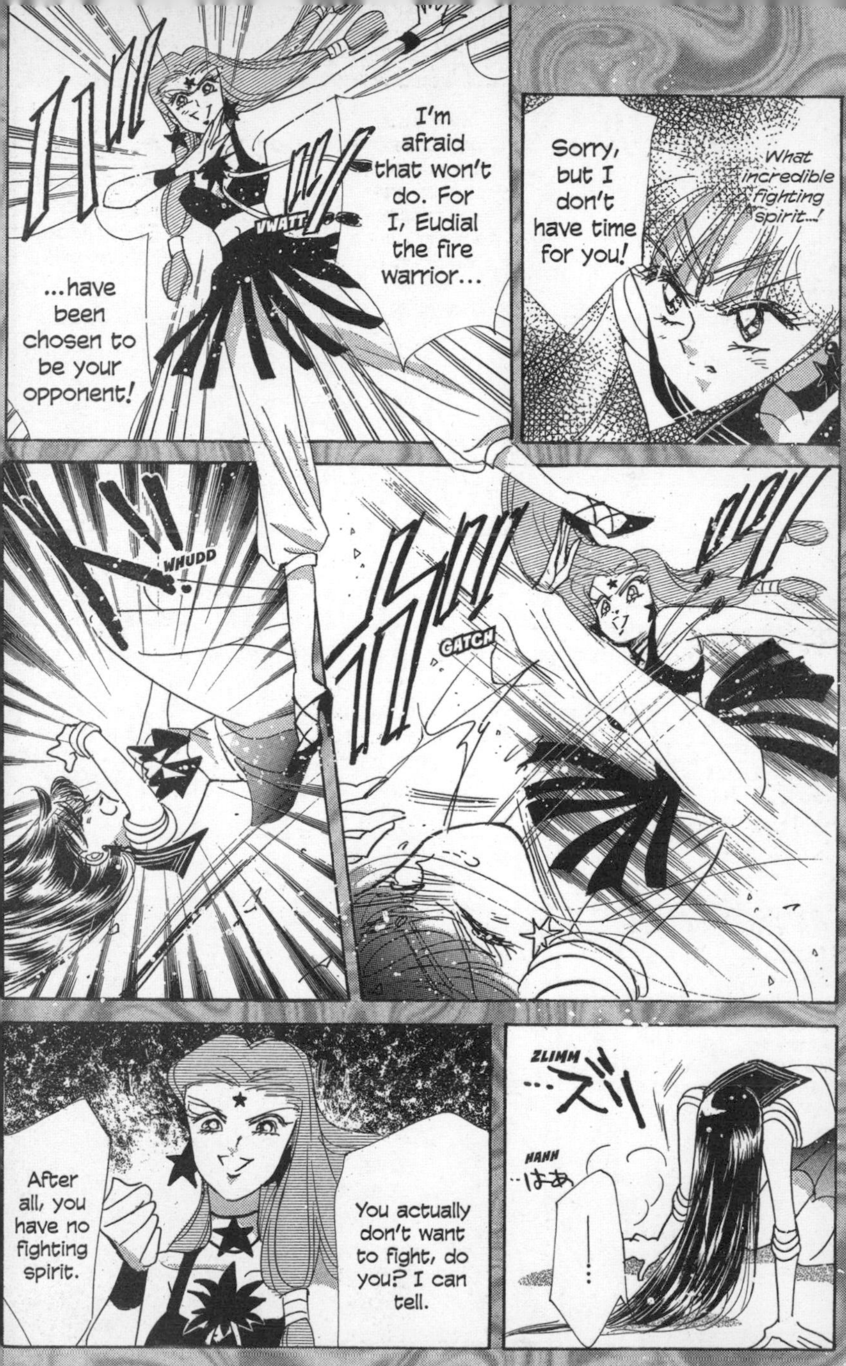
Sorry, but I don't have time for you!
What incredible fighting spirit...!
I'm afraid that won't do. For I, Eudial the fire warrior...
VWATT
...have been chosen to be your opponent!
GATCH
WHUDD
ZLIMM
...ズッ
HAHH
...はあ
...
You actually don't want to fight, do you? I can tell.
After all, you have no fighting spirit.

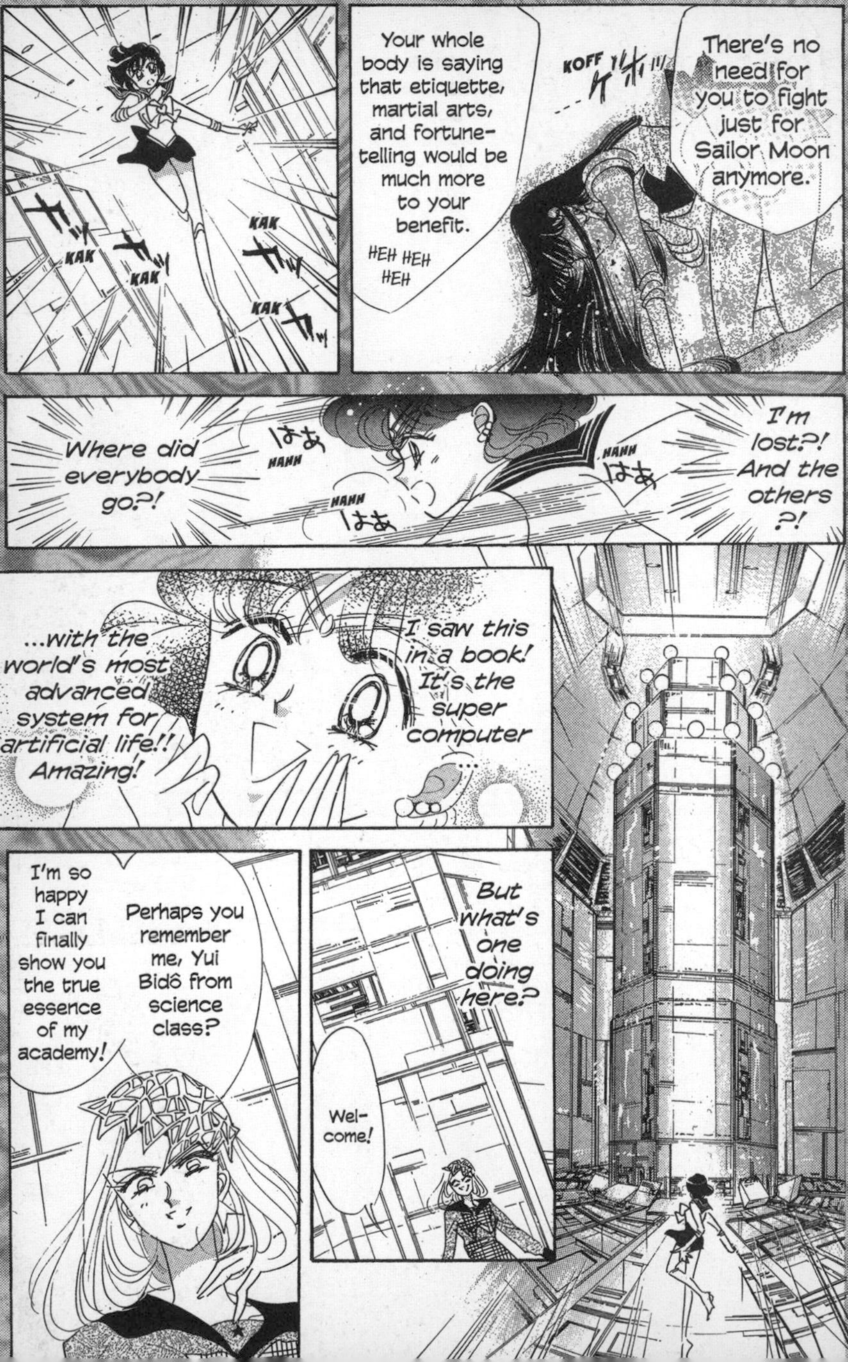
There's no need for you to fight just for Sailor Moon anymore.
KOFF
Your whole body is saying that etiquette, martial arts, and fortune-telling would be much more to your benefit.
HEH HEH HEH
KAK
KAK
KAK
KAK
I'm lost?! And the others ?!
HAHH
HAHH
HAHH
Where did everybody go?!
I saw this in a book! It's the super computer...
...with the world's most advanced system for artificial life!! Amazing!
But what's one doing here?
Wel-come!
Perhaps you remember me, Yui Bidô from science class?
I'm so happy I can finally show you the true essence of my academy!

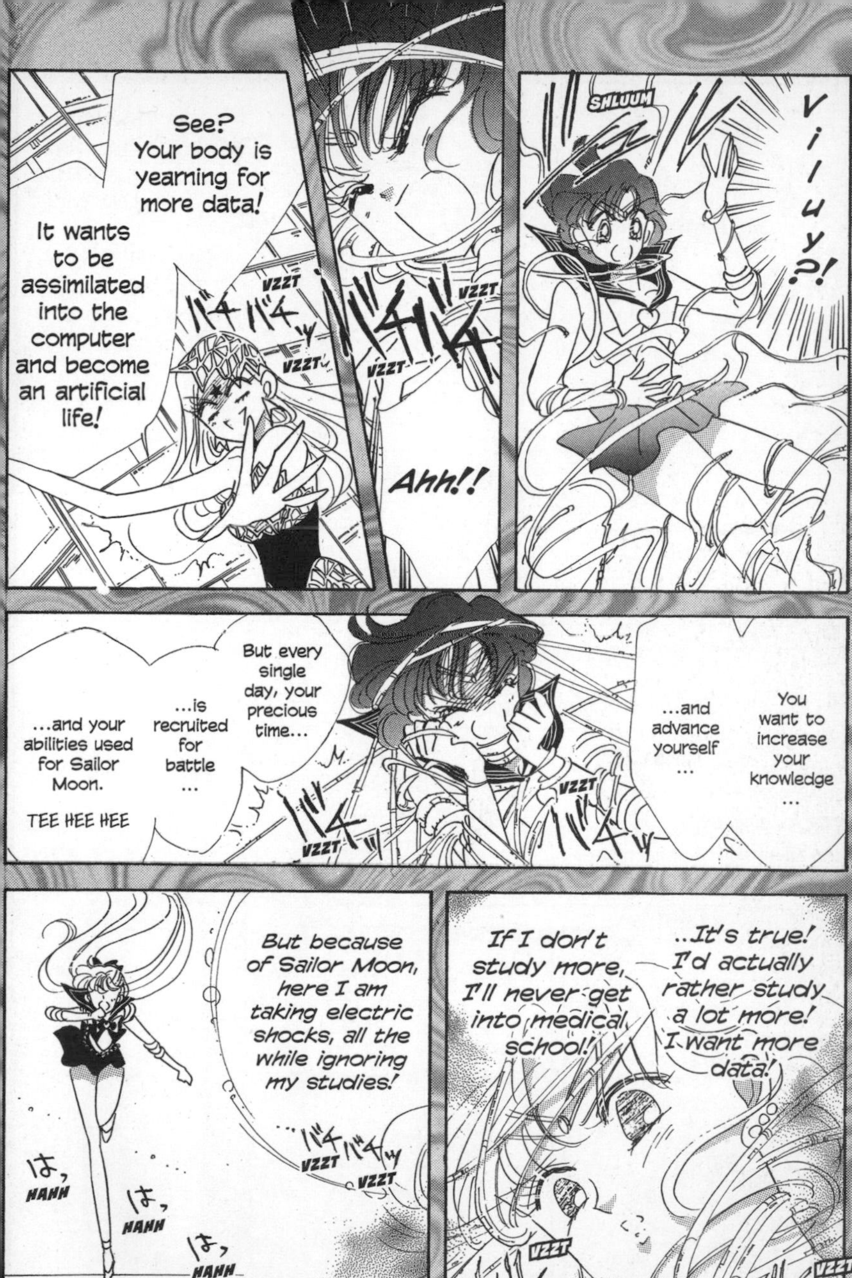

SHLUUM
Villuy?!
VZZT
Ahh!!
See? Your body is yearning for more data!
It wants to be assimilated into the computer and become an artificial life!
VZZT
VZZT
You want to increase your knowledge...
...and advance yourself...
VZZT
But every single day, your precious time...
...is recruited for battle...
...and your abilities used for Sailor Moon.
TEE HEE HEE
VZZT
...It's true! I'd actually rather study a lot more! I want more data!
If I don't study more, I'll never get into medical school!
VZZT
VZZT
But because of Sailor Moon, here I am taking electric shocks, all the while ignoring my studies!
VZZT
VZZT
HAHH
HAHH
HAHH

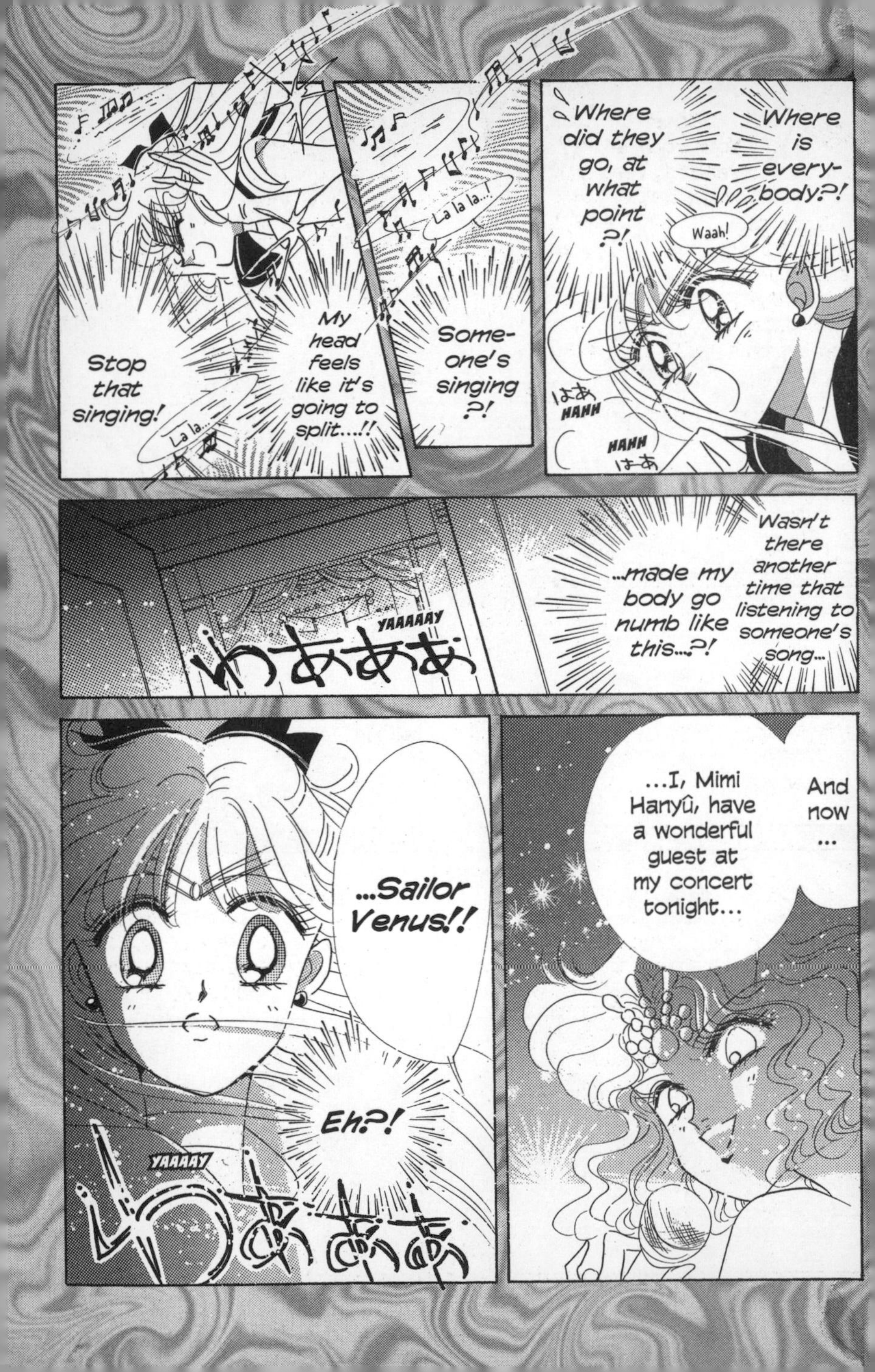
Where is every-body?!
Where did they go, at what point ?!
Waah!
はあ HAHH
HAHH はあ
Some-one's singing ?!
La la la...!
My head feels like it's going to split....!!
Stop that singing!
La la...
Wasn't there another time that listening to someone's song...
...made my body go numb like this...?!
わあああ
YAAAAAY
And now ...
...I, Mimi Hanyû, have a wonderful guest at my concert tonight...
...Sailor Venus!!
Eh?!
わあああ
YAAAAY

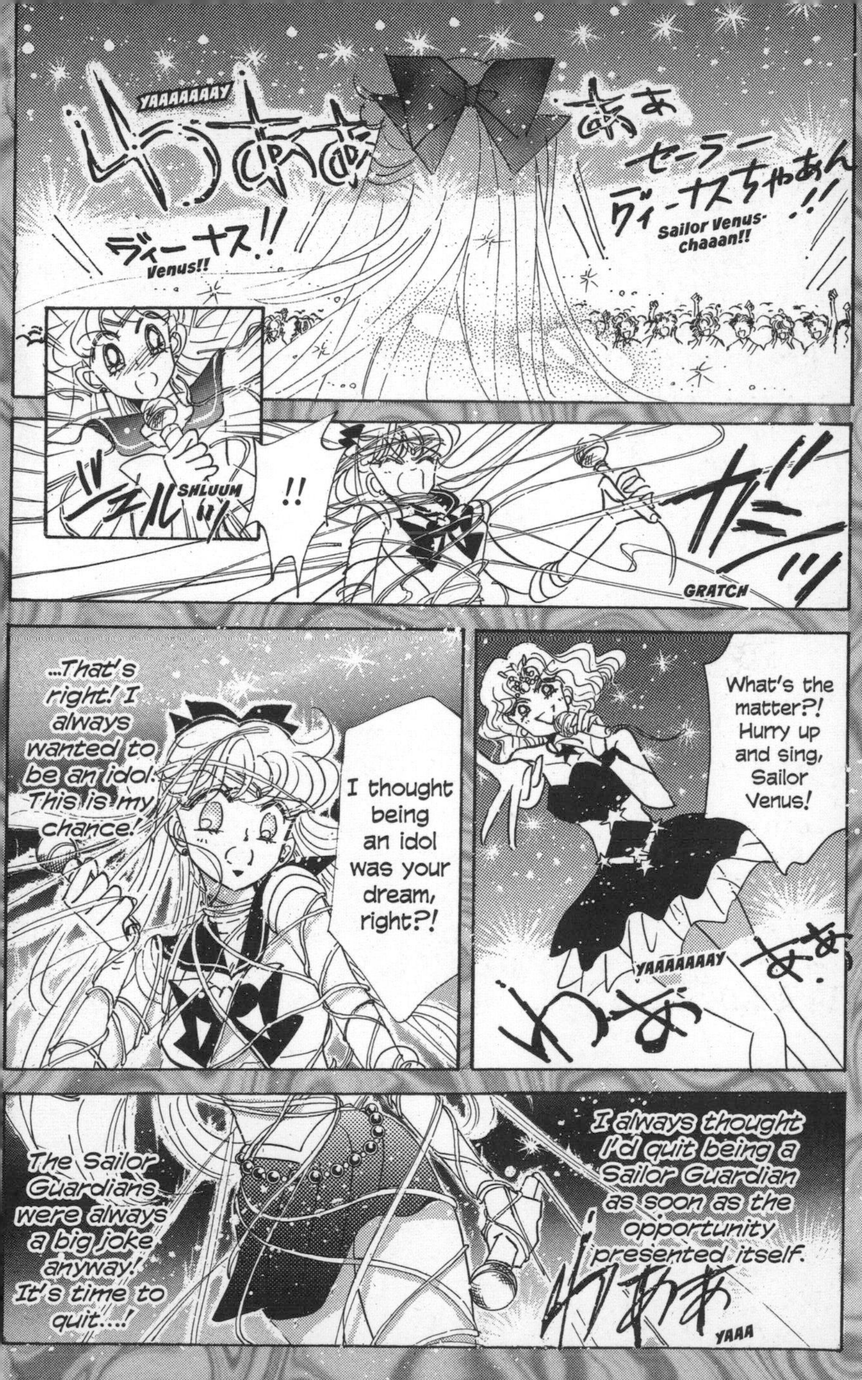

セーラーヴィーナスちゃあん!!
Sailor Venus-Chaaan!!
YAAAAAAAY
ヴィーナス!!
Venus!!
GRATCH
!!
SHLUUM
What's the matter?! Hurry up and sing, Sailor Venus!
YAAAAAAAY
I thought being an idol was your dream, right?!
...That's right! I always wanted to be an idol. This is my chance!
I always thought I'd quit being a Sailor Guardian as soon as the opportunity presented itself.
YAAA
The Sailor Guardians were always a big joke anyway! It's time to quit...!

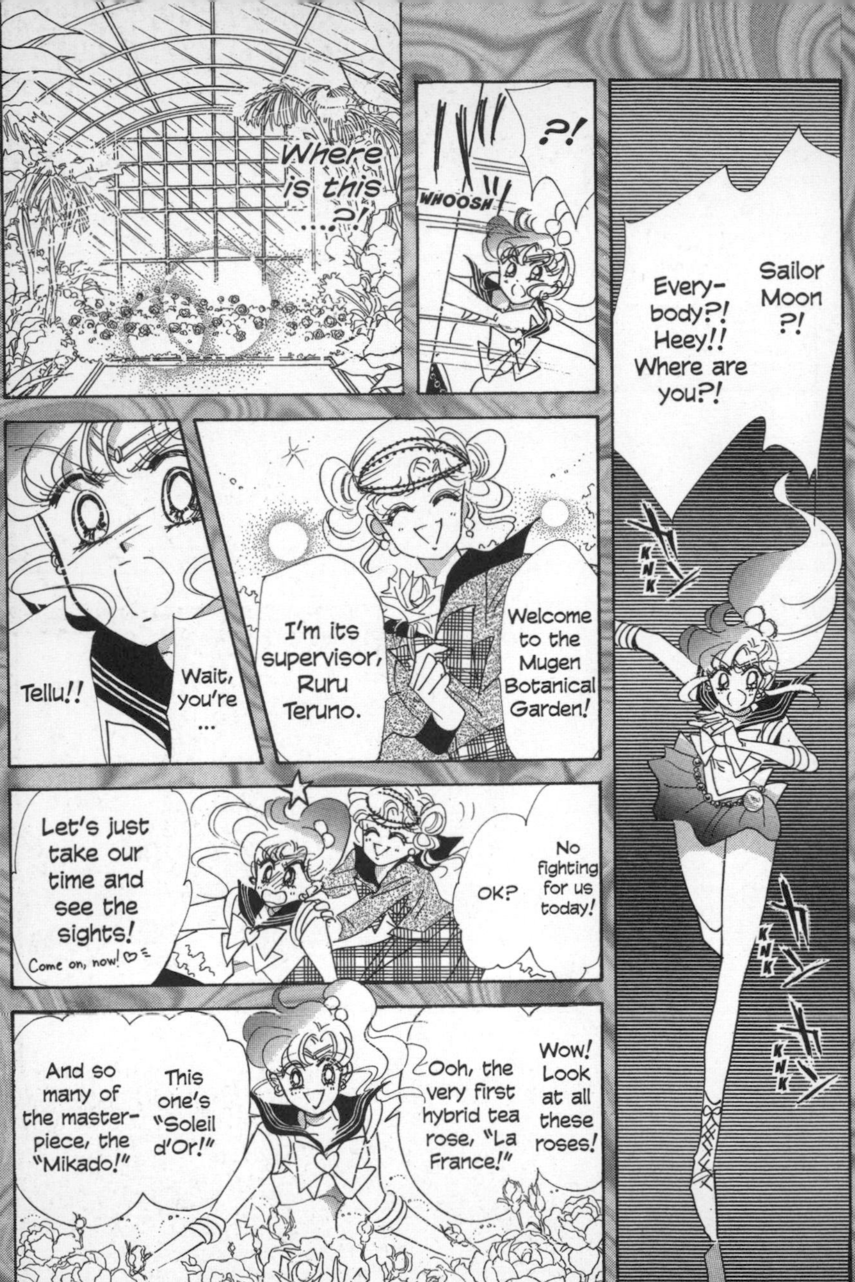
Sailor Moon?!
Every-body?! Heey!! Where are you?!
KNK
KNK
KNK
?!
WHOOSH
Where is this ...?!
Welcome to the Mugen Botanical Garden!
I'm its supervisor, Ruru Teruno.
Wait, you're ...
Tellu!!
No fighting for us today!
OK?
Let's just take our time and see the sights!
Come on, now!
Wow! Look at all these roses!
Ooh, the very first hybrid tea rose, "La France!"
This one's "Soleil d'Or!"
And so many of the master-piece, the "Mikado!"

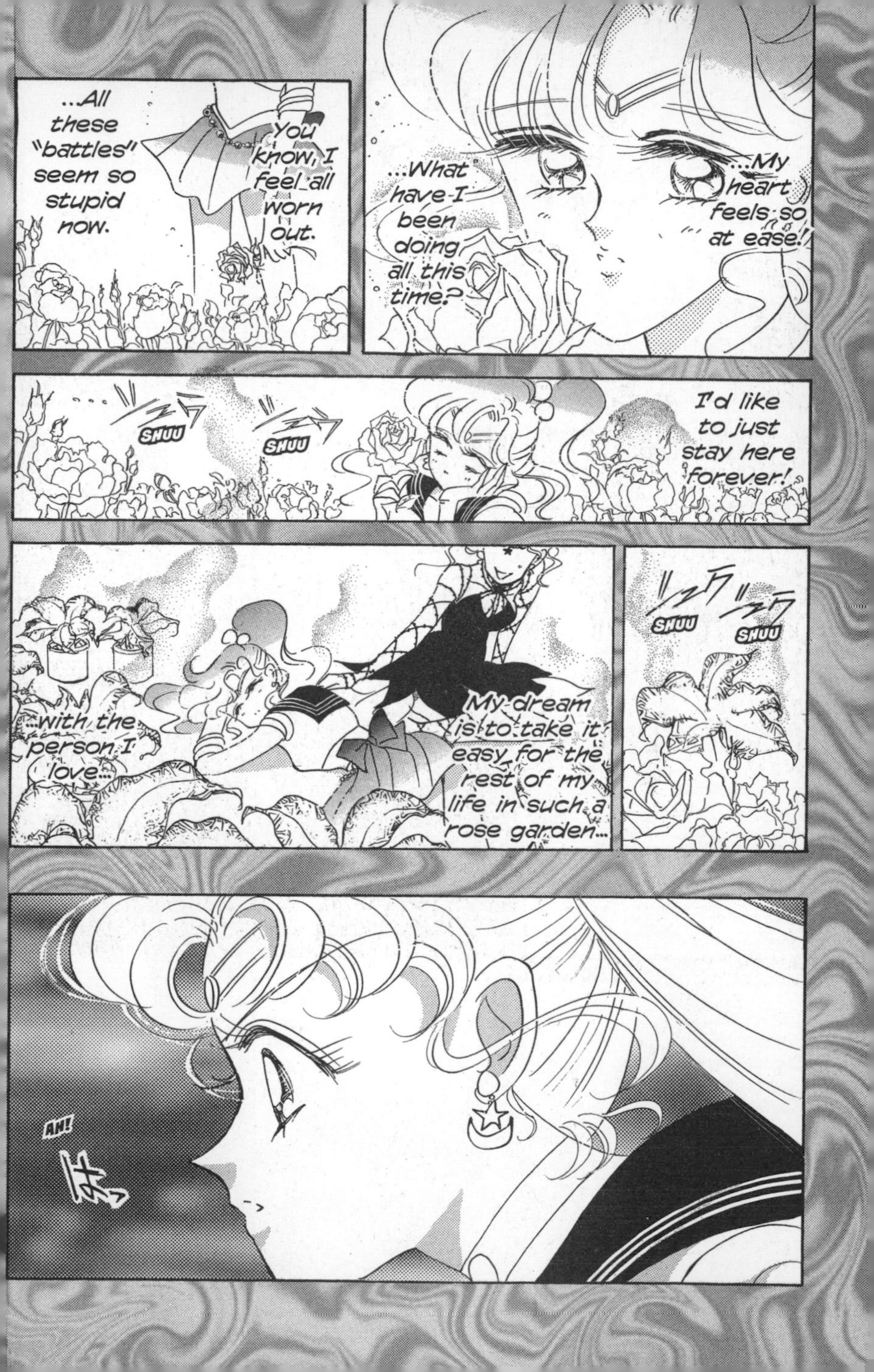
...My heart feels so at ease!
...What have I been doing all this time?
You know, I feel all worn out.
...All these "battles" seem so stupid now.
I'd like to just stay here forever!
SHUU
SHUU
SHUU
SHUU
My dream is to take it easy for the rest of my life in such a rose garden...
...with the person I love...
AH!

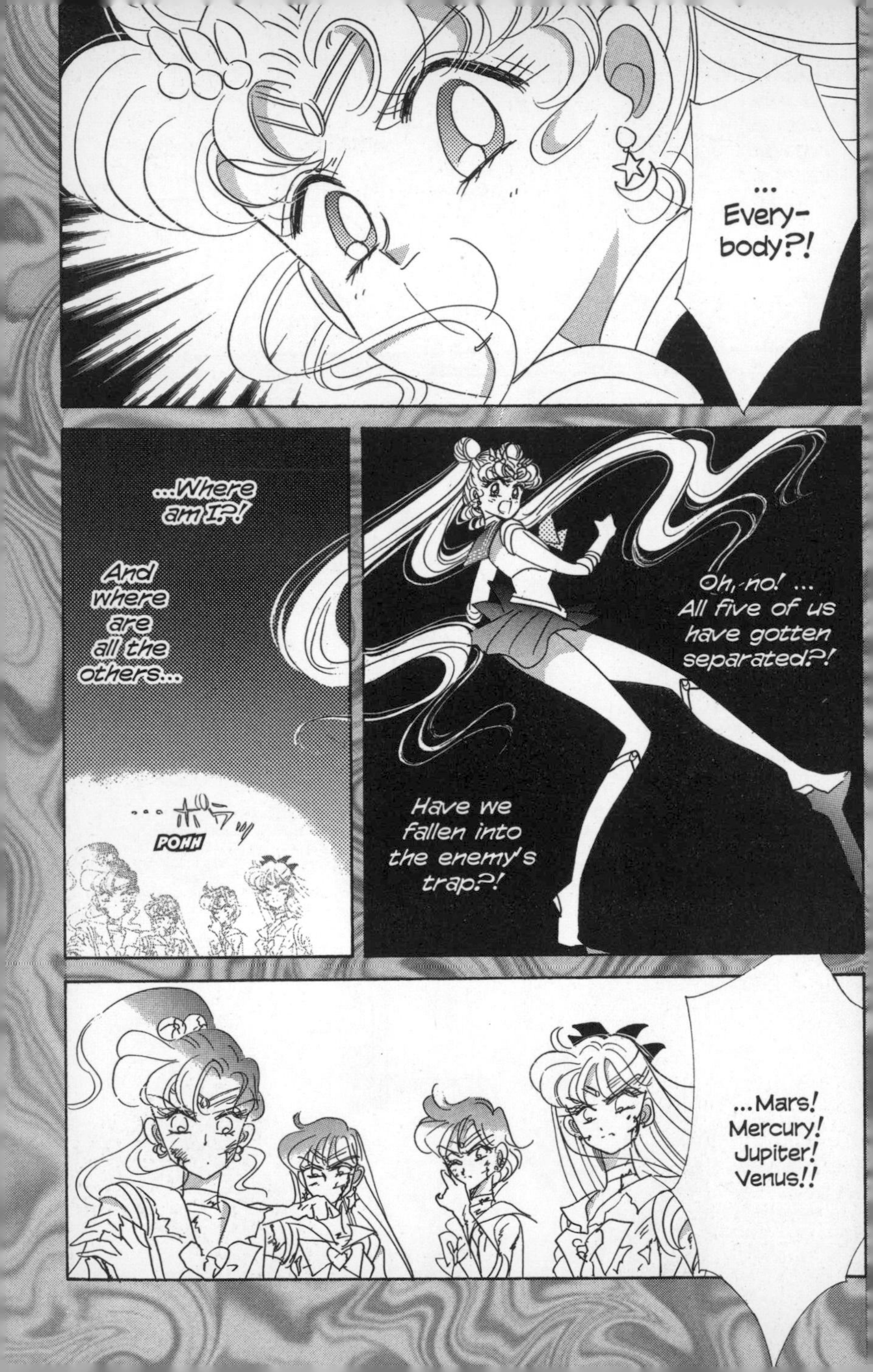

... Every-body?!
Oh, no! ... All five of us have gotten separated?!
Have we fallen into the enemy's trap?!
...Where am I?!
And where are all the others...
POHH
...Mars! Mercury! Jupiter! Venus!!

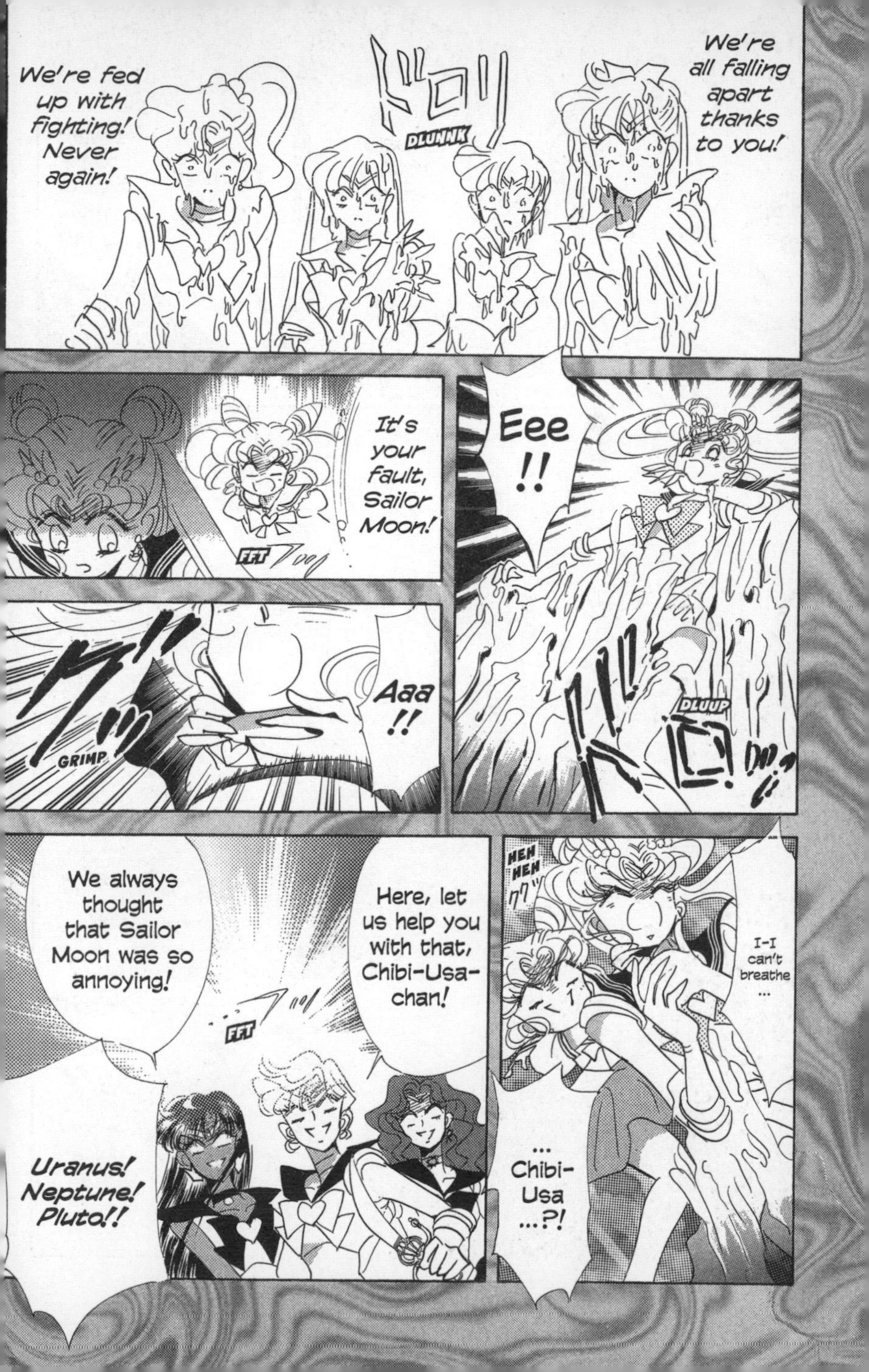

We're all falling apart thanks to you!
ドロリ
DLUNNK
We're fed up with fighting! Never again!
Eee!!
DLUUP
It's your fault, Sailor Moon!
FFT
Aaa!!
GRIMP
HEH HEH
I-I can't breathe ...
... Chibi-Usa ...?!
Here, let us help you with that, Chibi-Usa-chan!
We always thought that Sailor Moon was so annoying!
FFT
Uranus! Neptune! Pluto!!

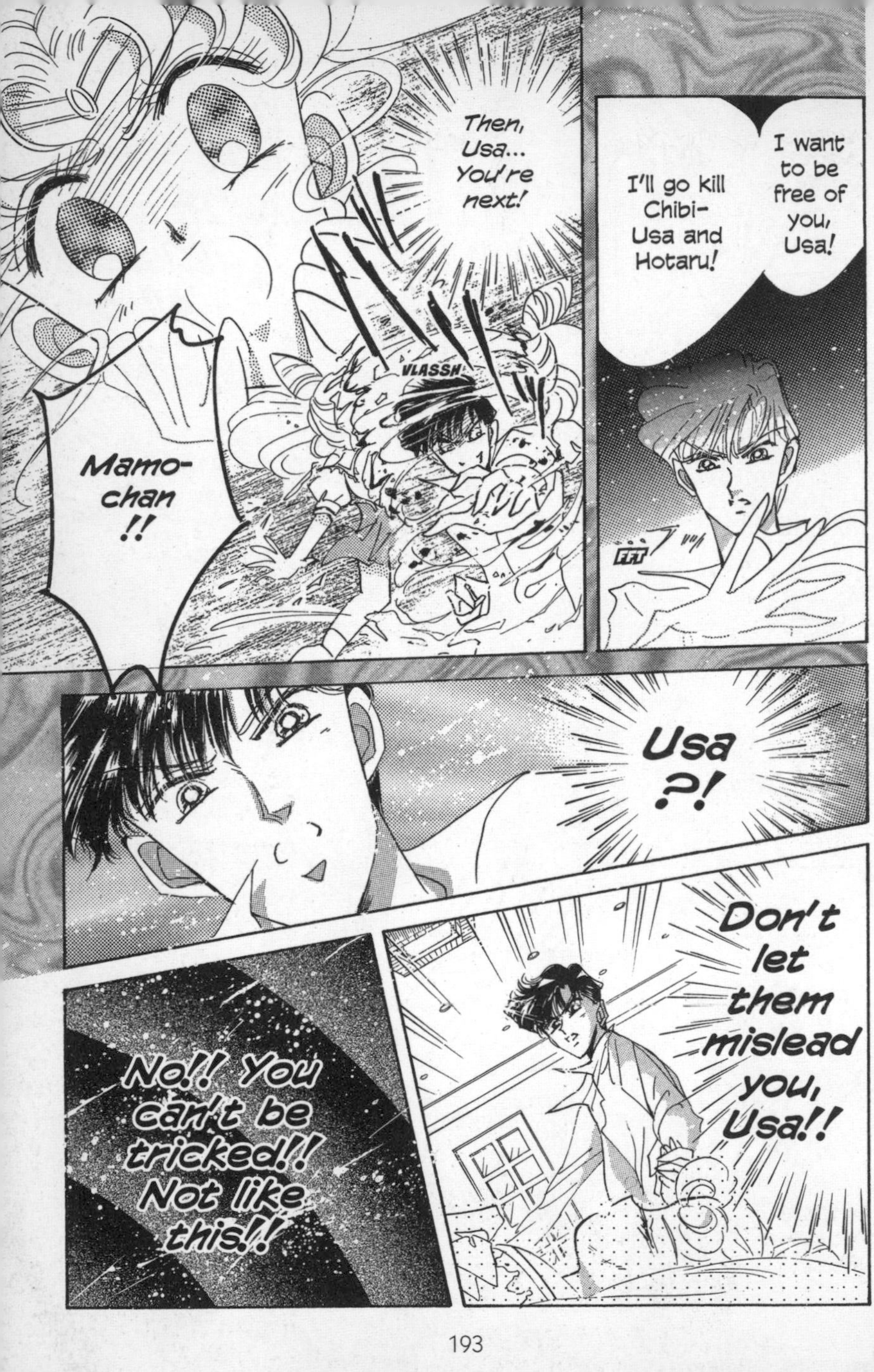
I want to be free of you, Usa!
I'll go kill Chibi-Usa and Hotaru!
FFT
Then, Usa... You're next!
VLASSH
Mamo-chan !!
Usa ?!
Don't let them mislead you, Usa!!
No!! You can't be tricked!! Not like this!!

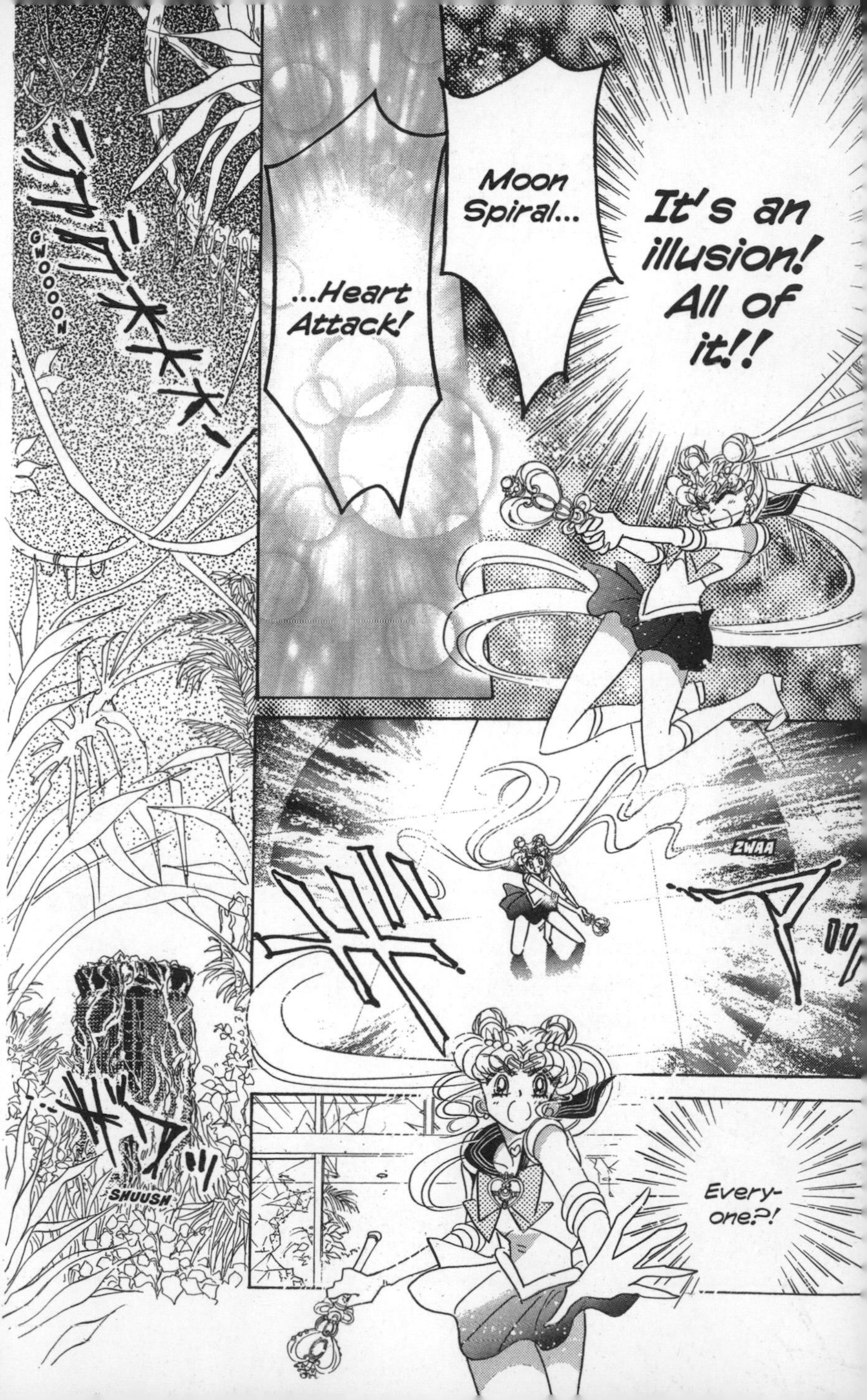
It's an illusion! All of it!!
Moon Spiral...
...Heart Attack!
ZWAA
Every-one?!
GWOOOOON
SHUUSH

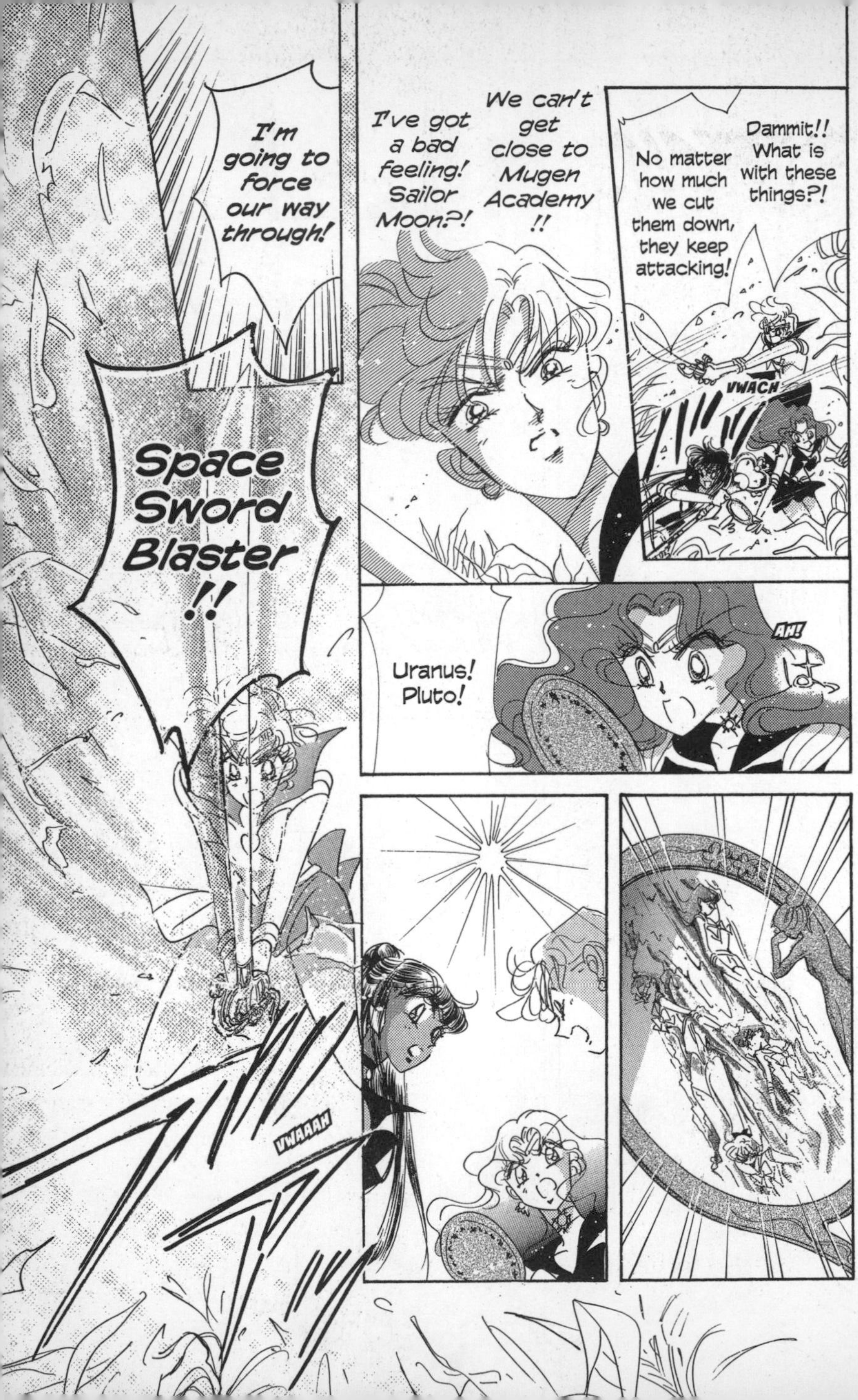
Dammit!! What is with these things?!
No matter how much we cut them down, they keep attacking!
VWACH
We can't get close to Mugen Academy!!
I've got a bad feeling! Sailor Moon?!
AH!
Uranus! Pluto!
I'm going to force our way through!
Space Sword Blaster!!
VWAAAH

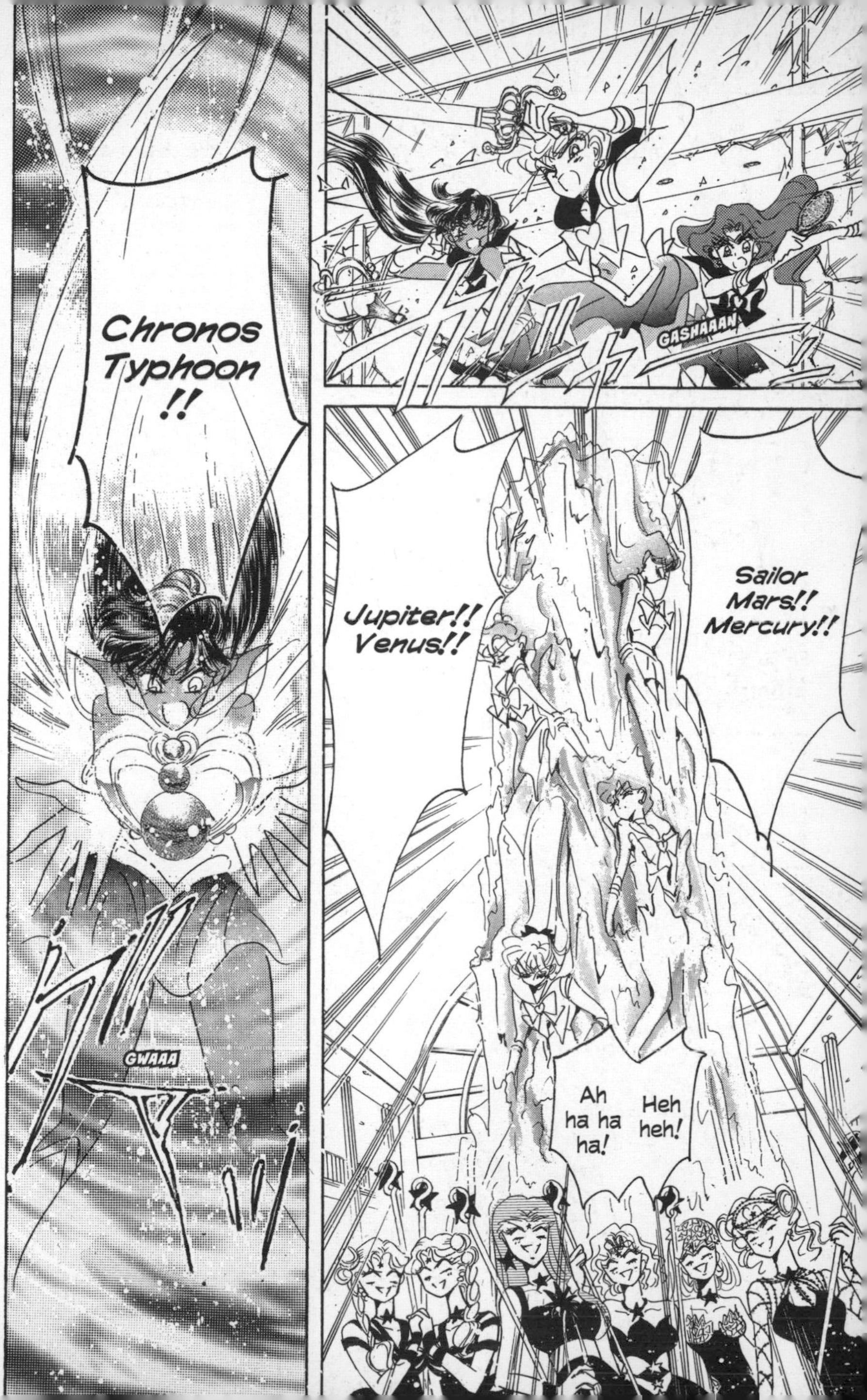
GASHAAAN
Sailor Mars!! Mercury!!
Jupiter!! Venus!!
Heh heh!
Ah ha ha ha!
Chronos Typhoon!!
GWAAA

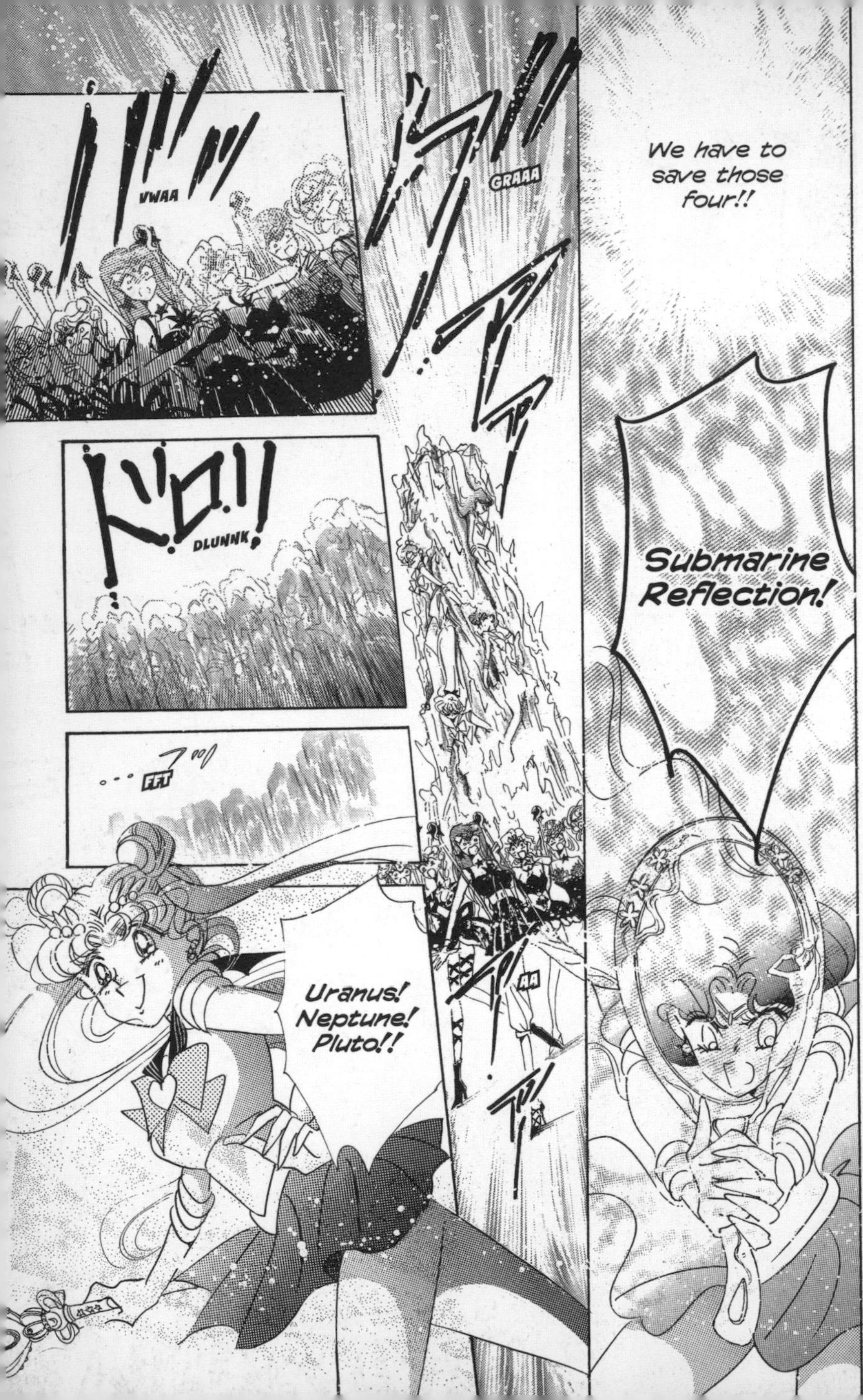
We have to save those four!!
Submarine Reflection!
GRAAA
AA
VWAA
DLUNNK!
...
FFT
Uranus! Neptune! Pluto!!

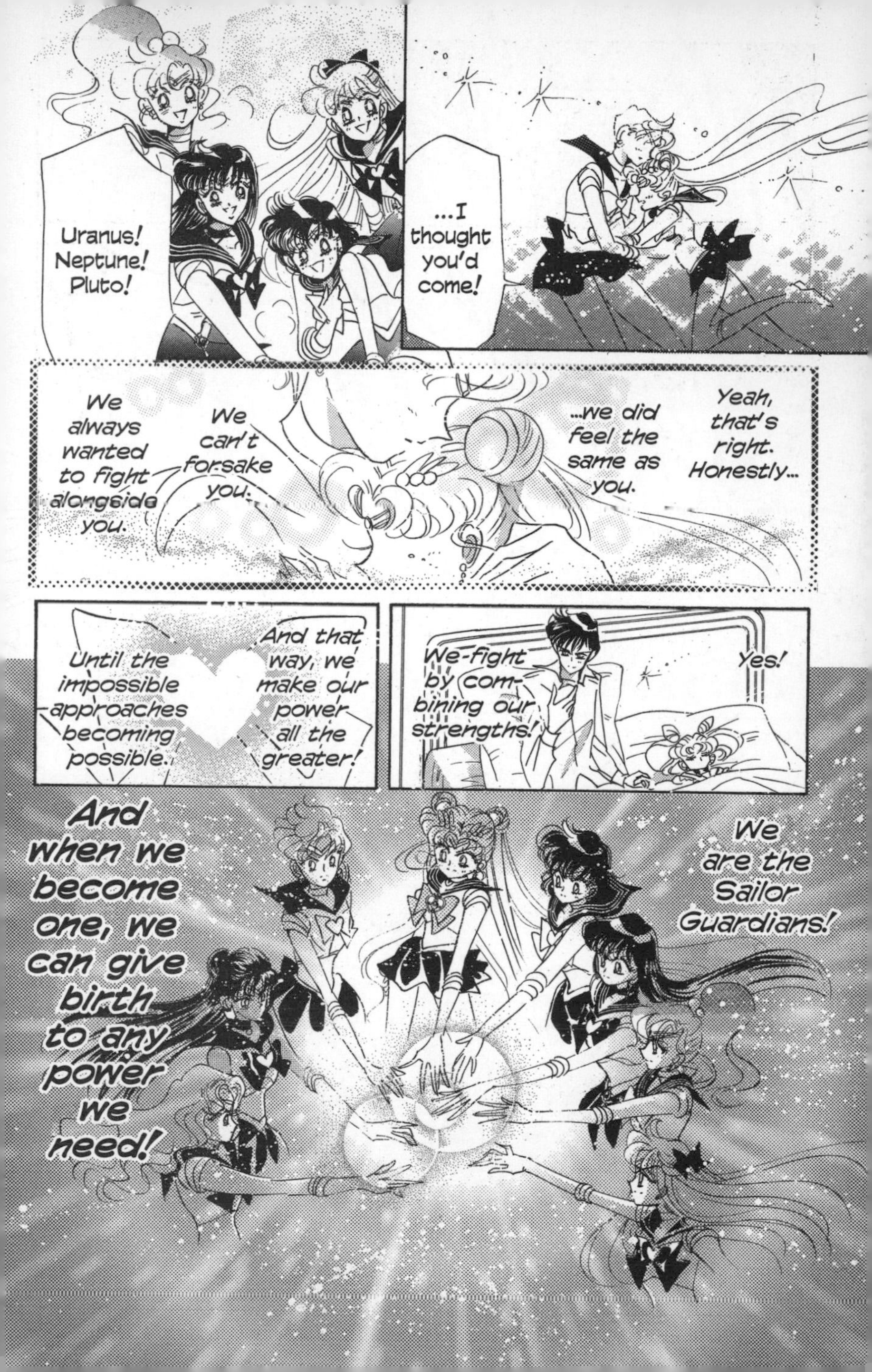

...I thought you'd come!
Uranus! Neptune! Pluto!
Yeah, that's right. Honestly...
...we did feel the same as you.
We can't forsake you.
We always wanted to fight alongside you.
Yes!
We fight by combining our strengths!
And that way, we make our power all the greater!
Until the impossible approaches becoming possible.
We are the Sailor Guardians!
And when we become one, we can give birth to any power we need!

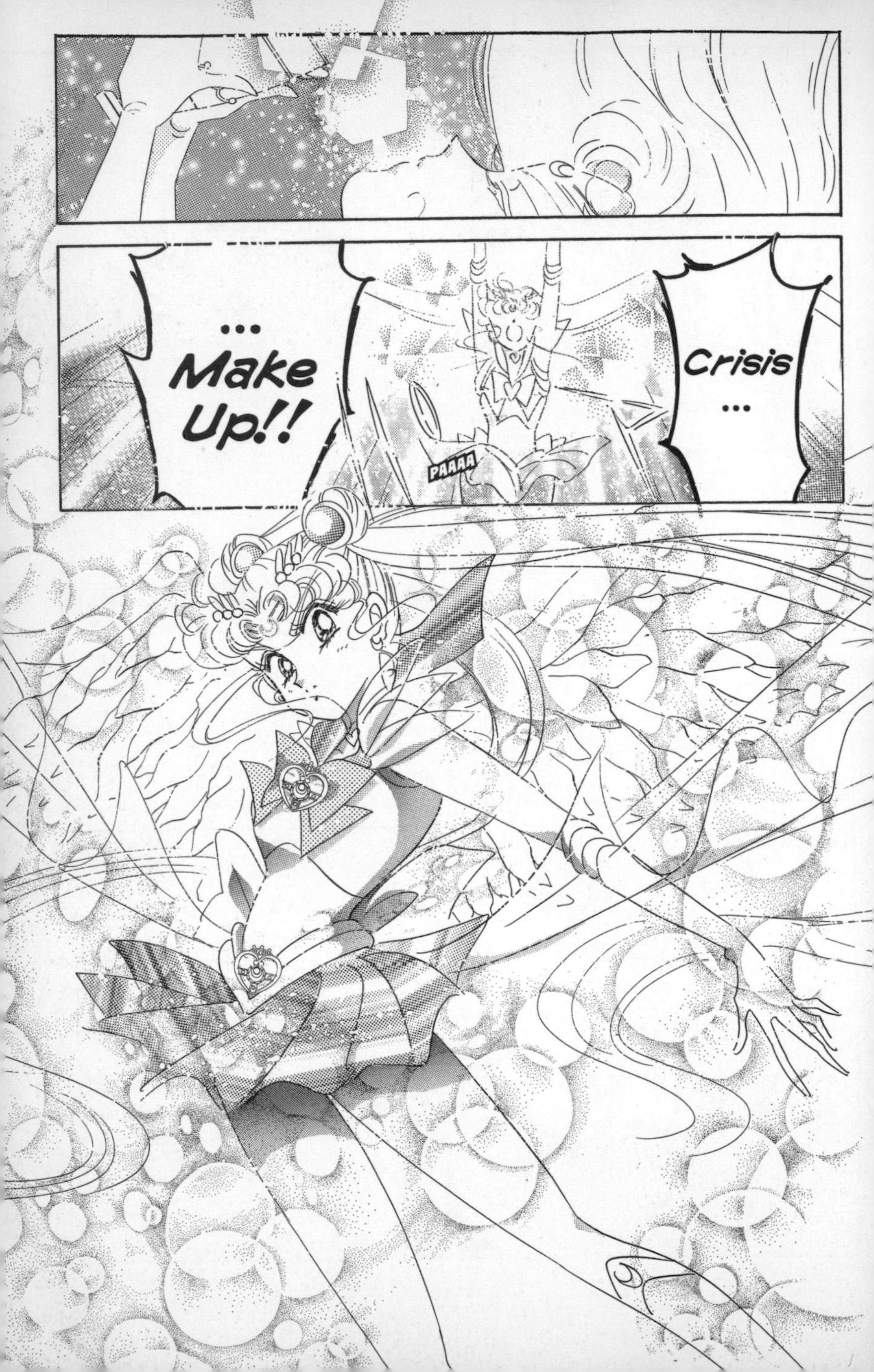
Crisis ...
PAAAA
... Make Up!!

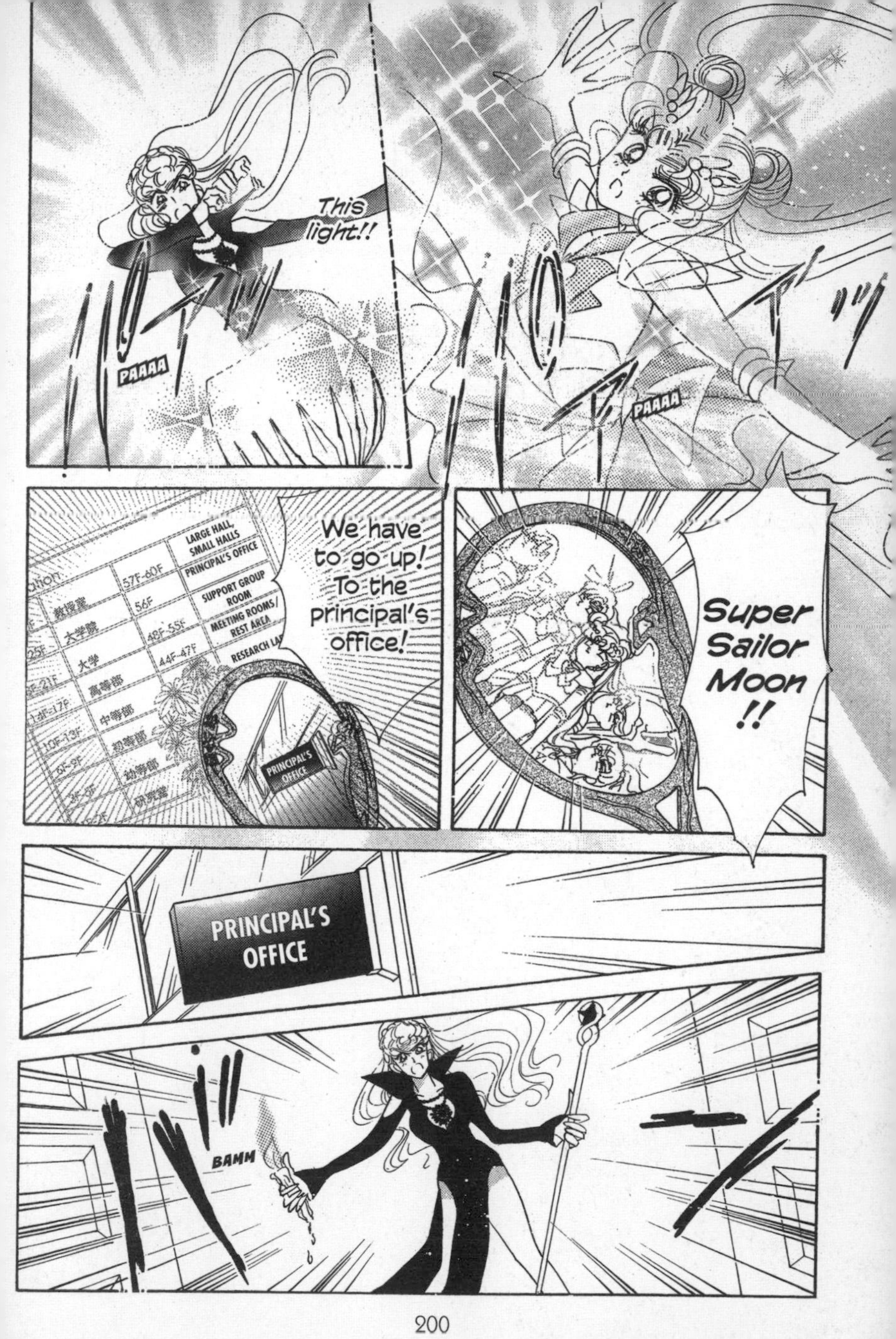
PAAAA
This light!!
PAAAA
Super Sailor Moon!!
We have to go up! To the principal's office!
LARGE HALL, SMALL HALLS
57F-60F
PRINCIPAL'S OFFICE
SUPPORT GROUP ROOM
56F
MEETING ROOMS/ REST AREA
48F-55F
44F-47F
PRINCIPAL'S OFFICE
PRINCIPAL'S OFFICE
BAMM

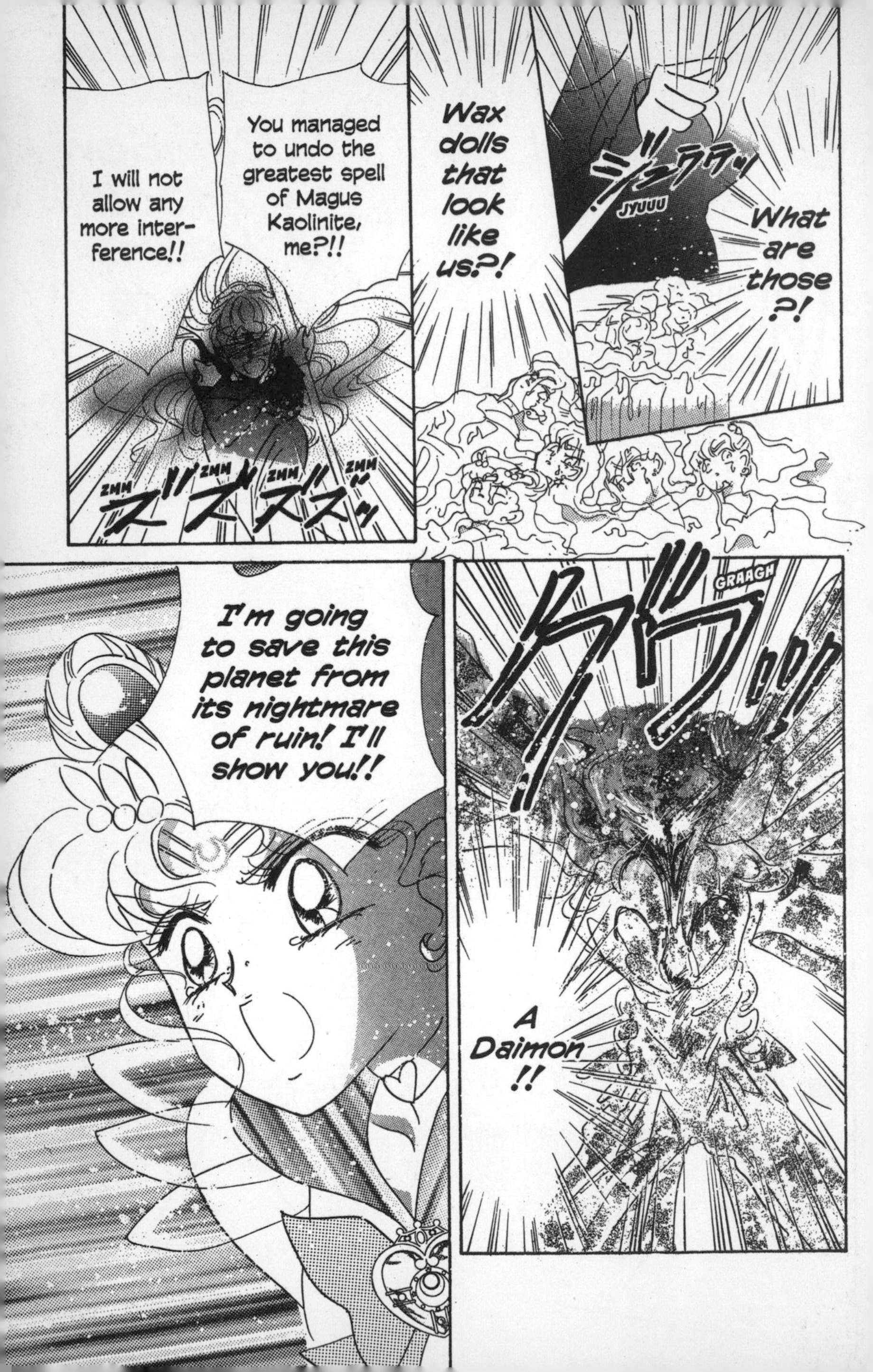
JYUUU
What are those?!
Wax dolls that look like us?!
You managed to undo the greatest spell of Magus Kaolinite, me?!!
I will not allow any more inter-ference!!
ZMM ZMM ZMM ZMM
GRAAGH
A Daimon!!
I'm going to save this planet from its nightmare of ruin! I'll show you!!

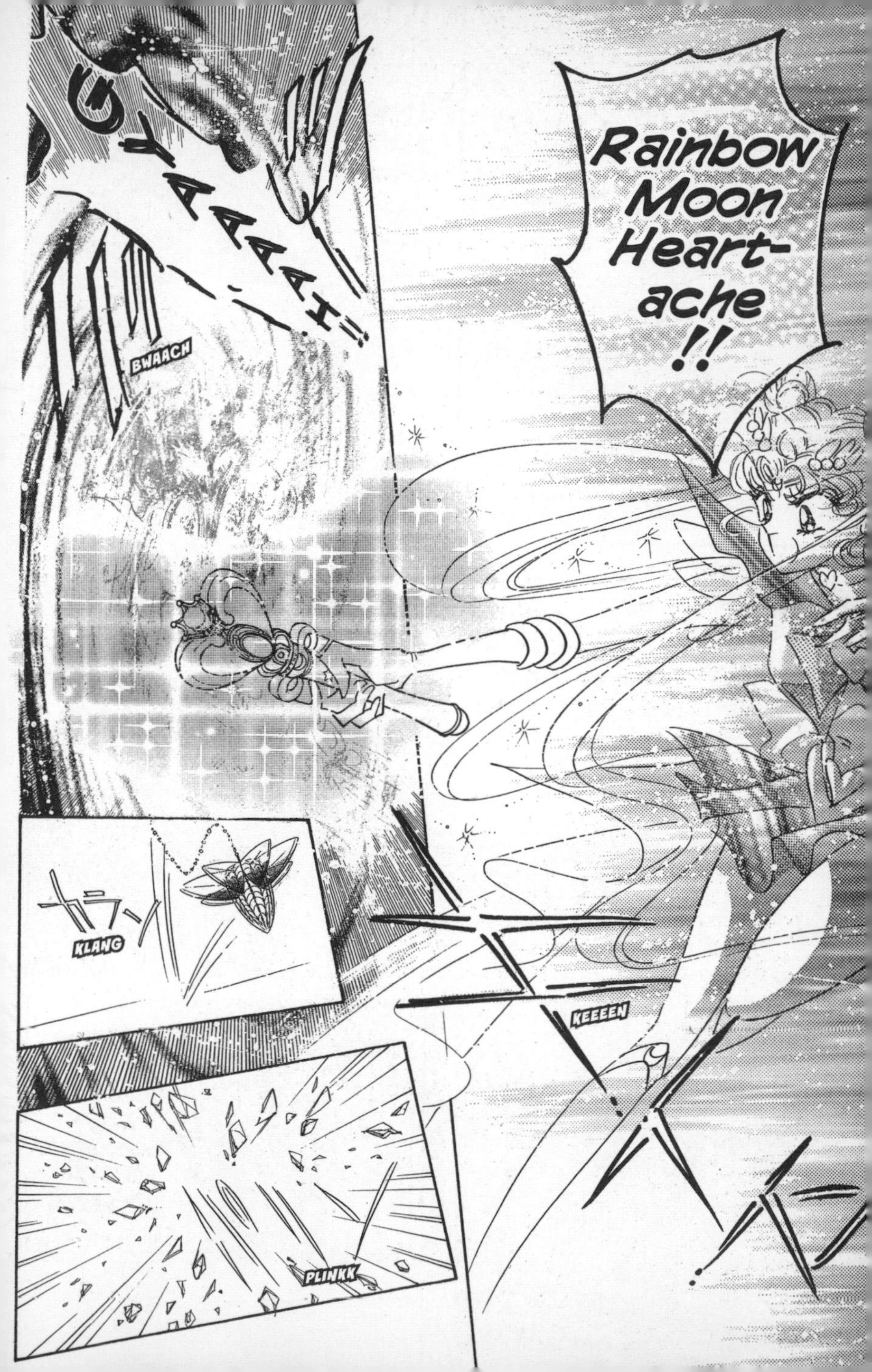
Rainbow Moon Heart-ache!!
KEEEEN
GYAAAAH!!
BWAACH
KLANG
PLINKK

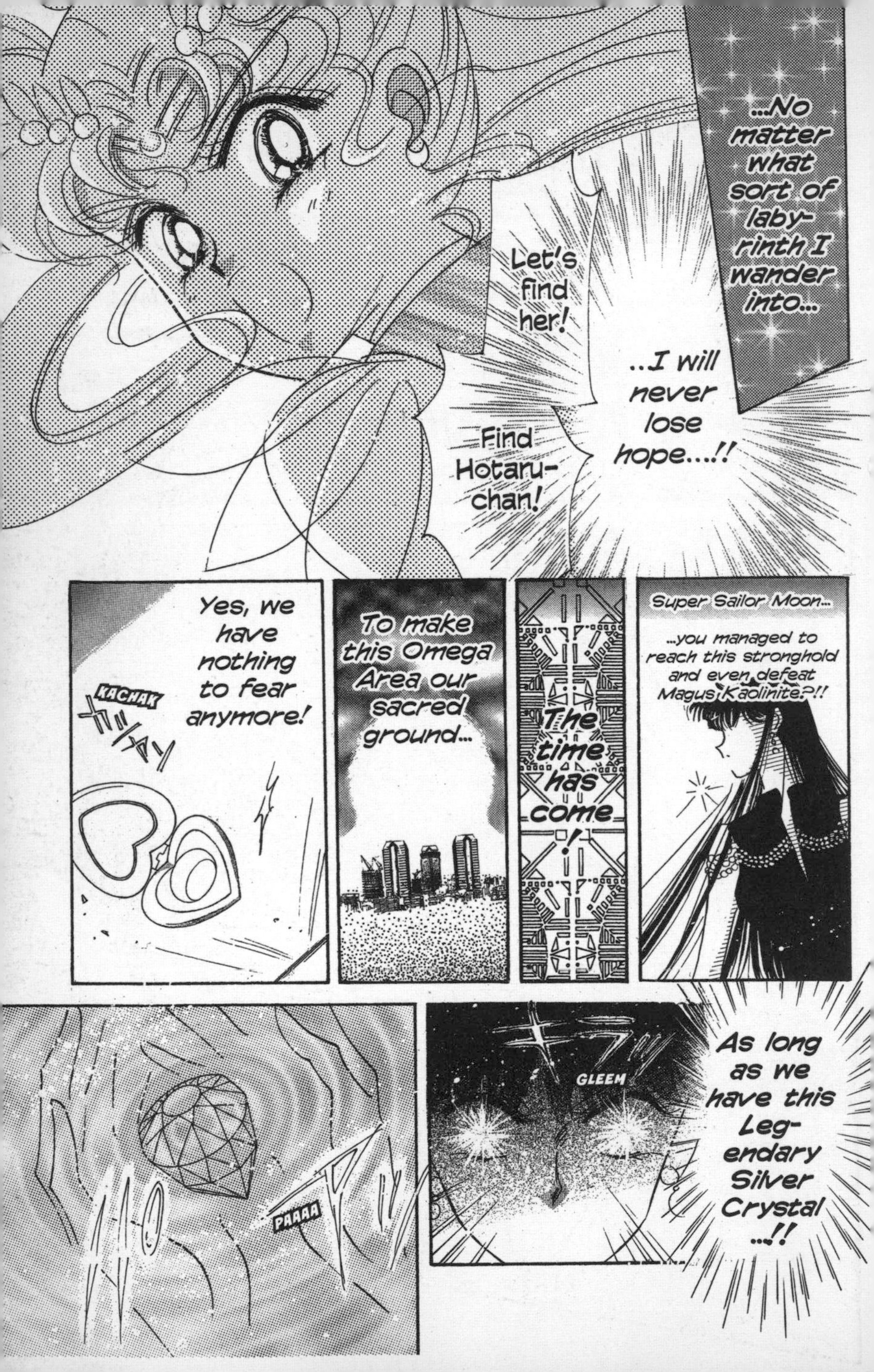
...No matter what sort of labyrinth I wander into...
...I will never lose hope...!!
Let's find her!
Find Hotaru-chan!
Super Sailor Moon...
...you managed to reach this stronghold and even defeat Magus Kaolinite?!!
The time has come!
To make this Omega Area our sacred ground...
Yes, we have nothing to fear anymore!
KACHAK
GLEEM
As long as we have this Legendary Silver Crystal ...!!
PAAAA

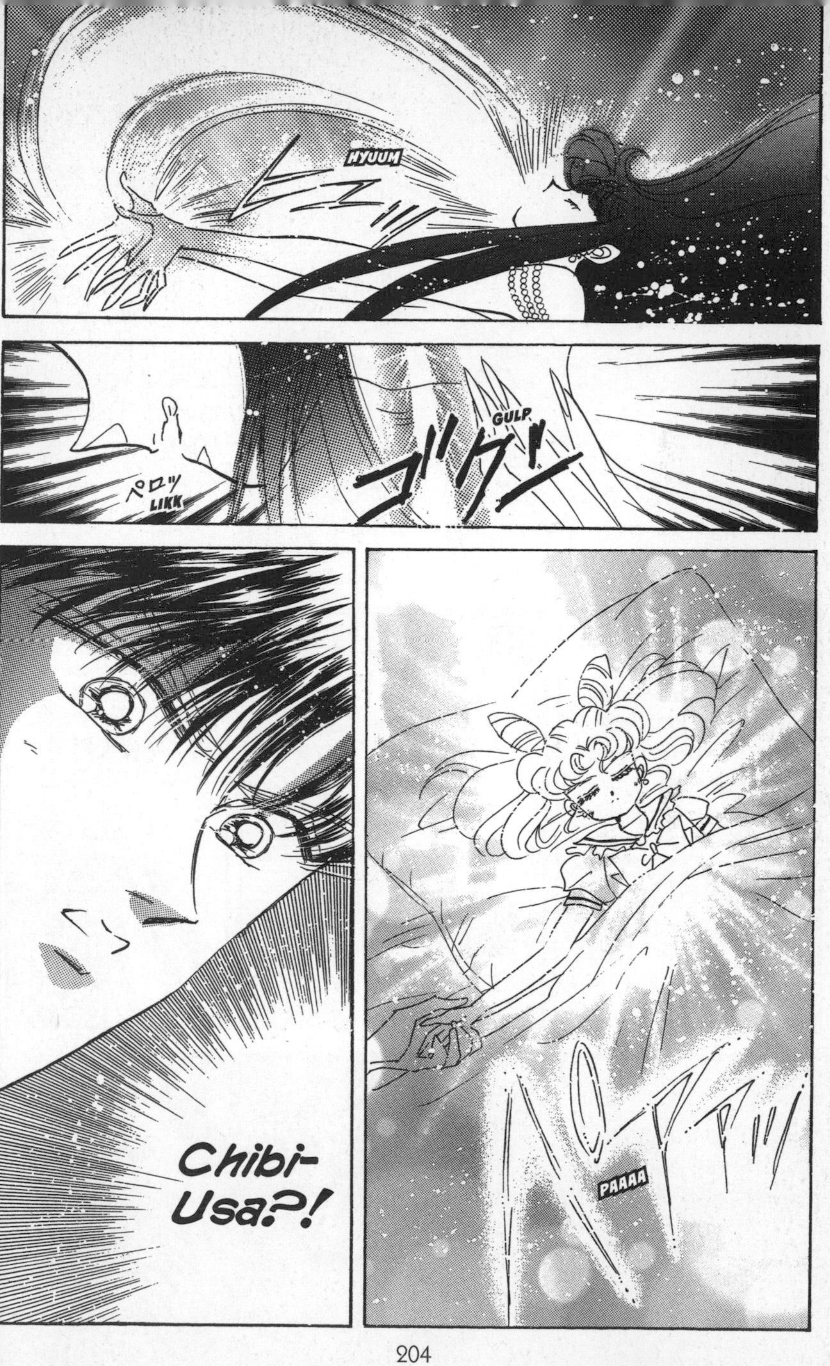
HYUUM
GULP
ペロッ
LIKK
PAAAA
Chibi-Usa?!

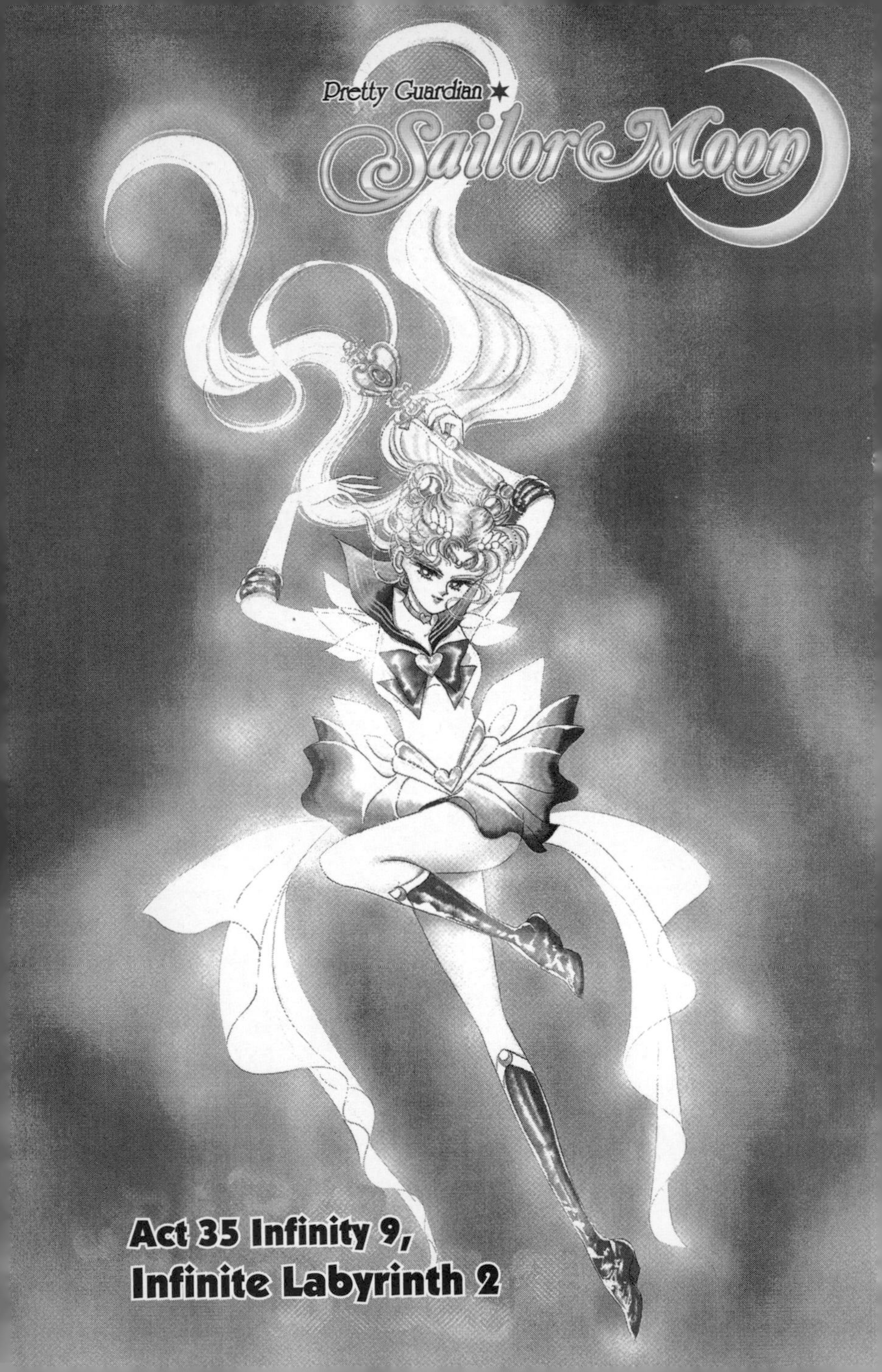

Pretty Guardian
Sailor Moon
Act 35 Infinity 9,
Infinite Labyrinth 2

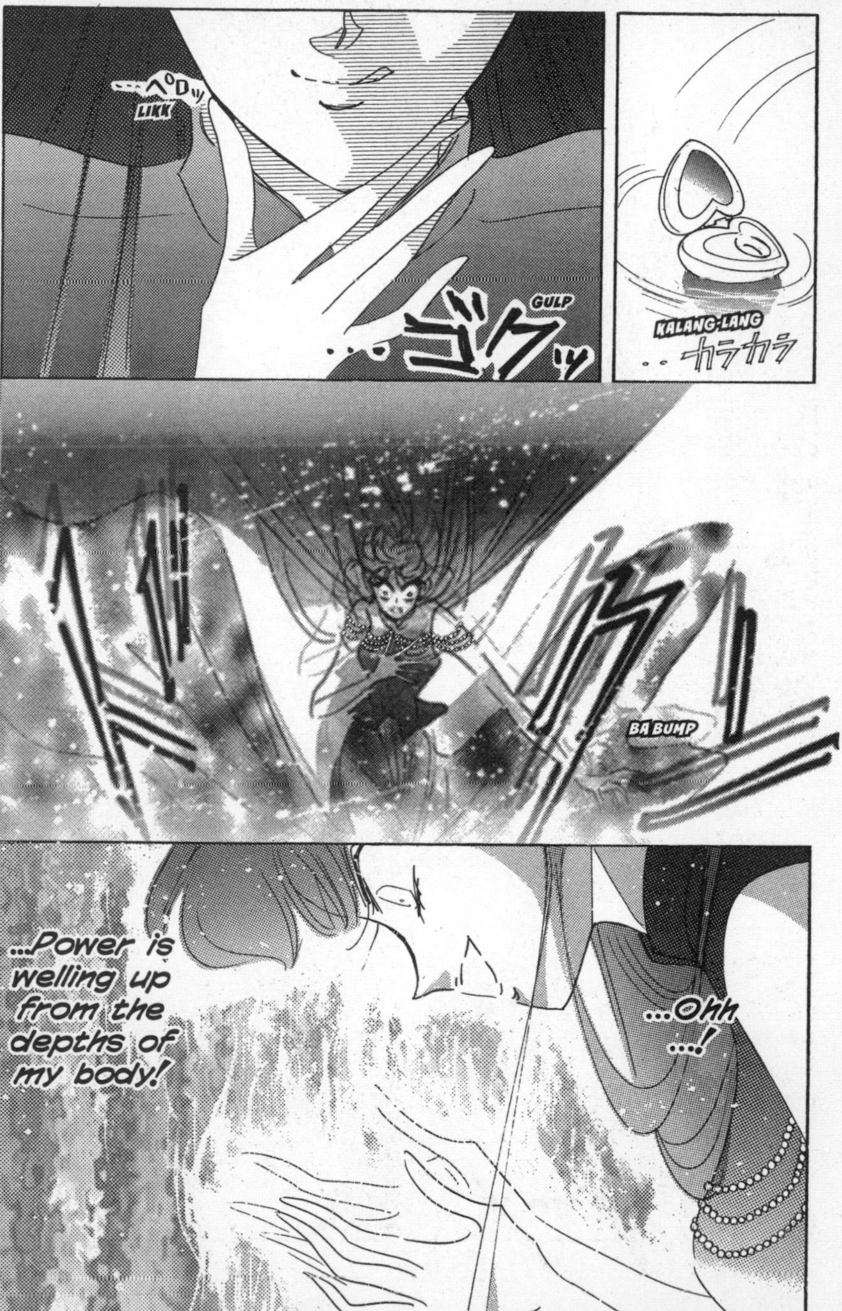
KALANG-LANG
..カラカラ
--ペロッ
LIKK
GULP
...ゴクッ
BA BUMP
...Ohh ...!
...Power is welling up from the depths of my body!

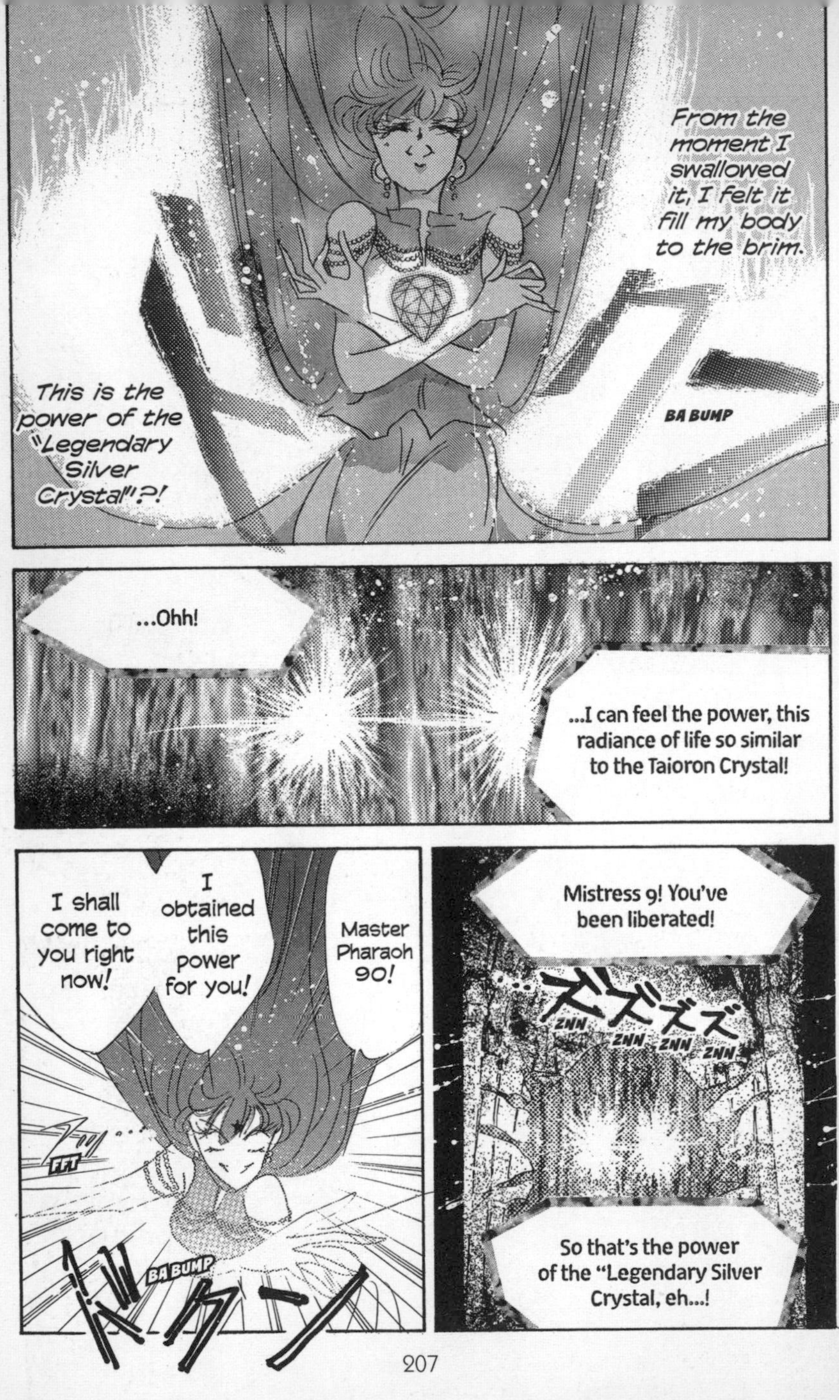
From the moment I swallowed it, I felt it fill my body to the brim.
BA BUMP
This is the power of the "Legendary Silver Crystal"?!
...Ohh!
...I can feel the power, this radiance of life so similar to the Taioron Crystal!
Mistress 9! You've been liberated!
ZNN ZNN ZNN ZNN
So that's the power of the "Legendary Silver Crystal, eh...!
Master Pharaoh 90!
I obtained this power for you!
I shall come to you right now!
FFT
BA BUMP

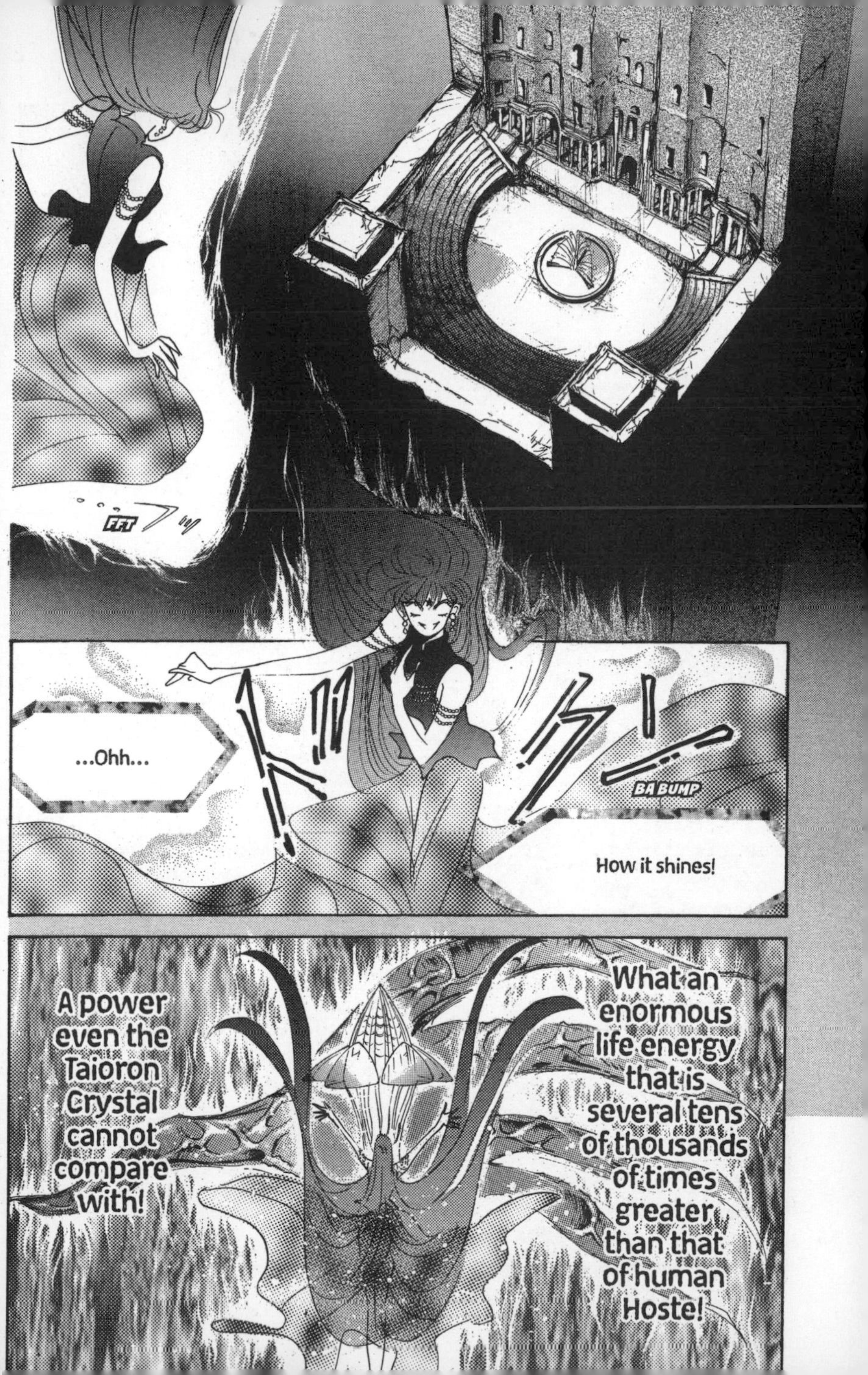
FFT
...Ohh...
BA BUMP
How it shines!
What an enormous life energy that is several tens of thousands of times greater than that of human Hoste!
A power even the Taioron Crystal cannot compare with!

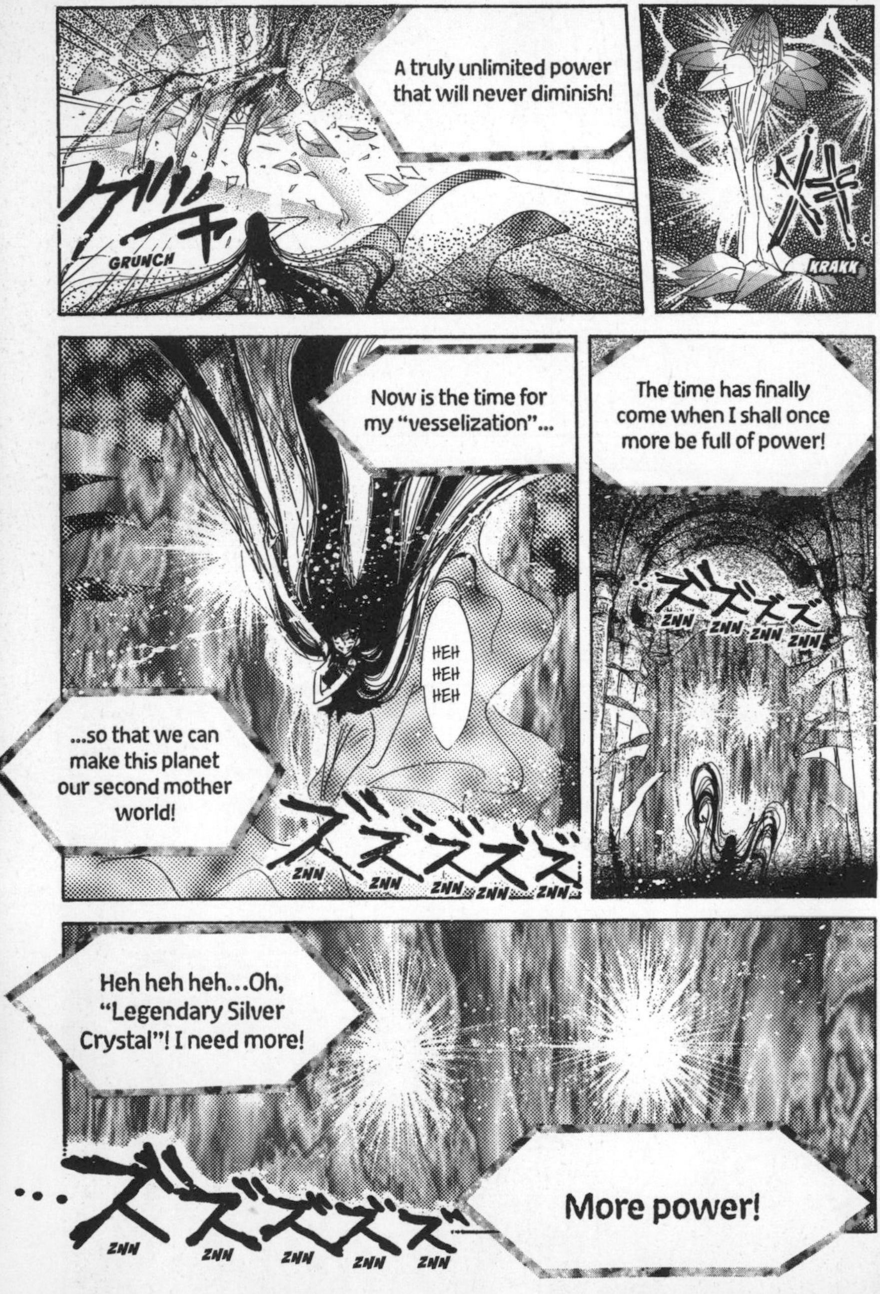
KRAKK
A truly unlimited power that will never diminish!
GRUNCH
The time has finally come when I shall once more be full of power!
ZNN ZNN ZNN ZNN
Now is the time for my "vesselization"...
HEH HEH HEH
...so that we can make this planet our second mother world!
ZNN ZNN ZNN ZNN ZNN
Heh heh heh...Oh, "Legendary Silver Crystal"! I need more!
More power!
ZNN ZNN ZNN ZNN ZNN

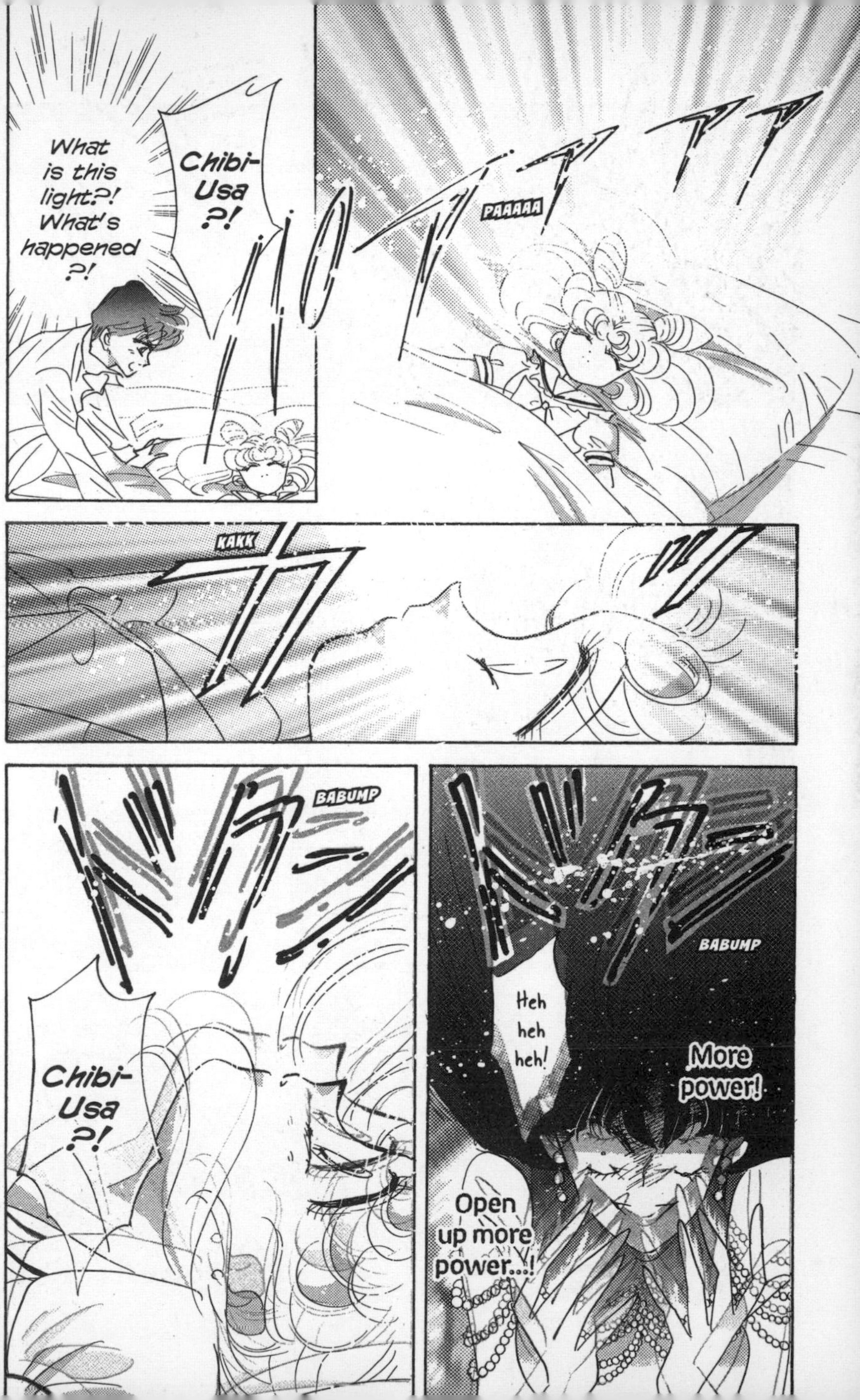
PAAAAA
Chibi-Usa?!
What is this light?! What's happened?!
KAKK
BABUMP
Heh heh heh!
More power!
Open up more power...!
BABUMP
Chibi-Usa?!

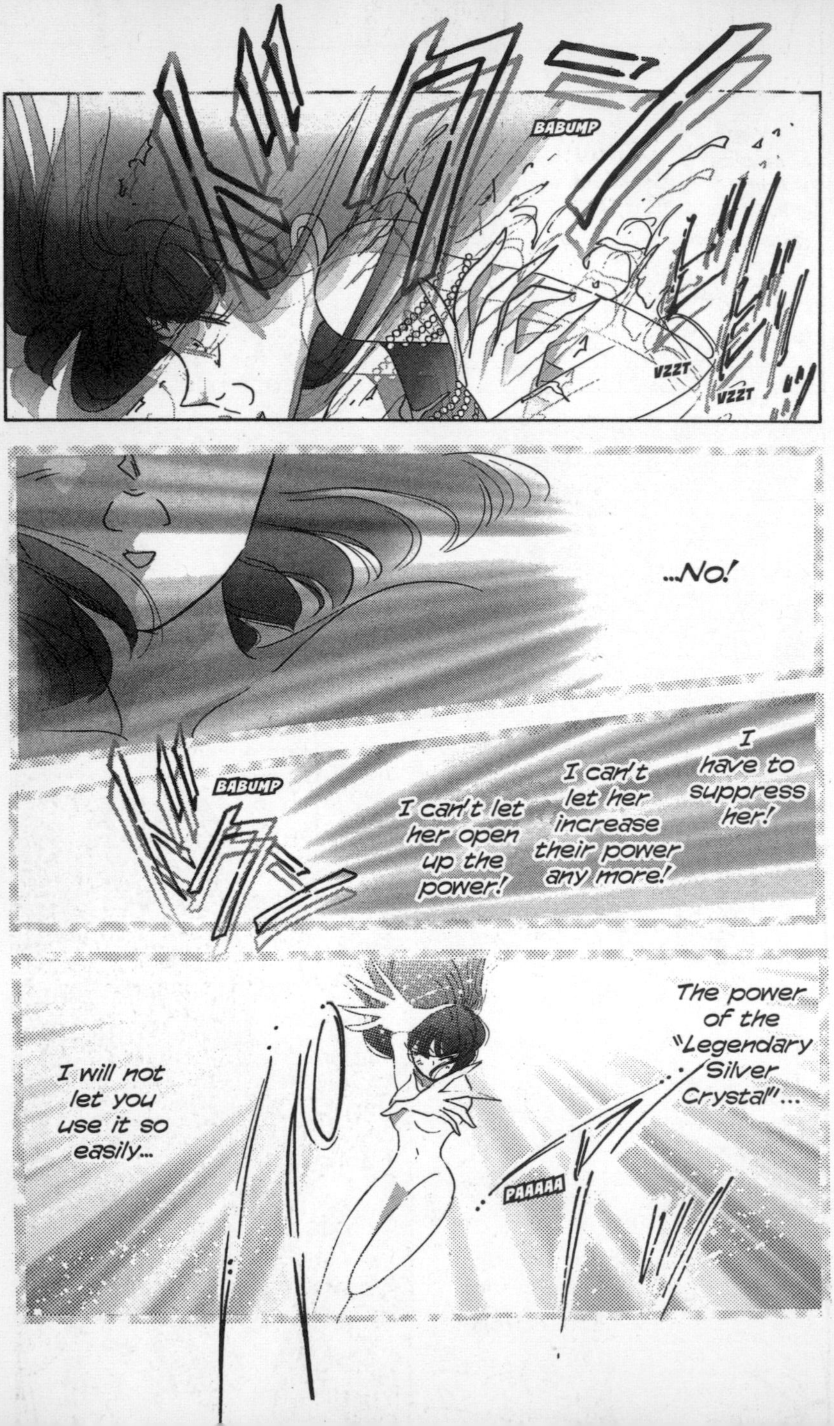
BABUMP
VZZT
VZZT
...No!
BABUMP
I have to suppress her!
I can't let her increase their power any more!
I can't let her open up the power!
The power of the "Legendary Silver Crystal"...
I will not let you use it so easily...
PAAAAA

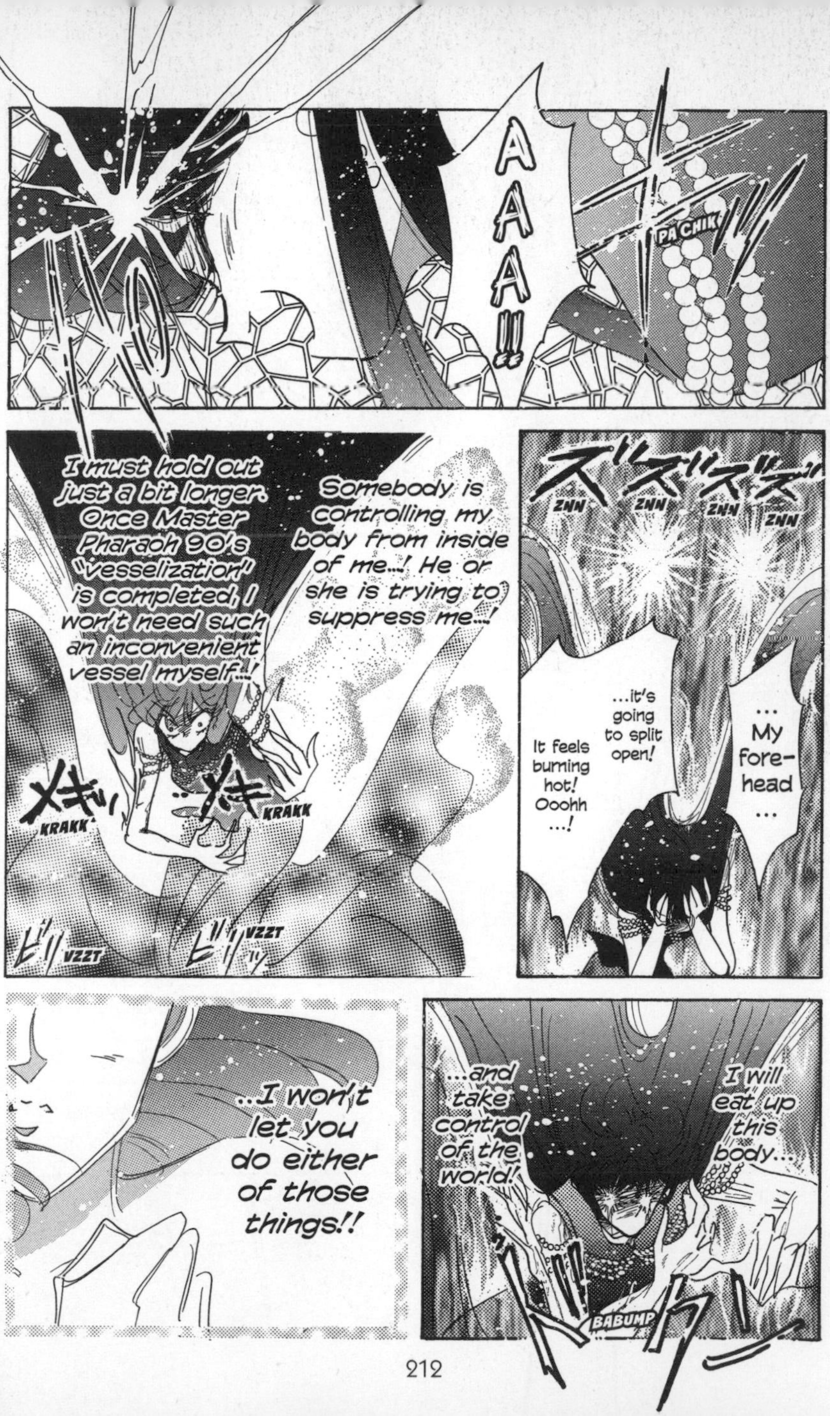
AAAA!!
PA CHIK
ZNN ZNN ZNN ZNN
... My fore-head ...
...it's going to split open!
It feels buming hot! Ooohh ...!
Somebody is controlling my body from inside of me...! He or she is trying to suppress me...!
I must hold out just a bit longer. Once Master Pharaoh 90's "vesselization" is completed, I won't need such an inconvenient vessel myself...!
KRAKK
KRAKK
VZZT
VZZT
I will eat up this body...
...and take control of the world!
BABUMP
...I won't let you do either of those things!!

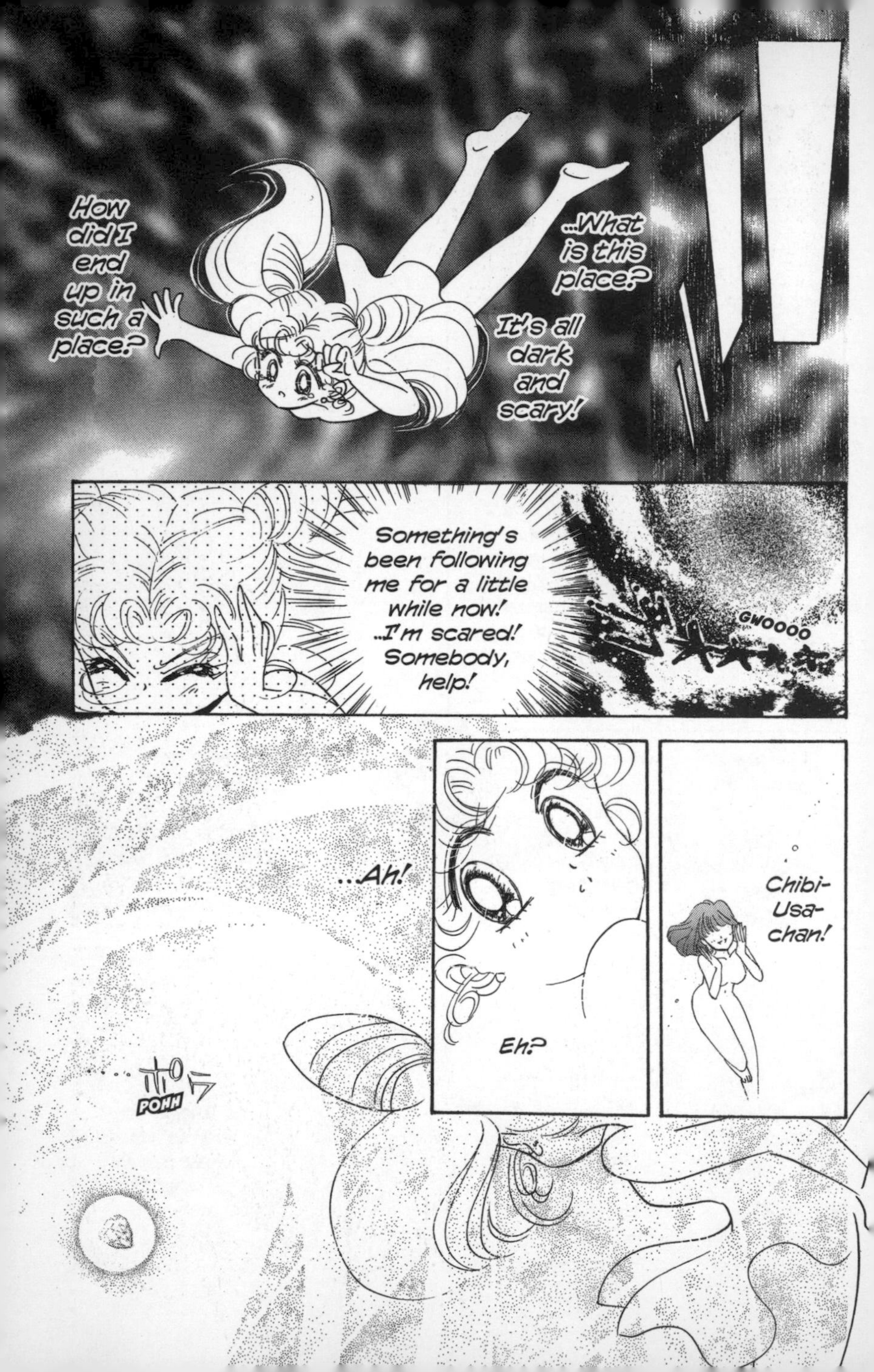

...What is this place?
It's all dark and scary!
How did I end up in such a place?
Something's been following me for a little while now! ..I'm scared! Somebody, help!
GWOOOO
Chibi-Usa-chan!
Eh?
...Ah!
POHN

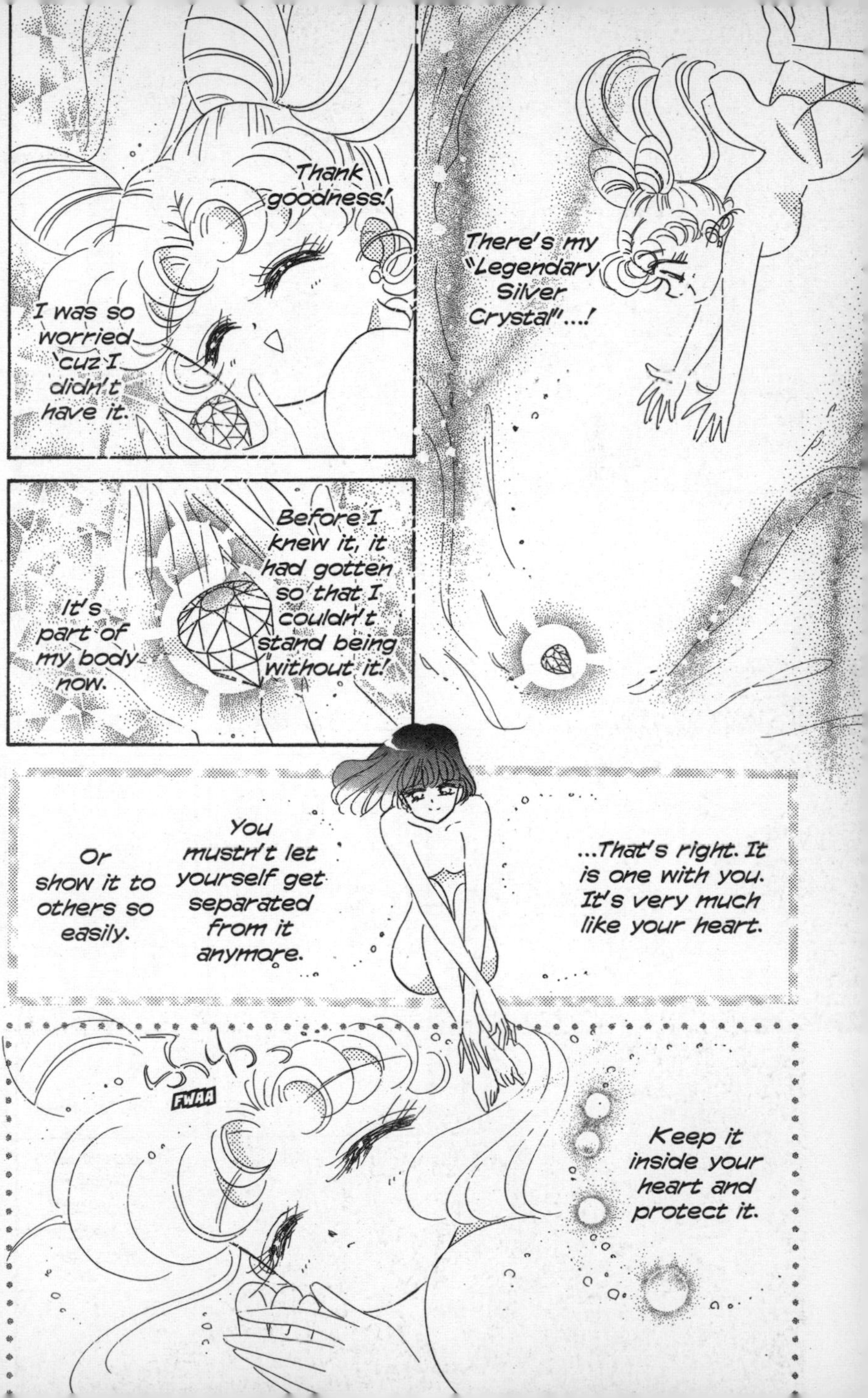

There's my "Legendary Silver Crystal"...!
Thank goodness!
I was so worried 'cuz I didn't have it.
Before I knew it, it had gotten so that I couldn't stand being without it!
It's part of my body now.
...That's right. It is one with you. It's very much like your heart.
You mustn't let yourself get separated from it anymore.
Or show it to others so easily.
Keep it inside your heart and protect it.
FWAA

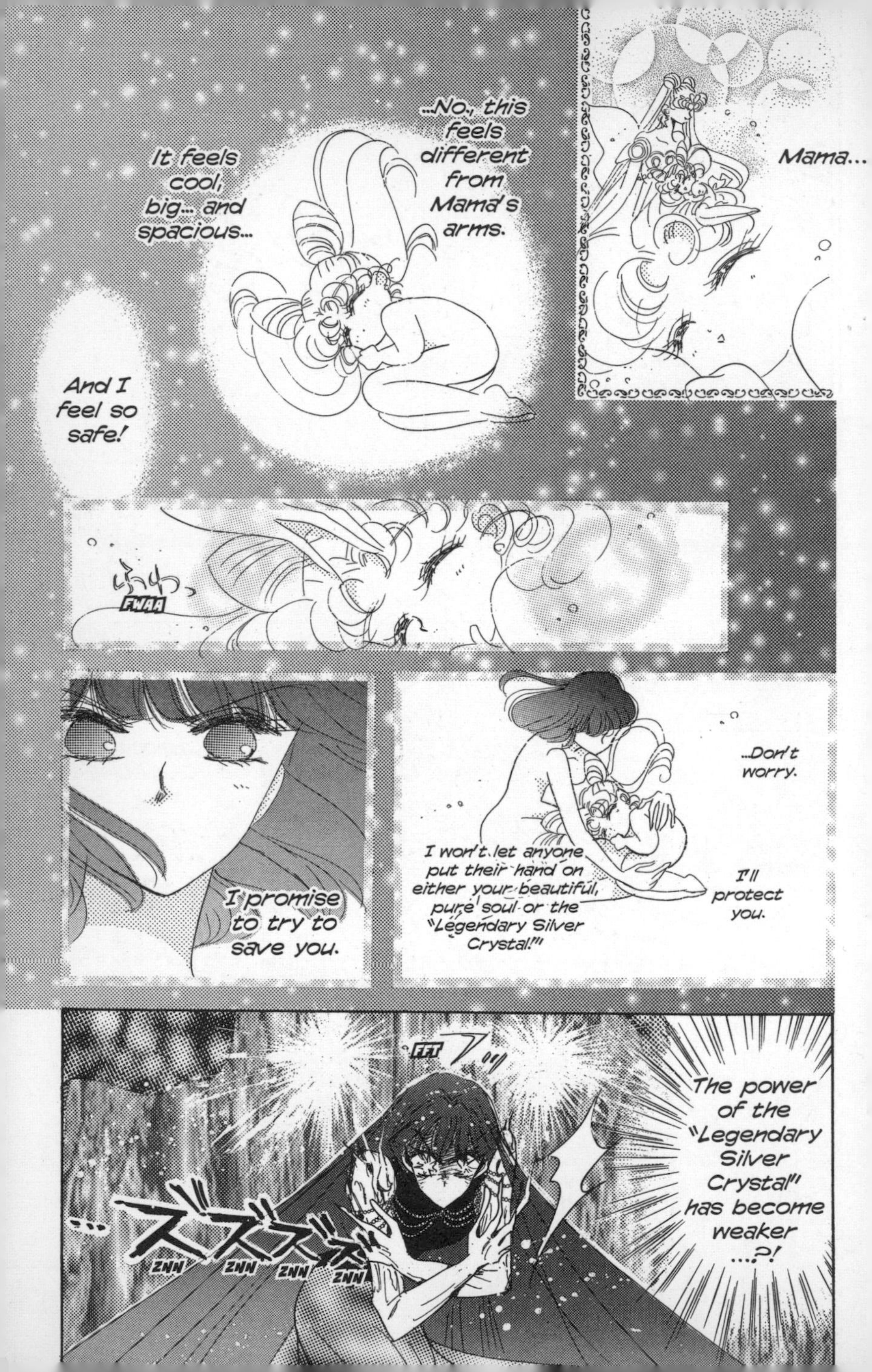
Mama...
...No, this feels different from Mama's arms.
It feels cool, big... and spacious...
And I feel so safe!
ふわっ
FWAA
...Don't worry.
I'll protect you.
I won't let anyone put their hand on either your beautiful, pure soul or the "Legendary Silver Crystal!"
I promise to try to save you.
フッ
FFT
The power of the "Legendary Silver Crystal" has become weaker ...?!
ズズズズ
ZNN ZNN ZNN ZNN

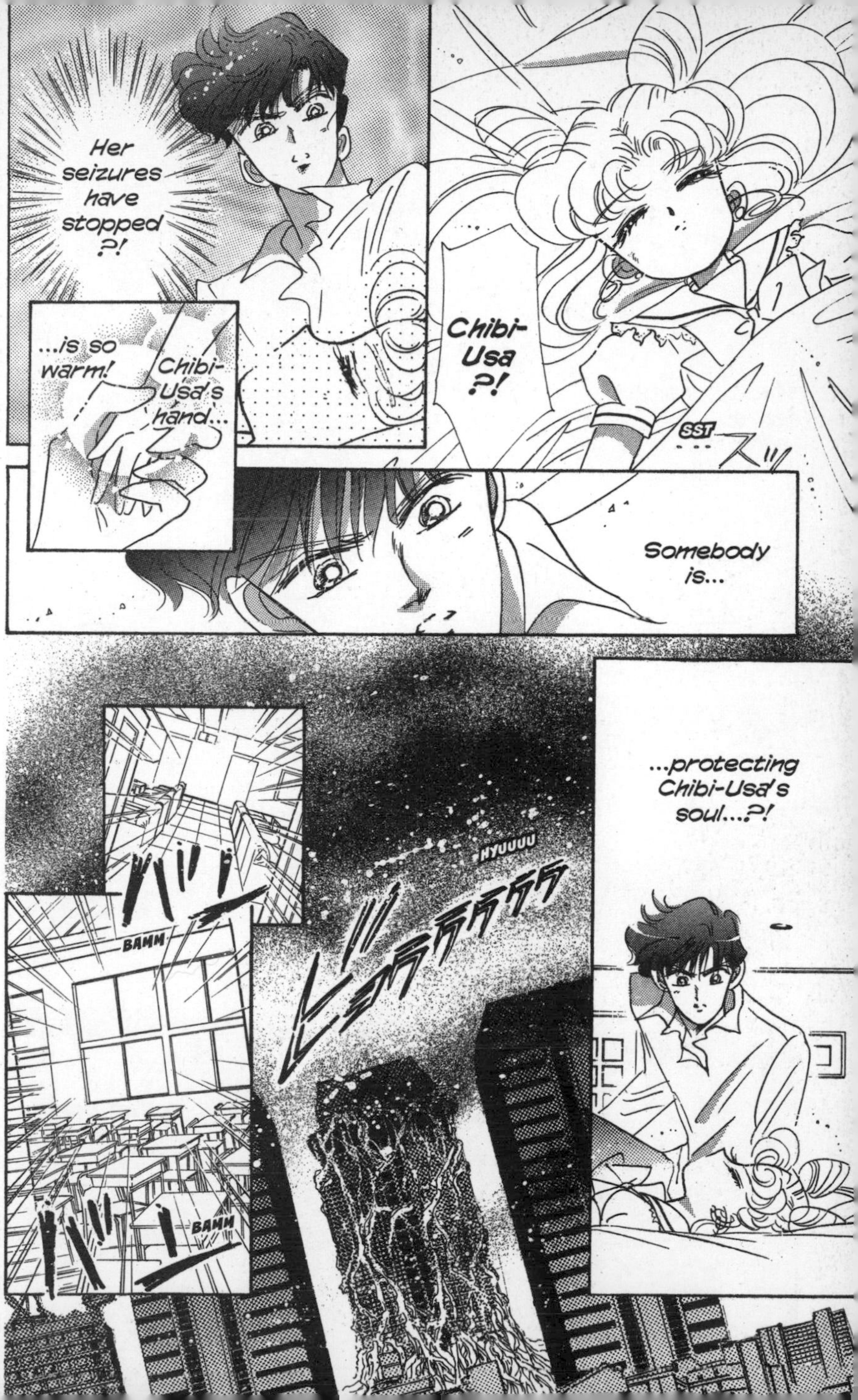
Chibi-Usa ?!
SST
Her seizures have stopped ?!
Chibi-Usa's hand...
...is so warm!
Somebody is...
...protecting Chibi-Usa's soul...?!
HYUUUU
BAMM
BAMM

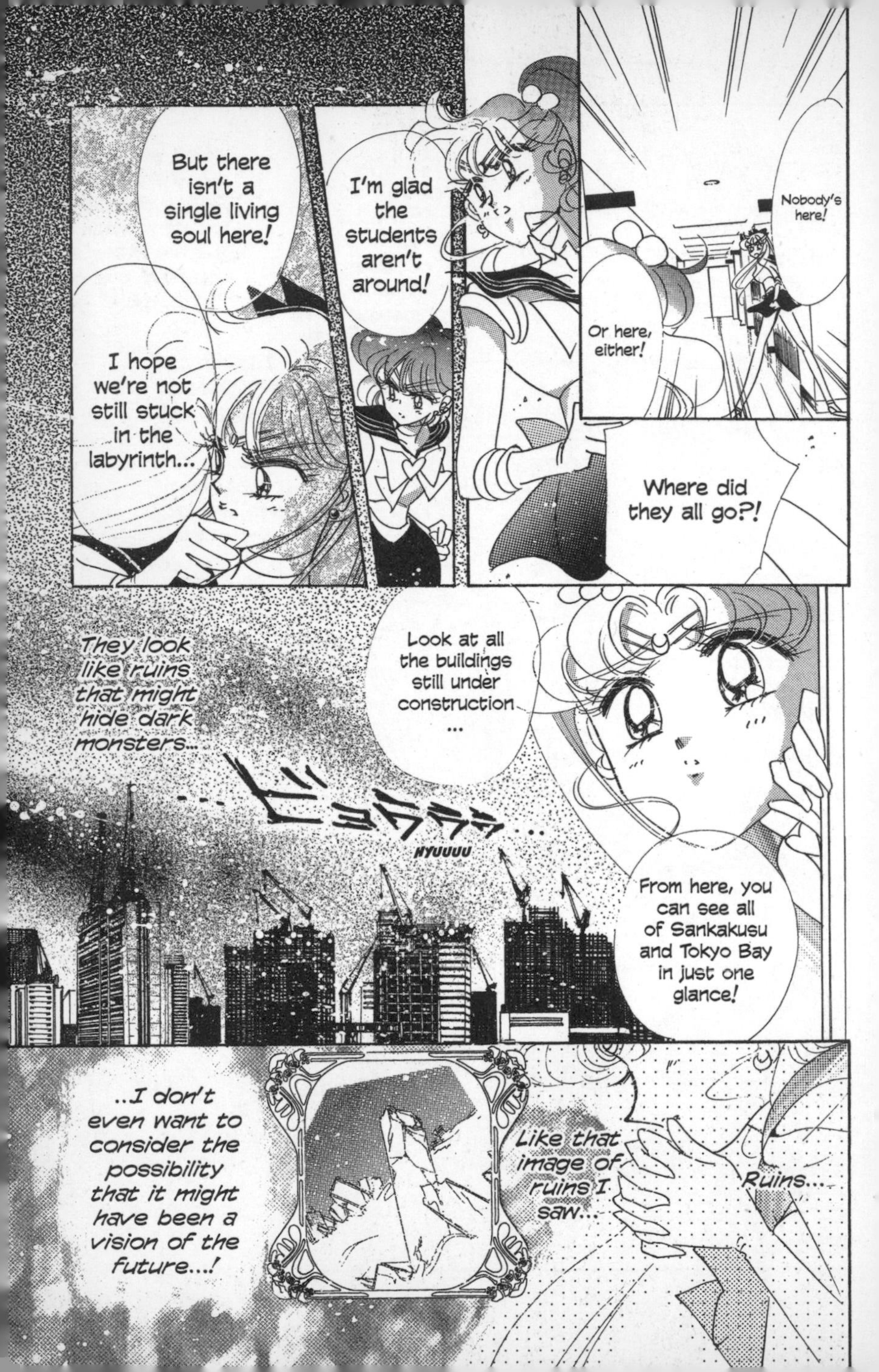
Nobody's here!
Or here, either!
Where did they all go?!
I'm glad the students aren't around!
But there isn't a single living soul here!
I hope we're not still stuck in the labyrinth...
Look at all the buildings still under construction ...
From here, you can see all of Sankakusu and Tokyo Bay in just one glance!
They look like ruins that might hide dark monsters...
HYUUUU
Ruins...
Like that image of ruins I saw...
..I don't even want to consider the possibility that it might have been a vision of the future...!

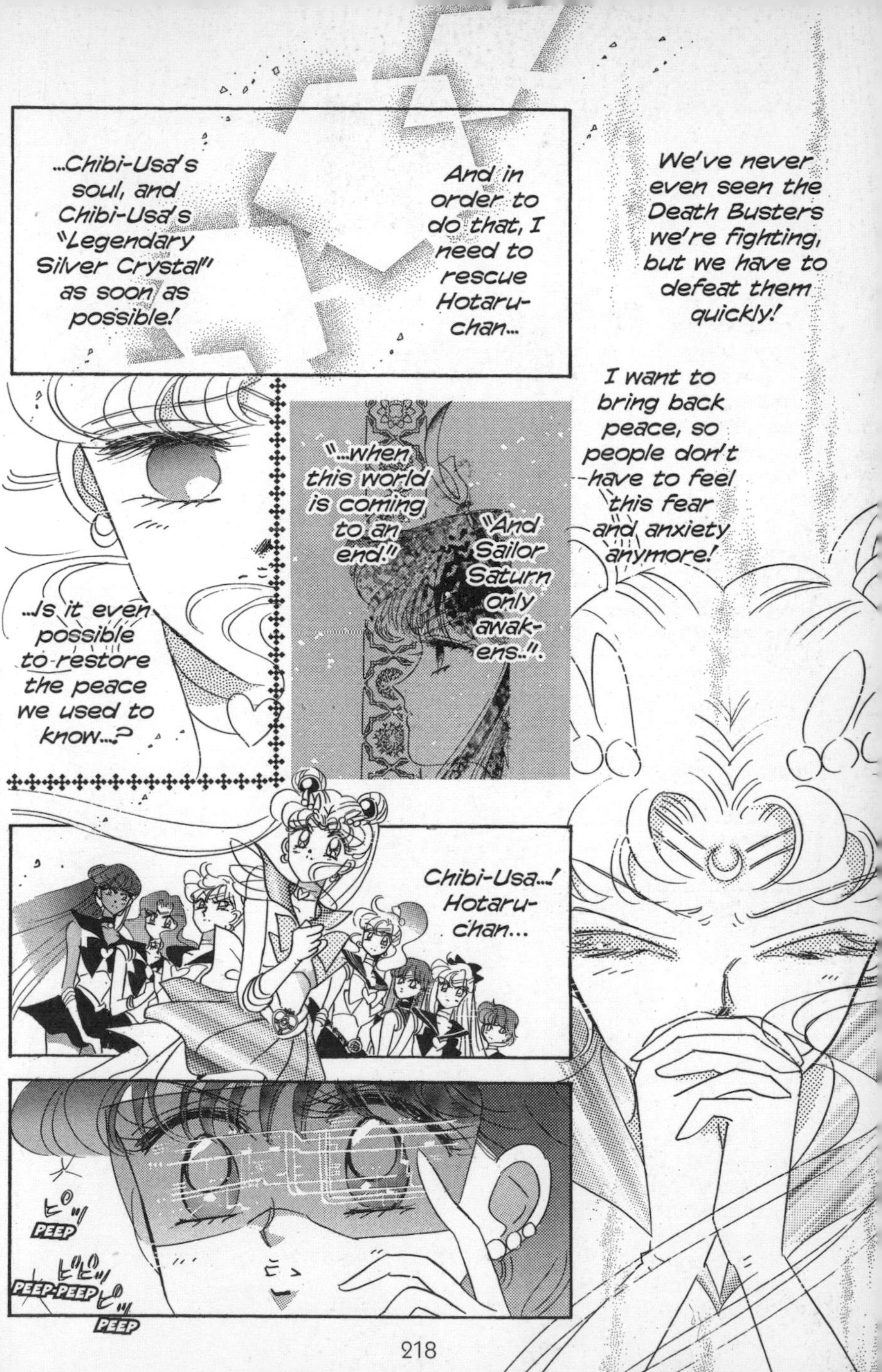
We've never even seen the Death Busters we're fighting, but we have to defeat them quickly!
And in order to do that, I need to rescue Hotaru-chan...
...Chibi-Usa's soul, and Chibi-Usa's "Legendary Silver Crystal" as soon as possible!
I want to bring back peace, so people don't have to feel this fear and anxiety anymore!
"And Sailor Saturn only awakens.."
"...when this world is coming to an end."
...Is it even possible to restore the peace we used to know...?
Chibi-Usa...! Hotaru-chan...
ピッ PEEP
ピピッ PEEP-PEEP
ピッ PEEP

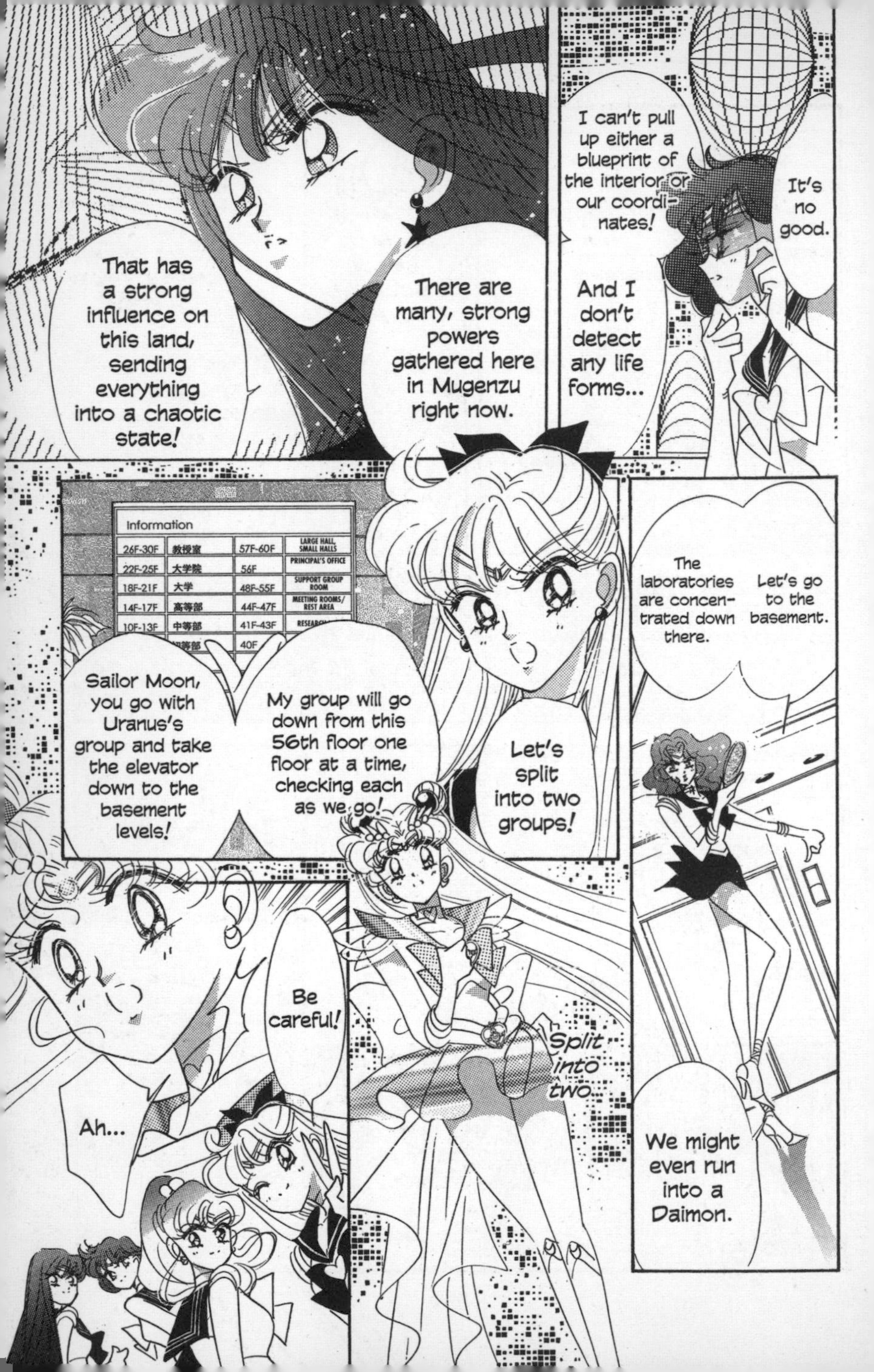
It's no good.
I can't pull up either a blueprint of the interior or our coordinates!
And I don't detect any life forms...
There are many, strong powers gathered here in Mugenzu right now.
That has a strong influence on this land, sending everything into a chaotic state!
Let's go to the basement.
The laboratories are concentrated down there.
We might even run into a Daimon.
Information
26F-30F 教授室 57F-60F LARGE HALL, SMALL HALLS
22F-25F 大学院 56F PRINCIPAL'S OFFICE
18F-21F 大学 48F-55F SUPPORT GROUP ROOM
14F-17F 高等部 44F-47F MEETING ROOMS/REST AREA
10F-13F 中等部 41F-43F
40F
Let's split into two groups!
My group will go down from this 56th floor one floor at a time, checking each as we go!
Sailor Moon, you go with Uranus's group and take the elevator down to the basement levels!
Split into two
Be careful!
Ah...

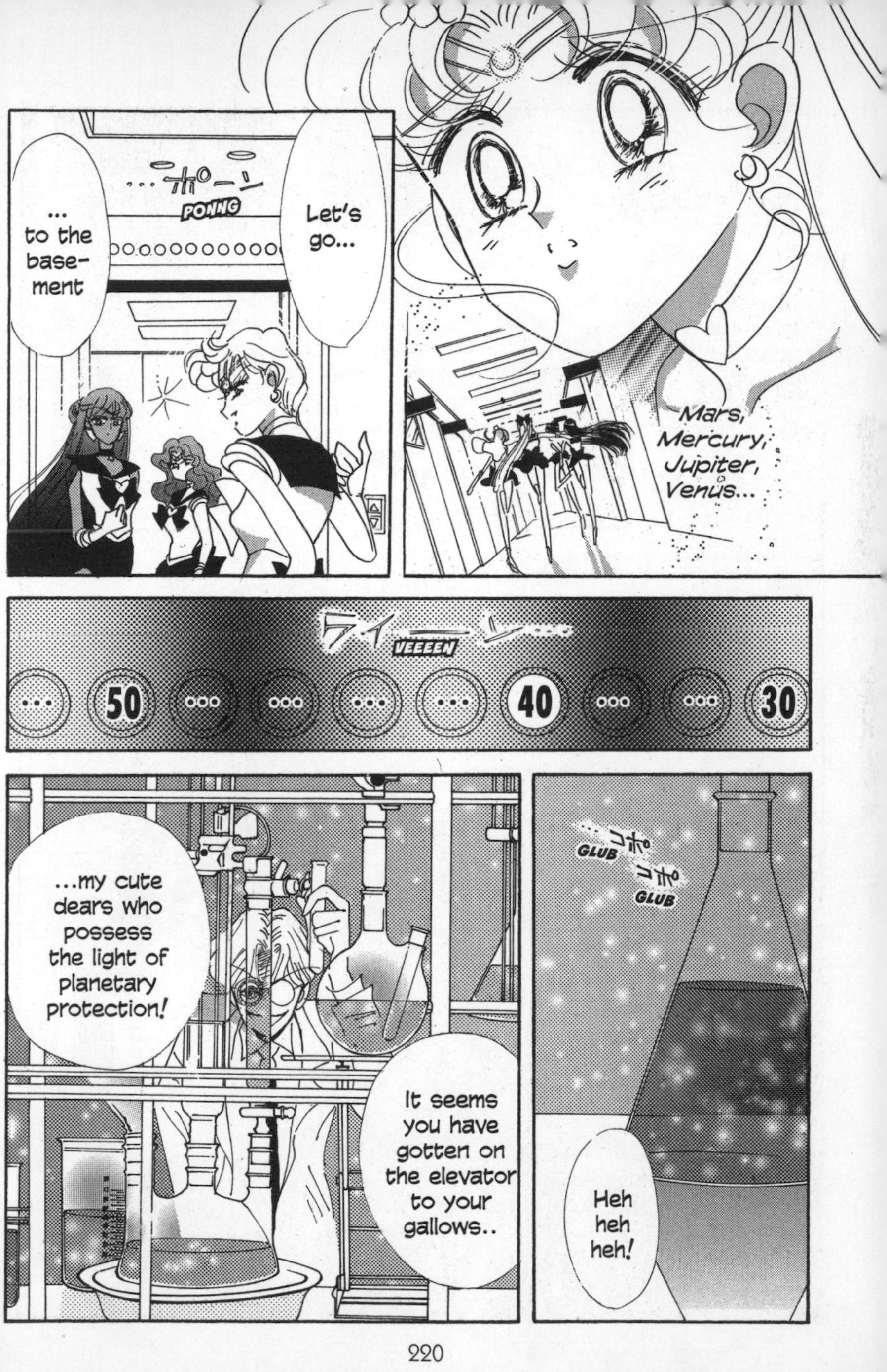
Mars, Mercury, Jupiter, Venus...
...ポーン
PONNG
Let's go...
... to the basement
ライーン...
VEEEEN
50
40
30
コポ
GLUB
コポ
GLUB
Heh heh heh!
It seems you have gotten on the elevator to your gallows..
...my cute dears who possess the light of planetary protection!

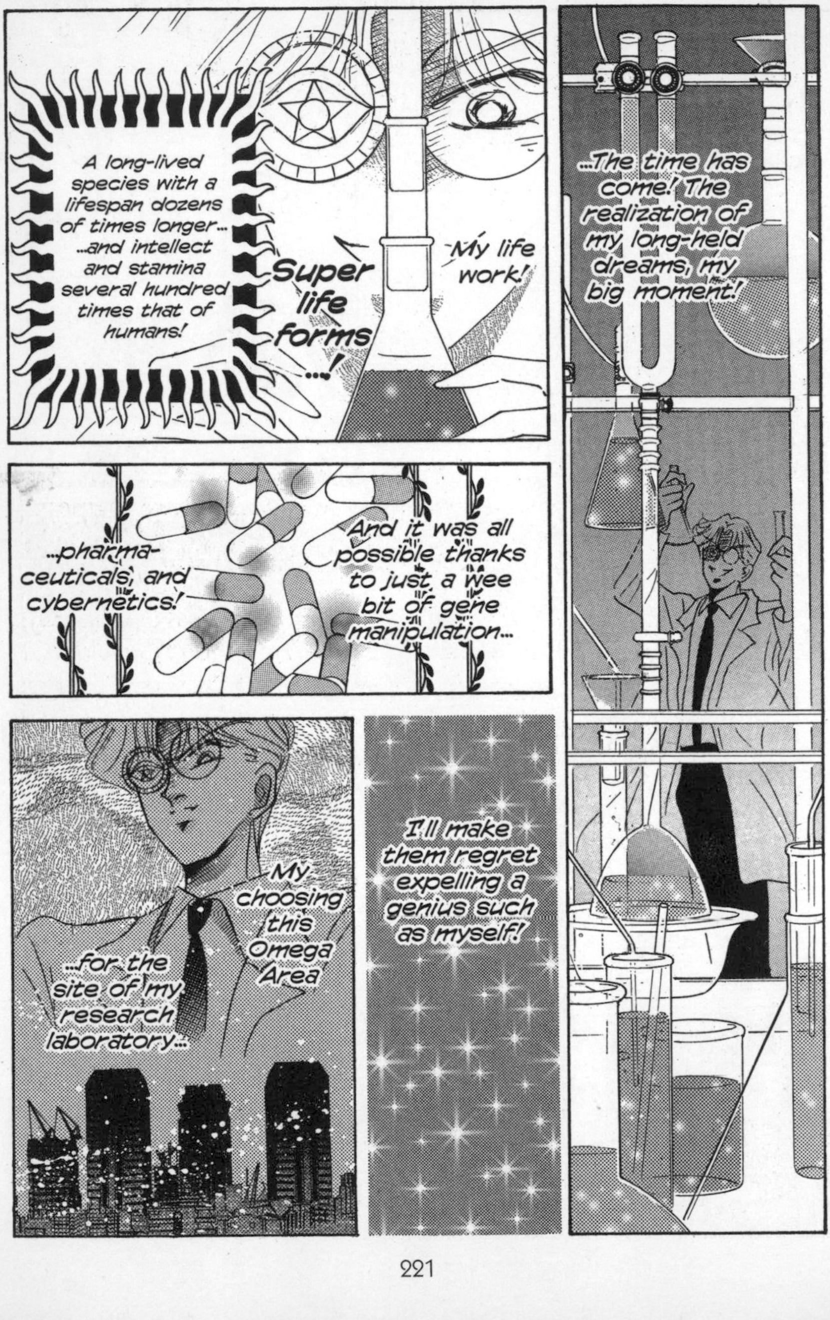
...The time has come! The realization of my long-held dreams, my big moment!
My life work!
Super life forms...!
A long-lived species with a lifespan dozens of times longer... ...and intellect and stamina several hundred times that of humans!
And it was all possible thanks to just a wee bit of gene manipulation...
...pharma-ceuticals, and cybernetics!
I'll make them regret expelling a genius such as myself!
My choosing this Omega Area
...for the site of my research laboratory...

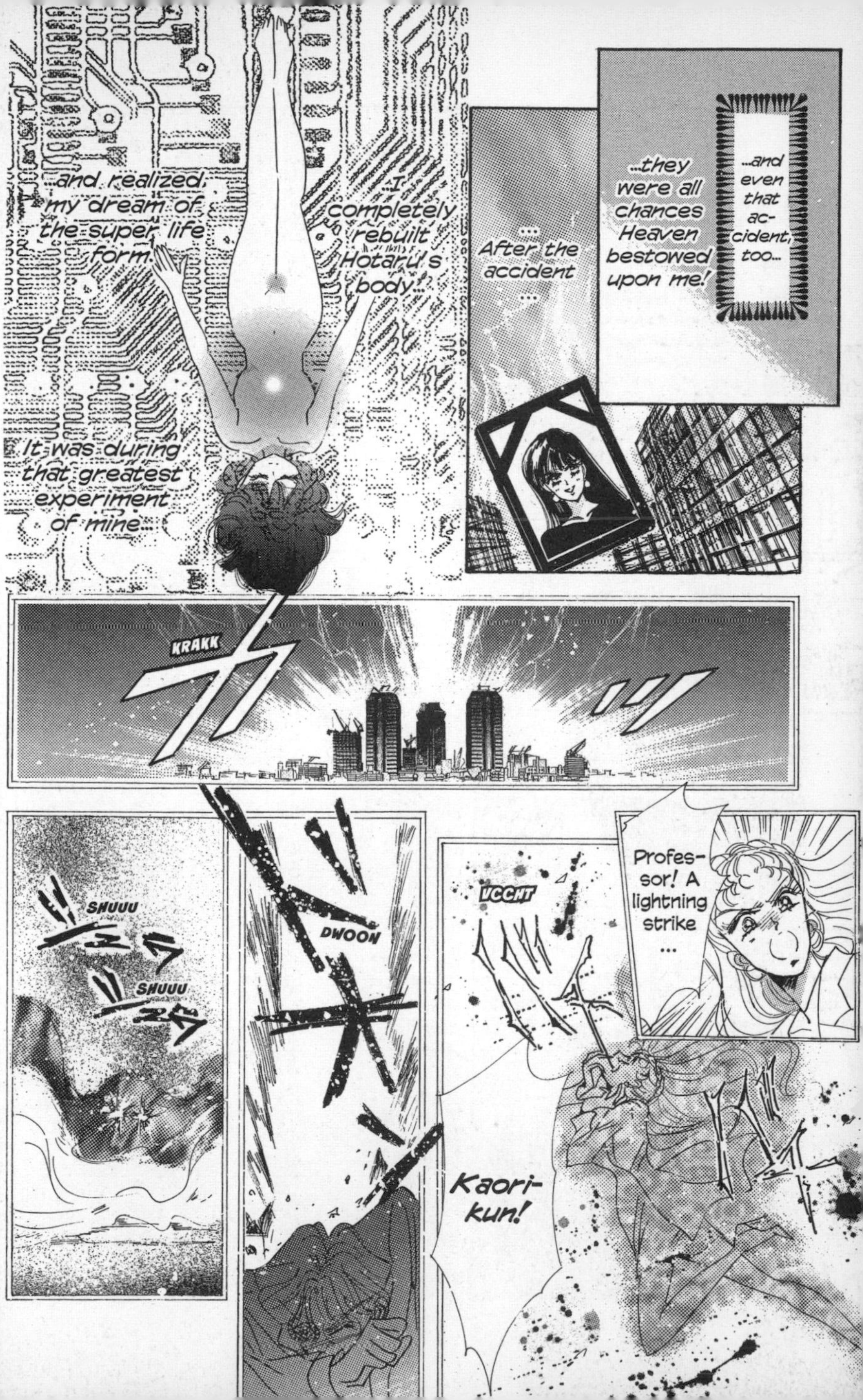

...and even that accident, too...
...they were all chances Heaven bestowed upon me!
... After the accident ...
...I completely rebuilt Hotaru's body...
...and realized my dream of the super life form.
It was during that greatest experiment of mine...
KRAKK
Profes-sor! A lightning strike ...
VCCHT
Kaori-kun!
DWOON
SHUUU
SHUUU

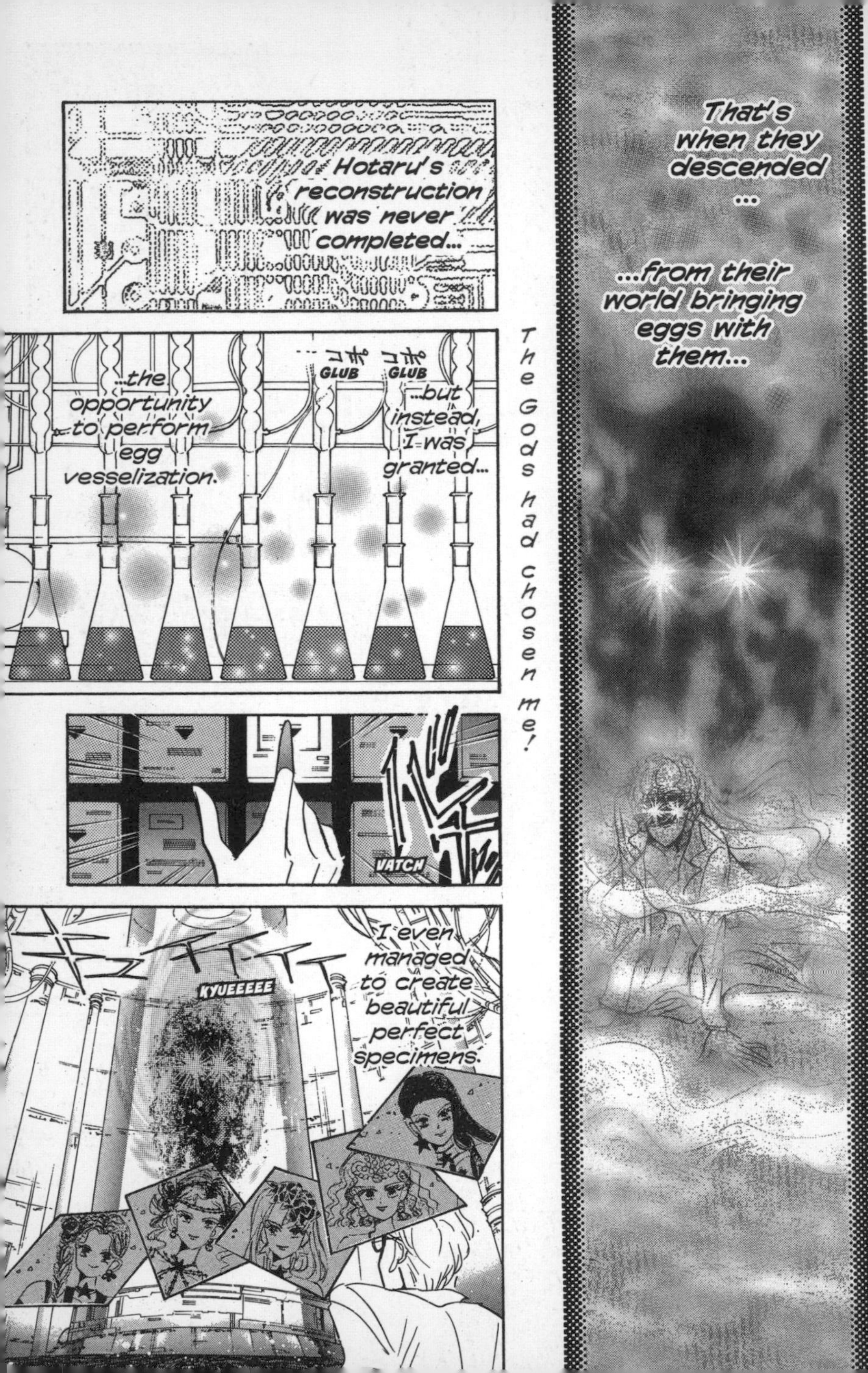
That's when they descended ...
...from their world bringing eggs with them...
Hotaru's reconstruction was never completed...
GLUB
GLUB
...but instead, I was granted...
...the opportunity to perform egg vesselization.
The Gods had chosen me!
VATCH
KYUEEEE
I even managed to create beautiful perfect specimens.

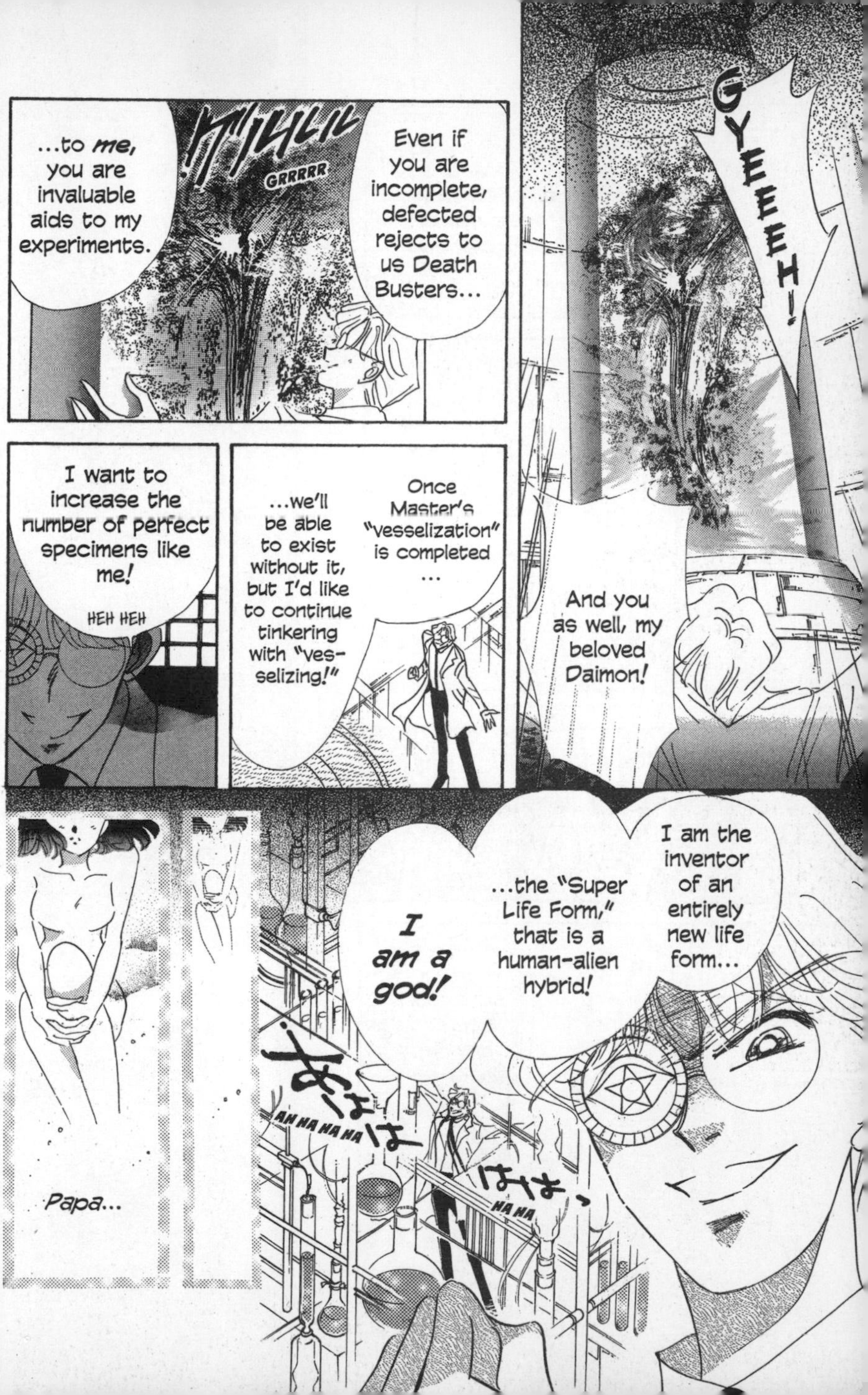
GYEEEEH!
And you as well, my beloved Daimon!
GRRRRR
Even if you are incomplete, defected rejects to us Death Busters...
...to *me*, you are invaluable aids to my experiments.
Once Master's "vesselization" is completed ...
...we'll be able to exist without it, but I'd like to continue tinkering with "vesselizing!"
I want to increase the number of perfect specimens like me!
HEH HEH
I am the inventor of an entirely new life form...
...the "Super Life Form," that is a human-alien hybrid!
I am a god!
AH HA HA HA
HA HA
Papa...

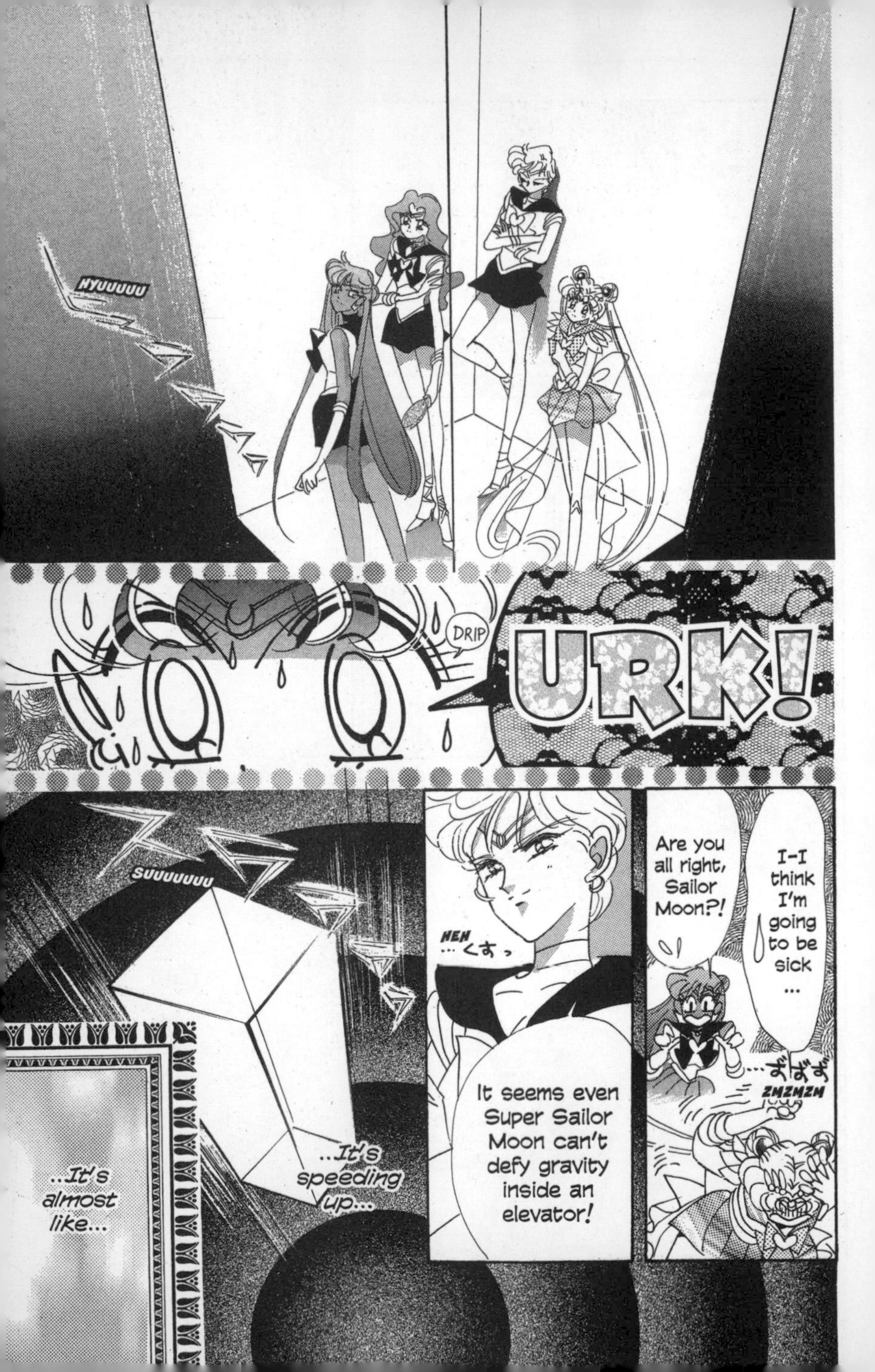
HYUUUUU
URK!
DRIP
I-I think I'm going to be sick...
Are you all right, Sailor Moon?!
ZMZMZM ずずず...
HEH... くすっ
It seems even Super Sailor Moon can't defy gravity inside an elevator!
SUUUUUUU
...It's speeding up...
...It's almost like...

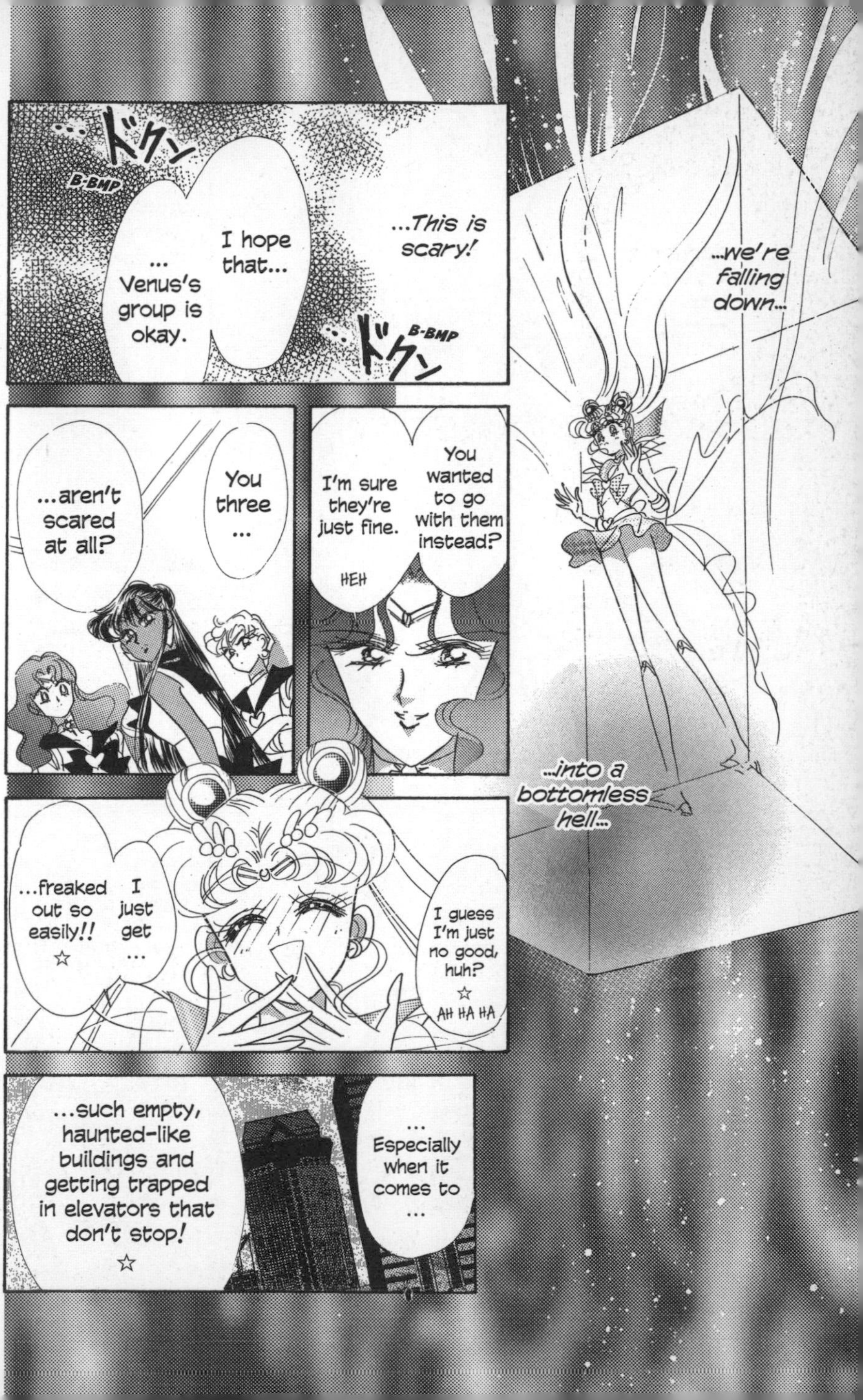
...we're falling down...
...into a bottomless hell...
ドクン
B-BMP
...This is scary!
I hope that...
... Venus's group is okay.
ドクン
B-BMP
You wanted to go with them instead?
I'm sure they're just fine.
HEH
You three ...
...aren't scared at all?
I guess I'm just no good, huh? ☆
AH HA HA
I just get ...
...freaked out so easily!! ☆
... Especially when it comes to ...
...such empty, haunted-like buildings and getting trapped in elevators that don't stop! ☆

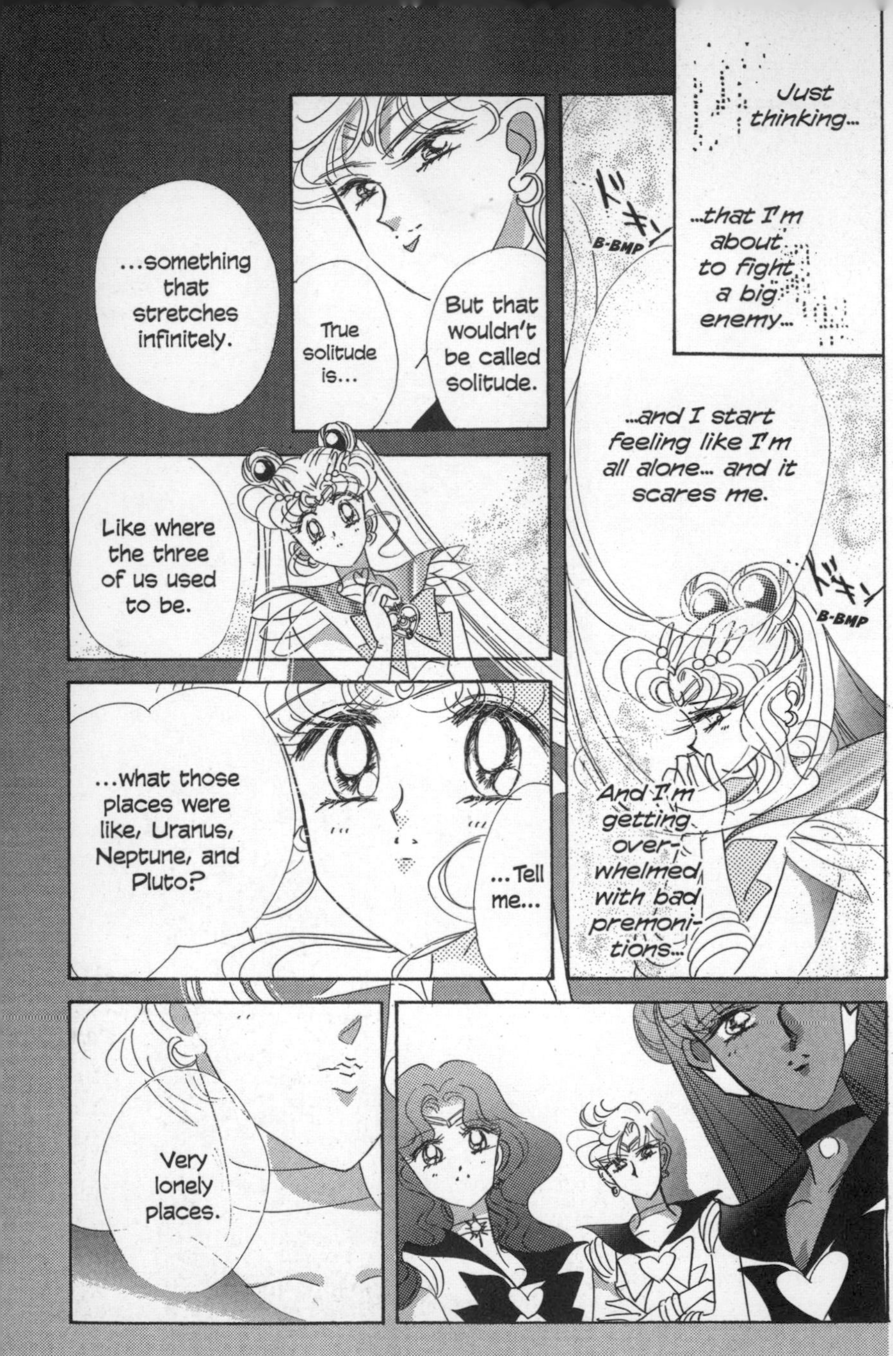
Just thinking...
...that I'm about to fight a big enemy...
B-BMP
...and I start feeling like I'm all alone... and it scares me.
B-BMP
And I'm getting over-whelmed with bad premoni-tions...
But that wouldn't be called solitude.
True solitude is...
...something that stretches infinitely.
Like where the three of us used to be.
...Tell me...
...what those places were like, Uranus, Neptune, and Pluto?
Very lonely places.

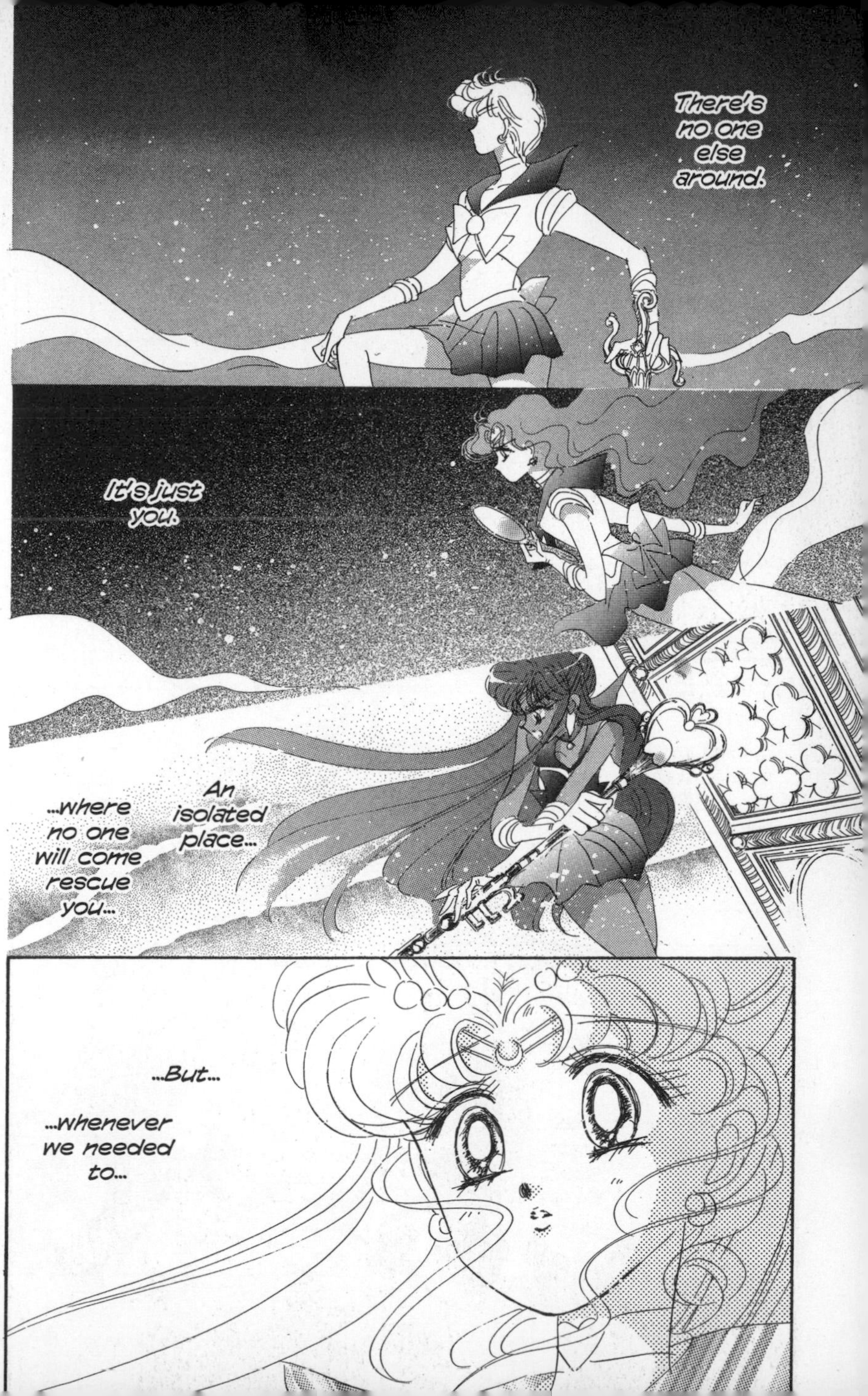
There's no one else around.
It's just you.
An isolated place...
...where no one will come rescue you...
...But...
...whenever we needed to...

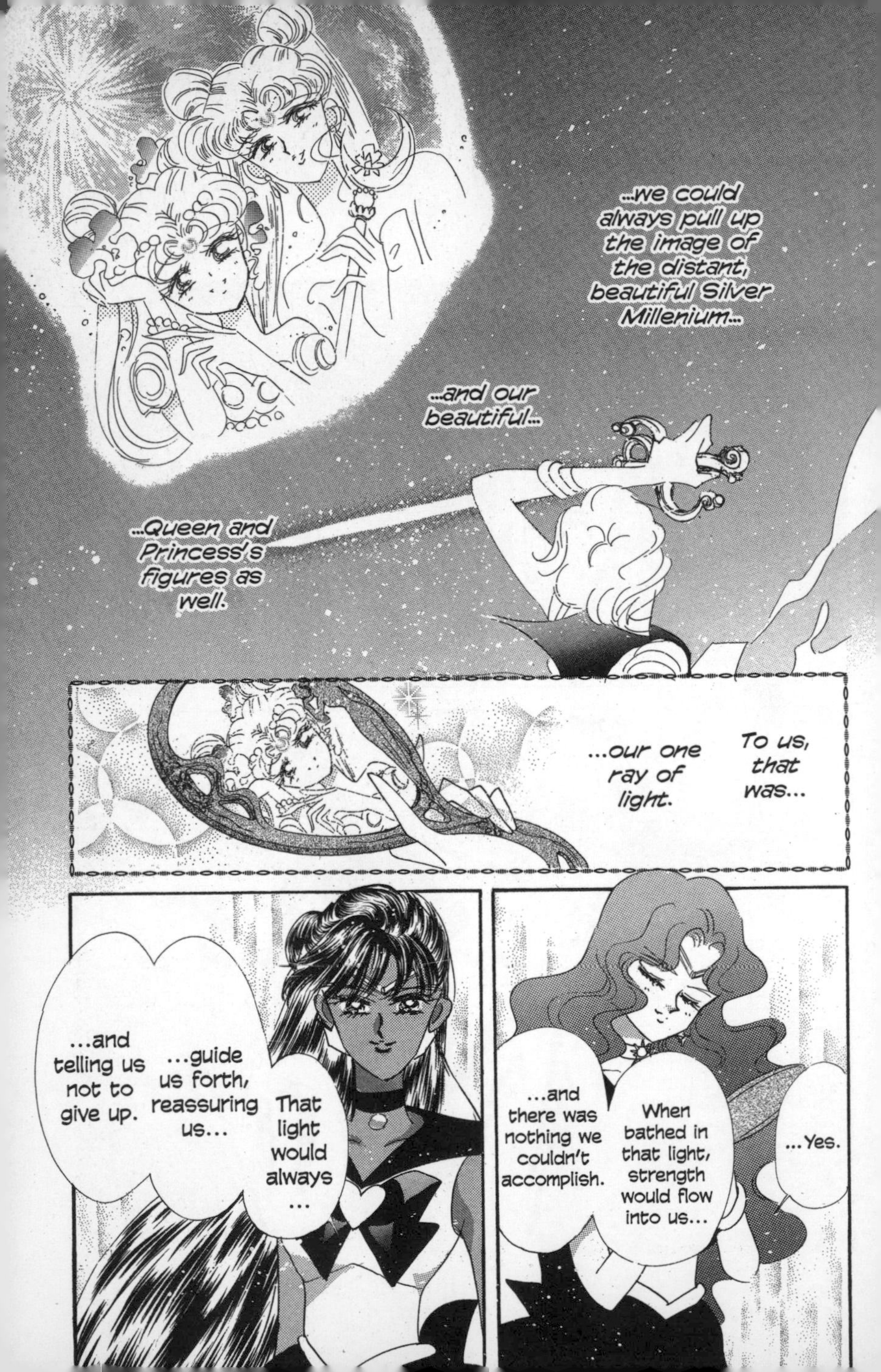
...we could always pull up the image of the distant, beautiful Silver Millenium...
...and our beautiful...
...Queen and Princess's figures as well.
To us, that was...
...our one ray of light.
...Yes.
When bathed in that light, strength would flow into us...
...and there was nothing we couldn't accomplish.
That light would always ...
...guide us forth, reassuring us...
...and telling us not to give up.

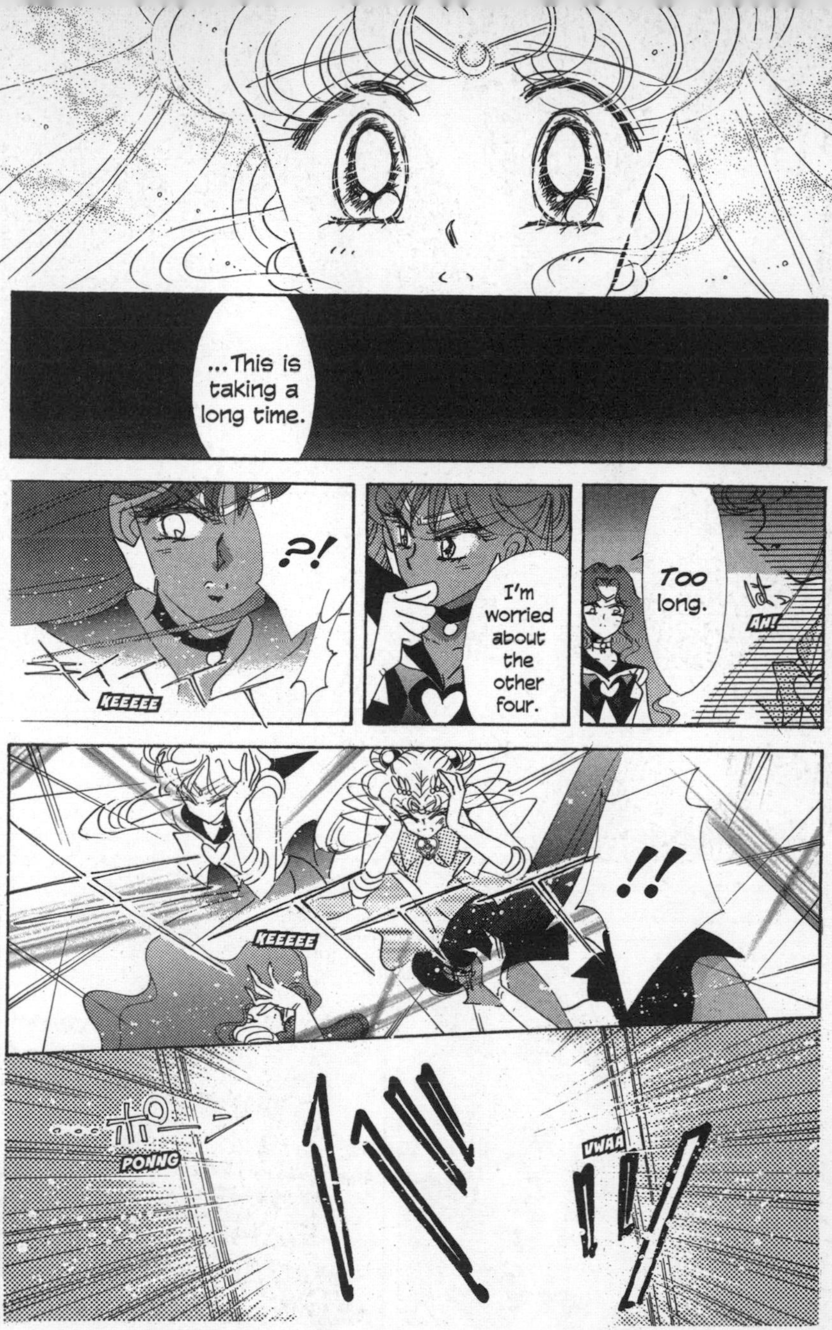

...This is taking a long time.
Too long.
はっ
AH!
I'm worried about the other four.
?!
KEEEEE
!!
KEEEEE
VWAA
PONNG

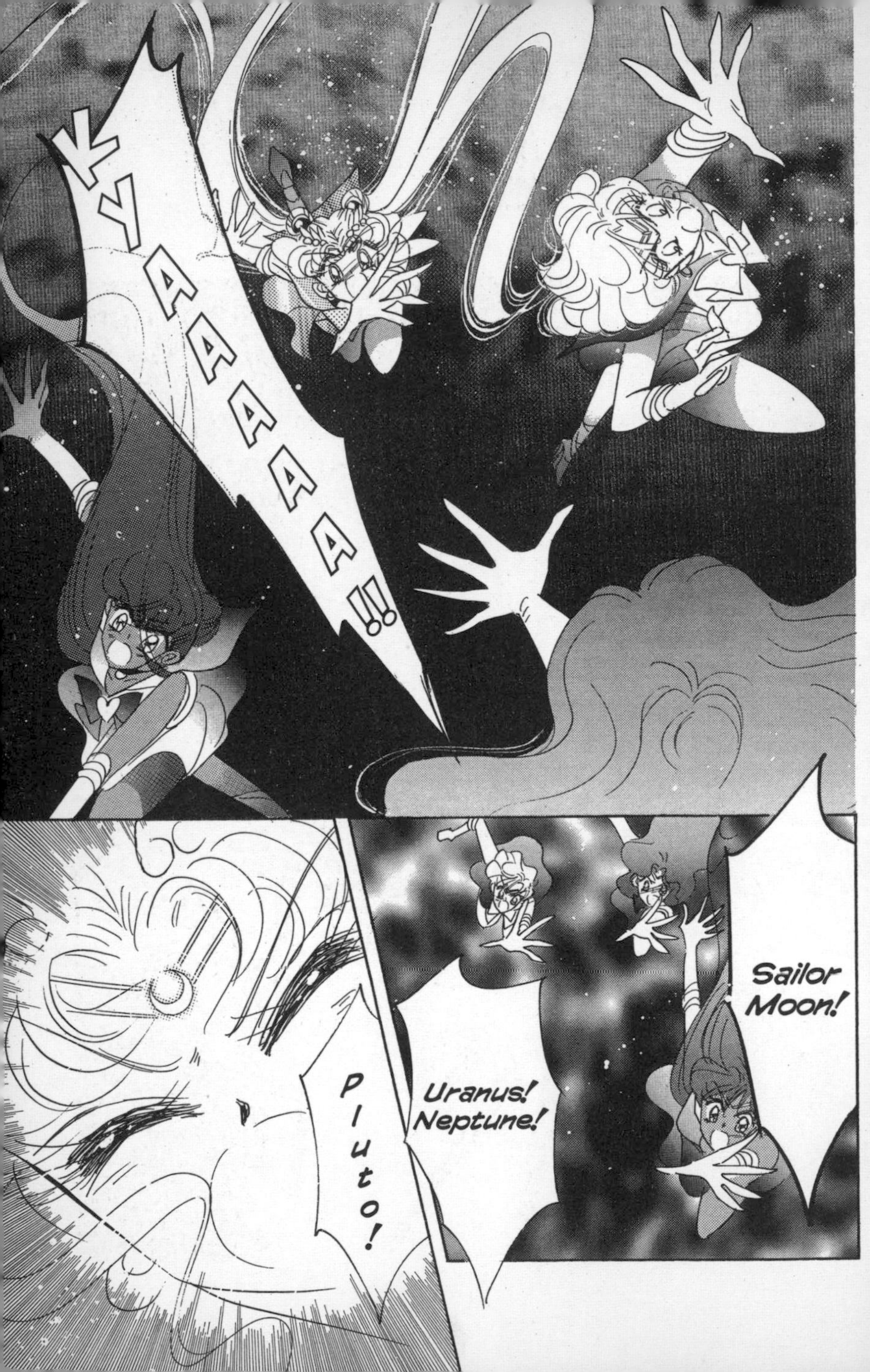
KYAAAAA!!
Sailor Moon!
Uranus! Neptune!
Pluto!

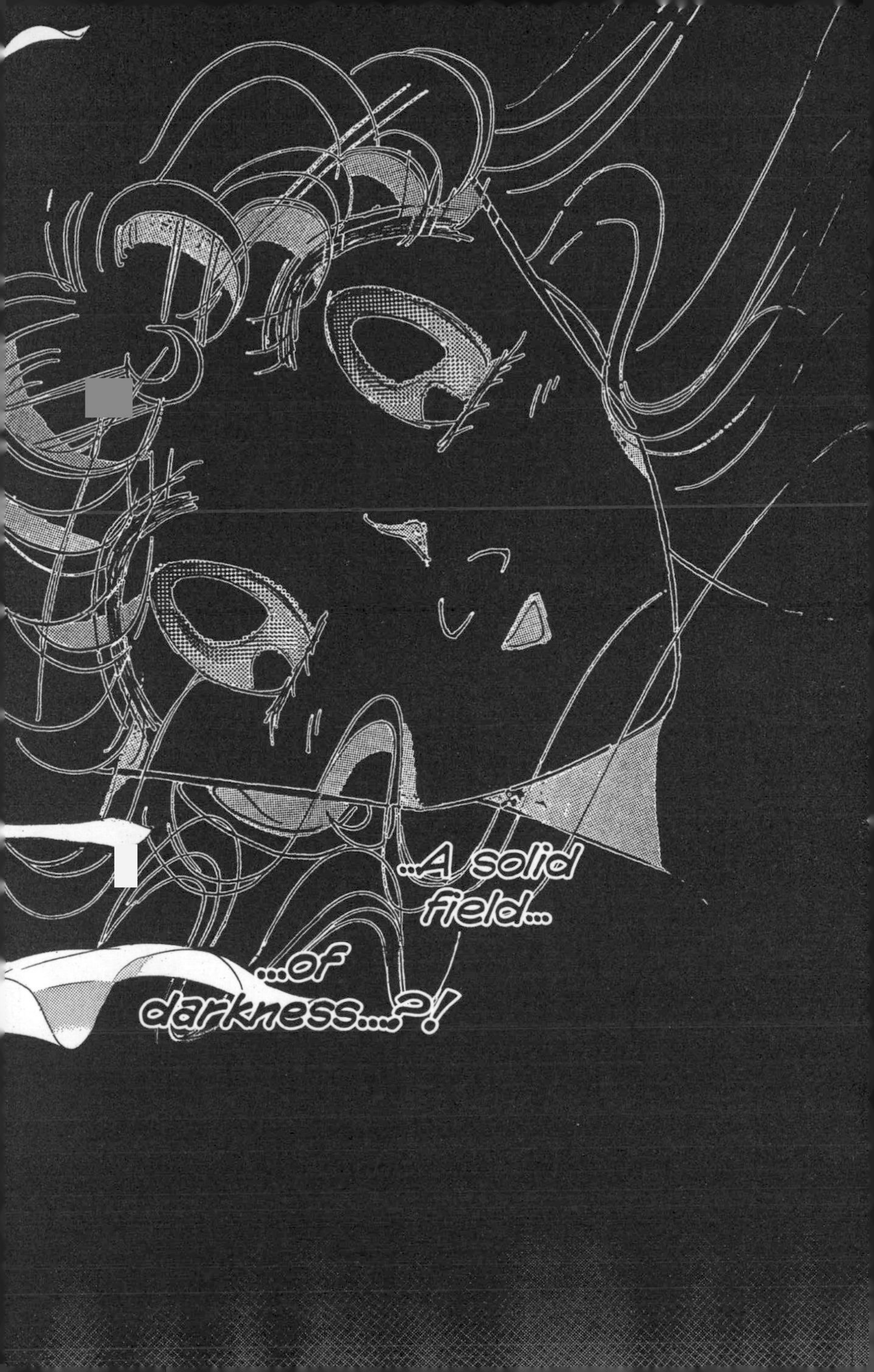
...A solid field...
...of darkness...?!

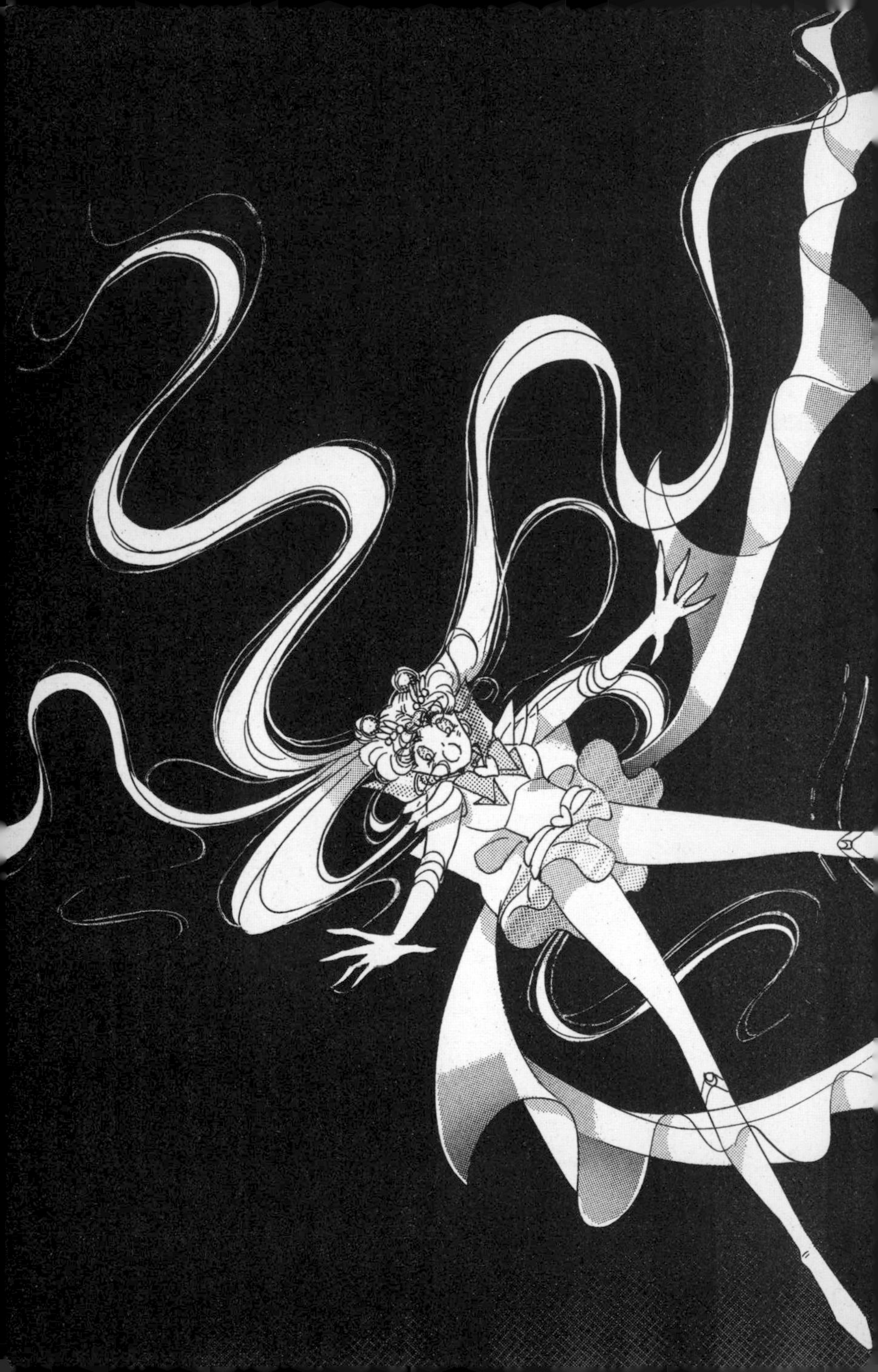

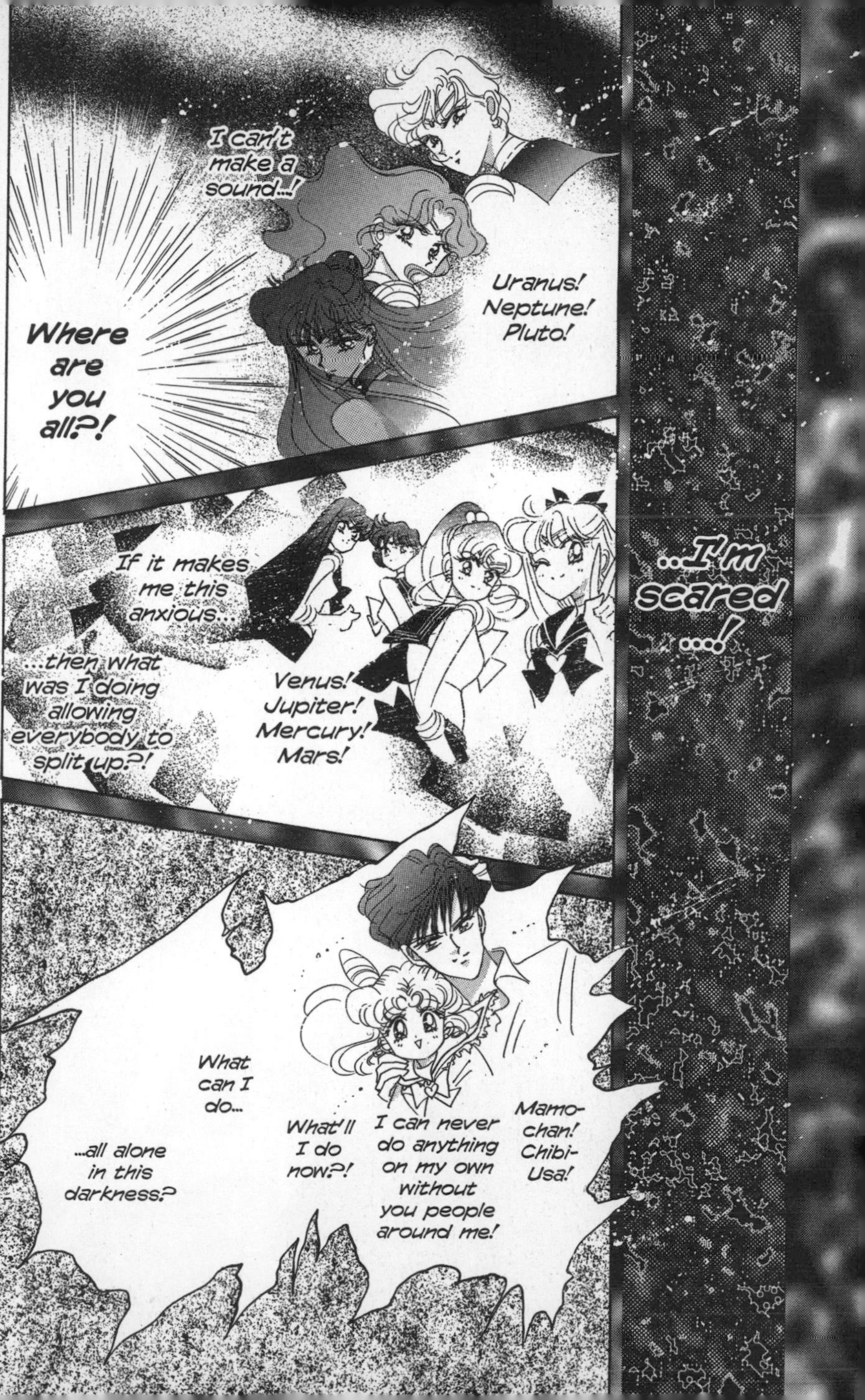
...I'm scared ...!
I can't make a sound...!
Uranus! Neptune! Pluto!
Where are you all?!
Venus! Jupiter! Mercury! Mars!
If it makes me this anxious...
...then what was I doing allowing everybody to split up?!
Mamo-chan! Chibi-Usa!
I can never do anything on my own without you people around me!
What'll I do now?!
What can I do...
...all alone in this darkness?

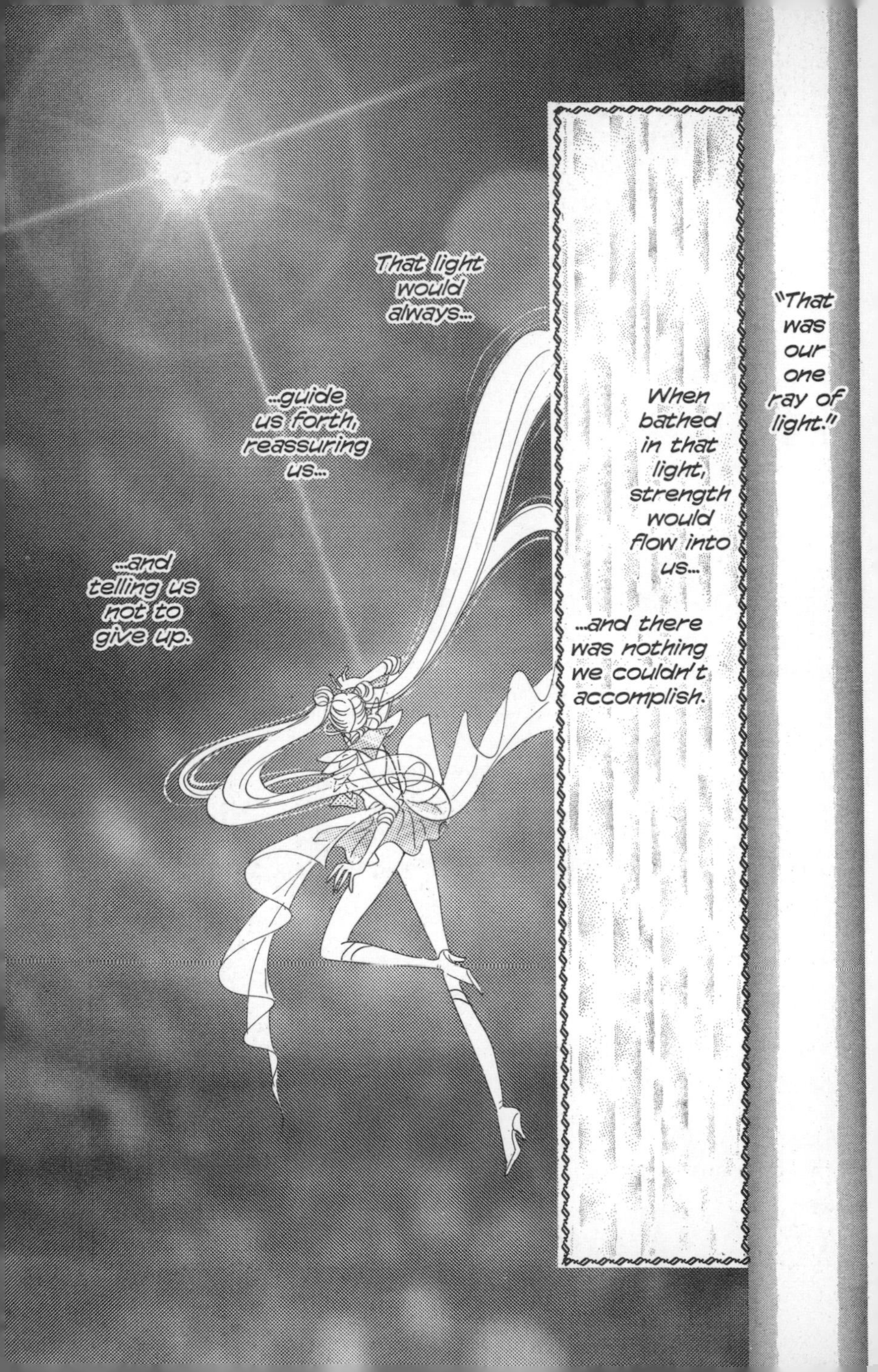
"That was our one ray of light."
When bathed in that light, strength would flow into us...
...and there was nothing we couldn't accomplish.
That light would always...
...guide us forth, reassuring us...
...and telling us not to give up.

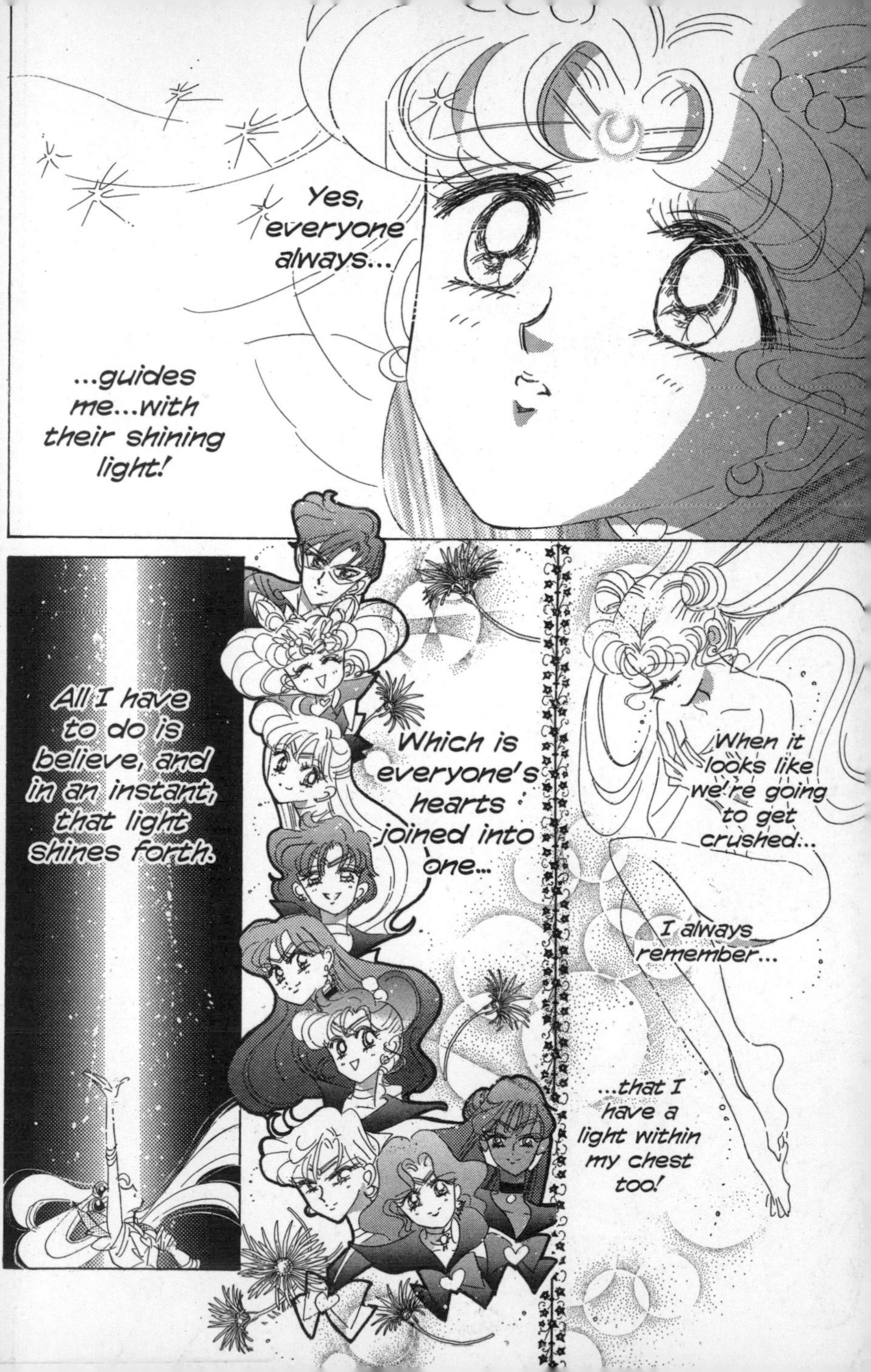
Yes, everyone always...
...guides me...with their shining light!
When it looks like we're going to get crushed...
I always remember...
...that I have a light within my chest too!
Which is everyone's hearts joined into one...
All I have to do is believe, and in an instant, that light shines forth.

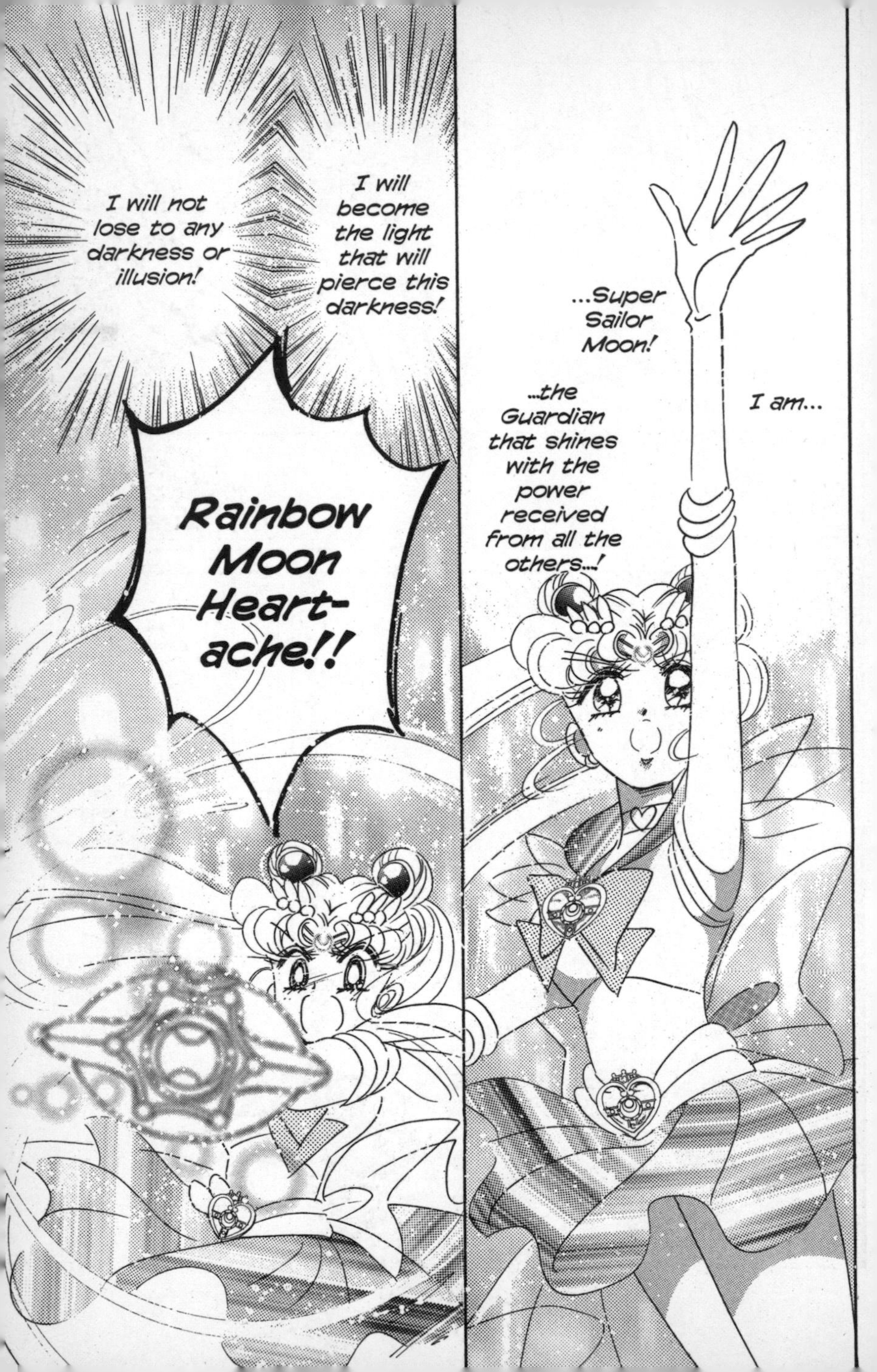
I am...
...Super Sailor Moon!
...the Guardian that shines with the power received from all the others...!
I will become the light that will pierce this darkness!
I will not lose to any darkness or illusion!
Rainbow Moon Heart-ache!!

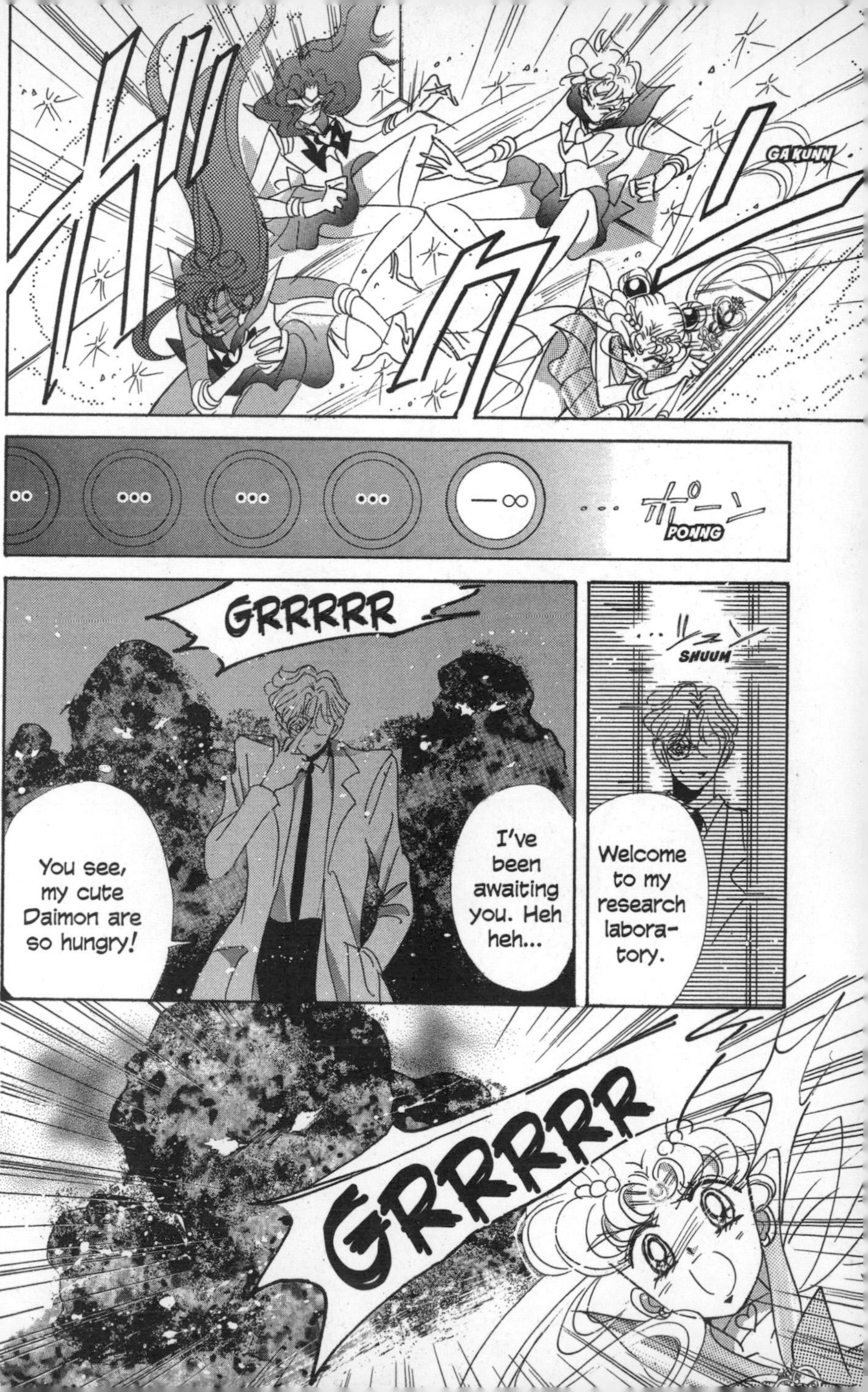
GA KUNN
PONNG
SHUUM
Welcome to my research labora-tory.
GRRRRR
I've been awaiting you. Heh heh...
You see, my cute Daimon are so hungry!
GRRRRR

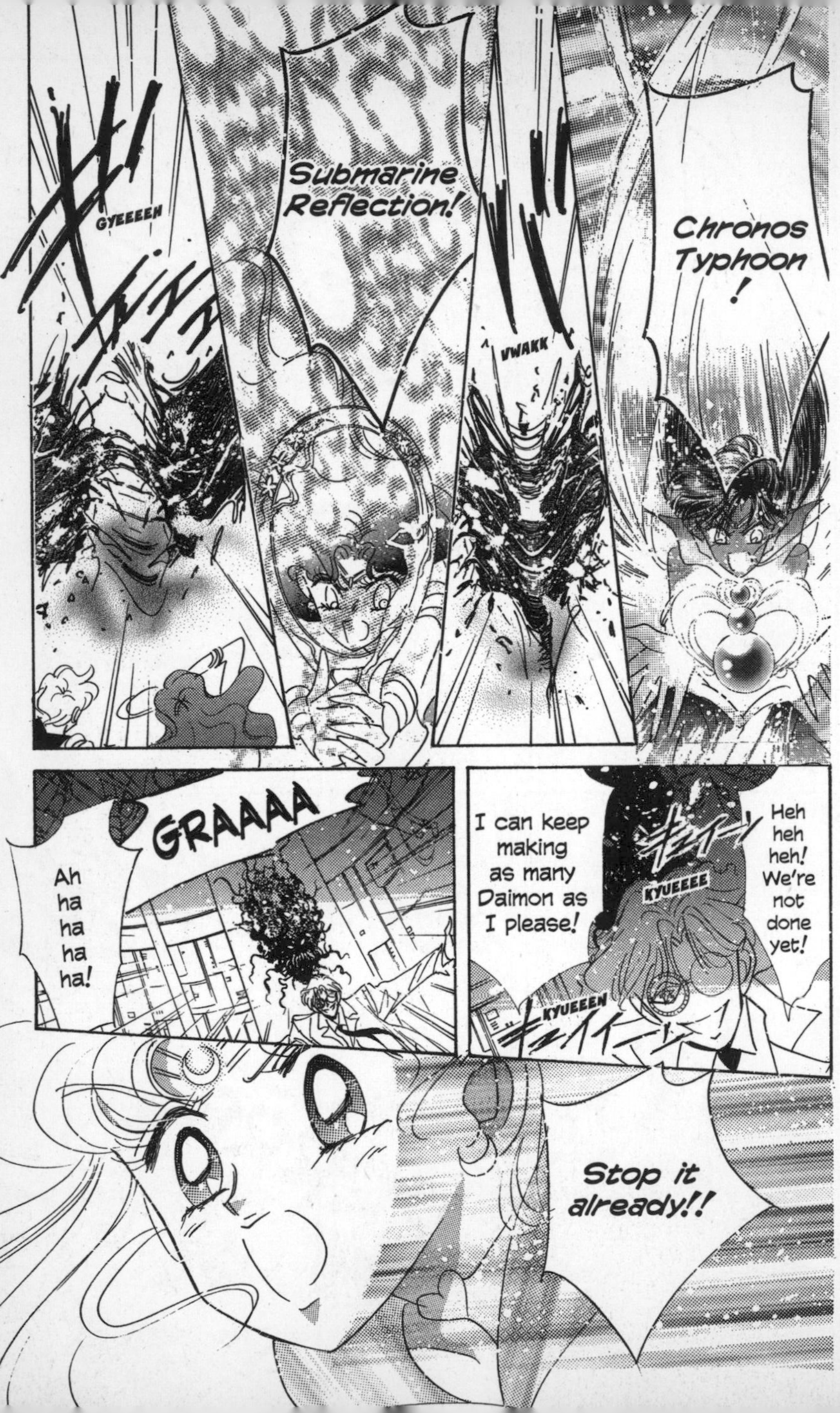
Chronos Typhoon!
VWAKK
Submarine Reflection!
GYEEEEH
Heh heh heh! We're not done yet!
KYUEEEE
I can keep making as many Daimon as I please!
KYUEEEN
GRAAAA
Ah ha ha ha ha!
Stop it already!!

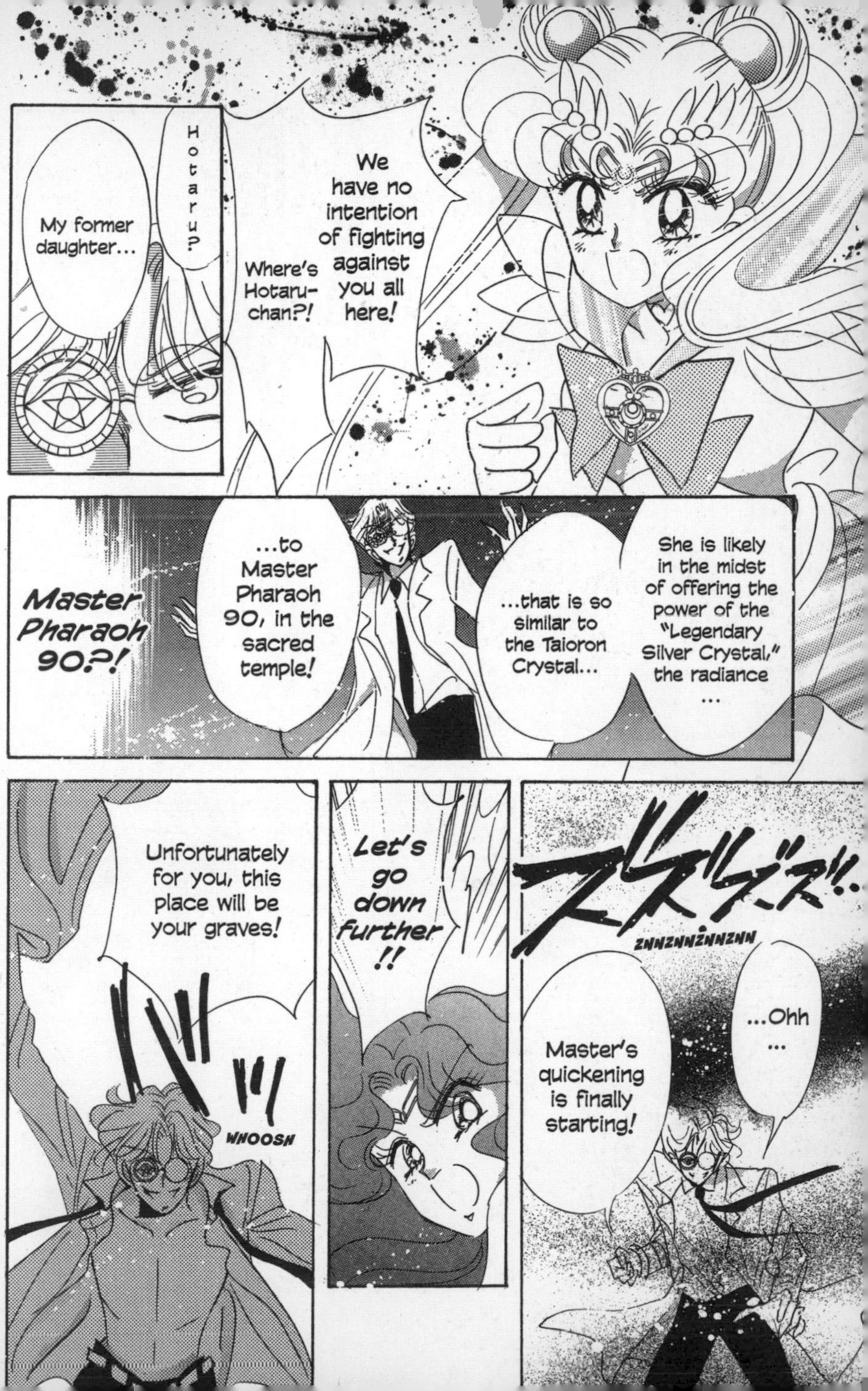
We have no intention of fighting against you all here!
Where's Hotaru-chan?!
Hotaru?
My former daughter...
She is likely in the midst of offering the power of the "Legendary Silver Crystal," the radiance ...
...that is so similar to the Taioron Crystal...
...to Master Pharaoh 90, in the sacred temple!
Master Pharaoh 90?!
ZNNZNNZNNZNN
...Ohh ...
Master's quickening is finally starting!
Let's go down further!!
Unfortunately for you, this place will be your graves!
WHOOSH

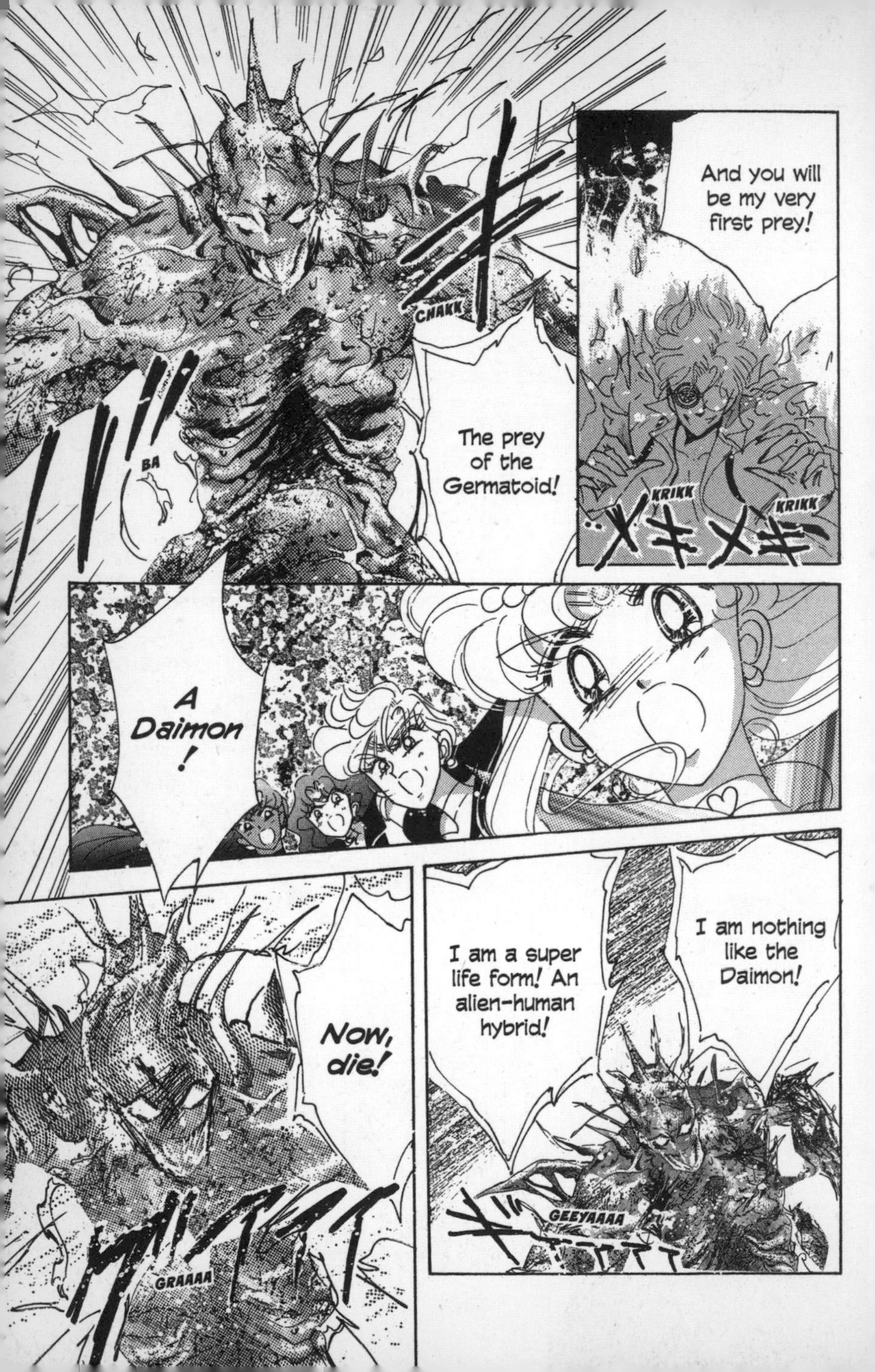
And you will be my very first prey!
KRIKK
KRIKK
CHAKK
The prey of the Germatoid!
BA
A Daimon!
I am nothing like the Daimon!
I am a super life form! An alien-human hybrid!
GEEYAAAA
Now, die!
GRAAAA

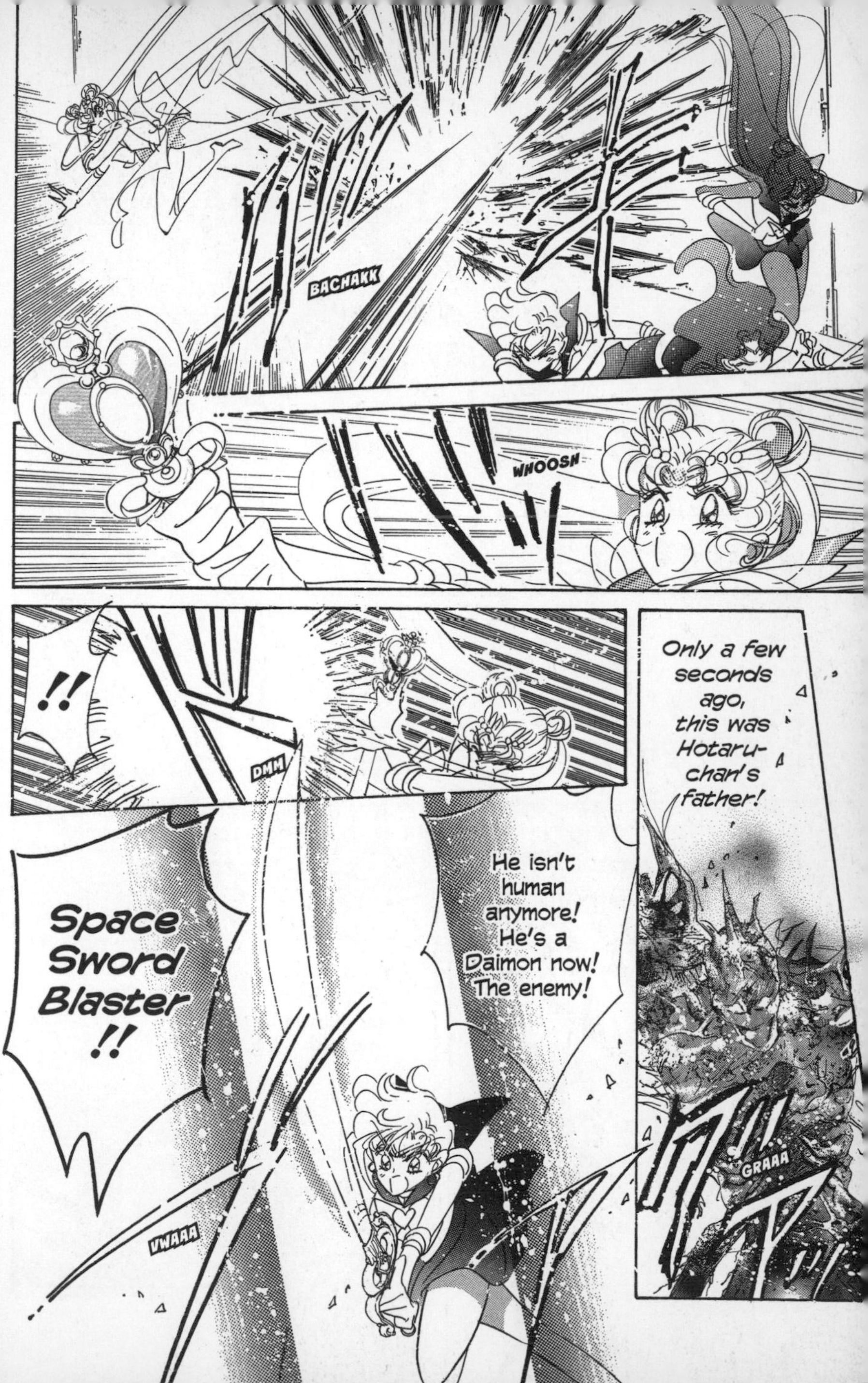
BACHAKK
WHOOSH
Only a few seconds ago, this was Hotaru-chan's father!
GRAAA
!!
DMM
He isn't human anymore! He's a Daimon now! The enemy!
Space Sword Blaster!!
VWAAA

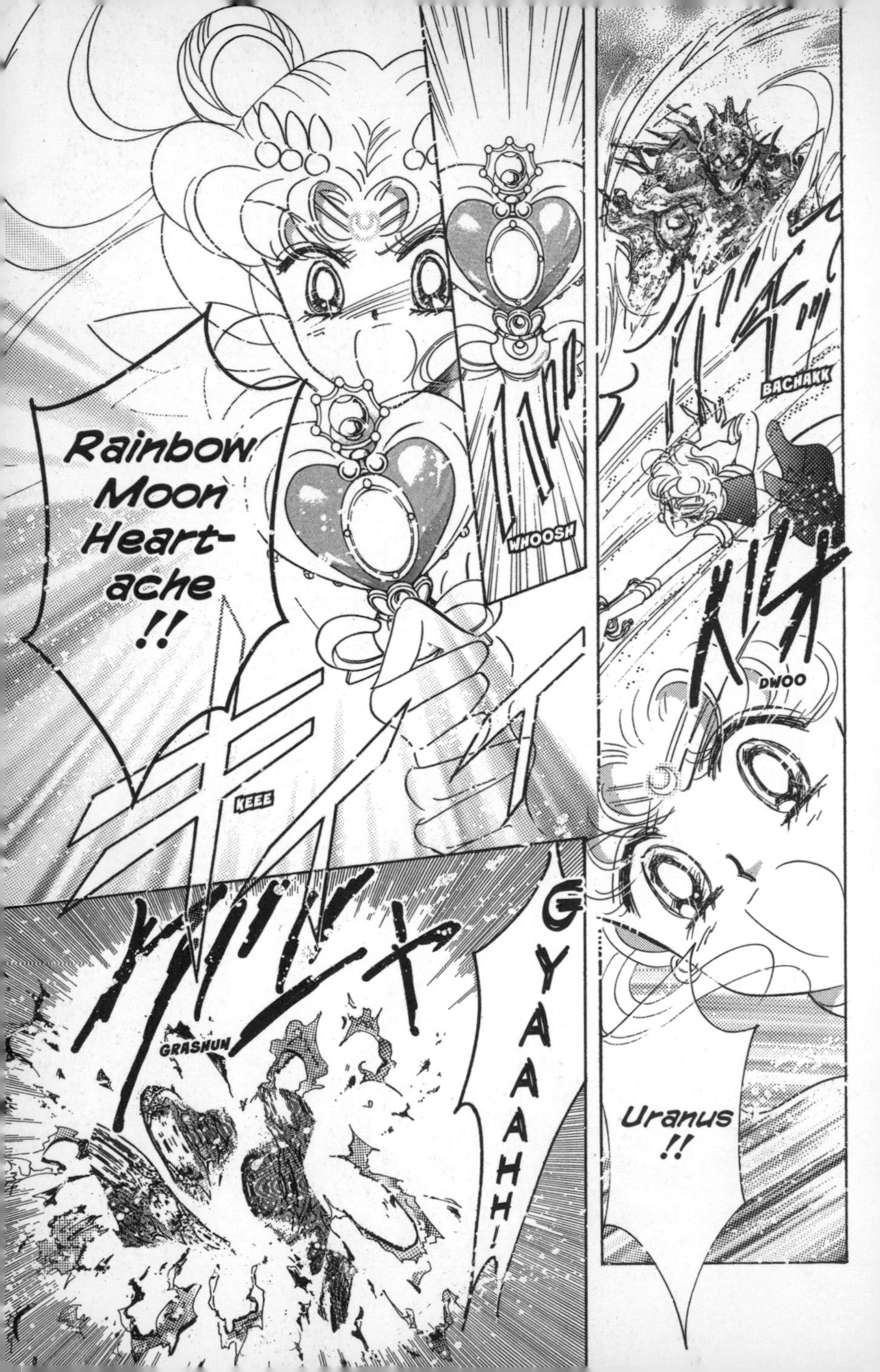
BACHAKK
DWOO
Uranus!!
WHOOSH
Rainbow Moon Heart-ache!!
KEEE
GRASHUN
GYAAAAHH!!

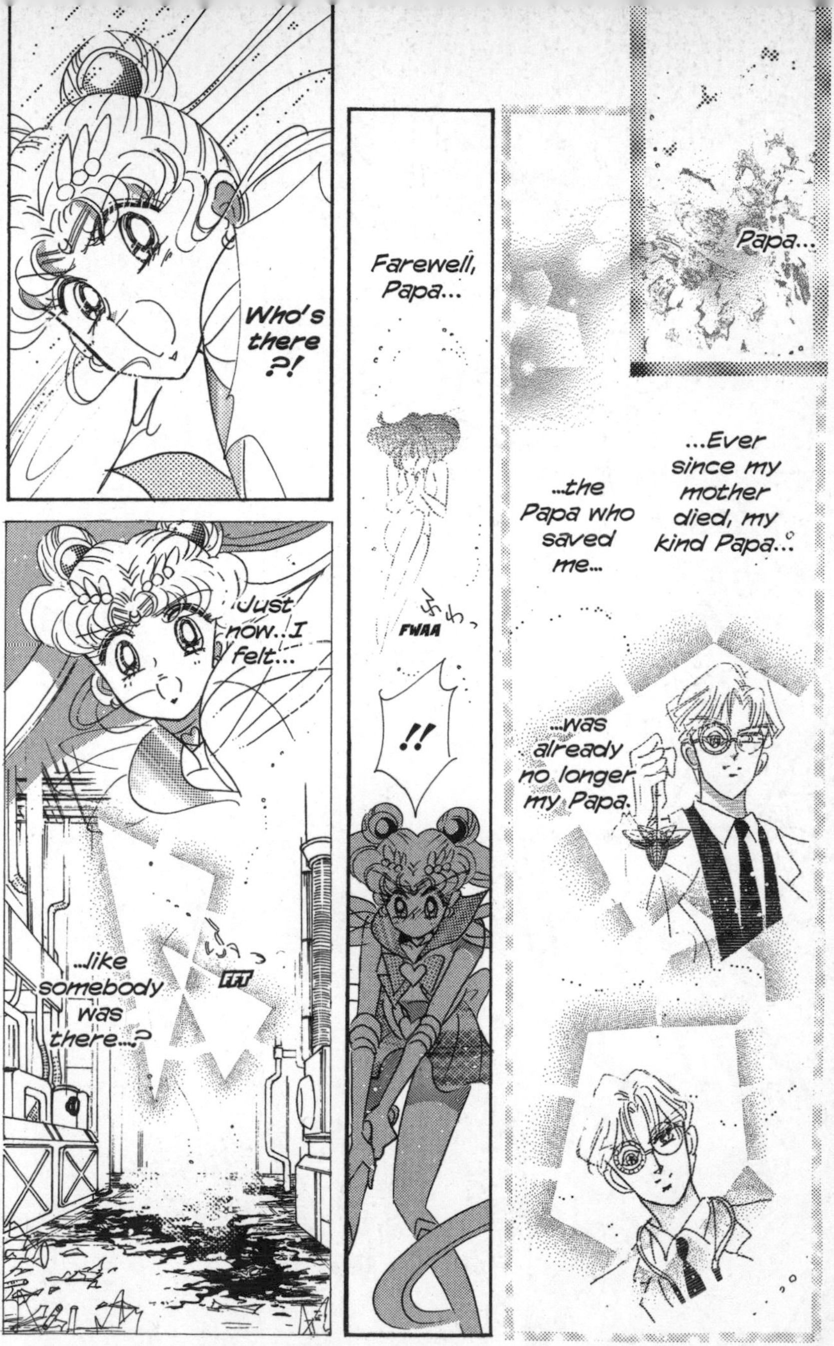
Papa...
...Ever since my mother died, my kind Papa...
...the Papa who saved me...
...was already no longer my Papa.
Farewell, Papa...
ふわっ
FWAA
!!
Who's there ?!
Just now...I felt...
...like somebody was there...?
FFT

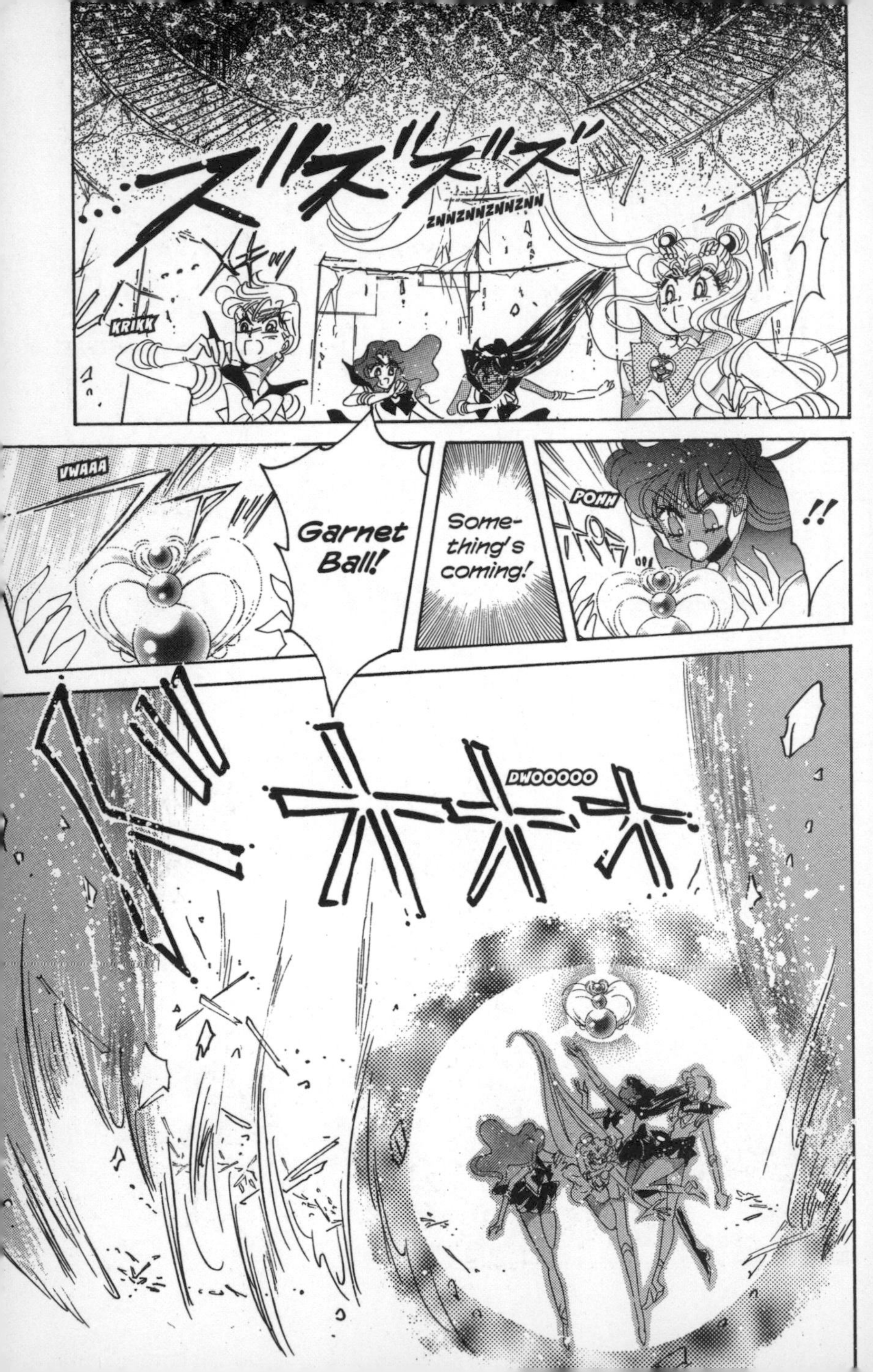
ZNNZNNZNNZNN
KRIKK
POHH
!!
Some-thing's coming!
Garnet Ball!
VWAAA
DWOOOOO

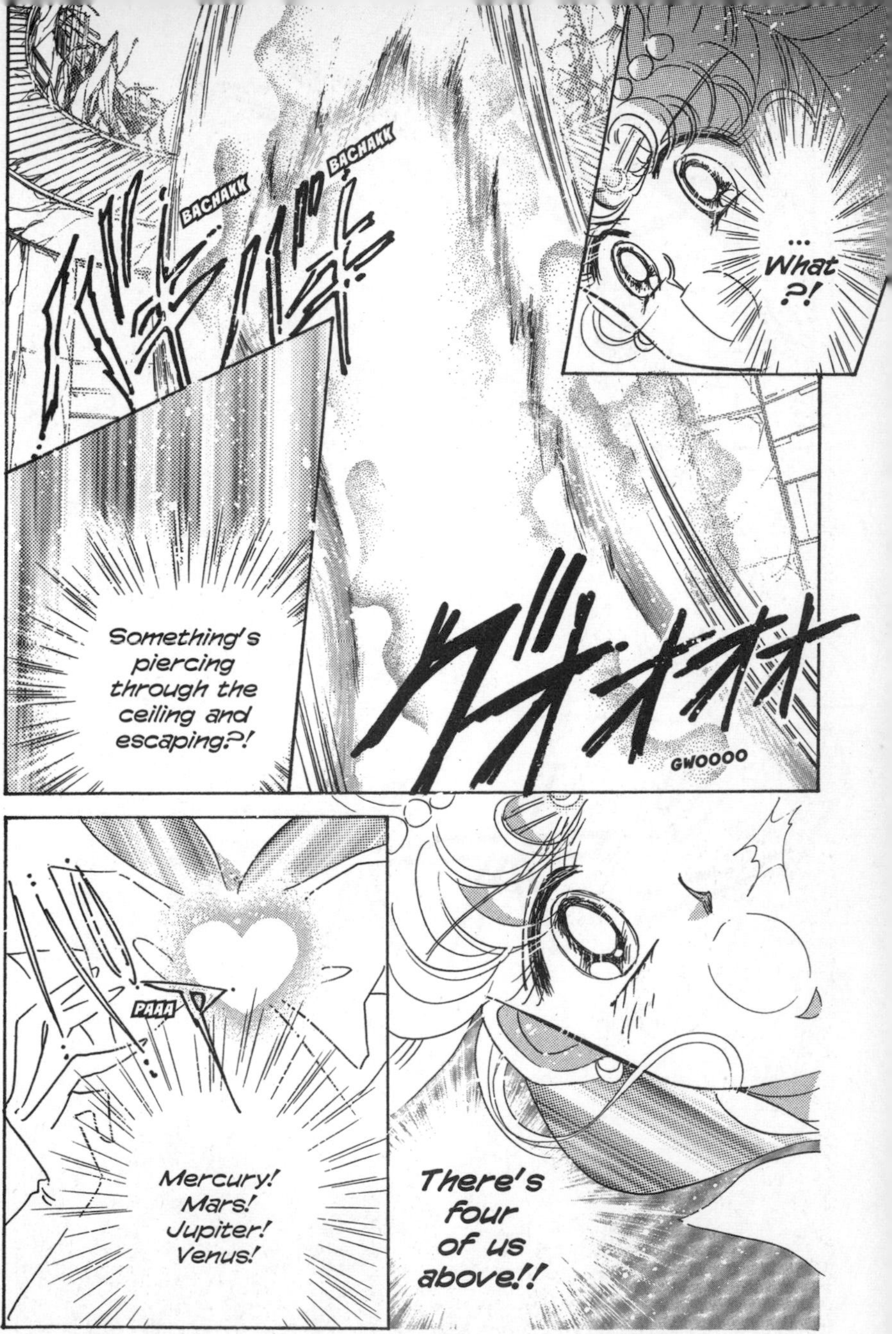

... What?!
BACHAKK
BACHAKK
GWOOOO
Something's piercing through the ceiling and escaping?!
There's four of us above!!
PAAA
Mercury! Mars! Jupiter! Venus!

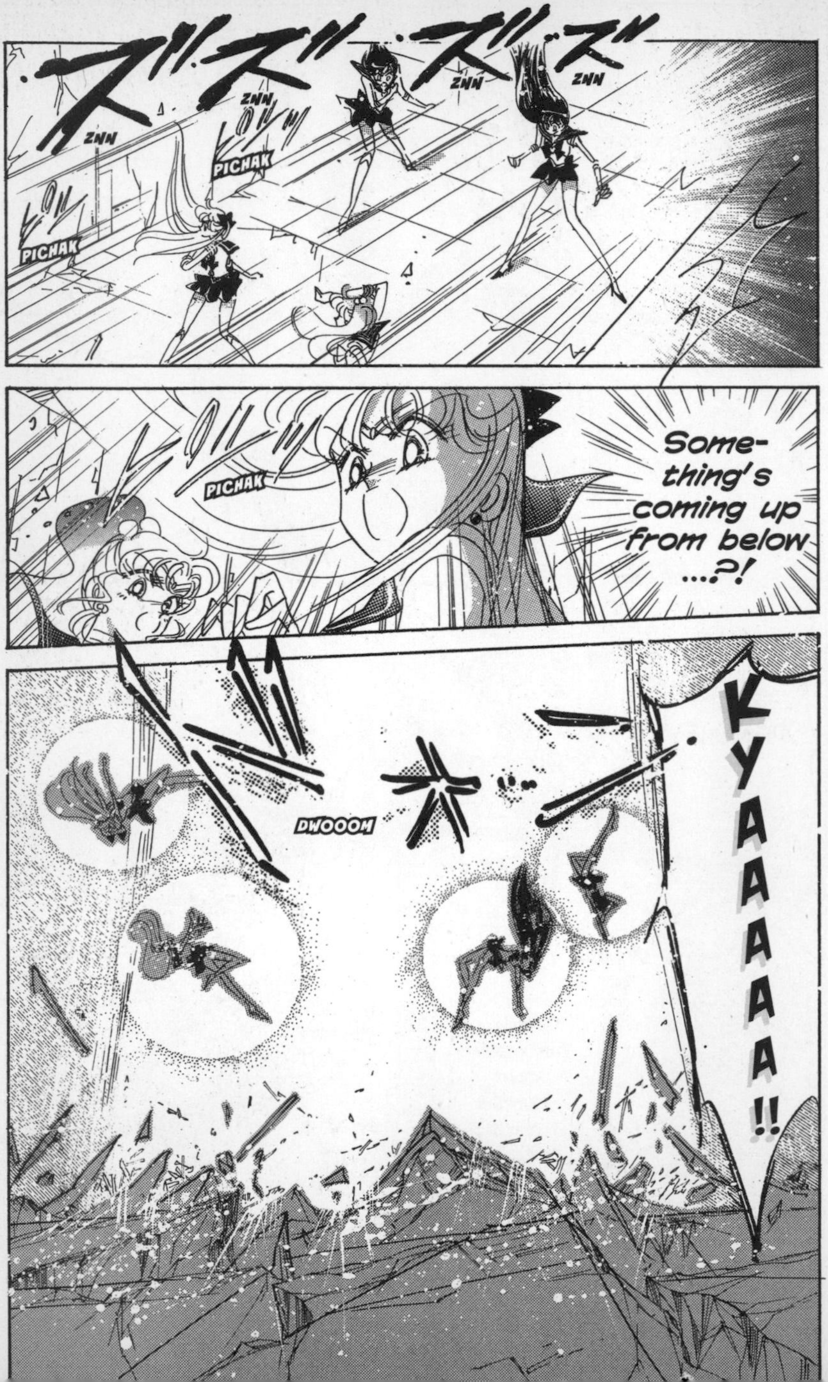
ZNN
ZNN
ZNN
PICHAK
ZNN
PICHAK
Some-thing's coming up from below ...?!
PICHAK
KYAAAA!!
DWOOOM

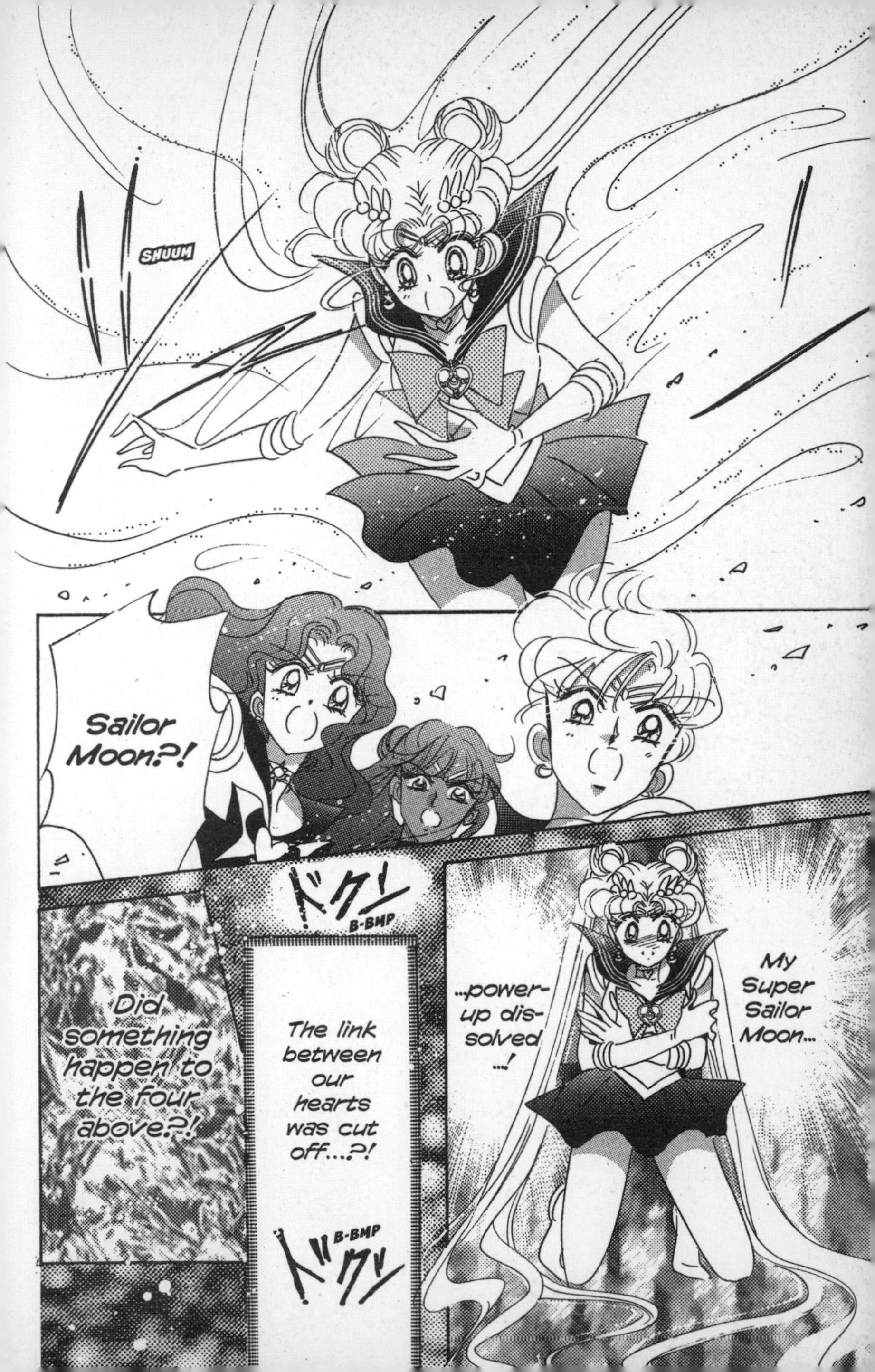
SHUUM
Sailor Moon?!
My Super Sailor Moon...
...power-up dis-solved...!
ドクン
B-BMP
The link between our hearts was cut off...?!
ドクン
B-BMP
Did something happen to the four above?!

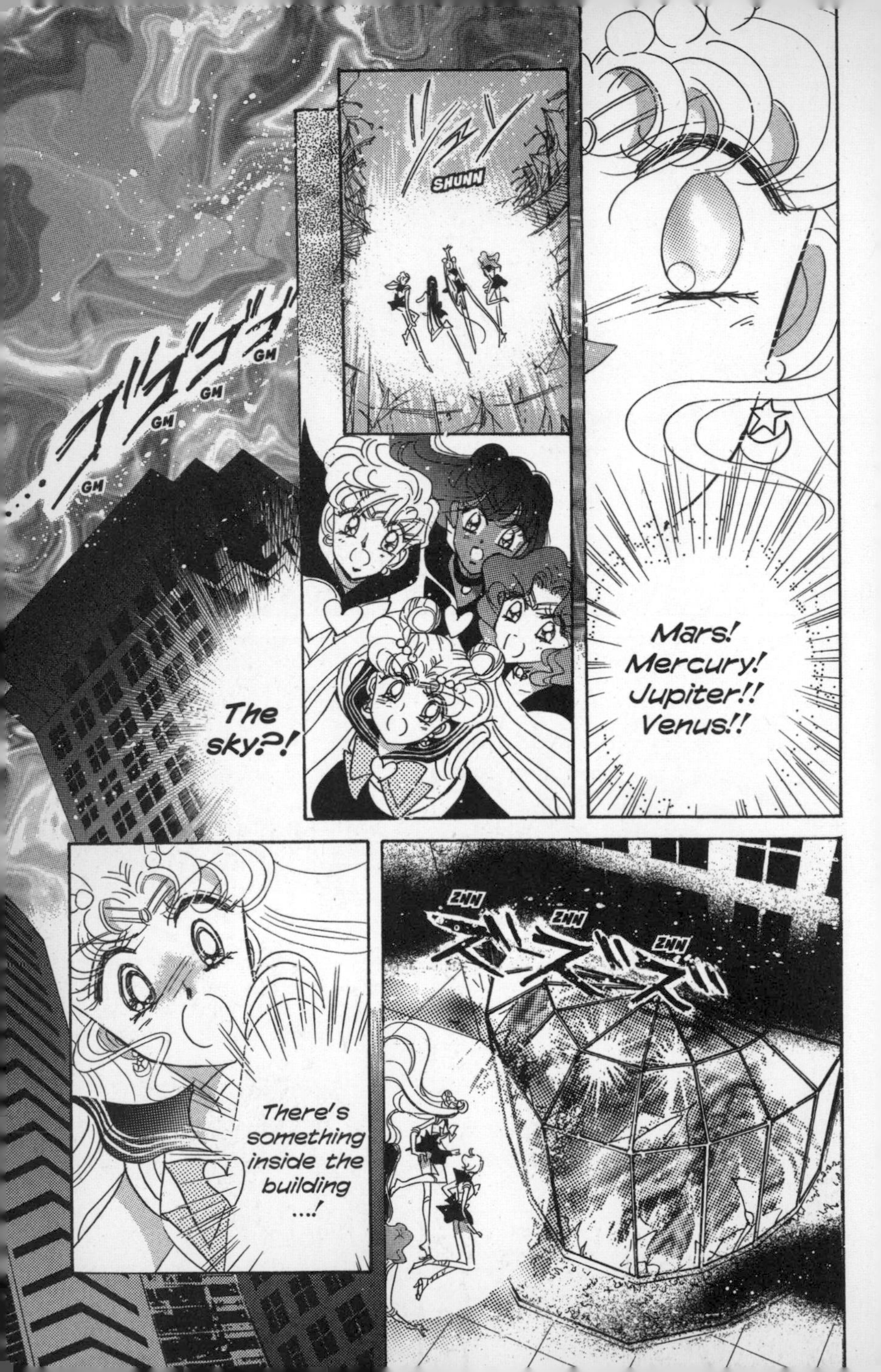

Mars! Mercury! Jupiter!! Venus!!
SHUNN
The sky?!
GM GM GM GM
ZNN ZNN ZNN
There's something inside the building ...!

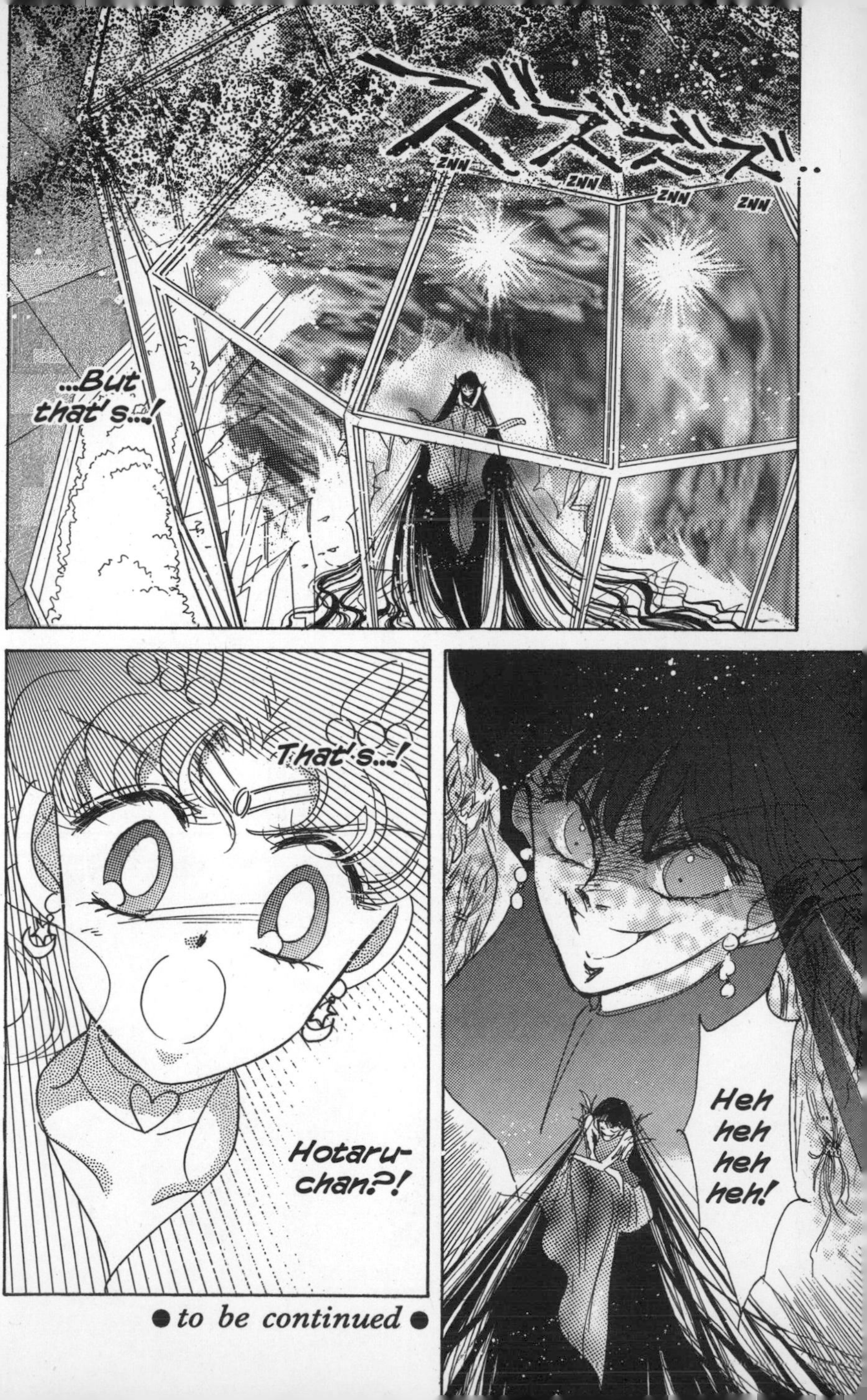
ZNN
ZNN
ZNN
ZNN
...But that's...!
Heh heh heh heh!
That's...!
Hotaru-chan?!

●to be continued●

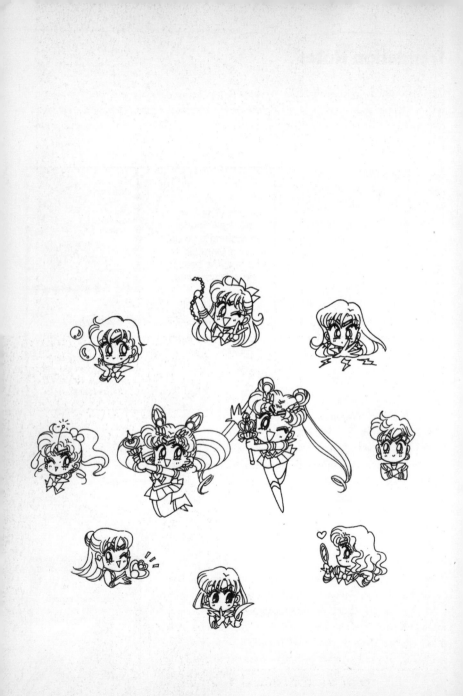

Translation Notes

Japanese is a tricky language for most Westerners, and translation is often more art than science. For your edification and reading pleasure, here are notes on some of the places where we could have gone in a different direction with our translation of the work, or where a Japanese cultural reference is used.

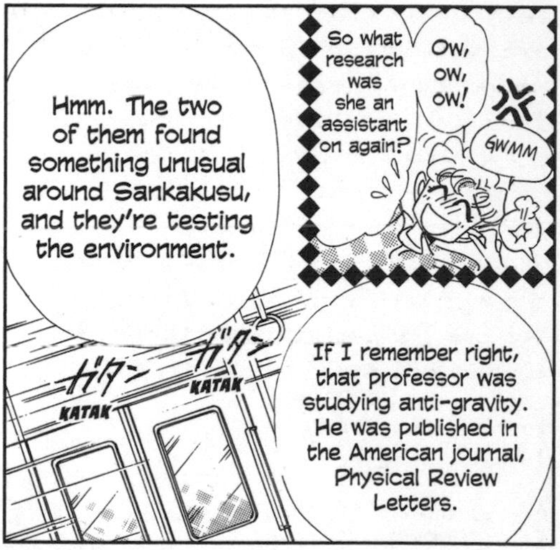
Ow, ow, ow!
GWMM
So what research was she an assistant on again?
Hmm. The two of them found something unusual around Sankakusu, and they're testing the environment.
KATAK
KATAK
If I remember right, that professor was studying anti-gravity. He was published in the American journal, Physical Review Letters.

Page 9, Physical Review Letters
Physical Review Letters is a real-world academic journal for publishing the results of scientific research. Originally, the publication printed letters to the editor of the journal, The Physical Review, but The Physical Review Letters itself became a very prestigious weekly publication. Now, it publishes short notes on fundamental research from all fields of physical science.

Page 9, Sankakusu
As mentioned in the notes for Volume 5, in Sailor Moon's world, there are several islands (Tenôzu, Kaiôzu, Meiôzu and Mugenzu) all arranged in a triangular formation. The region that comprises all four of these islands is called Sankakusu (the "su" and "zu" means "sandbar," but that meaning has expanded to mean small island). The word sankaku in Japanese means "triangle," referring to the shape the four islands encompass. In the real world, there is only Tenôzu (which is also called Tennoz). Although it is roughly rectangular shaped, it also houses upscale shopping, dining and condominiums.

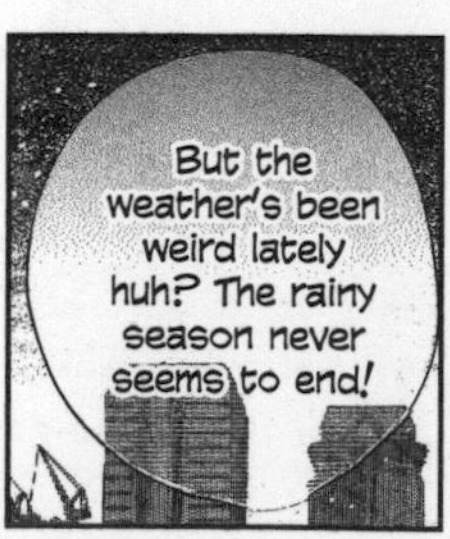
But the weather's been weird lately huh? The rainy season never seems to end!

Page 10 Rainy Season
June and the early part of July is traditionally the rainy season in Japan. It's about a month in length where it rains nearly every day. It is then replaced in later July and August with the extremely hot and humid weather of the Japanese summer. The continuous days of rain are depressing, promote mold and mildew in the house, make it difficult to dry one's clothes by hanging them out to dry, and invariably douse those who are caught outside without an umbrella

in bouts of rain and drizzle. Even with the hot, muggy weather of the Summer to look forward to, the Japanese tend to be very happy when the weather professionals tell them that the rainy season is over. It is very rare for the rainy weather to last in to late Summer as has in this story.

Page 12, Hoste

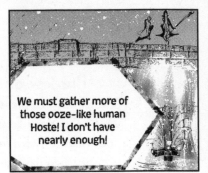

We must gather more of those ooze-like human Hoste! I don't have nearly enough!

In Japanese, the word is accompanied by kanji which mean "sacred body," and come along with the pronunciation guide "osuti." Checking on both the meaning and the pronunciation, I found that the wafer of leavened bread that represents the body of Christ in Catholic mass, the "host," was taken from word out of the old French language "hoste." The word comes from a Latin word meaning "enemy" or "stranger" because of an ancient pagan practice of the victors in war offering up the bodies of one's enemies up to their Gods. Somehow, the sound, the kanji meaning, and the story of the word's origin seemed to fit with the story.

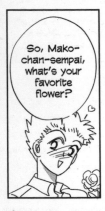

So, Mako-chan-sempai, what's your favorite flower?

Page 22 Mako-chan-sempai

This combination of contrasting honorifics is rather unusual in Japanese. As noted in the explanation of the honorifics, "chan" is a "cute" honorific while "sempai" is respectful. Honorific combinations in general are rare, but this contrasting combination is especially rare.

Page 81, Kaori-kun

Although the honorific -kun is most usually heard for school boy, it is not completely a male honorific. It's possible, or even necessary, to use -kun in the workplace where the one's rank is well known, and it would seem too familiar or inappropriate to use the diminutive honorific -chan. The honorific -san can and most often is used in times like this, unless the speaker wants to emphasize his/her higher status.

Page 130, A million yen

At the currents rates at the time of this translation, a rent of a million yen per month would come out to about 13,000 dollars per month. And Makoto's rent of 50,000 yen would come out to the more reasonable 650 dollars. But a good "rule of thumb" to get an idea of the amounts they talk about in manga would be a 100 yen per dollar.

Preview of *Sailor Moon 8*

We're pleased to present you with a preview from
Pretty Guardian Sailor Moon 8. Please check
our website (www.kodanshacomics.com) to
see when this volume will be available.

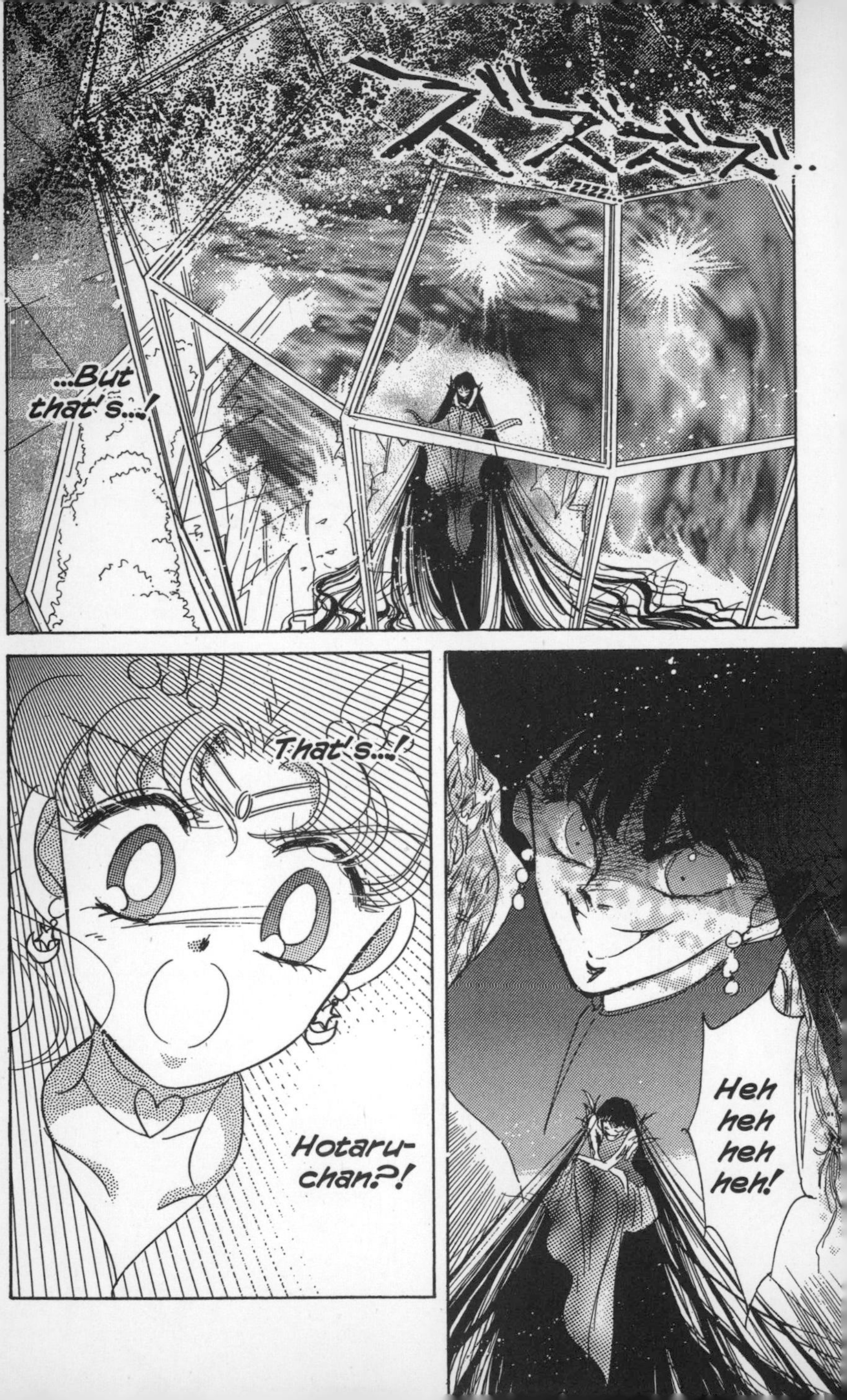
zzzz...
...But that's...!
Heh heh heh heh!
That's...!
Hotaru-chan?!

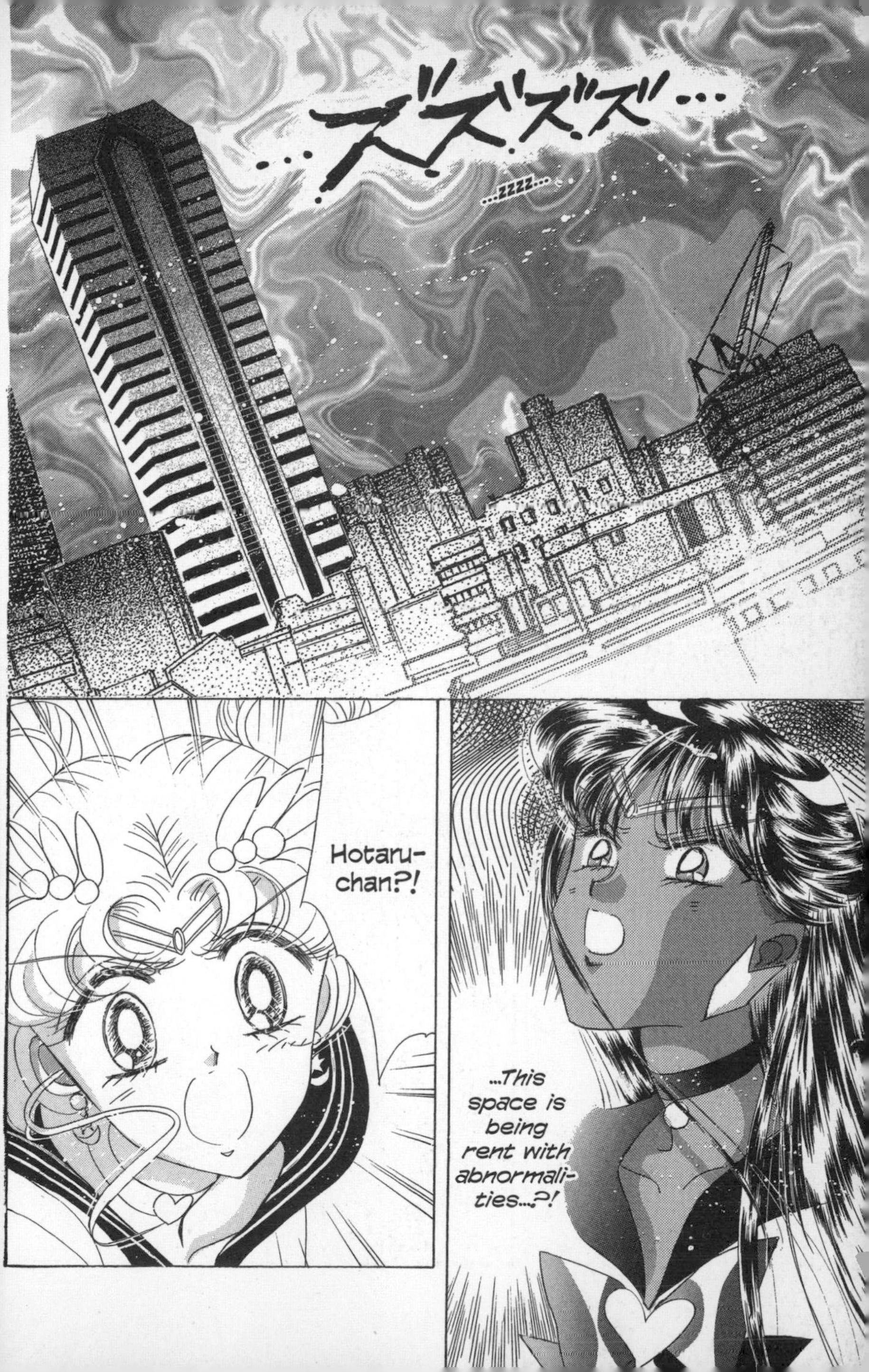
...ズズズズ...
...zzzz...
...This space is being rent with abnormalities...?!
Hotaru-chan?!

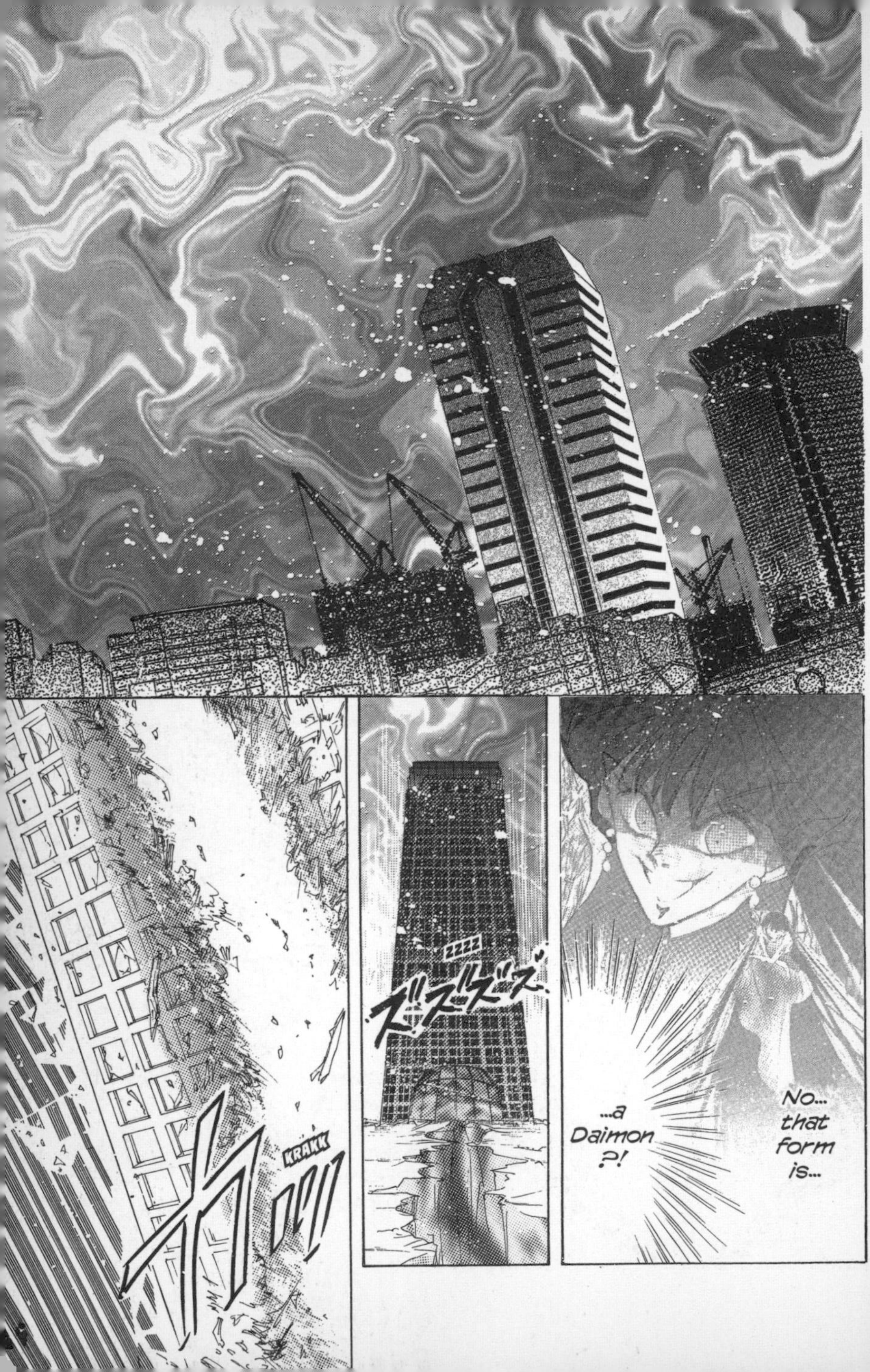
No... that form is...
...a Daimon ?!
KRAKK

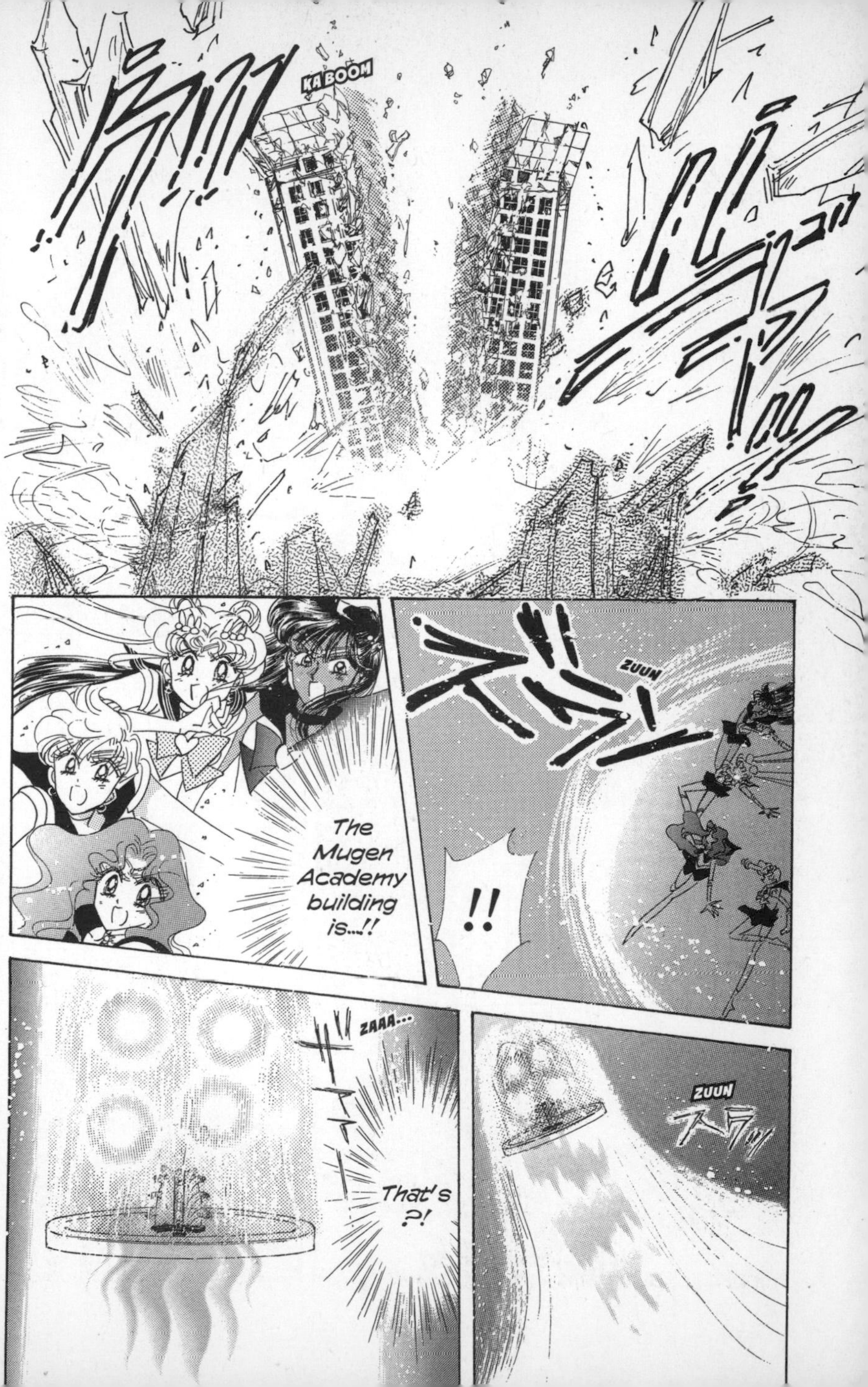
KA BOOM
ZUUN
!!
The Mugen Academy building is...!!
ZUUN
ZAAA...
That's ?!

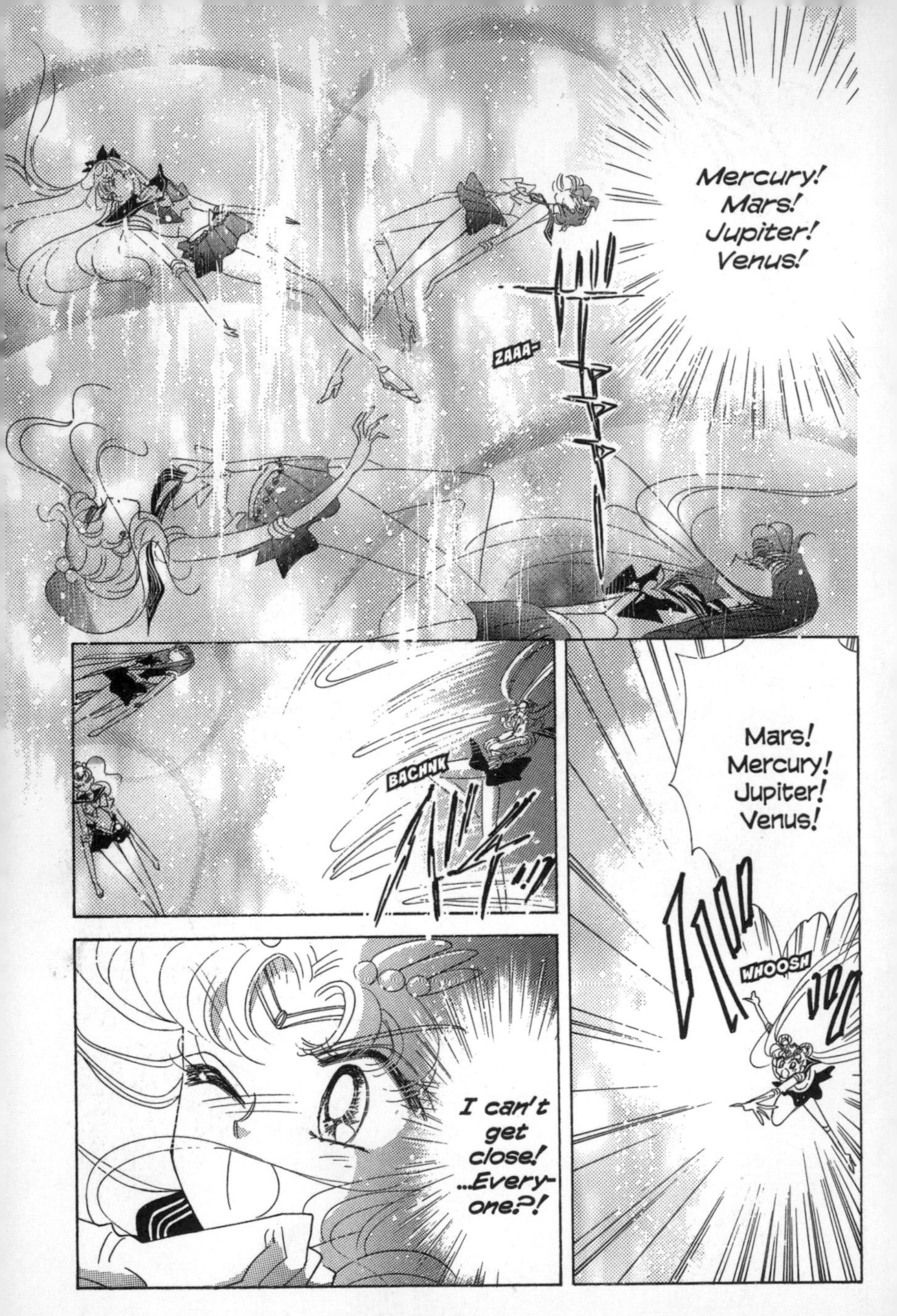
Mercury! Mars! Jupiter! Venus!
ZAAA-
Mars! Mercury! Jupiter! Venus!
WHOOSH
BACHNK
I can't get close! ...Every-one?!

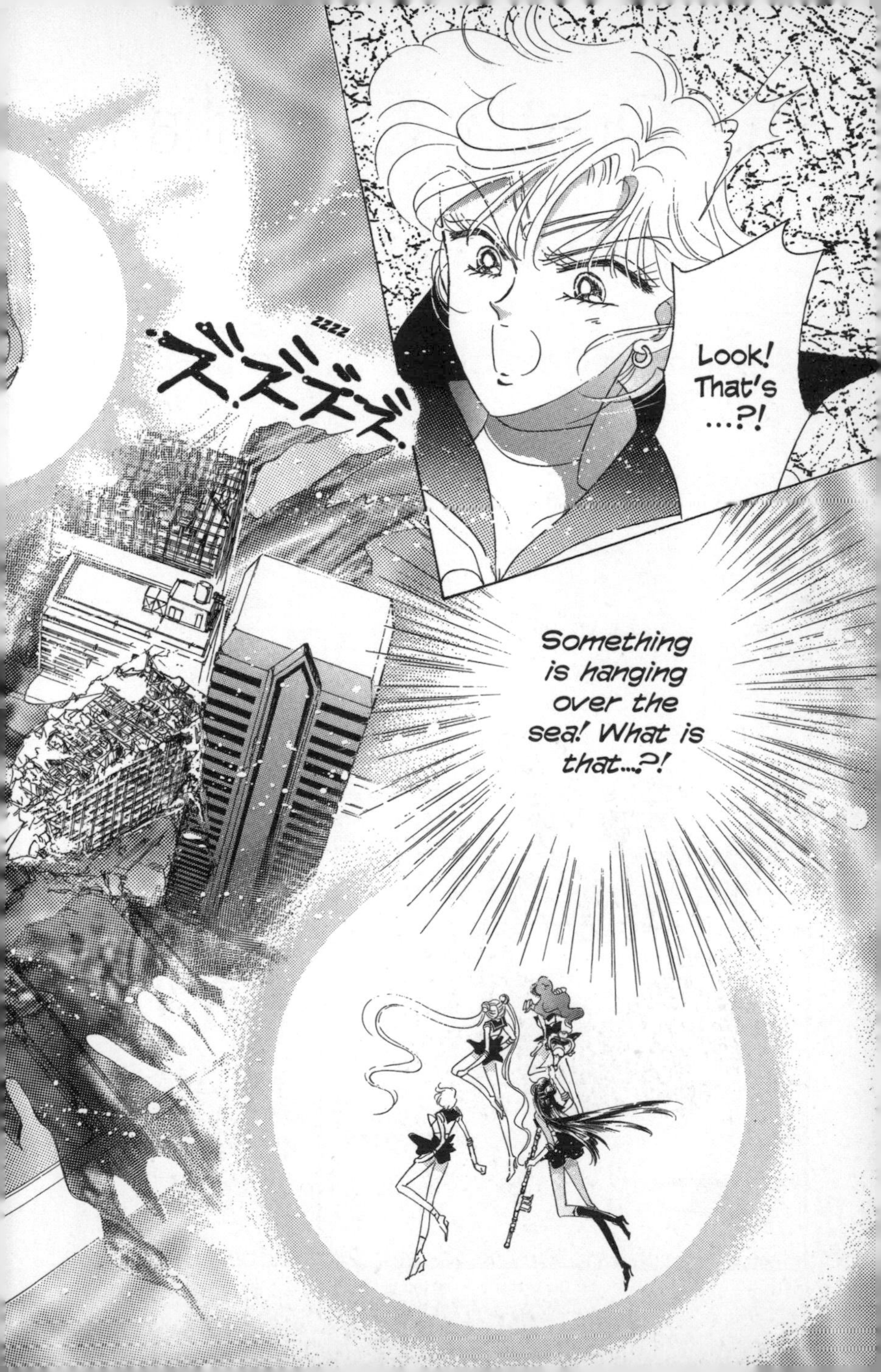
Look! That's ...?!
ZZZZ
ズズズズ
Something is hanging over the sea! What is that...?!

The Pretty Guardians are back!

✦

Kodansha Comics is proud to present
Sailor Moon with all new translations.

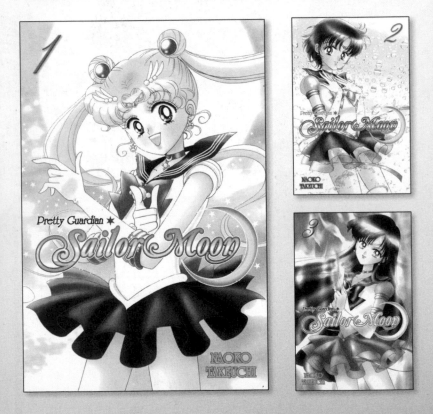

For more information, go to **www.kodanshacomics.com**

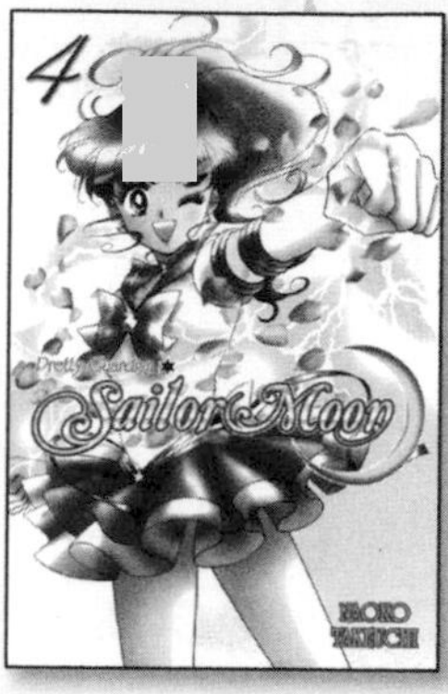
4
Pretty Guardian
Sailor Moon
NAOKO TAKEUCHI

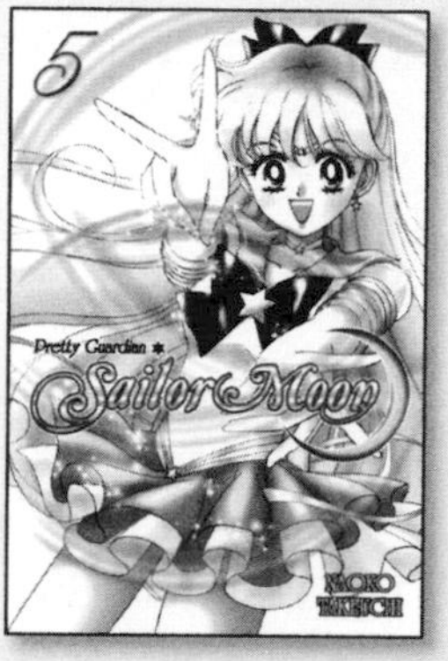
5
Pretty Guardian
Sailor Moon
NAOKO TAKEUCHI

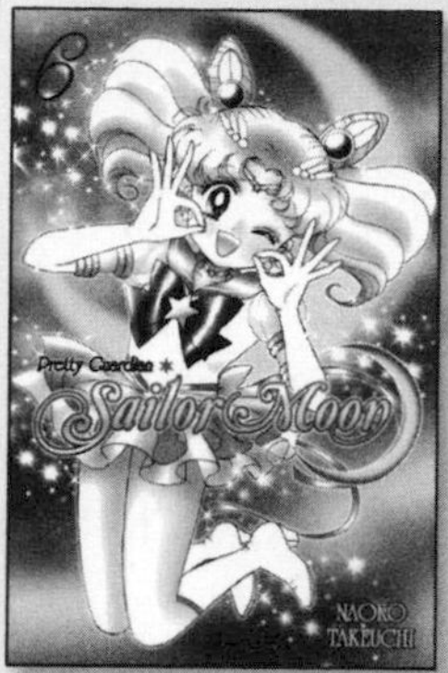
6
Pretty Guardian
Sailor Moon
NAOKO TAKEUCHI

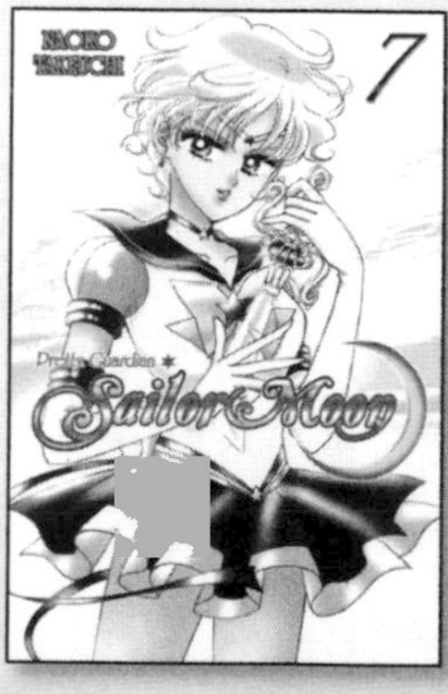
NAOKO TAKEUCHI
7
Pretty Guardian
Sailor Moon

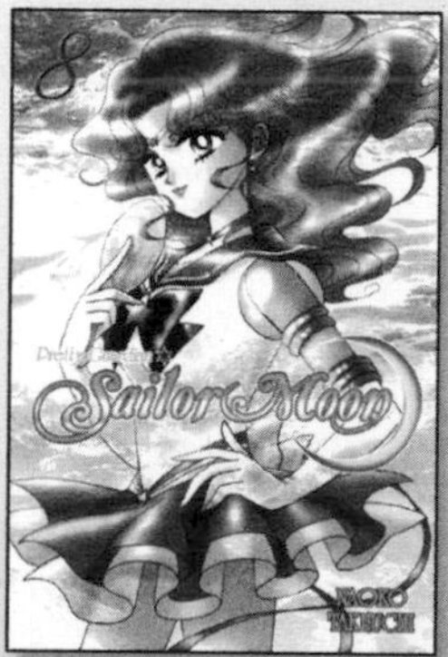
8
Sailor Moon
NAOKO TAKEUCHI

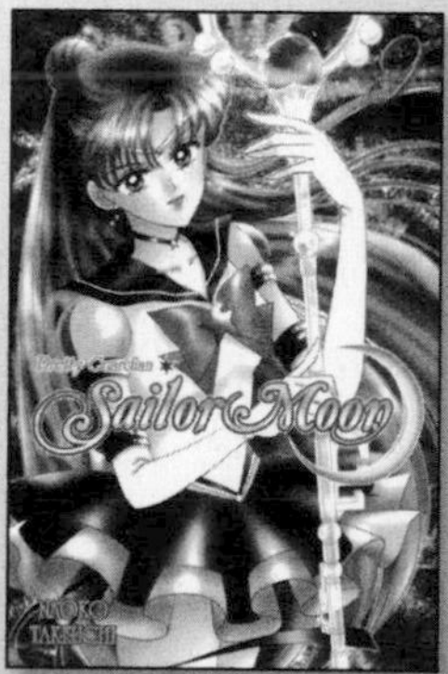
Sailor Moon
NAOKO TAKEUCHI

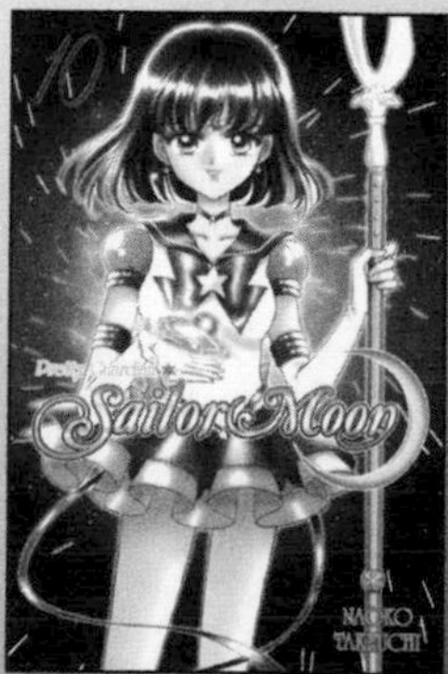
10
Sailor Moon
NAOKO TAKEUCHI

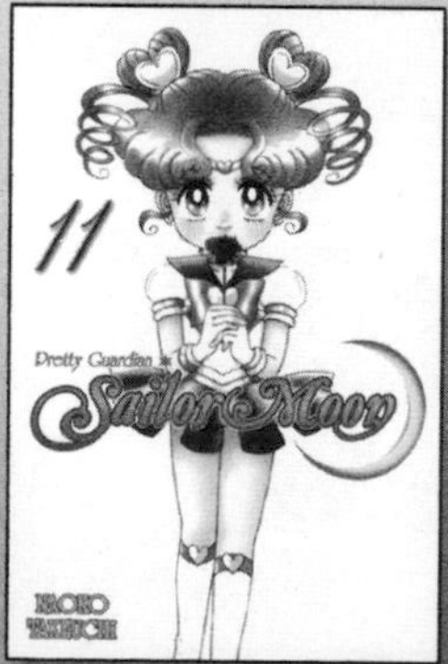
11
Pretty Guardian
Sailor Moon
NAOKO TAKEUCHI

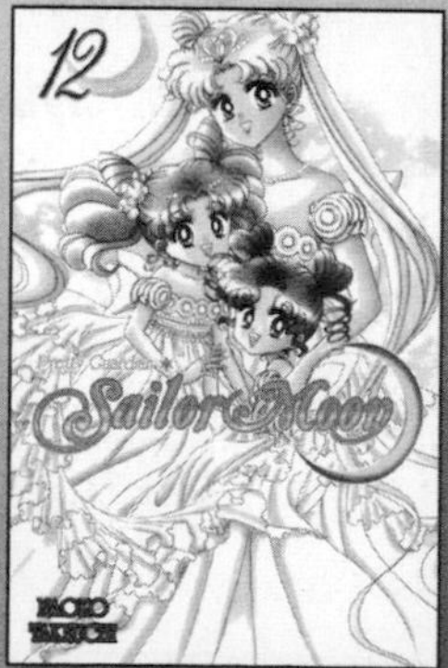
12
Pretty Guardian
Sailor Moon
NAOKO TAKEUCHI

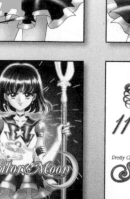

KC KODANSHA COMICS

A Kodansha Trade Paperback Original.

Published in the United States by Kodansha Comics, an imprint
of Kodansha USA Publishing, LLC, New York.

Publication rights for this English edition arranged through
Kodansha Ltd., Tokyo.

First published in Japan in 2004 by Kodansha Ltd., Tokyo, as
Bishoujosenshi Sailor Moon Shinsoban, volume 7.

ISBN 978-1-61262-003-9

Printed in the United States of America

www.kodanshacomics.com

9 8 7 6 5 4 3 2 1

Translator/Adapter: William Flanagan
Lettering: Deron Bennett

TOMARE!

止まれ

[STOP!]

You're going the wrong way!

Manga is a completely different type of reading experience.

To start at the *beginning*, go to the *end*!

That's right! Authentic manga is read the traditional Japanese way—from right to left, exactly the *opposite* of how American books are read. It's easy to follow: Just go to the other end of the book and read each page—and each panel—from right side to left side, starting at the top right. Now you're experiencing manga as it was meant to be!